GRAND STRATEGY IN THEORY AND PRACTICE

The Need for an Effective American Foreign Policy

This book explores fundamental questions about grand strategy, as it has evolved across generations and countries. It provides an overview of the ancient era of grand strategy and a detailed discussion of its philosophical, military, and economic foundations in the modern era. The author investigates these aspects through the lens of four approaches – those of historians, social scientists, practitioners, and military strategists. The main goal is to provide contemporary policy makers and scholars with an historic and analytic framework through which to evaluate and conduct grand strategy. By providing greater analytical clarity about grand strategy and describing its nature and utility for the state, the book presents a comprehensive theory and practice of grand strategy in order to articulate the United States' past, present, and future purpose and position on the world stage.

William C. Martel is Associate Professor of International Security Studies at The Fletcher School of Law and Diplomacy at Tufts University. His research and teaching interests are in international security and public policy. His most recent book is *Victory in War: Foundations of Strategy* (2011). Martel was a Professor of National Security Affairs at the Naval War College and served on the professional staff of the RAND Corporation in Washington. He served as an advisor to the National Security Council from 2002 to 2003 and from 2007 to 2010; as a consultant to the Defense Advanced Research Projects Agency, the Office of the Secretary of Defense, the U.S. Air Force, and the U.S. Air Force Scientific Advisory Board; and as a member of the Defense Department's Threat Reduction Advisory Committee.

Grand Strategy in Theory and Practice

THE NEED FOR AN EFFECTIVE AMERICAN

FOREIGN POLICY

William C. Martel
Tufts University, The Fletcher School

CAMBRIDGE
UNIVERSITY PRESS

CAMBRIDGE
UNIVERSITY PRESS

32 Avenue of the Americas, New York, NY 10013-2473, USA

Cambridge University Press is part of the University of Cambridge.

It furthers the University's mission by disseminating knowledge in the pursuit of education, learning, and research at the highest international levels of excellence.

www.cambridge.org
Information on this title: www.cambridge.org/9781107442214

First published 2015
Reprinted 2015

Printed in the United States of America

A catalog record for this publication is available from the British Library.

Library of Congress Cataloging in Publication Data
Martel, William C.
Grand strategy in theory and practice : the need for an effective American foreign policy / William C. Martel.
    pages   cm
ISBN 978-1-107-08206-9 (hardback)
1. United States – Foreign relations.   2. United States – Military policy.
3. Strategic planning – United States.   I. Title.
E183.7.M364   2014
327.73–dc23

                                                    2014027963

ISBN 978-1-107-08206-9 Hardback
ISBN 978-1-107-44221-4 Paperback

To my wife, Dianne

Contents

Acknowledgments

This book explores fundamental questions about grand strategy, as it has evolved across generations and countries. It provides an overview of the ancient era of grand strategy and a detailed discussion of its philosophical, military, and economic foundations in the modern era. This study investigates these aspects through the lens of four approaches – those of historians, social scientists, practitioners, and military strategists. The main goal of this book is to provide contemporary policy makers and scholars with a rigorous historic and analytic framework for evaluating and conducting grand strategy. By providing greater analytical clarity about grand strategy and describing its nature and utility for policy makers, the book presents a comprehensive analysis of the theory and practice of grand strategy. It articulates how many states, including the United States, define their past, present, and future purposes in the conduct of foreign policy.

For times of great strategic change, this work explores in a precise manner the concept known as grand strategy that the state seeks to formulate and implement. Even while scholars and policy makers debate grand strategy, we ambiguously use the term to describe both a general approach to policy as well as more specific policies that states may pursue in peacetime or war. What is missing from the debate, however, is a detailed analytic and historical examination of grand strategy, from ancient to modern times, as a useful guide for action or as a meaningful way to analyze the successes and failures of past policy. Fundamentally, grand strategy describes how the nation sees its role in the world and the broad objectives that govern its actions.

As the United States and other states struggle with the principles governing foreign policy, we enter the precise realm of grand strategy. With wars winding down in Iraq and Afghanistan, an insurgency spreading across Syria and Iraq, Russia's annexation of parts of Ukraine, Iran's efforts to acquire nuclear weapons, and the rise of China in Asia and Japan's role as a counterweight to China, now is the time to consider the strategy that governs what policies states pursue. Indeed, grand strategy is the center of gravity for policy makers and scholars who contemplate what ought to be done in foreign policy. From the time during the Cold War when the United States and its allies knew precisely what they ought to do – when they were guided by the grand strategy of containment – to the present, we find that states struggle most when they lack clarity about their grand strategy.

I have written this book because scholars and policy makers have failed to develop a grand strategy that guides their actions and communicates that strategy to allies and adversaries. If neither the state nor its allies and adversaries understand a state's grand strategy, we have a prescription for miscalculation, crisis, and war. In fact, the debates about whether and how to exit from Iraq and Afghanistan, and how to "pivot" the nation's attention toward Asia, were complicated by confusion about America's grand strategy. Nor is this a purely American problem, because many states in the West remain confused about the principles that should govern their foreign policy.

The more deeply I study the problem, the more obvious it becomes to me that we need to think carefully and analytically about the meaning and role of grand strategy. Although grand strategy identifies the broad purpose of foreign policy, this is not to say that a consensus will necessarily emerge. Certainly that is the preferred case, but modern societies, including the United States, are consumed by debates in deeply divided publics concerning what policies the state ought to pursue. We also see in numerous opinion polls that American society has waning enthusiasm for global involvement. Ultimately, the missing ingredient is a systematic framework – which is another way of saying grand strategy – that helps the public and policy makers articulate the broad principles governing the state's policies.

With these thoughts in mind, this book analyzes grand strategy, beginning with ancient societies and concluding with modern states, to illuminate its meaning and practice. By exploring grand strategy in theory and practice, it helps scholars and policy makers more effectively formulate principles guiding their political, economic, and military policies. This study, which builds on the existing scholarly and policy literature, explores the analytic foundations of grand strategy. It addresses the ancient and modern eras of grand strategy, the forces that shaped grand strategy in empires, and the influence of revolutionary ideologies and nuclear weapons on grand strategy development. The second part of the book explores the forces that shaped the development of American grand strategy by studying the policies of various presidential administrations. This analysis examines the administrations that made particularly critical contributions to grand strategy, beginning with the administration of George Washington and ending with the Bush and Obama administrations. The book concludes with a systemic framework of principles to govern American grand strategy in a world that has moved well beyond the ideas that governed foreign policy at the end of World War II.

I am deeply indebted to a group of individuals who made important contributions to this work. First, I would like to thank several colleagues at The Fletcher School, particularly Professors Richard Shultz, Robert Pfaltzgraff Jr., and Antonia Chayes and Dean Jim Stavridis, for their wisdom, support, and friendship. I am indebted to several anonymous reviewers whose critical comments and suggestions helped to sharpen the arguments and logic of this study. I also would like to thank Harry Kazianis at *The National Interest* for his insightful comments. A special note of thanks goes to Torrey Taussig, a doctoral student at The Fletcher School, for her critical insights and comments on the content and organization of the entire project. Her outstanding work had a decisive impact on this book. In addition, several graduate students at Fletcher – Nick Kenney (doctoral student), Jeff Bryan, Sean Duggan, Brennan Mullaney, and Sarah Schaffer – all made significant contributions to this work.

An enduring note of gratitude goes to my editor at Cambridge University Press, John Berger, whose support and encouragement were instrumental in bringing this project to completion. Having worked on three books with John, I deeply appreciate that he patiently gives me the time and freedom to finish the project at its own pace, and his wisdom and judgment are always immensely helpful. I also want to express a word of thanks to my copy editors for their unfailing attention to matters of logic, expression, and detail. All that being said, it is not possible to avoid the simple axiom that whatever shortcomings exist in this work are my responsibility.

Finally, I want to thank my wife, Dianne, for her love and support.

William C. Martel
Medford, Massachusetts
July 2014

1 Introduction

Why This Book on Grand Strategy?

There are several factors that influenced the decision to write this book on grand strategy. The first is the distinction that exists today with an earlier era in American foreign policy. From the late 1940s to the early 1990s, the U.S. grand strategy of containment was marked by a high degree of coherence that helped guide the conduct of foreign policy.[1] Several generations of American policy makers knew the fundamental purpose of the nation's foreign policy for dealing with the United States' central challenges and, more precisely, understood what had to be done to deal with them. The second factor, which features a dramatic contrast with the situation at present, is the corrosive effect on American foreign policy from the period of strategic incoherence that has prevailed since the collapse of the Soviet Union and the concomitant end of the Cold War. In the two decades since the early 1990s, it has been largely unclear what principles and purposes should guide the decisions of American policy makers as they deal with challenges to the nation.

With the end of the Cold War and the gradual collapse of the grand strategy of containment, the foreign policy establishment failed completely in its efforts to define a widely accepted and compelling successor grand strategy, much less broad concepts, to help the American people and their policy makers answer some of the fundamental questions about what choices to make in foreign policy. What is the condition in the world that we seek to achieve, what does the world look like that we want to help build and shape for future generations, at home and abroad, and what resources can we and should we devote to conducting American foreign policy to achieve these ends? Inherent in these larger questions is the matter of what our core interests are, what the most critical threats to the nation are, how we prioritize and counter them, and who our friends and allies are in our efforts to meet these challenges. In fundamental terms, grand strategy provides answers to all these and many other questions.

Despite operating without a coherent grand strategy, the United States has, since the early 1990s, found itself involved in numerous wars and humanitarian interventions, yet it has done so for reasons, while entirely plausible at the moment, that should be based explicitly on a clearly articulated strategy. However, one senses that American policy makers and the public have been operating on strategic autopilot as they make choices about where to intervene (Somalia, Haiti, Bosnia, Kosovo, Afghanistan, and Iraq, to name a few) and where not to intervene (Rwanda and Syria being two prominent examples). To complicate matters, American society is deeply polarized in terms of *what* the nation should do in its foreign policy. To a considerable extent, the nation and its leaders have lacked a basic consensus on grand strategy. Debates about grand strategy, war, and diplomacy reflect considerable confusion about the broad purposes that animate American foreign policy. This confusion is remarkable, and deeply distressing, when we consider the contrast with the broad consensus in the United States about the nation's grand strategy that existed in the decades following the end of World War II.

The third factor derives from these forces. The deep and persistent confusion and discord in the United States about the answers to the most basic questions about foreign policy is a source of weakness. In the end, there is no better way to resolve these questions than to begin at the beginning, which means to analyze what the United States ought to do in foreign policy, and this has its foundation in studying the intersection between grand strategy and the challenges that the United States faces in international politics. It is only then that the American people and their policy makers can reestablish some degree of order and coherence in the nation's foreign policy. This brings us to the purpose of this book, which is to conduct a high-level and systemic examination of the nature, meaning, and evolution of grand strategy; to use that framework to examine the broad patterns in American grand strategy; and then to examine where the United States is and is likely to find itself in its conduct of foreign policy.

What This Book Proposes to Do

This book explores several central questions about grand strategy that are critical to the scholarship on strategy and security and to the decisions of policy makers who confront practical decisions about what principles ought to guide the nation's foreign policy. The book is organized into three parts. Part I, Chapters 3 through 6, begins with a chapter on the conceptual foundations of grand strategy. It seeks to provide greater analytic clarity about the definition of grand strategy, describes its nature and utility for the state, and develops an analytical framework to help scholars and policy makers evaluate grand strategy – or what so often passes as such. The next two chapters examine the first two (out of four) historical eras in the evolution of grand strategy. Chapter 4 provides a brief overview of the ancient era of grand strategy as well as a more detailed discussion of the philosophical, military, and economic foundations of how states develop and conduct grand strategy in the modern era. Chapter 5 advances this logic by using several case studies to examine the success and failure of grand strategies – from the reign of Spain's Philip II to the fall of the Ottoman Empire – and thus to illustrate the practice of grand strategy in the modern era. Chapter 6 develops arguments about grand strategy along similar lines. This chapter examines the influence of the revolutionary and nuclear eras on grand strategy and also uses several case studies from those eras to make the applicable principles of grand strategy transparent.

Having established the analytic foundations of grand strategy in Part I, Part II of the book provides a detailed analysis of the evolution of grand strategy in the context of the conduct of American foreign policy, with case studies drawn from presidential administrations from George Washington to Barack Obama. What emerges from this study are patterns and themes that have animated the grand strategies of various states for millennia, which help draw particular attention to the principles and arguments that have shaped American grand strategy since the republic's inception.

Finally, Part III examines critical lessons learned about the conduct of grand strategy: the challenges for modern scholars and policy makers responsible for answering some of the most basic questions about how the United States should organize its foreign policy to deal with opportunities, aspirations, threats, and challenges to its interests and values. This book concludes with recommendations for articulating and implementing a grand strategy to help guide the decisions of the United States in the conduct of foreign policy in the early twenty-first century.

The narrative on grand strategy that unfolds in this book exists as two clearly separate elements or distinct tracks. The first focuses on the vast history going back millennia that encompasses the evolution of what we know as grand strategy, and the second examines the forces that have defined how the United States has defined its grand strategies in the past and present to help guide how modern policy makers make decisions about dealing with future challenges to the nation. The last chapter builds conceptual bridges between these case studies (which are drawn from several regions of the world), examines why these historical eras are crucial to understanding grand strategy, and outlines how they help inform the conduct of U.S. foreign policy.

A central argument in this book is to outline why, if the state's foreign policy is to be both successful and effective, it must derive from a coherent grand strategy. With its collection of case studies across several historical eras, this book will help inform how scholars and policy makers alike think about grand strategy as the nation moves forward to redefine grand strategy in the aftermath of the World War II and Cold War eras. The main purposes of this study are to show how grand strategy can be successfully articulated and implemented, and more generally how to move forward as nations seek to renew or redefine their grand strategy as a guide to the conduct of foreign policy. Essentially, the central purpose of this book is to look at grand strategy as a way to more broadly inform policy makers and scholars who are responsible for the formulation and implementation of American grand strategy. The audience for this study is scholars and policy makers as well as others who have a broad interest in the historical forces, trends, and ideas that influence how states formulate and implement grand strategy.

Why This Book Is Different

So many scholars and policy makers have examined the facets, contours, and principles of grand strategy that the subject is by no means new.[2] What is remarkable, however, is how unresolved the matter of grand strategy is in terms of providing an architecture for guiding the conduct of American foreign policy. For several reasons, this book about grand strategy differs from its predecessors.

To begin with, many studies of grand strategy focus on a discrete historical era, examining the nature of grand strategy as practiced by specific states in particular epochs. Others focus on the development of grand strategy in the twentieth century since World War II and the articulation of containment.[3] However, this study also discusses the historical foundations of grand strategy by examining the evolution of ideas that govern what we mean by grand strategy starting as far back as the governments in ancient Greece and China and encompassing both modern and contemporary approaches to grand strategy. Although the historical dimension is critical to developing the analytic foundations of grand strategy, it is critical for modern scholarship to explore how grand strategy has evolved across various historical eras. That is precisely how this study proceeds.

One reason for the failure to deal properly with grand strategy has been debates about the interrelationship between, and the failure to properly distinguish among, strategy, grand strategy, and foreign policy. To establish some definitional order, the term *foreign policy* as it is used in this study embraces all of the actions – guided by political, military, and economic objectives – undertaken by a nation in its relationships with other states. Some clarity about "strategy" is likewise in order. In practical terms, *strategy* for this study is the "science and art of using all the forces of a nation to execute the approved plans as effectively as possible during peace or war" as well as the "science and art of military command as applied to the overall planning and conduct of large-scale combat operations."[4] In recent centuries, the term *strategy* described the political, economic, and military means that policy makers use to accomplish the state's broad objectives.[5] In effect, strategy tells us *what* policies to pursue, whereas foreign policy is about the *how* to do so. Missing is the broad question of *why* the state pursues such policies using particular strategies, which is the precise function of grand strategy.

A central argument in this study is that grand strategy encompasses much more than war or military strategy, because it extends to all efforts undertaken by states to marshal their political, economic, and social resources to achieve a common goal. In practice, grand strategy incorporates all facets of state power, including notably domestic and economic policy, because these influence how the nation conducts its foreign policy. What this study seeks to develop is a deeper analytic basis for better understanding the theory and practice of grand strategy.

In its practical application, grand strategy is not and never has been simply about war or the conduct of war – in fact, war often represents a failure of grand strategy. Grand strategy goes far beyond war or the preparations for it, because it embraces all the actions and policies pursued by the state as it conducts foreign and domestic economic policies in both the short and long term. It also governs decisions about the state's priorities and capabilities. In theory and practice, grand strategy establishes and then balances the state's priorities in terms of the general framework within which the state accomplishes its foreign policy goals.

This Book's Core Arguments

This work develops a series of arguments that are central to understanding what grand strategy is, its promises and pitfalls, and the ways in which it helps policy makers make decisions about the political, economic, and military issues that confront the state as it conducts foreign policy.[6]

First, the evolution of grand strategy during the past several thousand years has been marked by significant and substantive trends in the history of strategy, warfare, and states. With these developments, the nature of grand strategy before the eighteenth century differs significantly from that existing since then. A critical factor in the evolution of grand strategy was the formation of the modern state and its impact on industrial warfare, as discussed in Chapter 4. This study examines the critical theorists and strategists whose ideas have contributed to the articulation and implementation of grand strategy since the times of ancient Greece and China, the formation of the modern state in the seventeenth century, the critical ideas and political philosophies that have influenced the evolution of grand strategy, and how changes in the conduct and technology of war throughout the centuries have shaped its foundations.

Second, grand strategy should and does, by its very nature, evolve and shift as the state's interests and the forces shaping the international system likewise change. Furthermore, when states undergo periods of change, particularly those that are dramatic, it is likely that their grand strategy similarly will (or should) change. With the end of the Cold War and the collapse of containment as the central organizing principle that guided the conduct of American foreign policy, the predictable outcome should be for the nation's grand strategy to undergo a period of renewal and redefinition.[7] Should a state not experience such a period of renewal of its grand strategy that puts it on a more prosperous and sustainable trajectory, it may enter a period in which its power and influence experience drift and decline.

Third, a state without an agreed-upon and coherent grand strategy will, as a matter of definition, suffer the penalties that follow from having a confused and chaotic foreign policy. The purpose of grand strategy is to define for policy makers the general goals that they want to achieve for the state and its role in the international system. In this sense, grand strategy provides a framework for outlining what kind of world the state seeks to build. What we arguably are witnessing in the case of the United States is the confusion that results when the state's grand strategy is in a period of flux. To remedy this failure, this study presents a clearer analytic basis for grand strategy as a way to smooth the transition to the emergence of principles that will help govern American foreign policy in the future. We also must consider the argument of whether states, particularly democracies, need an adversary to help stimulate how scholars and policy makers articulate and implement their grand strategy. Looking at the United States and its European allies in the aftermath of World War II is instructive, because it raises the question of whether they would have articulated such a coherent grand strategy without the pressure imposed and the focal point of attention provided by the Soviet Union. Later, the study considers the consequences that result from facing an adversary that is not a coherent and sovereign entity (as is the case with the current U.S. struggle with violent Islamic extremism).

Fourth, for those who follow the evolution of grand strategy and wonder about the forces that shape it, a central point is that grand strategy is defined by intense and often episodic debates among scholars and policy makers. Such debates, however, are likely to be more contentious in periods when the state is engaged in a redefinition and renewal of its grand strategy. Such is the case at this writing and likely will remain this way for the foreseeable future as individuals and communities struggle to answer pressing questions about foreign policy, notably what policies the state should pursue and why it should do so.

Lastly, the debate about grand strategy is not a surrogate for the argument that the United States is in decline or that the principles governing its grand strategy are similarly a prescription for managing America's decline.[8] To the contrary, this study advances the argument that the United States puts at risk the substantial economic and security advantages it now possesses if it fails to develop principles and precepts that build a coherent grand strategy while simultaneously providing some balance among its foreign and domestic priorities. The failure to advance such a grand strategy itself directly contributes to broad confusion about the role of the United States in world affairs as well as its domestic priorities.

Over time, states without a coherent grand strategy suffer from having a confused foreign policy, which contributes to shifting, confused, and discordant policies. American foreign policy since the end of the Cold War has suffered from a failure to articulate a coherent grand strategy, which is not a remnant of containment, and if this problem is not addressed, the United States will squander the ability to use its global power and influence to build a peaceful, prosperous, and stable twenty-first century. The effort to articulate a new grand strategy after the end of a major war or conflict is marked by a period of renewal and redefinition that, if successful, will generate a new set of long-term priorities to guide foreign policy and provide continuity in the midst of leadership changes. We can look at history to see different examples of states that were able to manage this period of renewal and redefinition successfully, just as others allowed themselves to drift into foreign policy incoherence and irrelevance.

This book is an effort to build the foundations of a process to renew and redefine grand strategy in a way that moves the discussion closer to constructive debates. Perhaps this process will help the United States and other nations forge a consensus on what their long-term international priorities should be and how to achieve them.

2 Contemporary Classics in American Grand Strategy

There are four disciplinary approaches to the study of American grand strategy. Each approach has a valuable contribution to make because each offers a different perspective on the key determinants of American grand strategy and then recommends certain policies on the basis of this analysis. The first approach is the study of grand strategy through the lens of American history. This historical approach is led by such academics as John Lewis Gaddis, Paul Kennedy, Walter Russell Mead, and Williamson Murray.[1] It could also be dubbed the Yale school of American grand strategy, since two of the professors (Gaddis and Kennedy) are in Yale's history department. They see the approach as developing not in accordance with some general social scientific theory, but evolving as part of the unique political, cultural, and social conditions that exist in each state.

In the second approach, social scientists study American grand strategy through the lens of theory. They use more deductive than inductive reasoning, which means that American grand strategy is best explained in terms of general theories rather than specific historical and evolutionary developments. Social scientists downplay, if not totally ignore, the exceptional nature of the United States as a government and treat it more or less like other states, each of which is rationally pursuing its own self-interest. Social scientists tend to treat states as equivalent and operating in an international system that is primarily characterized by the distribution of military and economic power. Although this represents an important level of analysis, it is not a complete framework for analyzing the evolution of grand strategy.

The third approach is the product of the practitioners – the policy makers who implement American grand strategy and find their role to go beyond simply articulating it. Their approach has the advantage of being deeply knowledgeable about the limits of implementation. Kissinger, for instance, has excellent insights into the role of domestic political traditions and institutions in shaping and constraining the options available to the nation's grand strategy. The drawback of the resulting works is that they tend to have a temporary relevance to the larger debate about American grand strategy because they are practically oriented to the more immediate concerns of the day. The practitioners often develop critical appraisals of the current administration's implementation of grand strategy rather than contextual analyses of the evolution of American grand strategy as a whole.

Finally, there are the military strategists. These are predominantly scholars who see grand strategy as primarily about, and through the lens of, military strategy. Their arguments are in the minority but nonetheless are very much worth noting, because they make a critical contribution to the debate about grand strategy. The military strategists' ideas link back to the early age of the evolution of grand strategy, the ancient to the modern, when the most important instrument of national power was, by and large, the military. As we will see later in this chapter, Robert Art defines *grand strategy* in terms of military capabilities and is one of the more influential thinkers about this approach to grand strategy.

This book is designed to draw from all four approaches. It takes from the historical approach the importance of understanding United States foreign policy as the product of unique historical experiences and conditions. It draws from the social scientists the conclusion that power remains a fundamentally important element of grand strategy. And it takes from the practitioners the need to be sensitive to domestic political and institutional factors as well as the willingness to engage with the policy-making community. Finally, the military strategic approach exerts significant influence in the sense that arguments about grand strategy often concern the proper deployment and use of military power globally.

Whereas all four approaches play an important role, the historical approach is still the most influential in terms of method. There is no substitute for examining history in detail, because although it does not necessarily repeat itself, it certainly rhymes, as Mark Twain put it.[2] Because patterns emerge, submerge, and reemerge, the purpose of this study is to reveal those patterns as they have slowly unfolded over many centuries of history and across continents. It is only by stepping back to see the broad sweep of historical evolution that we can understand what brings us to this point in the present and how best to position the United States for the future. This approach also is consistent with one of the purposes of the book, which is to help bridge the gap between how the scholarly and policy-making communities understand the evolution of grand strategy and its consequences for security.

The following review of the contemporary classics of grand strategy proceeds in three parts for each author. The first question is, How does this author approach and analyze American grand strategy? The second question is, Based on this approach and analysis, what are the author's recommendations for American grand strategy in the early twenty-first century? The third part provides a brief summary of how this book is similar to as well as different from these valuable and prior contributions to the study of grand strategy.

The Historians

Paul Kennedy's *The Rise and Fall of the Great Powers* is one of the most renowned studies of grand strategy. In it, Kennedy surveys 500 years of world history and tracks the patterns of interaction between economics and strategy in the rise and fall of modern empires, specifically the Ottoman, Dutch, Habsburg, Spanish, Napoleonic, and British Empires. His main finding is that each empire fell because of what he coins "imperial overstretch" (p. 515), which occurred not because of hubris or hyper-ambition, but because of a natural tendency of the Great Powers to face increasing numbers of security threats at the time when their share of the world economy is declining.[3] This "leads to the downward spiral of slower growth, heavier taxes, deepening domestic splits over spending priorities, and a weakening capacity to bear the burdens of defense."[4]

This downward spiral, however, though seemingly inescapable, does not exist as a historical necessity. His economic-historical approach leads to the recommendation that the United States should prioritize two principles if it is to prevent decline: first, it should keep its defense budget modest and manageable, and second, it should not overcommit itself in providing global security. In short, he recommends generally that the United States should strike a balance between its security ends and economic means.

The strength of Kennedy's approach is that it understands grand strategy within the context of the economic and political comparison of empires across centuries.[5] It benefits from a richly detailed analysis of broad economic indicators that portend long-term decline. The challenge with this approach lies in its application to the United States, since it is not a formal empire as are the subjects of the case studies he considers. The most similar case to the United States likely is that of the British Empire, but there remain significant differences. Thus, applying the lessons learned from Kennedy's book to American grand strategy in the early twenty-first century is problematic. For instance, unlike the cases of the Ottoman, Dutch, and Napoleonic Empires, the U.S. government does not have formal imperial frontiers to defend, and it has much more flexibility in its deployments of garrisons and basing.

Second, U.S. spending on defense has historically been much lower than that of most European empires. Kennedy shows that defense spending at the level of approximately 10 percent has historically been "excessive" and has led to imperial decline.[6] Yet, defense expenditures since the 1950s in the United States have declined from a high of around 10 percent to a post-9/11 average of under 5 percent of GDP.[7] The levels of defense spending that Kennedy cites as signaling unsustainability have not been seen in the United States since the 1950s and likely will not be seen anytime in the near future.[8] Kennedy, moreover, relies almost exclusively on more traditional indicators of domestic economic power: GDP growth rates, trade balance, and defense spending. One aim of this book is to understand the domestic sources of American national debt in several dimensions, including spending for infrastructure, innovation, and education, among other priorities.

John Lewis Gaddis is the preeminent American historian of the Cold War and therefore is broadly a crucial scholar of American grand strategy. His ideas, as with the arguments here, take the view that American grand strategy cannot be understood or analyzed apart from its deep traditions.[9] American grand strategy does not grow out of a single presidential administration, nor can it be implemented over such a short time horizon. By its very nature, grand strategy spans multiple presidencies and is deeply embedded in the diplomatic and military traditions of the United States. Thus, he argues that the grand strategy of one particular presidency – that of George W. Bush – has deeper roots than many assume.[10] Its reliance on primacy, preemption, and unilateralism, Gaddis argues, are not new, radical departures. They are based on old traditions of expansionism and preemption dating at least as far back as the Monroe Doctrine, when it established U.S. hegemony in the Western Hemisphere.[11]

What does Gaddis recommend American grand strategy should be in the early twenty-first century? Because he finds that George W. Bush's grand strategy as articulated in his 2002 National Security Strategy has deep historical roots in the American experience, he essentially advocates the Bush Doctrine as a grand strategy for the present. Nor is his defense without merit. He, for instance, demonstrates that George W. Bush actually *articulated* a grand strategy, in contrast to Clinton and George H. W. Bush, who left American grand strategy largely unstated and vague.[12]

Gaddis is right in his approach, but his conclusions leave considerable room for debate. While grand strategy does arise from deep historical roots in the American experience, his argument seems to exclude the possibility of evolution. The American tradition in grand strategy – as this book seeks to establish – is not static, but has evolved and will continue to evolve in response to the ever-changing political, economic, and security context of the times. His argument that Washington, Monroe, McKinley, and others were unilateralist uses a term from the twentieth century to understand the forces shaping grand strategy in the eighteenth and nineteenth centuries. These presidents were not thinking in terms of unilateralism versus multilateralism, but rather in terms of the basic survival of the Republic against threats both internal and external. The goal for the first phase of American grand strategy was not to act unilaterally for the purposes of altering the international system. By contrast, the essence of American grand strategy was always to stay sufficiently apart from, but to grow strong enough to fend off, European intervention.

This book differs from Gaddis's argument in two key respects. First, while Gaddis does not contrast the American tradition in grand strategy with Europe's, this book explores that relationship. True, America has responded to surprise attacks such as the burning of Washington, DC, in 1814, the Native American incursions on the frontier, and Pearl Harbor. But the central point is that the nation used these surprise attacks to stimulate a more activist foreign policy. Unlike the European experience, the evolution of American grand strategy as examined in this book does not have a bias toward transforming the international system in favor of establishing American hegemony.[13]

The second major counterargument that Gaddis could address is the explanation of the role of the slow and reluctant assertion of American hegemony in the early twentieth century. Unlike most European states, the U.S. government did not seek global hegemony, but reluctantly accepted it only after World War II eroded the power of all other Western candidates, especially Great Britain, and only after the threat of the Soviet Union required a superpower to counterbalance it. In short, a critical point from Gaddis's work is the distinction between a unilateralism of necessity and a unilateralism of choice. European grand strategy, especially on the Continent, has traditionally been a function of the latter, while American grand strategy has tended toward the former.

Walter Russell Mead offers an alternative and more comparative historical analysis of American grand strategy, because he includes the European experience.[14] He forcefully argues that American grand strategy cannot be understood apart from the American historical experience. Attempting to understand it in terms of what he calls the "Continental realism" of Europe's modern history is misguided. Continental realism rests on a set of assumptions that are not applicable to America. It assumes, for instance, that the balance of power in the system is the all-important calculation in grand strategy. It further assumes that the state – indeed, sometimes led by a small cadre of elite experts – constitutes the sole articulator and guiding implementer of grand strategy. In addition, the Continent has a long history of hegemonic bids for system transformation, since the time of Napoleon and culminating with Stalin. The United States, by contrast, does not share these assumptions or this experience in its foreign policy.[15] The arguments developed in this book align with this key point, which is that American grand strategy has its own unique traditions that derive from its exceptional history in the conduct of foreign policy.

However, the arguments here take a different view of the grand strategic traditions in American history. Mead describes four traditions: the Hamiltonian, Jeffersonian, Jacksonian, and Wilsonian. The Hamiltonian tradition is about building a strong alliance between big business and government, while the Jeffersonian tradition is one that looks inward as it seeks to safeguard democracy at home before engaging in expensive initiatives abroad. By contrast, the Jacksonian tradition focuses on the people's desire for basic security and economic prosperity, whereas the Wilsonian tradition is concerned with seeing American interests based morally in democracy. The latter prefers to spread democracy abroad instead of merely safeguarding it at home.[16] To be sure, all these ideas exist in American foreign policy, but they do not exert equal influence, nor do all of them rise to the level of traditions as argued here. Mead's argument, much like that of Gaddis, does not chart the *evolution* of American grand strategy as it rose in power and as the global context changed around and with it.[17] The purpose, here, of this study is to chart that evolution.

The historian Williamson Murray is the author and editor of a number of influential works on grand strategy. His critical works include *War, Strategy, and Military Effectiveness*, *The Shaping of Grand Strategy*, and *The Making of Strategy: Rulers, States, and War*.[18] Murray brings to bear the historian's perspective of judging grand strategy. For this scholar, the functions of grand strategy are to help the state deal with the most important challenges – notably to protect its citizens from the ravages posed by both short-term and long-term risks. It is with respect to the latter that the successful strategist will consider threats to the state that may occur in the future. As he writes, "some governments and their leaders have attempted to chart a course for their nations that have involved more than simply reacting to the course of events."[19]

For Murray, the first step in formulating grand strategy is to define precisely what we mean by that term. He is a proponent of the view that grand strategy is the domain of great states. In his words, "Grand strategy is a matter involving great states and great states alone." Murray's argument is that "no small states and few medium-sized states possess the possibility of crafting a grand strategy."[20] A second central argument for Murray is that a fundamental burden imposed on the state that practices grand strategy is the risk of overstretch. His reasoning, which parallels the arguments made by Paul Kennedy and many other prominent scholars of grand strategy, is that "strategy is about balancing risks [and] about insuring that the balance is right in those areas that matter most."[21] Third, he argues that truly effective grand strategies are designed to look and "act ... beyond the demands of the present." His view is that states and their leaders must take a "longer view" and must focus on the "great issue confronting them."[22] For Murray, great states that fail to follow these core principles of grand strategy will miss opportunities to relate the state's interests to critical developments in the world. With these ideas, this scholar makes critical, systematic contributions to the modern understanding of the evolution of grand strategy.

The Social Scientists

As noted previously in this chapter, the social scientists studying grand strategy reason deductively from theory to specific examples. They use generalized causal statements about the nature of international politics as a whole rather than about the nature of American political culture and history. Their goal is to explain grand strategy in universal terms, applicable across time and space, and to use these explanations to make predictions about the grand strategy and actions of states. The problem with this approach is that it tends to be reductionist. In its search for causal explanations, it misses the essential "ecological" nature of grand strategy, which rests on the necessity of seeing cross-disciplinary connections and contingencies. Nonetheless, these academics provide several conceptual insights.

Joseph Nye is perhaps the most famous social scientist to grapple with the current debates about American grand strategy. His work spans decades and is centered on the concept of soft power and its use of carrots and sticks in the form of economic incentives, as opposed to hard power's military force, to induce or coerce people to do something they would not otherwise do. He defines *soft power* as the power of attraction, the power to get someone to want the things you want.[23] It is noncoercive and not about material incentives but draws from varied sources, including diplomacy, persuasion, negotiation, and culture. The United States, he argues, possesses significant soft power resources in the attractiveness of its popular culture, its democratic values, and its economic success and reputation for being a place of opportunity and prosperity.[24] Nye advises U.S. policy makers to adopt a grand strategy that combines hard and soft power into what he calls "smart power," which uses contextual intelligence to exploit opportunities and adjust to context. Nye's theory also leads him to recommend that the United States does not need to view China's rise as threatening. He thinks realists who predict a U.S.-China conflict are falling victim to self-fulfilling prophecies because China's rise can be peaceful and not something that the United States can or should prevent.[25]

Nye's contribution is to see that power is not based solely on formalized structures, such as the economy and the military. It depends on ideas, leadership, and prestige, as well as the adaptability to context. The problem, however, is whether soft power is a cause or effect of a successful grand strategy. Nor is it clear how to measure and employ it as an instrument of national power over the long term. Furthermore, his concept of soft power is not placed within a specific historical context of American diplomatic history. When did the United States acquire soft power? Did different European states in their great power competition possess more or less soft power? Did soft power rise, decline, or stay steady through certain periods of American history? The answers to these questions remain unknown, and without the historical context, it is difficult to know how soft power has aided us in the past and how it can serve us in the future at the level of grand strategy.

John Mearsheimer is the foremost proponent of the offensive realist school of international relations theory. His basic argument is that great powers seek more and more power until they achieve hegemony in their own region, while preventing any other great power from becoming hegemonic in another region. Hegemony is the only way to achieve a stable level of security. Furthermore, the only reason states historically have stopped at regional hegemony is because of "the stopping power of water." The world's oceans are barriers to the projection of land power. Land power for Mearsheimer is the *sine qua non* of a state's overall national power because, without a large army, a state cannot be effective at the level of grand strategy.[26]

Mearsheimer, in the post–Cold War era, foresaw not the end of history as Francis Fukuyama argued, but a lull before the next great power confrontation, because great powers cannot help but compete militarily and violently. The unipolar moment of U.S. global hegemony is only a prologue to the next era in which a peer competitor or a coalition of states will balance against the United States to challenge its hegemonic status. China is the leading candidate to take on the role of challenger.[27] Mearsheimer's theory is clear, is concise, and offers useful insights and explanations of how grand strategy influences the behavior of some states.

The problem is that it rests on evidence largely from modern European history. It is a theory that does not account for changing global conditions. Realists tend to downplay historical development and instead emphasize the repeating patterns of political inter- action. One significant development is globalization, which has elevated the level of interdependence between great powers such as China and the United States. Indeed, Lawrence Summers argues that China and the United States are in a balance of financial terror, which arguably replaced the balance of nuclear terror.[28] China holds about $1 trillion in U.S. debt and cannot afford to dump all of it in order to wreck the U.S. economy. It is far too dependent on the American consumer market for its own economy. In effect, China and the United States are locked together for better or worse in a mutual hostage relationship. This is unlike the case of the European states on which Mearsheimer bases his theory, because the China-U.S. level of interdependence is unprecedented. One senses that for Mearsheimer, China and the United States are contemporary manifestations of the European great power states of the past.[29] This book makes the case that the traditions shaping American grand strategy make it different in ways that have always and will continue to shape U.S. foreign policy over the long term.

Robert Gilpin is the third social scientist used here who examines grand strategy through the lens of political economics.[30] His theory is arguably a generalized but more precise version of Paul Kennedy's historical thesis on the rise and fall of empires. Essentially, Gilpin's theory is that there are two inescapable laws of international relations. The first is the law of uneven growth, which holds that states do not rise in power at the same rate. States lose, maintain, or gain overall power (he defines *power* primarily in economic and military terms) at varying rates depending on the nature of technological innovation, economic competition, domestic politics, and trade. The second law is that of diminishing returns, which holds that hegemonic states tend to rise in power at slower rates or lose power relative to rising states. The reason is that the costs of maintaining the status quo rise more rapidly for the hegemon who carries the primary burden, while the domestic special interests of hegemons tend to capture resources that should be diverted to the interests of the state's grand strategy.[31] These two laws taken together specify that hegemons facing inevitable decline confront three options: to acquiesce, to reduce foreign and domestic demands on resources, or to wage a hegemonic war to eliminate rising rivals.[32] Gilpin argues that historically states have chosen the third option more often than not. As a result, he predicted a fairly high likelihood of a hegemonic war with the Soviet Union.[33]

This predictive failure is one problem with Gilpin's work. The other is that it treats states and the international system as stable, monolithic abstractions. One of the essential features of states is that they are rational actors that employ military and economic power when the benefits outweigh the costs, much like a firm would take a specified action as long as it promised more than the current net profit. An essential feature of the interna- tional system is that it is full of armed, rational actors involved in a zero-sum competition for prestige and power. This book critiques these premises heavily. Grand strategy is not purely a function of rational choice. Rather grand strategy is a function of foreign policy traditions, particularly in the case of states such as the United States that have a unique geopolitical advantage and a political culture that often emphasizes the attribute of exceptionalism. Similarly, the arguments in this book proceed from the premise that the international system is subject to change in its essential features. Power is not definable outside of a particular historical context, because it depends on a complex set of ideas, relationships, and structures.

Perhaps this underscores a significant problem with the social scientists' approach to grand strategy: they treat states as equivalent, monolithic, rational cost–benefit accountants and the international system's essential purpose as the distribution of military and economic power. Although this is part of the story and a necessary part for understanding grand strategy, it remains an incomplete framework for analyzing grand strategy.

The Practitioners

The practitioners do not suffer from reductionism. Because they are immersed in the daily grind of foreign policy making, they understand full well that grand strategy is not simply a product of rational cost–benefit analyses. And they have a deeper appreciation for the domestic bases of and constraints on effective grand strategic decision making in the American political system.

Henry Kissinger is the principal figure that straddles the academic and policy-making worlds of grand strategy. He is quite possibly the most influential American grand strategist in the twentieth century, second only to George Kennan. Their influence was far reaching and profound because they played crucial roles in both the articulation and implementation of American grand strategy. It is this dual-level role that gave them enduring prominence in the American foreign policy establishment. Kissinger wrote important scholarly texts, such as *A World Restored, Nuclear Weapons and Foreign Policy*; *Does America Need a Foreign Policy? Toward a Diplomacy for the 21st Century*; and his masterpiece, *Diplomacy*.[34] He was also a professor in Harvard's Department of Government before becoming President Nixon's national security advisor in 1968. He is the only person to serve in that post and as secretary of state concurrently, which he did from 1973 to 1975.

Kissinger is a preeminent American grand strategist, but the label deceives because he relies in part on a distinctly European view of America. He knows American politics intimately, but he sees it as an outsider, coldly objective and appreciative of its idiosyncrasies. For Kissinger, a grand strategy should follow the precepts of the balance of power as practiced in nineteenth-century Europe. The balance of power is about the equilibrium of the system, which remains stable as long as there is no revolutionary or revisionist power with the incentive and capability of upsetting the stability.[35] In *Diplomacy*, Kissinger laments that America's foreign policy traditions do not allow for the European-style practice of power politics. American voters believe that democratic values and norms, rather than simply national interest, should guide foreign policy. The proper practice of grand strategy, for Kissinger, comes from European history. His role models of grand strategic genius are Richelieu, Metternich, and Bismarck. American exceptionalism in its foreign policy is not something to be admired but avoided, because it leads to the extremes of isolationism or crusading interventionism.[36]

Furthermore, whatever may be said of Kissinger, he practiced what he published. Or, to employ the terms used in this book, he consistently implemented the policies that he articulated. As national security advisor and then secretary of state, he consistently sought to bring the concept of the balance of power back into a position of central influence in American grand strategy. Détente was an attempt to find equilibrium of influence with the Soviets. The withdrawal from Vietnam was conducted to minimize damage to the prestige of U.S. power. And, of course, Kissinger and Nixon's great move to reestablish diplomatic ties with China was part of a larger plan to create a flexible, multipolar system of balance among great powers that was driven not by ideology, but by their interest in preserving the status quo.[37]

Kissinger's oeuvre is unparalleled in its articulated clarity and consistency, and impressive in its implementation. But he lauds the European experience and dismisses and denigrates the U.S. tradition of grand strategy – to the detriment of his overall argument. Although Europe's balance-of-power system enjoyed a century of success after the Napoleonic Wars, it failed ultimately, setting the stage for two horrendous world wars. Kissinger would argue that this was because European statesmen forgot the importance of maintaining and respecting the balance of power.[38] Bismarck's ouster as chancellor by Kaiser Wilhelm II in 1890 was a momentous blunder in terms of Kissinger's underlying theory because it removed from the scene the one man who understood how to satisfy German ambitions without triggering a European civil war. Indeed, the concept of the balance of power has an alluring and comforting connotation, but it relies very heavily on deft diplomacy and the sure-mindedness of diplomatic geniuses. This reliance is arguably misplaced and has led to more instability and bloodshed in the international system. Niall Ferguson, for instance, persuasively argues that the British insistence on maintaining the balance of power on the Continent that led it to intervene in World War I was unnecessary and foolish. It transformed what could have been a short, regional war into a long and destructive world war.[39] In addition, advocates of the European style of balance-of-power politics see diplomacy and grand strategy as having universal rules whose application transcends history and geography.

This book argues the opposite. America's experience in grand strategy has been remarkably more successful than Europe's, but that success is in part due to a preference of the American public that the U.S. government not pursue idealistic crusades abroad. Kissinger overrates the amount of influence of Wilson's idealism on the American public's perception of foreign policy. This argument is explored in Chapter 8 in a discussion of how American grand strategy rose to power in the early nineteenth century.[40] Moreover, the deeper argument here is that grand strategy is not a purely rational enterprise, neatly separable from its political and historical context. It arises from a state's traditions and geopolitical attributes and is embedded in its institutions. Grand strategy does not depend on one person or a small group of elites. This is particularly true of America, and it has served the nation well, contrary to Kissinger's view. Finally, Kissinger's elevation of nineteenth-century European diplomacy as the gold standard of grand strategy ignores the basic fact that the twenty-first century provides a much different economic, political, technological, and cultural context.[41]

Zbigniew Brzezinski shares many similarities with Kissinger. Both are from the cockpit of European conflict – Kissinger was born in Bavaria, Brzezinski in Warsaw. Both were on the Harvard Department of Government faculty in the 1950s. Both view grand strategy as having universal rules that were developed in Europe. And both served as national security advisors in the turbulent 1970s when American power was viewed as in decline – Kissinger for Presidents Nixon and Ford from 1968 to 1975 and Brzezinski for President Carter from 1977 to 1981. But they are different in terms of their grand strategic outlooks and their recommendations for American foreign policy in the twenty-first century.

Whereas Kissinger is the quintessential scholar and practitioner of realpolitik, Brzezinski is a proponent of classical Mackinderesque "geopolitik."[42] Mackinder argued in the early twentieth century that grand strategy must be understood in terms of the relationship between geography and political power. For Mackinder, and thus Brzezinski, the Eurasian land mass is the center of the global chessboard.[43] The state that controls the heartlands of Eurasia – Eastern Europe and the Ukraine – is the state that has the basis for establishing hegemonic power. To be sure, Brzezinski realizes that the "heartland" thesis needs updating.[44] In *Strategic Vision*, he observes an unprecedented shift in the geostrategic center of gravity from West to East. Nonetheless, he maintains that the Middle East and Central Asia are the most important geostrategic areas, where the threats are most pressing. The heartland, then, has shifted to the east, but not that far. He does not agree with other commentators that China and the Pacific Rim will be the key power and financial centers of the near future.[45]

There are several areas of overlap between Brzezinski's work and this book. Brzezinski is right to note the troubling and long-standing drift in American foreign policy post-Cold War. Furthermore, his critique of post–Cold War presidents is very much in line with the views developed in Chapter 10 of this work.[46] His recommendations are quite similar to those proposed by Joseph Nye in which America needs to manage the global commons and provide public goods that allow for stability, peace, and prosperity. Unlike Nye and the arguments in this book, Brzezinski places a very strong emphasis on the nuclear proliferation issues of Central and Southwest Asia, and sees, for example, Russia and Turkey as pivotal states that must be incorporated into an enlarged concept of the West.[47]

This book departs from Brzezinski in terms of the analytical lens. He uses a concept of geopolitics that prioritizes threats and regions, whereas the arguments in this book rest on the idea that the sources of disorder – whether financial instability, terrorism, state failure, or nuclear proliferation – are more systemic and global than geographic and regional. Second, Brzezinski is Europeanist in the sense that he agrees with Kissinger that European diplomacy set a very high standard for making proper decisions about grand strategy. American foreign policy traditions are ignored for the most part, but they need to be understood if they are to be employed properly, as this book argues.[48] Finally, Brzezinski is much more pessimistic about the decline in relative American power because he sees the beginning of the end of American global hegemony as already underway.[49] The argument in this book, however, is that it is too early to make such a judgment and the outcome depends very much on whether the problem of drift in grand strategy can be resolved.

The final practitioner-scholar is Richard Haass. A senior National Security Council staffer for the Middle East during the First Gulf War and director of policy planning in the State Department during the Second Gulf War, Haass is currently the president of the Council on Foreign Relations. Having written widely on current issues in American grand strategy,[50] his newest book is *Foreign Policy Begins at Home*.[51] He is not unlike Brzezinski in this skepticism toward the efficacy of military power. But his recent prescription for America's grand strategic drift is for American policy makers to prioritize rebuilding the domestic foundations of American power to the near exclusion of dealing with external sources of disorder and maintaining alliances and strengthening local partners. His best book, however, is probably his memoir, *War of Necessity, War of Choice*, in which he uses just-war theory to analyze the quality of decision making on whether to use military force.[52] The First Gulf War was a war of necessity because it satisfied several just-war criteria: the cause was worthy (reestablishing regional stability in a crucial region, liberating an occupied territory and its people, and upholding the norm against unprovoked military aggression), there was a likelihood of success (a clear, defined objective of liberating Kuwait and protecting Saudi Arabia), and the legitimacy of authority was present to undertake the use of force (the United Nations along with a broad-based coalition, which included Syria). The Second Gulf War, by contrast, did not satisfy these criteria.[53]

Haass's use of just-war theory as a practical but not a moral guide for the use of force in U.S. foreign policy is laudable but only partly contextualizes this theoretical framework within American diplomatic history. The worthiness of the cause, for instance, depends not only on abstract definitions of U.S. vital interests, but relies heavily on those international norms that are inviolable in American foreign policy. Territorial conquest has a long history in European interstate relations. In American foreign policy, by contrast, territorial conquest and the annexation of other nation-states have always been regarded as unacceptable.[54] In other words, the contours of what constitutes a just or unjust war depend on the traditions established in a nation's grand strategy. This is an argument that Haass does not develop directly, but the current book implicitly raises the issue.

The Military Strategists

The final group in this review of literature is the military strategist camp, which has a particularly narrow but immensely important view of grand strategy. Robert Art defines grand strategy as the proper long-range and long-term use of military power for achieving all of the nation's foreign policy goals. For Art, foreign policy is the highest level of strategy because it concerns not only the use of military force, but also the use of all instruments of national power.[55] His prescription for American grand strategy is called "selective engagement," the grand strategy of military interventions in the most important parts of the world, which he designates as Europe, Northeast Asia, and the Middle East.

The strength of Art's approach is in its insistence on setting priorities. He offers a practical set of policies for preventing the imperial overstretch that Kennedy and Gilpin warn that all hegemonic powers are likely to experience. The weakness of the military strategic view is that it misconstrues grand strategy as the use of military power. This is critiqued in more detail later in this chapter, but the key point is that military power is actually less important in today's world than it was in the nineteenth and twentieth centuries. Economic, diplomatic, informational, and, to some extent, what Nye calls "soft power," are equally if not more important for influencing political outcomes.

Colin S. Gray is a British American historian and scholar of grand strategy whose most influential books are *War, Peace and International Relations*; *Modern Strategy*; and *Strategic Studies and Public Policy*. The one most relevant to American grand strategy is *The Sheriff: America's Defense of the New World Order*.[56] In this work, he uses the image of America as the guarantor of world order and stability much as a sheriff enforced law and order in the American West.[57] This image of America's role in the world is apt in some respects, while deeply flawed in others. First, it is apt in the sense that the world is much like the "Wild West" of the late nineteenth century. The rule of law is tenuous. Low-intensity violence and crime are constant, and the overarching sovereign state is one of many players attempting to assert itself politically. But it is wrong in the sense that in the world there is no shared sense of "law and order" and the values that they represent. A sheriff has the benefit of a citizenry who agree largely on what is best for the town – murders, stealing, drunken disorderliness, and random violence are clear violations of norms. Such is not the case in the international system. This is arguably changing over time, but America's role defined as the world's policeman implies that it has a monopoly on the legitimate use of violence for enforcing a set of legal norms that the vast majority of the population accepts. This is simply not the case in international relations. It is no surprise, then, that Gray dismisses the significance of intergovernmental organizations and alliances such as the United Nations.

Gray is on stronger ground with respect to the two major contributions of his work: the concept of strategic history and the relationship between technology and strategy.[58] He defines *strategic history* as "the history of the influence of the use and the threat of force."[59] Gray argues that strategic decision makers filter strategic options through "values, attitudes, and preferences derive[d] from a typically national, or tribal, process of historical education."[60] The idea of strategic history is used as a point of departure in this book for developing the concept of the history of grand strategy – the history of the behavior of states articulating their grand strategic aims and employing all the instruments of national power to implement them. This perspective provides a broader look at the evolution of grand strategy as a whole instead of limiting it only to the use or the threat of using military force. In addition, Gray notes a tension between the idea of strategy understood as a cross-cultural, universal discipline with a certain set of rules and the idea that strategy is inseparable and deeply conditioned by its political and cultural context.

The argument in this book rests on the latter idea – that strategy is historically and culturally conditioned. It depends on the state's particular geopolitical realities and the values of its people. As for technology, Gray is squarely against technological determinism, the theory that the technological innovations in military capabilities determine whether and how states wage war and whether technology shapes grand strategy.[61] Weapons are neither inherently offensive nor defensive, but depend on the intentions and strategies of the policy makers that use them. These intentions and strategies are determined by policy and politics and not by purely military considerations. Here, technology is also taken not as a determining factor, but as one that has to be considered in its political and grand strategic context.

The final military strategist examined here is Stephen Peter Rosen, whose most recent book is *Winning the Next War: Innovation and the Modern Military*.[62] His main argument is that military operational and technological innovations are very different from each other. Operational innovations are much easier in peacetime because there is more time to consider the nature and extent of enemy threats. In wartime, the lessons might not be obvious while commanders have a stronger preference for routine deviations from standard operating procedures. Technological innovations occur more commonly because of the perceived demands of the current or expected battlefield as those perceptions are shaped by intelligence estimates.[63]

Rosen's recommendations for American grand strategy, however, transcend his theoretical work on military innovation. He contends that the U.S. military should develop an ability to innovate and adapt at the time of a crisis. The U.S. government cannot afford to have a full range of off-the-shelf capabilities ready to go for every probable contingency.[64] The question, however, becomes, How does one foster the values of innovation and flexibility into military institutions that are built around rigidity and routine? Moreover, how much flexibility will be needed at the different levels of strategy? Flexibility in grand strategy is different from military strategic flexibility, which in turn is different from operational or doctrinal flexibility. Finally, this book argues that flexibility in grand strategy is more limited than a rational choice theorist would argue. In America, it is limited by its grand strategic traditions, which cannot be abandoned, ignored, or fundamentally altered in the short term. They are too deeply embedded in the value system of the electorate and in national security institutions. Instead, Rosen deals with the necessity of prioritization of capabilities as he estimates the amount of flexibility possible.[65]

Summary of Contemporary Classics in American Grand Strategy

This book is interdisciplinary in approach, but it relies most on the work of the historians and the practitioners. It is meant for both an academic audience that studies grand strategy as a historically conditioned phenomenon as well as for policy-making audiences who are grappling with how U.S. foreign policy should be shaped and operated within the complex, interdependent world of the twenty-first century. The social scientists are useful for specific conceptual insights – e.g., Nye's concept of "soft power," Mearsheimer's concept of "the stopping power of water," and Gilpin's law of uneven growth and law of the diminishing returns of hegemony.

There is, however, a fatal weakness in treating states as functionally equivalent units. They are very different, as this book maintains. Moreover, America's distinctiveness lies in the exceptionalism of its grand strategic history, which reflects the important contribution that the military strategists make to this study. The reason is that this work incorporates the military strategic approach but then builds beyond it to include a perspective that is in line with forces at play in the twenty-first century, in which other influences outside the military are addressed. These influences include such powerful examples as culture, values, and institutions, among others. These forces are well worth mentioning because the use and threat of force traditionally encompasses one of the most vital issues of grand strategy, dating as far back as Sun Tzu, who wrote as follows in the opening line of his famous treatise: "The art of war is of vital importance to the State. It is a matter of life or death, a road either to safety or ruin." Thus, military force remains an indispensably important part of the intellectual and policy traditions of grand strategy.

PART I

Makers of Grand Strategy

3 Foundations of Grand Strategy

The term *grand strategy* is relatively new to the lexicon of international politics and policy. To understand its meaning, it is essential to keep in mind that it is not a term that scholars of international relations and practitioners of statecraft have employed since the early origins of the literature on strategy and politics. To be sure, merely because the term did not exist in earlier times does not mean that we cannot use it retroactively to understand state policies during, for example, the Roman Empire. Edward Luttwak, in his famous study *The Grand Strategy of the Roman Empire*, does exactly that and achieves some fascinating, if heavily critiqued, insights into Roman political and military trends over time.[1]

The term *grand strategy*, if we export it to the past, has to be handled with some degree of sensitivity to the historical context. What was the nature of the state during this time period? What were the state's primary political purposes – e.g., security, prosperity, or justice? What was the range of the state's capabilities? What was the nature of the international system? The challenge is that thinkers and practitioners of grand strategy have not used the term in the same way and with the same meaning consistently through time. It has evolved, changed, and altered its meaning as the purpose of the state has changed, the breadth of its capabilities have expanded or narrowed, and the essential features of the international system have shifted. The threshold for inquiry into grand strategy, then, begins with defining the term in a precise, coherent, and contextualized fashion.

This chapter is intended to unify analytically the historical overview of the strategists, theorists, and case studies on grand strategy that are presented in this book. The discussion provides a simple descriptive overview and analysis of the "who, what, when, why, where, and how" of grand strategy. Who made grand strategy in Sun Tzu's time versus Clausewitz's time, for example? What did it consist of? Why was it made? Where and how – i.e., in what institutional context and with what processes – was it made? When did states tend to make it, revise it, discard it, etc.? The discussion also traces the evolution of the meaning, the practice (articulation and implementation), and the dimensions (political, economic, military, technological) of grand strategy. The purpose is specifically to highlight the central contributions that strategists and practitioners have made to our modern understanding of "grand strategy," while identifying the signposts that allow us to mark the long evolutionary development of grand strategy in the historical chapters that follow.

The chapter is organized into three parts. The first part explains how the term *grand strategy* grew out of the study of *strategy*, examines why these two terms are easily confused, and provides a detailed definition and analysis of grand strategy and its constituent elements. The second and third parts examine the two fundamental dimensions of grand strategy – what we call articulation and implementation – and establish the basic analytic framework for the study and evaluation of grand strategy. The concept of the articulation of grand strategy has three features: first, grand strategy and strategy must define and represent unified objectives and goals for the state; second, grand strategy is an ongoing, continuous process of articulation and revision that operates at all times along the war-peace continuum; and third, the elements that contribute to grand strategy – notably, policy, doctrine, strategy, and operations – must be properly distinguished and kept in alignment if a grand strategy is to be effective. The process of the implementation of grand strategy consists of two features: first, marshaling the domestic foundations of national power to strengthen the state's long-term interests, and second, the ability of the state to balance means and ends.

Origins of Grand Strategy

The first part of this chapter explains how the terms *strategy* and *grand strategy* are easily confused if we are discussing a time period in which the only source of state power was essentially its military, a situation that lasted until the nineteenth century. The other sources of power (economic, diplomatic, and informational) existed in one form or another, but the institutions for the accumulation and application of these types of power were relatively underdeveloped and miniscule compared to the advancement and strength of the state's military institutions. Thus, *strategy*, though it has traditionally meant for Earle "the art of military command, of projecting and directing a campaign," was synonymous with *grand strategy* when the state's main purpose was to project and direct military force against internal and external threats.[2] The result is that these terms (strategy and grand strategy) are easily confused if policy makers and strategists lack a proper awareness of the historical period and context.[3]

To be sure, some ancient theorists and practitioners can be considered "grand strategists" – e.g., Sun Tzu, Thucydides, Machiavelli, and Clausewitz. But that does not change the fact that they focused primarily on the military dimension of state power. For them, military power was the central, anchoring type of state power. Sun Tzu was a military commander. Many people read his *Art of War* for the sage strategic advice that transcended its original and narrowly defined military context. Yet, we should not forget that his *Art of War* is first and foremost about war and how to win one – ideally, how to win without fighting. It is not about business, leadership, strategy, or grand strategy, but governs the proper practice of the art of warfare at various levels of interaction ranging from the tactical to the strategic. This does not mean that Sun Tzu was not a theorist on grand strategy, only that he did not set out to write a book about grand strategy in the sense that we understand the term today.

The same holds true for Thucydides, Machiavelli, and Clausewitz, who are grand strategists implicitly but not explicitly. Thucydides is perhaps the closest we come to an ancient grand strategist, but his book, it should be remembered, is about the conditions prevailing in a particular war. It is much more than a military history, of course, but at its core it is concerned with politics in the midst of a terrible war between great powers. It is not about grand strategy in general, but about how war and military force have defined the scope of grand strategy for most of human political history. It is only recently that grand strategy has expanded boldly beyond the confines of the conduct of war and the use of the military. In short, for most of its history the language of grand strategy was inseparable from the language of strategy and war.

When did it emerge as a distinct concept? Who was the first person to coin the term? The origins of the term are obscure, but we do know that in the early phases of World War II, American and British thinkers began to conceive of how to think about strategy in more holistic terms as the war unfolded. These scholars, many of whom were primarily academics, saw a great, unmet need in their respective polities: the need for a grand strategy that looked forward to the peace after military victory, that considered that the best way to conduct war was to create a peace that would endure, unlike the failed peace of World War I, which in their minds led directly to the causes of the World War II. They saw that *strategy*, which had become too narrowly defined in terms of militarily defined ends and means, needed to look beyond the end of military victory and employ means beyond the armed services. And these scholars were living in a time when the modern nation-state had reached its full industrial might. The economic base of war and its crucial role in determining long-term strategic outcomes was clear and recognized, much more so than in World War I, when states did not anticipate the protracted struggle that it would become. Unlike in August 1914, when European leaders and their societies thought the war would be over by Christmas, in September 1939 all sides had a much better sense of the exhausting marathon of violence and suffering that lay ahead.

Economic power has moved to the center of strategy and so, too, did social power or the societal base for war. This power base had been expanding since the time of Napoleon, but it became even more central to a state's conduct of war as the civilian population base not only supplied the labor, military recruits, technological capabilities, and political support on the home front, but also became a direct part of the fighting itself as strategic bombing and other military strategies designated civilian populations as primary targets. In sum, at the opening of World War II, the modern industrialized state had a broader range of capabilities that relied more closely on society. As a consequence, *grand strategy* acquired the meaning it has today, which essentially expresses the highest level of strategy where all types of national power are mobilized to achieve the state's highest political ends. But the thinking about this type of grand strategy as a product of a diversified set of power resources was quite limited, if not nonexistent. The reason is that, although some scholars eventually stepped forward to fill the breach, most of the grand strategists were essentially from the ranks of war strategists.

Prominent among the former were H. A. Sargeaunt, Geoffrey West, and the founder of modern grand strategy, Edward Mead Earle. Sargeaunt and West published *Grand Strategy* in 1941; Earle published *Makers of Modern Strategy* in 1943.[4] Both of these works established the foundations for defining and conceptualizing what we mean in modern terms by grand strategy. Sargeaunt and West's book defines a state's grand strategy "as the highest type of strategy" (13), and as a product of the state, its society, and political values. Not every state, society, and value system can produce any possible grand strategy, because it depends on the nature of these factors, as Sargeaunt and West hold: "War and society condition each other" (7). The state and society set the parameters for the possible grand strategies that can be pursued. As Sargeaunt and West go on to argue, the grand strategies of the Allied powers reflected a different set of values from those of the Axis powers, for example, on the role of war in achieving the state's political ends. For the Axis powers, war was essential to their domestic and foreign policies. War was seen as a positive process for political consolidation of power at home and the expansion of power abroad. In contrast, the Allied powers saw war as a necessary but not preferred element of grand strategy. If war had to come, then let it do so, but the Allied powers did not articulate or promote grand strategies that rested on the premise of seeking war.[5]

Earle's classic work is even more instructive on the nature of modern grand strategy. His *Makers of Modern Strategy* draws the distinction between the historically narrow definition of strategy as the art of military command and the projecting and directing of campaigns and the broader definition that is more relevant to the problems faced at present by the industrialized state.[6] His definitional discussion is worth quoting at length because it slices through the confusion over strategy and grand strategy:

> Strategy deals with war, preparation for war, and the waging of war. Narrowly defined, it is the art of military command, of projecting and directing a campaign. It is different from tactics – which is the art of handling forces in battle – in much the same way that an orchestra is different from its individual instruments. Until about the end of the eighteenth century strategy consisted of the body of strategems and tricks of war – *ruses de guerre* – by which a general sought to deceive the enemy and win victory. But as war and society have become more complicated – and war, it must be remembered, is an inherent part of society – strategy has of necessity required increasing consideration of nonmilitary factors, economic, psychological, moral, political, and technological. Strategy, therefore, is not merely a concept of wartime, but is an inherent element of statecraft at all times. Only the most restricted terminology would now define strategy as the art of military command. In the present-day world, then, strategy is the art of controlling and utilizing the resources of a nation – or coalition of nationals – including its armed forces, to the end that its vital interests shall be effectively promoted and secure against enemies, actual, potential, or merely presumed. The highest type of strategy – sometimes called grand strategy – is that which so integrates the policies and armaments of the nation that the resort to war is either rendered unnecessary or is undertaken with the maximum chance of victory. It is in the broader sense that the word strategy is used in this volume.[7]

The scholars from the 1940s established the definitional groundwork for grand strategy, but their work has not led to a clear consensus among scholars as to the essential elements of the definition. There are three definitional approaches taken since the 1940s. The first is the one that establishes the roots of grand strategy in the problems and language of war. A second and closely related approach defines grand strategy in terms of its relationship within a hierarchy of concepts that define how states interact in strategic terms. And the third approach, the one favored in this book, is to understand grand strategy in its broadest, political, and hence nonmilitary sense.

War-Centric Definitions of Grand Strategy

The famed military historian and theorist, B. H. Liddell Hart, published his classic *Strategy: The Indirect Approach*, in which he defined grand strategy in terms of its role in coordinating and directing as "all the resources of a nation, or band of nations, towards the attainment of the political object of the war – the goal defined by fundamental policy."[8] In later editions, he revised the definition to allow for a political end that was not necessarily limited to war aims: "Strategy is concerned with the problem of winning military victory"; in contrast, "grand strategy must take the longer view – for its problem is the winning of the peace," or at least the efforts for achieving peace in the long term.[9] Yet, the emphasis on grand strategy as war strategy remains, nonetheless, a prominent theme in his work. This is unsurprising given his experience as a soldier in World War I and his extensive study of armored warfare in the interwar years.

Robert Art's definition of grand strategy is military-centric in the opposite sense and includes "the full range of U.S. foreign policy *ends*, both security and non-security in nature, but restricts the *means* considered to purely military ones."[10] Terry Deibel critiques Art's definition of grand strategy, which "is so narrow that it appears to differ little from the [military's or Joint Chiefs of Staff's] definition of military strategy." However, it encompasses the "national political objectives that the military strategist merely accepts as [those] handed down from higher authority."[11] One strength of the narrower definition of grand strategy is that it emphasizes the specific policies and instruments of power that the state must use as it implements its foreign policy.

In both cases, however, the narrow approach to the definition is outdated and departs too radically from the foundations that Sargeaunt, West, and Earle laid down in their definitions of grand strategy in the early 1940s.

The Hierarchy of Strategic Interactions

Edward Luttwak is the leading scholar on the hierarchical approach to defining grand strategy. His definition is useful for understanding grand strategy in relation to other levels of strategic interactions. The problem, however, is that these other levels of strategic interaction rely on military terminology. So, again, the language of grand strategy becomes intertwined with the language of military strategy, which can cause and remains a source of confusion. Nevertheless, it is worth reviewing Luttwak's hierarchy, as expressed in the subsequent chart, to clarify the place of grand strategy in relation to the competing domains of strategy, operations, tactics, and technology.

Luttwak argues that these levels "form a definite hierarchy" but do not imply that policy outcomes are directly or linearly "imposed in a one-way transmission from top to bottom." The reason, for these scholars and theorists, is that these levels directly "interact with one another" in various and often unpredictable ways to form some coherent whole that modern audiences understand as the field of grand strategy.[12] As discussed later, the concept of grand strategy, which is the product of these principles and ideas, directly influences whether scholars and policy makers define grand strategy in narrow or broad terms.

The Technological Basis of Grand Strategy

If we begin at the narrowest level, the argument is that grand strategy is shaped by technological or technical factors, which include "having special practical knowledge of a mechanical or scientific subject."[13] In this sense, the technical meanings and "effects" matter to the extent that they have "tactical" consequences for policy.[14]

These technical foundations of grand strategy have a critical effect on what choices policy makers believe are realistically available to the state.[15] In the study of grand strategy, this technical level of strategy has its own "importance [which may be more critical] now ... than in the past when change was slow and differences in technical capacities were of much smaller effect."[16] In practical terms, whatever principles of grand strategy policy makers articulate should never be divorced or isolated from the technical foundations of the state's capacities, particularly those scientific and technological foundations from which the state's power and influence derive to some extent. One risk, however, occurs when policy makers overestimate the extent to which new technologies can solve problems that arise with grand strategy. In effect, there are distinct "limits" to the relevance that technical matters have for the conduct of grand strategy as well as the other levels that exist in strategy.[17]

In the contemporary debate about post–Cold War grand strategy and its relationship to military strategy, one example of the relevance of the technical level is the argument made in 2009 by the former secretary of defense Robert Gates about defense strategy. When Gates discussed Pentagon procurement choices, he argued that "we will pursue greater quantities of systems that represent the '75 percent' solution instead of smaller quantities of '99 percent,' exquisite systems."[18] In this sense, the technical level of strategic interaction includes procurement strategies over the long term, while purely technical matters of strategy should be subordinated to broader political conditions. In this example, these political conditions include the advent of tighter budgetary restraints as governments make deep cuts in defense spending.

A related problem with relying on the technical level in shaping strategy is the "chronic dissonance" that exists between the technical and political spheres. This dissonance exists because states' political aims usually are "so distant and vague" that they do not "enter into [the technician's] calculations."[19]

The Tactical Level

In practice, the technical level of strategy has significant, but nonetheless limited, consequences for the state's grand strategy. One reason is that the next step in formulating grand strategy rises to the tactical level, which focuses on how "lesser" factors influence the ways in which policy makers articulate and implement policies. The concept of "tactical," which derives from "actions or means that are distinguished from those of strategy," is "less importan[t] to the outcome of a war" or to strategy in general.[20] In effect, this refers in the shorter term to the "science and art of disposing and maneuvering troops, ships, or aircraft in relation to each other and the enemy and of employing them in combat." It also includes "the art or skill of employing available forces" in order to achieve the "end [or strategy] in view."[21]

The origins of the term *tactical* derive directly from historical works articulated by strategists and leaders who, since the rise of ancient civilizations in China and Greece, have used this word in describing how states succeed in strategy, diplomacy, and war by making fine adjustments to the balance of power.[22] For a classic definition of *tactical*, a useful and "generally accepted criterion" or construct is the "general possession of the battlefield."[23] More elaborate definitions emphasize the tactical nature of strategy in the conduct of warfare. For example, during the Middle Ages, "decisive factors [included] disciplined troops and good leadership, quick thinking and the ability to make the most of an advantage, and an awareness of what one's forces could be expected to achieve."[24] In this study, tactical events signify or symbolize the extent to which smaller-scale actions or developments align with and thus support the larger purposes articulated in the state's grand strategy.[25]

Despite the overwhelming emphasis on military strategy and procedures that is evident when policy makers use the term *tactical* – for instance, Luttwak describes tactical skill as the "ability to make good use of terrain and weapons at hand" – the tactical level itself nonetheless has a significant effect on how policy makers articulate the state's grand strategy. When considering the tactical level of strategy, it is essential to understand how the "intangibles of skill, leadership, morale, discipline, and unit cohesion" (note the consistent usage of language in ways directly reminiscent of the field of military strategy) influence the state's articulation and implementation of grand strategy.[26] Of greater relevance to grand strategy is that the tactical level embraces the unique context of the "human dimension" and the role of "chance and probability."[27]

The Operational Level

In developing a more precise understanding of the concepts that influence the development of grand strategy, the next step for theorists and practitioners is to consider the "operational" level. In effect, the operational level – for scholars, such as Luttwak – embraces the "detailed particularities of context," which become less important as scholars and policy makers consider the higher levels of strategy. This level includes the "full array of rival forces" (political, economic, military, and technical, among others), rather than simply the forces "immediately opposed." The operational level in strategy deals with how campaigns and major operations, including policy initiatives, are planned, conducted, and sustained to accomplish the state's broader objectives.[28]

The operational level of strategy exemplifies the "middle level of thought and action" in which "generic methods of war contend and battles unfold in their totality."[29] For the strategist, the operational level focuses on disrupting the "entire supporting structure of the defense [and] unbalancing ... [its] command decisions," in order to cause the adversary to "misdirect" its counterattacks and have "disorganizing effect[s]" on its policies and actions.[30] For policy makers, what distinguishes the operational level of strategy from the technical and tactical levels is that the details are subordinated to the wider strategic situation. For the conduct of grand strategy, the role of the operational level is to ensure that activities and events are not "autonomous," but are tightly "governed ... by the broader interaction" of "armed forces" that exists "within the entire theater of warfare." Put differently, this governs the role of the state's resources in the conduct of strategy. To understand grand strategy on the operational level, the analogy "battles are merely parts of campaigns" is appropriate.[31] This means that actions are subordinated to broader policies, thus ensuring a close relationship between actions and goals.

In looking beyond the functional dimensions of strategy, the consequence for scholars and policy makers who articulate grand strategy is that it should be guided by a hierarchical process in which they build their strategy in a rational and progressive fashion from the technical level up through each subsequent level. The implication is that grand strategy is a highly stratified and hierarchical process in which events at the tactical and operational levels directly influence the state's grand strategy in significant and dynamic ways.[32] One inference is that grand strategy provides a broad framework that helps guide *all* elements of state policy.

The Level of Strategy

The penultimate step in formulating grand strategy is to deal with the realm of strategy itself. Derived from the Greek *stratēgía* to mean generalship, military leaders, or the leadership of troops, strategy encompasses "the science and art of employing the political, economic, psychological, and military forces of a nation or group of nations to afford the maximum support to adopted policies in peace or war." It also includes the "science and art of military command" that leaders use "to meet the enemy in combat under advantageous conditions."[33] In formulating strategy, policy makers use political, economic, and military means as these are guided by a coherent definition of the goals they seek to achieve and a reasonable expectation that success is possible. The intent is to promote the state's objectives, which may include, if necessary, defeating an adversary or building an alliance.[34] In practical terms, the purpose of strategy is to organize the state's policies and resources effectively for the purpose of achieving the goals articulated in its grand strategy.[35]

The Level of Grand Strategy

Practically speaking, *strategy* as an abstract concept, and not as a level of strategic interaction, describes "how something is done" and is best understood as "a plan for action" or "a plan for applying resources to achieve objectives."[36] Thus, all levels of strategic interaction involve matching means to ends. Not surprisingly, this describes one of the most basic functions of grand strategy, which is to define what we mean by *security* – or "the very meaning of security" when expressed in the "context of national policy and international diplomacy." This function can (and should) exist "only [at the] highest level of grand strategy."[37] From this reasoning, it follows that the essential task of grand strategy is to define at the highest and broadest conceptual level what central principles or objectives should guide the state's foreign policy. The following chart illustrates all of these levels in the hierarchy reviewed in this section.

Level	Geographic Scale	Temporal Scope	Types of Ends	Types of Power (Means)
Grand Strategy	Global	Long term (decades)	Highest political ends	All (diplomatic, informational, military, economic)
Strategy	All theaters of war (and conflict)	Mid term (years)	Overall military victory	Military, informational, economic
Operations	One particular theater of war	Short term (weeks to months)	Campaign victory	Military, informational
Tactics	Battlefield	Very short term (minutes to days)	Achievement of tactical objectives	Military
Technology	Home front/ academia Industry	Variable time horizon	Competitive advantage over enemies	Technical expertise

As we can see, grand strategy sits atop all the variables involved in calculations of strategic interactions. Its proper role is to help the policy maker organize the state's policies and resources so that the state can achieve success in both its broad and specific policies, including, but never subordinated to, war.[38] After seeing grand strategy in its hierarchical context, the next step is to define grand strategy, a subject to which we now turn.

Grand Strategy Defined

Grand strategy symbolizes what we mean by the highest level of strategy for the state in its operations and very existence. In effect, grand strategy resides at the most overarching, comprehensive level of statecraft, diplomacy, and politics. The strategist Luttwak defines grand strategy as the level at which "all that is military happens within the much broader context of domestic governance, international politics [and] economic activity."[39] The emphasis on the military domain – the subject of widely differing definitions and interpretations within scholarly and policy-making literature – has been a source of confusion in debates about the nature and practice of grand strategy. In practical terms, grand strategy includes the entire discipline of strategy from its mundane technical roots to matters of the highest strategic consequences. It is useful to keep in mind that the political-military-economic-technological dimension of strategy is far too narrow and that grand strategy transcends each of these individual domains. Without a grand strategy, the entire range of considerations, from the mundane to the sublime, simply cannot be organized into coherent policies.

Grand strategy, therefore, can be understood in terms of what it *should* accomplish. For the scholar Richard Hart Sinnreich, grand strategy expresses a "sense of the consistent execution over time of a preconceived strategic design."[40] Without a strategic design, he argues, the "formulation, let alone the prolonged execution, of grand strategy as [a] deliberate method seems to be uncommon at best" and often "impermanent."[41] Later in this study, we will consider the argument that grand strategy is highly impermanent precisely because it is subject to the effects of shifting events, ideologies, and interpretations.

Stephen Krasner sees grand strategy as a "conceptual framing that describes how the world is, envisions how it ought to be, and specifies a set of policies that can achieve that ordering." For this scholar, its purpose is broadly to "mold the international environment by regulating international regimes, influencing the foreign policy choices made by other states, and shaping or even determining the domestic regime characteristics of other countries."[42] While expansive, this definition embraces the concept in which grand strategy assists in the development of guiding principles that will help govern the overall contours of the state's foreign policy. Although it excludes the domestic component of grand strategy (a subject to which we turn later), it has a strong normative content because it specifies what policies the state *ought* to pursue. In the view of the scholar Walter McDougall, a "sound" grand strategy is defined as that "equation of ends and means so sturdy that it triumphs despite serial setbacks at the level of strategy, operations, and campaigns." In this sense, grand strategy is equivalent to "a logic [of] strategic interactions that [actors] sense" and then employ to guide their policies.[43] The scholar Terry Deibel defined grand strategy, at least as it applies to the foreign policies of the United States, as a "strategic logic to help it design policies that will frustrate its enemies." However, it also seeks to "protect . . . its liberties and [advance] its interests" in an increasingly "globalized world."[44]

The international relations scholar Hans Morgenthau was one of the first to develop a broad definition of grand strategy. According to Morgenthau, grand strategy is "the art of bringing the different elements of national power to bear with maximum effect upon those points in the international situation which concern the national interest most directly."[45] In the view of John Lewis Gaddis, "grand strategy is the calculated relationship of means to large ends," which provides a definition as elegant as it is broad: "[Grand strategy is] about how one uses whatever one has to get to wherever it is one wants to go."[46] According to Gaddis, the use of "calculated" describes "a deliberate as opposed to an accidental, inadvertent, or fortuitous connection" between the instruments of foreign policy and the state's grand strategy.[47] The utility of Gaddis's approach lies in its universality, because it opens the field of grand strategy beyond the realms of war and statecraft to encompass policies for dealing with any major challenges a state or individual may face. This definition, however, leaves open both the types of ends and the types of means.

Gaddis's colleague at Yale, Paul Kennedy, is more specific. He defines grand strategy historically as the extent to which states "sought to integrate their overall political, economic, and military aims and thus to preserve their long-term interests." However, in the context of contemporary debates, Kennedy argues that grand strategy translates to developing "the proper balance of priorities" to ensure that the state's long-term interests in an increasingly complex world are met, which in effect requires the full integration of political, economic, and military aspirations as well as resources.[48] This definition is useful because it directly and explicitly incorporates the concept of priorities. In theory and practice, grand strategy must set clear priorities, as this remains one of its primary functions, which will be incorporated into the definition presented at the end of this section and used throughout this book.

Stephen Biddle's definition also includes the element of both military and nonmilitary sources of national power. This scholar defines grand strategy as the articulation of the "the state's ultimate ends" as it uses "both military and nonmilitary (e.g., economic, diplomatic, social, and political) means" to achieve the ends articulated in its strategy.[49] For Biddle, grand strategy "integrates military, political, and economic means to pursue states' ultimate objectives in the international system."[50]

In presenting another interpretation of grand strategy, scholar Peter Feaver sought to demystify the "term of art from academia." In Feaver's view, grand strategy "refers to the collection of plans and policies that comprise the state's deliberate effort to harness political, military, diplomatic, and economic tools together to advance that state's national interest." Like Gaddis, he believes that "grand strategy is the art of reconciling ends and means." Feaver also describes grand strategy as involving "purposive action – what leaders think and want – [which] is constrained by factors leaders explicitly recognize (for instance, budget constraints and the limitations inherent in the tools of statecraft) and by those they might only implicitly feel (cultural or cognitive screens that shape worldviews)."[51]

Based on the most important parts of the definitions given in this section, the definition of grand strategy used here in this study is the following:

> Grand strategy is a coherent statement of the state's highest political ends to be pursued globally over the long term. Its proper function is to prioritize among different domestic and foreign policy choices and to coordinate, balance, and integrate all types of national

means – including diplomatic, economic, technological, and military power – to achieve the articulated ends. In effect, grand strategy provides a framework of organizing principles that in a useful way help policy makers and society make coherent choices about the conduct of foreign policy.

In essence, grand strategy provides an overarching guide for the policies that the state should implement. Some scholars and policy makers may choose to organize our thinking by focusing on particular categorizations of challenges, such as the *states*, *transnational issues*, or *regions* that pose the greatest challenges. The central problem is that we need a more agile definition of grand strategy and a more helpful approach to dealing with a "fragile, fragmented and disordered world." The first step, as discussed later in this chapter, is to define the "sources of disorder" and then to articulate policies for dealing with them.[52] The definition given here has several statements worth elaboration.

Grand Strategy is a coherent statement of national purpose.

The first element states that grand strategy must provide "a coherent statement" of what the state seeks to achieve in foreign policy. This statement does not necessarily have to be written in one document or articulated by one person at a particular time, but it does have to be clear and reducible to a set of guidelines concrete enough to provide real guidance and signal to implementers what is expected. If the state's grand strategy is not clear, then that grand strategy will fail to provide coherence to the state's foreign policy over time, undermine its policies, and ultimately weaken the state.

Grand strategy articulates the state's highest political ends.

A grand strategy articulates "the state's highest political ends," which is another way of saying "the most vital priorities of the state." These ends are typically, but not necessarily, related to the highest security threats. Because grand strategy involves the most abstract and decisive level of thinking about the nature and direction of state policy, the matters it entails sit at the top of the hierarchy of principles that govern what policy makers will seek to achieve in foreign policy. Luttwak holds this view when he argues that "grand strategy [exists at] the conclusive level" in which all other matters [in the technical, tactical, operational, and theater-strategic] "dimensions finally come together to acquire a definite meaning."[53] In effect, grand strategy represents the highest and most abstract expression of state policy as policy makers consider what they want to achieve in foreign policy and what steps they will take to accomplish it. For Luttwak, such matters exist at the level of grand strategy where "interactions of the lower, military levels, their synergisms or contradictions, yield final results" as part of a process that shapes how the state conducts its foreign policy.[54]

The argument that grand strategy resides at this level was implied by the scholar Stephen Biddle, who writes that "grand strategy and military strategy, organizational adaptability, administrative skill, or politico-military coordination are all clearly important." However, his argument that "operations and tactics ... are more proximate to realized capability"[55] implies that matters pertaining to grand strategy cannot be resolved, much less "explained *without* considering the operational and tactical levels of war."[56] This reasoning is consistent with the earlier discussion about the intimate relationship between strategy and grand strategy, in which the articulation and implementation of grand strategy builds on the other instruments of state power. This scholar, for example, observes that the "effects" of grand strategy are "felt largely via its influence on preponderance and technology."[57]

Operating at the highest and most conclusive level, grand strategy rests for Biddle on such "central grand strategic tasks" as "denying allies to one's opponent and securing them for oneself, providing the economic basis for a large war effort, while denying resources to one's opponents, or ensuring domestic political support for mobilizing resources." As Biddle argues, "grand strategy is largely about creating material," which is quite distinct from the ways in which grand strategy makes its effects known on such matters as "military strategy, operations, and tactics."[58] Grand strategy, nevertheless, provides the broad background to and context for all actions and policies pursued by the state.

Grand strategy operates on a global scale.

Grand strategy exists and is designed to operate on a global scale that encompasses all aspects of the international system, and not simply one part of it. It deals with all the variables at play among the different components of the international system, whether it is rival states, non-state threats, or international institutions. For this reason, only states with a global reach can truly have grand strategies. Great powers possess the true grand strategies, and though lesser states can have overarching strategies, these tend to operate on a regional scale.

Grand strategy has a long-term time horizon.

Grand strategy is designed to operate over the long term, which equates roughly to decades but also can mean years. For instance, the U.S. grand strategy that governed its policies during World War II spanned about four years. It was in effect less than a decade, but Presidents Roosevelt and Truman and their advisors, nonetheless, designed it to operate over the long term at the outset, not knowing how long the war would last. Grand strategy, in short, is supposed to be sustainable and stable against shifting political fads and passing interests. It is a statement of the nation's long-term strategy for governing the conduct of its foreign policy.

Grand strategy encompasses all instruments of national power.

Grand strategy encompasses all the types of national power that are available. It is not only about military power, especially in today's world, but includes the use of diplomatic, economic, and technological instruments of power. This book relies primarily on a threefold classification of the instruments of power. First, states use their diplomatic (or political) power to guide how their political and economic influence can be used to defend the nation's interests. Second, the state's economic and technological power determines the nation's resources that can be used to help achieve its policies and objectives. Third, grand strategy relies on the state's military power, which in turn rests on the extent to which the state can employ military force to achieve its national ends. All three – including to a somewhat lesser extent informational and soft power – are critical instruments of grand strategy in the modern era.

> The four functions of grand strategy are to prioritize, coordinate, balance, and integrate.

The first of the four essential functions of grand strategy is to prioritize among ends. For scholars and policy makers who study grand strategy, a central challenge is how to "choose [among the] most important and doable goals," while avoiding the problems of dissipating "energy and resources" on otherwise "worthwhile efforts, only to see none of them succeed."[59] Although scholars and policy makers articulate a coherent grand strategy for managing the many objectives and challenges they face, it is nevertheless true that no state can accomplish all of the tasks it sets for itself – "even if one's power seems overwhelmingly preponderant." A critical function of grand strategy is to help policy makers make prudent choices among reasonable priorities in the face of the many compelling demands that are competing for the state's attention.[60] The difficult issue of prioritizing and selecting among competing issues is explored in Chapter 10.

This priority-setting function is accomplished by articulating a coherent statement of the highest political ends to which the state is committed and then directing the state's institutions to set priorities based on those ends. But this function is also accomplished by prioritizing regions and issues that affect various states and parts of the globe. The key to grand strategy is to have a geostrategic framework that helps policy makers navigate the political terrain of a world in which challenges are not always marked by the actions of clear adversaries. One can see that without a coherent grand strategy, the state will find it immensely difficult to articulate and implement policies in a coordinated and prudent fashion. Grand strategy is the framework within which all actions of the state are taken.

The scholar Gaddis argues that this geostrategic reality derives from the cartography of grand strategy, or what he calls that "necessary simplification that allows us to see where we are, and where we may be going."[61] For example, the Truman Doctrine's division of the world between the forces of democracy and totalitarianism was a useful, if perhaps necessary, simplification of the prevailing geopolitical realities in the late 1940s and early 1950s.[62] As Gaddis explains, "it was an exercise in geopolitical cartography" that defined international politics "in terms everyone could understand." Of greater significance, this architecture also "prepared the way for the more sophisticated strategy of containment" that was soon developed by the Truman administration.[63] In effect, as policy makers and scholars articulate grand strategy on the basis of familiar features in international politics, this approach provides a conceptual road map that helps guide a society as it balances threats with the resources that it is willing and able to mobilize.

The second function of grand strategy is to coordinate the actions of the state among and between different types of national power. Diplomatic initiatives, for example, should be conducted without working at cross-purposes to military operations. The idea of defining grand strategy in terms of its relationship to the coordination of the state's resources is discussed in the work of Otto von Bismarck in his dispatches while he was serving as ambassador to the Frankfurt Diet in the 1850s. One theme from Bismarck's writings is, as Craig and Gilbert write, that he saw strategy as a "classic illustration of the effective coordination of force and statecraft for the attainment of [the state's] political aims." The emphasis on "coordination" is an important signal that the state, if it is to successfully develop and implement its grand strategy, must prudently manage its resources that are essential to attaining its strategic goals. What Craig and Gilbert describe is "a more recent example of a systematic and carefully coordinated national strategy," which is seen in how President Truman dealt with the problems that emerged between 1947 and 1950.[64] His grand strategy was based on using "a shrewd determination of the nature of American interests in the postwar world," along with "the effective mobilization of public support for its European commitments and the skillful use of economic resources to gain its objectives."[65]

The third function of grand strategy is to balance means and ends in ways that do not allow the means to be too costly so as to make the ends politically self-defeating. Grand strategy in the era of nuclear weapons exemplifies this balancing of means and ends. It makes no rational sense to initiate a nuclear war for reasons of grand strategy if this action produces a "military victory" at the cost of seeing the destruction of major urban areas in a retaliatory strike and leads to a war that brings an end to civilization itself. This cost would be too high, would violate the principle of striking a proper balance of means and ends, and would never gain public support.

This classic means-ends balance is of central prominence as policy makers struggle daily with how to articulate and implement the state's grand strategy in the face of what always are serious economic and political constraints. This problem presents a lesson in the perils of overreach, which is an all-too-common consequence when states miscalculate what their grand strategy calls for or when policy makers find that the society is unwilling to support that strategy.

The role of balancing ends and means in grand strategy was apparent in historian B. F. Liddell Hart's ideas about the fundamental differences that separate strategy and grand strategy. Drawing heavily from the ideas of Clausewitz, Liddell Hart argues that if war is a continuation of policy, which is governed and directed by a central political objective, then war and grand strategy must be governed by a coherent vision of the postwar outcomes and benefits that policy makers seek to achieve and expect that their policies will produce. As Liddell Hart warns, "A state which expends its strength to the point of exhaustion bankrupts its own [grand strategy]."[66] To emphasize this point, he uses the example of the post–World War I era in which grand strategy not only failed to achieve the condition of an ideal peace, but contributed arguably to the outbreak of World War II.[67] His suggestion is that the strategic deliberations of scholars and policy makers must be guided by a "thorough re-examination of the whole problem of the object and aim [of war and strategy]."[68]

In principle, the state's overall policies must ensure that its actions are guided prudently by the conditions and outcomes it seeks to achieve. The ability of policy makers to articulate a grand strategy that provides a coherent and rational explanation of (1) the dangers facing the state, (2) what objectives its policy makers seek to achieve, and (3) the opportunities presented is the *sine qua non* to ensuring that strategy – whether in the form of formulating peacetime policies or the conduct of war – is governed by constant regard for the desired condition, which remains the state of peace.

For this British strategist, in keeping with his war-centric definition of grand strategy, policy makers must possess clear goals of the ends that they seek to achieve – in effect, what the postwar policy environment should look like. As Liddell Hart writes, "it is the responsibility of statesmanship never to lose sight of the post-war prospect in chasing the 'mirage of victory.'"[69] The fighting instinct is necessary to win battles or political struggles, but "the statesman who gives that instinct its head loses his own; he is not fit to take charge of the fate of a nation."[70] For Liddell Hart, there are powerful reasons why the conduct of war needs to be (but often is not) controlled by a rational grand strategy.[71]

The central argument in Liddell Hart's analysis is how important it is for those who articulate and implement grand strategy to rein in the dangerous imbalance that so often exists between means and ends – between the conduct of policy or war and the ability to achieve the state's political aims in the conditions or peace that follows.[72] The inescapable logic for Liddell Hart is that scholars and policy makers routinely fail to strike the proper balance between ends and means as they articulate and subsequently put their grand strategy into practice. When this failure occurs, policy makers learn the painful consequences of the perils that exist when the state engages in what Paul Kennedy called "overreach," which is a common failure when states miscalculate what their grand strategy calls for.[73] This critical balancing between means and ends in grand strategy was evident in Kennedy's writings, and his conclusion was that it is "critical for those [tasked with] formulating grand strategy to balance economic and manpower resources [so that the state can] sustain the fight and avoid damage to a future state of peace (the ultimate end goal)."[74]

The fourth, and perhaps most difficult, function of grand strategy is to integrate the different types of national power that are available to the state. Policy makers must ensure that they are not merely avoiding the negative consequence of working at cross-purposes but are actually accomplishing positive results by using the elements of power to put the strategy into practice. In modern parlance, the objective is to ensure that these elements of power become force multipliers for each other. The economic base of supply, for instance, can become a force multiplier in supplying the state with a war-fighting capability.

Articulation of Grand Strategy

The first step in achieving an effective grand strategy is to clearly articulate its principles and objectives, which may take the form of written documents or policy statements, speeches, or simply the clear expression in thought of the state's dominant policy makers or grand strategists. What is clear, however, is that this articulation must satisfy certain requirements if it is to produce an effective grand strategy.

Grand strategy and military strategy must be unified in their objectives and goals.

A central theme is the relationship between grand strategy and strategy as broadly defined, particularly in terms of whether the state is able to strike the right balance between the two. The argument is that war, which is governed generally by the principles of strategy in a narrower sense, must be in general agreement with the state's broad policy goals – another way of describing its grand strategy. In practice, there must be a conceptual or intellectual unity between the state's grand strategy and its conduct of policy, which may include its strategy for war. In effect, the two must be in close unity and therefore governed by some degree of conceptual and practical coordination.

Drawing heavily from the ideas of Clausewitz and writing at a time when discussions of strategy were fixated on World War II and its aftermath, Liddell Hart argues that if war is a continuation of policy that is governed and directed by a central political objective, then war and grand strategy must be guided by a coherent vision of the postwar outcome and benefits that policy makers seek to achieve. As he warns, "A state which expends its strength to the point of exhaustion bankrupts its own policy [grand strategy]."[75] To emphasize this point, Liddell Hart uses the example of the post–World War I era in which grand strategy failed to achieve the condition of an ideal peace, suggesting that scholars and policy makers must conduct "a thorough re-examination of the whole problem of the object and aim [of war]."[76] In principle, the state's overall policies must ensure that its actions are guided by the political conditions it ultimately seeks to achieve. According to Liddell Hart, policy makers must possess clear goals of the ends they seek to achieve – in effect, grand strategy should guide policy makers as they determine what principles should govern politics in the post-conflict environment.

The strategist Bernard Brodie explored the matter of whether the state's policies are consistent with its grand strategy. In the final chapter of *War and Politics*, he examines directly the ability of strategic thinkers, planners, and policy makers to establish a unified approach to the state's grand strategy. In Brodie's view, the basic argument is that "war [and thus strategy] must be in unity with its object,"[77] and he goes on to assert that civilian decision makers are better able to reach this unity than military leaders. It is difficult, he argues, for military leaders to give strategic advice because their basic conceptual orientation is shaped by both their organizational bias and a deep sense of loyalty to their service.[78] This tension is most acute when their advice runs contrary to the interests of their organization. As Brodie writes, "The skills developed in the soldier are those of a fighter, and not of the reflector on ultimate purposes."[79] Second, Brodie observes that military commanders "may too readily confuse the prestige of the nation with" what is best for one's "own forces."[80]

This argument is germane in terms of understanding the forces that influence the ability of policy makers to keep their policies in general unity with the state's grand strategy. As Brodie sees the problem, "Strategy is a 'how to do it' study, a guide to accomplishing something and doing it efficiently." But beyond its role as a guide to action (which, parenthetically, is one definition of *ideology*[81]), the essence of strategy – or "strategic thinking, or 'theory' if one prefers" – for Brodie "is nothing if not pragmatic." His emphasis on the practical aspects of strategy suggests that the central question with strategy is Will the idea work? According to Brodie, the "more important" consideration is whether this strategy will "be likely to work under the special circumstances under which it will next be tested."[82]

Bernard Brodie views the articulation of grand strategy as more art than science because he sees "strategic theory" as a "theory for action."[83] Since the end of World War II, many "civilian strategists" have tried to answer the questions presented here, but Brodie harshly criticizes some of these and the organizations with which they are associated, focusing in particular on the work that emerged in the 1950s and 1960s from the RAND Corporation. The nature of his criticism is that their preferred method for formulating and evaluating strategies is to rely on the cost–benefit method outlined in systems analysis, which, though "bound at best to be imperfect, [is] also likely to be far superior to anyone's simple, intuitive judgment."[84] Based on Brodie's earlier criticisms of the extent to which military leaders influence policy making, it is easy to see how organizational interests could distort the ability of policy makers, whether civilian or military, to articulate a grand strategy that remains in close balance or unity with the state's broad foreign policy objectives.

The question of maintaining unity with the state's strategy generates debates about whether the formulation of grand strategy belongs in the realm of art or the realm of science. Brodie clearly and forcefully agrees with those who believe strategy is closer to art than science. Writing in the Cold War era when strategy was heavily influenced by systems and cost–benefit analyses, he was dismissive of those "who yearn [for] a true science or theory of strategy, replete with principles that are both immutable and deeply meaningful." The risk, in Brodie's view, is that those who rely on this logic demonstrate "a basic misunderstanding of their subject [of how to articulate strategy properly]."[85]

In his defense of the argument that strategy is more art rather than science, Brodie (relying on observations from Clausewitz) opposed any "conception of tightly worded 'principles' [of strategy, grand or otherwise] that suggest a computerized tabulation or keyboard where pressing the right button produces the right answer."[86] Thus, the best approach for dealing with strategy is to rely on generalizations, which may not always be useful. Analytically, Brodie sees strategy as "a catalogue of principles [that] must be recognized for what it is," which is "a device intended to circumvent the need for months and years of study of and rumination on a very difficult subject."[87] Whether approached as art or science, strategy is a complex subject that requires careful study and reflection by scholars, strategists, and policy makers, and is not reducible to formulaic or mechanistic solutions.

Paul Kennedy is largely in agreement with Brodie in that he sees the articulation of grand strategy as a constant reassessment of ends and means at all levels of strategy and grand strategy. According to Kennedy, pressing to preserve a sense of unity in the state's goals is equivalent to arguing that strategy is designed to guide the state toward the best possible ends in its foreign and domestic policies. This principle suggests that the conduct of strategy [or war] must be guided by the search for a positive outcome in policy, which includes the condition of peace.[88] From this it follows that the "success or failure of any grand strategy" is a direct product of "the constant and intelligent reassessment of the polity's ends and means."[89] The emphasis on aligning the state's strategy with its broad goals reaffirms that the fundamental purpose of grand strategy is to balance the state's instruments of power, while imbuing its foreign policy with a deep sense of unity and purpose.

In contrast, Robert Art sees that the articulation of grand strategy should be focused on the ends of the state's military capabilities. He distinguishes between grand strategy and foreign policy, noting that these differ in one fundamental respect. In Art's view, the purpose of foreign policy is to "lay out the full range of goals that a state should seek in the world," and only then to "determine how all of the instruments of statecraft – political power, military power, economic power, ideological power – should be integrated and employed . . . to achieve those goals." By contrast, grand strategy also "deals with the full range of goals that a state should seek, *but it concentrates primarily on how the military instrument should be employed to realize them*."[90] With these ideas, Art's approach returns us to the distinction addressed earlier between broader and narrower definitions of grand strategy. Yet, for Art, grand strategy also "prescribes how a nation should wield its military instrument to realize its foreign policy goals." In practical terms, the failure to define grand strategy precisely means that the state will find it difficult to achieve a unity or balance between its grand strategy and its specific policies.[91]

David Baldwin, in his study *Economic Statecraft*, examines the relationship between grand strategy and the process by which the state chooses its strategic goals. He uses the term *statecraft* to describe how policy makers choose the "means for the pursuit of foreign policy goals." In this sense, his construct is clearly distinct from grand strategy because the function of statecraft is to "consider the instruments used by policy makers [as they] attempt to exercise power, i.e., to get others to do what they would not otherwise do."[92] Grand strategy, by contrast, outlines the broad goals that define what the state seeks to accomplish in foreign policy, rather than the "how" or more mechanical aspects as policy makers consider how to translate grand strategy into specific policies and actions. This concept of grand strategy, as articulated by Schwenninger, frames grand strategy as a "road map" that helps the state choose its "most important foreign policy goals and the most effective instruments and policies for achieving those goals." In the case of U.S. grand strategy, he writes that it "contains a vision for America's role in the world based on America's domestic needs and ... the international challenges the country faces."[93]

To return to arguments made earlier in the chapter, grand strategy – in sharp contrast with foreign policy and the conduct of statecraft – helps guide policy makers as they "establish" priorities and provide "focus to an otherwise volatile foreign policymaking process."[94] As a consequence, a central theme in the study of grand strategy is the search for the unity or coherence between the state's overall grand strategy and the specific strategies and policies statesmen used to put it into practice.

> Grand strategy is an ongoing, continuous process of articulation and revision
> along the war-peace continuum.

One theme in the scholarly and policy literatures is that grand strategies tend to arise from and are the product of periods that are shaped by great struggles or confrontations among states. The fact that most grand strategies often evolve during and are shaped by such moments suggests that states often articulate grand strategies in response to specific problems or challenges, which reinforces the argument that grand strategies often have a reactive or adversary-centric quality to them. The question of when, how, and why states articulate grand strategy seems to be a recurring theme, as grand strategies often are articulated in response to new strategic challenges. At some point, the state's grand strategy can be overtaken by events and then must inevitably be reworked. The society could redefine its grand strategy or on a more mechanical level engage in a large-scale reorganization of its policy machinery. Facing such shifts, scholars and policy makers must outline the principles that help them deal with the ongoing tension in grand strategy that always exists between long-term and short-term solutions to problems.

In effect, states face this permanent dynamic in the articulation and implementation of grand strategy, which illuminates why the strategist Edward Luttwak defines grand strategy as operating along a continuum. As he argues, because the "dynamic logic of strategy has no end[,] all outcomes – even victory and defeat sealed by formal treaty – are only interim results." Critically, these "interim results" will produce changes that alter the state's grand strategy and call for its refinement.[95] Because strategists are always refining their grand strategy in response to new domestic and international developments, for scholars and policy makers there never will be an end to the process of articulating grand strategy. It is a never-ending cycle for policy makers and scholars.

Because there never will be an end to the cycle of reformulating and adapting grand strategy to ensure that it fits current circumstances and that its principles continue to endure, strategists and policy makers should recognize, for example, that although no particular grand strategy has a formal ending, except when a major adversary is defeated in a war or collapses, it is bound to constantly evolve in the face of changing circumstances.[96] For example, the current American grand strategy still is influenced by the country's experiences during the Cold War.[97] If scholars and policy makers believe that any given grand strategy is "final," this finality can only exist in the sense "that [ideas about grand strategy only] mark a completion of [a phase of] the ... process" as policy makers evaluate the principles behind it and judge its ability to effectively guide the state's foreign policy.[98]

Building on the principle that each state evaluates "results differently so that the same outcome ... may be deemed highly successful by one government and a crushing failure by another," the belief that there is an objectively correct grand strategy or that grand strategy derives from a particular interpretation by one individual or state is open to criticism. The more useful argument is that grand strategy symbolizes "the net outcome of the technical, tactical, operational and theater-strategic" factors – all of which develop "continuously" to reflect all of the interactions between and among states. Furthermore, this process operates more or less continuously, and in practice, it includes but is not limited to "what is done or not done militarily" as well as politically and economically by any state or collection of states.[99]

One consequence for scholars and policy makers is that grand strategy must be articulated and pursued constantly at all times – in both peace and war. This is a central conclusion that emerges from the works of such strategists as Paul Kennedy and B. H. Liddell Hart.[100] Building on the argument that grand strategy is a never-ending process as states struggle with policies for war and peace, Luttwak contends that grand strategy is akin principally to the conduct of "everyday strategy," whose "dynamic workings continue even in the absence of warfare."[101] From this principle it follows that grand strategy operates as a continuous process as individuals and states struggle with what policies the state should pursue and what must be done to achieve those ends in the face of political, economic, and military realities.

Debates about grand strategy are influenced by the tension between continuity and change as states engage in the unending work of formulating and refining their grand strategy. In the end, scholars often conclude that debates about grand strategy never completely fade away, but reappear in different forms and fonts.[102] Broadly speaking, the scholar Peter Feaver suggests that we see vastly more continuity than change in grand strategy, particularly in the case of the United States in the decades after World War II. In the case of modern politics, "it is possible to imagine Obama continuing in broad strokes what George W. Bush, of the second term, developed." However, the dynamics surrounding grand strategy lately have failed to produce the bipartisan consensus that many scholars and policy makers often wish were the case.[103]

According to the historian Edwin Mead Earle, grand strategy operates equally well in managing the problems states confront as they deal with the war-peace continuum.[104] In *Makers of Modern Strategy*, Earle writes that "strategy, therefore, is not merely a concept of wartime, but is an inherent element of statecraft at all times."[105] This dynamic leads, for Earle, to "the highest type of strategy – sometimes called grand strategy – [which] so integrates the state's policies and armaments that the decision to resort to war is rendered unnecessary or gives the state the maximum chance of victory."[106] We can trace the origins of this argument to the 1940s, when Earle defined grand strategy as the principles that help policy makers "[integrate] the [nation's] policies and armaments."[107] But this definition is problematic because, in Earle's view, "most writers using the term grand strategy discard this limitation," which effectively limits their thinking to applying "strategic thinking to peacetime security [and] planning for or fighting a war."

Defining grand strategy in these terms is dangerously parochial and ultimately self-defeating.

A historical example that illustrates the peril of failing to adapt one's grand strategy is the case of imperial Spain, as discussed in Paul Kennedy's *Grand Strategies in War and Peace*, which relates to the much-debated question of the reasons for the fall of the Soviet Union in the late 1980s and early 1990s.[108] This debate, which was provoked in large measure by Paul Kennedy's *The Rise and Fall of Great Powers*, raises questions about whether and how well great powers can sense and then manage their decline.[109] In the case of Spain, failure to prosper contributed to its political, military, and economic decline, largely because it was unwilling to change its grand strategy, which was based on military and economic expansion. The source of that failure, for the scholar Elliott, was the ruling class of the seventeenth century in Spain, whose inflexible and traditional adherence to attitudes, values, and geopolitical orientation made it unable to adjust its policies and strategy to match the realities of Spain's declining economic and military power. In effect, it was unable to manage its decline in a graceful fashion.[110]

Another example from Kennedy's *Grand Strategies in War and Peace* is the case of Great Britain in the eighteenth century, from which several important themes emerge.[111] In this research, Kennedy evaluates the states' success or failure precisely in terms of how well they integrated their overall political, economic, and military aims into preserving their states' long-term interests central to their grand strategy. One case was London's need to preserve alliances while minimizing the unwelcome and distorting consequences that alliance entanglements create, particularly as it related to Great Britain's failure to achieve victory against the colonists in the American Revolutionary War.[112] London's decision to preserve its alliances highlights the tension that always exists between the cost of conducting war and the cost of premature or overambitious campaigns. This case also identifies the adverse consequences for British grand strategy that occurred when London failed to deal effectively with significant constraints on its resources. It illustrates the importance of being flexible when formulating and conducting grand strategy, which in turn argues why it is imperative for the state to engage frequently in critical self-assessments if it is to achieve and sustain a coherent and balanced grand strategy.

> Grand strategy, policy, doctrine, logistics, and operations must be properly distinguished.

Recalling the hierarchical approach to defining grand strategy, a principle in the scholarly literature and policy making treatises is that grand strategy does not exist in isolation. The argument is the deep "interrelatedness" or "connectedness" in grand strategy that governs how the state manages its affairs in dealing with issues that fit in the realms of policy, doctrine, strategy, and operations. As one might surmise, grand strategy should contribute to and be central to developing and perpetuating a systematic approach to and broad guidance about how the state should conduct its foreign and domestic policies. As they confront practical decisions about what policies to pursue, it is essential for theorists and practitioners to examine precisely how grand strategy relates to these matters.

The first step is to establish some definitional and conceptual clarity to guide discussions about grand strategy. The logical place to begin is with the concept of policy. *Policy* is defined as "general objectives that guide the activities and relationships of one state in its interactions with other states," and it may be described as "the art or science of government."[113] The related but more expansive term is *doctrine*, which is "a formulation of the principles on which a government proposes to base its actions or policy in some matter, especially in the field of international relations."[114] For an expansive definition of doctrine, Kissinger suggested that doctrine "defines the challenges which it [the society] will meet in its relations with other societies and the manner of dealing with them." In the context of grand strategy, doctrine in Kissinger's view "plays the role of education for the individual: it relates seemingly disparate experiences into a meaningful pattern."[115] It is common in discussions of grand strategy and foreign policy to use the term "doctrine" to describe the principles that define the state's actions and intentions, which is a subject to which we shall return later.[116]

The argument of "relatedness" builds from the idea that grand strategy is a unique discipline that derives from but ultimately transcends ideas about strategy, policy, operations, and tactics. The problem is that scholars and policy makers, *before* they move to articulate and implement a broad strategy, need concepts and arguments to help them answer fundamental questions about how the state should organize its policies and institutions for developing and managing threats and challenges to its interests. It is worth noting, however, that the inertia surrounding these matters often overcomes the contributions that grand strategy should make to the conduct of policy.

The principle that grand strategy is based on and provides guidance to these interrelated and yet highly dependent concepts is evident in the writings of numerous scholars and policy makers. When Paul Kennedy argues that "the crux of grand strategy [is] in policy," his interpretation reflects the broader definition of grand strategy, one that encompasses "the capacity of the nation's leaders to bring together all of the elements, both military and nonmilitary" to preserve and strengthen "the nation's long-term best interests." For Kennedy, grand strategy is not, however, a "mathematical science but a difficult art" that "*operates at various levels* that are in constant interaction with each other." Although this logic applies to all states and extends to the many variables that are at play when the state articulates its grand strategy, the corollary, in Kennedy's view, is that "grand strategy can never be [an] exact or foreordained [practice]."[117] Whether dealing with peace or war or doctrine or policy, policy makers must pay constant attention to the political outcome or "the peace you desire" as they articulate and implement policies. According to Kennedy, this means that the success of failure of grand strategy depends on "the constant and intelligent" evaluation of the state's "ends and means."[118]

In arguing that these concepts are intimately related, Kennedy presents a series of historical case studies (focused on European powers, which somewhat limits the scope of his work) of grand strategy in *Grand Strategies in War and Peace*.[119] For modern students, these case studies lend support to Kennedy's conclusions about the forces that have had an enduring effect on shaping grand strategy.

In the fourth case in Kennedy's *Grand Strategies in War and Peace*, Elliott considers the role of Germany during the twentieth century.[120] What is remarkable about this case is how the German "genius for war," as measured by its ability to plan for and conduct war, did not extend to the realm of formulating and putting into practice an effective grand strategy. German strategic thought, as Showalter argued, "devolved downward, toward the tactical and operational levels, rather than upward" toward the broader level on which the fate of the grand strategy depends.[121] One lesson from this case is that the German military establishment, which was highly effective when it came to formulating highly organized plans to win campaigns (operations), utterly failed when it came to building a strategy that would permit it to win wars. Success, then, at the lower levels of strategic interaction does not guarantee that the state will achieve success when it operates at the higher level of grand strategy. This devolution downward of Germany's plans shows how distinguishing between success at the level of operations versus success at the level of grand strategy is critical to articulating grand strategy. The fundamental conclusion is that Germany overinvested in articulating its operational-level plans but underinvested in dealing with the means and ends of its grand strategy.

The last of the case studies in Kennedy's *Grand Strategies in War and Peace* examines the failure of the Soviet Union to properly articulate and implement a grand strategy during the Cold War. A central argument that emerges from this case study is that the influence on Soviet strategy of a holistic and universal ideology contributed to both *doctrinal* rigidity and *tactical* inflexibility.[122] The Soviet belief system not only viewed politics, society, economics, and warfare itself through the lens of the class struggle, but also predicted that it would transcend all power relationships within and among society.[123] This outlook contributed to the Soviet leadership's inability to articulate a coherent grand strategy that would not seriously weaken the Soviet leadership's ability to handle problems and crises when circumstances did not align with Marxist theory. The lesson is that an ideologically rigid doctrine for governing policy can lead to a massive failure of the state's grand strategy.

By examining the contemporary debate about the state's obligation to properly balance priorities, Kennedy is outlining the essential function of grand strategy for the state. Even in peacetime, states must make preparations for war in ways that effectively distinguish its grand strategy from the daily debates about policy, doctrine, and operations if it is to ensure that these contribute to its long-term strategy and power. The crux of the argument about the relatedness of grand strategy to these other domains is that states always face scarce national military and nonmilitary resources and that policy makers must set priorities to ensure that their grand strategy directly guides the other domains.

What makes grand strategy crucial is its role in an intricate, if clearly not scientifically derived, hierarchy of concepts and principles that cumulatively define the state's foreign policy and its relationship to domestic policies. In the view of one scholar, Richard Betts, the relationships between the supporting elements of grand strategy deal specifically with the matter of means and ends. These components "span several levels of analysis," ranging from "maneuvers of units in specific engagements through larger campaigns, whole wars, grand strategies, and foreign policies." Ideally, the relationships between these levels should "govern the one below and serve the one above."[124]

This hierarchical approach to coordinating the various elements of grand strategy was pursued from the earliest days of the Cold War, first with the emphasis on systems analysis and policy analysis and later with strategic planning frameworks that sought to develop, albeit with only limited success, logical links between these.[125] The intent to link grand strategy logically to these supporting components is consistent with the views of Gaddis, who argues that strategy involves the search for ways to establish formal relationships between means and ends. This is, according to Gaddis, the "all-important center, the iron linkage of strategic thought."[126]

To better understand how strategy developed historically and connects to foreign policy, particularly in cases involving the use of force, Michael Howard developed a framework based on the historical development of strategy and warfare over the past two centuries that he applies to the strategic posture of the West.[127] Howard begins with an examination of Clausewitz, who defined strategy (in contrast to the broader meaning of grand strategy) as the "use of engagements for the object of war." *Strategy* thus means the deliberate decision to apply military means to achieve specific political ends. Clausewitz took a deliberately simplistic approach when he referred to war as a "remarkable trinity" consisting of political objectives, operational instruments, and social (or societal) forces. While earlier theorists (as examined in Chapter 4) were interested primarily in raising, equipping, moving, and maintaining armed forces in the field, Clausewitz held that this approach to strategy was about as relevant to fighting battles and wars as the skill of the sword maker is to success in a duel.

For Howard, the fact that Clausewitz drew several questionable conclusions about strategy had unfortunate consequences. One is that Clausewitz paid insufficient attention to the logistical side of strategy. Although he concedes that in the Napoleonic era operational skill was more important than logistical planning, the commanders that he admired (such as Napoleon and Frederick the Great) could never have enjoyed such operational successes without understanding that logistics is a critical element in strategy. This is particularly true in the modern era when states must mobilize their economies to support war or during long periods of political competition, strategic confrontation, and hostility.[128] In the modern era, the American Civil War provides an important example. However, the role played by logistics and the general understanding of it by scholars and policy makers has changed dramatically since Clausewitz's time. But this raises an important counterargument: Southern generals in the American Civil War were highly flexible and imaginative during battles and campaigns, and yet they lost in part because logistics and supply were more significant in the long term as the conflict shifted to a war of attrition.[129] The second error in Clausewitz's conclusions relates to the fact that strategy in Clausewitz's era was not heavily influenced by significant differences in technology. In Howard's view, Clausewitz likely did not understand the extent to which strategy was influenced by technological superiority.

With this framework for understanding the historical development of strategy, Howard observed several noteworthy changes in the nineteenth and twentieth centuries that are relevant to contemporary debates about grand strategy. To begin with, there was the disappearance of "limited wars of pure policy fought by dispassionate professionals."[130] In the modern era, policy makers have at their disposal large volunteer-based armed forces and must deal with the powerful influence of the media and public opinion. According to Clausewitz, logistical power is rooted in the people, who in democratic societies not only control resources but also can decide whether to wage war or intervene. Furthermore, pure numbers in manpower, firepower, and popular support are only partially decisive, all things being equal, in the development and implementation of grand strategy. Moreover, after the dawn of the twentieth century, the four dimensions that dominated strategy were operational, logistical, social, and technological. For Howard, successful grand strategies must take these factors into account, while noting that any one of these may dominate at any given moment.

The study of grand strategy also must take into account the dominant strategies that emerged in World War II. For instance, some thought that airpower would eliminate the operational dimension of war because no society arguably could withstand a punishing air campaign, a view outlined at the turn of the century by the airpower theorist Giulio Douhet.[131] For such theorists as Douhet, grand strategy ultimately rested on the ability of military forces to strike directly at the enemy's social and economic strength. "Social strength" means the will and capacity of the public to support war, including the public's ability to inflict punishment and absorb deprivation.

By 1915, Douhet had propounded a theory of total war in which the function of strategy was to guide the state in crushing the morale of the civilian population by targeting the people directly from the air. As a critical advocate of the "destruction of nations" from above,[132] Douhet is foremost among the preeminent theorists who studied the influence of airpower on modern strategy.[133] However, this development raises several problems for grand strategy. One is that airpower technology was not sufficiently developed at the time of Douhet's theory to accomplish his stated objective in war. Consider, for example, the fact that British and German morale were not effectively destroyed by the air campaigns in World War II. Whereas technology certainly influenced the nature of warfare, it arguably did not fundamentally transform the nature or development of grand strategy.

Other strategists, however, believed that the technological dimension of warfare would dominate grand strategy because it would restore the relevance of operational decisiveness in war as practiced by Napoleon. In the modern era, nuclear weapons are arguably so decisive that they may overwhelm the need to take into account the social basis of grand strategy or even the capacity of opposing forces. In World War II, however, technology did not totally eliminate or undermine the conduct of operational strategy, and it has not so done today. Grand strategy still depends on other political and economic dimensions even though technology remains a significant element.[134] That being said, the impact of technology on strategy will probably be felt most as states seek to improve the capabilities of operational weapon systems and the logistics that makes their deployment possible.

The third major argument about the interrelated nature of the elements of grand strategy focuses on the role of nuclear weapons. According to Howard, calling for deterrence or crisis management is not enough, because strategists must consider what will happen to their grand strategy if deterrence fails. In addition, scholars and policy makers must consider the effects of public opinion on the state's grand strategy, including how public opinion shapes the government's will and capacity to make decisions. It is incumbent on policy makers to consider the social and operational dimensions when formulating the state's policies for deterring nuclear war and its broad grand strategy.

In studying grand strategy, credibility in matters related to nuclear strategy is not just about the perceived balance or imbalance in weapons, but also about perceptions regarding the society's willingness to support a grand strategy in which nuclear weapons play a decisive role. The problem is that a grand strategy based on the threat to use nuclear weapons may erode with time. Growing opposition to, or at least discontent with, a grand strategy based on nuclear deterrence means that the state will see diminished public support for policies that emphasize the role of such weapons. However, we also should consider the enemy's strategy and how it interacts with its opponents, which cannot be articulated in the absence of such considerations. As Howard observed, American and Soviet conclusions about each other during the Cold War often led to "ignorant caricatures."[135]

It was during the public debates in the late 1970s and early 1980s about nuclear weapons that Howard argued that the West altogether ignored the social ramifications of a strategy based on nuclear weapons. As a practical matter, the public was less likely to support and was overwhelmingly opposed to any strategy that rested on using nuclear weapons. Because the employment of nuclear weapons is so devastating, the problem was that neither side could articulate a grand strategy that was able to move beyond policies that rested on conventional options. The point is that just as in the past with the Civil War, World War I, and World War II, the societal dimension heavily influences whether the state's grand strategy is effective.

Implementation of Grand Strategy

The second step in creating an effective grand strategy is its proper implementation. It is not enough to articulate a grand strategy. Grand strategies are not self-executing but require steady, persistent efforts of implementation given the friction of war, the bureaucratic inertia in government that prevails in peacetime, and the unavoidable shroud of uncertainty that governs the final outcomes.

> The implementation of grand strategy depends on marshaling the domestic foundations of national power to strengthen the state's long-term interests.

One theme in the study of grand strategy is the ability of the state to marshal its resources as a way to advance its long-term interests. The challenge for scholars and policy makers is to understand how this idea translates to policies that help the state coordinate its resources into an effective grand strategy.

One well-developed argument that appears throughout historical and contemporary studies of grand strategy is how to effectively organize the state's resources to support its strategy. For instance, D. Clayton James distinguishes the concept of grand strategy in terms of the national and military strategies that were employed during the Pacific War in the 1940s. He defines national strategy as utilizing "all necessary resources – political, diplomatic, military, technological, economic, propagandistic, and others" – to achieve "the objectives of national policy." Bearing in mind its direct relationship to the broader definition of grand strategy, James argues that military strategy refers "to the employment of armed services to secure the ends of national policy by force or the threat of force."[136]

This broader approach to conceptualizing grand strategy for guiding how the state should organize its resources emerges clearly from the work of Gordon A. Craig and Felix Gilbert. They write, "strategy is not merely the art of preparing for the armed conflicts in which a nation may become involved," but it more broadly encompasses "planning [how to] *use ... its resources* and the deployment of its forces in such a way as to [produce] success." For these scholars, grand strategy exists "*in a broader sense,* [as] the modern equivalent of what was, in the seventeenth and eighteenth centuries, called ... *raison d'etat.*" The reasoning by Craig and Gilbert is that grand strategy represents the "rational determination of a nation's vital interests," which properly encompasses all "things ... essential to its security [and] its fundamental purposes" in relations with other states – including the nation's "priorities with respect to [the state's] goals." To help guide the deliberations of contemporary scholars and policy makers, these thinkers describe a "broader form of strategy," which if successful will "guide the narrower strategy of war planning and war fighting."[137]

The idea of defining the implementation of grand strategy in the broader terms of its relationship to marshaling the state's domestic foundations of power is a key but largely ignored teaching from the literature on grand strategy. How "the Truman administration responded to the challenge of the years 1947–1950" is what Craig and Gilbert describe as "a more recent example of a systematic and carefully coordinated national strategy." In the late 1940s, Truman's grand strategy used "a shrewd determination of the nature of American interests in the postwar world," along with "the effective mobilization of public support for [U.S.] European commitments and the skillful use of economic resources to gain its objectives."[138]

The end of the Cold War elevates a central principle in grand strategy, which holds that the state must effectively marshal its resources to support its policies. The reason is that the post–Cold War world left the United States without an obvious adversary for the first time since the end of World War II. For more than half a century before then, the principal motivation of American grand strategy was to articulate a coherent strategy to help guide how Washington allocated resources to deal with its principal adversary. The risk is that the failure to identify an imminent, singular threat does not mean that significant threats do not exist. And failure of American grand strategy to articulate coherent principles will coincide with a drift into a period of ineffective policies. As Gaddis contends, the end of the Cold War era "by no means implies an end to American involvement in whatever world is to follow." Building from the risks that follow when the purpose of American foreign policy is not clear, the function of grand strategy is to articulate a framework that helps policy makers navigate in the unfamiliar terrain of a world that is not marked by the actions of clearly defined adversaries.[139]

Because marshaling resources to support the state's long-term interests is critical to grand strategy, how states balance the countervailing forces of integration and fragmentation within and among societies has a dramatic influence on foreign policy. In the early years after the Cold War came to an end, the search for a new geopolitical cartography (i.e., the Gaddis view of grand strategy) often began with analyses of the balance between the forces of integration and fragmentation in international politics. According to some scholars, the forces of integration are evident from the "connectedness" that follows from the communications revolution, increasing economic integration and interdependence, ideas about a common security regime under the auspices of the United Nations, and building peace among the Great Powers, among others.[140]

However, the forces of fragmentation can be so powerful that they simultaneously resurrect and bolster old and new barriers between nations and peoples. In contemporary politics, nationalist pressures for self-determination have contributed to fragmented societies in the East and the West alike. Protectionist economic policies constitute another cause of fragmentation beyond that of the modern resurgence of extremist ideologies. Yet, fragmentation also exists within societies. In the case of the United States, domestic fragmentation is occurring as a result of a shrinking middle class and an anemic economic outlook, uncontrolled immigration, the drug crisis, the breakdown of the education system, the emergence of a seemingly permanent social and economic "underclass," and the effects of a rising axis of authoritarian states on foreign policy.[141] All of these forces directly influence the formulation of grand strategy.

Whereas the forces of integration may be more benign, Gaddis argues that the trend toward integration runs contrary to America's long-standing ability to maintain the balance of power in a world dominated by diverse rather than uniform interests. However, the contradiction between balancing and integrating power calls for states to reassess the resources they marshaled to support their post–Cold War geopolitical strategies. As one scholar argues, the end of the Cold War "brings not an end to threats, but rather a diffusion of them."[142] The struggle between "integration and fragmentation presents us with difficult choices," including questions about "which tendency we should want to see prevail" or the scale of resources the state should organize to support its strategy.[143]

In considering what resources are necessary to support the state's grand strategy, scholars such as Gaddis call for returning to economic and strategic solvency, while chiding the American public for their reluctance to bear the costs of maintaining national security. As former secretary of defense Robert Gates argues, a central challenge for the United States is how to maintain security without undermining the nation's fundamental values and institutions or destroying the very foundations of the society we seek to defend. This theme emerged in Eisenhower's insistence in his farewell address on January 17, 1961, when he warned, "we must guard against the acquisition of unwarranted influence, whether sought or unsought, by the military-industrial complex." His fear was that "we must never let the weight of this combination endanger our liberties or democratic processes," because the nation "must avoid the impulse to live only for today, plundering for our own ease and convenience the precious resources of tomorrow."[144] To ensure that the state's decisions on spending resources are guided by a coherent strategy, Gaddis held that "bearing the full pain of what one is doing [is the best way to] discipline our conception of the national interest." While acknowledging that this approach may be "constantly annoying, [it is] intellectually bracing [because of its] demands of stringency." In effect, linking grand strategy directly to resources produces "less grandiose visions, but more sustainable policies."[145]

In debates about grand strategy, scholars generally argue that the grand strategy must take into account three conditions: the nation's interests, priorities, and instruments of power. However, the ability to integrate these conditions is a difficult political process that calls for understanding not only the intensity of the state's interests but the extent to which successfully achieving them depends on using certain instruments of power and striking a proper balance among them.[146] When considering how its interests influence how the state organizes its resources to support its grand strategy, a general principle is that the state's interests generally fall into two distinct categories of vital interests.

Donald Nuechterlein outlines a framework for grand strategy that helps analyze and categorize U.S. interests. First, there are survival interests that come into play when the physical existence of the state is at risk. Second, we have vital interests that encompass those interests in which serious harm would occur unless action is taken (often and more specifically by the use of military force). A third category includes the state's major interests, which embrace its economic, political, and social well-being that may be adversely affected but in whose defense the use of military force is not necessarily the proper or best course of action. Lastly, all states have peripheral interests that may or may not be affected by any specific decision or policy outcome and are unlikely to generate direct actions by the state.[147] By combining these categories of interests, the policies the state uses to defend and promote these interests form the basis for what policy makers call the "interest dimension" of grand strategy.

Although this argument about the elements of grand strategy is relatively straightforward, the problem is how to organize the state's resources in ways that effectively protect and promote its interests. In effect, this effort falls into the purely practical realm of how to organize, analyze, and prioritize those interests into a coherent grand strategy. The difficulty with analyzing interests, according to Nuechterlein, involves drawing the line on when the state is willing to use force or other significant policy instruments, such as economic sanctions, and when it responds to challenges to its vital and major interests.[148] Scholars understand that distinguishing between "vital" and "major" is an important but fundamentally difficult undertaking. In the case of the United States, we should consider that the nation has not faced a serious threat to its territorial interests since the Civil War.[149] In practice, the formulation of American grand strategy must deal with the more difficult challenges beyond territorial threats, and these fall essentially between vital and major interests.

Grand strategy must deal with the matter of national objectives and priorities. Once policy makers determine what the state's interests are, the next steps are to prioritize those objectives and then articulate a grand strategy. Even though scholars concur that "ends must be determined by available means,"[150] it is always difficult to determine when the public's willingness to support the strategy reaches the threshold where it is permissible for the state to take action. In the case of the United States, scholars suggest that a latent tendency toward isolationism is so engrained in American political culture that it effectively restrains the nation's desire to take action. President Washington expressed this sentiment in his farewell address, when he said that "Europe has a set of primary interests which to us have none; or a very remote relation."[151] More recently, during the Cold War, nuclear weapons posed a direct threat to American society and hence to its vital interests, but in the calculus of grand strategy, these threats were still so distant as to be almost unthinkable, except during times of direct superpower confrontation such as the 1962 Cuban Missile Crisis.

The challenge for scholars and policy makers is to define the national instruments of power in ways that help implement the state's grand strategy by explaining what actions and policies are covered by the strategy. One approach to translating this concept into grand strategy is to use a threefold classification of the instruments of power. First, grand strategy relies on the state's military power, which in turn rests on the extent to which military force can be employed to achieve its national ends. Second, there is the state's economic power, which specifies the national resources that can be used to achieve its policy objectives. Third, states use their diplomatic (or political) power to guide how their political and diplomatic influence can be used to defend the national interests. All three are critical determinants and instruments of grand strategy.

Joseph Nye and other scholars have identified other types of power as well: soft power ("the ability to affect others through the means of coopting and then framing the agenda, persuading, and eliciting positive attraction in order to obtain preferred outcomes"[152]); cyberpower ("the ability to obtain preferred outcomes through use of the electronically interconnected information resources of the cyberdomain"[153]); and informational power ("the spread of information will mean that power will be more widely distributed and informal networks will undercut the monopoly of traditional bureaucracy"[154]). These secondary types of power are important but should be seen as supplements to the three primary types of power. A state's grand strategy is reliant primarily on military, economic, and diplomatic power – at least that is what history teaches, as there has yet to be a great power whose grand strategy was based primarily on soft power, cyberpower, or informational power.[155]

Policy makers, however, confront several problems when they use these instruments of power to bolster the state's grand strategy. In a democratic society, the extent to which these instruments can be used is greatly restricted by the separation of power among the various branches of government and by the powerful constraints imposed on policy makers by public opinion. Furthermore, calculating the proper use of these factors is less an exact science (i.e., which types of military forces should be used in a given circumstance) than it is closely aligned with being an "art." In reality, since policy makers rarely confront situations calling for them to mobilize just one instrument of power, they struggle with determining how to strike the right balance when using the instruments of power. To complicate matters, the fact that each county has a different history, a different culture, and different interests reinforces the tendency of policy makers to rely on different instruments at different times for varying reasons. Furthermore, the emphasis that individual states and policy makers place on each of the instruments of power varies significantly over time.

Nevertheless, the decisions that policy makers make, while scholars evaluate how best to advance the state's interests using the various instruments of power, all dramatically impact the effectiveness of the state's grand strategy. One determinant of whether a grand strategy is successful is how effectively the state mobilizes its resources – notably its economic and military power and public support – to defend its interests. Several scholars, including Edward Mead Earle, Gordon A. Craig, and Felix Gilbert, in their *Makers of Modern Strategy: Military Thought from Machiavelli to Hitler* (1973), examine the development of modern strategy, which encompasses both grand strategy and war strategy, through an analysis of the influence of various strategists whose works date back to the sixteenth century, if not earlier, in the annals of strategy. The intellectual pillars of strategy, which are explored in Chapters 4 and 6, include such theorists as Machiavelli, Jomini, Clausewitz, Adam Smith, Alexander Hamilton, Friedrich List, Engels, Marx, Churchill, Hitler, Stalin, Ho Chi Minh, and Liddell Hart, among others. The ideas of these and many other strategists and theorists who have studied the nature of war have built the foundations directly and indirectly for what we know today as grand strategy.[156]

Earle's analysis of strategy rests on what the state does both conceptually and practically to deal with the conduct of war, preparations for war, and *mobilizing its economy and society*. Until the end of the eighteenth century, plotting and scheming on how to use military force and alliances to gain the territory and material resources of another state dominated the evolution of strategy. However, Earle argues that as the techniques of war were refined and societies developed, strategy increasingly incorporated a number of nonmilitary factors, of which economic, psychological, moral, political, and technological considerations are essential determinants. In effect, the function of grand strategy is to provide a coherent framework within which the state is able to mobilize all these factors, which, as Earle asserts, are relevant in more than simply the conduct of war. This remains "an inherent element of statecraft at all times." Drawing on the logic of this modern theorist, strategy is linked to grand strategy when we define the former as "the art of controlling and utilizing the resources of a nation – or a coalition of nations – including its armed forces [so] that its vital interests shall be effectively promoted and secured against enemies, actual, potential, or merely presumed."[157]

In implementing a nation's grand strategy (using, in this case, the example of the United States), its policies should be "formulated by [such political actors as] the President and the General Staff and implemented by acts of Congress."[158] In times of war, democracies require the efforts of their leaders to build support for the nation's grand strategy, which reflects decisions about what resources the citizens are willing to devote to supporting the strategy. That strategy also must be understood and embraced by all members of the society. As Earle writes, "Even the private soldiers and the junior officers of an embattled democratic society must know the purposes for which they risk their lives."[159] Earle cites the example of Winston Churchill as a supremely effective leader whose "magnificent speeches" about Great Britain's grand strategy told the British people precisely why their sons and fathers were dying on faraway battlefields.[160] Drawing on Churchill's compelling and vivid explanations of the underlying reasons for the war – which he presented in his May 20, 1943, address to the U.S. Congress – Earle gives some credit to Churchill for his ability to persuade a previously divided American public that its vital interests called on it to actively support Great Britain's efforts to defeat Germany first before shifting to fight against Japan in the Pacific theater.[161]

When the prospect of war aligns with the state's grand strategy, the implementation of the strategy will require a significant effort on the part of society. Facing this circumstance, Earle argues that the public must embrace the reality that the path charted by the state's grand strategy is one they share. His reasoning is that "the very existence of a nation depends on its concept of the national interest and the means by which the national interest is promoted." The imperative for democratic societies is to ensure that their citizens "understand the fundamentals of strategy."[162] Properly articulated and implemented, the state's grand strategy should communicate more-or-less precisely what efforts the members of the society are willing to make to support its grand strategy.

Another scholar who contemplated the relationship between national interests and the society's ability to mobilize its resources in support of grand strategy is Samuel Huntington. His works studied how to redefine the concept of America's "national interest" once the power and influence of the Soviet Union was no longer a defining consideration. In this scholar's view, the lack of a coherent American identity contributed to the erosion of a consensus on the clearly defined interests of the nation.[163] The problem for Huntington was that foreign policy is vulnerable to the criticism of being disjointed because, without a clear threat, it tends to reflect the priorities of particular interest groups. The implicit argument is that the nation's grand strategy must reflect and embrace a societal identity, which Huntington argued is increasingly elusive.

Writing in the late 1990s, Huntington observed that the American identity is in a state of gradual disintegration. Since a nation's interests follow from its national identity, he argued that the United States has a significantly "weakened sense of national purpose," which will cause its national identity to fragment and will gradually undermine its grand strategy. His argument is that the American identity historically was based on culture (notably based on the English language, church/state relations, ideas about the individual's place in society) and creed (a set of universal ideas and principles such as liberty, equality, democracy, and constitutionalism, among others). These sources of the American identity are changing because, with "the end of the Cold War and social, intellectual, and demographic changes in American society," the society faces increasingly profound "questions about the validity and relevance of both traditional components of American identity." For Huntington, the intersection of these forces contributes to a serious problem: "without a sure sense of national identity, Americans have become unable to define their national interests." In practical terms, the confluence of "subnational commercial interests and transnational and nonnational ethnic interests" will increasingly control the formulation and implementation of American grand strategy.[164]

One reason for the weakening sense of national identity is the absence of external threats, which Huntington said makes it more difficult for policy makers in Washington to articulate a grand strategy that permits them to build a public consensus and mobilize the resources necessary to support it. To further complicate matters, the disintegrative effects that emerged at the end of the Cold War were reinforced by two trends in American society: changes in immigration and the rise of multiculturalism. Not only do the "ideologies of multiculturalism and diversity reinforce and legitimate these trends,"[165] but more dangerously, according to Huntington, these ideologies undermine the "central element in the American Creed" because these "[substitute] for the rights of individuals the rights of groups, defined largely by terms of race, ethnicity, gender and sexual preference."[166] Because immigrants founded the nation, one counter to his argument is to note that multiculturalism and diversity are fundamentally engrained in the American experience. However, the central point, according to Huntington, is that the absence of an external threat amplifies the tendency within the American political environment to emphasize the views of special interest groups.

The unifying element that is necessary for mobilizing the proper level of resources to implement the state's grand strategy is properly defining its national interests. In practical terms, a national interest is "a public good of concern to all or most Americans," and "a vital national interest is one on which they are willing to expend blood and treasure to defend."[167] During the Cold War, the Soviet Union and communism were widely seen as direct and serious threats to both American security and values, which Huntington said created a "happy coincidence" between the demands of power politics and the demands of morality. It did, however, create a dilemma: "instead of a need to find the power to serve American purposes, there is a need to find purposes for the use of American power." The American foreign policy establishment searches for a "new sense of purpose that would justify a continuing U.S. role in world affairs comparable to what Washington followed during the Cold War,"[168] but the central missing ingredient is a consensus on the purposes that drive the nation's grand strategy and the resources needed to support it.[169]

One argument in scholarship is that the implementation of grand strategy depends on a clear articulation of agreed-upon goals. In an article in *Foreign Affairs* in 2000, Condoleezza Rice argued that states need a disciplined and consistent approach to foreign policy, which helps policy makers distinguish between the important and the trivial, while not seeking to assuage the concerns of all interest groups. Although Rice's article appeared one year before the September 11th attacks altered American security and hence its grand strategy, her main argument was that the national interest, which consists of more than humanitarian interests and the interests of the international community (which she does not wholly discount), should govern the state's grand strategy and drive the mobilization of the resources needed to support it.[170]

Rice's argument rests on several key points. To begin with, for this former national security advisor and secretary of state in the Bush administration, humanitarian concerns and a strong desire to appeal to the international community distracted policy makers' attention during the Clinton administration – from formulating grand strategy and achieving a societal consensus on the resources needed to defend and promote the nation's central national interests. In effect, inconsistencies in grand strategy can be problematic in highly pluralistic democracies when "the absence of an articulated 'national interest' produces a fertile ground for those wishing to withdraw from the world or creates a vacuum to be filled by parochial groups," which often are driven by "transitory pressures." Thus, for U.S. grand strategy, the challenge is to mobilize resources as a way to promote a unified conception of U.S. national interests along several dimensions.[171]

According to Rice, what ultimately matters in grand strategy is having the power to implement it. The problem is that discomfort with using power politics to create a stable balance of power led to the conclusion that international law and norms and institutions, as embodied in the United Nations, are necessary instruments for bounding the legitimate and effective exercise of the state's grand strategy.[172] However, whereas Rice argues that "there is nothing wrong with doing something that benefits all humanity," this remains, in Rice's view, a "second-order effect." An enduring requirement of American grand strategy is to mobilize the resources needed to pursue U.S. national interest so that the nation can create "conditions that promote freedom, markets, and peace." Rice argues that historically American grand strategy – based on the "pursuit of national interests after World War II" – was instrumental in permitting the United States to build a "more prosperous and democratic world."[173]

This is not to argue, however, that the architects of American grand strategy should reject the principle that humanitarian values motivate the state to intervene. The reason is that policy makers should have the freedom to intervene when they believe that the United States has a strategic or moral obligation to do so. However, when our values are attacked in areas that reside lower on the scale of strategic priorities, the decision to intervene must be balanced with the view that an excessive commitment to humanitarian conflicts can weaken the consensus on what resources the society should mobilize in defense of its grand strategy. This phenomenon, known as "mission creep," puts the state's grand strategy at risk, because it can dissipate the nation's consensus, particularly if policy makers pursue an "overly broad definition of America's national interest." This approach to grand strategy, for Rice, would "be a mistake."[174]

Finally, Rice addresses the problem that rogue states pose for the state's grand strategy, notably the cases of Iraq before 2003 as well as North Korea and Iran. According to Rice, U.S. grand strategy must be implemented in a decisive and resolute approach, beginning with "a clear and classical statement of deterrence," followed by efforts to defend against nuclear, chemical, and biological weapons and to expand the nation's intelligence capabilities.[175] In summary, Rice argues that the problem with American foreign policy "is not an absence of bipartisan spirit in Congress or the American people's disinterest . . . [but] the existence of a vacuum" on what the state seeks to accomplish. The point is that "unless grand strategy helps a society define what resources it should devote to foreign policy, the result will be confusion and discord."[176] Accordingly, for Rice, a state's grand strategy should be firmly rooted in the national interest rather than reflect the interests of an "illusory international community."[177] What is at stake is the balance between the pursuit of national interests and the desire to promote international norms and values.

These arguments highlight the difficulties that exist when policy makers are tasked with formulating a grand strategy that marshals the domestic foundations of national power required to support it but seeks to avoid policies that will bankrupt the state economically or weaken its morale. In the case of World War II, the scholar Jim Lacey writes that "Roosevelt sold the American people on the idea that the United States was to become the vast 'arsenal of democracy' that would save the world."[178] However, it took some time before war planners would "determine exactly what victory in a global war against Germany, Japan, and Italy would require in terms of munitions and equipment" that the nation must mobilize.[179]

Beyond the example of the highly successful American grand strategy in World War II, scholars such as Stephen Krasner contend that the broader problem is that so many efforts to articulate grand strategy simply end in failure. Noting that grand strategy "provide[s] resources – diplomatic, bureaucratic, ideational, military, economic – for specific policies," the reason so many attempts fail is, for Krasner, an imminently practical one. In effect, scholars and policy makers find it inherently difficult "to align vision, policies, and resources" with the state's grand strategy.[180] Those who study how to align the state's resources with its grand strategy well understand that this challenge is so daunting that it explains why so many efforts failed historically, for reasons we examine later.

One case study from Kennedy's *Grand Strategies in War and Peace* shows how marshaling the domestic sources of national power depends on both nonmaterial and material factors. In examining the French military's utter collapse in the face of Nazi Germany's military pressure in World War II, Douglas Porch argues that this result was the product of several factors.[181] Not only were political intrigues and poor planning among its politicians to blame. Strategists also must consider the role of pessimism and the general lack of faith in the country that gripped the middle classes as well as much of the country and its leadership. Furthermore, the low productivity, selfishness, and lack of patriotism of the trade unions, as well as the failure of the French officer corps to critically analyze their own prejudices, all contributed to France's collapse.[182] From this case emerges the argument that internal domestic political forces in a society and its leadership can contribute decisively to the failure of the state to build and marshal the domestic foundations of national power that are necessary to support its grand strategy.[183]

Implementing grand strategy also depends on balancing means and ends.

The classic means-ends balance is of fundamental prominence as policy makers struggle with how to articulate and implement the state's grand strategy in the face of the always-serious economic and political constraints. The problem of striking a balance between means and ends presents a lesson in the perils of overreach, which is all too common when states miscalculate what resources and public support their grand strategy calls for.[184]

The role of balancing ends and means in grand strategy was apparent as the British historian Sir Basil H. Liddell Hart outlined his ideas about the fundamental differences that separate strategy and grand strategy. The central argument in Liddell Hart's analysis is how important it is for those who articulate and implement grand strategy to rein in the dangerous imbalance that so often exists between means and ends. In the extreme case, this imbalance exists between the conduct of war and the ability to achieve the state's political aims in the peace that should follow.[185] The inescapable logic in the view of Liddell Hart is that scholars and policy makers routinely fail to strike the proper balance between ends and means as they articulate and subsequently put their grand strategy into practice. When this failure occurs, policy makers will learn the consequences of the perils that exist with what Paul Kennedy describes as "overreach."[186]

This critical balancing between means and ends in grand strategy was emphasized in Kennedy's writings, and his conclusion was that it is "critical for those [tasked with] formulating grand strategy to balance economic and manpower resources [so that the state can] sustain the fight and avoid damage to a future state of peace (the ultimate end goal)."[187] Christopher Layne, who defines grand strategy primarily as "the process by which a state matches ends and means in the pursuit of security," concurs with this line of reasoning. He argues that grand strategy in peacetime is tasked with "defining the state's security interests; identifying the threats to those interests; and allocating military, diplomatic, and economic resources to defend the state's interests."[188]

The overwhelming responsibility for scholars and policy makers of grand strategy is to ensure, above all else, that the state's grand strategy expresses fairly and accurately a broad conception of the state's interests and objectives. Only then can the state balance its available means with ends. Gaddis builds on this means-ends argument when he writes that strategy "is nothing more than the calculated relation of ends and means." Critically, he uses the adjective "calculated" to imply "a deliberate as opposed to an accidental, inadvertent, or fortuitous connection" between the two.[189] Such arguments are central to how well the state articulates and implements its grand strategy.

The classic example of the failure to balance ends and means is the case of the Roman Empire. In Kennedy's *Grand Strategies in War and Peace*, Arther Ferrill examines the failure of the Roman Empire's grand strategy.[190] His argument is that Rome's grand strategy centered on maintaining the empire through a forward-deployed troop posture and the clear demarcation of its frontiers. A distinguishing feature in Roman grand strategy was that it was understood implicitly to mean the expansion of the Roman world and the subjugation of the non-Roman world. The Romans' grand strategy was fundamentally about expanding the territorial reach of Roman control over uncivilized and "inferior" cultures. Although this strategy was successful for some time, the failure of Rome's grand strategy derived from its dramatic inability, as it emerged over several centuries, to match ends (the maintenance and expansion of the empire) with the means available (i.e., the forward deployment of Roman forces). One conclusion from this case was that Rome's policy resulted in the failure of imperial defense and overreach, leading eventually to its collapse as an empire.[191]

Conclusion

This chapter advances the argument that grand strategies are best evaluated along two axes: articulation and implementation. Articulation involves forging a conceptual unity between strategy and grand strategy, which properly distinguishes between grand strategy, policy, doctrine, logistics, and operations. Implementation is equally important and consists of the recognition that (1) grand strategy is an ongoing process along the war-peace continuum, (2) any successful implementation will require the marshaling of the domestic foundations of national power, and (3) grand strategy is a process of balancing and rebalancing means and ends over time. The next three chapters trace the origins of these elements in the works of the major theorists and practitioners of grand strategy. Then we turn to the evolution of American grand strategy in the second part of the book. Once this foundation for understanding grand strategy is in place, the last part of the book proposes a working outline for American grand strategy in the twenty-first century.

4   Ancient and Modern Eras of Grand Strategy

Chapter 4 provides an overview of the evolution of the theory of grand strategy as it developed, from its roots in ancient China and Greece to prominent theorists who contributed to the philosophical, military, and economic foundations of grand strategy since the seventeenth century. These scholars and strategists laid the foundations for understanding the forces that shape the articulation of grand strategy and its development as a discipline for guiding how the state implements its policies and strategies.

Grand Strategy in the Ancient Era

The development of grand strategy can be traced back to ancient China, Greece, and Rome. To understand how the thinkers of those eras contributed to the evolution of grand strategy, this chapter analyzes prominent strategists whose ideas and principles helped articulate the defining concepts of strategy from which the discipline and principles of grand strategy are derived. The ideas developed by these thinkers influence primarily how we as modern scholars and policy makers think about the nature of the articulation of grand strategy and, to some extent, its implementation.

Ancient China – Sun Tzu

Scholars are not certain when Sun Tzu lived. Most, however, think it was during the Spring and Autumn Period of Chinese history (ca. 771–476 BCE). Experts believe that Sun Tzu lived at the end of this era of upheaval and reform (ca. 544–496 BCE). However, his book *The Art of War*, which was not completed until later – in the Warring States Period (476–221 BCE) – is probably a compilation of strategic thought from various authors.[1]

In *The Art of War*, Sun Tzu does not discuss grand strategy directly, nor does he use that term in his book. *The Art of War* is written in brief, almost poetic sentences and deals largely with the tactical element of war and the importance in strategy of terrain, maneuver, logistics, and supply. Despite Sun Tzu's detailed discussions and analysis of military operations and tactics, several sections are highly relevant to the origins of grand strategy. In particular, *The Art of War* provides some enduring insights on the articulation and implementation of grand strategy.

His implicit argument about the formulation of grand strategy is that, first, it is a process that arises from the security demands of dealing with the state's most pressing threats and conflicts. Second, it emerges from a continuous process along the war-peace continuum that should be, but is not always, based on the *rational* calculation of interests, challenges, and opportunities. And third, the best grand strategies are those that "attack the enemy's [grand] strategy." To attack the enemy's grand strategy is to take into account the enemy's tendencies and likely reactions, and then to incorporate those calculations into the state's grand strategy. In terms of implementing the state's grand strategy, Sun Tzu emphasizes the necessity of balancing the means with the ends.

Sun Tzu's Articulation of Grand Strategy

To begin with, Sun Tzu understood that grand strategy is often articulated in response to a period of instability and struggle. The Spring and Autumn Period was a period of intense and frequent interstate wars in the Yellow River basin, because there, premodern states developed organized military capabilities and competed for power and influence over territory and people. Thus, one theme in the development of grand strategy is that the process by which it emerges often is triggered by periods of great struggle or confrontation within and among societies. Further, even though grand strategies can possess a reactive or defensive quality, they also can simultaneously provide offensive principles that guide the state as it promotes, aggressively if necessary, the broad objectives in its foreign policy. This balance between offense and defense constitutes a fundamental tension in grand strategy that applies equally to states in times of both war and peace.

This line of reasoning sheds light on how Sun Tzu contemplated the field of what we call grand strategy. A critical part of his argument is the role of conflict, which implied for this strategist that the principal objective of strategy (and, by extension, of grand strategy in modern terms) is to achieve success in political and military endeavors. Success, as Sun Tzu wrote, "is the main object in war. If this is long delayed, weapons are blunted and morale depressed." At the same time, this process of articulation is emotionally charged for the very same reasons. Periods of struggle and upheaval stir powerful human emotions that can interfere with coherent and purposeful thinking about the best way to pursue one's grand strategy. The risks for the state increase when its grand strategy is influenced by emotions, because these all too often affect adversely the decisions of policy makers. To cite Sun Tzu, "A sovereign cannot raise an army because he is enraged, nor can a general fight because he is resentful." His analysis continues as he writes about an enduring principle of strategy that holds that, "while an angered man may again be happy, and a resentful man again be pleased, a state that has perished cannot be restored, nor can the dead be brought back to life." In effect, he is affirming the principle that the formulation and conduct of grand strategy must be driven, first and foremost, by reason and analysis and never by one's emotions or passions.[2]

One function of grand strategy is to articulate the value of offensive principles that describe what objectives should fundamentally guide what the state accomplishes in foreign policy and how it should do so. Sun Tzu's foremost principle in strategy, which strategists and theorists cite approvingly, is that "what is of supreme importance . . . is to attack the enemy's strategy." This logic applies equally well to the conduct of grand strategy. The state's strategy may rest on either the offensive or the defensive as long as its core purpose is to define the nation's strategy in a way that undermines or attacks the adversary's overall strategy while advancing its own. Although the state may seek to defeat or destroy the adversary in military terms, Sun Tzu advises policy makers and strategists alike that "to capture the enemy's army is better than to destroy it; to take intact a battalion, a company or five-man squad is better than to destroy them." In effect, Sun Tzu is outlining the principle of minimizing risks and damage as core elements of strategy.[3]

In all cases, the superior strategy is to attack the source of the enemy's power and the fundamental strategy that guides its behavior. If that approach is not possible, as Sun Tzu proposed, "the next best [strategy] is to disrupt his alliances."[4] His argument is that the power of the state matters, particularly when it defines its own strategy as an instrument for defeating that of its opponent. For Sun Tzu, "when a Hegemonic King attacks a powerful state he makes it impossible for the enemy to concentrate [because he] overawes the enemy and prevents his allies from joining him." If the state does not clearly understand the enemy's strategy, it is in a less advantageous position because "one [who is] ignorant of the plans of neighboring states cannot prepare alliances in good time."[5]

A cardinal principle of strategy for Sun Tzu is to encourage the state to take advantage of opportunities that present themselves. To put this strategy into practice, he directs policy makers to consider what the enemy may value and what crucial steps it may take to ensure that its strategy prevails. Thus, the policy maker should "anticipate [that the adversary will seize] something he values and move in accordance."[6] Lastly, it should be noted that beyond supporting the central importance of the offensive in strategy, Sun Tzu also defended the value of the principles of moderation and damage limitation when the state acts to promote its strategy. This philosophy was evident from his argument that "generally in war the best policy is to take the state intact; to ruin it is inferior to this."[7] Although he does not express it in precisely these terms, Sun Tzu's concern for moderation and limiting collateral damage underscores a central argument in this book about grand strategy. Notably, grand strategy and strategy ("war" in Sun Tzu's terms) must be in close unity with the state's goals. Why should the state bother losing precious blood and treasure to achieve success over territory that has been destroyed or desecrated in the process – or simply is not worth the effort? No strategy is worth absorbing unnecessary losses.

Sun Tzu's Implementation of Grand Strategy

In practice, Sun Tzu introduces two cautionary principles to guide how states should articulate grand strategy. The first focuses on balancing the strategy with an analysis of the state's interests and resources: "If not in the interests of the state, do not act. If you cannot succeed, do not use troops. If you are not in danger, do not fight." A central principle for Sun Tzu is that the strategy must align with the state's interests and resources.

A second and related principle is that the risks for the state increase if its strategy encourages it to engage in protracted wars or struggles.[8] The danger is that a strategy relying on the use of a protracted struggle can lead to the state's physical and psychological exhaustion. In Sun Tzu's view, the "acme of skill [is not] to win one hundred victories in one hundred battles [but to] subdue the enemy without fighting." Here, Sun Tzu explicates the concept of the indirect approach, which later would be advanced by Liddell Hart.[9] As the ancient Chinese strategist observed, "those skilled in war subdue the enemy's army without battle." The essence of strategy, for Sun Tzu, is to "capture his cities without assaulting them and overthrow his state without protracted operations."[10] Implicit, however, is Sun Tzu's view of an ideal condition in grand strategy: to let the enemy defeat itself and avoid the costs of war as much as possible.

In speaking about implementing the state's grand strategy, Sun Tzu outlined approaches that do not rely purely on the sheer size or number of military forces or of resources, and he warned against relying on military dominance alone to secure success. For Sun Tzu, numbers alone provide no inherent advantage in strategy. The scholar Michael Handel, in his *Masters of War*, argues that unlike Clausewitz and Jomini who strongly favored risk-taking in strategy, "Sun Tzu's preferred center of [strategic] gravity implies the need to avoid the risks associated with the use of force if possible."[11] What this means for strategy, using the words of Sun Tzu, is that the "victorious army wins its victories before seeking battle [since] an army destined to defeat [still] fights in hope of winning." His preferred approach was to articulate strategy to ensure that it accurately reflects whether the state's power and influence are sufficient to permit it to achieve success. As Sun Tzu notes, a policy maker should seek to achieve "his aims [by using] his ability to overawe his opponents," which in the classic sense constituted a strategy often based on taking "the enemy's cities and overthrow[ing] the enemy state."[12]

Sun Tzu identifies several fundamental factors – moral influence, weather, terrain, command, and doctrine – that have a decisive effect on strategy and the state's ability to prevail. As this Chinese strategist states plainly, "Those who master [these fundamental factors] win [while] those who do not are defeated."[13] Whereas such issues as weather, terrain, command, and doctrine are tangential to the study of grand strategy, these operational elements for Sun Tzu form a hierarchy of less critical concepts. However, the idea of moral influence directly influences how states articulate grand strategy, which for Sun Tzu is directly relevant to its implementation. He judges the factor of moral influence to be a fundamental determinant of the success of a grand strategy. In his language, moral influence encompasses "that which causes the people to be in harmony with their leaders."[14] The reason moral influence is critical derives from the reality that when policy makers or leaders seek to persuade the society to follow their policies, they often rely on moral injunctions to influence public sentiment. In Sun Tzu's view, moral conditions impose a constraint on public support and constitute a central influence on how well states articulate and implement strategy.

Finally, Sun Tzu was a strong proponent of the argument that the state and its policy makers must articulate their strategy so that it adheres to the principle of adaptability. To help scholars and policy makers understand how well the state responds to unexpected challenges and opportunities, Sun Tzu defended the concept of adaptability, or agility, as the "strategist's key to victory." Adaptation is a principle that bridges the articulation of grand strategy between the continuous, rational process along the war-peace continuum and the balancing of ends and means that occurs in its implementation. Since policy makers can never know all possibilities in advance, and the policy maker must, "when confronted by the enemy, respond to changing circumstances and devise expedients," Sun Tzu emphasizes that the principle of adaptation is critical to successfully articulating and implementing a state's strategy.[15] In the end, the concept of adaptability calls for adjusting one's strategy to match the decisions and actions of the enemy. To quote Sun Tzu, "the crux of military operations lies in the pretense of accommodating one's self to the designs of the enemy."[16]

With these ideas, Sun Tzu has exerted a powerful influence on subsequent generations of scholars and policy makers, principally because he was a preeminent advocate of the indirect approach to strategy. This approach relates to the ideas of the scholar Handel, who attributed the "longevity and preeminence of *The Art of War* and *On War*" to two central factors: "the underlying logic of human nature, and by extension of political action, [which] has not changed throughout history," and "the greatly increased complexity of modern warfare." Sun Tzu and Clausewitz, according to Handel, "viewed war as infinitely complex … but modern technological developments have added an entirely new dimension of uncertainty," often by "[obfuscating] the fundamental principles of strategy [which in] the post-industrial age is now impossible."[17] In addition, the principle of letting the enemy defeat itself and its own strategy became a central pillar of various grand strategies, including that of containment.[18]

Ancient Greece – Thucydides

The ancient Greek historian Thucydides (ca. 460–400 BCE) was an influential strategist who wrote about the Peloponnesian Wars that raged between the ancient Greek city-states of Athens and Sparta.[19] (He had served Athens, unsuccessfully defending the colony Amphipolis, and wrote in exile.) His major contribution to the literature of grand strategy, *History of the Peloponnesian War*, is rightfully revisited in civilian and military academic and policy circles for its portrayal of the perils that protracted war can visit on democracies. The parallels between Thucydides's narrative of Athenian democratic, economic, and naval power against Sparta's authoritarian government but conventionally superior military capabilities is often used in the modern era to illuminate the characteristics of the strategies that operated in such historical events as the Union and the Confederacy in the American Civil War, the dynamics between the Allied and Axis powers in World War II, and the interactions between the superpowers during the Cold War.

Like Sun Tzu, Thucydides does not discuss grand strategy directly, nor does he use the term in his book. That being said, it is clear from a careful reading of the *History* that for Thucydides, grand strategy is the result of the outcomes that derive from both tactical and strategic successes that occur among contending states. As one of the preeminent strategists who wrote during the Peloponnesian Wars, Thucydides's ideas translated directly into much of the early thinking about grand strategy, particularly in terms of the critical motifs that this study explores. In the case of the articulation of grand strategy, it governs the relationship among strategy, policy, and doctrine in the struggle among states for influence. As to implementation, Thucydides returns repeatedly to the art of striking the right balance between means and ends in grand strategy. As with Sun Tzu, Thucydides held that grand strategy is shaped by the competitive tendencies among powerful states. This perspective derives from seeing grand strategy as the product of many influences, including the various ways in which allies help or hinder the state as it pursues its objectives.

Thucydides and the Articulation of Grand Strategy

In terms of the articulation of grand strategy, the key for Thucydides was to translate policy deliberations into prudent strategy. As outlined in Pericles's Funeral Oration and in Diodotus's speech during the debate about whether to punish Mytilene for revolting, Pericles warned that "instead of looking on discussion as a stumbling block in the way of action, we think it an indispensable preliminary to any wise action at all."[20] For those who contemplate the articulation of strategy, Diodotus (a moderate Athenian who supported Pericles's policies) argues that "the two things most opposed to good counsel are haste and passion; haste usually goes hand in hand with folly, passion with coarseness and narrowness of mind."[21] The problem, however, is that years of protracted war caused great dissatisfaction within the Athenian democracy, and this proved to be a catalyst for Athens' descent into oligarchy. It also effectively amplified the extent to which "haste and passion" figured prominently in the deliberations among Athenian policy makers. Recalling Sun Tzu's insight about the benefits that follow from the rational calculation of grand strategy, Thucydides saw the decline of rational politics as the war dragged on year after year, until it finally degraded Athens' ability to make prudent decisions about its grand strategy.

It is essential for there to be a strong degree of unity between the state's grand strategy and the policies it pursues, particularly in the case of war. As Thucydides writes in the *History of the Peloponnesian War*, Pericles argued that in order to defeat Sparta and maintain the Athenian empire, Athens must avoid new conquests and unnecessary risks until the war was over – if the goal was to ensure that war was consistent with Athens' foreign policy goals. To cite Pericles, "I have many other reasons to hope for a favorable outcome, if you can consent not to combine schemes of fresh conquest with the conduct of the war."[22] Athenian general and politician Nicias tried to dissuade Athens from the Sicilian expedition, given the other pressing challenges that Athens faced. His argument was that "a man ought, therefore, to consider these points, and not to think of running risks … or of grasping at another empire before we have secured the one we have already." In effect, Nicias faults Athens for losing its ability to focus on its primary strategic objective.[23] In the end, Athenians disobeyed the strategic guidance outlined by both Pericles and Nicias when they made the decision to invade Sicily, which contributed to Athens' strategic overstretch and eventually to its defeat in the war. In this case, we have a lesson in the perils of overreach that threaten all too commonly when states miscalculate the ends-means balance in their grand strategy.

Thucydides affirmed that Pericles "rightly gauged the power of his country [and] the correctness of his foresight concerning the war became better known after his death." Pericles's advice was "to wait quietly, to pay attention to their marine, to attempt no new conquests, and to expose the city to no hazards during the war." Despite his advice on limiting the ends of Athens' grand strategy, Athenian leaders took the "contrary" path, which permitted "private ambitions and private interests, in matters apparently quite foreign to the war, to lead them into projects unjust both to themselves and to their allies."[24] Pericles suggested that Athens should let the Peloponnesians commence hostilities, presumably so that they could paint the Spartans as the aggressors and at the same time demonstrate that Athens was a benevolent hegemon: "We shall not commence hostilities, but shall resist those who do commence them."[25] In addition to formulating a less overtly aggressive grand strategy, Pericles, in his Funeral Oration, praises Athenian democracy for its openness to the world and declares that its military conduct differed markedly from that of Sparta.[26]

As the war progressed, this policy of openness was steadily undermined, which demonstrates the effects that a protracted war can have on a state's grand strategy. The Mytilenian Dialogue presents two opposing views on how the strategy for and conduct of war must be in unity with their objectives. In the first view, Cleon argued that because Athens' empire depended on receiving tribute from its allies, by force if necessary, Athens should have shown no mercy in punishing those like Mytilene, who betrayed Athens and attempted to undermine its empire. As Pericles urged, "Punish them as they deserve, and teach your other allies by a striking example that the penalty of rebellion is death."[27]

The second view is that of Diodotus, who argued that because Athens' empire depended on receiving tribute through the willful acquiescence of its allies, Athens should have demonstrated political adeptness by distinguishing between the elites of Mytilene, who instigated the revolt, and its people, who should have been spared the costs of war. In effect, Thucydides extols the virtue of moderation in grand strategy, despite the fact that Diodotus's argument carried the day.[28] Benevolence on behalf of Athens early in the war stands in contrast with the bloodthirstiness and desire for total war that emerges as the war drags on. This dialogue speaks of the consequences of a drawn-out war on a nation's resources and character, and most decisively on the integrity and prudence of its grand strategy.

Thucydides and the Implementation of Grand Strategy

It is also useful to consider how, for Thucydides, the ability of policy makers to marshal the domestic and international foundations of power affects the implementation of grand strategy. At the beginning of Thucydides's history, the Athenian empire's grand strategy was to rely on tribute and commerce to maintain the state's position of power and influence on the peninsula. For this strategy to succeed, the Athenians had to secure the allegiance of their allies, which they accomplished by their largely just and moderate rule. As the Athenians said to the Spartans, the "empire we acquired [was] not by violence, but because ... the allies attached themselves to us and spontaneously asked us to assume the command."[29] In principle, mobilizing the state's resources should not be pursued if it is done at the risk of undermining the state's own principles. However, the Corinthians urged the Spartans to wage war by undermining Athens' base of support and persuading their allies to break away from the Athenians. Although they had various means for "carrying on the war, such as revolt of their allies, the surest method [was] depriving them of their revenues,. ... the source of their strength."[30]

Grand strategy, for Thucydides in the context of politics on the Greek peninsula, focused on organizing the state's resources. This emphasis on means was evident when the Corinthians characterized the Athenians and Spartans as opposites in terms of how they dealt with the means of grand strategy. As Thucydides warned, "The Athenians are addicted to innovation, and their designs are characterized by swiftness alike in conception and execution; [Sparta] has a genius for keeping what you have got, accompanied by a total want of invention, and when forced to act you never go far enough." This analysis resonated with the views of Spartan king Archidamus, who argued that Sparta should delay going to war with Athens, which was far superior to Sparta, both materially and financially. He identified how compelling the difference was in terms of the comparative power of the adversary: "Unless we can either beat them at sea, or deprive them of the revenues which feed their navy, we shall meet with little but disaster." The better strategy for Sparta was to delay going to war, because that would give it more time to further "develop our home resources." Then, as now, his point, which is germane to policy makers who seek to link ends with resources, is that strategy is inextricably governed as much by "arms as ... money."[31] Furthermore, the marshaling of a state's resources was as central to grand strategy as is harnessing technological innovation.

The Corinthians, in fact, urged Sparta to marshal the resources of its entire coalition before confronting Athens. As they noted, "We have in Athens an enemy that is a match for our whole coalition, and more than a match for any of its members." When the

Spartans failed to realize this, they warned that "unless as a body and as individual nationalities and individual cities we make a unanimous stand against her," we will be "easily conquer[ed]" and "divided . . . city by city."[32] What the Corinthians understood is that highly effective strategies historically rely on coalitions of states rather than individual states to marshal the requisite resources for presenting a unified front against a common enemy. Such, for example, was the grand strategy of the West in its post–World War II struggle against the Soviet Union.

The argument about the relationship between resources and strategy has significant consequences for modern practitioners and students of grand strategy. Whereas the Athenians began the war seeking to co-opt or coerce allies to support them in order to provide tribute to subsidize expanding their empire, their strategy ultimately was to defeat Syracuse. But as Thucydides observed, their strategy led to defeat, because the Athenians "were beaten at all points and altogether; all that they suffered was great; they were destroyed . . . with a total destruction, their fleet, their army – everything was destroyed."[33] A central lesson for Thucydides was that an effective grand strategy requires the state to carefully balance means and ends or risk defeat, if not annihilation.

A further element in Athens' grand strategy, writes Thucydides, was the role of allies and their ability to decisively influence the outcomes of struggles among states. In fact, the Mytilenians asked Sparta to receive them as allies on the grounds that if they did so, Sparta would undermine the foundations of Athens' tactics and strategy (which was based on contributions from allies, sea power, and the Athenians' perceived benevolent rule). As he wrote in his *History of the Peloponnesian War*, "It is not in Attica that the war will be decided . . . but in the countries by which Attica is supported [and from which] the Athenian revenue is drawn from allies."[34] The appearance of Athens' overwhelming power when it invaded Sicily later in the war prevented it from achieving its strategy of convincing all city-states on the island to ally with it. The size of the expedition frightened other Sicilian city-states and induced them to unite with Syracuse. In fact, Hermocrates forewarns of this: "Nor is the greatness of their armament altogether without advantage to us."[35]

Thus, there is an inherent tension between marshaling and deploying the state's resources to their utmost and attracting allies to support the strategy. The appearance of overwhelming power invites counterbalancing, and can sometimes actually provoke it. Thucydides, as a keen observer of political actions and reactions at the level of grand strategy, understood this tension and exposes it in his *History* for his readers to recognize and respect.

In addition, there is a moral dimension to this tension between using awe-inspiring power and attracting allies. As Thucydides describes in the debate over whether to attack Mytilene, Diodotus argued that it is a failure of strategy to completely vanquish cities, because this would violate the principle of proportionality among means and ends. As he asks, "How can it be otherwise than hurtful to us to put to the expense of a siege, because surrender is out of the question; and if we take the city, to receive a ruined city from which we can no longer draw the revenue which forms our real strength against the enemy?"[36] During the debate, the Athenians noted that because they were strong, they could employ whatever means they wished in pursuing their desired ends. Thucydides and others observed that this speech marks the beginning of the decline of Athens' once-benevolent rule. As Thucydides wrote, however, ". . . you know as well as we do that right, as the world goes, is only in question between equals in power." In a memorable phrase, he writes that "the strong do what they can and the weak suffer what they must."[37] The principle of proportionality and the prudent use of resources emerge as central elements of an effective grand strategy.

Later in the war, during the Melian Dialogue, the Athenians attempted to persuade the Melians to surrender and not to do battle with Athens because the means that they would employ (overwhelming force) would not align with either of their respective ends (for Melos, it was the integrity of their city, whereas for Athens, it was keeping the riches of Melos intact). As the Athenians said to the Melians, "You would have the advantage of submitting before suffering the worst, and we should gain by not destroying you." During the Melian Dialogue, the strategy for Athens is to wage battle on Melos to keep the respect of its subjects and maintain its empire (its desired end): "Besides extending our empire we should gain in security by your subjection; the fact that you are islanders and are weaker than others render[s] it all the more important that you should not succeed in thwarting the masters of the sea." In effect, the Athenians tried to sway the Melians to "think over the matter therefore, after our withdrawal, and reflect once again that it is for your country that you are consulting . . . and that upon this one deliberation depends [your] prosperity or ruin."[38]

As this observation makes clear, the overall strategy in the Athenian wars against both Sparta and Syracuse, which were meant to secure the Athenian empire, was beginning to exhaust the Athenian economy. In effect, continued stress on the Athenian military and economy was wreaking havoc on Athens' desired ends.[39] For a state's grand strategy to be effective, it must carefully balance the expenditure of the state's economic and political resources with its overall ends. Athens, it would seem, violated this inviolable principle of grand strategy.

In the sixth year of the war, Sparta proposes peace with Athens. Spartan envoys point out that real peace must arise through generosity (in the form of a diplomatic peace settlement) and not through military success, which so often spawns a desire for revenge.[40] However, Athenians who are swayed by the demagogic Cleon reject the peace offer in hopes of gaining a more advantageous outcome. Alcibiades, the Athenian statesman and general, argues that the grand strategy of the Athenian empire requires it to act like an empire, for doing otherwise will lead to atrophy and loss of its empire. (These arguments in defense of a more assertive grand strategy may not accord well with a unity between grand strategy and the avoidance of unnecessary wars.) Alcibiades, who supported the Sicilian campaign, proposed a largely expansionist grand strategy: "We cannot fix the exact point at which our empire shall stop; we have reached a position in which we must not be content with retaining what we have but must scheme to extend it for, if we cease to rule others, we shall be in danger of being ruled ourselves."[41]

Nicias finally accepts that Athens will go to war with Sicily, but he argues that if the Athenian goal is total conquest of that city-state, it must have overwhelming power to succeed. As Nicias notes, "Even if we leave Athens with a force not equal to the threat of the enemy except in the number of hoplites in the field, but even at all points superior to him, we shall still find it difficult to conquer Sicily or save ourselves." A cardinal point is that policy makers should not underestimate the difficulties of conquest in their strategy: "We must not disguise from ourselves that . . . he who undertakes such an enterprise should be prepared to become master of the country the first day he lands, or failing in this to find everything hostile to him."[42]

This leads to a fundamental observation about the perils of implementing grand strategy when the state is at war. In attempting to defeat the Spartans and expand the empire, Athens turned its back on the qualities that made it great (a democracy based on free trade with minor tribute from its allies). The risk was that the means required to support its strategy increasingly were at odds with the available ends, which ultimately sought to bolster its democracy by building it on empire. However, this grand strategy was destined to failure even though Athens bowed to necessity by adopting an oligarchy and hoping for the future return to democracy. As a consequence, the fall of democracy led Athenians to be suspicious of one another, which severely hampered their war effort and fatally weakened Athens' overall grand strategy.[43]

Grand Strategy in the Modern Era

This section examines the critical thinkers whose ideas contributed to developing the modern discipline of grand strategy in its philosophical, military, and economic aspects. These thinkers are the source of the three major developments in grand strategy for the modern era. First, there are the political philosophers – Machiavelli, Hobbes, Locke, and Kant – who developed the concept of national interests as understood in the context of the ultimate ends of the state. According to all four of the major philosophers discussed in this chapter, the state's interests are defined in terms of political ends rather than religious or moral criteria. Second, Jomini and Clausewitz, among other strategists, introduced the proper use of the military instrument of national power as the state moves to implement its grand strategy. Finally, Smith, Hamilton, and List defined the essential function and dynamics of the economic foundations of national power.

Philosophical Foundations of Modern Grand Strategy

Niccolò Machiavelli

Italian political theorist and statesman Niccolò Machiavelli's (1469–1527) books and treatises on the nature of national policy, diplomacy, and military operations are indispensable to studying the development of grand strategy.[44] The primary expression of his thoughts about strategy was outlined in the book *Dell'arte della Guerra* (*The Art of War*), which examines how rulers achieve and maintain power as they develop a grand strategy to govern the actions of the city-state.[45]

Since societies and military institutions and practices were in the midst of significant political and economic changes prior to Machiavelli's emergence, a fuller understanding of his work on strategy requires that we appreciate the environment in which he lived in Florence, Italy. The rapid expansion of the money economy shook the agricultural basis of medieval society and moved Europe toward early industrialization; the effects on the development of modern military institutions had equally immediate and significant consequences. In the military sphere, one influence was a decline in the role and power of knights in the feudal system and a concomitant rise in the number of soldiers looking for money as mercenaries. As historian Felix Gilbert writes, policy makers and strategists had to deal with "adventurers and ruffians who wanted wealth and plunder, [while] men who had nothing to lose and everything to gain through war, made up the main body of the armies."[46]

In the rich Italian cities such as Florence, prosperity and stability had increased to the point where the emerging view among the leaders of city-states was to see war as a thing of the past. In 1474, an ambassador from Florence stated, "Stability has increased so much that, if nothing unexpected happens, we shall in the future hear more about battles against birds and dogs than about battles between armies." However, in 1494 when the French invaded and conquered much of Italy, it undermined the existing view of politics and reshaped the conduct of statecraft and grand strategy.

Wars among city-states or dynasties during this period were deliberately limited in scope politically and militarily to prevent strategy from being defined in ways that would lead to the pursuit of absolute policies and thus to the state's destruction. This strategy was consistent with an era in which the economic and military resources available to fifteenth-century princedoms were severely limited. It was also a time when decisions about the conduct of strategy were not guided by the principle of mass mobilization.[47] To ensure that strategy produces gains for the state, Machiavelli noted, "victories [from the proper conduct of strategy] after all are never so complete that the victor must not show some regard, especially to justice."[48] In following this principle, he argued that the all-out pursuit of one's strategy was dangerous, states should use moderation in their pursuit of their strategy, and a prudent strategy must rest on more than its ability to annihilate the enemy or achieve total aims.[49] Machiavelli did not argue that states should *disavow* the principle of success, but held that the costs of an overly ambitious grand strategy could overwhelm and ultimately impoverish the state, particularly when its statesmen aspire to achieve maximal gains.

In Gilbert's view, "It is only when, through some shattering political event, the traditional prejudices and presumptions have collapsed, that the inadequacy of existing political concepts becomes evident, and the way is cleared for a completely new appreciation and evaluation of the political situation."[50] From the late fifteenth century on, grand strategy increasingly came to be viewed as a concept that constantly governs the shifting continuum between war and peace. To complicate matters, the Italian city-states lost the desire and political will to possess strong military forces.

Although the Italians were rich culturally and economically, Machiavelli believed that they were weak militarily and too focused on financial matters. He attributed the defeat of the Italians at the hands of the French to the poor state of the military system that flourished in the fifteenth century, writing that the "prevalence of financial considerations determined the nature of the military organization as well as the conduct of war in Italy during the fifteenth century."[51] To remedy this failure, Machiavelli proposed forming an army of foot soldiers, using general conscription along the lines that governed the Roman army. This type of military organization was difficult to implement because it first required political reforms, a change in how people thought about their role in society, and a shift in the state's power and its control over society.

In effect, Machiavelli's ideas rested on the revolutionary principle that political, rather than military, objectives are the foremost guide to grand strategy. The proposition that strategy should not be governed by the pursuit of total objectives aligned with an era in which princes in the pursuit of their strategy were discouraged from using all of their resources to defeat the enemy or achieve their objectives. In practical terms, we see the origins of the rational calculus of strategy in which achieving lesser and deliberately limited objectives is more likely to produce strategic successes. Yet, Machiavelli's ideas also reinforce the principle that states should use great caution when they make decisions about how and toward what ends they should pursue their strategy.

According to Gilbert, Machiavelli believed that "the basis of political power is military power, and money contributes to political power only if it is in fact transformed into military strength."[52] The lack of fighting spirit coupled with a preoccupation with money and personal well-being is, according to Machiavelli, the basis of the strategy that led to Florence's military defeat. This reasoning affirms that Machiavelli likely saw strategy and politics as heavily intertwined.[53] Due to the importance of strategy in war, militaries must prepare for battles, which means that the central purpose of a military organization is to win battles quickly and decisively as a way to put the adversary at its mercy. This principle guides Machiavelli's view of strategy in instrumental terms as a guide to the state's policies: "Efficient preparation for battle was the only criterion for the composition of an army ... [P]olitical institutions, in their spirit as well as in their form, must be shaped in accordance with military needs."[54] In his view, the function of strategy is to marshal all of the state's resources – political, monetary, and military – to preserve and enhance the state's long-term interests.

The historical development of grand strategy was shaped decisively by Machiavelli's writings; he was a prominent defender of the principle that the ultimate purpose of strategy is to dominate one's enemy. He provided the intellectual foundation for strategy that subtly shifted how statesmen thought about the nature of state policy. Machiavelli's ideas, which made decisive contributions to strategy despite the fact that these often were in direct contradiction to the prevailing fashion of the fifteenth century, elevated the principle that viewed managed military campaigns and wars as limited, almost procedural exercises, rather than events whose outcomes had significant consequences for the state, its prosperity, and its very survival. Later, his ideas helped link the state's military, economic, and technological resources into a coherent grand strategy for guiding its policies and actions. Machiavelli's principles also contributed to the emerging framework for grand strategy precisely because he urged the state to organize and marshal all of its resources to support its policies.

In Machiavelli's view, a state could survive and prosper only if it possessed a strategy that guided how it used its influence and power in a single-minded, disciplined manner designed to support its strategic ends.[55] As he wrote in *The Prince*, published in 1513, "A prince ought to have no other aim or thought, nor select anything else for his study, than war and its rules and discipline."[56] He is calling directly for a clear linkage between strategy and all actions undertaken by the state. At the same time, Machiavelli warned about the high costs of strategy for the state when policy makers are forced to make the tradeoffs between gains and losses that all states must bear.[57] This line of reasoning is central to the concept of Pyrrhic victory, which describes losses so great that they undermine the state's strategy. It also contains an implicit warning that statesmen may become so careless after achieving successes that they suffer subsequent setbacks despite initial gains from their strategy.[58] Building from these ideas, Machiavelli implied that a strategy is more effective if it expends the state's scarce resources with great care. His reasoning was that it is easy to overestimate one's power, miscalculate the likelihood that the strategy will be successful, and pursue policies that effectively weaken the state.[59] Machiavelli's writings also strengthen the argument that elements of a state's grand strategy must be closely aligned with its goals.

After Machiavelli, the seventeenth- and eighteenth-century political theorists Thomas Hobbes, John Locke, and Immanuel Kant decisively shaped modern thinking about the nature of political institutions and ideas.[60] More importantly, these thinkers, whose ideas build indirectly on many of the ideas articulated by Machiavelli, are indispensable to understanding the formation of the modern state system and the evolution of grand strategy itself. A critical feature of this analysis is how the ideas of these Enlightenment thinkers defined the purpose of the state, described the forces that govern how states function internally and in conjunction with other states, and set the parameters for what the political ends of grand strategy should be. In strict terms, Machiavelli, Hobbes, Locke, and Kant remain among the most critical of the political theorists who built the modern foundations of grand strategy.

One scholar, Charles Hill, in *Grand Strategies: Literature, Statecraft, and World Order*, explores the relationship between political ideas and their influence on the development of grand strategy.[61] To illustrate, during the Enlightenment, several prominent themes influenced how we think about the state. As Hill argues, it is essential to focus on several groundbreaking developments in modern political theory:

> the idea of "the social contract" as the foundation of state governance and a way to tame power, the beginning of the end of the "divine right" to rule, the idea of religious freedom, the importance of "grand strategy," and inquiry into the positive and negative attributes of a variety of kinds of governance within a state.[62]

Thomas Hobbes

The English philosopher Thomas Hobbes (1588–1679) made fundamental contributions to the prevailing concepts that govern our understanding of the international state system and one of the foundational theories of international relations, that of realism.[63] Hobbes is known for his contributions to social contract theory, in which free and rational humans establish principles and organize themselves into governments by ceding some of their liberty to a recognized "sovereign" in exchange for the security that the sovereign's power provides. Hobbes's ideas were influenced by the ideas of Thucydides, who implicitly theorized in his *History of the Peloponnesian War* about how the concept of sovereign power guides the decisions and actions of the state. Hobbes, as it turns out, translated Thucydides's work early in his career.[64] These ideas are important, because they frame how states operate in international politics as they articulate and implement grand strategy.

When Hobbes was writing, thinking about the modern international system was in its early formative stage. (The 1648 Treaty of Westphalia was signed about halfway through his life.) Hobbes played a definitive role in formulating the "purpose of the state which would influence all subsequent international thought under the rubric of *realism*, and become a leading doctrine of modern statecraft."[65]

Hobbes articulated principles of governance that he believed would lead to greater harmony and peace within and among societies, but this is not to say that states would articulate grand strategies that excluded the use of war as an instrument of policy. To the contrary, Hobbes argued that war was inherent in the anarchic structure of the international system. Implicitly, then, if war was inherent in the structure of international politics, then any state seeking to survive had to articulate and implement a grand strategy that accounted for the use of state-directed violence.

Hobbes's most famous work, *Leviathan or The Matter, Forme and Power of a Common Wealth Ecclesiastical and Civil* (1651), outlines his influential theory of the social contract, "under which citizens confronted by the horrors and chaos of 'a war of all against all' voluntarily give up their rights to a sovereign who is then bound to use his monopoly on the use of force to protect the people from violent death." The central argument in *Leviathan*, which makes highly relevant contributions to the evolution of grand strategy as an instrument of statecraft, is the fundamental need for societies to be guided by a strong central authority. Such an authority must be able to create political order and social stability in the midst of the anarchic structure that exists in international politics.

Building on the fact that the Treaty of Westphalia "legitimized the state as the unit of international order," Hobbes took the next step in the *Leviathan* when he articulated "a political theory [that would] justify and explain the necessity of sovereign state authority."[66] Although *Leviathan* addresses the problems of legitimacy, authority, and governance *within* the state, the same rules arguably apply to relations among states. In the end, according to Hobbes, the most prudent strategy for the state is to gain as much power as possible while articulating a grand strategy that guides how that power should be applied in the international system.[67] With his ideas, Hobbes articulates the concept of an anarchic, competitive international system in which the power of the state creates an organizing principle on which states are able to build some degree of international security and the basis for national security.[68]

In his argument that individuals need a strong central government and political order if they are to avoid the state of chaos and strife in societies, Hobbes articulated one of his most famous concepts: the state of nature. His argument was that without an overarching political sovereign, individuals would find themselves in the "state of nature," in which the absence of government would lead to lives that were, using Hobbes's famous phrase, "solitary, poor, nasty, brutish, and short."[69] The principal strategy by which individuals could avoid this condition is to form themselves into societies with a strong central authority that is mutually agreed upon or contracted.

This is the "social contract" between state and individuals. Without some organizing authority – which for Hobbes is a product of the state's ability to exercise sovereign power – the state of nature would easily transform itself into what he called the "state of war," where it is a "war of all against all," another of Hobbes's more well-known sayings. The escape from the state of nature was possible at the domestic level with the establishment of a central, sovereign authority, but this likely would not be possible, according to Hobbes, at the international level. States in the anarchic international system – a system that lacks its own sovereign authority – are therefore in a state of nature, in a state of "war of all against all," even when war is a possibility but not a reality. The threat of war under Hobbes's realist theory is ever present and always near the surface of interstate relations. In sum, Hobbes outlined the principles that govern how states interact as they use their grand strategies to compete for the highest stakes in a world prone to conflict.

When Hobbes's ideas are applied to grand strategy, we can see three major philosophical contributions. First is the primacy of internal security. Hobbes establishes that the state's first priority in its grand strategy is to establish its own domestic basis for stability against the natural tendency of societies to drift toward the condition of widespread chaos and violence between individuals. Without internal security, a state cannot articulate or implement a grand strategy. In effect, it can do nothing but seek to create the basis for orderly social relationships.

The second contribution that derives from the Hobbesian view on grand strategy is the concept of limits on the ability to create external security. Whereas in the domestic realm states can achieve a relative level of stable, long-term security, as Hobbes defined international relations, the best states can achieve is to avoid the "war of all against all" as they pursue grand strategies that produce a temporary respite from violent conflict. According to Hobbes, the ends of grand strategy should be articulated very modestly, because the best they can hope to achieve is to prolong temporary respites from destructive wars. If war is the natural default of state-to-state relations, the state's grand strategy is well advised to pursue very modest political ends. A state cannot transform the system itself, but it has to work within its constraints and keep its most violent aspects from overwhelming the domestic sphere of peace and security.

Third, Hobbes implicitly elevates the military instrument of national power to a privileged position. The military is important for domestic security but even more important for conducting policies successfully in the state of nature that is the essence of the international system. Hobbes's philosophy suggests that a state should invest heavily in its military capabilities, because, in the final analysis, it is the use of force that will determine the success or failure of that state and its grand strategy in an anarchic system. Moreover, this means that under Hobbes's philosophical system all other forms of national power must serve, for the most part, to strengthen the state's military capabilities. Thus, economic power is important primarily insofar as it can be converted into military power, and the same holds for diplomatic power. For Hobbes, nonmilitary types of power likely would be seen as having limited utility for the conduct of grand strategy. Long before Mao wrote in his "Little Red Book" that "power grows out of the barrel of a gun," Hobbes established that the state's power is reliant first and foremost on its military and security services.

To summarize, Hobbes is a prominent architect of the realist school in international politics who built his formal ideas upon the premise that the human condition is one in which individuals incline naturally toward struggles and conflicts. This theory is known for its more pessimistic assessment of human nature, which has profound implications for how the state conducts itself and ultimately the nature of its grand strategy.[70] According to Hobbes, the maintenance of domestic security is the primary purpose of the state and should always take precedence in grand strategy. Grand strategy can never aim to achieve complete external security in an anarchic interstate system, but military power is a crucial type of state power that should be supported by other forms of state power. We return in later chapters to these philosophical foundations because they set the foundations for the articulation and implementation of grand strategy.

John Locke

Following in the intellectual tradition of Hobbes, the English philosopher John Locke (1632–1704) is another highly influential Enlightenment thinker whose political ideas added decisively to the contributing principles of the American Revolution and whose intellectual lineage we see in the language adopted in the American Declaration of Independence. His ideas had a decisive effect on the principles espoused by Alexander Hamilton, Thomas Jefferson, and James Madison, among other early architects of the political and constitutional order in the United States. In fact, his ideas constitute the basis of liberalism.

Locke's view of human nature is more sanguine than Hobbes. Whereas Hobbes argued that human nature is characterized by highly competitive behavior with no standards of morality, Locke believed that humans tend to cooperate for mutual interest as much as to engage in conflict for individual gain. In addition, for Locke, cooperation and conflict do not occur within a context of amorality as Hobbes claimed, but rather within some sort of morality based in reason.

The distinction between Locke's view of the state of nature and Hobbes's view is subtle but highly significant. In both cases, individuals have license to do what they want for their own best interest because they have absolute freedom. But the difference is that this freedom under Locke's conception is exercised within some set of moral standards. For Locke, human beings have an innate sense of "natural law" – that basic fairness and equity that exists apart from any overarching sovereign. This does not mean that individuals in Locke's state of nature exist in a utopian place of perfect harmony. Individuals still conflict, but not because they live in fear and dread of everyone around them, but rather because they have no overarching authority to rule in an unbiased way on the standards of morality that should govern human relations. They have no way of entering into enforceable agreements and therefore have no basis for trust. The sovereign exists not to provide security, but to provide the contractual basis for prosperity. By this logic, the state of nature is less a state of war and more a state of constant disagreements and misunderstandings about who owes what to whom on the basis of this or that principle.

Consequently, although human nature in the state of anarchy has powerful competitive qualities, individuals establish societies precisely because they want to build a more prosperous political order.[71] In his highly influential work the *Second Treatise of Government* (1690), John Locke articulates the necessary elements that are required, as he put it, to "begin the world anew."[72] The first element, as already noted, is to create the conditions for mutual gain through economic transactions. The second element is to secure the rights of its citizens, who as the governed possess the right to revolt when the government destroys the liberty and security that it was intended contractually to create and sustain.[73] The necessary elements align with the purposes of the state, which are twofold: to protect individual liberties and to create conditions conducive to prosperity. In contrast, for Hobbes, the purpose of the state is singular: to provide security. Locke, in further contrast with Hobbes, contends that the two purposes of the state constitute the basis for its political legitimacy. A government that fails to secure the individual liberties of its citizens and/or violates the rights of property is a government that has lost its right to rule. As such, it can and must be overthrown by force or otherwise.

What are the implications of Locke's philosophy for grand strategy? The first major implication is that a state's grand strategy must rest on political legitimacy and economic vitality. The reasoning that the state's domestic relationship with its citizens is paramount applies for Hobbes as well. For both, there must be a strong domestic foundation for national power. But Locke sees this foundation in terms of the state's ability to safeguard its citizens' rights and to create a vibrant, growing economy. In effect, freedom and property are the supporting pillars for any grand strategy.[74] If a state fails to provide freedom, then it is vulnerable to internal dissent and even rebellion. Similarly, if a state lacks a strong economy, its citizens will not only be dissatisfied but also will be unable to contribute to the implementation of a grand strategy. Under either condition, a state cannot hope to act in a coherent and purposeful fashion, but will find that its policies are more erratic and haphazard.

Second, the views of the two theorists as to the implications for the international system are quite different. Hobbes sees an anarchic structure leading to war as the default tendency, whereas Locke sees anarchy as much less threatening. In such a structure, states can cooperate as well as conflict when they see opportunities for mutual gain and when there is some unbiased enforcement mechanism for dealing with agreements. Treaties and international law, then, are much more central to how Locke's ideas contribute to grand strategy, because they have the potential to produce the value for individuals and states that results from cooperation. To be sure, Locke would agree with Hobbes that the interstate system was anarchic, but his disagreement with Hobbes would be over the extent to which international politics would be prone to conflict simply because of its inherently anarchic structure. The limits of cooperation are not set by human tendencies to see threats everywhere but instead derive from the human proclivity to withhold trust in agreements that do not rest on some legal basis for enforcement.

Third, the most important type of national power for Locke is not the military but the domestic economy. The economic foundations of national power are important in and of themselves not simply because they can support military capabilities, but because they are one of the core purposes of the state's economy that contributes most directly to the well-being of its citizens. This is not to argue that Locke saw no place for military power in a state's grand strategy. But it is to suggest that he saw military power as a necessary cost that should be minimized, while the domestic economy should be the highest priority as the state makes strategic investments in human and financial capital.

In short, grand strategy for Locke is about seizing opportunities within and among societies as humans cooperate for mutual gain. The interstate system is a positive-sum game where states can be better off for having cooperated rather than refusing to cooperate. In Hobbes's view, grand strategy is essentially about dealing with threats. The interstate system is a zero-sum game in which one state's gain must inevitably become another state's loss.[75] In Part II, we discuss the history of American grand strategy in terms of how Locke's ideas on the domestic foundations of national power implicitly shaped its political institutions and early American grand strategies and contributed to arguments about what is known as American "exceptionalism." As Hill writes, "Locke's political philosophy provides a basis for American 'exceptionalism,' which is a theme that reappeared across American diplomacy from colonial times to the present: that America at once is, and is not, a part of the international state system."[76]

Immanuel Kant

In looking beyond the influence of such preeminent political philosophers as Hobbes and Locke, another critical thinker to arise during the Enlightenment age was the German philosopher Immanuel Kant (1724–1804). Kant believed that "superstition," which is the main cause for mankind's intellectual immaturity, ideally should be replaced with a framework based on "rational inquiry, scientific standards of progress, toleration, and secular politics."[77] In formulating ideas that directly strengthen the foundations of grand strategy, theorists during the Enlightenment played a prominent role as they challenged existing ideas about diplomacy, war and peace, and religion.[78]

In his essay "What Is Enlightenment?" Kant wrote that people would leave behind their "self-imposed immaturity" and give up such moral and intellectual guides as religion and tradition, because this would liberate the mind and help individuals approach old problems in a new way. Kant proposed problem solving from the ground up, which he called *ab initio* (meaning "from the beginning"), by formulating his famous "categorical imperative," which defines the nature and realm of proper actions without reference to outside authority.[79] Kant defined the state not as a "piece of property" but as a "society of men whom no one else has any right to command or to dispose except the state itself."[80] Importantly, Kant did not see "the state of nature" as a state of conflict, because for him human nature was progressing toward a more civilized, less violent stage of political development. Human nature, therefore, was a product not of inherent tendencies but of the context provided by institutions, incentives, and education. As will be seen, these concepts align directly with modern concepts about the nature and purpose of grand strategy.

Kant differed from previous political philosophers who had focused on developments *within* the state but devoted little attention to the ungoverned areas that exist beyond their sovereign borders. Generally, problems in international affairs remained largely beyond the attention of major philosophers at the time.[81] But Hobbes, who believed that only the stark law of nature as the constant striving for self-preservation could provide the basis for ruling the international arena, and Rousseau, whose social contract was one between all individuals and "The People" as a whole, not between the individual and the state, declared that their proposed political systems could not extend beyond a particular political community. Kant, however, applied the Enlightenment principles of starting from the ground up while disregarding blind adherence to traditional authority, to write his work *Perpetual Peace: A Philosophical Sketch* (1795). He concludes that "the state is the basic unit of the international system"[82] and held that the nature and purposes of the state affect the nature of the international system as a whole.

As to the inherent tendencies of human nature that predispose humans toward conflict, Hobbes and Kant agree on many fundamentals. Kant's ideas about human nature derive from the principles outlined by Hobbes. Indeed, one sees the influence of Hobbes on Kant's thinking when he describes the "perverseness of human nature which is nakedly revealed in the uncontrolled relations between nations." Kant recognized that states possess the means for "making war, together with the inclination to do so on the part of rulers." He also agreed with Hobbes that this "inclination . . . seems inborn in human nature [and serves as a] great hindrance to perpetual peace."[83] As Kant wrote, "the state of peace among men living side by side is not the natural state [because] the natural state is one of war." He does not imply the condition of "open hostilities, but at least an unceasing threat of war." The result, for Kant, is that the state of nature often leads to war, which is "the sad recourse in the state of nature . . . by which each state asserts its right by violence."[84] He said that "a war of extermination, in which the destruction of both parties and of all justice can result, would permit perpetual peace only in the vast burial ground of the human race."[85]

The difference between Hobbes and Kant is that Kant held that this unceasing threat of war was not an inescapable trap. There was a way out for humankind. To remedy the consequences of this conflict-prone side of human nature, Kant proposed "a league of a particular kind . . . [to maintain security and freedom] of the state itself and of other states in league with it."[86] From these ideas of Kant, we see the basis for the argument that states need international institutions to help them embrace unifying and organizing principles, which serve to regulate international affairs if we are to avoid the condition, relying on the language of Hobbes, of a "war of all against all."

Locke and Kant agree on several fundamental issues. They both argued that the state exists to safeguard the liberty of its citizens and to provide an environment in which commerce can flourish. Locke, however, focused more on the domestic implications of these purposes; Kant's *Perpetual Peace* concerns the international consequences of these purposes and the influence of domestic institutions. First, according to Kant, the more democratic governments there are in the world, the less likely war is to occur. Peace will become more typical and war more rare because in democracies citizens have to vote for or against war: "If the consent of the citizens is required in order to decide that war should be declared ... nothing is more natural than that they would be very cautious in commencing such a poor game." Without a popularly based government, "a declaration of war is the easiest thing in the world to decide upon, because war does not require of the ruler ... the least sacrifices of the pleasures of his table."[87] Since citizens would carry the burden of doing the fighting, Kant surmises that they will go to war only when they feel it absolutely necessary and they will be doubly reluctant to wage war against a fellow democratic republic. Thus, the anarchic international system is not trapped under the shadow of perpetual violence and its threat.

A late-twentieth-century form of this argument, *democratic peace theory*, also suggests that the rise of democratic governments decreases the chance of war. Democracy, as it spreads, can transform the system, at least with respect to relations between democracies, and have a powerful influence on how states develop grand strategies. Although the democratic peace theory was not rigorously studied until the 1960s, the basic principles have its foundations in Immanuel Kant. Scholar Michael E. Brown, in *Debating the Democratic Peace*, argues that through liberal democracies, which are based on similar political values, "an understanding of the legitimate rights of all citizens and of all republics comes into play."[88] Furthermore, there is now a "moral foundation" for peace among democracies since they have a respect for one another.

The second consequence for the international system is that as states create vibrant domestic economies, they will seek more trade opportunities with other states. These trade relationships, Kant reasoned, will foster closer ties of material, mutual self-interest, ultimately making war less and less likely. As he specifically writes, "the spirit of trade ... sooner or later ... dominates every people." For Kant, this means that the state's "financial power may be the most reliable in forcing nations to pursue the noble cause of peace (though not from moral motives)." The combination of more democracies and increased trade, Kant concluded, would serve as potent social forces for moving parts of the world towards perpetual peace, which was a far cry from Hobbes's vision of a "war of all against all."

What implications does Kant's philosophy have for the articulation and implementation of grand strategy? Critically, Kant's ideas establish a relationship between grand strategy and the form of government of the state. In particular, democracies by their very nature operate on the basis of a fundamentally different logic for their grand strategy than do those of nondemocracies. This difference in grand strategy arises from the fact that democracies, in theory, rest on the consent of the governed. Therefore, the government's policies, including its overall grand strategy, reflect the consent of the governed as well. Grand strategy in Kant's philosophical system is not something to be articulated behind closed doors by a small clique of experts. It is, by contrast, a body of work that requires the input of the entire society – at least as expressed by public opinion – particularly because any grand strategy must account in the extreme case for the use of force. This is a decision in which the citizens who do the fighting have a direct interest in influencing, if not directly sanctioning, by their consent.

The second point pertains to the international system. Unlike for Hobbes and Locke, the essential purpose of grand strategy for Kant ultimately should be to establish "a state of peace."[89] Since democracy and trade are the causes of this peace, these should be the central political ends of a state's grand strategy. Kant's ideas lead ineluctably to the principle that a state's grand strategy should, all things being equal, promote "world order, peace, justice, and progress." It is the view of some scholars that Kant's ideas provide the basis for an international system that "make[s] progress toward peace [by increasing] the number of republics – democracies."[90] As for trade, Kant articulated ideas that contribute to building a more peaceful world, largely by emphasizing the principle that "those in commerce with each other won't want to spoil their trade by war."[91] With this reasoning, Kant establishes the idea that economic forces are a powerful determinant of the grand strategy that each state articulates.

This leads to the final point: the implementation of a grand strategy should rely on international institutions and diplomacy because these provide an instrument for moderating hostile competition among states. Although Kant suggests that truly global governance is unlikely, given the diversity of peoples and geography, he argues that a "federation of free states" across international borders is ideal since the propensity for peace would be stronger than that for war.[92] Although Hobbes exercises an important role in developing the foundations of grand strategy given that he established the role of power in societies, Kant's contribution is to establish the principle and role of institutionalized cooperation. Ideas and values have real, political consequences, while sharing democratic values brings societies closer together and empowers them to take steps that will avoid the outbreak of war, especially if those ideas and values find expression in the institutions of governance. These ideas remain central to the study of grand strategy.

In effect, these three thinkers – Hobbes, Locke, and Kant – made critical contributions to ideas that helped define and then broaden the definition of grand strategy, which was based on using different types of national power (military, economic, and diplomatic) to steer the nation in a particular direction that aligns with its interests. Their views also reflect and incorporate the enduring philosophical debates about the principles that drive the foreign and domestic policies of the state, including fundamental decisions as to what course the state should pursue as it articulates and implements its grand strategy.

Military Foundations of Modern Grand Strategy

In regard to the contributions of seventeenth- and eighteenth-century political theorists, Antoine-Henri Jomini and Carl von Clausewitz both had decisive effects on shaping modern ideas about the military foundations of grand strategy.[93] The concepts put forward by these two strategists are indispensable to understanding the formation of the principles that govern how grand strategy has evolved. Critically, these strategists definitively defined the military element of grand strategy in their respective studies.

Antoine-Henri Jomini

Antoine-Henri Jomini (1779–1869) of Switzerland served with the French army under Marshal Ney and later as a military adviser to Czar Nicholas of Russia. A prominent thinker who established many fundamental principles of strategy, Jomini focused more on the nature and conduct of military strategy than on grand strategy per se. Yet, his work explores how Napoleon and other statesmen wielded the critical innovation in grand strategy, the concept of levee en masse, so effectively. Building on the view that the mass army "is the truly significant inheritance we have received from those troubled years,"[94] Jomini shaped the literature on what today constitutes the military foundations of grand strategy. Some aspects of Jomini's ideas are, surprisingly, not obsolete, but his principal contribution to grand strategy remains his ability to clarify "the basic concepts of military science [in] his definition of the sphere of strategy."[95] It is essential to understand the role and influence of modern military strategy on statecraft if we are to grasp the intellectual forces that shaped the evolution of grand strategy.

The strategist Jomini contributed to the refinement of many of the concepts that are central to the theory and practice of military strategy in the eighteenth century.[96] A critical argument in his *Précis de l'art de la guerre* (*The Art of War*) is the value of permanent principles in strategy, which are those whose "eternal validity can be comprehended and formulated by the human mind." Another of his prominent contributions is the view that determining the nature of strategy is in practice a highly rational, if not scientific, form of inquiry. The scholar Azar Gat emphasized this view when he observed that "war, like all fields of nature and human activity, was susceptible to a comprehensive and systematic theoretical study."[97] For Jomini, strategy, just like war, is governed by its own internal logic based on rational, scientific laws that provide rules for action. When states follow those rules, success will follow in a logical and orderly, if almost deterministic, fashion. Jomini's philosophical approach to strategy was to follow a series of fundamental axioms whose rules had an exclusively military flavor to them. In effect, he emphasized the nonpolitical (meaning the military) dimension of grand strategy.[98]

The function of strategy, as Jomini saw matters, was to encourage the state to "fight battles in a truly scientific fashion."[99] His strategy rested on the principle – along with the concept of "lines of operation" (which run from the base of operations to the objective) – of applying the greatest force or resources at the right moment and place to achieve success.[100] In practice, strategy for Jomini was influenced by the state's ability to conquer an opposing state – or capture its territory – along lines that were entirely consistent with the principles governing European warfare in the eighteenth and nineteenth centuries, when campaigns were waged strictly within the geographic confines of the European continent.[101] His fundamental contribution to strategy was the argument that destroying the military forces of the enemy is necessary for the state to conquer its opponent successfully.[102]

Jomini's ideas strengthened the central role of territorial conquest, which itself had a decisive effect on strategy in the nineteenth century. Although his ideas about strategy became increasingly less relevant toward the end of that century – as the growth of centralized governments and highly industrialized economies prompted a shift in military strategy toward the principle of total war – he remains an influential strategist today.[103] For all practical purposes, the universal theory of war as a unified effort by the state espoused by Jomini remains his central contribution in modern terms to the theory and practice of grand strategy.[104] As explored in an earlier work, all of these considerations relate to the nature and meaning of success in strategy.[105] However, the strategist Clausewitz, in *On War*, criticized the presumed universality of Jomini's strategy.[106]

Carl von Clausewitz

As perhaps the most significant military strategist, the Prussian army officer and war-college director Carl von Clausewitz (1780–1831) rightly has been heralded as the preeminent nineteenth-century strategist. His principle governing the relationship between war and the state often is summed up in the well-known, if sometimes mis-interpreted, phrase "war is a mere continuation of policy by other means,"[107] which implies that grand strategy must be governed ultimately by its ability to achieve the state's political objectives.

Clausewitz defined the state's overall strategy in fundamentally political terms as "an act of force to compel our enemy to do our will."[108] Here, Clausewitz overturned the "accumulationist" assumption in strategy dating back to the Romans, which holds that there is no necessary causal relationship between military and political objectives because it depends on the context and whether the leaders have correctly linked their actions to the state's overall strategy.[109] His approach was consistent with the prevailing trend in contemporary German philosophy of evaluating strategy in the prevailing political and social context.

Clausewitz developed an intellectual framework in which the state's pursuit of clearly defined principles provides the basis of what constitutes, in modern terms, its grand strategy. By never deviating from the view that the state's fundamental strategy is to disarm and overthrow the enemy as the step toward achieving its political objectives, he argued that war is state-controlled violence guided by the political ends of its strategy.[110] In practice, Clausewitz built the foundations of a strategy of total war that had been theoretically possible since Machiavelli's writings in the sixteenth century but was never systematically put into practice. For Machiavelli and subsequent generations of theorists, the essential function of grand strategy is to guide the state in achieving its political goals, rather than fixating on gaining territory or destroying the enemy.[111]

Clausewitz presented his ideas about strategy in the three-volume work *Vom Kriege* (*On War*), published posthumously in 1832. The sheer scale of his intellectual efforts is evident from the wealth of literature on Clausewitz's works and his overall influence on strategy for nearly two centuries.[112] He did not develop a universal theory of strategy,[113] principally because he was skeptical about whether it was feasible, as he expressed in *On War*.[114]

Despite the intellectual momentum that gained ascendancy during the Enlightenment to base strategy on the use of scientific principles, Clausewitz defined strategy more broadly as an enterprise whose central purpose is to achieve the political goals of the state or organization.[115] In effect, the fundamental purpose of strategy – by which in this case we mean grand strategy – is to achieve political successes. It is important to note that Clausewitz saw strategy as an inherently *political* phenomenon that operates on several levels. For this Prussian strategist, the natural objective of strategy for the state is to establish peace on favorable terms, not necessarily conquering territory or overthrowing the enemy's government but rather achieving what have been defined as its fundamental political objectives. These objectives may well not include the resort to war.[116] This is consistent with the principle that holds that a grand strategy can be effective if it reflects a unity of purpose between its political and military elements.

Writing in an era when Europe was dominated by interstate wars, Clausewitz realized that if the ends of strategy were not confined to essentially limited problems or contests, states would find themselves drawn into conflicts that would put their interests, if not their existence, at risk.[117] As with many strategists, he understood that the conduct of grand strategy in the nineteenth century, if based on resort to war, could destroy Europe's reigning territorial, political, military, and social order. In effect, states whose strategies are uncontrolled or in pursuit of unlimited objectives can destroy the status quo and ultimately disrupt the international system.

Nonetheless, Clausewitz argued that the "complete or partial destruction of the enemy must be regarded as the sole object of strategy in war."[118] Using the logic advanced by the military strategist Bernard Brodie, Clausewitz saw "the conquest of the enemy's ground [as] a 'visible sign of victory.'"[119] In its "pure" form, the purpose of strategy is to "overcome the enemy and disarm him," which may include "the destruction of the enemy's armed forces" and "the conquest of his territory."[120] According to Clausewitz, the proper strategy for the state is to accomplish the "gradual exhaustion of [the enemy's] physical and moral resistance."[121]

By the time of the French Revolution in 1789, the predominant approach for the state was to successfully use its military, economic, human, and technological resources to support its overall grand strategy. This development heralded the beginning of an era in which modern states possessed the means and increasingly a highly coherent strategy for waging total war.[122] Now that war had moved well beyond the limited dynastic aims that had dominated European politics since the Middle Ages, strategy, in Clausewitz's view, was conducted on the two discrete levels of territorial conquests and complete overthrow of the enemy. In modern terminology, these describe the strategies for limited and total war, respectively.[123] In the case of limited war, the purpose of strategy is to defeat enemy forces through attrition, whereas the aim of strategy in total war is to destroy the opponent's ability to support war, which often is accomplished through a strategy of annihilation.[124]

Because the loss of territory theoretically weakens the state's ability to mobilize its economy and military forces for war, such losses and the prospect of military defeat are likely to weaken the states' will and ultimately undermine its grand strategy.[125] When territory has been captured, the state has been disarmed to such an extent that its ability to continue the struggle is compromised. In Clausewitz's view, wars between modern states do not need to be total because strategy is defined above all else to be governed, and ideally constrained, by the state's political objectives, which in turn must be kept limited. Since strategy does not necessarily call for the destruction of another state in every case, there is a prominent place in grand strategy for limited war and limited objectives. Still, with his emphasis on the role of annihilation and territorial conquest in strategy, Clausewitz canonized the principle that strategy often calls for – but is not necessarily equivalent to – totally defeating a state. Indeed, his writings contain political arguments about the limiting nature of strategy that are familiar to modern readers.

Clausewitz defined grand strategy as the guiding principle that expresses the state's political aims: "Tactics teaches the use of armed forces in the engagement; strategy, the use of engagements for the object of the war."[126] And grand strategy by this logic should guide the state when it is appropriate to engage in war. Finally, he sought to judge strategy on the basis of whether it rests on a rational calculus that policy makers can use to evaluate decisions about war and peace.[127] Thus, he framed strategy in strictly political terms, arguing like his intellectual predecessors Sun Tzu and Machiavelli that the costs of a strategy may outweigh its benefits.[128] In addition, when he referred to capturing territory or the enemy's capital, or defeating the enemy's army, he was merely pointing to indicators that a strategy may be successful if it helps the state attain its political objectives. In the end, Clausewitz was skeptical that strategy on any level should be reduced to "universal principles."

To understand Clausewitz's ideas about the implementation of strategy in *On War*, Gat made the point that "war was affected by innumerable forces, dominant among which were political conditions and moral forces; it was saturated with the unknown and incalculable, and was changing throughout history."[129] It is on the basis of these arguments that Clausewitz made significant and enduringly modern contributions to the evolution of grand strategy. When his ideas about strategy and those of other German military strategists combined with new technologies emerging in the mid-nineteenth century, their ideas solidified into a construct for grand strategy that could, on occasion, promote, if not encourage, the conduct of total war.[130]

The central argument about strategy in Clausewitz's time was that wars were "no longer fought over dynastic claims of limited scope [because] they involved the very existence of nations concerned and ... involved opposing principles, opposing philosophies of life."[131] Clausewitz was keenly aware of the changing structure of war. As the historian Rothfels writes, "Clausewitz was certainly correct ... [that] since the time of Bonaparte, war had become 'an affair of the whole nation,' and that the integration of new social forces resulted in war approaching 'its absolute perfection.'"[132]

More broadly, the genius of Clausewitz – which contributes to the conclusion that his work is still powerfully pertinent today as scholars and policy makers study grand strategy – is his skepticism about the existence of universally binding theories.[133] Clausewitz believed that all military events are integrally tied to their sociopolitical preconditions. "War," Clausewitz said, "is nothing else than a continuation of political transactions intermingled with different means." He qualifies this argument by saying, "We say intermingled with different means in order to state at the same time that these political transactions are not stopped by the war itself, are not changed into something totally different but substantially continue, whatever the means applied may be."[134] His decisive argument is framed as a question: "Is not [the strategy for] war only a different method of expressing their thought, different in writing and language? [This strategy for war] admittedly has its own grammar but not its own logic."[135]

Clausewitz was intimately interested in the interconnectedness of grand strategy with politics and war. Strategy needed to (and still must) take into account the changing nature of war and politics, especially in an age when nationalism and mass ideological movements were on the ascent.[136] He also was keenly interested in the consequences for grand strategy when states wage "wars of coalition." According to one scholar, Clausewitz "points out that a state engaged in war against an alliance is confronted with the problem of deciding which of the allies, the stronger or the weaker, should be first overthrown." The state's strategy for defeating any enemy means, for Clausewitz, that the state's grand strategy must be based on understanding the enemy's "center of gravity."[137] In Clausewitz's view, a core principle in strategy was not "mere physical killing," because "the main battle involves the killing of the enemy's courage rather than of the enemy's soldiers."[138]

In effect, Clausewitz's principal contribution to grand strategy is to warn the state and its policy makers that their approach to policy ultimately must be guided by highly coherent and yet strictly limited political objectives. In an age when grand strategy can on occasion embrace the idea of totally defeating an adversary, Clausewitz imposes a limiting factor on what the state can do in pursuit of its policies. As will be examined, nuclear weapons have imposed a similar limit on what states can do as they articulate and conduct grand strategy in the twenty-first century.

More broadly, when the role of clear political objectives in Clausewitz's ideas about strategy are integrated with Jomini's emphasis on the role of rules or principles to guide the conduct of strategy, it has significant consequences for the articulation and implementation of grand strategy. It means that there is a powerful relationship between the state's political objectives and the pursuit of grand strategy as an orderly, logical exercise that seeks to produce conditions that serve the state's interests. Both of these military theorists helped shape the argument that an effective grand strategy must be pursued in a highly coherent fashion, which places considerable emphasis on how their ideas about the role of politics and principles derives from their study of military strategy.

Economic Foundations of Modern Grand Strategy

A critical theme in the literature on grand strategy is how it rests ultimately on matters of statecraft, diplomacy, and the military foundations of strategy. Political philosophers, as discussed, have made precisely this argument. The problem, however, is that during the past several centuries, the study and practice of grand strategy increasingly emphasized the central importance of economic power on grand strategy.

As discussed in Chapter 3 concerning the literature on the intellectual origins of grand strategy, Machiavelli's work on strategy correctly anticipated that the state's economic power and technological capabilities are central – and, some might argue, decisive – elements in shaping the state's grand strategy. Politics and wars among city-states or dynasties during the Middle Ages and the Renaissance were deliberately limited in scope politically and militarily, largely because the economic and military resources available to fifteenth-century princedoms were dramatically reduced in scope in comparison with the resources that could be mobilized starting with the time of the French Revolution. Prior to the era of Napoleon, political units, or city-states, simply were not organized to maximize the use of mass political and economic mobilization.[139] This limit, however, clearly faded by the middle-to-late eighteenth century as strategists and statesmen grasped that they could harness the state's immense human, economic, and industrial resources to support their grand strategy. In this process, the ideas that govern the conduct of statecraft were redefined.

This reasoning about the relationship between grand strategy and economic power eventually culminated in the strategy of what became known as total war.[140] This approach stands in sharp contrast to the grand strategy of Frederick the Great, who opposed total war and policies that call for the annihilation of the enemy state.[141] The approach of Frederick the Great rejected grand strategies in which the state would enact strategies that ultimately could lead to the depletion of its economic wealth and human resources; strategists anticipated the fate that befell Germany during World War I and World War II. More broadly, ideas that contributed to grand strategy in the nineteenth century aligned quite well with significant developments in how states organized and prepared themselves for war. As a result of Napoleon's ability to capitalize on the social and economic forces at play in the French Revolution, the practice of grand strategy focused increasingly on unifying and coordinating all of the state's human and economic resources. As it evolved during the nineteenth century, grand strategy increasingly reflected the principle that states should harness all of their human, economic, industrial, and technological resources to support the pursuit of its policies.

The shift in grand strategy from limited wars between ruling dynasties in the Renaissance to the era of unlimited, national wars between modern European states in the nineteenth and twentieth centuries was made possible precisely because strategists called for harnessing all of the state's economic resources. The French Revolution and Napoleon's reign altered irrevocably the relatively limited bounds established in grand strategy since antiquity, which had rested on using only some of the state's economic power. From that era on, states had to deal with a categorically different genre of total war. With the state's economic power at least as important in the conduct of grand strategy as military forces, the increasingly tight linkage between economic and military power contributed to the devastation produced during each of the two world wars of the twentieth century.[142] During the nineteenth century, the gradual ability to mobilize entire economies transformed grand strategy into an exercise in which states no longer waged wars for limited objectives. From that time on, strategy evolved to the point where policy makers learned how to conjoin economic and military power into policies that called for annihilating another state in support of its grand strategy.

By the time of the French Revolution in 1789, the focus of grand strategy rested on using the state's economic, industrial, and human resources along with its military power to animate its policies, including the ability to wage wars. This development in grand strategy marked the onset of an age in which modern states were increasingly seen as instruments of total war as the state defined its overall strategy to support policies of expansion and conquest.[143] Building on foundations established by such military strategists as Jomini and Clausewitz, the intellectual and philosophical discussions about grand strategy and statecraft – as well as narrower analyses of the conduct of war and how to achieve victory – encompassed by the mid-nineteenth century the broad relationship in grand strategy between the state's economic and military sources of power. Some strategists argued that the emergence of national, trade-based economies in Europe after the 1500s slowly reshaped grand strategy to instill economic competition between and among societies as a fundamental aspect of interstate relations and politics. To explore how economic power contributes to the evolution of grand strategy, this section examines the ideas of several critical theorists who contemplated the enormous impact that economics would have on the state's power and its grand strategy.

The scholar Edward Mead Earle begins his work "Economic Foundations of Military Power" with the argument that "only in the most primitive societies, if at all, is it possible to separate economic power and political power."[144] For Earle, "In modern times – with the rise of the national state, the expansion of European civilization throughout the world, the industrial revolution, and the steady advance of military technology – we have constantly been confronted with the interrelation of commercial, financial, and industrial strength on the one hand, and political and military strength on the other."[145] This relationship lies at the heart of what we mean by modern grand strategy.

To frame the discussion about the differences that exist between the guiding principles of mercantilism and that of democracy on the conduct of grand strategy, Earle begins with the argument that "when the guiding principle of statecraft is mercantilism or totalitarianism, the power of the state becomes an end in itself." The implication, as he writes, is that "all considerations of national economy and individual welfare are subordinated to the single purpose of developing the potentialities of the nation to prepare for war and to wage war." The problem, for this scholar, is that "democratic peoples ... dislike the restraints which are inherent in an economy based upon war and the preparation for war." In the case of grand strategy, this principle establishes a political preference for an economic system that is "predicated upon individual welfare rather than upon the overweening power of the state." The practical reason for this preference is that state power in these terms represents "an inherent threat to their long established liberties."[146]

In his study of the economic foundations of military power, Earle reaffirms the inseparable nature of economic and political power when it comes to understanding the state's overall influence. In studying the evolution of grand strategy – which encompasses "the rise of the national state, the expansion of European civilization throughout the world, the industrial revolution, and the steady advance of military technology" – policy makers must be aware, bearing in mind Earle's words, of the close relationship between "commercial, financial, and industrial strength on the one hand, and political and military strength on the other." This relationship between the economic and political foundations of power is a "critical and absorbing problem of statesmanship." The reason, for Earle and other theorists, is that security broadly defined, as well as the nation's general liberty and well-being, hinge on how well the state articulates and implements its grand strategy.[147] This, in turn, depends on the ability to closely integrate the state's political, military, and economic power.

To explore this relationship between economic and political sources of power and its consequences for grand strategy, the ideas of economic theorists – specifically, Adam Smith, Alexander Hamilton, and Friedrich List – are examined.

Adam Smith

In the late eighteenth century, Scottish philosopher-economist Adam Smith (1723–1790) argued that the state's economic resources, including markets, determine to some significant extent its political and military power.[148] Smith was a prominent architect of capitalism, and his ideas about the economic foundations of state power contribute directly to capitalism's overall influence and thus to how states develop and pursue their grand strategy. According to this economist, the state's military power directly depends on the size and sophistication of its economy and trade, which means that states with weak economies will be less powerful and less influential in the pursuit of their grand strategies than states whose economies are more powerful and dynamic.[149]

This line of reasoning by Smith raises questions about the role of government as it makes decisions about grand strategy. It also reinforces the belief that governments whose policies are guided by economic interests will articulate their grand strategy with deliberate attention to building and maintaining the economic foundations of the state's power.[150] For Smith, economic power is not only a source of power that animates the state's grand strategy, but also serves as a powerful check on its ambitions as other states similarly pursue commerce and trade. To complicate matters, some thinkers – most notably the statesman Alexander Hamilton (1757–1804), as examined later in this chapter – argued that economic competition is a permanent source of wars between states.

Although economic considerations always have exerted a powerful influence on grand strategy, a central theme during the eighteenth century was the close relationship between armies in the field and the state's overall economic output. Statecraft always was concerned with wars whose objectives included, at least in part, the destruction of the armies and the productive capacities of the opposing state or principality. Consider, for example, the devastation wrought in what is now Germany during the Thirty Years' War (1618–1648) or the devastation inflicted on Germany and Japan during World War II.[151] One principle in grand strategy that gained ascendancy in the mid-to-late nineteenth century was that of destroying the enemy's economic sources of power as a critical step to destroying its military capabilities.

Proceeding from the principle that the state involved in a war will seek to destroy the enemy's civilian economy, grand strategists from the mid-to-late nineteenth century who focused on the economic implications of strategy were guided by the argument that a state must possess significant economic and industrial resources if it is to be a great power in the political struggle with other states. The meaning is clear: economic power is important, because it provides the basis for the state's ability to achieve the ends in its grand strategy. As a consequence, one determinant of grand strategy rests on the state's ability to develop significant economic and technological sources of power.[152]

When Adam Smith published *An Inquiry into the Nature and Causes of the Wealth of Nations* (*The Wealth of Nations*) in 1776, his argument was that "the time was ripe in Britain for a robust critique and reconsideration of the theories and practices of mercantilism."[153] Even though Britain had lost control of the American colonies, it was still undisputedly the most powerful state in the world. Because Britain had no rival, there was no need to pursue a zero-sum economic game as conceived under mercantilism. Instead, and as an integral part of Britain's grand strategy of political expansionism, there was a deliberate push to increase trade with its neighbors as a means of relieving the burden of war debts. As Adam Smith noted, "the wealth of a neighboring nation, however dangerous in war and politics, is certainly advantageous in trade."[154] And trade strengthens the state.

An adamant supporter of free trade, Smith disagreed with the conventional notion that the best way for a state to become wealthy was to accumulate great amounts of bullion. Instead, Smith believed that "fleets and armies are maintained, not with gold and silver, but with consumable goods."[155] As his ideas gained currency, the nature of economic power based on trade rather than gold reserves increasingly influenced how theorists and policy makers viewed grand strategy.

As a resolute advocate of free trade, Smith believed that the state should interfere with trade and use its economic power as a weapon only when absolutely necessary for the state's defense. As an enduring principle of its grand strategy, Great Britain's ability to control the seas was essential to maintaining its military and economic superiority. As Lord Haversham said in the House of Lords, "Your fleet and your Trade have so near a relation and such mutual influence on each other, they cannot well be separated [as] *both together are the wealth, strength, security and glory of Britain.*"[156] Smith would agree with Haversham's statement, finding nothing wrong with the Navigation Acts, which limited the use of foreign shipping in trade between London and its colonies. As Smith wrote in *The Wealth of Nations*, "The act of navigation is not favourable to foreign commerce, or to the growth of that opulence which can arise from it . . . the act of navigation is, perhaps, the wisest of all the commercial regulations of England."[157]

However, Smith was criticized by individuals such as Frederich List, who understood that free trade could be a powerful instrument for bolstering the grand strategy of wealthy states. Those who criticized Smith's notion of free trade argued that Great Britain utilized the mercantilist system to achieve its current level of wealth. Now that Great Britain was undisputedly the wealthiest and strongest military state in the nineteenth century, its policy makers supported the idea of utilizing free trade as a deliberate instrument of grand strategy precisely because it would help the state increase its wealth, while maintaining the political, economic, and military status quo.[158]

Smith was also a proponent of an idea that many British citizens found abhorrent yet essential to Great Britain's grand strategy: a standing professional army. For Earle, "there is a long standing and deeply rooted Anglo-American prejudice against 'standing armies.'"[159] Despite considerable debate in Parliament about the merits and dangers of a standing army, Smith believed that a standing army was not only good for the state but also absolutely essential to its security and ability to defend its interests.[160] With these arguments, Smith articulated the relationship that exists between the state's economic and military power and that relationship's intimate connection to grand strategy.

Alexander Hamilton

The development of ideas about how economic and military power intersect with grand strategy raises questions about how these forms of power influence the military power of the state. Some practitioners of grand strategy – most notably secretary of the treasury, statesman, and philosopher Alexander Hamilton (1757–1804) – argued that economic competition was a permanent source of wars between states.[161] The inescapable logic of Hamilton's reasoning is that economic interests exert a powerful influence on how states articulate and implement grand strategy.

For the scholar Earle, Alexander Hamilton was "the most influential single member of Washington's cabinet, roaming far afield from his own duties as Secretary of the Treasury." Predictably, Hamilton agreed with Adam Smith's ideas about the wisdom and necessity of maintaining a professional army, as well as those about the relationship between how "economic policy ... related to national defense."[162] In what became central elements of the emerging American grand strategy (see Chapters 7 to 10), he also sought to promote America's economic strength as an instrument for building the foundations of state power and establishing its economic independence. When Hamilton wrote the "Report on Manufactures," submitted to Congress on December 5, 1791, his stated goal was to promote manufacturing so that it would "render the United States independent of foreign nations for military and other essential supplies."[163]

In defining principles that were central to the formation of American grand strategy, Hamilton believed that newer states – including, notably, the United States – should carefully protect their economic interests if they want to compete with established countries such as Great Britain. As Hamilton wrote, "To maintain, between the recent establishments of another country, a competition upon equal terms ... is in most cases, impracticable." In effect, he argued that the industries of newer countries should receive "extraordinary aid [from] and protection of the government."[164] With these thoughts, Hamilton articulated the principle of economic self-sufficiency that became a critical element in American grand strategy.

This element of grand strategy included a strong national navy and merchant marine fleet, which Hamilton argued were a *sine qua non* to the ability of the United States to become a great power. The naval forces Hamilton envisioned would not only be able to protect American ships and strengthen the U.S. economy, but also greatly enhance the standing and power of the United States in the event of wars with other nations. In *Federalist Paper No. 11*, entitled "The Utility of the Union in Respect to Commercial Relations and a Navy," Hamilton writes that the ability to "influence ... the conduct of European nations ... would arise from the establishment of a federal navy." His argument is that "we may hope ... to become the arbiter of Europe in America, and to be able to incline the balance of European competitions in this part of the world as our interest may dictate."[165] Evidently, Hamilton saw powerful connections between economic power and the state's ability to develop those military forces that were necessary for the state to defend its interests and project power in implementing its grand strategy.

Hamilton was a strong proponent of building a unified and diversified economy in the United States. As Earle writes, Hamilton "visualized a nation in which sectional economies would interweave themselves into a common national economy and interest."[166] With these ideas, Hamilton linked the diversity of the state's economic system to the effectiveness of its grand strategy, which in turn established a framework that gave the United States the necessary financial options to exercise its independence from other states.[167]

Like Adam Smith, Hamilton was a firm proponent of a standing army. With European powers surrounding the United States and hostile Indian tribes adjacent to many early American communities, Hamilton observed that it would be irresponsible to wait for an enemy to strike the first blow. In *Federalist No. 25*, entitled "The Powers Necessary to the Common Defense Further Considered," Hamilton argues that without a standing army, "we must receive the blow, before we could even prepare to return it."[168] Even Thomas Jefferson, who was an ardent pacifist and free trader, came to agree with Hamilton about the essential relationship between economics and grand strategy. In an 1815 letter from Jefferson to the French economist and free trader Jean Batiste, Jefferson wrote, "Experience has shown that continued peace depends not merely on our own justice and prudence, but on that of others also ... and to the other distresses of war adds the want of all those necessaries for which we have permitted ourselves to be dependent on others, even arms and clothing."[169]

A cardinal principle of Hamilton's philosophy was the central role of economics on grand strategy. The question for the state, in Hamilton's view, reduces ultimately to "whether profit or preservation is the first interest of a State."[170] Since the state's survival depends directly on its economic power, Hamilton promoted the principle that economic power is a fundamental determinant of the state's grand strategy and its ability to promote its interests, even in the face of fierce competition with other states.

Frederich List

The German economist Friedrich List (1789–1846) advanced the idea that there is a direct and powerful relationship between the state's economic power, particularly the development of its economic and industrial infrastructure, and what we know as grand strategy. His fundamental argument was that the state's economic power and the influence of its grand strategy ultimately depend on developing a significant economic and industrial base.[171] This theorist anticipated in the late eighteenth and early nineteenth centuries that the state's power and influence were measured by its ability to harness its economic infrastructure to use that power to support its grand strategy in peacetime and wartime. List proposes that a critical step for the state is to develop significant *industrial* resources if it is to be a great military power – and if it is able to achieve the objectives outlined in its grand strategy.

As a proponent of linking the state's economic power to its grand strategy, including the conduct of war or total war, List argued that the railway system could transform the state into an integrated and organized entity that is better able to promote its grand strategy in both peace and war.[172] Not surprisingly, List's ideas about the economic foundations of grand strategy influenced in both theoretical and practical ways the policies that contributed to the great wars of the twentieth century, in which states successfully mobilized their industrialized economies and military forces to conduct total war with devastating consequences. List is among those theorists who correctly anticipated that the state's entire economic infrastructure eventually would be harnessed to support its grand strategy, including prominently the case of its military machine in times of war.

A top priority for List was to unite Germany into a strong economic and military power. In effect, List espoused mercantilist policies, which describe a direct relationship between the state's economic resources – including the influence of available markets and military power – and its ability to conduct its grand strategy successfully.[173] During his time in exile from Germany, which he spent in the United States, List was so influenced by the writings of Hamilton that it could be said that his thoughts about a diversified economy relate directly to those espoused by Hamilton.

List may have been jealous of Great Britain and the power it attained throughout the world, perhaps believing that Germany must unite and use its power to colonize others.[174] With these ideas, List advanced, along with other thinkers, the central role that economic power played in grand strategy when states pursued the policies of imperial expansion that dominated international politics in the nineteenth century. List wanted to expand the use of railroads throughout the entire world. Earle writes, "[List] seems to have been the originator of the Bagdad railway idea," which was a proposal to build a network of railway and steamship lines that would reach from the Americas to China and thus build the basis for global economic commerce.[175]

One of List's enduring contributions to the evolution of grand strategy is his argument that the development of railways powerfully influences the nation's economic and military power – and therefore its grand strategy. He was prescient in terms of his vision of how railways could transform the nation, which in the words of Earle would "transform the whole territory of the nation into one great fortress" that could readily be defended.[176] List also believed that the construction of railways would help Germany achieve greatness.[177] As an ardent nationalist, List promoted the development of railways in Germany because he believed this would help accelerate German unification and support its grand strategy of political and military integration.

Conclusions about Grand Strategy in the Modern Era

Each of these thinkers contributed to the development of grand strategy in the modern era in significant ways. Machiavelli established the concept of political interest as distinct from religious and moral values, arguing that its political interest should define the ends of the state's grand strategy. Jomini's core idea is that the state has to invest in military expertise, which itself is rooted in scientific principles. Clausewitz, like Jomini, believed that military power is of primary significance to the survival and success of the state.

However, he illuminated the proper relationship between military means and political ends and, unlike Jomini, thought war was as much art as science.

Finally, the economists of the modern era each emphasized a different aspect of the relationship between the state's economic power and grand strategy. Smith emphasized trade as opposed to sovereign wealth, whereas Hamilton emphasized the role of the state in pursuing policies to encourage an economy to develop greater overall efficiency and growth. Finally, List emphasized the importance of industrialization, in particular the value of investments in transportation infrastructure such as railroads. Taken together, these six thinkers define many of the core ideas that we find in contemporary debates about grand strategy.

Before turning to the revolutionary ideologies and nuclear eras in grand strategy, it is useful to summarize the central features of the modern era of grand strategy, whose influence remains very strong today. First, political competition imposes a set of rules that exerts a powerful and enduring influence on the development of grand strategy. The centrality of political power in the calculations of grand strategy is the principal contribution of the realist school, whose architects include Machiavelli and Hobbes. Locke introduced the importance of property, economic prosperity, and the consent of the governed. As a consequence, grand strategy is not the exclusive purview of a privileged elite, but involves not only many domestic interests but also a consensus among these, because by its very nature grand strategy directly affects the interests of all members of society. Kant emphasized how trade and democratic institutions can change the context of grand strategy by bringing states closer to a social relationship and further away from the inherently violent state of nature.

As for the military features of the modern era, the central concept is to ensure the proper subordination of the military to the dictates of the state's political leaders and the ends they designate. This is Clausewitz's fundamental insight, which seems obvious today only because it is so deeply embedded in all of our assumptions about grand strategy and foreign policy. Jomini makes an important contribution to grand strategy by virtue of his understanding of the techniques of war and strategy and the professionalization of the skills that it requires to succeed. And, finally, the economic theorists introduce the indispensability of having a strong economic base if the state is to implement an effective grand strategy, including war. The ideas of these economic theorists are crucial for seeing that any grand strategy in the modern era cannot succeed unless it provides economic growth, development, and technological innovation.

5 Grand Strategies of Empire in the Modern Era: Sixteenth to Twentieth Centuries

Chapter 5 builds on the conceptual discussion in Chapter 4 about the modern era of grand strategy by providing a series of case studies on the implementation of grand strategy by states and leaders throughout modern history. This chapter explores how states and statesmen have articulated and implemented grand strategy in ways that reflect, yet also sometimes diverge from, the theoretical foundations of strategy by scholars, as discussed in the earlier chapters. These cases focus on how grand strategy evolved during several historical periods starting with the reign of Philip II of Spain in the sixteenth century and ending with the fall of the Ottoman Empire in the twentieth century. Furthermore, this chapter identifies specific, common lessons across the case studies that are discussed later in the book as well as observations on the relationship between the scholars of strategy and the actual strategies pursued by states and statesmen.

Grand Strategies of the Modern Era: Philip II, Frederick II, and Napoleon

These cases on grand strategy were selected for several reasons. The first was to represent a broad swathe of the history of grand strategy – from the early modern era with Phillip II to the early twentieth century with the end of both the Ottoman and British Empires. Another criterion for selection was to focus on statesmen that made major contributions to or marked historical turning points in the evolution of grand strategy. Finally, this selection of case studies includes both examples of failures of grand strategy (e.g., Phillip II and Napoleon) and successes (e.g., Metternich and Bismarck). The success or failure experienced by each of these grand strategists derives from the analytical framework presented in Chapter 3. It also considers whether the leader in question understood the historical context and its consequences for grand strategy. To become a successful grand strategist in the modern era, one has to discern the political, military, and economic foundations of modern grand strategy, as outlined in Chapter 4. This discussion also includes more incisive observations on the relationship between scholars of strategy and the actual strategies that were pursued by states and statesmen. This includes the extent to which statesmen and states have heeded (or even concerned themselves at all) with the writings and theories of scholars who write on strategy.

To review, for articulating grand strategy, a state or leader must keep in mind the following principles: grand strategy must articulate unified objectives and goals; grand strategy is an ongoing, continuous process of the articulation and revision of policies that operates at all points along the war-peace continuum; and grand strategy must be carefully and properly distinguished from the realms of policy, doctrine, logistics, and operations, all of which compete for the attention of policy makers. To implement the state's grand strategy, the two central, guiding principles are, first, to marshal the domestic foundations of national power to strengthen and support the state's long-term interests and, second, to achieve the proper balancing of means and ends to ensure that the state's strategy does not exceed its grasp.

Philip II of Spain: A Grand Strategist Operating behind the Times

The grand strategy of Philip II (1527–1598), who reigned from 1556 to 1598, was primarily based upon maintaining the vast empire that he inherited from his father, Charles V.[1] This section presents a case study on the failure of Philip's grand strategy. Although Philip did not destroy the Spanish Empire, it began to fade during his reign. Some scholars point to the failed attempt by the Spanish Armada to invade England in 1588 as one reason for Spain's downfall, but the Armada exemplifies the larger problems that weakened Philip's empire.

Philip II ruled at a time of the emergence of the modern nation-state and the modern era of grand strategy. He is an example of a ruler who failed to understand the importance of the two principles that shape the implementation of grand strategy. First, he failed to marshal the domestic foundations of national power by creating a state bureaucracy that could effectively and efficiently implement his grand strategy. In short, he did not properly delegate the burdens that must be managed when implementing a state's grand strategy. Not only did he attempt to make all critical decisions by himself, but his failure also was a product of his worldview. This failure of execution in grand strategy derives from the relatively new development in the origins of states in which the state apparatus could carry out the orders of the king. Known as the divine right of kings to rule, it meant that kings had a divine obligation to govern, which in turn placed a very heavy burden of leadership on the individual who wore the Spanish crown in the sixteenth century.[2] In relative terms, the Spanish Empire was the most powerful empire in the world at that time, but also one beset with great challenges and threats.

Second, he failed to balance the political ends of his grand strategy with the financial means available to Spain. Again, Philip was a product of his era because economics and finance were not well-developed disciplines at the time; rulers could not routinely rely on experts in the field of budgetary management. These ideas simply did not exist as common knowledge or even in the remotest sense as they do today. In the sixteenth century, balancing budgets was a relatively new skill still in its earliest stages of development.

These two shortcomings in implementation were symptoms of a wider problem in Philip II's grand strategy – notably the influence of religious zealotry and ideological rigidity. His value system and way of thinking about the political world were largely outdated. Philip II lived in the modern era of grand strategy but still practiced the art of grand strategy as it existed during ancient times when states were smaller, their capabilities were less varied, the geography of international relations was far more proximate, and the time horizon for decision making operated on a short-term basis.

In terms of a clear and articulated grand strategy, many historians argue that Philip did not have one. As the scholar Paul Kennedy states, "had the Hapsburg rulers achieved all of their limited regional aims ... the mastery of Europe would virtually have been theirs."[3] Philip's empire, which was truly the first empire in history upon which the sun never set, stretched from the Philippines in the East to Mexico in the West.[4] However, Philip's ability to execute his duties as a leader and maintain his empire was so lackluster that it undermined his grand strategy, which was based on imperial expansion.

His failure to implement his grand strategy relates to the lack of managerial and administrative skill – above all to the failure to delegate authority and responsibility. The problem was that Philip did not greatly increase the number of councils, which meant that the timeliness of bureaucratic work in supervising the affairs of the empire greatly deteriorated during his reign.[5] At a time when other states, such as England, were bureaucratizing at a faster rate,[6] Philip wanted to ensure that he made important decisions on his own, and thus he delegated very little authority to his subordinates. By making decisions in this way, he delayed actions that were already slow to take effect because of the vast reach of his empire and the bureaucratic difficulties associated its far-flung geography. There are numerous complaints from his subordinates that Philip simply took much too long to make decisions.

To put the magnitude of the administrative load into perspective, for example, "in the month of March 1571 … over 1,250 individual petitions, an average of over 40 a day, arrived for the king's consideration.… In addition, the king read, and if necessary emended, the text of outgoing letters; and at least until the 1570s, he seems to have signed in person every order, however minor, issued in his name."[7] Another explanation for the problem with administration was "that his system of government required [that] all these processes be carried out by the king in person." Facing such centralized policy making, Philip "insisted that all the councils and juntas at the centre – like the various ministers, institutions and corporations on the periphery – should wait to receive their orders from the king in person."[8]

As Don Juan de Silva – a page, soldier, ambassador, and councilor who served Philip for over 50 years – complained, "His Majesty's brain … is not capable of organizing the multitude of his affairs without making some division between those that he should deal with himself and those that he cannot avoid delegating to others." The predictable result was that "he leaves nothing entirely alone and takes from everyone the material that should be delegated (concerning individuals and details), and so does not concentrate on the general and the important because he finds them too tiring." One explanation for the failure of Philip's grand strategy was the inability of individuals to take "responsibility for the most important matters."[9] What we see in the case of Philip II is the failure to organize the government's administrative apparatus properly, his inability to set and enforce priorities, and the general inefficiency that is endemic to all bureaucracies. All of these bureaucratic weaknesses contributed to the gradual failure of his empire's grand strategy.

A second explanation concerns difficulties that relate to financial planning and imperial overreach. A central problem was Philip's failure to balance financial means with political ends and to conduct wars with objects and goals that preserved and enhanced Spain's long-term interests. In practice, Philip had difficulty understanding the financial implications of engaging in the protracted wars fought across his expansive empire and in managing these far-flung enterprises. As Paul Kennedy notes, "The Hapsburgs simply had too much to do, too many enemies to fight, too many fronts to defend."[10] In terms of Spain's military power, "the Spanish troops in battle could not compensate for the fact that these forces had to be dispersed in homeland garrisons, in

North Africa, in Sicily and Italy, and in the New World, as well as in the Netherlands."
Kennedy draws the obvious parallel to the problems that plagued the British Empire
several centuries later when he observed how "the Hapsburg bloc was a conglomeration
of widely scattered territories, a political-dynastic tour de force which required enormous
sustained resources of material and ingenuity to keep going." In comparative terms, how
Philip badly managed Spain's empire represents "one of the greatest examples of strategic
overstretch in history."[11]

To maintain this empire, Philip needed to have either a firm understanding of
financial matters or the ability and willingness to delegate the empire's finances to
financial experts, yet neither occurred. For the scholar Geoffrey Parker, "Philip's greatest
failure ... lay in his inability to understand his finances." In fact, Philip himself
complained about how poorly he understood financial matters: "I have already told
you on other occasions how little I understand of these matters – and in this case I
certainly understood very little, almost nothing, of this paper, although I have read it
more than twice."[12]

An obvious lesson for grand strategy emerges from the reign of Philip II: despite "its
impressive military and administrative achievements, the Spanish Empire was showing
obvious signs of strain during the second half of the reign of Philip II." The problem was
that government "expenditure[s] in the last years of Philip II had been dramatically
outrunning resources."[13] Philip's lack of financial understanding and his reliance on a
micromanagerial style contributed to a serious economic downturn. In order to finance
his wars, he borrowed heavily at a time when the empire's expenditures exceeded
revenues, thus illustrating how crucial it is in the implementation of grand strategy for
the state to ensure that its ends and means are in balance. By the early 1570s, Spain's
deficit was approaching 50 percent. In 1560 Philip's debts were nearly 20 million ducats,
whereas by the early 1580s Spain's debts had increased fourfold to approximately 80
million ducats.[14]

The principal observation by the scholar J. H. Elliott was that we were seeing the
consequences and perils of economic overreach.[15] According to Kennedy, the economic
complications were too great for Spain to carry: "The much larger flow of income from
American mines – around 2 million ducats a year by the 1580s compared with one-tenth
of that four decades earlier – rescued the crown's finances, and credit, temporarily."
However, the Armada in 1588, which "cost 10 million ducats ... represented a financial
as well as a naval disaster."[16]

Spain could not afford the burdens of empire that were required by its grand strategy,
and thus "by 1596, after floating loans at an epic rate, Philip again defaulted." To put the
scale of Spain's debts in perspective, at the time of Philip II's death, "his debts totaled an
enormous sum of 100 million ducats, and interest payments on this sum equaled about
two-thirds of all revenues."[17] From the time of Thucydides to the present, a recurring and
powerful theme in grand strategy is to preserve the health of the state's financial and
economic affairs while keeping it in balance with the ends articulated in the state's grand
strategy.

A third explanation for the failure of Philip II's grand strategy was his imperialism and a
heavy-handed approach to policy, along with the ideological rigidity exhibited by many
officials in his court. During Philip's reign, the number of Protestants was increasing
throughout England and the Netherlands. As Philip fought both Protestants to his north
and Muslims to his south, he believed that he was doing the work of God, hoping to

return Protestants to Catholicism. Philip's belief was that he was doing God's will and therefore would be successful if he was steadfast: "You can assure his Holiness that rather than suffer the least injury to religion and the service of God, I would lose all my states and a hundred lives if I had them for I do not intend to rule over heretics."[18] The rise of religious zealotry had a major influence on Spain's decline because Philip was unable to act in Spain's best interests when he was distracted by what Geoffrey Parker calls the impulse of "Messianic Imperialism."[19]

We see signs of an imperial ethos in Philip's policies.[20] In effect, his dogmatic Catholicism points to an orthodox or apocalyptic mindset, which was typical of many sixteenth-century Christians who relied more on divine intervention than serious strategic planning and tangible contingency plans. To put this argument is rough terms, when good fortunes fell his way, Philip would praise God, and when he fell into trouble, he would call on God for assistance.[21] One observation is that such ideological principles likely undermined Spain's ability to pursue prudent policies that would keep its interests aligned with its grand strategy.

Philip's grand strategy was designed to maintain his vast empire and at the same time ensure that it remained under the influence of Catholicism for reasons related to both patronage and religious zealotry. However, Philip failed to understand that constant wars against Protestants weakened his empire and led to its eventual demise. He fought the rebels in the Netherlands for nearly thirty years largely because he refused to moderate his claims to fit their religious desires,[22] and this decision to engage in continual warfare helped bleed his empire of its financial strength. In the end, Philip's grand strategy, which was marked by poor financial management and religious zealotry, contributed to Spain's secular decline. For scholars and policy makers, Philip's policies provide an enduring example of how the failure to implement a coherent and prudent grand strategy can have truly devastating consequences for the state.

Frederick II (the Great) of Prussia: Grand Strategic Scholar and Master of Swift, Decisive War

One thinker whose ideas have had a decisive influence on the prevailing theory of strategy is Frederick II of Prussia (1712–1786). Also known as Frederick the Great, his most significant writings are his *General Principles of War* of 1746 and his *Military Testament*, composed in 1768 after the conclusion of the Seven Years' War. His body of work is significant.

As both a scholar and a practitioner, Frederick combined his intellect and propensity for action, which provides one reason for his successes in grand strategy. As he reflected on the critical conditions of his times, he was able to articulate an effective grand strategy. During his reign, Frederick acted as a European state leader vying for relative power, while also understanding the art and science of how to implement an effective grand strategy. His genius was in being able to step back to observe the political and military context and then to step back in decisively to influence that context in ways that bolstered the state's grand strategy.

The best way to understand Frederick's contributions to grand strategy is to consider the shift that occurred during this reign, from the conduct of siege warfare to the mobile, industrial-scale conflict occurring in the late eighteenth century. This shift, which was in reaction to trends already in motion, altered how theorists contemplated the nature and development of grand strategy. Drawing on Machiavelli's ideas about the total nature of war as a political enterprise and departing from the siege-centric views of earlier theorists, such as Vauban, Frederick was well ahead of his time.[23] Understanding that he lived in an era in which grand strategy was radically different from what existed during the ancient era of city-states, he not only grasped the nature of grand strategy in his era but also the geopolitical realities facing his state, Prussia.

For Frederick, the size and power of Prussia and the composition of its forces directly contributed to his grand strategy. Noting Prussia's significant territorial and military constraints as well as its relatively small population and territory, Frederick favored a strategy based on short, quick wars in which Prussia sought to make small but consistent and measurable gains.[24] What emerges from these principles are the outlines of the argument that the proper grand strategy for Prussia was to balance prudently the physical constraints on its power with limited and tightly constrained political ends. In contrast to Philip II, Frederick's grand strategy emphasized the principle of limits on the political ends the state should choose (articulation) and how it should pursue those ends (implementation).

Frederick's principal contribution to grand strategy was his ability to focus on the organization and configuration of forces that are necessary for the state to defeat other states and build the domestic foundations of its power. His fundamental legacy was to outline the precepts of what later became known as the strategy of blitzkrieg that emerged as an instrument for achieving "quick successes" in war.[25] By understanding that strategy is based on tactical victories whose value increases as they are achieved more quickly, his genius was to articulate how such tactical successes contribute to the state's grand strategy. In practice, he linked tactical accomplishments on the battlefield or in politics to the grand strategy of expanding Prussia's territorial influence and control.

As a critical architect of a more moderate or limited notion of strategy, Frederick the Great's ideas became less relevant as strategy shifted to the conduct of total war, whose outlines gradually began to take shape during the French Revolution and continued to gain momentum during the twentieth century. In his time, the state's strategy was to use cavalry charges in which armies attacked first in order to achieve such decisive results that the enemy was compelled or persuaded to negotiate.[26] In his "Military Instruction to His Generals," Frederick proposed that the "most certain way of insuring victory is to march briskly and in good order against the enemy, always endeavoring to gain ground."[27] Although the central purpose of strategy for Frederick was to accomplish the "entire destruction of your enemies," he cautioned that "to shed the blood of soldiers when there is no occasion for it, is to lead them inhumanly to the slaughter." We see here the principle of prudent limits imposed on the policies pursued by the state.

However, strategy for Frederick was governed by the principle that "war is decided only by battles, and it is not finished except by them."[28] Despite his emphasis on the role of the offense in strategy, Frederick opposed strategies that drove the state inexorably toward the conduct of total war, because he rejected any philosophy that called on one state to annihilate another. In a decisive contribution to the development of grand strategy, he rejected the concept of protracted wars or struggles because these inevitably would exhaust the state's (in his case, Prussia's) economic wealth and human resources – and this is essentially the fate that befell Germany almost two centuries later during World Wars I and II. This case illustrates the principle that grand strategy, to be effective, must reflect a unity between the state's military objectives and its political ends, whether in pursuit of war or peace.

Frederick's enduring contribution to grand strategy is the principle that the state must generate specific, decisive political results rather than simply destroy or obliterate the enemy. From that argument, Frederick fostered the idea that success in grand strategy does not necessarily require totally destroying one's adversary. Importantly, unlike Philip II, Frederick's grand strategy – which took active account of the constraints of his time, including physical resources, public support, and minimizing civilian involvement – allowed him to balance military means with political ends. For him, the roots of strategy existed in the civilian population. As one who held patriotism in high regard, he believed that because citizens fought with honor and courage, "with such troops one would defeat the whole world." Importantly, he understood that it would be necessary to radically change the nature of his kingdom if he were to wage war effectively using an army comprised wholly of citizens.[29]

A critical element of his approach to grand strategy was the dictum that it is prudent for the state to minimize the extent to which the civilian population is required, through conscription, to participate in military activities. In implementing the state's grand strategy, Frederick sought to keep the number of Prussians fighting in the Prussian army to an absolute minimum. His reasoning was that "useful hardworking people should be guarded as the apple of one's eye, and in wartime recruits should be levied in one's own country only when the bitterest necessity compels."[30] This understanding of the human and economic basis for strategy stands in sharp contrast to the failures that resulted from Philip II's approach to grand strategy.

Napoleon Bonaparte: Operational Genius and Grand Strategic Blunderer

We conclude this first section with one of the most ambitious rulers in Europe. As general and emperor, Napoleon Bonaparte (1769–1821) made significant contributions to formulating the idea that states should mobilize their societies by developing the mass armies that would allow them to conduct total wars as part of implementing grand strategy.[31] Napoleon sought to master war at the tactical and operational levels, believing that this would help the state achieve the objectives outlined in its strategy.[32] He serves as a cautionary example of the consequences of focusing too heavily on the operational level, because he fatally allowed the objectives of his military strategy to diverge from the goals of France's grand strategy.

Although it can be argued that Napoleon defined the success of strategy in mechanistic terms of combat between armies and the tactics that govern their actions, his ideas also contributed to the broad concept of grand strategy – one that the state supports by harnessing all of its resources. It was Napoleon's view that strategy should proceed from the tactical vantage point that dictates that actions in battle build the basis for a strategy seeking to totally defeat the enemy state.[33]

Napoleon's principal contribution to the evolution of grand strategy was to outline the factors that led to success and failure in the modern era. He enshrined the principle that a state that mobilized its entire society and most of its economy for war – *la levée en masse* – could attain success on an historically unprecedented scale, even in comparison with Genghis Khan's conquests during the Middle Ages and the devastation inflicted on Europe during the Thirty Years' War. Grand strategy as it emerged in the later nineteenth century reflected the influence of Napoleon's precept that states should use all of the human, economic, industrial, and technological resources at their disposal to ensure that their overall grand strategy prevails.

The shift from limited wars between ruling dynasties in the Renaissance to unlimited, national wars between modern European states in the nineteenth and twentieth centuries unquestionably influenced the evolution of modern ideas about grand strategy.[34] The type of limited struggle that had prevailed since antiquity to shape grand strategy was transformed by the French Revolution and Napoleon's leadership into the categorically different genre of total war between states, which culminated in the devastation produced by World Wars I and II.[35] During the nineteenth century, the effects of technological progress in weaponry and the ability to mobilize entire economies contributed to long and intense wars often fought for more unlimited objectives in the state's grand strategy. This era contributed to a redefinition of the principles of grand strategy, which often were governed by the desire to annihilate the enemy state.

Metternich, Bismarck, and the Formation of Germany: Building Stability

Nineteenth-century European politics was important to the development of a multilateral grand strategy as the great states of Europe sought to build a stable international political order. In the aftermath of the Napoleonic wars and as a prelude to even greater wars to come in the twentieth century, several statesmen played a critical role in building the foundations of grand strategy dedicated to achieving a delicate, artful balance of power on the European continent. In effect, this shift replaced the beliefs of the previous era in which warfare and political struggles had dominated politics for centuries.

One of the most influential critical statesmen was Prince Klemens von Metternich (1773–1859), who served as the chancellor and foreign minister of the Austrian Empire from 1809 to1848. His system of diplomacy, which was marked by numerous international congresses, rested on a firm commitment to maintaining a stable balance of power on the Continent. Metternich was a master of the use of diplomatic power – which at its heart is about making the right alliances at the right times – while avoiding making the wrong enemies at all times. Metternich made alliances and unmade them but above all made sure Austria was never vulnerable to another Napoleon through an ongoing process of consultation about grand strategy through the Concert of Europe mechanism. He understood that grand strategy was an ongoing process of articulation and constant revision and refinement along the war-peace continuum. His genius was in managing this process to accomplish Austria's grand strategy of maintaining a balance of power in Europe without relying too heavily on military power.

Otto von Bismarck was a contemporary statesman who, as the prime minister of Prussia, became the country's first chancellor in 1871. His ideas are synonymous with the *realpolitik* approach to diplomacy that he used to engineer the unification of Germany.[36]

Both Metternich and Bismarck were involved in building the foundations of a grand strategy that guided a new political order in Europe in the nineteenth century. At the center of this evolving strategic landscape were two major geopolitical shifts. The first was to weaken France enough so that it would not bid again for hegemony after the defeat of Napoleon in 1815, but not so much so as to give free rein to the other great powers in Western Europe. The second, which occurred later in the century, was to form a unified Germany whose political, economic, and military power would permit it to challenge the power of Great Britain, France, Austria, and Russia. In time, the emergence of Germany so altered the balance of power in Europe and globally that it compelled states to develop grand strategies whose purpose was to moderate and, as some might argue, contain Germany's power. This section examines how the ideas and policies of Metternich and Bismarck significantly contributed to the articulation and implementation of grand strategy during the highly dynamic political landscape that marked politics in nineteenth-century Europe.

Before examining the influence of Metternich on grand strategy, it is first useful to review the concept of the balance of power in international politics and its consequences for grand strategy. One scholar, Henry Kissinger, contributed important insights to help us understand this issue. In his *A World Restored* (1957), he analyzed how the precepts of peace, stability, and legitimacy influence the formation and conduct of grand strategy.[37]

The defining principle for Kissinger is that of stability. As he argues, "Whenever the international order has acknowledged that certain principles could not be compromised even for the sake of peace, stability based on an equilibrium of forces was at least conceivable." Kissinger writes that stability results "not from a quest for peace but from a generally accepted legitimacy." However, he warns that "legitimacy," which refers to "an international agreement about the nature of workable arrangements," should not be confused with justice. The implication, for Kissinger, is that the acceptance of this "framework of the international order by all major powers [provides stability], at least to the extent that no state is so dissatisfied that, like Germany after the Treaty of Versailles [it] expresses its dissatisfaction in a revolutionary foreign policy."[38] Although a legitimate and stable order will not prevent conflicts altogether, it can help limit their extent and destructiveness when conflicts occur nonetheless. If grand strategy expresses the principles that define the state's fundamental purposes and policies in its foreign policy, then the concepts of peace, stability, and legitimacy that emerged during the era under discussion evolved for many into enduring principles in the evolution of grand strategy.

For Kissinger, the principles of legitimacy and stability are the fundamental conditions to which all policy makers should aspire as they articulate their grand strategy and put it into practice. "Diplomacy in the classic sense," argues Kissinger, "is possible only in 'legitimate' international orders."[39] Thus, Kissinger's study of the contributions of Prince Metternich (1773–1859) to grand strategy derives directly from that Austrian statesman's efforts to "legitimize" and "stabilize" the conduct of foreign policy in Europe.

Prince Klemens Wenzel von Metternich: Deft Use of Diplomatic Power

There are two critical actors, for Kissinger, who more than any others shaped the balance of power politics in nineteenth-century Europe: Lord Robert Stewart Castlereagh (1769–1822) of Great Britain and Klemens von Metternich of Austria (1773–1859). These statesmen helped formalize the rules for a stable balance of power on the Continent.[40] Like Frederick the Great, Metternich's decisions provide a case study of the success of grand strategy. The difference is that, unlike Frederick and Napoleon, he relied on diplomatic power primarily – a feat arguably more intellectually challenging than the use of military power. Diplomacy, by its nature, is not exclusively coercive. It has elements of persuasion, manipulation, and timing whose implementation require a subtle mind that can judge both the role of individuals and the broader structural forces at work around them.

The problem for Metternich and Castlereagh, as Kissinger writes, was to determine in the conduct of diplomacy how best to "reconcile what is considered just with what is considered possible." Predictably, such a balance depends on many factors, including "the domestic structure of his state" and the "resources, determination and domestic structure of other states."[41] In the end, a coherent grand strategy is no more than an orderly framework that helps guide how policy makers align their ultimate goals with the resources available to the state.

Castlereagh, confident of England's safety as an island empire, directed his strategy of preventing *overt* aggression as a way of promoting stable relations in Europe after the era of Napoleonic Wars. Metternich, as the leader of the much-less-insular Austria, aspired to minimize the likelihood of conflicts that would lead to instability on the Continent. As Kissinger argues, while England pursued a doctrine of "non-interference" in the domestic affairs of other states, the Austro-Hungarian Empire pursued a strategy of maintaining stability based on a "generalized right of interference" whose purpose was to "defeat social unrest wherever it occurred."[42] A critical concept for grand strategy from this era is that, "because the balance of power only limits [but does not prevent] the scope of aggression ... Metternich sought to buttress the equilibrium by developing a [grand strategy based on] legitimacy." For him, it was entirely legitimate to intervene in order to pursue stability on the Continent.[43] In practice, Metternich's strategy of perseverance (when integrated with Castlereagh's influence) contributed to a period of peace that lasted nearly one hundred years and came to an end with the outbreak of two world wars in the twentieth century.

Metternich's concept of "a doctrine for universal interference," which he articulated in order to limit the risks of a perpetual "world revolution," depended on his own importance as an international mediator. Metternich's pursuit of this role, which allowed him to dictate the terms of agreements, largely reflected the limits of his country's geographic location and power.[44] Situated in the middle of Europe, Austria, unlike England, did not have the option of pursuing a more insular policy. The consequence, according to Kissinger, is that, "for Napoleon, everything depended on exhibiting his continuing omnipotence, [whereas] for Metternich [it rested] on demonstrating the limitations of French power."[45] In contrast with Napoleon's military approach, Metternich pursued a more diplomatic approach, which existed "within the larger context of Coalition politics, national self-interest, and the grand strategy" of other Continental powers.[46]

Austria offered to serve as a mediator to Napoleon "precisely because no power could be more interested in the restoration of the [political] equilibrium than the state whose geographic position condemned it to devastation in any war."[47] As this reasoning reflects, Metternich's answer to the problem of how to articulate a grand strategy that would build a stable international order was to pursue "an equilibrium" based on a broad "legitimizing principle."[48] Thus, for Kissinger, Metternich's grand strategy rested on the principle "of status quo *par excellence*," which involved not "marshaling a superior force, but ... obtaining a voluntary submission to his version of legitimacy."[49] Kissinger is an adherent of Metternich's belief that the goal of preserving stable relations in Europe transcends the desire for revolution. In building the foundations for an enduring grand strategy, he defends the argument, drawn directly from the writings of Metternich as well as Thucydides and Machiavelli, of how critical it is for interstate solidarity to be guided by shared interests.[50]

In effect, Metternich articulates a critical principle in grand strategy in which states must collaborate if they are to achieve mutually agreeable policies. As Kissinger writes, Metternich proposed "a policy which today we would call 'collaboration,'" which depends on the state being "certain of its moral strength or overwhelmed by the consciousness of moral impotence."[51] The source of Metternich's policy likely was his belief that conquest was incompatible with a stable and organized international system, his distrust of both Russia and international alliances, and his view that the preferred outcome was to achieve a condition in which universal laws are inevitable elements of international politics.[52] This strategy of collaboration reflects the enduring principle of grand strategy in which the state marshals available resources – political will as much if not more so than physical military assets – as it pursues the national interests that it holds in common with other states.

The grand strategy articulated by Metternich and Castlereagh proved effective after the Congress of Vienna (1815) because it promoted a system of collective security among European states.[53] Many states and their leaders were interested in a system of security, based on a common interest in maintaining peace and security, particularly as they contemplated the wars and disruptions attributed to Napoleon. In the end, it was his defeat and the later restoration of peace that brought security to Europe. Ultimately, however, disagreements over the purpose of the Alliance, after its primary objectives were achieved, undermined Metternich's grand strategy of collaboration.[54] By mid-century, as the Concert of Europe stitched together by Metternich began to unravel, Bismarck used this approach to grand strategy to consolidate the German states under his guidance.

Otto von Bismarck: Expanding the Prussian State through Short Wars and Skillful Diplomacy

If Metternich was the master diplomat of the status quo, Otto von Bismarck (1815–1898), who as Chancellor oversaw German unification, was the master revisionist.[55] He remade the map of Europe, positioning Germany as the most powerful state on the Continent – and did so without a major hegemonic war. He had a reputation for possessing remarkable insights into politics and an ability to exercise influence that had dramatic consequences for European politics in the latter half of the nineteenth century. He was a revolutionary in the sense that his grand strategy, which differed dramatically from that of Metternich, was designed to solve the problem of German unity. For the scholar Williamson Murray, Bismarck, just "like Napoleon [had an] instinctive understanding of operational art," and his "grasp of strategy was that of a genius: intuitive, decisive, and in almost all cases effective."[56]

Proceeding from the argument that grand strategy should seek to build a balance of power or equilibrium on which all states can build stability, Kissinger observes that the conditions in Germany following the Napoleonic Wars were the key to building the European equilibrium. The European order established by Metternich permitted peace in Europe, which in turn depended on an overall balance of power, or equilibrium, *between* the German principalities and kingdoms, all of which were united by a consensus on the fundamental value of preserving a stable balance of power. The argument is not that these states articulated a joint grand strategy, but that their grand strategies were united by the common principle that Europe in the aftermath of the turbulent Napoleonic era would be well served by a stable political order. By the early 1850s, this system helped to define European politics "for the indefinite future."[57]

Bismarck's grand strategy continued to evolve during his tenure as chancellor, but he did not begin "with a clear idea of the route or the political and international framework within which he was going to have to work." In practice, Bismarck's policy was governed by several long-term goals, notably "the political security, internal as well as external of the Prussian monarchy." But in the end, Bismarck sought to "unify ... the 'Germanys,' southern and northern" as the strategy to "secure Prussia."[58]

Bismarck's strategy presented a theoretical challenge to the prevailing domestic structure in Metternich's regime. Believing that Prussia's domestic structure was uniquely invulnerable to domestic upheaval, Kissinger writes that under Metternich, "Prussia's policy of repression was even more effective than that of Austria because it was not leavened by Austrian inefficiency."[59] The aim for Bismarck was to articulate and implement a grand strategy that was designed to overthrow the Metternich system within Germany. In terms of grand strategy, Kissinger notes that "Bismarck fought domestic upheaval because he wanted Prussia to focus on foreign policy." His reasoning was that this approach would enable Prussia's domestic institutions to evolve to match the nation's foreign policy needs. By this logic, Bismarck adopted a revisionist approach because it entailed a sudden departure from his previous acceptance of and longstanding adherence to the precepts outlined in Metternich's grand strategy.[60]

Perhaps Bismarck's most famous expression is that "policy is the art of the possible, the science of the relative."[61] The distinctive feature of Bismarck's ideas was his concept that the state should base its foreign policy "not on sentiment but on an assessment of strength," which means that the state's policy should reflect the forces of "calculation, not emotion."[62] The reason, for Bismarck, was that "the perfect flexibility of international relationships [was] limited only by the requirements of national interest."[63] Whereas Metternich believed legitimacy was critical to security and stability, Bismarck sought to articulate principles that built strategic equilibrium based not only on the state's power and interests but on the evolutionary principle that the most fit will survive. In effect, Bismarck began the conceptual shift "from the rationalist to the empiricist conception of politics" in which the statesman pursues utility over legitimacy, while noting that power creates a unique source of legitimacy.[64] Bismarck's primary influence on grand strategy in the second half of the nineteenth century was to maintain relative peace in Europe even after Germany had been unified. This unification represented a shock to the system in Europe, which now faced a unified and consequently vastly more powerful Germany.

One imperative in Bismarck's grand strategy is that the state should base its decisions on classic realist calculations of power and that this principle constitutes a fundamental determinant of relationships among states.[65] Although Bismarck succeeded in maintaining peace in Europe for a generation, his grand strategy did not provide the requisite degree of flexibility for guiding diplomacy because it was itself guided by "maxims that presupposed the infinite adaptability of the principal actors."[66] In Bismarck's view, how the state promoted its national interests was sufficiently ambiguous to give states some flexibility as they define their grand strategy and the policies that support it.[67]

The extent of Bismarck's legacy in grand strategy and his role in encouraging conditions in statecraft contributed to Germany's tragic experience in the twentieth century with the rise of Hitler and Nazism.[68] Bismarck biographer Otto Pflanze, however, challenges this argument. He concedes that Bismarck's "career heightened the already dangerous adulation of power in Germany and accentuated the popular belief that what matters in the employment of power is success." However, he argues that Bismarck's approach to articulating and implementing Germany's grand strategy was entirely consistent with the realities of nineteenth-century diplomacy. During that era, leaders did not so much aim to reshape the world or align it with the dictates of religious or political ideologies as they did endeavor to strengthen their states without provoking hegemonic wars. In line with this reasoning, Bismarck's grand strategy was not designed "to unify the German cultural nation, but to expand the Prussian state" in ways that were consistent with the nature of the balance of power in Europe during the nineteenth century.[69]

Scholars argue that Bismarck was a man beyond his time because he was the first statesman to recognize that the popular movements emerging across the European continent required states to develop a new kind of grand strategy – or face a continent ablaze with popular unrest. As Pflanze explains, "No longer could the masses be ignored in the conduct of either domestic or foreign affairs [because] the doctrines of legitimacy and divine right no longer sufficed to justify authoritarian rule." Once it was clear that monarchical institutions had to be rooted in and eventually displaced by national senti-ment, Bismarck understood that moral forces were means rather than ends – "objects to be manipulated rather than ... [practical] guides for political action." In fact, some credit Bismarck's ability to manipulate national sentiment for his own political purposes to his keen understanding of the origins of German nationalism. This moral sensibility even-tually moved public sentiment, changed the political center of gravity in Europe, and altered the geopolitical landscape of the twentieth century. In discussing these conse-quences of Bismarck's legacy in grand strategy, scholars hold that the German chancellor was a deeply moral person who was devoutly religious in his personal life. The problem, however, was that "the priority he gave to might over right in both domestic and foreign affairs established an unfortunate precedent in German history upon which men of other aims and other conscience were eventually to capitalize."[70]

A critical component of Bismarck's pragmatic view of politics, known as *realpolitik*, follows from the argument: "There is no exact science of politics ... one has to reckon with given and unknown factors, but there are no rules and formulations with which to sum up the results in advance."[71] Bismarck dismissed the role of popular will when he defended the role of "legitimacy" in governance, arguing that pursuing the state's interests gave its authority greater legitimacy. Finding in Darwinism a better framework for understanding the relationship between science and society, he rejected the meta-physical idea that natural laws govern societies. When Bismarck described politics, he saw politics as "less a science than an art ... [which] is the capacity to choose in each fleeting moment of the situation [the] least harmful or most opportune."[72] From this principle, we see the concept of limiting damage emerge as central to realism.[73]

For Bismarck, patience, timing, intuition, and a careful and accurate evaluation of one's opponents were the key principles that must guide the state's grand strategy. An equally important dimension of Bismarck's approach to grand strategy was the constant generation and exploration of alternative courses of action. Often, Bismarck would simultaneously explore multiple solutions to political problems, while waiting to choose a course of action until the last possible minute. The value of exploring alternatives "enabled him to gain and retain the initiative ... [and] by monopolizing the alternative possibilities which the situation afforded, he often severely restricted his adversary's sphere of action."[74]

Bismarck believed in the necessity of using coercion, for either the threat or actual use of violence, to achieve one's aims. Coercion, including violent coercion, even if it should lead to war, was merely a means of accomplishing a political end that is articulated by the state's grand strategy. This logic aligns well with Clausewitz's reasoning about strategy, but Bismarck gave the highest priority to the national interest in the struggle against revolutions (particularly against the Napoleonic dynasty at the time). Addressing why large states go to war, Bismarck famously quipped in a December 1850 speech defending the Olmütz agreement, "The only sound basis for a large state is its egoism and not romanticism; this is what distinguishes a large state necessarily from a small one."[75] Although not hesitant to engage in hostilities, Bismarck was adamant that going to war, particularly should it be against two of the three biggest Continental powers, required an eminently worthy cause and a clear connection to the state's national interests. Building on the framework for grand strategy in this study, Bismarck's beliefs align quite closely with the principle that a nation should go to war only when the urgency and gravity of the nation's interests warrant doing so and, in the terminology of this book, when the state's military strategy is consistent with the grand strategy that guides its actions.

One scholar, Marcus Jones, concludes from his study that Otto von Bismarck was the greatest modern master of diplomacy. In studying grand strategy through the lens of the particular qualities that made Bismarck so successful, Jones argues that "Bismarck's great genius as the founder of a Prussian-dominated German nation lay not in his adherence to a systematic program or plan." What marked Bismarck's acumen in grand strategy was his ability to handle "uncertain events through intuition and broad experience."[76] He understood, like Metternich, the need for adaptability in the constant process of articulating and revising the state's grand strategy to deal with the challenges posed by war and peace.

One of Bismarck's critical strengths was his excellent written and oral communication skills, which allowed him to deliver messages in a style that was persuasive and direct, yet elegant. Thanks to his diplomatic career, including years spent in St. Petersburg and Paris, Bismarck was fluent in Russian, French, English, Italian, and Latin. All in all, it was the combination of Bismarck's unique intellectual personal traits and his professional diplomatic experience that helped him be such a successful grand strategist.[77] Significantly, Bismarck had a special gift for carefully balancing alternatives without losing sight of the state's preeminent long-term interests. He also possessed an intellectual capacity far beyond that of his counterparts, which allowed him to quickly distinguish the most salient aspects of critical problems.

In articulating the state's grand strategy, Bismarck adroitly addressed the state's urgent needs without losing sight of its long-term objectives. This Prussian statesman was attuned to exercising caution in the conduct of grand strategy. What distinguished Bismarck as a "strategic actor," for Jones, "was his moderation and prudence ... [because he] never set his country on a course that his mind had not cautiously explored beforehand."[78] Bismarck's actions were marked by an unwavering loyalty to the interests of the Prussian state. In addition, Bismarck was keenly aware of Prussia's vulnerable geographic exposure and political position, as demonstrated by his "consistent moderation in defining and pursuing Prussian interests." In practice, his skepticism about the effects and limits of romantic nationalism, which distinguished him from his political contemporaries, translated into his conviction that in pursuing the state's grand strategy, "military and diplomatic hubris could result not just in failure but also in disaster."[79] In his desire to avoid unnecessary risk, Bismarck demonstrated that he possessed a conservative outlook in statecraft.

With regard to grand strategy, Bismarck was notable for his keen ability to focus, to the exclusion of other distractions, on the state's most critical long-term goals. Yet he acknowledged that the unpredictable nature of diplomacy and warfare makes flexibility and adaptability perhaps the cardinal principles of statecraft. Scholars emphasize that flexibility was an integral part of Bismarck's strategic personality.[80] Quick to reevaluate and redefine the state's objectives when confronted by shifting threats and challenges, his actions emphasized why it is critical for policy makers to constantly rebalance the state's priorities and interests as they articulate and implement its grand strategy.

The conclusion is that Bismarck comprehended the essence of international politics so well that, in formulating Prussia's grand strategy, he was guided by an exquisitely "clear notion" of Prussia's interests.[81] His ability to grasp the strategic environment – to know when to use the tools of both force and diplomacy to pursue and advance the state's long-term national interest – was the hallmark of Bismarck's highly coherent and effective grand strategy for Prussia. His mastery of both how to articulate and implement grand strategy brought Germany to within reach of great power status.

British Imperial Geopolitics before World War I: Preserving and Clashing Empires

The previous cases studies concerned the actions of individuals who were involved in crafting grand strategies, whereas the next two case studies focus on the grand strategies pursued by imperial states. From the mid-nineteenth century to the early twentieth century, the European great powers were engaged in a global struggle for empire. It was during this age of imperial empires when these states expanded their spheres of influence through the systematic pursuit of colonies. This also was the age when states started to challenge the hegemonic power and influence of Great Britain. During this era, the deliberations about grand strategy among the European powers reshaped the conduct of geopolitics and led ultimately to the conditions that contributed to the outbreak of World War I.

British Grand Strategy: Offshore Balancing and Economic Power

Beginning in the late seventeenth century, the British increasingly took strategic advantage of the unique benefits afforded by their island geography and political stability. London gradually built a vast global network of colonies as part of an empire that was committed to geopolitical influence and trade[82] that drew from its naval strength and superior technological knowledge. As the historian Paul Kennedy writes, these policies sustained "the country's continuing growth, making it into a new sort of state – the only real world power."[83] In economic terms, Great Britain's industrial power contributed to its "ascendancy in commerce and finance and shipping," and its unprecedented economic power formed the basis of London's "naval supremacy."[84]

In shaping Britain's grand strategy, its geographical position as an insular state, which essentially eliminated the chance of overland attack, contributed to a form of political stability quite unlike that of any other European powers at the time. Great Britain took such advantage of its geography that between 1815 and 1865 it had established itself as an unprecedented global economic power. The years between 1815 and 1865, known as *Pax Britannica*, saw Britain gain enormous wealth and holdings of overseas territories.

To understand the economic dimensions of British grand strategy, by the middle of the nineteenth century, Britain produced "two-thirds of the world's coal, about half its iron, five-sevenths of its steel, two-fifths of its hardware and about half of its commercial cotton cloth." In addition, it produced roughly "40 percent of the entire world output of traded manufactured good[s]."[85] Economic power on this scale had dramatic consequences for other states, particularly those with "land frontiers such as Spain, France, and even the Netherlands," which were forced to focus "their resources and attention upon the wider world" and the threats it posed.

By contrast, however, Great Britain was so well positioned to exploit changing patterns of international trade that it was able to leverage the advantage that flowed from its insularity – and to do so at very low risk of overland attack. Shielded by its powerful fleet, Great Britain could both protect itself against invasion and dominate the world's shipping lanes. During this era, British foreign policy makers articulated and implemented the grand strategy that permitted the country to wield extraordinary influence, while simultaneously building the foundations of London's economic domination of the globe.

To put the influence of economics on grand strategy into perspective, Great Britain's rise to superpower status was not merely due to clever tactical political or military maneuvers by its political leaders, but also to its ability to merge the nation's economic and military arms into a coherent grand strategy. As the scholar Kennedy writes, "Aristocrats and gentry joined with city merchants in financing overseas trading companies and in ensuring that the government provided the necessary martial support to keep foreign rivals at bay."[86] Of greatest importance, Kennedy writes, was the "'sense of common identity in those who wielded [the] economic, social, and political power,'" [which trumped the] "necessity of preserving and enhancing Britain's place in the world." What is significant is how Great Britain's economic and military power merged into "mutually supporting organs of a grand strategy predicated upon commercial expansion, colonial exploitation, domestic stability, and insular security."[87]

The scholar and prominent proponent of modern naval power, Alfred T. Mahan, examined the relationship between economic production, sea power, and colonies in his seminal work, *The Influence of Sea Power Upon History, 1660–1783*. In that book, Mahan argued that Great Britain harnessed "*production*, with the necessity of exchanging products, *shipping*, whereby the exchange is carried on, and *colonies*, which facilitate and enlarge the operations of shipping and tend to protect it by multiplying points of safety."[88] By taking advantage of these conditions, Great Britain strengthened an already powerful cycle in which shipping, commerce, and economic growth underpinned its colonial expansion and prolonged the duration of its imperial dominance.

The only limitation of Britain's grand strategy existed on the Continent itself. It was "only in Europe itself," Kennedy writes, "where armies were the ultimate arbiters of international disputes, [and] British power [was] limited."[89] "'We are fish,' [Prime Minister] Salisbury often remarked." As long as the "continental balance [of power] was maintained, the British could remain offshore islanders."[90] In effect, Great Britain's grand strategy derived from a status quo orientation in which it sought to preserve the foundations of geopolitical stability. To the extent that one can describe it, the "English [political] ideology" was based on "adroitly [fusing] Liberal progressivism with a Conservative respect for law and order and 'good form.'" In the end, it rested on the desire to avoid extremes, while relying on "commonsense and compromise."

Lastly, the emphasis on economic power had a pervasive influence on British policies. Consider for example that in 1865 "about 52 per cent of MPs were merchants, industrialists and men of finance (whereas only 8 per cent of the members of the 1871 Reichstag came from such circles)."[91] Britain's ability to successfully integrate the middle classes into its political system was reflected in how its foreign policy used trade as an instrument for preserving the Continental balance of power.

The Fall of Britain's Empire

By the latter half of the nineteenth century, however, nations that possessed greater human and economic resources slowly were beginning to challenge Britain's hegemony. With the spread of technology (in the categories of steel, steam, and rail), the United States, Russia, and Germany had reached the point where they could credibly challenge Great Britain's uncontested position as the leader of a global empire. The American, German, and Russian grand strategies that emerged during this era sought in part to restrain Great Britain's imperial power, and London's corresponding grand strategy was designed to counter those efforts. Indeed, Britain's dominant grand strategy of offshore balancing meant that it sought to prevent the rise of a hegemonic Continental power that could challenge it. In effect, Britain's foreign policy establishment consistently acted in ways that sought to counterbalance any such rising threats.

In response to the threat posed by rival nations – and as it attempted to maintain the status quo while preserving its preponderance of wealth and power – successive governments in London formed tighter bonds with Britain's self-governing dominions (notably, Canada, Australia, New Zealand, and South Africa). The dominant belief in British politics was that the nation had an obligation to expand its influence across the globe, for two reasons. The first was to maintain Great Britain's economic power and strength by maintaining its position in the global markets, and the second was to continue its duty, with both self-imposed and paternalistic roots, to "uphold and extend the standards of . . . civilization" in cultures around the world.[92] Despite intense domestic political debates between liberals and conservatives over the moral and practical consequences of the policy known as imperialism, Great Britain's grand strategy of projecting its power and maintaining its economic and territorial holdings was the central defining principle that animated British foreign policy – regardless of which prime minister was in power.

For intellectuals, businesspeople, and statesmen during the late nineteenth and early twentieth centuries, the theory of social Darwinism was used to propagate and justify the principle that it was Europe's and North America's duty to colonize what were perceived as "inferior cultures" and provide them with the expertise to run their own societies (often called the "White Man's Burden").[93] Cecil Rhodes (founder of Rhodesia, De Beers, and the Rhodes Scholarship) expressed this sentiment quite starkly in 1892 when he observed that, "in view of the fact that these islands can only support six out of their thirty-six millions, and in view also of the action of the world in trying to exclude our goods, we cannot afford to part with one inch of the world's surface which affords a free and open market to the manufacture of our countrymen."[94]

This ideology was central to Great Britain's ability to marshal the domestic foundations of national power into economic power that supported its military (and particularly its naval) power. Rhodes was a vocal proponent of this ideology and set up a trust "to and for the establishment, promotion and development of a Secret Society whereof shall be the extension of British rule throughout the world . . . especially . . . the entire continent of Africa, the Holy Land, the Valley of the Euphrates."[95] This "foundation" for its power would be so "great [that it would] render wars impossible and promote the best interests of humanity."[96] One British official, Sir Frederick Lugard (governor of Hong Kong and governor-general of Nigeria), likened Britain's colonial policies to those of the Roman Empire.[97]

The sentiment that it was Britain's obligation to govern other societies was expressed well by Lord Rosebery, British prime minister and liberal statesman. It is, he said, "our responsibility and our heritage to take care that the world, as far as it can be moulded by us, shall receive an Anglo-Saxon and not another character."[98] The rhetoric of Great Britain's imperial defense was evident when Lord Rosebery declared in 1893 that "an Empire such as our[s] requires as its first condition an imperial race – a race vigorous and industrious and intrepid." As British military historian Michael Howard writes, "Britain's imperial aims helped British citizens reclaim their individual and collective strength."[99]

As stewards of the political, economic, and military status quo, policy makers in Britain worked to preserve the balance of power on the European continent, while simultaneously maintaining London's preeminence in naval affairs. In implementing this grand strategy, London formed alliances first with Japan and later, in what would become far more fateful alliances in the early twentieth century, with France and Russia. When confronted with the threat of a rising and increasingly powerful German nation, Britain engaged in a naval arms race with Germany, which ultimately contributed to the conditions that culminated in World War I and contributed to severely weakening Britain.

The shift from Britain's dominance to its subsequent geostrategic demise involved a complex mix of internal and external forces. By 1870, we see evidence that Britain's position as the preeminent world power was showing signs of deterioration. Other nations with larger populations and greater natural resources were beginning to catch up to Britain in terms of its industrial power and maritime strength. To put this development of the late 1800s into perspective, the maritime strategist Mahan used six characteristics that help explain how Germany, Russia, and the United States were able to achieve strategic parity with Great Britain. Mahan's list includes the state's geographical position, physical conformation, territory, population, national character, and government policy.[100] As various rising powers achieved parity and then overtook Great Britain in these crucial categories, their increasing economic and military power eroded Britain's unchallenged hegemony in various strategically critical domains.

A crucial factor was the proliferation of railroads, which gave nations with vast natural resources – such as Russia, Germany, and the United States – a distinct economic advantage over Great Britain.[101] As the British recognized this worrisome trend, they began to lean more heavily upon their self-governing dominions to provide more money and resources to help maintain London's power. But as a result of industrialization, mass transportation provided by railroads, investment, and new techniques for agricultural and mining production, the balance of power shifted "inexorably" toward such powers as those on the Continent – notably Russian and Imperial Germany – as well as the United States.[102]

Britain's declining share of global manufacturing capacity in the late nineteenth century is a telling trend. By 1870, London possessed "32 per cent of the world's manufacturing capacity [which] was down to 15 per cent by 1910; and although its share of world trade was 25 per cent in 1870, by 1913 this had shrunk to 14 per cent."[103] Because Britain's grand strategy depended in part on economic expansion, industrial wealth, and military power, a shift in these elements of power was not a positive development for the nation. For some scholars, the conclusion is that this shift reflected the beginning of the end of Britain's inability to compete unless it could marshal the resources of its colonies.[104] As the extent of Great Britain's economic dependence on its colonies became apparent, its policies sought increasingly to more closely integrate the colonies with London. As Joseph Chamberlain (an influential British statesman) asked in 1888, "Is there any man in his senses who believes that the crowded population of these islands could exist for a single day if we were to cut adrift from the great dependencies which now look to us for protection and assistance and which are the natural markets for our trade?"[105]

Great Britain's grand strategy was based on the principle that London would resist getting involved in military affairs on the continent of Europe. Some of the reasons included the domestic populace's widespread distaste for the horrors of war, their objection to the costs of global military commitments, and their desire to focus on domestic political issues, including for a time the case of parliamentary reform. This led to a policy of British neutrality in European conflicts, precisely along the lines of the policies London adopted during the Franco-Prussian War (1870–1871). Because Britain sought to remain free from entangling alliances, its grand strategy was designed to maintain the existing balance of power on the European continent as a way of preventing wars and protecting its prosperity. As with many British policy makers, Lord Salisbury argued that "defence of the Empire [was] the most important task facing British states-men in the last quarter of the nineteenth century."[106] Great Britain's experience during this era reaffirms the principle that grand strategy is an ongoing, continuous process of articulation, implementation, and revision as the state balances its policies between war and peace.

The scholar J. A. S. Grenville argued that Prime Minister Salisbury's objective was not simply to defend London's imperial interests, but was governed by the broader objective of preventing rival powers from challenging Britain's interests.[107] Yet Salisbury under-stood, unlike many other architects and supporters of imperialism, that the expansion of Britain's territory through the acquisition of colonies should be seen not "as the end of a problem but as its beginning."[108] This sentiment foreshadowed many of the difficulties that Britain and the other European colonial powers experienced as their empires progressively deteriorated and gradually came to an end during the twentieth century. Indeed, this issue was at the heart of the struggle between President Franklin Delano Roosevelt and Prime Minister Winston Churchill, given their dramatically opposing views on the fate of Britain's imperial empire after World War II.[109]

In the struggle between the contending grand strategies of the various European powers, Salisbury's "achievements were undeniably impressive" because, as Grenville observed, Bismarck "never got the better of him." As another example of his accomplish-ments, "the partition of Africa was accomplished without war and Britain got the lion's share." Ever the pragmatist, Salisbury was interested in preserving the balance of power without recourse to war because conflict was "the ultimate misfortune." Salisbury believed that Britain's "permanent interests were better defended by the careful culti-vation of harmonious relations than by a pedantic insistence on the individual points of a particular dispute."[110] In exercising restraint in Great Britain's overall conduct of its grand strategy during the early twentieth century, Prime Minister Lord Rosebery argued that Britain should abstain from involving itself in the First Sino-Japanese War (1894–1895).[111] In reasoning based on economic realities, he said that "our commerce is so universal and so penetrating that scarcely any question can arise in any part of the world without involving British interests." Pragmatically he commented, however, that if "we [did] not strictly limit the principle of intervention we should always be simultaneously engaged in some forty wars."[112]

Early in the twentieth century, British statesmen questioned the value of London's grand strategy of remaining unaligned with the European great powers. For these policy makers, the need for Britain to reexamine its historical isolation from the Continent led London to establish treaties with Japan and the United States, which were designed to maintain peace and protect British interests. But this shift in grand strategy inevitably produced its own complications. For example, in order to stabilize its interests in China against Russian expansion, Britain attempted to enter into an agreement with Germany. This strategy failed, however, because "Berlin insisted that any alliance should not be with Germany alone but with Austria-Hungary and Italy." The problem was that this alliance would link "Britain to the defence of central Europe,"[113] and worryingly to an unending series of conflicts. In 1902, Britain signed a treaty with Japan that pledged "mutual aid in the event of the other being engaged in a conflict over China or Korea with *two or more* countries, but benevolent neutrality if it was a conflict with only one country."[114] By the turn of the century, Great Britain developed closer ties with Washington to foster mutual cooperation as part of its strategy to balance China's influence, while responsibly withdrawing its strategic and political influence over Latin America.

The problem was that intensifying Anglo-German animosities precluded any peace agreement with Germany. In turn, this led to the signing of the *entente cordiale* between Britain and France in 1904. For the British, the *entente* pacified yet another challenger to London's strategic position. It was a source of "immense satisfaction to many in Britain and France that Berlin could no longer take advantage of the colonial tensions between the two western powers."[115] In addition, the *entente* helped Britain manage the "Asiatic factor," because an agreement with France likely would have increased Britain's chances of dealing with its defense challenges in India. By 1900, as Kennedy observes, "with the majority of the Cabinet seeking an Anglo-German accord, even an acute student of foreign affairs could hardly have imagined that within seven years Britain would have drawn closer to France and Russia and would be regarding Germany as its most dangerous enemy."[116]

The growing clash between the British and German grand strategies culminated in competition between their naval forces. The naval arms race between Great Britain and Germany was driven by Germany's expansion and Britain's fear of it. The British wanted peace, which for them required maintaining the status quo based on their naval superiority and empire. London feared that reducing its naval supremacy would not only harm its ability to conduct the trade that was the lifeblood of Britain's economy and global power, but would directly weaken the military security of the British Isles. As Howard argues, "Like most members of the 'Peace Lobby' at the time and since, [many] identified 'peace' with the maintenance of the status quo." The problem was that "foreigners, unfortunately, saw things differently." Britain's reasoning on this issue was sound because policy makers understood that the country relied on its fleet for trade *and* security. The leadership of the British Royal Navy steadfastly adhered to the view that "neither invasion nor blockade was feasible so long as Britain maintained command of the sea." In practice, Great Britain's grand strategy depended on its ability to "exercise command of the sea [which] depended on the possession of a superior battle fleet."[117]

By the late nineteenth and early twentieth century, Germany's grand strategy was in direct competition with Great Britain's over primacy in Europe and globally. This rivalry produced the basis for a clash: Germany's grand strategy to be a Continental power, with its increasing naval might, versus Britain's grand strategy to maintain its existing maritime and global power. London's view was that Germany's growing naval power threatened Britain's vital interests, and Germany believed that it had every right to expand its navy. Because the British government could not settle its differences with Germany, these clashing views contributed to Great Britain's decision to become involved in World War I. For reasons of politics and geography, "neither an American fleet expansion, nor Japanese, threatened Britain's vitals: Germany's navy did." When the prospect of a "rising German battlefleet in the North Sea cast doubt upon British naval supremacy in home waters,"[118] Germany's expansionist grand strategy clashed directly with London's grand strategy of naval supremacy.

The results of this clash are painfully clear. The realization that the grand strategies of London and Berlin were directly competing for supremacy and economic prosperity influenced Britain's decision to enter World War I. As Kennedy argues, there was "fear of what might happen if Britain stayed out," but even greater fear that "the Germans would win and then, all-powerful in Europe, resume their naval challenge with greater energy and resources than before." The fundamental source of this clash was their opposing grand strategies whereby Britain sought to preserve its empire, while Germany wanted to expand its power and influence as a great power.[119] This is a case of the pattern in grand strategy in which a rising state seeks to challenge an established power.[120] The inescapable observation is that the scale and duration of World War I – and later of World War II – derived in part from the Anglo-German competition in which interactions among their grand strategies had dramatic consequences for the two states.

The British case is a study in success with regard to both articulation and implementation. The principle of offshore balancing and the importance of trade and economic power were articulated again and again in the government's debates about its grand strategy. Generation after generation in the British foreign policy establishment internalized its meaning and used it to guide their thinking. Yet, each generation was capable of adapting this internalized guideline to the demands of their own time. Thus, the British shifted their economic focus to the colonies in the late-nineteenth century to keep pace with the rapidly growing economic power of the Continental challengers. Furthermore, their ability to use these twin guideposts effectively balanced the ends of grand strategy with the means of national power. The British never sought to rise to supremacy and yet they did so because they kept the political ends of their grand strategy – the prevention of a Continental hegemon and the protection of global trade – at a prudently sustainable level.

So, then, the question of why the British Empire declined remains an important lesson from the case for modern policy makers and scholars.[121] Even the pursuit of an optimal grand strategy will not prevent great power decline. It is a law of international politics that state power grows, expressed by the law of uneven growth, at differential rates. Eventually, the British Empire failed not because its grand strategy failed, but rather because other states simply outpaced London in economic, military, and political terms. But this loss of empire occurred after the British helped win two world wars and acquired a standing in the world that allowed them to hand off their legacy to a close ally, the United States, whose democratic system and economic policies continued in many ways some features of the project the British left unfinished. It is for this reason that Great Britain's grand strategy remains of such interest today.

The Rise and Decline of the Ottoman Empire: Adapting Too Little, Too Late

The Ottoman Empire holds a unique place in history that rivals some of the most powerful and longest-standing empires.[122] The empire's hold on power continued for more than six hundred years, as it enjoyed a continuous period of growth and expansion for more than one hundred of those years. At the height of its power, the Ottoman Empire extended over three continents, controlling much of southeastern Europe, western Asia, and North Africa. This tremendous amount of amassed territory allowed the Ottoman Empire to stand at the center of interactions between the Eastern and Western worlds and intercontinental trade for six centuries. These lands extended from the Balkans and the Black Sea region through Anatolia (Asia Minor), Syria, Egypt, and most of the North African coast until World War I.[123]

Although it is important to focus on the failures in the grand strategy of the sultans in the seventeenth and eighteenth centuries, it is equally critical to discuss their adept ability to fashion a society defined by flexibility and general tolerance. Social flexibility, military power, and the development of a strong state-centric bureaucracy led to the extended period of Ottoman successes. To attain this success, the Ottoman Empire's grand strategy articulated a coherent relationship among the state or empire's political, military, and economic policies. The implication is that the grand strategy of the Ottoman Empire did not exist in isolation, but instead reflected a coherent relationship among all of its policies and doctrines as it coordinated its military and nonmilitary sources of power.

The Ottoman Empire's most prominent ruler by many accounts was Suleyman I, also referred to as Suleyman the Magnificent, who ruled from 1520 to 1566 and reigned over the Ottomans' greatest period of territorial expansion and economic prosperity. By the end of his reign, the empire was a dominant naval force, controlling much of the Mediterranean Sea and firmly establishing itself as a political and military power that many scholars compare to the Roman Empire. The Ottoman Empire's military prominence, however, cannot alone account for its durable and flexible hold on power that lasted for centuries. Economic and commercial development played an equally important role, allowing the sultans to sustain continuous streams of state revenue and further integrate their territory politically.

Pragmatism and Adaptability: State Intervention in Economic Development and Expansion

For much of the empire's existence, Ottoman economic institutions and policies were shaped to a large degree by the priorities of a central bureaucracy. However, the empire was comprised of zones with varying degrees of administrative control.[124] One concrete example of its ability to rely on markets and local practices outside of its centralized and bureaucratic control is in Ottoman monetary practices.

Until the sixteenth century, the Ottoman territories operated a unified monetary system based on gold, silver, and copper coins. As expansion continued throughout the sixteenth century, it became clear that this system could not continue in its traditional form. The newly conquered territories, all of which were subject to different patterns of trade, already had their own well-established currency systems. Therefore, whereas the gold *sultani* remained the only gold coin in the empire throughout the sixteenth century, the central government allowed newly conquered territories to use existing silver coinage – with exchange rates set by market forces – to avoid economic disruption that would fuel popular discontent.[125] In this sense, the Ottomans were highly flexible and pragmatic from the start, allowing the "central bureaucracy to co-opt and incorporate into the state social groups that rebelled against it." This approach constituted a source of success in terms of the empire's "willingness and ability to adapt, to utilize talent and accept allegiance from many sources, and to make multiple appeals for support."[126] The openness and adaptability also extended to encouraging technological innovation and showing a willingness to borrow institutions from conquered territories.

As one scholar writes, "The Ottomans conceived an ideal order that included balances between such social groups as the peasantry, the guilds, and the commercial sector."[127] Sitting at the top of this political order were the sultan and the central bureaucracy, while the government attempted to "preserve as much of the traditional structure of employment and production as possible." However, this approach weakened the empire economically because the "rapid accumulation of capital by merchants, guild members or any other interests [constituted] a potential disruption of the existing order." Although Ottoman society and government bureaucracy remained rigidly opposed to changing the economic-political order, some "institutional change in selective areas – for example, military technology and organization and public and private finance" – undoubtedly helped perpetuate the rule by the Ottoman Empire.[128]

Overall, the sultans' ability to implement long-term changes to the empire's economic institutions, as well as to its economic performance, provides evidence of the state's pragmatism, flexibility, and willingness to compromise. These characteristics enabled the empire to endure and to grow, despite its many internal and external challenges, particularly at a time when its contemporaries in Europe and Asia were still unable to modernize.

The Ottomans' Gradual Decline

Although it succeeded for several centuries, the Ottoman Empire ultimately did not articulate and implement a grand strategy that would work effectively within the prevailing geopolitical climate. Beginning in the seventeenth century, the empire began a gradual period of decline that culminated with its partition and eventual dissolution in the decade following World War I. As the scholar Fawaz writes, "By the second half of the eighteenth century Ottoman power had weakened, and the government began to rely more and more on local governors to maintain order and implement Ottoman policies."[129] Before its dissolution, however, it managed to conquer and survive for over six hundred years against rivals that included some of the longest-standing empires. In the end, the Ottoman Empire's grand strategy failed to articulate a coherent relationship among the empire's political, military, and economic policies.

The reason for the rise and eventual decline of the empire lies principally in the areas of economics and strategy. In the economic domain, one central factor is the role of the "Capitulations of the Ottoman Empire," which was a series of treaties established between the Ottoman Empire and European powers, particularly France, that gave

European states the ability to trade freely in the Ottoman territories.[130] The Capitulations, initiated at a time when the Ottoman Empire possessed significant military and economic dominance, were designed and encouraged as a way of promoting open trade. However, as the European states grew in strength relative to the Ottoman Empire, the Capitulations essentially weakened the Ottoman economy, leading to gradual declines in the empire's governmental effectiveness, military strength, and economic power. Furthermore, susceptibility of both military and government officials to corruption is attributed to the erosion of the central government's ability to exercise effective control over its vast and diverse territories, which eventually came to span much of Europe and parts of the Middle East and Asia.

A lack of diplomatic relations and the inability to interact with their European counterparts, for reasons related partially to language differences, was another factor that contributed to the Ottoman decline. As the dominant Eurasian power between the fourteenth and sixteenth centuries, the Ottomans were not persuaded that it was necessary or useful to maintain a degree of "connectedness" to the rising states in Europe, as measured by the level of diplomatic engagement that embassies provide. Whereas the European states were rising in importance and power, the grand strategy of the Ottoman Empire was marked by some degree of insularity. This insularity was not a critical problem during the time of Ottoman prominence, but it eventually undermined the ability of Ottoman Empire leadership to comprehend the momentous changes taking place in Europe – including significant improvements in European military strength and economic power – or more importantly to undertake the necessary reforms in economics, military forces, and diplomatic interaction with Europe. By the time the Ottoman Empire had begun to make necessary reforms, the European states already possessed military and technological advantages. In effect, the grand strategy of the Ottoman Empire did not evolve at a pace and scale that enabled it to keep pace with rival powers.

A related complication for the Ottoman Empire was that potential reforms often met with powerful internal resistance from the empire's military, government, and religious officials.[131] Such officials, largely satisfied with the status quo, consistently opposed reforms that arguably might have weakened their political and economic influence. The significant extent of the opposition to change from influential elements within Ottoman society prevented the government from taking the steps necessary to preserve and enhance the empire's power, and hence its grand strategy and role in the world. The failure of the Ottoman Empire relates in part to its inability to engage in an ongoing review of its grand strategy.

In the language of grand strategy, the decline of the Ottoman Empire was governed by the intersection of powerful external and internal factors. In an external sense, the military, economic, and political power of the European states from the sixteenth to the nineteenth centuries grew dramatically, in sharp contrast to the economic and political stasis that afflicted the Ottoman Empire.[132] Although elements within the Ottoman intelligentsia may have grasped this uncomfortable reality, the overwhelming majority of the influential political and military officials who resisted reforms were so successful in their resistance that it severely hampered the society's progress. In economic terms alone, the Ottoman Empire saw its overall indebtedness to European financiers increase dramatically. Internally, the empire was so vast and diverse that dissatisfaction among minority populations, predominantly European Christians, posed a constant threat to peace and stability.[133] In practice, strong external forces and the political weakness that occurs within states that are divided among sharply opposed groups fatally weakened the Ottoman Empire.

Free Trade Becomes a Detriment

The economic structure of the empire was defined by its geopolitical structure. The Ottoman Empire's territory contained the major land trade routes between the East and the rival powers of Portugal and Spain in the West. Following the Ottoman conquest of Egypt in the early sixteenth century, the state interventionist model of administering the spice trade led to decades of surprisingly dynamic innovation. In practice, the Ottomans "experimented with strategies designed both to increase the total volume of the spice trade, and to maximize the state's share of its revenues."[134] All of this, when combined with the natural advantages of geography and the goodwill of Muslim traders in the Indian Ocean, enabled the Ottomans to use the spice trade to develop economically and build a formidable empire. Ultimately, territorial control over land trade routes to the Indian Ocean forced the Spanish and Portuguese to explore new sea routes around the territory controlled by the Ottomans and to bypass the Middle East and the Mediterranean – a development directly linked to the eventual decline of the Ottoman Empire.

Several other external factors, in particular the penetration of European merchant capital into the empire, contributed to an accelerating weakening of the Ottoman economy. By the late sixteenth century, raw materials from the Ottoman Empire that "normally channeled into internal consumption and industry ... increasingly [were] exchanged for European manufactured products."[135] Although this trade benefited Ottoman merchants, it was a significant factor in the long-term decline of the textile manufacturing base and thus of revenues. In turn, this situation led to dramatic shortages of the raw materials the empire needed for domestic consumption. Facing rising costs of scarce materials, the Ottoman Empire suffered bouts of inflation, which made it increasingly difficult to procure sufficient revenues to meet its expenses. Without such revenues, many of the institutions that constituted the foundation of the Ottoman system, in particular its armed forces, entered into a period of long-term economic decay and decline.[136]

As a result, a fundamental problem for the Ottoman Empire was economic. Along with the gradual diffusion of manufactured goods from European states, those states increasingly dominated the scale and extent of commerce in the Ottoman Empire. One reason for this shift in and decline of the empire's economic power was, as noted earlier, the Capitulations.[137] The first of these, signed with France in 1536, was significant because it effectively permitted French merchants to trade freely at Ottoman ports, to be exempt from Ottoman taxes, and to import and export goods at discounted tariff rates. The Capitulations, which were established at a time when the empire's military power was greatest, were designed to encourage commercial trade and exchanges between the Ottoman Empire and Europe.

However, as the economic balance of power between the Ottomans and the European powers shifted progressively toward Europe, it had dramatic military consequences for the empire. One such consequence of the Ottoman Empire's declining economic power was the government's increasing inability to afford to invest in the new military technologies and weapons it needed to compete effectively with the growing military power of the European states. Moreover, the empire could not afford to pay the Janissaries, which were the infantry troops that guarded the sultan's household and constituted a significant source of political power in the empire. Both factors were harbingers of the gradual erosion of the once-dominant position that the Ottoman Empire's military forces had maintained for centuries.

Furthermore, the European merchants, backed by the economic power of their states, gradually exploited the Capitulations to the disadvantage of the Ottomans, who could no longer count on their superior military power to maintain the balance of power in their favor. Ultimately, these treaties had "a devastating effect on the Ottoman economy," because the Capitulations led to revenue shortages and rising inflation, both of which signaled the gradual economic and military decline of the Ottoman Empire in contrast with the growing power of its European counterparts.[138] Equally debilitating, the government was exposed to cycles of political intrigue, corruption, and military coups, which progressively weakened the empire.[139]

Internal Disruptions

Looking beyond the effects of these economic problems on grand strategy, the Ottomans had to deal with the broader problem of revolutions that originated from within the empire, predominantly from Christian subjects who felt the rising force of nationalism in Europe. The ascent of nationalism, whose guiding principle was that populations speaking the same language and sharing similar secular traditions should have state representation, helped undermine the religious foundations of the Ottoman Empire's power. The spread of nationalism among its Balkan peoples exposed the empire to a series of regular uprisings, all of which were in effect politically and strategically debilitating.[140] Although the Ottoman army could defeat individual nationalist rebellions, these became so widespread across the empire that it was increasingly difficult to deal effectively with them. In effect, as the Ottoman Empire experienced the growing forces of "gradual territorial dismemberment and ethnic cleansing," this undermined the political, military, and economic foundations on which its grand strategy depended.[141]

In the case of Greece and other regions in the Ottoman Empire, the decay of central authority contributed to increasingly inefficient and capricious government policies. This, in turn, coincided with the rise in Turkey and Greece of local *derbeys* (local chiefs or landlords) whose control over the land often led to the exploitation of the peasants. In effect, the people's gradual alienation from the Ottoman government was accompanied by the emergence of a new nationalism that further accelerated the decline of the empire.[142] The fact that the Ottomans increasingly "came to be seen as alien oppressors, not imperial protectors," contributed to the empire's dissolution.[143]

In considering the relationship between these political forces, the reign of Suleyman I (1520–1566) emerged as a critical period in the evolution of the Ottoman Empire's grand strategy. According to Ottoman scholar Gabor Agoston, the Ottoman grand strategy initially combined elements of an "imperial ideology and a universalist vision of empire." It also sought to collect "information both within and outside the borders of the empire [to help integrate the Ottomans] into European politics and political culture." Lastly, it called for mobilizing the empire's human, economic, and military resources to support the empire's policies.[144]

The Ottoman Empire became quite powerful in comparison with the European powers largely because it adhered to the principle of mobilizing support. However, with the expansion of Ottoman-controlled territory during the fifteenth and sixteenth centuries, the sheer enormity of the empire increasingly challenged and eventually exceeded the government's ability to manage its dominions effectively. Scholars see Sultan Selim III as a force for reform and his reign (1789–1806) as a pivotal period in the history of the Ottoman Empire, because he established the foundations for a "full-fledged reform movement by his successor [Mustafa IV]." Despite Selim III's downfall, "his reign" came to be seen as an "important bridge between the old and the new." When he became sultan, the Ottoman Empire was waging what would become "another losing war with Austria and Russia."[145]

This campaign taught the sultan that if the Ottoman Empire failed to improve its military capabilities dramatically, the empire itself would be unable to defend itself and would eventually collapse. The lesson was obvious: the military needed to undertake significant technical and organizational innovations if the empire was to survive in the face of the steadily growing military and economic power of the European states. In the wake of the 1792 Treaty of Jassy that brought to an end the Russo-Turkish War of 1787 to 1792, Selim III adopted a series of reforms whose purpose was to reorganize and hence modernize the empire's armed forces along the lines of modern European militaries. In particular, he created in 1797 "an entirely new infantry corps … called the *nizam-i jedid* (meaning, the new order)." His purpose was to persuade the Janissaries to accept new methods of military organization, which included raising their salaries and rebuilding barracks. However, Selim III's policies and initiatives "aroused their suspicions" and ultimately the Janissaries were able to oppose his reform efforts.[146]

A fundamental challenge for the grand strategy of the Ottoman Empire was how to deal with the growing difficulty of managing its interests during a time of relative peace. In the language of the framework examined in this study, the problem was how to articulate the empire's grand strategy in dealing with issues along the war-peace continuum. One element of the Ottoman Empire's grand strategy was to engage more broadly in serious diplomatic efforts. Thus, when Selim III moved to build more permanent Ottoman embassies throughout Europe, his strategy was designed to open "new channels for the transmission of knowledge about the West into educated Ottoman circles." Until the very end of the eighteenth century, the Ottoman Empire had no permanent diplomatic representatives, but this failure was reversed between 1793 and 1796, when permanent embassies were established in London, Vienna, Berlin, and Paris.[147]

One critical aspect of Selim III's efforts was that it represented a radical break from the policies followed by previous leaders of the Ottoman Empire. In a practice dating back to the origins of the Ottoman Empire and during its period of military conquests, a powerful imbalance characterized the interactions between European societies and Ottoman governments. Whereas Europe became increasingly active in commerce and diplomacy, the opposite was true for the Ottomans, who clung to the view that their system of politics and economics was superior to that of the Europeans. In part due to this worldview, the Ottoman Empire did not reciprocate through mutual exchanges with the commercial and diplomatic overtures of their European counterparts.[148] During times when the Ottoman Empire was clearly the dominant geopolitical force in Eurasia, the disadvantages to this imbalance in interactions were of no great consequence. However, by the time of Selim III's reign, the imbalance in diplomatic and cultural interaction and familiarity increasingly became a serious impediment to the empire's ability to achieve economic prosperity and to survive, if not gain strength, as a serious political force.[149]

Prior to Selim's reforms and the gradual opening to the West, the people of the Ottoman Empire were not sufficiently knowledgeable about Europe's political, economic, military, and technological achievements that emerged during the periods of the Renaissance and the Reformation.[150] The fatal flaw of adhering to a highly insular approach to international politics ultimately weakened the empire's grand strategy and contributed to its decline as a central force in Eurasia.

In the case of the internal dynamics of the regime, one problem was the ability of influential groups within the Ottoman Empire to prevent Selim III from marshaling in a coordinated fashion the totality of the empire's resources to support its grand strategy. To cite one example, the decision to form and later expand the new infantry corps (known as the *nizam-i jedid*) generated significant opposition within Ottoman society, particularly from groups whose gains in power and influence coincided with the decline in the Ottoman government's central authority. The Janissaries, who were elite forces, were deeply suspicious of Selim III's military reforms because they believed these reforms represented a direct "threat to their independence."[151] Similarly, the Ottoman Empire made little attempt to expand its naval presence in the Atlantic despite the greatly increasing naval expenditures and policies of large-scale exploration that the European powers were following.[152] By failing to establish themselves as a growing power in the Atlantic, the Ottomans forfeited the material resources and advantages in terms of having the military bases from which other European powers benefitted, which further contributed to the empire's relative decline.

In the end, the Janissaries played a central role in deposing Selim III and in selecting his successor, Mustafa IV, who promised that he would not interfere with the privileges to which the Janissaries were accustomed.[153] The strategic error in this policy was its return to the insularity that marked the Ottoman Empire's grand strategy. With the political rise of Mustafa IV, the empire returned to the policies in which "embassies in Europe were dismantled, the *nizam-i jedid* troops [which were designed to absorb lessons from the European militaries] were dispersed, and the deposed sultan ... was murdered."[154] The problem for the Ottoman Empire, which Selim III sought to reverse, was its failure to articulate a grand strategy that marshaled in a coherent fashion the political, military, and economic instruments of power available to the Ottomans.

The reign of Sultan Mahmud II (1808–1839) served as a transition period in which the Ottoman Empire started moving toward reform. Although the Ottoman Empire lost considerable territory during Mahmud II's reign, the sultan's harsh measures forced the empire to reform and also allowed him to retain highly centralized control. As Cleveland writes, Mahmud "saw the need to act decisively against the centrifugal political forces that continued to paralyze royal authority." In practical terms, his reforms included curbing the autonomy of the *derbeys*, destroying the power and influence of the Janissaries, and reorganizing the bureaucracy to make it more dependent on and responsive to the sultan's direct authority.[155]

The reign of Mahmud II provides several insights into the challenges that faced the Ottoman Empire's grand strategy. Mahmud first sought to diminish the power of entrenched groups and interests within the government. Given the dominant role played by the *derbey*-ulama-Janissary coalition that had overthrown Selim III, it was imperative that Mahmud II proceeded cautiously. Mahmud used the Janissaries, whose loyalty he secured with bribes, to move against the *derbeys* to break their power. By the 1820s he had taken the decisive step of creating a new "European-style army corps." As the Janissaries demonstrated against his reforms, "Mahmud II had prepared for the rebellion [using] his new troops to crush it." Within several hours on June 15, 1826, "thousands of Janissaries were massacred on the streets and in their barracks," which eliminated them and eradicated a major political and institutional obstacle to reforming the government and society.[156] In effect, Mahmud's strategy was to reorganize and rebuild the army – i.e., the Janissaries – along the lines of how the major European powers had organized their militaries and to train the new military with the help of Prussian, French, and British officers and advisors.

The second step for Mahmud was to make the state more administratively efficient and to "reestablish royal authority" in the day-to-day affairs of the state.[157] Mahmud reorganized the bureaucracy by abolishing old offices, introducing new lines of responsibility as part of an effort to "create European-style ministries," and raising salaries as part of a strategy to diminish, if not end, the corrosive effects of bribery on government and society. In bureaucratic form, Mahmud established in 1838 two institutions for training government officials, whose curriculum included both "standard and secular subjects." In a significant departure from past tradition, he built this curriculum on the basis of instruction in French. This effort was significant in light of how the relative insularity of the Ottoman Empire from European traditions and languages effectively impeded the empire's ability to conduct foreign affairs (discussed earlier). To remedy the fact that relatively few Ottoman officials knew European languages or were familiar with political, economic, and military conditions on the Continent, Mahmud increased the language proficiency of Ottoman diplomats and officials as a way of reversing the detachment that had weakened the empire.[158]

The period in the history of Ottoman Empire reforms was known as the Tanzimat (1839–1876). It means, literally, reorganization and refers to the laws, regulations, and reforms introduced in Turkey during the nineteenth century, the aim of which was to align society with the conditions in modern European states. The Tanzimat was most influential in the nineteenth century when the reformist impulse reached its zenith in the Ottoman Empire. This period of reform was inspired not by the sultans but by Ottoman bureaucrats who were heavily influenced by European institutions that emerged during the reign of Mahmud II. Thus, we see the motivation from within the empire's intelligentsia to redefine the empire to deal with growing political, economic, and military pressure and competition from Europe. Mahmud II's reform met with some success, but it was too little, too late. By that point European states were simply too far ahead of the Ottomans in terms of institutional, economic, and military development.

As to economic efforts, Tanzimat reformers in the government pursued a series of new and quite costly programs and initiatives precisely when the revenues available to the state were not growing. The Ottoman Empire "began to take out loans on the European money markets ... to cover its annual budget deficits."[159] In effect, the empire diverted "more and more funds ... from the operating budget," which it used to pay interest on loans. Predictably, the economic consequences for the empire's grand strategy were considerable: at the beginning of the 1860s approximately 10 percent of the state's total expenditures went to servicing the debt, by 1874 that figure rose to nearly 60 percent, by 1875 the empire essentially declared bankruptcy, and in 1876 it stopped almost all payments.[160] Although not entirely attributable to the reforms, the empire's efforts to modernize itself contributed to its bankruptcy.[161] As a result, the Europeans gained "a privileged economic position within the empire," because they now operated "under the jurisdiction of their own consuls rather than the Ottoman courts."[162]

The geostrategic pressure of Russia's expansion into Ottoman areas increased the motivation for reformers to reorganize the government and society to make it more competitive with its European counterparts.[163] Moscow's grand strategy was to use "its religious ties with Greek Orthodox subjects of the empire to gain influence in Ottoman internal affairs."[164] However, the relationship between the Ottoman Empire and Russia had other geostrategic effects. In the face of increasing Russian involvement in the Ottoman Empire, Britain's Middle East strategy was increasingly threatened, which nearly led to war between Russia and Britain until Chancellor Otto von Bismarck brokered a peace. Later, at the Congress of Berlin, the European powers maintained a fragile peace among themselves by awarding each other pieces of Ottoman territory.[165] Not unexpectedly, as the power of the Ottoman Empire declined and it suffered significant territorial losses, these forces redrew the political map of Europe. This action was a symbol of the Ottoman decline, convincing Ottoman government officials that a modern military was "not a luxury but a basic requirement for survival."[166]

In the early twentieth century, the Young Turks (1908–1918), a secular nationalist reform party calling for the return of absolute monarchy in the Ottoman Empire, came to power during a period of revolutions waged by those who supported European-style political institutions and counterrevolutions by those calling for a restoration of the shari'ah. In 1909, the army deposed the sultan, Abdul Hamid, replacing him with his brother, Mehmet V, who was little more than a figurehead. The defeat of the Central Powers in World War I and the division of the Ottoman Empire among the victors at the San Remo Conference in 1920 stymied efforts by the Young Turks to implement their preferred governmental and societal reforms.

Prior to gaining power, various reform groups, such as the Committee of Union and Progress (CUP), were committed to the concept of "Ottomanism." It held that the way to preserve the empire was through a constitutional government that "would limit the power of the monarch and guarantee the rights of non-Muslims."[167] The young Turks understood that they had to abolish the religious distinctions between Muslim rulers and non-Muslim subjects if a reform strategy was to succeed. However, the CUP was not successful in translating the principle of equality into practice. Once the CUP assumed power, its nationalist emphasis called for "the hegemony of Turkish-speaking Moslems over all others."[168] It called for members of the international community to "respect the Ottoman Empire's territorial integrity, but this never came to pass."[169]

The disintegration of the Ottoman Empire was in full swing as revolts in Ottoman lands within Europe had dramatic consequences for the empire's survival. The scale of the geographic decline can be described as follows: In 1912 "Ottoman domains in Europe totaled 65,350 square miles inhabited by an estimated 6.1 million people." When the Balkan Wars came to an end in September 1913, "the Ottoman Europe had been reduced to 10,882 square miles and a population of 1.9 million people." In terms of manpower, revenue, and productivity, the losses suffered by the Ottoman Empire were extraordinary. More critically, the empire and its military suffered the humiliation of being occupied "by the armies of the small states inhabited by former subject peoples."[170]

The other element of the strategy of the reform group CUP was to find a strong European ally that would serve as a protector of the empire. The Young Turks believed that allying with a great power was the only prudent strategy if the Ottoman Empire was to defend itself against further territorial losses, also giving it the time and space necessary for domestic reforms.[171] After an internal debate within the CUP leadership, the CUP decided to ally with Germany after the Germans agreed to protect Ottoman territory. Although the Germans were not initially receptive to this alliance, the CUP persuaded them that an alliance was in their best interests.

The decision to seek a protective alliance with Germany bought time for reforms to take hold, while balancing against the threat posed by the Triple Entente that consisted of Great Britain, France, and Russia. The leaders of the Ottoman Empire realized that marshaling economic resources was critical because "so much of the empire's trade and investment was in the hands of firms from the Entente powers whose governments were at war with the Ottomans." Consequently, in 1914 the CUP unilaterally abrogated the Capitulations, made foreigners subject to Turkish laws and courts, and raised customs duties on foreign imports.[172] This announcement was paired with moves toward establishing an eventual alliance with Germany against Russia, Great Britain, and France.

Political rivalries in the nineteenth century among the great powers of Europe had restrained them from conquering or occupying Ottoman territory. This geopolitical balance of power collapsed with the establishment of the Triple Entente, which acted as a counterweight to the Triple Alliance among Germany, Austria-Hungary, and Italy. However, the Triple Entente carried the burden of efforts among the Great Powers to dismantle the Ottoman Empire. In response to this strategic alignment, the leaders of the Ottoman Empire took two actions: First, its leaders reenergized their efforts at military reform. Second, as noted earlier, the Ottoman leadership actively sought to strengthen their political, military, and economic relationship with Germany, believing that such ties would serve as a deterrent to aggressive moves by the Triple Entente.[173]

In military terms, the armies of the Ottoman Empire "performed much more effectively throughout the war than their opponents had anticipated." In the aftermath of the Second Balkan War (1912–1913), the Ottoman government moved to modernize and strengthen the empire's military forces.[174] During World War I, the Ottoman Empire not only faced opposition from its Christian subjects, but also from its Arab Muslim subjects. The British strategy was to "recognize an independent Arab state after the war" to induce a "revolt against the Ottomans and to recognize an Arab caliphate should one be proclaimed."[175] In effect, this strategy called for an "all-out armed uprising and a denunciation of the Ottoman regime as an enemy of Islam."[176]

After World War I the Ottoman Empire reached its terminal phase. The end of the Ottoman Empire was cemented on October 31, 1918, when the "government in Istanbul signed the Armistice of Mudros." This was essentially a document of unconditional surrender that imposed an armistice, effectively ended the war in the Middle East, and signaled the demise of the Ottoman Empire. With Great Britain now occupying "most of the Arabic-speaking provinces" and with French military forces stationed in Beirut, the Ottoman Empire ceded control of its territories to the Allied powers.[177]

The formal dissolution of the Ottoman Empire occurred at the San Remo Conference, which was held in Italy on April 19–26, 1920. The decision of representatives from Great Britain, France, Italy, and Japan was to remove the "Arab provinces from Ottoman authority and apportion them between Britain and France." The former provinces of the Ottoman Empire "were divided into entities called mandates," which one scholar describes as "little more than nineteenth-century imperialism repackaged to give the appearance of self-determination."[178] The allocation of the empire's former provinces had important consequences for modern geopolitics because "Britain received the mandates for Iraq and Palestine, France the mandate for Syria." Worse, "Iraq was a completely new state created out of three Ottoman provinces – Basra, Baghdad, and Mosul – that had little in common." In strategic terms, Great Britain significantly strengthened its power in the Middle East and the Persian Gulf, bolstered its position in India, and improved its access to oil.[179] This success for Great Britain's grand strategy was achieved directly at the expense of the Ottoman Empire.

Predictably, this realignment had profound consequences for the Arab provinces, which once were part of the Ottoman Empire but at this time came under the direct administration of Great Britain and France. World War I and the dissolution of the Ottoman Empire remains a source of antipathy and bitterness for the Arab peoples, who feel a deep sense of antagonism because the European states betrayed and maltreated them in the aftermath of the war in a failure to give them independent status.[180] The decisions of Great Britain and France to occupy Arab lands incited a palpable sense of mistrust and anger that remains a powerful theme in the narrative of modern Middle East politics.[181]

In conclusion, the dissolution of the Ottoman Empire derives from its failure to adapt its grand strategy to modern conditions, a circumstance that continues to reverberate in the Middle East and in international politics. It also suggests a failure to articulate a grand strategy that was in rough balance with the strategies of adjoining states. As we saw with the the lack of balance in the empire's relationship with the great powers in Europe, the failure to articulate a coherent grand strategy can contribute to the demise of a great empire.

Conclusions about the Grand Strategy of Empire

This chapter examined seven case studies of grand strategy in the modern historical era, beginning with Philip II of Spain and ending with the Ottoman Empire. They illustrate the core principles of grand strategy, as outlined in Chapter 3. Some of the case studies demonstrate the failure of grand strategy that can result when states violate these principles. For example, Napoleon's confusion of operations with grand strategy was a clear violation of principle 3, which calls on policy makers to clearly distinguish operations, doctrine, policy, and logistics from the field of grand strategy. His error in judgment rested on the belief that operational-level successes automatically translate into success at the level of what we call grand strategy. Finally, the case of the Ottoman Empire is a cautionary tale of what occurs when a state fails to adapt its grand strategy to the realities of the emerging geopolitical conditions. The leadership of the Ottoman Empire clung for centuries to an outdated grand strategy that worked in the premodern era but failed utterly in the age of modern nation-states. In both the Spanish and Ottoman cases, their leaders thought about grand strategy in premodern terms, but only belatedly realized that they had been surpassed by formerly weaker states.

The cases of success are equally instructive. Frederick II and Bismarck, for instance, both carefully cultivated a unity between the means of Prussia's strategy and capability and the ends of its grand strategy. In the case of the British Empire, the grand strategy of trade promotion and offshore balancing were effective over the long term in marshaling the domestic (and colonial) foundations of British power on a global scale. The next section examines four cases from the twentieth century to understand how the emergence of revolutionary ideologies and nuclear deterrence influenced the development of grand strategy.

6 Revolutionary and Nuclear Eras of Grand Strategy

To continue the overview of the evolution of grand strategy begun in Chapter 4, this chapter covers the revolutionary and nuclear eras of the nineteenth and twentieth centuries. The scholars and strategists presented here established the foundations for understanding the articulation of grand strategy and developing it as a discipline for guiding the implementation of state policy in the presence of revolutionary ideologies and the influence of nuclear weapons and deterrence. This chapter also examines a range of case studies on the design and implementation of grand strategy by states and statesmen throughout the revolutionary and nuclear eras. It begins with the rise of authoritarianism and its critical leaders during World War II, continues with the revolutionary leaders during the Cold War, and concludes with the struggle between contending grand strategies during the Cold War and its aftermath. The five cases from the twentieth century help build an understanding of how the emergence of revolutionary ideologies and nuclear deterrence influenced the development of grand strategy.

This chapter examines two principal themes that governed the evolution of grand strategy in the twentieth century. One is the struggle between contending ideologies, and the other is the development of nuclear weapons. Of particular note in this discussion is how the transformation of Marxist ideology and the opposing ideology of democracy and capitalism formed the basis of the contending grand strategies that guided the policies pursued by the Soviet Union, the United States, and many other states during the Cold War. This chapter then examines the design of the West's grand strategy during the Cold War at a time when government policies were influenced directly by how nuclear weapons were being developed and managed.

A powerful theme in the evolution of grand strategy was the advent of revolutionary war, which also is known as insurgency.[1] The theory of insurgency fundamentally altered the use of political violence by shifting the focus from violence per se to the political use of violence, which had dramatic consequences for grand strategy. After millennia spent trying to understand and identify the fundamental rules that govern strategy, societies saw much of that thinking nullified by what transpired at the end of World War II and in its aftermath – notably, the development and proliferation of nuclear weapons.

With the advent of thermonuclear weapons, classic approaches to strategy became largely irrelevant, having lost any practical meaning in the face of intolerable urban destruction, if not the annihilation of societies and humanity itself. This development effectively shifted strategy from its historical foundations of how to win wars to how to avoid wars. However, most, but not all, of the revolutionary theorists predated the nuclear era. This chapter explores how the development of revolutionary ideas and nuclear weapons altered the foundations of grand strategy.

The Revolutionary Era

The Cold War ideological struggle between democratic and totalitarian states had a significant influence on the conduct of grand strategy, but perhaps to a lesser degree than did the debate about nuclear weapons as explored later in the chapter.[2] The concept of grand strategy in a revolutionary war, which is interpreted as seizing political power within or against a state by force, was more meaningful at a time when states in Europe, Asia, and Latin America were engaged in struggles whose strategy was to defeat – to use the language of communism – the ruling classes and the institutions under their control.

Contrary to the consensus that the ability to conduct grand strategy in the nuclear age was severely restricted, as discussed later in the chapter, it *was* quite possible for revolutionary groups to define strategies that would succeed, as did North Vietnam against South Vietnam and Fidel Castro in Cuba. Revolutionary wars involved a new approach, in which a grand strategy of the weak – notably in the form of insurgent groups – proved to be highly effective when the population was politically alienated from the incumbent government. External, interventionist states (e.g., the United States in Vietnam and the Soviet Union in Afghanistan) waged these revolutionary wars by basing their strategy on the accumulation of many lesser successes. However, what they overlooked was the extent to which success in a revolutionary war was not based on success at lower levels of strategic interaction (i.e., at the levels of military strategy, operations, and tactics), but on altering the purposes that defined the grand strategy of the state or revolutionary movement.

To complicate matters, revolutionary wars often involved states or factions within states that were allied with great powers, which played a direct supporting role in these struggles. The prospect that the defeat of a state by a faction supported by a major state might escalate into a crisis involving the great powers undermined the sponsoring state's credibility and resolve. This was not simply a theoretical possibility, as witnessed in active debates in the Johnson and Nixon administrations about whether the escalation of American involvement in Vietnam would pull the Soviet Union or China into the war.[3] Earlier, policies pursued by President Truman during the Korean War were influenced by similar concerns about the influence of Soviet and Chinese involvement on the ability of the United States to successfully implement its grand strategy of containment.[4]

Here, we examine the principal architects who articulated the concepts of revolutionary politics and class struggle, which had decisive consequences for the development and conduct of grand strategy. These individuals represent the principal thinkers and practitioners who articulated the critical ideas that evolved into the practice of revolutionary political and class struggles. These thinkers also made significant contributions to the articulation and implementation of grand strategy in the struggle between states and revolutionary movements. The provenance of many of these ideas clearly derive from Marxist arguments, which hold that political affairs in and among societies are defined in fundamental terms by the concept of class struggle. Since revolutionary forces within societies decisively shape the conduct of international politics (and hence of grand strategy), all politics is the product of economic forces, and, thus, these forces, endemic to all societies, constitute a permanent and decisive influence on how states articulate and implement their grand strategy.

Karl Marx and Friedrich Engels

Perhaps no two theorists have had a more dramatic effect on philosophy, politics, and economics in the twentieth century than the nineteenth-century political theorists Karl Marx (1818–1883) and Friedrich Engels (1820–1895). The ideas developed by these theorists had a historically significant degree of influence on how societies, scholars, and policy makers think about how to articulate and implement the state's grand strategy.[5] Karl Marx and Friedrich Engels outlined their principles in *The Communist Manifesto*. Marx is also famous for works such as *Das Kapital* (volume 1: 1867; volume 2: post-humously, 1885; volume 3: posthumously, 1894) and *The Eighteenth Brumaire of Louis Napoleon* (1852). From this and other works emerge several themes, which are emblematic of how their thoughts contributed to the evolution of ideas about the nature of grand strategy and its implementation by the state and revolutionary movements.[6]

Through their theoretical works on socialism, Marx and Engels had a powerful effect on how modern thinkers understand the practical meaning of revolutionary politics and class struggle. But they also made significant contributions to the development of grand strategy, in particular through its relationship to the role played by revolutionary ideology in shaping politics and the use of political violence within and among societies.[7]

According to Marx and Engels, the bourgeois system of capitalism rests on an unending and uninterrupted quest for new markets and the derivative exploitation of the proletariat. By implication, "the bourgeoisie cannot exist without constantly revolutionizing the instruments of production [and] the whole relations of society." Marx holds that the foundations of economic power rest on the "constant revolutionizing of production, uninterrupted disturbance of all social conditions, everlasting uncertainty and agitation [that] distinguish[es] the bourgeois epoch from all earlier ones." For Marxists, this equates to the "need of a constantly expanding market for its products [which] chases the bourgeoisie over the whole surface of the globe."[8]

Marx and Engels held that the exploitation of the proletariat occurs in phases:

> [T]he proletariat goes through various stages of development. With its birth begins its struggle with the bourgeoisie. At first the contest is carried on by individual labourers, then by the workpeople of a factory, then by the operatives of one trade, in one locality, against the individual bourgeois who directly exploits them.[9]

This argument is critical because it identifies a constant process of change and class struggle within and among societies, which manifests itself in the development of grand strategies whose aim is to foment and win revolutions. This antagonistic process that drives historical change is called dialectical materialism and rests on the Hegelian conflict between opposing forces that we know as the antagonism between a thesis and its antithesis, which leads to a new synthesis. For example, capitalism as a political-economic system emerged from a previous class conflict between feudal nobility and the landless peasantry. In theory, these class struggles can lead to a "veiled civil war, raging within existing society, up to the point where the war breaks out into open revolution." In the era of the capitalist state, Marx and Engels believed the next class struggle would lead to "the violent overthrow of the bourgeoisie [and] lay the foundation for the sway of the proletariat."[10]

In the face of capitalism's more oppressive characteristics that gained prominence during the nineteenth century, the theory of communism gained universal attention for its suggestion that the complete destruction of governments is equivalent to a historical inevitability. As such, it becomes a moral imperative for the proletariat and its vanguard or elite to ensure this outcome. Twentieth-century revolutionaries, armed with this absolute philosophical mandate, promoted the idea that governments must be defeated totally; i.e., this means the destruction of the state's existing political and economic institutions and its armies in the field.

The state finds itself approaching its extinction through the development of transnational revolutionary movements whose guiding principle – as enshrined in its grand strategy – is the destruction of existing states and their institutions.[11] To achieve this outcome, the bourgeoisie "have forged the weapons that bring death to itself [and] called into existence the men who are to wield those weapons – the modern working class – the proletarians."[12] Despite these ideas about the concept of a permanent revolution, Marx clearly did not "hold a mechanistic theory of history," since he argued that the history of a "proletarian revolution shows that revolutions do not happen automatically."[13] He did, however, articulate ideas that contributed to the evolution of grand strategy as a concept for promoting revolutionary movements.

Marx discussed the role of war as an essential feature of human existence: "Up till now, violence, war, pillage, murder and robbery, etc., have been accepted as the driving force of history."[14] When, Marx and Engels believed, ideologically based mass movements reached the stage where they could harness the technology of the modern state – which would occur as new railways and naval vessels traversed and controlled large geographic areas – this development would profoundly alter the nature of war, the essential meaning of grand strategy, and ultimately how the state conducts its grand strategy.[15]

Because their philosophies dealt primarily with the struggle between classes, these ideas deemphasized the function of state borders or interstate relations and transcended borders in what they envisioned as a global, class-based struggle. To be sure, statesmen and theorists who studied Marx and Engels later integrated and stretched their philosophies to fit more comfortably with the necessities of international politics. In practice, the principle of grand strategy that rested on the necessity of a global revolution assumed concrete form in the first decades of the twentieth century. It did so again when the concept of total war reemerged during the Cold War when the Soviet Union allocated most of its economic power and national wealth to the defense sector to implement its grand strategy of defeating the capitalist powers.[16]

The ideas of Marx and Engels are not routinely associated with the study of grand strategy, but in practice they had significant consequences for how societies and governments contemplated the nature of politics, strategy, and war. Their first contribution, which accelerated the development of grand strategy, emphasized the point in theory that the conduct of politics and of war were seen as absolute endeavors by the state. One argument is that because Marx and Engels, as theorists, had such a decisive impact on social theory writ large, and because grand strategy deals with such a broad set of social concepts, they had by extension a significant impact on the conduct of grand strategy. The case can certainly be made that their philosophy and guiding ideological principles were integrated directly into the grand strategies of many countries. In effect, the ideological imperative that so directly influenced grand strategy was the desire to totally defeat the opposing state and its grand strategy. But in the case of revolution, the "opposing state," at least initially, can be elements within one's own state. In terms of articulating a grand strategy, the political ends espoused by revolutionary ideologies are transformative and far-reaching, even having a utopian quality. Marx and Engels contributed to the language of grand strategy in which the nature of political struggle redefines societies and then proceeds to alter the nature of international politics itself. For these theorists, the ultimate function of grand strategy was to destroy the old economic and political order while constructing a radically new political-economic system to replace it.

Second, Marx and Engels saw class as the basic unit of political-economic analysis, which stands in sharp contrast to Hobbes, Locke, and Kant, all of whom saw the state as the basic unit of political analysis. As a result, for Marx and Engels, the concept of "grand strategy" becomes that of particular classes. The bourgeoisie class has a grand strategy of constant market expansion, profit seeking, and labor exploitation, all of these attributes being inherent in the structure of capitalist states, which cannot help but have a grand strategy that derives from these principles. In the language of revolutionary ideologies, grand strategy is driven implicitly and explicitly by the underlying economic system. The grand strategy of the proletariat is directly opposed to that of the bourgeoisie, unified by its purpose of eliminating private property and the state and instituting a socialist system in its stead. Marx and Engels saw a proletarian grand strategy as the organization of people and trade unions that form an ever-growing body of workers whose ideology transcends national boundaries. This organization also constitutes a universal force that governs how all states articulate and implement a revolutionary strategy. The essence of the struggle, for Marx, "lies, not in the immediate result, but in the ever-expanding union of workers."[17] Furthermore, the "immediate aim of the Communists is the same as that of all the other proletarian parties: formation of the proletariat into a class, overthrow of the bourgeois supremacy, [and] conquest of political power by the proletariat."[18]

Indeed, to postulate that a single socioeconomic class can have a "grand strategy" may be to dilute the concept of grand strategy, which traditionally involves the *state*'s mobilization of all resources (and hence, all classes) within a society. Nevertheless, the Marxist foundations of grand strategy for revolutionary societies were based on a degree of fatalism about the struggle against capitalism, since "it perfected an analysis that showed that the forces underlying capitalism [would lead to] socialism of their own accord." For Marx and Engels, "capitalism's very success produces a constantly growing proletariat, which is forced by its dependent position to destroy capitalism and create socialism in its place."[19] This tension highlights one of the central ambiguities of Marx's work: If the proletarian revolution is inevitable because capitalism sows the seeds of its own destruction, then why should proletarian leaders actively work for revolution? Lenin argued that a "vanguard of the proletariat,"[20] essentially a group of revolutionary elites, is necessary for the revolution to proceed, but Marx left the question largely unanswered. In his view, the grand strategy of the proletariat will arise automatically and naturally from the political-economic dynamics occurring between classes as capitalism develops.

The third contribution of Marx and Engels to grand strategy is to highlight the immense power of a revolutionary ideology. Power comes from the increasing suffering and exploitation of the proletariat masses. In effect, Marx and Engels argue that it is possible to harness the forces of social and economic history to one's advantage. The proletariat, in resisting the state and private property, are using the dominant trend in human history to influence societal revolutions. Using language that underscores the revolutionary aims of the Marxist elements of grand strategy, Marx writes that communists "openly declare that their ends can be attained only by the forcible overthrow of all existing social conditions."[21] This hostility derives from the oppressed classes, the antagonism among classes, and the emancipation of the oppressed class that occurs when a new society is created.[22] For any revolutionary movement to achieve success, its grand strategy must seek to create an inevitable sense that the future holds "impending bloody conflicts," which "workers [will win against the state] by their courage, determination and self-sacrifice."[23]

Revolutionary movements have political and social dimensions that call for radical change in and among societies. The source of this condition is the antagonism that exists between the "proletariat and the bourgeoisie classes," which represented for Marx "a struggle which carried to its highest expression is a total revolution." When framed using this language, a grand strategy that is influenced by the prospect of a revolution will be the source of "brutal" struggles over the nature of politics in societies and the relationships among those societies.[24] This is an interesting argument because it focuses on the very real possibility that a Marxist revolutionary philosophy will be incorporated as a central feature of a state's grand strategy. Marx and Engel reoriented the foundations of grand strategy when they argued that a revolutionary ideology provides a guide to action, which, if successful, transforms how states articulate and implement their grand strategy. What is key here is that Marxist revolutionary philosophy is not considered grand strategy itself when narrowly defined, but it serves as a potential ingredient in the development of a state's grand strategy, as we saw with the cases of the Soviet Union and China.

For Marx, the endgame in a grand strategy based on revolutionary change occurs when the proletariat eventually uses "its political supremacy to wrest, by degrees, all capital from the bourgeoisie, to centralize all instruments of production in the hands of the State, i.e., of the proletariat organized as the ruling class."[25] The outcome for grand strategy, derived from the ideas of Marx and Engels, involves a sociopolitical condition within societies that preserves and strengthens the long-term interests of the socialist societies and strengthens their ability to defeat capitalist societies – at least in theory.

Vladimir I. Lenin

If Marx was the great architect of the principle of a class-based understanding of how human political development occurs within and among societies, Lenin was its great implementer who gave Marxist abstractions real political effects. Even before the establishment of Marxism as the official state ideology of the Soviet Union, theorists such as Vladimir Lenin (1870–1924) articulated critical ideas about the relationship between ideology and grand strategy.[26] As one of the more prominent social theorists and revolutionary theorists, Lenin defined grand strategy and essentially all aspects of state policy entirely in the context of the forces leading to political and economic revolutions.[27] His contributions to revolutionary ideology in terms of its influence on grand strategy are historically significant and perhaps without parallel.

As a first principle, Lenin believed that revolutions would evolve in stages, and for revolutions to succeed, the Russian proletariat had to adopt and follow several immediate objectives (see the discussion that follows). Each stage of revolution was infused with the themes explored in this study of grand strategy – notably, the relationship between political, military, and economic types of national power, and the articulation of grand strategy as a never-ending process of struggle. Lenin also believed that the success or failure of applying Marxism to the Russian context in the late nineteenth and early twentieth centuries required leaders who could take local conditions into consideration and use them to guide the society toward a successful revolution.

Taken together, we see that Leninist grand strategy was rooted in the forces that lead to and sustain revolutions within societies, which produce dramatic changes in those societies and have wide-ranging effects on international politics as they spread across societies. In this way, Marxist ideology is linked directly to the articulation and implementation of a state's, in contrast with a class's, grand strategy. In this way, Marxism-Leninism is one variant of a revolutionary grand strategy in contrast to the pure Marxism articulated by Marx and Engels.

For Lenin, the "principal and fundamental" objective of his political theory – noting that political theory provides the general basis for the design and conduct of grand strategy – was to develop a theoretical and practical basis for the state's policies and broad strategy.[28] In this sense, the ultimate purpose of grand strategy was to "facilitate the political development and the political organization of the working class."[29] For this to happen, it was necessary to create a "durable revolutionary organization among the factory, the urban, workers," which, as Lenin argued, represents "one of the first and urgent tasks that confronts the Social Democrats."[30] The historical mission of the working class was "to emancipate itself and the whole of the Russian people from political and economic slavery."[31] To put this theory into practice, Lenin believed that "the proletariat must strive to form independent, political workers' parties, the main aim of which must be: the capture of political power by the proletariat for the purpose of organizing socialist society."[32] In building the foundations of a great revolutionary movement, Lenin argued that the "most urgent task ... is to strengthen" the connection between the "Russian working-class movement and Russian Social-Democracy."[33]

What, then, was the basis of Lenin's grand strategy when he was a revolutionary, non-state leader? Lenin's ultimate goal was to overthrow the capitalist class, which itself was animated by his intention to reorganize the nature of politics within and among societies. However, he likely believed that several stages in the proletarian revolution had to take place before this condition and outcome could be achieved. Lenin's revolutionary grand strategy relied on mobilizing a radical peasant movement as well as the proletariat, unlike that of Marx and Engels, who believed the urban proletariat of an industrialized society alone would form the revolution's rank and file as the instrument for guiding a grand strategy committed to successful revolutions within and across societies.

Lenin wrote about the "The Stages, Trends and Prospects of the Revolution," which he organized into six discrete steps. First, "the labor movement rouses the proletariat immediately under the leadership of the Russian Social Democratic Labor party and *awakens* the liberal bourgeoisie: 1895 to 1901–02." Second, "the labor movement passes to open political struggle and *carries with it* the politically awakened strata of the liberal and radical bourgeoisie and petty bourgeoisie: 1901–02 to 1905." Third, "the labor movement flares up into a direct *revolution*, while the liberal bourgeoisie has already united in a Constitutional Democratic party and thinks of stopping the revolution by compromising with Tsarism; but the *radical* elements of the bourgeoisie and petty bourgeoisie are inclined to enter into an alliance with the proletariat for the *continuation of the revolution*: 1905 (especially the end of the year)."

Fourth, "the labor movement is victorious in the *democratic* revolution, the liberals passively temporizing and the *peasants* actively assisting. To this must be added the radical republican intelligentsia and the corresponding strata of the urban petty bourgeoisie. The uprising of the peasants is victorious, the power of the landowners is broken." Fifth, "the liberal bourgeoisie, temporizing in the third period, passive in the fourth, becomes downright counterrevolutionary, and organizes itself in order to filch from the proletariat the gains of the revolution. The whole of the well-to-do section of the peasantry and a large part of the middle peasantry also grow 'wiser,' quiet down and turn to the side of the counterrevolution in order to wrest power from the proletariat and the rural poor, who sympathize with the proletariat."

Sixth, "on the basis of the relations established during the fifth period, a new crisis and a new struggle blaze forth; the proletariat is now fighting to preserve its democratic gains for the sake of a socialist revolution. This struggle would be almost hopeless for the Russian proletariat alone and its defeat would be as inevitable as the defeat of the German revolutionary party in 1849–50, or as the defeat of the French proletariat in 1871, if the *European socialist proletariat* should not come to the assistance of the Russian proletariat."[34]

Lenin's ideas about revolutionary movements align quite well with what grand strategy is. One reason that his ideas contributed so significantly to grand strategy in the early twentieth century was his belief that it is as much about ideas that reshape not just societies and relationships between individual states or collections of states but also the political and economic foundations of the global political system itself.

Lenin adhered unwaveringly to the principle that revolutionary movements, if they are to be successful, must be based on a close relationship between political and military objectives. For instance, as he wrote, "a revolutionary army and a revolutionary government are two sides of the same coin ... equally necessary for the success and the uprising and for the consolidation of its results."[35] In terms of the linkage between political and military power, he proposed that the revolutionary army is required for the military struggle and the political leadership of the masses is required to direct the revolutionary army in its opposition to the incumbent bourgeoisie regime.

Of greater significance for the development of grand strategy, Lenin emphasized the primacy of military power: "The revolutionary army is needed because great historical questions can be solved only by violence, and the organization of violence in the modern struggle is a military organization."[36] Lenin's view that violence was the critical instrument that transcends and supersedes all other mechanisms of power provides insights on how his grand strategy based on revolutionary movements should operate. What he was describing was a world in which the struggle between the working class and the capitalist class must necessarily be a violent one.[37] From here, it is a short step intellectually to a world where, as a primary instrument of grand strategy, violent revolutions will govern international politics until the remnants of capitalism are destroyed.

Lenin also adhered to the view that to be successful, a strategy for revolutionary movements, and its corollary of how grand strategy guides the conduct of the state's foreign policy, must reflect a tight relationship between political and economic objectives. As he noted, "economic and political agitation are equally necessary in order to guide the class struggle of the Russian workers, for every class struggle is a political struggle." His reasoning was that "economic and political agitation are equally necessary for the development of the class consciousness of the proletariat."[38]

Lenin's grand strategy, which was designed to undermine all the pillars of the tsar's power in order to further the revolution, identifies the extent of the state institutions arrayed against his forces: "Against the revolution are rallied the autocracy, the court, the police, the government officials, the army and a handful of the higher aristocracy."[39] For the class struggle to succeed, Lenin argued, it "must necessarily combine the political and economic struggle [that] has permeated the very flesh and blood of international Social Democracy."[40] In Lenin's view, the value of the revolution's ultimate goal demanded significant sacrifice, which the historian Edward Mead Earle noted in Lenin's message to American workers: "He is no Socialist who does not understand that the victory over the bourgeoisie may require losses of territory and defeats. He is no Socialist who will not sacrifice his fatherland for the triumph of the social revolution."[41]

Lenin's views on grand strategy when he became a state leader as the new ruler of the Soviet Union were consistent with his views as a revolutionary leader. As Earle argues, Lenin viewed revolutionary policy as a never-ending process that applies at all times, in both peace and war: "Lenin was a convinced believer in *Realpolitik*. Peace to him was not an end in itself; on the contrary, peace, like war, was an instrument of policy."[42] This philosophy, of course, traces to the ideas of Clausewitz. This war-mindedness, which helps one understand the nature of Soviet ideology and its relationship to grand strategy, influenced the Soviet social system because it created a public perpetually prepared for, if not in, a state of war.

Like Marx, Lenin also sees class conflict as inevitable: "The revolution itself must not by any means be regarded as a single act ... but as a series of more or less powerful outbreaks rapidly alternating with more or less intense calm."[43] What is decisive about the ideological foundation of grand strategy as formulated by Lenin is the central role of conflict within societies, which is inseparable from conflict between governments: "The workers' struggle against the capitalists must inevitably bring them into conflict with the government." Lenin proposes that a perpetual state of conflict will exist, in part because the government does "its utmost to prove to the workers that only by fighting and by united resistance can the workers influence the state."[44]

The ability to implement this strategy of revolution meant, for Lenin, that the vanguard must make "a sober and strictly objective estimation of *all* the class forces in a given state (and in neighboring states, and in all states the world over) as well as of the experience of revolutionary movements."[45] This explicit emphasis on "neighboring states" was a reference to the relationship between Lenin's ideas about revolutionary movements and their intimate connection to grand strategy – that is, how grand strategy contributes to the spread of revolutionary struggles from within one society to others, and thus permanently alters the foundations of international politics. His language about how political and economic forces influence the "affairs of state" is crucial to understanding how revolutionary ideologies are part and parcel of the articulation and implementation of grand strategy.[46]

As noted earlier, Lenin drew heavily on the work of Clausewitz, particularly his idea that war is an extension of politics by forcible means. Earle reflects on reasoning articulated by Lenin when he notes that "the Marxists have always considered this axiom as the theoretical foundation for the meaning of every war." Lenin also believed "that there was an intimate connection between the structure of the state and the system of government, on the one hand, and military organization and the conduct of war on the other."[47] Furthermore, Lenin was a student of the lessons articulated by Marx and Engels on the realities of power politics. Thus, for Earle, Lenin "was aware that warfare is not only military, but also diplomatic, psychological, and economic in character." In reasoning that reaffirms how powerfully his ideas contribute to the development of grand strategy, Lenin promoted the view that "war and revolution were in [such a] continuous and fundamental relationship with one another . . . to paraphrase Marx, that war could be midwife to revolution."[48]

In the context of Lenin's ideas and their influence on the development of Soviet grand strategy, Earle describes the Soviet concept of marshaling all the resources of the state or movement to support the revolution. Returning to the broad definition of grand strategy, as Earle writes, "Soviet Russia has never given up the waging of war by all available means – political, economic, psychological, and military."[49] The idea of marshaling all resources, particularly for the purposes of arming the population, was reiterated in a statement of the Sixth World Congress of the Communist Party in 1928.[50]

In practice, Lenin's ideas about mobilizing all of the state's resources to conduct its grand strategy align quite well with his arguments about how to promote the state's long-term interests. On the principle that political, economic, and social conditions differ in each society, Lenin believed that the success or failure of the revolution in each state and throughout the international system depended on correctly gauging whether local conditions were ripe for revolution. Marxist-Leninist revolutionaries advanced the view that having an accurate understanding of the underlying conditions in societies was essential to successfully fomenting a revolution, and hence to knowing how the state configures its grand strategy to deal with these forces in other societies. Lenin expressed this principle in his essay on "Left Wing Communism": "The art of politics (and the Communist's correct understanding of his tasks) lies in correctly gauging the conditions and the moment when the vanguard of the proletariat can successfully seize power."[51] In practical terms, Lenin proposed that a "revolution is impossible without a nationwide crisis (affecting both the exploited and the exploiters."[52] With these ideas, Lenin underscored a common quality that exists in all grand strategies: that they are often reactive in nature and must recognize and exploit windows of opportunity as they emerge.

In building the basis for the state's grand strategy, Lenin wrote, "Victory cannot be won with the vanguard alone." He essentially proposed that the ability to reshape politics in a society or on an international scale depends on knowing when the circumstances are right and on when to use the "vanguard" in a proper and decisive fashion.[53] In the end, the ability to decipher when conditions are right and how revolutions spread across societies is of strategic importance for the success of a revolution within a society. This is particularly true when the state's grand strategy calls for reorganizing the rules that govern how international politics is organized.

Leon Trotsky

Another prominent revolutionary theorist in the Soviet Union, Leon Trotsky (1879–1940), was an advocate of the principles outlined in the theory and practice of pure Marxism, which was based on using the instrument of proletarian revolutions in the state's grand strategy. These lines of thought converged to become "Trotskyism," based on the concepts of "permanent revolution" and "proletarian internationalism."[54] Both of these concepts were integral to Trotsky's socialist worldview and revolutionary strategy. In one of his famous, if altered, aphorisms that underscored the importance of strategy in politics and revolutionary movements, Trotsky said that "you may not be interested in strategy, but strategy is interested in you."[55]

Drawing on arguments that align with Clausewitz's theory of total war, Trotsky, as People's Commissar of War and Supreme Commander of the Red Army during the Russian Civil War, held that revolutionary ideologies are designed to destroy the political foundations of a society.[56]

In terms of historical background, from 1923 to 1928, Trotsky was seen as "both political leader and intellectual guide of the left opposition groups in Russia which attacked the growing despotism of the Stalin regime."[57] He gained fame in Russia and internationally after publicly denouncing Stalinism for its betrayal of the basic tenets of Marxism-Leninism, which act led Stalin to force him into exile in 1929. A Soviet agent murdered Trotsky in Mexico City in 1940.

Trotsky is most prominently identified, perhaps more so than any other Russian revolutionary thinker, for his concept of the "permanent revolution." Trotsky believed (as did many revolutionary thinkers at the time) that the social and economic conditions in Russia during the early 1900s had "not yet ripened for a socialist economy."[58] Therefore, his argument, which is familiar for the theme of how grand strategy influences international politics, is that "the socialist revolution thus begun in a backward country [such as Russia] cannot be completed within national limits." Furthermore, as he argued, "power could be held and steps toward socialism taken only if there speedily followed victorious revolutions in the advanced European countries."[59] In building support for revolutions and promoting their spread to other societies, Trotsky advanced the notion that revolutionary governments in economically successful parts of Europe would lend support and aid to their Russian brethren. The success of the Russian revolution fundamentally depended on support from other societies, which led Trotsky to defend the need for a "permanent revolution."[60]

As Trotsky concluded, "the bourgeois-democratic revolution could be completed in a backward country only under the leadership of the working class, small and inexperienced though it may be."[61] Thus, Trotsky held that "the democratic revolution grows over immediately into the socialist, and thereby becomes a *permanent* revolution."[62] This line of thinking was familiar with the ideas of Lenin, who similarly advanced the theory of "permanent revolution."[63]

By the mid 1920s, the Russian Civil War and World War I had decimated the Russian economy, industry, and population. In Trotsky's view, the fractured society that resulted made true socialism in Russia impossible. In its place, Stalin pursued collectivization programs, while consolidating power through the establishment of a totalitarian Soviet bureaucracy (this bureaucracy "freed itself from political control of the masses"[64]). These steps were in direct contrast to the original goals of Lenin's ideal of the Social Democrat Party. Though impossible to determine whether aid from other successful revolutionary countries in Western Europe could have furthered the cause of pure socialism in Russia, Trotsky's prediction that the Russian revolution would fail without outside assistance eventually came to pass.[65]

In contrast to Stalin's doctrine of "socialism in one country" (i.e., the belief in Soviet self-sufficiency), Trotsky advanced the concept of "proletarian internationalism" (which emphasized the idea of proletarian international solidarity as part of coordinated efforts to articulate an ideology that produced a coherent grand strategy for defeating the capitalist global system). Conceptually, proletarian internationalism was a key aspect of the "permanent revolution" and had a key economic dimension. Because of Russia's weak industrial capability and relatively low labor productivity, Trotsky believed that the "superiority of post-capitalist economies ... would depend on their reaching a higher level of labour productivity than that attained by the leading imperialist economies." For these reasons, the views of Lenin and Trotsky closely align. But when considering grand strategy as an instrument of international change, Trotsky believed that the "prospect of fully constructing socialism in a single country (or in a group of countries) was, right from the start, completely utopian."[66]

In arguments that align perfectly with the evolution of grand strategy as a unified global phenomenon, Trotsky proposed that "it is impossible to complete the construction of socialism, of a classless society, in one country." For Trotsky, "As long as the socialist revolution has not spread to at least the leading industrialized nations of the world, the non-capitalist economy and society of the USSR remains threatened both militarily and through the pressure of the world market."[67] Trotsky acknowledged that the revolutionary ideology of Marxism-Leninism, when embellished with Trotskyism, has expansionist elements that rest on hostility to capitalism in other states. His ideas encapsulated the confrontational ethos of Marxism-Leninism, which both established the basis for the arguments about the inevitability of revolutions in other societies and motivated the West to resist. In effect, Trotsky's ideas contributed to a concept of grand strategy that is animated by a revolutionary ideology that transcends national borders and operates globally to change the nature of societies and international politics.

Harold Nelson, author of *Leon Trotsky and the Art of Insurrection 1905–1917*, highlighted how Trotsky's ideas shaped the conduct of grand strategy: "[Trotsky's] recognition of the fact that a country's military resources themselves are the product of economic resources and political decisions increased his ability to weigh the feasibility of military alternatives ..." Thus, he argued that Trotsky developed "conclusions [that operate] in the realm of 'Grand Strategy' where consideration of all factors that may influence the course of a campaign can render the campaign unnecessary or inevitably successful."[68]

In arguments familiar to scholars of revolutionary movements, "Trotsky's theory brings to light ... all the major elements (economic, political, class, psychological, ideological, and organizational) of a historical mechanism at work."[69] The grand strategy of global revolutionary movements embraced the ethos of using ideology to mobilize the masses to support the overthrow of their governments. When Trotsky writes that to overthrow tsarism "it was necessary to arouse scores upon scores of millions of the oppressed for a heroic, self-sacrificing, reckless, supreme revolutionary onslaught," we see the outlines of a grand strategy that emphasizes the value of ideological revolutions pursued on a global scale.[70]

When Trotsky was appointed People's Commissar for Military and Naval Affairs of the Soviet Union from 1919–1925, scholars argued that this position consequently gave his "reporting a degree of dispassionate objectivity." The reason was that it allowed him to discern "the fundamental relationships between military resources and the successful pursuit of governmental interests which are the essence of strategy."[71]

However, Trotsky (reflecting on the forces at play in the seventeenth-century English revolution) was wary of the military's role in politics, in particular with the risks of forming a parallel sovereign entity within the state that could weaken the state itself. He feared that the military could interfere "powerfully ... in the [state's] social life, not merely as an armed force, but as a Praetorian Guard," and, more strategically, could serve "as the political representative of a new class opposing the prosperous and rich bourgeoisie." According to this revolutionary theorist, the danger was that the military "creates a new state organ" that transcends "the military command" by establishing itself as "a council of soldiers' and officers' deputies."[72] Nonetheless, scholars describe Trotsky as "one of the outstanding figures of modern military history," who was "the directing genius of the Soviet armies" during the Russian Civil War. However, for Trotsky, the civil war was only "a miniature war, judged by the size of the armies engaged," and "the small war differed from a big one only in scale." The scholar of grand strategy, Earle, draws the conclusion that "the civil war demonstrated anew that revolutionary strategy must be related to military efficiency and even to orthodox military methods."[73]

Trotsky, who was one of the most influential of the Soviet revolutionary theorists in the early twentieth century, understood and forcefully defended the argument that the state's political and economic (and ideological) objectives must remain tightly and centrally coordinated. Trotsky not only clearly had in mind forces that could unleash momentous change, but he also envisioned the more dramatic outcome that history would soon know as the birth of totalitarianism.[74]

The argument about the relatedness of the forces behind revolutions suggests that Trotsky's ideas had a direct impact on the development of grand strategy. Furthermore, the international focus of his ideas about building concepts that would encourage revolutions on a global scale, in part by coordinating forces within the society and its institutions such as the military, reaffirms why these concepts are directly relevant to the study of grand strategy. Focusing on how revolution influences military institutions, Trotsky agreed "that the Revolution, and the Bolshevik propaganda which preceded it, had destroyed the army."[75] For Trotsky, "In capitalist countries the problem is that of maintaining the existing army – strictly speaking, of maintaining a cover for a self-sustaining system of militarism."[76]

Accordingly, he planned to destroy the old military and build a new one during the revolution. In a highly controversial move, Trotsky enlisted the services of officers of the former army to take advantage of their technical expertise. In order to assuage his critics, but also "to keep a constant vigil over officers of the old army, to carry on propaganda and party work among the rank and file, to educate the peasantry concerning the objects of the revolution and the civil war, and to do other non-military work," Trotsky appointed political commissars to each Red Army unit.[77] The commissars were not allowed to interfere in military operations but were held accountable for the morale and loyalty of their commands. In terms of its effects on military strategy, Earle observes that "Trotsky's work of organizing, supplying, officering and even personally commanding the Red Army is one of the outstanding achievements of modern military history."[78] However, he faced fierce opposition (led by Stalin) to his policies – especially the practice of employing former tsarist officers. Trotsky's opponents also criticized his centralized army, which they considered a characteristic of a capitalist state.[79]

Trotsky's policies sparked debate regarding military theories, military strategy, army organization, and whether a Marxist military doctrine existed. Although "Trotsky readily admitted that Marxian doctrines might determine the broad strategy of the Bolshevik Revolution in world politics . . . he was opposed to amateur and ideological approaches to military theory, without reference to the experience of other countries and of the old regime in Russia." According to Trotsky, "when strategy is developed from the viewpoint of young revolutionaries, the result is chaos."[80]

In the end, the ideas of Marx, Lenin, and Trotsky were instrumental in formulating the principles that translated grand strategy into an instrument for guiding revolutionary movements against incumbent, noncommunist regimes.

Mao Tse-tung

As the principal theorist of the communist revolution in China, Mao Tse-tung (1893–1976) was the influential founder of the People's Republic of China (in 1949). By virtue of the intellectual and political influence of the major revolutionary theorists on Mao (Marx and Engels defined the nature of class-based struggles, whereas Lenin and Trotsky articulated the ideas of ideologies and permanent revolution), it is clear that Marxist-Leninist ideology exerted a powerful influence on Mao's ideas about grand strategy, particularly in terms of the role of mass revolutionary movements.[81]

Mao's concept of grand strategy rested on what he believed was necessary if states or ideological movements are to prevail against the opponents of communism and social-ism.[82] As with his ideological contemporaries, Mao defined *strategy* in terms of defeating his ideological enemies, which would be accomplished by mobilizing mass armies of peasants.[83] For Mao, strategy meant that the state and revolutionary cadres – depending on one's position and stage in the revolutionary cycle – could prevail only when they understood "the actual circumstances of war, its nature, and its relations to other things."[84] The intellectual lineage of Mao's ideas about grand strategy unquestionably derives from the writings of Lenin, who observed that there could be "no victory for the revolution without armed struggle."[85] It also draws from the Chinese declaration of solidarity with the Soviet Union against the West, or what Mao called the "People's Democracies," and the ensuing struggle between these ideological camps.[86]

For Mao, leaders of ideological movements must understand the "laws of war" if they are to properly conduct the movement's or the state's grand strategy.[87] Mao often relied on the term "annihilation," which he frequently used in the narrower case of defeating an enemy division or describing the broader outcome of grand strategy.[88] It was his view that the role of strategy is to guide the revolutionary cadres both within a society and across all societies so that they can develop "a war of total resistance [conducted] by the whole nation."[89] Mao was a strong proponent of the view that success or failure in war or strategy "is decided . . . by the military, political, economic, and geographical conditions, by the character of the war, and by international support on both sides."[90]

A number of preeminent theorists contributed to thinking about the nature and conduct of guerrilla and revolutionary warfare.[91] In essence, grand strategy, for Mao, rests on a condition of revolutionary change that occurs when the leadership is able to mobilize the peasant population against the state. Thus, he noted that a "national revolutionary war as great as ours cannot be won without extensive and thoroughgoing political mobilization," also noting that this "is the most fundamental" [condition for success].[92] As Mao argued, "the central task [of strategy] is to mobilize all the nation's forces for victory in the War of Resistance," because the "key" to success "now lies in developing the resistance . . . into a war of total resistance by the whole nation."[93]

The concepts of demoralizing an enemy, encouraging the people, and eventually annihilating the enemy form the core principles of Mao's strategy of revolutionary change. His ideas about guerrilla warfare directly ". . . influenced deeply . . . how revolu-tionary leadership should be organized."[94] Mao believed that "political mobilization and winning the sympathy of the masses [are] indispensible to the success of the military struggle." For his grand strategy of promoting successful revolutionary movements around the world to succeed, however, Mao "still believed, as he proclaimed in 1938, that 'political power grows out of the barrel of a gun.'"[95] Scholars and policy makers understand that from Mao's perspective, "armed struggle in China" is, in essence, peasant war [while] the party's relations with peasantry and its close relation with the peasant war are one and the same thing."[96]

Mao's grand strategy rested on the principle of an agrarian communist revolution, which in turn was built on the basis of a peasant military force. Many in the Chinese Communist Party leadership, such as Li Li-san, criticized Mao's vision as un-Marxist, asserting that "without urban working class leadership (that is leadership exercised from the urban areas under Central Committee Control) there likely would be 'a complete destruction of the revolution and the Party.'"[97] Lenin similarly envisioned a role for the peasantry in revolutionary grand strategy, but it was coupled tightly with the proletariat. One of Mao's contributions to the revolutionary era was to focus on the rural peasantry alone as the principal political base of support. Ultimately, Mao's vision of a peasant or agrarian revolution prevailed as the ideological basis of the Chinese communist movement.

As have other theorists of grand strategy, Mao believed in a close relationship between political and military objectives when implementing a strategy of revolution, both during the Chinese Civil War and later in formulating China's strategy toward the rest of the world. As Mao wrote, it is essential first to "discuss the relationship of guerrilla warfare to national policy." Noting his focus on the "resistance of a semi colonial country against an imperialism," he argued that "hostilities must have a clearly defined political goal and firmly established political responsibilities." For Mao, the conduct of guerrilla operations should "not be considered as an independent form of warfare," because these represent "but one step in the total war [and] one aspect of the revolutionary struggle."[98]

Like Marx, Mao's grand strategy for guiding revolutionary movements also anticipated that the coming communist revolution in China was inevitable: "We shall also see that the high tide of revolution against the imperialists, the warlords, and the landlords is inevitable, and will come very soon."[99] Because grand strategy involves a delicate balance between war and peace, Mao emphasized the ability to assess political and strategic conditions, "not only before the formulation of a military plan but also after." Importantly, Mao argued that a successful grand strategy begins the "moment [the plan] is put into effect [and continues until] the end of the operation," which means that the effectiveness of a state's or a movement's grand strategy depends in large measure on the ability of revolutionary leaders to guide and implement it – what Mao called "the process of practice."[100]

Mao's grand strategy of revolution depended on winning over the Chinese people, in particular the agrarian-peasant class. Therefore, Mao's tactics (or means) were designed to further that end. As he writes, "the tactics we have derived from the struggle of the past three years are indeed different from any other tactics, ancient or modern, Chinese or foreign." By using "our tactics the masses can be aroused for struggle on an ever-broadening scale, and no enemy, however powerful, can cope with us. Ours are guerrilla tactics."[101] To restate Mao's grand strategy, he was calling for "the use of guerrilla warfare tactics to defeat the ruling political classes" in *all* societies.[102] In this vein, Mao used his famous reference to the "fish" in the struggle against the regime[103] to articulate the principle on which his revolution could spread to other societies and thus form the basis of his unified approach to grand strategy as a revolutionary force.

Strategy, for Mao, was "the study of the laws of a war situation as a whole." In formulating a grand strategy whose objective was to govern all aspects of revolutionary movements, state policies, and war, Mao held that the purpose of the "science of strategy is to study those laws for directing a war that govern a war situation as a whole." As with other ideological theorists, Mao's thinking operated along the lines of "the science of campaigns and the science of tactics," because this would motivate revolutionaries "to study those laws for directing a war that govern a partial situation."[104]

With these thoughts in mind, the fundamental purpose of grand strategy for Mao was to provide "the guiding principles" for military operations, which in turn "grow out of the one basic principle: to strive to the utmost to preserve one's own strength and destroy that of the enemy." The emphasis on preserving one's strength and weakening that of the enemy was an important concept for Mao in revolutionary wars. In the case of China's war of resistance against Japan, the "basic political principle . . . [or] its political aim" was to eliminate "Japanese imperialism and build an independent, free and happy new China." To implement a grand strategy, Mao was saying that it was permissible to use "armed force to defend our motherland and to drive out the Japanese invaders." Later, Mao would apply these principles of grand strategy to challenge "the militarily and economically strong United States."[105]

In practice, Mao's reasoning proceeded from the argument that "revolutionary experience," when governed by an "integrated and comprehensive strategy," would enable the revolutionary cadres to achieve "political gains [even] from a position of military inferiority." It also permitted him to "achieve highly ambitious objectives with initially meager means in a protracted struggle."[106] Restated, Mao's approach to grand strategy sought to overcome or rebalance one's military and economic weaknesses with the greater power that comes from being guided by a revolutionary ideology that mobilizes a broad base of political support from within the society.

As with other Marxist-Leninist theorists, Mao believed that the success of a grand strategy was measured by its ability to promote ideologically inspired revolutions. This would require the movement and its leaders to marshal all available resources to promote the best interests of the revolutionary movement or the state. Thus, he wrote about the "objective material conditions, i.e., the military, political, economic, and natural conditions" that determine whether the state or movement could achieve the goals outlined in its grand strategy.[107]

Mao also developed the concept of stages or levels of strategy as he discussed the Party's "changes in strategy" through the period of the Chinese Civil War (beginning in 1927) through the "War of National Resistance" against the Japanese (beginning in 1937). He was referring to the changes in the Party's (and the Red Army's) military strategy for conducting regular warfare, irregular warfare, and then, again, regular warfare.[108] In the case of grand strategy, Mao noted that some military strategies are more appropriate than others in certain stages of a conflict. For instance, "of the three stages (the defensive, the stalemate, and the counter-offensive) in the entire process of the war . . . the first and last are stages in which regular warfare is primary and guerrilla warfare supplementary." By contrast, "in the intermediate stage guerilla warfare will become primary and regular warfare supplementary, because the enemy will be holding on to the areas he has occupied and we will be preparing for the counter-offensive but will not yet be ready to launch it." In the case of the "anti-Japanese war," the best strategy was to use "regular warfare" as the primary means and "guerilla warfare [as the] supplementary." Mao's reasoning was that "only regular warfare can decide the final outcome of the war."[109]

Thus, Mao "pursued a three-phase revolutionary strategy during China's protracted war against Japan: Strategic Defensive; Preparation for Counteroffensive; Strategic Counteroffensive."[110] Mao also examined how irregular forces and strategy evolve into regular forces and strategy, noting that during a long struggle, "guerrilla units and guerrilla warfare will ... develop to a higher stage and evolve gradually into regular units and regular warfare." His point, which reinforces how grand strategy has evolved and is put into practice, is that guerrilla warfare permits revolutionaries to "build up our strength and turn ourselves into a decisive element in the crushing of Japanese imperialism."[111] For Mao, military strategy was as important to the success of grand strategy as the classic political, ideological, and economic instruments of power.

Mao emphasized that China's revolutionary war could be won only if revolutionary leaders took local conditions into consideration as they articulated their grand strategy. When he argued that "China's revolutionary war, whether civil war or national war, is waged in the specific environment of China," Mao was warning that it would have "its own specific circumstances and nature distinguishing it both from war in general and from revolutionary war in general." Using words that directly influenced the evolution of grand strategy in an era dominated by revolutionary ideologies, Mao concluded that "different laws for directing different wars are determined by the different circumstances of those wars."[112]

In looking beyond Mao's strategy in the Chinese Civil War, his greater challenge was to develop the outlines of a grand strategy that would govern China's foreign policy after the revolution. This would develop after 1950, when China under Mao's control struggled as a unified state against the rest of the world. At that moment, the concept of grand strategy at its highest level was most relevant because it was built from the argument that the instruments available to the state for implementing its grand strategy vary by circumstance. This is a remarkable deduction for a revolutionary theorist such as Mao, who, steeped in the concepts of Marxism-Leninism, concluded that there are no uniform principles that apply in all cases in which the state seeks to articulate and implement its grand strategy. In the modern vernacular, generic rules for articulating and implementing grand strategy simply do not exist.

Early on, Mao's ideas formed the basis for his strategy for successfully guiding China during its civil war, but this raises the different question of the development of Mao's grand strategy post-1950. Arguably, it was during the post-1950 phase, when China under Mao was struggling to define its role as a unified state in a struggle against the rest of the world, that the concept of grand strategy at its highest level is most relevant. Equally important is how China's history impacted Mao's understanding of his nation's role, which fundamentally focused on the principles and conduct of its grand strategy. Under Mao's guidance, the ideology and statecraft of communist China was the product of seeking to guide China's revival as its leadership sought to reattain its historical greatness after the "century of humiliation" at the hands of imperialist powers. Arguably, this nationalist motivation, along with the impetus provided by revolutionary ideology, prompted China to pursue policies that were central to its grand strategy in the decades after its civil war.

Hitler: Elevating Military Strategy over Grand Strategy

The objective of the strategy of Adolf Hitler (1889–1945), as Earle writes, was "to unite all Germans, and 'to lead them, gradually and safely to a dominating position' in the world."[113] As we see from these comments, Hitler's grand strategy rested on using the principles of expansionism and aggression as the instruments for building Germany into the dominant European, and perhaps global, power. Subsequent events in World War II, including the invasions of Poland, France, and Norway; the occupation of most of Europe; and the invasion of the Soviet Union, along with the genocidal policies pursued by the Wehrmacht and Waffen SS, all reaffirm that the concept of expansionism was central to Hitler's grand strategy.

Scholars focus on the role of Hitler as political leader in contrast with his influence on Germany's military leadership as they seek to understand the origins of German grand strategy. Earle, for example, notes that although any head of state depends on his general staff for guidance on developing and implementing the state's strategy, "it is highly improbable that the [German] high command could have effected the moral, psycho-logical, and emotional mobilization of the German nation which was so essential to its plans." Nor could Germany's military leadership by itself have "waged the political, economic, and ideological war – the 'white war' – of 1933–1939." The obvious source of these policies was unquestionably Hitler and the Nazi Party, the latter of which was "largely" a creation of Hitler.[114] German successes against Poland, Norway, and France were "the result of an extraordinarily effective combination of imaginative and daring *military* strategy and imaginative and daring *political* strategy." Once these political and military elements of Germany's grand strategy were in place, Hitler had at his disposal "new military techniques [which, when] combined with revolutionary audacity," were able to "produce a devastating force."

But as the diplomatic dimension of Hitler's grand strategy gradually fell away, he increasingly based his grand strategy almost exclusively on the use of military force. Grand strategy was not conducted along a continuum of war and peace but was conducted as a perpetual state of war. According to Hitler, war was not the continuation of politics by other means; it was all about politics and control in terms of both his domestic rivals and foreign adversaries. Hitler's ability to implement his grand strategy, which was made possible by the totalitarian nature of the German state under his control, enabled him to closely coordinate the various facets of his policies. The Nazi concept of war and hence of grand strategy was marked by the central and close "coordination of army and party," which was the product of the "expenditure of much blood in the purge of 1934 and by continuous political tight-rope walking thereafter."[115] The general strategy in Germany in the 1930s was to build a war machine that would permit Hitler to put his expansionist and destructive grand strategy into practice. One practical step for Hitler, as he described it in *Mein Kampf*, was that the "motorization [of the military] will be overwhelmingly decisive" in the next war.

Broadly defined, his strategy was to build a German motor industry that would serve primarily as an instrument for waging war and would be without any close rival in Europe. As Earle explains, Hitler's approach to strategy, which was implemented by the "unity, ingenuity, and daring of the high command," was "centered in and personi-fied by Hitler." He was able to guarantee by virtue of his "totalitarian powers" the ability to conduct "the perfect coordination of all arms," which is another way of saying the strategy, operational, and industrial foundations of German power. All of these were "regarded as essential to success in modern war."[116] In the case of Germany under Hitler, we see how the strict coordination and centralization of all facets of political, economic, and military power were aligned tightly with Germany's overall grand strategy. In effect, Germany's totalitarian political system, very much like that of Stalin's Soviet Union, permitted a degree of control over grand strategy that is without parallel in democratic societies – even when one considers the degree of mobilization and central government control in American and British societies during World War II.

An important argument for Earle, as he writes in *Makers of Modern Strategy*, first published in 1943, was that "there is not much evidence available to show that Hitler's military strategy will compare favorably with his triumphs in the realm of psychological and political warfare."[117] What was revolutionary and demonstrably used for sinister purposes was Hitler's ability to marshal all of Germany's resources – economic and military, and particularly the will to fight – to support his vision of a political and military campaign against the rest of Europe and the other major powers. As Earle explains, the essential "first step in the war of nerves" was to unify the German people into an instrument that was "terrifying to the outside world."

Hitler's grand strategy, which called for mobilizing Germany's resources into a highly effective war machine, was achieved by the "ruthless suppression of all internal dissent from the Nazi program." At the same time, it was guided by the highly "skillful [use of] propaganda of press and radio, reinforced by party discipline and appeals to national pride." As Hitler and his cadre of leaders unquestionably understood, they used the concepts of "militarism, Pan-Germanism, anti-Semitism, racial superiority, worship of the state, and other features of Hitler's program," all of which "were [so] deeply rooted in Germany history [that these could be] exploited by Nazis to their own ends."[118] Thus, the means Hitler used to marshal the domestic foundations of German power locked Germany into a rigid grand strategy. As a result, German foreign policy could not be adapted and moderated but instead relied on wars of expansion and brutality against the rest of Europe.

This reasoning was evident when we examine Hitler's language in *Mein Kampf*, where he wrote that "any resurrection of the German people can take place only by way of regaining external power." But the expansionist impulses in German grand strategy and its rebirth always were evident in the use of language that evoked military power, attacks on the bourgeois leaders, and the people's morale. Hitler (quoted directly) said that "the prerequisites for this are not arms, as our bourgeois 'statesman' always babble, but the forces of will power." He believed that "the best arms are dead and useless material as long as the spirit is missing which is ready, willing, and determined to use them." As a result of the psychological and emotional mobilization and rejuvenation of the German population in the aftermath of World War I and the Treaty of Versailles, Hitler deliberately "bred in the hearts of all classes a consuming sense of injustice over the *Diktat* of Versailles." He was able to arouse "among large numbers of Germans ... a spirit of vengeance"; and in the case of Germany's younger population,. "he developed a cult of Spartanism, a fanatical German nationalism, and an unquestioned loyalty to the Führer which boded no good for the peace of the world."[119]

These forces were essential to implementing a grand strategy whose objective was to control Europe and later much of the world with all-too-well-known destructive consequences. Further, Hitler was able to keep Germany unified even as the Allies conducted an immensely destructive air campaign that should have decimated the sense of unity in Germany.[120]

A critical principle in German grand strategy was the concept of total war.[121] Hitler's grand strategy was designed not only to mobilize the German people's will to fight, but also to mobilize the economy for war as well as accomplish the complete militarization of the German economy.[122] As one scholar writes, "from the general staff the Nazis took over the idea that the 'total' war of 1914–1918 was not total enough [while] the home front must be solidified economically, as well as psychologically, in support of the war effort which was to come."[123] These policies align with the principle that the state's grand strategy cannot be implemented unless the economy and industry are similarly mobilized, which is precisely what Hitler instituted in the 1930s as he sought to energize Germany's economic potential for war.[124] As Earle argues, while total war was "inherent in their theories of the totalitarian state," the role of "force alone ... was never considered by Hitler to be an effective weapon." The principle was that "force and the threat of force must be supplemented by words, slogans, ideas." The critical conclusion, which found its way directly into the design and execution of Germany's grand strategy, was that "only the ideological offensive – a fanatical belief in one's own view of life – can give victory" to a state's grand strategy.[125]

War emerged as the highest form of politics, not as a necessary means to an end. In practice, however, the logic of war and expansionism replaced the logic of strategy. As Earle writes, the strategy of Nazi Germany "drew no clearly defined line between war and peace [because it] considered war not peace the normal state of society." This idea directly relates to the Nazi embrace of the concept of total war: "Since war to the Nazis no longer consisted solely, or even primarily, of military operations, the policy of the state in time of so-called peace was only a 'broadened strategy' involving economic, psychological, and other nonmilitary weapons." For Hitler and his entourage, the purpose of grand strategy was to engage constantly and ruthlessly in the act of "political warfare."[126]

The implication for grand strategy is that Hitler employed "both in peace and war ... a strategy of terror." In his struggle to gain power in Germany, "he won the 'battle for the streets'; in order to stay in power he tortured and imprisoned and murdered his opponents; in order to have his way in Europe he projected the same methods beyond the boundaries of the Reich."[127] With his record in mind, the conduct of grand strategy for Hitler was an absolute undertaking in which the state used all instruments at its disposal and without regard to moral constraints on behavior to conduct total war.

The role of the principle in grand strategy of the balance between the means and the ends in the practice of the Nazi concept of war requires closer scrutiny.[128] Since Hitler was a firm believer "in his destiny ... in both the military and political spheres," it follows that his willingness to take risks vastly exceeded what most German military officials viewed as reasonable, to say the least. In Earle's view, "No other chancellor in modern German history has been so thoroughgoing a militarist." When one considers "Hitler's contemporaries, only Stalin showed, before the collapse of France, the same single-mindedness of purpose."[129] In a decisive departure from the policies of such predecessors as Frederick the Great and Bismarck, Hitler's strategy was to ensure that Germany would be the only military power in Europe. Accordingly, as he told the German people, "we must undertake every sacrifice which may help bring about a nullification of the French drive for European hegemony." Earle expressed this logic when he wrote that the "central and controlling aim of Hitler's policy [was] the total and permanent elimination of France as a great power." Notably, this meant in practice for Hitler that "only by the destruction of France could Germany be assured uninterrupted conquest of eastern Europe."[130]

Despite skepticism in Germany about the value of alliances, in part because of the German people's experience in World War I, Hitler understood that pursuing a strategic relationship with England was key to his plans – despite Churchill's absolute rejection of such cooperation.[131] As Hitler was quoted, "To 'gain England's favor, no sacrifice should have been too great' in the years before 1914, and none was too great for the Third Reich if such sacrifice led to unchallenged control of the continent."[132] Such a statement stands in sharp contrast to Churchill's when, in a speech in Cyprus on February 1, 1943, he spoke about fighting "until unconditional surrender is extorted from those who have laid the world in havoc and ruins."[133]

Nevertheless, the means available to Germany for achieving the destructive ends in Hitler's policies were guided by the following strategy. In order to isolate and defeat France, "Hitler pursued a well thought out policy of whittling away rather than demolishing at one blow, the sources of her strength." His grand strategy was designed to destroy smaller states "one at a time [while] . . . the sapping of French power was to be piecemeal, always avoiding a *casus belli*.'" To follow this logic, "an intelligent victor will, whenever possible . . . present his demands to the vanquished in installments." In the end, the principle in German grand strategy was to make "sure that a nation which has become characterless – and such is every one which voluntarily submits – will no longer find any sufficient reason in each of these detailed oppressions to take to arms once more."[134] In effect, Germany's grand strategy was designed to whittle away at the opponent's will to resist and then defeat it militarily.

In conclusion, Germany's grand strategy before and during World War II was based on policies whose effects continue to be studied for their ruthlessness and inhumanity. As the instrument of the grand strategy that guided Nazi Germany, its armed forces were "only the cutting edge of the war machine." Hitler transformed the entire German state and society into a war machine, which eventually lost the capability to articulate and implement a grand strategy beyond that of an expansionist war and only continued as a failed war strategy.

Ho Chi Minh: A Revolutionary's Grand Strategy of Avoiding Defeat

Ho Chi Minh (1890–1969) was the principal revolutionary leader in Vietnam, serving as prime minister and president of the Democratic Republic of Vietnam (North Vietnam).[135] Before examining how his ideas contributed to the evolution of grand strategy, one must first understand his influence during the American involvement in the Vietnam War.

As the guiding ideological force in developing the political and economic ideas that shaped North Vietnam's strategy for defeating the United States in the Vietnam War, Ho's success demonstrated the power of a determined insurgency, especially one driven by a highly coherent revolutionary ideology and supported by another superpower.[136] This lesson coincidentally aligns somewhat with the American experience in its own revolution in the eighteenth century.[137] Not surprisingly, this ideological dimension in the case of the Vietnam War and more generally during the twentieth century has significant consequences for the study of grand strategy.[138]

To complicate matters, the Vietnam War was perhaps the only significant defeat in U.S. military history.[139] Although the reasons are debated, for one scholar, "the key to U.S. defeat was a profound misunderstanding of enemy tenacity and fighting power."[140] In the end, Ho Chi Minh's contributions to North Vietnam's revolutionary ideology played a decisive role in the war's outcome as it evolved into a strategy that produced a highly resilient and adaptive adversary. His strategy vastly complicated – which is to say dramatically weakened – the ability of American policy makers to sustain public support for the war.

Ho as a Nationalist and Communist

Ho Chi Minh, born Nguyen Sinh Cung and also known as Nguyen Ai Quoc, was a fierce advocate of Vietnamese national liberation. He believed that Vietnam's struggle was more important than the global socialist revolution being advocated by Moscow and Beijing. In contrast to some who paint Ho Chi Minh as either a wholehearted nationalist or a wholehearted communist, many scholars contend that Ho saw Vietnam's national emancipation as a necessary precondition to successful Marxist revolutions. In effect, his strategy was guided by nationalism *and* communism.

According to Ho Chi Minh biographer Pierre Brocheux, Ho saw "national liberation as a prerequisite to social emancipation."[141] For Ho, only after all imperialist powers were expelled could Marxist-Leninist ideals and principles become a prominent feature of the Vietnamese leadership's grand strategy, whose central purpose was to organize Vietnamese society along the lines outlined by prominent revolutionaries and spread that revolution among neighboring countries. However, his focus on national liberation was a source of great tension between Ho Chi Minh and other communist leaders who argued that proletarian internationalism and unity should transcend allegiance to individual national struggles. Despite these disagreements, Ho continued to receive large-scale political and financial support from Moscow and Beijing because of his commitment to the anti-imperialist (read: anti-French and anti-American) struggle. In theory and practice, Ho's grand strategy harnessed the power of Vietnamese society (and more than just the proletariat class) to expel the French and then the Americans as part of his strategy to unite Vietnam. Ho and his successors deftly combined a highly effective political and military strategy, while waging a protracted "people's war" against first the French and then the Americans. In the end, his strategy prevailed against the superior military and economic power of both Paris and Washington.

Perhaps more than any other communist leader, Lenin's anticolonialist writings and theories about ideological movements and his belief that these inevitably would succeed decisively influenced Ho Chi Minh's grand strategy of revolution. National liberation and Vietnamese sovereignty were the primary objectives of Ho Chi Minh's grand strategy rather than simply goals to further the global communist struggle. His strategy placed the national interest above all other elements in the global struggle against capitalism. In Ho's view, as Brocheux described the situation, "independence was the most important of all political values [that] would lead to the freedom of [his] people." Ho's writings present a complex balance between the demands imposed by nationalism and the desire to promote social revolution along the lines suggested by such revolutionary theorists as Lenin.

His ideological mentors in Moscow and Beijing arguably viewed Ho Chi Minh as less than ideologically committed to the success of Marxism-Leninism. For many ideologues, it was "commonly believed that [Ho Chi Minh's] policy of national unity exalting a nation's past was heretical to the internationalism of the Comintern" (or Communist International).[142] But Ho Chi Minh's decisive contribution to revolutionary ideology was to help found the Viet Minh, a coalition that formed to support independence for Vietnam. In effect, Ho's grand strategy combined "the dynamism of nationalism and that of international communism."[143]

Ho's strategy was that "revolution would be an alternative to the slow and legal path of reforms" and would provide an alternative to depending "on the great powers to decide the fate of the world," which, as Ho argued, often did not align with "the will of the people involved."[144] Scholars have observed that policy makers in Moscow viewed Ho Chi Minh "as a maverick in colonial countries in Asia" who believed that "national liberation from colonial rule had to take precedence over revolutionary transformation."[145] Some argue that Ho Chi Minh's commitment to "nationalism and social revolution" contributed to his "slippery maneuverings to be all things to all people that he engaged in throughout his adult life."

The question is, what were Ho Chi Minh's "core political beliefs," and how did those influence his grand strategy, beyond that of defeating the United States? Scholars, such as Brocheux, do not accept "the simplistic extremes of doctrinaire Marxism and simple patriotism," but defend the argument that Ho possessed a more "balanced portrait of an astute mind capable of weaving together the strands of nationalism and social revolution into a complex strategy."[146] To quote Ho Chi Minh directly, "I didn't understand what you said about strategy, proletarian tactics, and other points. But there is one thing that I understood clearly: The Third International is interested in ... liberating the colonies."[147] In effect, Ho's grand strategy balanced the demands of nationalism with the imperative of social revolution as a way to help Vietnam gain its independence and retain a strong allegiance to the Marxist-Leninist revolutionary movements that were an important source of his own ideas.

What is unclear about Ho's influence is the extent of the Vietnamese Communist Party's autonomy in terms of the ideological guidance and policy dictates provided by Moscow and Beijing. The experience of Mao Tse-tung and the Chinese communists in their relationship with Moscow deeply influenced Ho Chi Minh's grand strategy of promoting a revolution in Vietnam and adjacent states. Ultimately, he was persuaded to support a policy of greater detachment from and less dependence on Moscow. Seeing how Moscow's attempts to internationalize the Chinese communist cause weakened the influence of China's Communist Party, Ho surmised that in the case of Vietnam, international support often evolved into entanglements that would pose a serious threat to successful national liberation movements. For this reason, Ho Chi Minh supported the principle of an autonomous communist party, which was a defining feature of his revolutionary grand strategy.

The scholar Brocheux discusses these ideas about Ho, in particular the conclusion that "events in China must have helped [Ho] form his own strategy for the Indochinese revolution, especially the failure to establish the united front with the Nationalists." Facing these circumstances, Ho's conclusion was that "Indochina needed to have an autonomous communist party."[148] Scholars have observed that "the Chinese experience taught [Ho] that he would have to ... ease the tension sparked by the confluence of colonialism and communism." For Ho, studying the Chinese communist revolution under Mao's guidance emphasized just how important it is to mobilize "the peasantry and its revolutionary potential in [the largely agrarian] countries where urban workers were a minority (.5% of the Chinese population in the 1920s)."[149]

In formulating his grand strategy, Ho's "strategic goal for the early 1940s" helped shape his dealings with China. In broad terms, it was to "drive out the French and the new Japanese aggressors to establish a 'new democracy.'"[150] Scholars observe that Ho was "disappointed by recent events in China" because "the Leninist alliance between Nationalists and Communists had ended in a bloody massacre of CCP militants." As a consequence, communist revolutionary movements and parties in colonial empires "were now instructed to reject alliances with bourgeois nationalist parties." The reason was that "the native bourgeoisie" that had abandoned the "revolution . . . could no longer be trusted as an ally of the proletariat."[151]

Like Mao, Ho Chi Minh was convinced that communist revolutions in Indochina would succeed only if the agrarian/peasant class (and not simply the proletariat class) played a prominent role. Although Ho believed that the peasantry "represented a revolutionary potential . . . that absolutely had to be mobilized," his conclusion was that the success "of the proletarian revolution is impossible . . . unless the proletariat is actively supported by the bulk of the peasant population."[152] For his grand strategy to succeed, Ho likely believed that revolutionary movements must marshal human capital to the greatest extent possible. In conclusion, Ho saw that the "revolution would be achieved through armed struggle led by the party," which would lead to the liberation of "all Indochinese peoples . . . including the Khmer and Lao."

The success of Ho's grand strategy depended on the ability of the Communist Party to "broaden its influence and multiply its organizations among the urban working class and peasants." In addition, he stressed how essential it was "to recruit and train cadres from the proletariat."[153] Although this guidance is consistent with Lenin's concept of the vanguard of the proletariat to steer the revolution, Ho was not "ready to abandon entirely the broad Leninist united front approach" that was so central to his revolutionary beliefs.[154] In practice, Ho borrowed Lenin's "idea of a multiclass united front of progressive classes to bring about the first stage of the revolution."[155] To express his commitment to revolutionary theorists, Ho once said that "I am committed to making sure that in the future we will make the principles of Lenin and Sun Yat-sen the guiding light of the Vietnamese revolution."[156]

Ho and Insurgency as Grand Strategy

Apart from esoteric debates among Marxist-Leninists in the early twentieth century about whether to involve all classes in a social revolution, Ho demonstrated that a revolutionary movement could defeat, if not simply wear down, much more powerful adversaries, even a superpower. In measuring the strategic significance of Ho's ideas, his contributions to grand strategy existed within the microcosm of the larger ideas and forces that were at play in the struggle against capitalism.

For Ho Chi Minh, as with many prominent theorists of revolutionary ideologies, a central principle was that a successful grand strategy based on a communist revolution had to be part of a coherent political and military strategy. Further, it has to be conducted as a drawn-out struggle. In effect, Ho's grand strategy, to be successful, had to be waged as a protracted struggle in which the revolutionaries used the full range of political, military, and economic instruments of power available to them. In formulating the precise mix of instruments, Ho Chi Minh, as reported from Politburo debates, described "his preference for a protracted war strategy that applied a mixture of political struggle, propaganda, and guerrilla warfare to wear down the enemy on a gradual step-by-step basis." Proceeding on the basis of these ideological foundations, Ho advanced the view that success in revolutionary struggles depends to a significant extent on the patience of revolutionary leaders in contrast with others who make the mistake of seeking to achieve success as soon as possible.[157]

How Ho Chi Minh came to these views is a matter of debate. It is clear that communist party leaders in Vietnam and throughout Asia who had read the works of Mao expressed "an interest in applying [Mao's] strategy" of conducting "guerrilla warfare in the countryside, [including] inside Vietnam." Ho Chi Minh, who had, as one scholar expressed it, "developed some familiarity with Mao's ideas on revolutionary warfare," concluded that "Mao's concept of a 'people's war' [was highly] suitable as a weapon to carve out a liberated base area in his own country."[158] Thus, Ho drew directly from Mao's ideas, which provided the foundation of Ho's grand strategy in terms of his dedication to bringing to a successful conclusion a revolutionary movement in Vietnam. It is similarly evident from Mao's works that the success of such movements depended significantly on whether the revolutionary cadres possessed sufficient political will and resources to conduct the revolution on a protracted basis. The success of a grand strategy that seeks to promote and spread revolutionary movements is highly contingent on allowing the forces within society to evolve at their own pace and scale.

In sum, the guiding principle for Ho Chi Minh's grand strategy was to conduct a protracted ideological and political struggle based on mobilizing the masses and using violence to create a successful revolutionary movement. When we consider the litany of revolutionary movements that occurred during the second half of the twentieth century, the grand strategy advanced by Ho Chi Minh was immensely successful in defeating a superpower whose commitment to defending its own grand strategy appeared to be less than Ho's commitment.

The Nuclear Era

The atomic bomb changed the ultimate nature and purpose of strategy and its consequences for grand strategy.[159] What emerged gradually in the postwar era was the realization that the conduct of grand strategy in the presence of nuclear weapons had to be redefined radically if policy makers were to develop policies that would lead to strategic stability in the form of stalemate rather than mutual annihilation. This section builds on the previous one on revolutionary strategists and includes analyses of the case of Stalin as well as the Cold War case of statesman Henry Kissinger. First, let us look at a set of strategists and theorists who illustrated how grand strategy would forever be changed by the advent of nuclear weapons.

Bernard Brodie, Herman Kahn, Paul Kecskemeti, Raymond Aron, Vasily D. Sokolovskii

For Bernard Brodie (1910–1978; at the RAND Corporation, 1951–1966), in *The Absolute Weapon* (1946), the eminently rational logic of *deterrence* might be an immensely useful element to formulating grand strategy: "The general idea is that if the enemy hits us, we will kill him."[160] Deterrence as an instrument of grand strategy ultimately rests on the ability to "eliminate the cities of the other," which is "tantamount" to success "provided always [that one's] own cities are not similarly eliminated."[161] As Brodie observed, the only sensible principle for the nuclear powers was that "thermonuclear war between them is simply forbidden."[162] And as he famously wrote in 1946, "Thus far, the chief purpose of our military establishment has been to win wars. From now on, its chief purpose must be to avert them."[163]

Herman Kahn (1922–1983), a military strategist at the RAND Corporation, presented a somewhat opposing view in *On Thermonuclear War*. There he argued that, "when governments are informed of the terrible consequences of a nuclear war, they will realize there could be no victors."[164] Yet, when Kahn emphasized the concept of survivability in nuclear war as a way to avoid having to distinguish between the concepts of victory and defeat, he became a proponent of the view that it was possible for the state to conduct a rational grand strategy in which nuclear weapons played a central role.[165] In contrast, the economist and arms-control theoretician Thomas C. Schelling (1921–) argued in *Arms and Influence* that nuclear weapons undermined strategy as a practical instrument of diplomacy because they could inflict "monstrous violence to the enemy without first achieving victory."[166] In effect, Schelling discounted classic approaches to grand strategy as a practical option for governing the actions of nuclear-armed states.

The Hungarian-born sociologist Paul Kecskemeti (1901–1980) defined the classic principle of strategy in his 1958 RAND analysis, *Strategic Surrender*: "One side achieves a monopoly of armed strength and the other is reduced to defenselessness."[167] Arguing that the state can achieve the ends outlined in its strategy by either "disruption" (i.e., overcoming enemy resistance in pitched battle) or "siege or attrition," Kecskemeti suggested that military leaders would choose disruption when the enemy's "entire strength is concentrated in a field army." However, the development of nuclear weapons, he noted, rendered forever obsolete the classic strategy of attrition among conventional forces that governed the military strategies of states (8). For Kecskemeti, nuclear weapons are so destructive that "the losses they cause must far outweigh any political advantage that might be derived from victory." In practical terms, the state's grand strategy "will be meaningful . . . only in wars that are nontotal" – that is, wars that do not involve the use of nuclear weapons.[168]

Building on these observations, Kecskemeti pointed out a fundamental feature of strategy that many apparently have missed: "Victory, defeat, and stalemate, when used to characterize the final outcome of wars rather than the outcome of military engagements, are not absolute, but relative, concepts" (20). He also noted that whether a state can be said to have achieved the goals outlined in its strategy is always bounded by uncertainty (208). Thus, although Germany suffered the defeat of total war and strategic surrender in 1918, the Allies' complete "victory" after World War I (232–234) had no permanent value for England and France, both of which had suffered extraordinary human losses in the course of "winning" (121–125). In World War II, Kecskemeti argued, the Allies' grand strategy was based on defeating the Axis powers, while mandating the terms of peace and refusing to negotiate with them (215). Yet, theirs was a "hollow victory" (234) because their strategy forced the Axis powers to fight a war of attrition to a point at which the Allies also were exhausted physically and economically.[169]

Nuclear weapons forced strategists and policy makers to wrestle with what it means for one's strategy to be shaped by the presence of absolute weapons. The French philosopher, political scientist, and sociologist Raymond Aron (1905–1983) concluded that the only coherent strategy would be to avoid war because the "spoils of victory could no longer be commensurate with the cost of battle." The obvious reason, for Aron, was that there are "ways of conquering that quickly transform victory into defeat."[170] The broader point for Aron was that "it was rationally conceivable to aim at absolute victory in terms of disarming the enemy and thereafter to limit the fruits of victory"; however, in the nuclear age, it is "no longer necessary to disarm a country in order to annihilate it."[171] In other words, the conduct of grand strategy in classic terms in an age dominated by nuclear weapons is no longer rational. Whereas Sun Tzu and Thucydides recognized the power of human emotions to cloud rational thought about grand strategy, Aron sees technology itself as reaching a destructive potential that makes the old ways of thinking about grand strategy seem irrational.

One of the more influential works by Soviet strategists was *Soviet Military Strategy*, published in 1963 and edited by the marshal of the Soviet Union Vasily D. Sokolovskii (1897–1968), who was a key figure in resisting and repelling the German invasion of 1941. Soviet strategists during the Cold War subordinated all considerations in strategy to the conditions that are necessary to achieve "world-wide historical victories of the international revolutionary movement of the working class."[172] As he argued, any war between the "opposing world social systems . . . will inevitably end with the victory of the progressive, communist social and economic system over the reactionary, capitalist social and economic system, which is historically doomed to destruction."[173] In Sokolovskii's formulation, grand strategy aims, to the absolute extent possible, to gain political power from the use or threat of using force.

During the pre-nuclear age, Soviet leaders equated strategy with the total overthrow of the existing social and political structure of power within societies and throughout the international system.[174] Soviet-era strategists and ideologists consistently defined grand strategy as the triumph of socialism over capitalism. During the early decades of the twentieth century, Soviet strategists emphasized the "annihilation and total defeat of the enemy."[175] Thus, the purpose of Soviet military strategy was to "defeat the enemy forces, occupy his territory, crush his will to resist, and achieve final victory" (235).

The Soviet or communist position that based strategy on the triumph of socialism over capitalism through military means grew increasingly unrealistic in the face of the development of nuclear weapons and the growing emphasis among Western theorists on avoiding rather than waging wars. Writing during the nuclear age, Soviet strategists contended that a state could not necessarily "achieve a victory in a war with an opponent who did possess such [nuclear] weapons" (101). Yet, such a war, if there were one, would be waged by "massive missile blows to destroy the aggressor's instruments for nuclear attack and, simultaneously, to destroy and devastate on a large scale the vitally important enemy targets . . . [so as] to attain victory within the shortest possible time" (313). Therefore, Soviet thinkers thought – at least, initially, perhaps – that nuclear weapons could be used as a real instrument of the state's grand strategy, which was based on radically divergent ideologies and the threat of confrontation.

Although both numerical superiority and morale may contribute to the state's ability to achieve its strategy, neither can guarantee it. As noted in *Soviet Military Strategy*, "Victory in war is determined not only by superiority in the military and technical sense . . . but also by the ability to organize the defeat of the enemy and make effective use of available weapons" (314–315). A related tenet in Soviet thinking was the importance of the "maximum mobilization of their [economic] resources and strength in order to gain victory" because, as affirmed in *Soviet Military Strategy*, "Lenin showed that once it comes to war, *everything* must be subordinated to its interests" (emphasis added, 274). In terms of the influence of morale on strategy, Sokolovskii cited Lenin's observation that "our proletariat, weak in numbers, exhausted by calamity and privation, was victorious because it was strong in morale" (123–124). This belief that military strategy should consume all other state interests is one of the reasons for the fall of the Soviet Union.[176] Its grand strategy failed to build other sources of national power, especially its economy, and consequently did not balance ends and means. It thereby overinvested in its military and underinvested in its society and economy, with devastating results.

Grand Strategy Altered

Based on the belief that the conduct of grand strategy was vastly more complicated in the nuclear age, some defined strategy in terms of achieving political and military outcomes in struggles short of war. When the historical purpose of strategy, in the case of the United States, was to achieve victory, it had stimulated policies calling for mobilizing all of the nation's economic capacity to produce sufficient numbers of weapons to destroy the enemy's will and ability to fight.[177] However, as Kecskemeti warned, the "worst strategic outcome will no longer be defenselessness but utter destruction of the entire society."[178]

Policy makers soon realized that diplomacy in the nuclear age was fundamentally incompatible with traditional definitions of grand strategy. Although total war was no longer a useful instrument of the state's grand strategy, lesser forms of success might be relevant in the limited sense of a state seeking to prevent the enemy from gaining victory.[179] As General Curtis LeMay remarked in a speech at the National War College in April 1956, "The most radical effect of the changes in warfare [i.e., nuclear weapons] is not upon how wars are won or lost, but upon how they will start."[180]

The consensus among strategists and policy makers was that basing grand strategy to some extent on the threat of nuclear war imposes an irrational objective on the state, which by its nature should persuade policy makers to avoid war in the first place. The strategic dilemma of the Cold War superpowers, as Robert Oppenheimer wrote in *Foreign Affairs* in 1953, was a situation equivalent to "two scorpions in a bottle, each capable of killing the other, but only at the risk of his own life."[181] As a result of this debate, the theory and practice of deterrence entered the lexicon of grand strategy as an instrument for managing the well-understood calculus of risks and for displacing the by-now discredited classic concepts of strategy.[182]

Once strategists and policy makers understood that nuclear weapons undermined the relevance of how states and policy makers approached the problem of grand strategy, the debate shifted to the development of the strategy of limited war.[183] One of the more prominent thinkers was Robert E. Osgood (1921–1986), whose *Limited War* focused on an analysis of the nature of and distinctions between limited, unlimited, and total war. The American strategy for war, he argued, has been to achieve "clear-cut, definitive" victories as effectively and quickly as possible and then to return to "politics as usual."[184] Osgood argued that less-than-total victories tend to leave problems unresolved: "Military victory, no matter how it comes about, at least provides the nation with the opportunity to solve its political problems later."[185] With a tradition of "unpreparedness, mobilization, overwhelming offensive, total victory, and demobilization," the United States had shown by the late 1950s – and continues to show – a remarkable potential for organizing itself to defeat a traditional enemy.[186] Yet, despite its record of achieving overwhelming victories against its enemies, the United States altered its grand strategy once nuclear weapons entered the equation because the constraints they imposed on action undermined and invalidated the classic meaning and relevance of strategy.

At the beginning of the nuclear age, the efforts of scholars and policy makers to manage the challenges that nuclear weapons pose for strategy were dominated by the theory of strategic bombardment. The debate began with the observation – itself drawn from the literature on air power – that the nature of strategy in war is to attack the opponent's political, economic, and military targets. However, when it was understood that nuclear weapons nullified these ideas, the foreign policy establishment concluded that nuclear-armed airplanes could not lead to meaningful outcomes for the state's grand strategy.[187] This view, as expressed by Michael Howard, was that "it became almost impossible to visualize any political objective for which the use of such weapons would be appropriate."[188] The technological means for pursuing one's strategy eclipsed any reasonable ends of grand strategy, which explains why nuclear weapons are arguably most useful when they are not used. It was possible, however, for states to conduct wars during the nuclear age as long as policy makers recognized the limitations imposed on strategy by this technology.

Once policy makers accepted that these weapons made the classic structure and conduct of grand strategy impossible, traditional approaches to strategy were seen as an inherently irrational and dangerous line of inquiry – despite spirited discussions among strategists over the decades.[189] Early in the nuclear age, systematic discussions about strategy rightly disappeared from the literature, as the idea of achieving successes in grand strategy became increasingly outmoded intellectually.[190] With the role of nuclear weapons firmly entrenched in strategy, scholars and policy makers understood that states have a profound obligation to deter their use, while still pursuing the ends of their grand strategy. It was this concept that dominated how the administrations of all Cold War presidents – from Harry S. Truman to George H. W. Bush – translated the ideas of nuclear deterrence into a grand strategy that allowed the United States to defend its vital interests without undermining public support or engaging in a mutually annihilative war. Beginning with the concept of massive retaliation and proceeding through the various theories of nuclear strategy – that is, mutual assured destruction, flexible response, limited nuclear war, counterforce strategies, and so forth – the conduct of grand strategy was to rely on deterrence as an instrument for avoiding the use of this weaponry.[191]

Nuclear arms dominated strategy during the Cold War as scholars and policy makers debated the role and importance of conventional military forces in helping states deter war and defend their interests.[192] Facing the strategic stalemate that these weapons produced, some theorists argued that the strategy for managing political struggles was to shift the discussion to conventional war. It was understood, however, that the prospect of defeat could instantly trigger the nuclear war that states initially sought to avoid and which would instantly destroy the grand strategy that animated the state's policies.[193]

As societies grappled with total war in the nuclear realm, classic approaches to strategy as a practical instrument of diplomacy were undermined by the consequences that failure would bring. No longer could scholars and policy makers take grand strategy in the nuclear age as a serious enterprise other than to deter war. Indeed, B. H. Liddell Hart argued in his 1950 *Defence of the West* that relying on nuclear weapons for one's strategy rested on the risky proposition that victory in *any* form could emerge as the outcome of a struggle between nuclear-armed antagonists.[194]

Recall that Liddell Hart's principal argument about strategy, articulated in the pre-nuclear age, rested on the proposition that "military victory is not in itself equivalent to gaining the object of war."[195] By this, he meant that attaining tactical or even operational victories would not necessarily produce successes for one's grand strategy. Raising the question of the costs and benefits of actions dictated by the state's grand strategy, Liddell Hart contended that for aggressors, a strategy based on the "pursuit of victory is likely to bring them more loss than gain" (177). These ideas regarding the limits on grand strategy are of interest particularly because they are so familiar to modern audiences.

Josef Stalin: Realist and Revolutionary

As the leader of the Soviet Union for more than two decades, including during World War II, Josef Stalin (1879–1953) is a critical example of a leader who articulated and implemented a grand strategy whose ideological roots were defined by such revolutionary theorists as Lenin and Trotsky, as examined earlier in the chapter. There is a debate within the scholarly community over the influence of Marxist-Leninist ideology on the formulation of Stalin's grand strategy after World War II.[196] Some scholars contend that Stalin's post–World War II grand strategy was geared toward advancing the spread of global communism, based largely on the principles articulated in Marxist-Leninist ideology.[197] Others, by contrast, contend that Stalin's grand strategy in the aftermath of World War II was based primarily on asserting and defending Russia's fundamental national interests.[198]

Stalin, however, was also a grand strategist of both the revolutionary and nuclear eras who pushed the Soviet Union to acquire nuclear weapons after World War II even when his people desperately needed the state to undertake a broad reconstruction of their economy. He prioritized the Soviet nuclear weapons program because he knew that the USSR could not compete as a superpower with the United States unless it also had nuclear weapons that it could use to counter American intimidation of Soviet client states and deter aggressive moves by Washington. Stalin anticipated the balance of terror that would arise once both superpowers possessed nuclear weapons, which would produce some semblance of stability in the dangerously hostile bipolar system. Thus, Stalin had two somewhat paradoxical aims in his grand strategy: to alter the status quo by spreading communist revolution, and to maintain the status quo by preventing the U.S. government from adopting a rollback strategy of Soviet influence.

Stalin as a Revolutionary Grand Strategist

For Stalin, the essential principle in Marxist ideology was to guide the state's strategy toward the destruction of the enemy's military forces, seize the sources of its economic power, and expand the popular base of one's ideology.[199] While the origins of Stalin's grand strategy remain open to analysis and debate, it is important to note that Stalin's desire to maintain Soviet power and influence was universally recognized as a central guiding principle in his grand strategy, regardless of which interpretation prevails.

One side of the debate contends that Stalin's foremost contribution was to advance the principle that the proper strategy for revolutionary movements and states was to promote communist revolutions overseas and expand the sphere of influence in the near abroad. In practice, the uniquely Marxist-Leninist grand strategy that emerged under Stalin's reign was more absolute, comprehensive, and ruthless than many in the West perhaps understood in the 1930s.[200] Just as states had responded in the nineteenth century to the territorial and military ambitions of Napoleon, for example, the Western democracies similarly were forced to articulate grand strategies to counterbalance the policies articulated by Stalin and the Soviet leadership during the Cold War.

For Marxist ideology, the fundamental political end of strategy in interstate struggles is to completely destroy the state's political, military, and economic means of power by mobilizing the people on the basis of the principle of class struggle. Both Lenin's and Stalin's strategy for internal revolutions called for destroying the fundamental political and economic organization of the state as the basis for overthrowing the ruling classes who oppressed the working classes. In contrast with Lenin's focus on guiding the state toward a domestic revolution in what would become a step in the progression toward a series of revolutions on an international scale, Stalin by the 1930s was concerned with the imperial expansion of Russian power and institutions as a natural extension of Marxist-Leninist ideology. In effect, Stalin and Lenin pursued strategies that were unified by similar ideological goals, but Stalin went beyond Lenin's theoretical foundations in order to defend and promote Russia's national interests in Eurasia.

Stalin's grand strategy of letting the capitalist states destroy themselves was well reasoned in terms of articulation but failed in implementation. Just as "Hitler's ideology blinded him to the potential strengths of the Soviet Union and the United States throughout the war," scholars argue that the same holds true for "Stalin's miscalculation in his grand strategy about the nature of Nazi Germany and the threat that it posed to the Soviet Union."[201] This failure of grand strategy "entirely resulted from an analysis based on Marxist ideology," wherein Stalin's decision to sign the Nazi-Soviet Non-Aggression Pact in August 1939 signaled his belief "that the capitalist world would fight itself to exhaustion, as had been the case in World War I, and leave the Soviet Union and its Red Army to pick up the pieces."[202]

In articulating Soviet grand strategy, Stalin's analysis of the capitalist world, whose strengths he grossly underestimated, constituted an error of dramatic proportions. This error, however, would continue for fifty years, and its ultimate consequences would be fulfilled in 1991 with the Soviet Union's collapse. From Stalin's worldview, which contributed to the view that the Soviet Union was "permanently (until ultimate victory) at war, or warlike peace, with capitalist societies," it was ideologically evident to him that "Truman and America were enemies by definition and conviction."[203] Such values had a profound effect on Stalin's grand strategy toward the West.

In ideological terms, Stalin's grand strategy derived entirely from the belief in the inevitable struggle that existed between socialist or communist and capitalist societies. As Stalin said, "The war is going on between two groups of capitalist states (the poor vs. the rich ones in terms of colonies, sources of raw materials, and so on) for a redivision of the world and for world domination!" Using language directly tied to principles central to Marxist-Leninist ideology, Stalin warned that "Hitler himself does not appreciate this fact nor does he wish to, but he is demolishing and undermining the capitalist system."[204] As Stalin's comments reveal, his grand strategy drew inspiration from Marxist-Leninist revolutionary principles, which defined the broad struggle against capitalism and contributed to the origins and overall hostility that defined the Cold War.

As with Lenin and Trotsky, Stalin's policies consistently adhered to the belief that systemic forces in capitalist economies would ultimately lead to their collapse and defeat. According to Stalin, the collapse of international capitalism was a philosophical and scientific necessity, as outlined in and governed by the laws of dialectical materialism.[205] In the aftermath of the 1917 revolution, Bolsheviks advanced the "belief that international capitalism, or imperialism, was a profoundly evil system [and] must be eradicated from the face of the globe by violence." When Stalin and the Soviet leadership accepted this principle, it profoundly influenced Russia's "grand strategy" because it "dictated that the country, in the words of Josef Stalin, serve as 'base for the overthrow of imperialism in all countries' or as a lever for the further disintegration of imperialism."[206] Stalin and other Soviet leaders held to this view of grand strategy with the degree of conviction and inevitability associated with immutable scientific laws.

The belief in the inherent flaws of capitalism had powerful consequences for the design and execution of Soviet grand strategy. From 1939 to 1941, "several of Stalin's closest aids ... spoke explicitly and assuredly of 'extending the frontiers of socialism' on the wings of the 'inevitable,' coming war." For this view, "war, deemed 'inevitable' by Marxist-Leninist ideology and often reiterated by Soviet spokespersons," provided the philosophical and practical justification for an expansionist and confrontational grand strategy. It became, in effect, "a self-fulfilling prophecy for the expansionist aims of the communist leadership." Such thinking was evident several years before the outbreak of World War II, when "Stalin predicted ominously: 'war will surely unleash revolution and put in question the very existence of capitalism in a number of countries, as was the case of the first imperialist war.'"[207]

For decades, the argument advanced by many scholars was that Marxist-Leninist ideology and its views on the inevitable triumph of international communism convinced Stalin that the forces of history were clearly on the side of the Soviet Union. As noted, this belief lent an air of scientific assurance to their revolutionary ideology and their grand strategy. In contrast with the "gangsters of Nazi Germany, who believed that history was working against them," a central principle in Soviet grand strategy was that "adventurism could be a sin against the prudence that their theory of historical change endorsed."[208]

Edward Luttwak wrote that only three conditions were required to ensure the rise of the Soviet Union: control of capital by the state, enthusiasm of the public, and peace. Thus, the key element of Soviet grand strategy was to avoid war, which would put at risk any gains that Marxist-Leninist ideology was likely to produce. More ominously, it would "interrupt the Soviet Union's steady ascent to the centrally planned millennium" and threaten "eventual worldwide political victory." In effect, Luttwak argues, Soviet leaders "followed a genuine peace policy, at least until 1939."[209] This conception of Soviet strategy led George Kennan to contend in his essay "The Sources of Soviet Conduct" that containment was the best long-term strategy for dealing with the Soviet Union.[210]

Stalin the Realist

The countervailing view among scholars is that Marxist-Leninist ideology played a less significant role in shaping Stalin's post–World War II grand strategy than might otherwise seem to be the case. Edward Luttwak expressed this argument when he noted, "The true successor of the Tsars was Stalin rather than Lenin, because during Lenin's tenure transnational communism remained the true ideology." The implication for Luttwak was that the "Russians and their power were supposed to serve the interests of worldwide communism." However, as Luttwak argues, it was "Stalin who turned the proposition right around by first establishing a clear priority for Soviet state interests over the world-wide revolutionary cause ('Socialism in one country'), and then going on to exploit for all they were worth the powerful loyalties that transnational communism could attract."[211] While the importance of Marxist-Leninist ideology to Stalin's grand strategy is considerable, the opposite argument is presented here, suggesting that the precise origins of Stalin's grand strategy are subject to debate and conjecture.

Recent Soviet documents reveal that Stalin's posture toward Hitler's Germany was not as entirely defensive in nature as historians have often portrayed. Nor was Stalin's behavior after World War II guided solely by the principle in Marxist-Leninist ideology of nonadventurism. Rather, the scholar Albert Weeks uses Soviet documents of the post–World War II era to describe a new "offensist" school, which he argues "presents fresh evidence that strongly indicates that Stalin all along was secretly plotting an offensive war of his own – above all against Germany but ultimately against all of 'capitalist-imperialist' Europe."[212] This research offers some evidence that Stalin, in formulating his grand strategy, arguably elevated nonideological, power-centric interpretations of Soviet national interests above global communism's ideological aspirations or principles more than is commonly believed.[213] During Stalin's rule, "fundamental national interests seemingly [caused] contradictions between *raison d'etat* and Moscow's official ideology." By implication, when Stalin and other Soviet leaders articulated their grand strategy, "ideology [was] relegated to secondary importance in favor of other, larger national considerations," and those considerations "do not neatly fit ideological dogmas."[214]

Evidence of Stalin's realpolitik grand strategy is particularly abundant when it comes to his views on the nuclear era. Stalin was arguably one of the first grand strategists to understand the full political import of the immense destructive power of nuclear weapons. When Truman first heard the details of the successful test of the first atomic bomb in Alamogordo, New Mexico, in July 1945, he had an upbeat and almost cheerful reaction. He saw the new weapons as a way to quickly end the war with Japan. It is clear from his memoirs that Truman understood that the atomic bomb would fundamentally alter the nature of international politics.[215] Scholars debate whether Truman's decision to drop the atomic bombs on Hiroshima (August 6, 1945) and Nagasaki (August 9, 1945) was motivated in part by a desire to intimidate the Soviets. The historical evidence is inconclusive, but what we do know is that Stalin interpreted the bombs that way and understood the signal, while Truman likely did as well.[216]

Thus, when Stalin's agents reported on the destruction of Hiroshima and Nagasaki, he moved immediately to accelerate the Soviet nuclear program. He had initiated it in October 1942 but kept it as a lower priority. Stalin's reasoning was prescient as he told Lavrenti Beria, his ruthless chief of military intelligence, "we should not allow any other country to have decisive superiority over us. Tell Comrade Kurchatov [head of the Soviet nuclear program] that he has to hurry with his parcel [i.e., the atomic bomb]. And ask him what our scientists need to accelerate work." Later, he told his scientists, "Hiroshima has shaken the world.... The balance has been broken. Build the bomb – it will remove the danger from us."[217]

Stalin had a sophisticated realist understanding of that "danger." It was not the danger of invasion or actual attack, because he was not worried that the United States would actually use an atomic bomb against the Soviets. Instead, his highest concern was that it would be used to coerce him in postwar negotiations by the threat of its use. Stalin grasped early on that the immense political power of atomic and later nuclear weapons was not in their use but in the credible threat of their use. Moreover, Stalin understood that grand strategy in the nuclear age rested on a secure second-strike capability. Consequently, even though the United States and its allies, the United Kingdom and Canada, had a monopoly on nuclear weapons technology, that monopoly was politically less valuable as long as they could not guarantee that a first strike would wipe out the Soviet Union's military capabilities to retaliate.

Indeed, Stalin's intelligence sources kept him well informed about the low inventory of the West's nuclear weapons stockpile. As of March 1947, when Truman announced the Truman Doctrine, the United States had no more than fourteen devices, which was grossly insufficient to launch a preventive war against Stalin's state.[218] In fact, the Pentagon had studied this scenario and concluded that even the destruction of seventy major Soviet cities would not result in a decisive first strike given the vast landmass and huge population reserves of the Soviet empire. Stalin knew this, which allowed him to articulate a policy of defiance. In the immediate postwar period, Soviet foreign policy became not less but more unwilling to compromise, in a calculated effort not to appear intimidated by the West's nuclear weapons.[219]

But Stalin also knew that he must have his own nuclear deterrent before the West's inventories grew.[220] So he turned production into a crash program under Beria in August 1945; it achieved its objective of a successful test by August 1949, several years before the Central Intelligence Agency thought it would acquire the technology.[221] The pace of the program was all the more extraordinary because most of the Soviet Union's economy and infrastructure were desperately rebuilding from the ruins of war. The CIA estimated that by 1950 the Soviet nuclear program was employing between 330,000 and 460,000 people, ranging from manual laborers in the Gulags to the most talented scientists in the country.[222]

One argument is that revolutionary ideology was a factor in Stalin's grand strategy pre-World War II. But the war itself and the advent of nuclear weapons appear to have altered Stalin's views on grand strategy. He realized that a new era of grand strategy was approaching even before it had arrived.[223] Yet ideology played little role in the direction of Stalin's postwar grand strategy. Stalin's strategy was to "let nothing get in the way of the enhancement of the country's military might and security," and thus he moved to commit "vast resources to the acquisition of his own A-bomb and to the subjugation of eastern and east-central Europe to the Kremlin."[224]

For historian Gabriel Gorodetsky, Stalin's basic attitude toward Marxism and Leninism was that "Stalin was little affected by sentiment or ideology in the pursuit of foreign policy." He concludes that Stalin's "statesmanship was rooted in Russia's tsarist legacy [which] responded to imperatives deep in its history." By this reasoning, "It is not surprising that in the execution of his foreign policy Machiavelli rather than Lenin was Stalin's idol."[225] To put matters more directly, the German scholar and historian Andreas Hillgruber rejected the idea that Stalin relied on Marxist-Leninist ideology alone to articulate and implement his grand strategy. Whereas Weeks notes that "Stalin never made decisions about 'grand policy' on the basis of Bolshevist revolutionary ideology,"[226] Hillgruber, by contrast, argues that Stalin "practiced above all a rationally calculated power politics [whose] aim was to expand . . . the Soviet empire by exploiting the war that began in 1939 among the 'imperialist' powers."[227] In practice, ideological concerns, which Hillgruber calls "Social revolutionary transformation in newly won territories," always were "subordinated to strategic security."[228] The implication is that ideology, while undoubtedly important, was not as decisive in the formulation and conduct of Soviet grand strategy as many in the West may have believed.

In studying Stalin's grand strategy, one must ask what ideas and principles shaped his priorities. Various scholars, including Colin Gray, argue that Stalin's priorities were "(1) the security of his personal power, (2) the security of his state, (3) distantly and with mixed emotions, [make] progress in the historical process of global Communisation."[229] But in studying the sources of influence on Soviet grand strategy during Stalin's reign, Luttwak discerns a "gradual discovery" under Stalin that "the Soviet Union was a state much more bureaucratic than socialist, devoted more to the policeman than to the worker, and more of a vehicle for Russian imperialism than for transnational socialism."[230] Luttwak is essentially arguing that Soviet grand strategy during Stalin's era was governed less by the desire to transform the world according to the principles of socialism and more by the desire to strengthen the power and influence of the Soviet Union.

There is persuasive evidence to support the argument that Stalin elevated Russian imperialism over ideology, while Marxist-Leninist beliefs were not as influential as more nationalistic concerns in the formulation and conduct of Stalin's grand strategy. As we have seen so far and although scholars debate his priorities, it is predictably difficult to evaluate the sources of influence on Stalin's grand strategy. This case highlights just how difficult it can be to discern the ideological and political foundations of a state's grand strategy. In effect, Soviet grand strategy derives directly from policies, defined in terms of both ideology and power politics, whose purpose was to defend Soviet revolutionary prerogatives while advancing Soviet national interests.

Henry Kissinger and Grand Strategy in the Nuclear Era

The German-born Henry Kissinger (1923–) served first as national security advisor and then as secretary of state during the Nixon and Ford administrations. In his *Nuclear Weapons and Foreign Policy* (1957), he articulated one of the basic principles that came to dominate strategy during the nuclear age: "nuclear stalemate can be taken to mean that victory in all-out war has become meaningless."[231]

As one of the principal architects of the postatomic strategy of limited war, Kissinger observed that the strategy for total victory severely restricted the state's ability to conduct its grand strategy.[232] The central problem for Kissinger was that the U.S. strategic doctrine governing the relationship between diplomacy and military matters "recognized few intermediate points between total war and total peace," principally because the prevailing strategy was "based on the necessity of total victory" in the ideological struggle between the United States and the Soviet Union.[233] The problem, as Kissinger argued, is that states need "a [strategy or] strategic doctrine which gives our diplomacy the greatest freedom of action."[234] As he noted, "[m]any familiar assumptions about war, diplomacy, and the nature of peace will need to be modified before we have developed a theory adequate to the perils and opportunities of the nuclear age."[235]

With the development of nuclear weapons, Kissinger argued that strategists, policy makers, and military officials – such as General Douglas MacArthur, who wanted to rain atomic bombs on China in retaliation for its direct involvement in the Korean War – denied "the existence of any middle ground between stalemate and total victory" (34). He thereby rejected the dominant principle in U.S. strategy, which held that the state's objective is to "break the enemy's will to resist and its reliance on the decisive role of industrial potential" (104). For this strategist, the prevailing American strategic doctrine since World War I rested on possessing "forces-in-being at the beginning of a war [that] need only be large enough to avoid disaster" because "mobilizing our industrial potential [would crush the enemy] after the outbreak of hostilities" (107). To use the terminology of this study, Kissinger believed that the obsession with a grand strategy that rested on the premise of mobilizing for total victory against a nuclear-armed opponent would extinguish the state's ability to balance political ends and military means. His argument was that the state should develop a range of responses, depending on the scale of the threat from the enemy, that can be used to achieve the ends in its military strategy. In effect, strategists such as Kissinger are arguing in defense of a grand strategy that encourages policy makers to think and operate with greater flexibility.

Setting the Stage in the Cold War Era

The U.S. experience with grand strategy in World War II, while highly successful, was in desperate need of greater refinement if it was to provide useful guidance for managing geopolitical tensions during the Cold War. Although strategic hostility between the United States and the Soviet Union lasted more than forty years, neither state directly fought the other. While we might conclude that the countervailing orthodoxies about grand strategy were static during a condition of relative peace, the opposite was the case. In fact, the Cold War was a time of great strategic and intellectual ferment as policy makers and scholars wrestled with how to conduct grand strategy at a time when states were armed with nuclear weapons.

The Cold War began shortly after the end of World War II and by the late 1940s with the emergence of the Truman Doctrine was a period marked by intense strategic hostility and ideological competition between the United States and the Soviet Union.[236] It was increasingly understood by the late 1940s, and certainly by the early 1950s, that the combination of nuclear weapons and the ideological struggle between democratic and totalitarian states had effectively destroyed the conceptual foundations of strategy, which had been reified by the success of World War II as the fundamental doctrine governing how states conduct politics and war.[237]

During the Cold War, the U.S. experience with strategy pointed to a historically unique and unfamiliar problem for U.S. policy makers: there are few, if any, circumstances in which the United States would risk nuclear war with the Soviet Union.[238] The Korean War was the first conflict during the Cold War to demonstrate why nuclear weapons impose demonstrable limits on strategy. As these and other events slowly but predictably eroded the post–World War II and modern conception of strategy, scholars and policy makers drew the obvious conclusion: there was no rational or practical strategy for using nuclear weapons that did not lead ultimately to annihilation.[239] For the first time in history, it dawned on the post–World War II generation of strategists and policy makers that a new form of weaponry – both fission-based atomic bombs, such as those used on Japan, and the later fusion-based (i.e., thermonuclear) hydrogen bombs – totally undermined the theory and practice of strategy. While other strategies for employing nuclear weapons were developed, the logic of nuclear devastation was not altered.[240]

During the climate of the Cold War, the only rational "strategy" for nuclear weapons was to deter war and preserve peace, but certainly not to fight to win.[241] This logic was evident to President Eisenhower, who observed that with nuclear weapons "there is no alternative to peace."[242] By the late 1950s and early 1960s, the consensus in the U.S. government was that the objectives of deterrence, punishment, and limited wars were more rational than any competing strategy based on direct confrontation among nuclear-armed states. Even if started indirectly by a conflict between allies of such states, the result still would be mutual suicide. Central to Kissinger's work, therefore, is his recognition of the importance and difficulty of controlling escalation in crises, despite the tendency for nuclear-armed states to avert being drawn into a full-scale nuclear war (176–177). He argued that it is imperative for leaders to "understand that total victory is no longer possible" (143) given that any strategy that "search[es] for absolute victory ... paralyzes by the vastness of its consequences" (196).

Kissinger and the 1973 Yom Kippur War

Kissinger's approach to grand strategy in the nuclear era was evident in his handling of the Yom Kippur War. On Saturday, October 6, 1973, Egypt and Syria launched a surprise attack on Israel that was timed to catch the Israelis off guard – when many of their military personnel were on leave for the holiest day of the Jewish calendar, Yom Kippur, the Day of Atonement. In the initial stages, Egyptian and Syrian forces rapidly advanced deep into Israeli-held territory. Egypt captured the famed Bar-Lev Line in the Sinai, while Syrian forces rolled deep into the Golan Heights to the north.[243]

Kissinger saw the crisis as an opportunity and a threat. It was an opportunity to drive the parties toward negotiation if he could engineer a military stalemate. At the same time, it posed a significant threat to his policy of détente and building stable relations with the Soviets. In viewing the 1973 War through the lens of grand strategy during the Cold War, Kissinger's overriding objective was to avoid turning a regional military crisis into a nuclear confrontation with the Soviets. Thus, he and President Nixon took steps to help the Israelis recover military momentum, and then to launch a counteroffensive, principally by sending a shipment of arms to Israel at a crucial time in the fighting.[244] Yet once Israel had regained the initiative, he moved quickly through several rounds of shuttle diplomacy between Jerusalem, Cairo, and Damascus to broker cease-fires and finalize military disengagement agreements.[245] Kissinger implemented ideas about grand strategy that he had articulated in his writings and speeches. Specifically, he moved to prevent a total, one-sided victory by either side, and he used diplomatic steps to prevent the escalation of the war into a nuclear confrontation between the Cold War superpowers.

Concluding Observations on the Nuclear Era of Grand Strategy

Beyond the powerful influence that nuclear weapons exerted on grand strategy during the Cold War, the conduct and eventual outcome of the Cold War highlights several critical conclusions about the U.S. experience with strategy.

The first is that if a viable objective of war and military intervention is to ensure that the state's fundamental political and economic *ideas* prevail over those of another, then the outcome of the Cold War can be interpreted as a success for American grand strategy –

particularly because conflict between Washington and Moscow was averted.[246] With the Soviet Union's political and economic collapse, the prevailing ideas promoted by the United States and its allies about the value of democratic values and free markets were legitimized. The winning strategy in this case led to the establishment of democratic governments, the development of free-market economies, and the emergence of foreign policies on the part of Russia and other former Soviet republics that were generally less hostile to the United States – at least until the recent resurgence of hostility between Moscow and Washington.

A second conclusion is that the conduct of grand strategy during the Cold War involved far more than military confrontation with the Soviet Union. Because nuclear weapons deterred conflict between Washington and Moscow, this case represents an important historical anomaly: this is a rare example in which a grand strategy was not (and could not be) the result of military victories on the battlefield. Neither is it clear whether the proxy wars contributed decisively to the success or failure of grand strategy.

Third, the nuclear era of grand strategy made possible the revolutionary era of grand strategy. The revolutionary grand strategies of rebel groups rested on the premise of protracted war. Nuclear weapons made protracted struggles possible because nuclear annihilation was the likely outcome of direct military confrontation between the two superpowers. In the proxy wars, there were severe constraints placed on the state's strategy: a proxy could not be defeated entirely without raising the risk of "catalytic nuclear war" to intolerable levels.[247] The argument here is that the Cold War combined two interacting and overlapping eras – those of nuclear weapons and revolutions – in the conduct of grand strategy.

Conclusion to Part I

Part I presents several key points worth summarizing here. First, grand strategy has two basic dimensions – articulation and implementation. The articulation phase emphasizes the theory of grand strategy: how to think about it in contrast to strategy (the use of military force) and to distinguish it from doctrine, operations, policy, and logistics. The process of articulation occurs continuously over the war-and-peace continuum. The reason is that grand strategy had to be reassessed and revised precisely because threats and opportunities in international politics are in a constant state of flux. By contrast, implementation is no less important because it involves both marshaling all instruments of national power and balancing those instruments (means) with the political ends articulated in the state's grand strategy. These principles have operated throughout the four eras of grand strategy defined in this study – the ancient, modern, revolutionary, and nuclear eras.

These four eras, explored in Chapters 4, 5, and 6, mark the major periods in the evolution of grand strategy from the writings of Sun Tzu until the twentieth century. In general, the articulation and implementation of grand strategy has become much more complex and multidimensional as the state has become more complex in terms of its bureaucratic structure and the types of power at its command. In effect, both the means and the ends of grand strategy have evolved to become more multifaceted and intricate. This is a central reason why grand strategy today is so much more difficult than it was in ancient times: the variety, intensity, and interactive complexity of the means and ends have evolved to a remarkable level.

For ancient theorists, the central purpose of grand strategy was measured by the ability of the state to successfully conquer territory. Until the 1500s, strategists emphasized the conditions necessary to defeat armies in the field. With the rise of the industrial age and its emphasis on mechanized warfare, however, societies mobilized their total economic and industrial resources to accumulate the costly tactical victories that would be necessary to achieve the objectives outlined in their grand strategy. The objective was to win a "complete victory" and permanently vanquish their enemy rather than waste their resources on lesser endeavors.[248]

The prevailing concept of grand strategy in the early nineteenth century, which called for the state to wage total war, was based on the idea of organizing the state by mobilizing its people, military, and economy. We see the beginnings of the shift to a modern approach to grand strategy in the writings of Clausewitz. This thinker, who was the first to distinguish explicitly between the military means and political ends of war, marked the turning point in the evolution of the field that we now know as grand strategy.[249]

In the modern era, the function of grand strategy was to organize the state for waging the total wars that would come to dominate policy during the twentieth century. For many prominent strategists, Germany's defeat in the world wars reinforced the belief that grand strategy had to reflect far more than organizing for total war, if the state were to achieve its political ends – which is, after all, the central function of grand strategy. In the nuclear era, the development of weapons that could make military victory meaningless had a profound effect on shaping the grand strategies of the major antagonists in the Cold War. Grand strategy shifted from winning war to avoiding war. Concurrent with the nuclear era was the development of the revolutionary era of grand strategy, where conventionally weaker actors leveraged political power to defeat militarily stronger adversaries.

These four eras bring this study to the era of the Cold War, which lasted from the late 1940s to early 1990s and encompassed the overlapping eras of the influences of revolutions and nuclear weapons on grand strategy. Throughout this period, U.S. grand strategy rested on containing the spread of revolutionary communism along with its political and military influence and power.[250] Containment as the American grand strategy during the Cold War depended upon nuclear weapons, while massive military establishments deterred "hot" war between Washington and Moscow. For more than forty years, both states were divided by a deep ideological and geographical chasm with regard to the nature of political and economic freedom and state power. The two states, in occupying center stage in international politics, were the architects of a global bipolar order whose hallmarks were geopolitical confrontation and ideological hostility. During the latter half of the twentieth century, Washington and Moscow maintained that international order and avoided direct confrontation by building trust through a combination of deterrence and effective diplomacy with sustained contact.

Containment, as articulated by George F. Kennan, emerged from the prevailing conditions at the end of World War II to represent an evolutionary, and perhaps radical, departure for U.S. grand strategy. In response to geopolitical competition, ideological hostility, and the division of Europe after World War II, the United States was transformed from a historically detached state to its current position as the most significant actor on the world stage. One corollary of the global responsibilities inherent in containment, which persists to this day, is the lasting expectation – both in domestic and international circles – of U.S. policy makers and the public that America is obligated to play a central role in resolving the world's fundamental problems. Now, however, as we face far more complex, potentially dangerous, and largely unfamiliar problems, this logic is somewhat less compelling.

The next series of chapters in Part II examines the historical foundations of American grand strategy. Beginning with the administration of George Washington and concluding with the administration of Barack Obama, the purpose of Chapters 7 through 10 is to outline in detail the enduring themes that have dominated the development of the nation's grand strategy. While we do not study all forty-four administrations, these chapters focus on the most important administrations by virtue of their contributions to how policy makers over the span of two centuries have balanced the domestic and foreign elements of grand strategy. What emerges is a pattern, evolved over the two centuries, of grand strategies that range from building the domestic foundations of national power to dealing with foreign threats and finally to requiring grand strategies practiced jointly among allies. The evolution of American grand strategy will reveal that the most effective administrations are those that articulated and implemented a grand strategy tailored to their era and its most pressing national security problems.

Introduction to Part II

Part I concerns the evolution of grand strategy as a concept for organizing the foreign policies of states in Europe and Asia, whereas Part II shifts to the separate but closely related evolution of American grand strategy. American grand strategy, beginning in the eighteenth century, has developed across the modern, revolutionary, and nuclear eras of grand strategy. The history of the United States is no less a part of world history than are the histories of the states discussed in previous sections. But its geography, political culture, and history have given it distinctive features, which have, in turn, shaped the evolution of its grand strategy. These features of American history have created what some refer to as the exceptionalism of its grand strategy and foreign policy, which is reflected in three long-term and deep-seated traditions in U.S. foreign policy.

But first, what is American exceptionalism and how does it relate to grand strategy? It would be helpful to discuss the concept of exceptionalism and its evolving role in American history before moving on to its application to American grand strategy.[251] Exceptionalism, according to the Merriam-Webster Dictionary, is defined simply as "the condition of being different from the norm." To elaborate further, one of the foremost thinkers on this subject, Ian Tyrell, refers to American exceptionalism in the classical sense as "the special character of the United States as a uniquely free nation based on democratic ideals and personal liberty."[252] Exceptionalism when applied to a region or nation is inherently synonymous with a sense of nationalism, which all states across the world espouse to a certain degree through a sense of loyalty, devotion, and pride. Indeed, the exceptionalist tradition is notable for its propensity to concentrate on national differences, while "American exceptionalism presents a special case of the more general problem of history written from a national point of view."[253] That being said, it is a concept often evoked by policy makers in order to gain popularity in electoral campaigns or to amass domestic support for a specific policy or initiative abroad. Despite the fact that all nations promote an element of exceptionalism, America has consistently and prominently featured this concept throughout its history.

Exceptionalism has been a part of the country's narrative from the settlement days of John Winthrop's shining city on a hill to westward expansion and the great frontier. American presidents over the course of the nation's history have deemed America to be exceptional and have never wavered in sharing its values with the world. Therefore, before applying the idea of exceptionalism to the evolution of American grand strategy, readers must understand that American exceptionalism as a concept has a long and storied history in the nation's narrative. And it remains one that continues to gain domestic support when policy makers propose to take certain actions (or refrain from action) in international affairs. Furthermore, the concept of exceptionalism is deeply ingrained within the American national identity, expressing in a visceral sense how many Americans – and policy makers – view the country's global leadership role. As discussed in this book, it is possible to use this lens to view the rise of the United States in fundamentally different terms than that of other great powers.

The theme of exceptionalism in the evolution of American grand strategy emerges in each of the four eras developed in Part I. The exceptional aspect of American grand strategy in the modern era is that the United States was free to build the domestic foundations of national power in a geopolitical context that was relatively free from interference by enemies and external threats. Early in its history, the United States focused almost exclusively on building its territorial, economic, military, and political foundations of national power, with relatively little concern for land or naval invasion. This is truly unlike the historical experiences of modern European nation-states in the development of their grand strategies. The British experience comes closest to lacking a constant threat on its borders, but even in this case the threat of a cross-channel invasion haunted the British official mind and was the driving concern for its grand strategy, which focused on offshore balancing and naval supremacy, as elucidated on the case study in Chapter 5 on the British Empire. Thus, there is this strong tradition in American grand strategy of building the foundations of its national power without foreign interference or entangling alliances abroad. This will be covered in more detail in Chapter 7, which covers the evolution of grand strategy from the administrations of George Washington to Abraham Lincoln.

The second exceptional aspect of American grand strategy emerges in the revolutionary era in the late nineteenth and early twentieth centuries. As discussed in Chapter 8, America has a strong tradition of acting as a status quo power in the conduct of its foreign policy. This might seem paradoxical given its origins in a revolution against a colonial power, but it is nonetheless consistently evident in American foreign policy. The nation's grand strategy, for the most part, has never sought aggressively to transform the international system radically and rapidly. There has never been a Napoleon or Hitler who mobilized the American state and society as part of a strategy to make a bold bid for hegemonic power. Hegemony is not something the United States necessarily sought, but rather was something it accepted, almost reluctantly. This too is unlike the history of grand strategy as a whole. In the cases of Philip II, Frederick the Great, Napoleon, Bismarck, and the British Empire, grand strategy rested on promoting the idea of seeking and keeping hegemony.

From Theodore Roosevelt to Franklin Delano Roosevelt, what defines American grand strategy is the remarkable lack of disruption caused by America's rise to power. Indeed, as we will see in Chapter 8, from Theodore Roosevelt to Franklin Roosevelt there was a consistent effort to restrain the forces of disorder and disruptive revolution in the system. These revolutionary forces included communists, to be sure, but also anarchists, fascists, and even socialists. Indeed, as the elements of free markets and capitalism became more deeply engrained in America, the maintenance of peace, and the promotion of democracy and free trade, also became critical means for promoting American interests.

In the evolution of grand strategy, a rising power adopts a grand strategy that the current power perceives as threatening. War ensues as the two states battle for hegemony in the system. This is Thucydides's argument in which the fear of a rising power is unavoidably destabilizing in an anarchic system. But America never chose a grand strategy based on the path of a disruptive, rapid rise.[254] There is a powerful status quo bias within American foreign policy because its institutions, political culture, and people generally eschewed transformative agendas and adhered to making modest changes to the global political and economic system.

Finally, the history of American grand strategy in the nuclear era is marked by the exceptional attributes of alliance and partnership. The United States never unilaterally leveraged its advantage in nuclear weapons technology to coerce other states and transform the system. This is closely related to the second principle of restraining the forces of disorder and disruption, but it is distinct. It is distinct because nowhere in the annals of grand strategy has a state possessed an overwhelming military technological advantage that it did not exploit to its furthest extent. Whereas America did drop two atomic bombs, the United States did not exploit its military advantage against the Soviet Union. American grand strategy in the nuclear era was never a grand strategy of unilateralism. Instead, what developed in the Cold War was the principle in grand strategy of reinforcing alliances and partnerships to make nuclear weapons a technology for peace or at least for deterring war. Some might argue that this is not evidence of American exceptionalism because, as discussed in Chapter 6 on the nuclear era of grand strategy, all states with nuclear weapons have used them as deterrence technologies, not as offensive technologies. While this is true generally for the nuclear era, in the initial phase of this period, from 1945 to 1949, the United States had a monopoly on the possession and use of nuclear weapons.

In short, American grand strategy has evolved in exceptional ways against the backdrop of the larger, contextual evolution of grand strategy. With the evolution of American grand strategy, it has developed three enduring principles: (1) building the domestic foundations of national power; (2) the exercise of leadership to restrain the forces of disorder and disruption; and (3) reinforcing alliances and partnerships to address mutual threats and challenges. Each presidential administration discussed in the following chapters contributed in different respects to each of these three principles. Furthermore, each has strived to build on these principles using resources and tools to match the circumstances of the moment. But simply having the right principles is only part of the equation. Many periods throughout American history can be characterized by an overemphasis on the domestic or foreign arenas of statecraft, though administrations at the time saw the effectiveness of their grand strategy wane as a result. As most observers would expect, a society and its policy makers must carefully balance how they put those principles into practice. This is a struggle the following administrations undertook while attempting to build a world based on peace and security, while guided by the consent of the people.

We now turn to the first of these principles: the building of the domestic foundations of national power. The presidential administrations discussed in upcoming chapters were selected on the basis of their contributions to the three principles in grand strategy. Left out are the presidents who accomplished little in terms of articulation or implementation. James Buchanan, for instance, was known for letting the slavery issue fester and failing to create a political process for its gradual elimination. Herbert Hoover instituted shortsighted economic policies that worsened the Great Depression, and Gerald Ford merely served as a transitional caretaker as the nation recovered from the travails of Watergate. These were not consequential presidencies in the study of grand strategy, because they were instead consumed with short-term and narrow interests rather than broad matters that affect the long-term security and prosperity of the nation.

Finally, there is a constant tension between how the nation articulates and implements its grand strategy. Throughout these case studies, the reader will find references to the principles of the articulation-implementation framework that was introduced in Chapter 3 and is applied throughout Part I. This framework is still important for understanding the broad evolution of American grand strategy, but the goal here is less to elucidate grand strategy as a concept and more to show the unique contours and patterns of the history of America's grand strategy. It is about identifying the intellectual, political, and economic traditions in American foreign policy rather than about critiquing the process by which a given presidential administration went about articulating and then implementing the grand strategy for guiding the nation's foreign policy.

PART II

Makers of American Grand Strategy

7   Building Domestic Foundations of American Power: Washington to Lincoln

This chapter examines American grand strategy from the nation's founding to the Civil War. It illustrates how policies centered on building the domestic foundations of national power developed along three axes. First, America's power grew throughout the nineteenth century due to a period of dramatic territorial expansion. Second, the federal government grew in its political power over the separate states to create a much more centralized yet still federalist system; it also built a modern, professional military in this period and created the capability of projecting power globally beyond its borders and its hemisphere. Third, the economic basis of American power grew tremendously in this period as the nation shifted from being primarily an agrarian economy to a modern, industrial economy. This chapter also examines the slavery issue through the lens of grand strategy. It was a fundamental domestic constraint that all of America's leaders faced as they articulated and implemented the nation's first grand strategies. Territorial expansion eventually disrupted the balance of power between slave and free states, to the point at which the Union could not hold, and a bloody civil war ensued.

The First Principle: Building Domestic Foundations of National Power

The first principle of American grand strategy is to build the domestic foundations of national power. This is the focus of this chapter, which covers the administrations of George Washington through Abraham Lincoln. To the three types of domestic power – political, military, and economic – discussed in Chapter 4, we now add a fourth, territory, which is the basic necessity for the building of the other three foundations of power.

The political foundation of national power in the history of American grand strategy involves the establishment of internal security through a stable system of democratic government. This means that the federal government had to be strong enough to coerce states and individuals when necessary, while remaining consistent with the Hobbesian concept of a Leviathan, as discussed in Chapter 4. And yet it also meant that the government's strength must rest on the consent of the governed, echoing the liberal social contract theory of the political thinkers Locke and Kant. Recall that Hobbes, Locke, and Kant developed the modern theory of the social contract that exists between society and the state. It is the concept of the social contract, as its terms and meaning evolved in the modern era, that provides the political basis for the development of modern nation-states and their ability to articulate and implement grand strategy. Grand strategy in the modern era, as discussed in Chapter 4, now rests increasingly – some might say definitively – on the consent of the governed. It is that consent that allows the state to mobilize the resources of society, and it is emblematic of the historical shift from states that fought with mercenaries in the ancient era to states that mobilize and fight together with their citizens. The latter became the standard for the conduct of grand strategy, despite the persistence of authoritarian regimes on a global scale.

The military foundations of the modern era were rooted in the development of a modern, professional military institution that is directed and controlled by the political leaders of that state. This development flows from Clausewitz's fundamental idea of modern grand strategy in which the ends of grand strategy are fundamentally driven by political rather than military objectives. Grand strategy ultimately seeks to accomplish the highest political ends, whereas achieving solely or even largely military ends is always subordinated to the political. The military ends can be used rationally only as an instrument for achieving the ends designated by politics. In the evolution of American grand strategy, presidents consistently sought to professionalize and depoliticize the military to affirm that it is an instrument or means for achieving political ends. The American military foundation of power was never an end in itself and always secondary to grand strategy, and thus remains subject to the dictates of civilian control.

Finally, the economic foundations of national power are based on the idea of the state creating the conditions for an economic system, which establishes the technological and financial innovations that permit the state to fund and supply wars. Friedrich List, for instance, emphasized the importance for modern states to have railroads so that they could move troops and supplies. The transportation network was important for the economy and also essential for the state to be able to compete militarily in great power clashes. Moreover, in terms of the development and evolution of grand strategy, the economic foundations of national power became important in the modern era not only for its value in funding military capabilities but also because it was a source of national power in and of itself. The economic thinkers, Hamilton and Smith in particular, saw capitalism as the best system for creating this source of national power that in turn fueled the state's grand strategy.

What is exceptional about American grand strategy in this era is that it benefited from the fact that the nation had the time and space to concentrate on developing the three foundations of domestic power without significant or dramatic interference from foreign powers, principally those in Europe. Unlike the experiences that shaped the development of European states, the United States was not plagued with the constant competitive pressures from threats of invasion as well as political subversion by subnational groups that could have weakened its ability to build the foundations of power. This "splendid isolation" was a product of the nation's geographic distance from Europe and of the ocean barriers on both sides of the American territory that kept the United States isolated from European politics.[1] But it was also the result of a far-reaching precedent in grand strategy – established by President Washington and continued until World War I – of staying detached from the turmoil and war that routinely engulfed European politics. And so we turn to America's first president, George Washington, to understand how his administration shaped the fundamental characteristics of grand strategy that endure to the present.

George Washington – Setting Enduring Policy Precedents

As the first president of the new republic, George Washington (1789–1797) set the policy precedents for building the domestic foundations of American power that continue today.[2] Washington established the broad conceptual and policy overtones that would guide American grand strategy for more than two centuries.[3]

Washington's grand strategy balanced three complementary initiatives: enhancing the powers of the federal government, ensuring American neutrality during a period of revolutions and wars in Europe, and expanding control of what became the territory of the United States. All of these priorities were designed to ensure that the U.S. government had the authority, time, and resources to engage in the process of political, economic, and social development. Washington, however, chose to leave the divisive issue of slavery unresolved in order to preserve the fragile unity of the new nation. This decision bought the nation precious time to strengthen itself enough to confront the issue and survive the resulting political conflict that engulfed and nearly wrecked the nation during the Civil War.

Enhancing the Federal Government's Power

The central problem facing the country from 1781 to 1789 was that the Articles of Confederation, which vested all meaningful powers in the thirteen states, left the federal government without the ability to raise revenue, regulate commerce, or conduct foreign policy. Without these powers, the states were a loose confederation of likeminded mini-states, and the U.S. government existed in theory but not in practice. This was a problem of the highest order for the nation's grand strategy because each state was weak individually. (As proven in the War of Independence, however, when united they can become truly formidable.)

Political Foundations

There remained a fundamental tension in the early American republic: the effective executive power that was "politically essential for a viable American nation was ideologically at odds with what it claimed to stand for." As the scholar Ellis continues, "Washington believed that America's hard-won independence would be short-lived unless the 'United States' became a singular rather than a plural term." His argument related to one of his other grand strategic priorities – avoiding foreign interference and entanglements. "A mere confederation of states would become ... 'the dupes of some [foreign] powers and, most assuredly [gain] the contempt of all.'"[4]

Similar fears shared by other Founding Fathers led them to call for the Constitutional Convention. Washington was initially reluctant to participate, but his strong Federalist leanings persuaded him to accept the unanimous vote electing him president of the 1787 Philadelphia convention. One lesson that Washington learned while "commanding the Continental Army [was that] American independence, if it were to endure, required a federal government capable of coercing the states to behave responsibly."

It was at the Constitutional Convention that Washington took great care over his ceremonial and impartial role as head of state. Renouncing local and regional ties, as scholar Don Higginbotham states, "Washington knew he must remain above divisive issues in Congress, and he must eschew affiliation with any faction or party and avoid emphasizing his membership in Freemasonry and the Society of the Cincinnati since both were controversial in some quarters, especially the Cincinnati."[5] Furthermore, Washington knew that this impartiality was crucial to getting the American people to identify with America as a nation and persuade states to recognize national authority.

In his 1796 farewell address, Washington expressed this view when he affirmed his belief "that the centralizing impulses of the American Revolution were not violations but fulfillments of its original ethos." He defended the need for a stronger central government: "I am decided in my opinion that if the powers of Congress are not enlarged, and made competent to all *general purposes*, that the Blood which has been spilt, the expence that has been incurred, and the distresses which have been felt, *will avail in nothing*; and that the band, already too weak, which holds us together, will soon be broken; *when anarchy and confusion must prevail.*"[6]

For the conduct of both domestic and foreign policy, Washington believed that "both individual citizens and sovereign states often required coercion to behave responsibly." To continue this argument, Washington worried that the Articles of Confederation could lead to a debilitating system of near-anarchy. Without an overarching, central, and sovereign authority as articulated by Thomas Hobbes that could establish security and stability between individuals and the various states, the system would degenerate into chaos and anarchy. Furthermore, the government needed to expand its power to tax and establish decisive "control over fiscal policy." If the United States did not possess these powers, "Washington believed that 'the Confederation appears to me to be little more than an empty sound, and Congress a nugatory body which, in their current weak condition could only give the vital stab to public credit.'"[7]

The problems of governance in the immediate aftermath of the revolution remained a significant impediment to articulating and implementing effective policies. Although the nation "encompass[ed] a domain that was gigantic by European standards, the Confederation lacked a strong central authority and was a military dwarf." As scholars note, "The states refused to yield any of their sovereignty to the central government, and in particular refused to grant it the right to tax."[8] As American political culture slowly took shape, the forces of "parochialism and ideological distrust of centralized power [began to decisively] shape [American] strategic culture." These forces were detrimental to establishing an effective grand strategy, because they "undermined military preparedness at the federal level by prohibiting large standing forces and organized military planning." As the scholar Williamson Murray writes, the forces of "limited coercive powers, a reluctance to deprive citizens of their property via taxation, and a concern for the voters' approbation" all severely weakened the government's ability to mobilize resources."

Scholars argue that Washington was convinced that the "strategic stakes" in building the nascent American nation were "huge, stretching geographically across a continent and chronologically across the next century."[9] The problem, as Murray continues, was that the necessary coordination could only be "achieved by a federal government fully empowered to harness and manage the enormous energies and resources entailed in such a large-scale imperial project."[10] By moving first to build a strong central government, Washington helped establish the domestic institutional foundations of national power on which his and subsequent grand strategies would rest.

Beyond lacking a central governmental authority, the United States also lacked the social and political coherence necessary to become a powerful nation. As Ellis notes, "there was no such thing as a viable American nation when [Washington] took office as president." Even more seriously, "the opening words of the Constitution ('We the people of the United States') expressed a fervent but futile hope rather than a social reality." In this political climate, Washington likely saw the "American Revolution as a moment to establish both American independence *and* American nationhood," but he "did not believe you could have one without the other." In contrast with taking central government control away from Great Britain, this scholar argues that Washington feared, "not ... excessive federal power reminiscent of Parliament's arbitrary and imperial policies, but ... a weak confederation reminiscent of the Constitutional Congress's woefully inadequate performance during the war."[11] Washington understood that the first necessity for building the foundations of American power was having a central government strong enough to articulate and implement policies that could create a stable political system, a growing economy, and a strong military.

Economic Foundations

Several states had accumulated considerable public debt, both before and during the Revolution. Borrowing additional funds from international creditors, if there were another war with a European power and without a federal guarantee to repay further loans, would lead to unbearable interest rates that could seriously weaken the nation in its infancy. Secretary of the Treasury Alexander Hamilton's efforts to consolidate the collective debt of the states helped put the nation on a path to solvency. As historian James MacGregor Burns notes, "Hamilton's Report on Public Credit, presented to Congress in January 1790, was a typically bold initiative" in which he called for "a plan to establish the sound credit of the country as well as provide a source of capital for significant industrial projects."[12]

Hamilton's strategy was "for the new federal government to assume the nation's revolutionary foreign debt, domestic debt, and also the states' debts, totaling well over $70 million." For Washington, writes Burns, the obvious benefit of Hamilton's economic policy was to "chart a path" that would allow Washington to achieve his "goal of national cohesion and strength." Hamilton saw the connection between avoiding war and attaining financial stability: "'If we can avoid War for ten or twelve years more,' [Hamilton] wrote, 'we shall then have acquired a maturity, which ... will authorize us [to make] national decisions [on a] higher & more *imposing* tone.'" As the historian Burns notes, this economic strategy established the "groundwork for American military ascension."[13] In effect, the first steps for Washington and Hamilton for building the foundations of American grand strategy were based on establishing the government's creditworthiness while avoiding the expensive wars with stronger powers that would weaken the nation.

Military Foundations

Another challenge facing the United States under Washington's leadership was the Continental Army, which, despite its recent victory over the British, was a small force that had a doubtful ability to wage and credibly fight another war with a major European power. Scholars have observed that Washington believed that "security, stability, order – the nation's ability to survive, that is, its very *life* – constituted the supreme value" upon which all elements of national power and influence rested.

The broad argument was that the "other high principles [found in the Constitution and the Bill of Rights] could not be established and expanded except in an environment free from fear and tumult."[14] Washington believed this environment "free from fear and tumult" could only be established with a standing federal army. His experience commanding the Continental Army taught him that militias were useful as supplementary units but were no substitute for a professional, well-trained, and reliable corps of troops. During the Revolutionary War, he told Congress that he needed troops who would serve the length of the conflict, not "[m]en just dragged from the tender Scenes of domestick life, unaccustomed to the din of arms." He found these recruits difficult to discipline and bad for the morale of the regulars.[15]

Thus, Washington and Alexander Hamilton were squarely on the side of having a strong federal military. This was the Federalist position. Jeffersonian Democrat-Republicans, however, were suspicious of a central government that possessed a standing army, which they thought could be used to threaten state sovereignty and limit the liberty of their citizens. At the Constitutional Convention in 1787, Elbridge Gerry proposed that no standing army be larger than three thousand troops. Washington reportedly submitted a sarcastic counter-motion that no foreign country would invade the United States with more than three thousand troops. The Federalists won the argument in the end, and the Constitution authorized the federal government to raise and maintain a standing army to deal with enemies, both foreign and domestic.[16] But Democrat-Republicans in the new Congress continued to resist implementation; in the early 1790s, the standing army was very small, numbering only 500 men.[17]

Yet there were two insurrections against the federal government that bolstered the Federalist argument that a standing army was needed to maintain order. The first was Shays' Rebellion in western Massachusetts, 1786 to 1787, a tax revolt in which American farmers protested against state and local tax collections. Driven by poor harvests, high taxes, and an economic downturn, its leader was Daniel Shays, an officer from Massachusetts in the Continental Army. State militias easily suppressed it, but it was used as evidence in the constitutional debates mentioned earlier to highlight the necessity of an effective military.[18]

The second insurrection was the Whiskey Rebellion, 1791 to 1794. Washington's leadership illustrates the importance he attached to the military foundation of American power. At the beginning of the rebellion by whiskey distillers who refused to pay taxes on their wares, the national army was too small to restore order in western Pennsylvania and parts of Kentucky.[19] Unlike Shays' Rebellion, this insurrection was seen within the context of the revolutionary "disorder" sweeping across France. The rebels were setting up mock guillotines, waving their own flag, establishing their own courts, and talking of marching on the state capital of Pittsburgh to seize arms.[20] After trying to solve the problem with negotiations, Washington invoked the Militia Act of 1792 to mobilize men from the states. The army of 15,000 that he called up from the states of New Jersey, Pennsylvania, Maryland, and Virginia was larger than any he commanded during the Revolutionary War, and it was much larger than it needed to be for the actual suppression of the whiskey tax rebels. Washington, however, wanted to show the world that the new U.S. government was capable of wielding significant military power.[21] He led them in putting down the rebellion, proving that the young republic could enforce its writ and maintain domestic security. After this successful military action, Washington managed to convince Congress to allow for a standing army of about three thousand men. Indeed, the size of the army would continue to grow as Democrat-Republicans began to see its necessity in deterring European invasion and maintaining internal order.[22]

In this debate, Washington had a clear and consistent position in favor of a capable and professional federal military, and he left a legacy of building the military foundation of American power. It was a legacy that Adams, Hamilton, and others would carry on, including the Democratic-Republican James Madison, who was one of the original opponents of a standing army. Later, he would convincingly demonstrate the utility of a standing army in the War of 1812.

Ensuring American Neutrality

Washington's second enduring precedent in grand strategy was to build a foreign policy based on the twin principles of isolation and neutrality. In terms now famous in American foreign policy, Washington warned, "Tis our true policy to steer clear of permanent Alliances, with any portion of the foreign world."[23] His concern for entangling alliances was expressed in his farewell address when he stated, "Europe has a set of primary interests, which to us have none, or a very remote relation." From this we see that Europe is "engaged in frequent controversies, the causes of which are foreign to our concerns." Thus, as Ellis argues, Washington was confident – "as history eventually proved him right – that America's long-term interest was best served by steering a neutral course that avoided war with any of the European powers."[24]

In practical terms, Washington's decision to focus on the expansion to the west while avoiding being distracted by events in Europe was decisive in shaping American grand strategy. In fact, this logic would endure until forces in the twentieth century pulled the United States into two major wars on the European continent. Later, American grand strategy was reoriented as the policy of containment became the defining principle in American foreign policy in Europe and Asia after 1947.

Westward Expansion

A policy of American neutrality enabled Washington and his successors to pursue westward expansion as part of the overall architecture of the nation's grand strategy. Many, including Washington, believed that the American West, rather than Europe, was the primary theater of American interests. In effect, Washington viewed Europe as no more than a "sideshow," and American policy makers sought to ensure that events in Europe did not "divert attention from the enduring strategic interests of the United States."[25] Guided by this logic, Washington likely believed that the principal task of his foreign and domestic policy was to establish control of the territories to the east of the Mississippi River.[26]

Washington's convictions about the American West were firmly established well before the Revolution. Indeed, prior to the war, Washington came to believe that "the interest of the American colonies and the interest of the British Empire, so long presumed to be overlapping, were in opposition on [the question of westward expansion]." He believed that the power of the United States lay in its expansion to the west. Washington strongly believed, as Ellis writes, "that the future lay in those wild and wooded lands of the Ohio Country that he had explored and fought over as a young man."[27] For Washington, "gaining control of the vast American interior ... had been the central achievement of the French and Indian War."

According to scholar Don Higginbotham, "Washington's experiences exploring the interior led him to know more about the trans-Appalachian domain than any other American leader." Washington went on numerous journeys through Ohio, first in 1753 as Virginia's emissary to order the French out of the long-disputed region and then when he defended Virginia's extensive borderlands in the French and Indian War. In the decade following the war, Washington went on to own thousands of acres in the interior. He found great possibility in the "inland navigation of these united States . . . & could not but be struck with the immense diffusion & importance of it." Moreover, when Washington spoke of the nation, "he had always meant more than the original thirteen states. He had included the vast western regions extending to the Mississippi River." W. W. Abbot describes the situation well: "The West first stretched Washington's mind beyond his native Virginia. His association with that domain, more than anything else, except the war itself, served to prepare him for the role of nation builder."[28]

Setting Slavery Aside

The other issue that directly shaped the formation of American grand strategy during Washington's administration was slavery. Washington consciously avoided resolving the dispute between the Northern and Southern states over the matter of slavery both before and during his administration. This decision will always remain controversial. As Ellis argues, "what strikes us as a poignant failure of moral leadership appeared to Washington as a prudent exercise in political judgment."[29] Regardless of Washington's "personal views on slavery," one view is that his most important consideration as president was to build the foundations of the nation's power. One of Washington's most important objectives was to help the United States emerge as a unified nation from its origins as thirteen colonies.[30] In terms of grand strategy, Washington's policy toward slavery had serious moral problems that continued to trouble American society and led, eventually, to the civil war.[31]

Washington's Legacy in American Grand Strategy

In the end, the goal of Washington's grand strategy was to build the nation's political institutions along with the economic and military foundations of its power. His challenge was to design policies and strategies to guide the United States as it dealt with the range of challenges that would reoccur in subsequent centuries. Washington's three grand strategic priorities were centralizing the government's power, expanding westward to the Mississippi River, and maintaining American neutrality in the face of European and other foreign entanglements. These principles guided the nation over the next century and produced the threads of continuity amid many apparent changes in policies.

Another of Washington's legacies was in how he passed along his views. His farewell address was his most well-known speech, because in it he articulated explicitly the precedents that he believed should guide the conduct of American foreign policy going forward. His successors took his words to heart and, although not blindly following his policies, they adapted his precedents to their own times as they pursued his three goals with a remarkable degree of consistency and sense of purpose. In fundamental terms, the grand strategy of the United States today reflects the positions taken by Washington in the late eighteenth century.

Thomas Jefferson – Continuities in Grand Strategy

The nation's second president, John Adams, continued the policies in Washington's grand strategy in the tradition of the Federalists.[32] What is surprising is that Thomas

Jefferson, the nation's third president (1801–1809), fundamentally adhered to the broad outlines of Washington's grand strategy even though he led the opposing Democratic-Republican Party.[33]

In practice, Jefferson's grand strategy rested on the following three principles: enhance the power of the federal government, avoid entangling alliances and wars with Europe, and expand the nation's territory westward. Jefferson's approach to grand strategy is remarkably consistent with the themes followed by Washington and Adams. In addition, Jefferson saw slavery exactly as Washington did – as an issue in which morality demanded immediate action but political practicalities demanded delay until the federal government and American society were strong enough to survive resolving this highly disruptive controversy.

Jefferson presided over a politically polarized nation. In contrast to the Federalists, Jefferson's Republicans called for stronger state governments and favored revolutionary France over Britain.[34] The political atmosphere was so tense that many worried whether "Federalists and Republicans [were] on the verge of civil war." Federalists, who were predominantly Northerners or wealthy businessmen, were losing power as the nascent Republican Party, comprised mainly of Southerners and "new egalitarian-minded" Northerners, gained in popularity.[35]

Jefferson and his followers were concerned that a strong central government, as supported by the Federalists, threatened the guiding principle of the Revolution's commitment to limiting the powers of government and promoting individual freedom. At the same time, Jefferson continued to focus on the same three central principles that animated Washington's approach to grand strategy. The logical inference is that we see more continuity rather than change in the grand strategy pursued by the first three presidencies, despite the growing divisions, largely along partisan lines.

Expanding Federal Power

Moving to the more domestic element of debates about the development of the United States and its overall strategy, the problem for administrations responsible for formulating grand strategy was how to define and then balance the "proper strength and role" of the federal government in American society. As Mead writes, "Hamiltonians see a strong central government as the indispensable guarantor of national freedom [whereas] Jeffersonians have generally seen a strong central government as ... a necessary evil and, at worst, as the most dangerous enemy of freedom."[36] In this debate, Jefferson's approach to government authority resonated with those who feared that Hamilton's ideas would "re-create the kind of government and society that many Americans thought they had destroyed in 1776." In effect, many feared that the rise of a "hierarchical society" would eventually "destroy the integrity and independence of the republican citizenry."[37]

Jefferson and the National Debt

Related to the issue of the role of the federal government was the size of the national debt. Jefferson sought to shrink the debt, as this "went to the heart of the Republicans' conception of [limited] government." Jefferson and the Republicans believed that a government's ability to borrow money was the principal means by which the state is able to wage wars. But during each year of Jefferson's time as president, he sought to further reduce the debt. In warning about the dangers of a great and growing public debt, Wood writes how Jefferson "warned ... 'we shall be committed to the English career of debt, corruption and rottenness, closing with revolution. The discharge of debt, therefore, is vital to the destinies of our government.'" Worried about the risks that debt posed to the United States, Jefferson argued that holding down the debt was a "matter of preventing a present generation from burdening its descendants [and] of reducing the wherewithal of waging war." In building the domestic foundations of American power, Jefferson believed that eradicating debt was essential to building an "entirely new kind of government."[38] In Jefferson's view, unrestrained growth in the national debt would weaken the United States, undermine its democratic values, and call into question the principles over which the Revolution was fought and won.

Professionalizing the Military

Despite his Republican view that the federal government should be smaller, not larger, Jefferson decided to establish West Point for the development of a professional and nonpolitical military. This was a momentous decision because it meant that the military would be kept out of domestic politics and domestic politics would be kept out of the military. This principle of civil-military relations remains a defining element of American democracy.[39] It also meant the government would have a body of experts to help civilian policy makers make judgments on the proper use and projection of military power, which is a key determinant of the nation's ability to effectively implement its grand strategy.

Following Jefferson's 1800 electoral victory, there was some doubt as to whether "Federalist military institutions," notably the army, would survive the transition to the Jefferson presidency. One reason was Jefferson's strong criticism of Federalist programs that sought to increase the nation's military preparedness. At a time when Federalists dominated the army officer corps, Jefferson made farsighted reforms, which involved dismissing the most ardently partisan Federalist officers and persuading the rest to become loyal to the Republican administration for nationalist and decidedly not partisan reasons. Although "Jefferson in the 1790s had opposed the creation of a military academy," Wood writes, "he now favored the establishment of one at West Point as a means of educating Republican army officers, especially those whose families lacked the wealth to send their sons to college."[40] Jefferson was well aware of the risks associated with politicizing the military leadership. As president in 1801, Jefferson's response to "the Federalists' partisan military buildup," was to "depoliticize and reduce drastically the size of the army." This was the origin of Jefferson's decision to establish in 1802 the United States Military Academy at West Point.[41]

Jefferson's Republicanism conflicted with his belief that the world is dangerous ("predatory" in Jefferson's words) and "military weakness invited aggression." Here we see that continuity in American grand strategy trumped partisan beliefs as Jefferson's views shifted from wanting to eliminate the federal army to wanting "to relax the Federalist grip on the officer corps."[42] Of greater importance, his views reflected realism about the powers the federal government must possess if the nation is to compete effectively in international politics.

Preserving Precarious Neutrality and the Nation's Early Naval Wars

During Jefferson's presidency, the central foreign policy debate was about the Napoleonic Wars and how to deal with Great Britain and revolutionary France. This foreign policy debate reflected the domestic debate discussed in the previous section about the proper role and size of the federal government and the meaning of American democracy.[43] Jefferson's other major foreign policy decision to build a navy to defeat the Barbary pirates.

At the turn of the century, the political balance of power between the United States and Europe was precarious. The collapse of the Peace of Amiens in 1803, which temporarily ended hostilities between France and Great Britain during the French revolutionary wars, was followed by the British naval victory at Trafalgar and the French army's triumph at Austerlitz. As a result of these military events, as Wilentz writes, "Britain [was] the commander of the Atlantic, France the commander of the European continent, and the United States a neutral with no military leverage whatsoever."[44]

Although both Hamiltonians and Jeffersonians wished to avoid war, they differed in their view of the proper policy toward international alignments. The Federalists were more "inclined to risk war with France," whereas the Republicans were more "inclined to risk war with Great Britain." The proponents of these arguments, Alexander Hamilton and Thomas Jefferson, respectively, also were strong supporters of free trade in principle. In practice, however, Hamilton opposed any trade restrictions that were hostile to England, while actively favoring such restrictive policies toward France. By contrast, Jefferson opposed trade embargoes against France but supported them against England. These diverging positions revolved around opposing views of what types of governments the United States wanted to support – whether conservative constitutional monarchies or revolutionary democracies – as well what strategy would help the United States increase its relative power and influence.

Hamilton believed that the United States should adopt "a more British style of evolution." Jefferson, by contrast, was willing to "accept a greater [level of] dependence on France" precisely because he wanted "to achieve what he considered [the] more important [objective of] independence from Great Britain." Importantly, throughout this debate Jefferson and Hamilton's judgments about American grand strategy were defined precisely in terms of their views of "what America should become, both at home and abroad."[45]

The origins of the debate lie at the beginning of the nineteenth century, when the principal architects of American foreign policy articulated clear, if diametrically opposed, visions of what kind of nation the United States should become and how it should act. Such competing visions produced discord, which exists to the present, over what principles should guide the nation's foreign policy. Federalists interpreted the French Revolution as destructive and mindless populism as their anxiety grew when they heard reports of "the rioting in Paris and elsewhere, the horrific massacres in September 1792 of over fourteen hundred prisoners charged with being enemies of the Revolution, the news that Lafayette had been deserted by his troops and his allies in the Assembly and had fled France." Federalists believed these events confirmed their prediction that the French Revolution was degenerating "into popular anarchy."

More dangerous still, as the Federalists rightly worried, "American enthusiasm for the French Revolution" could lead the United States itself into "anarchy." Although "no

Republican was a more ardent supporter of the French Revolution than the party's leader, Thomas Jefferson," Jefferson's enthusiasm for the French Revolution would be tested by events. When the revolution turned into a dictatorship under Napoleon, Jefferson hoped that this would "result in . . . a free French republic." In his public life, Jefferson's "affection for France and his hatred of England never dimmed." Jefferson held that "France . . . was the Americans' true mother country since she has assured to them their liberty and independence," and, in contrast, described the British as "our natural enemies."[46]

In 1805, following naval incidents involving the British warship HMS *Leander* against U.S. merchant and naval ships, Jefferson decided to take action. Facing serious economic constraints on American policy, Jefferson – with strong support from "Secretary of State Madison (and despite the personal opposition of Treasury Secretary Gallatin)" – supported what was called "commercial coercion" but which we now call, in modern parlance, the practice of economic warfare. In December 1807, Jefferson imposed on the British what was in effect a "boycott" that would "prohibit all oceanic trade with foreign nations." Facing the choice between an economic embargo and war with Great Britain, Jefferson opted for "what he called . . . the 'least bad'" option.[47]

Jefferson viewed the embargo as an effective instrument of American policy that provided a way of "starving our [British] enemies."[48] Historians agree that the embargo was a risky option because it sought to build support for American neutrality. By embracing a strategy of neutrality, Jefferson and Madison thought they could influence British and American public opinion, hoping that "Britain's sensible businessmen would . . . come to their senses and demand respect for American neutral rights." While the British political opposition supported the Americans, the embargo hit the American economy "quickly and hard." In effect, it reduced "American shipping by as much as 80 percent and [caused] severe hardship among craftsmen and laborers in the seaport cities and neighboring farmers."[49]

The domestic political consequences were predictable. In New England, the Federalists were furious about the embargo. Since the Northeast bore "the brunt of the enforcement, they urged resistance and civil disobedience."[50] Soon there was political pressure by Republican members of Congress from the Northeast to lift the embargo. One unintended casualty of the embargo for the historian Gordon Wood was the "unity of the Republican party," since eventually "Congress voted to end this liberal experiment in peaceful coercion." As part of the emerging narrative on American grand strategy, Jefferson and Madison worried that they had lost an opportunity to give other states a better option for managing wars and conflicts.[51] The embargo ended on March 4, 1809, the same day on which James Madison was inaugurated as the fourth president of the United States. Nonetheless, the United States remained neutral during Jefferson's tenure; he followed the policies established by Washington far more than he departed from them.

The Barbary Wars

The Barbary Wars was an early test of the young republic's military power.[52] Prior to 1783, Kagan writes, "American merchants plying the Mediterranean had enjoyed the protection of the British flag." The British navy, in response, effectively restrained the Barbary powers, which were the "North African principalities nominally under the control of the Turkish Porte [who] made their living by piracy." This was, as Kagan notes, "the eighteenth-century version of 'rogue states.'" When the Americans defeated the British in the Revolution, the British no longer felt compelled to provide a "protective umbrella for American trade." Having lost this British protection, American merchant vessels became the principal targets of Mediterranean pirates, for several reasons.[53]

First, the Americans attempted to bribe the Barbary leaders, but predictably, these efforts failed as the pirates kept raising the ransom price. Second, Jefferson launched U.S. naval forces to fight the Barbary pirates. As Kagan observes, "In June 1801 a squadron of three frigates and a schooner sailed for Tripoli as the beginning of a naval campaign that would continue without interruption for the better part of four years." In what became the first case of a protracted American military intervention, this campaign did not end piracy in the Mediterranean, but it was highly successful strategically because the United States "earned the respect of the European great powers." Further, it established Jefferson's long-sought objective of establishing a "permanent and influential [American] presence in the Mediterranean."[54]

Territorial Expansion through Diplomacy and Displacement

The signature event in the new nation's grand strategy during the Jefferson administration was the Louisiana Purchase. In 1803, the United States paid approximately $15 million for 800,000 square miles in what became one of the largest land deals in history. Although Jefferson originally opposed establishing a strong central government because of its harmful effects on states' rights, the decision to acquire so much westward land was consistent with the early American grand strategy of establishing a territorially distinct nation whose power would eventually rise.

With Jefferson's decision, the nation gained an enormous expanse of territory, which doubled the size of the country, and did so "without firing a shot."[55] Not surprisingly, many historians consider the Louisiana Purchase to be "one of the luckiest strokes in the history of American diplomacy." When viewed from the perspective of France's efforts to gain world supremacy, the Louisiana Purchase was a "minor episode," but for the American people it was "a virtual second Declaration of Independence."[56] However, Napoleon's decision to sell Louisiana to the Americans related directly to France's difficulties as it attempted to conquer the island of Santo Domingo (present-day Haiti) and the risk of imminent war with Great Britain. He likely concluded that it was "better to sell Louisiana to the Americans and cement a friendship with a 'numerous, warlike' people who might prove useful in a war with Britain."[57]

In practice, the Louisiana Purchase fulfilled Jefferson's "greatest dream of having sufficient land for generations of yeoman farmers." It also removed America's greatest sources of danger at the time. "Neither France nor Britain could now threaten New Orleans and America's Mississippi outlet to the sea,"[58] and the Louisiana Purchase legitimized the strategy of expanding the United States into Spanish territories along the Gulf Coast. More importantly, since this decision prevented France from containing the United States, Jefferson's move was strategically decisive because it gained control of nearby territory and strengthened the nascent nation's border security.

As an early architect of American grand strategy, Jefferson was for some historians "the most expansion-minded president in American history." Wood argues that although "Alexander Hamilton always faced east, toward Europe," Jefferson "faced west, toward the trans-Appalachian territory and even the lands beyond the Mississippi." In following Jefferson's strategic thinking, moving westward was the only way the United States could preserve its "republican society of independent yeoman farmers and avoid the miseries of the concentrated urban working classes of Europe." For Jefferson, the term "'Empire' . . . did not mean coercive domination of alien peoples [but] a nation of citizens spread over vast tracts of land."[59] His principle of expansion was central to how Jefferson viewed the nation's role in international affairs and the precepts he promoted to guide his grand strategy.

Territorial expansion was inextricably tied to the "policy of Indian 'removal,'" which scholars normally attribute to Andrew Jackson. In reality, however, this conception is somewhat misleading because it was "Jefferson [who] pushed the Indians off hundreds of thousands of square miles of territory." When Jefferson came into office, vast swaths of Tennessee, Mississippi, Alabama, Florida, Indiana, Illinois, Arkansas, and Missouri had substantial Native American populations. By the time Jefferson left office, the United States had gained "nearly two hundred thousand square miles," which "flanked the remaining Indian-held lands with established white settlements on the east and west."[60]

` The historian Wood writes that Jefferson "had no doubt of the superiority of white agricultural society to the 'savage' state of the native peoples of America." This sentiment was clear in his first annual message to Congress in December 1801, when Jefferson wrote "that he would continue what he took to be the successful efforts of his predecessors to introduce among 'our Indian neighbors ... the implements and the practice of husbandry, and of the household arts.'"[61] Scholars describe "Jefferson's policy toward the Indians [as] tragically simple: let the natural demographic growth and movement of white Americans take their course." These policies were consistent with a grand strategy that promoted the political and territorial foundations of the new republic above all else, even above moral considerations that touched on matters of the highest order.

Keeping Slavery Unresolved

Arguably, no issue posed a more significant threat to American domestic political harmony and stability than slavery. During the Revolution, British offers of freedom to slaves fueled fears among Southern slaveholders and generally in American society of the possibility of a slave uprising that could destroy the nation's political stability.[62] These political disputes contributed to fears about the power of the Republic and its ability to survive and determine its destiny.

The obvious problem was that the position of the Southern states on slavery was diametrically opposed to that of the Northern states. In terms of population statistics, the numbers are telling: "In 1790 black slaves constituted 30 percent of the population of Maryland and North Carolina, 40 percent of that of Virginia, and nearly 60 percent of that of South Carolina." Furthermore, more than 90 percent of the slaves in the United States lived in the Southern states, which indicates the deep reliance of the Southern economy on slavery and its tendency to inhibit the growth of the white, middle-class artisans.[63] On this issue, Jefferson stated that "he would go to great lengths to end slavery 'in any *practicable* way ... we have the wolf by the ear, and we can neither hold him, nor safely let him go. [J]ustice is in one scale, and self-preservation in the other.'"[64] As Jefferson undoubtedly realized, the failure to end slavery posed a moral and existential threat to the Republic. He realized that the democratic value of equality embodied in the

"Revolution had unleashed anti-slavery sentiments." Jefferson disagreed with the proponents of race equality, believing "that the two peoples could not live side by side as equal citizens."[65]

Still, in 1807, despite significant opposition from Southern slaveholders, both Federalist and Republican, Jefferson convinced Congress to outlaw the transatlantic slave trade. This decision he defended on the basis of "'violations of human rights which have been so long continued on the unoffending inhabitants of Africa, and which the morality, the reputation, and the best interests of our country have long been eager to proscribe.'"[66] This policy change imposed high political costs on Jefferson in the South.

Jefferson's Legacy in American Grand Strategy

Looking back on Jefferson's legacy in grand strategy, it clearly rests on a series of complex and at times contradictory developments. First, some historians contend that Jefferson betrayed his principles because he expanded federal power territorially with the Louisiana Purchase and militarily with the building of a navy and the founding of West Point. Others critique Jefferson for betraying the moral principles he articulated in the Declaration of Independence and accuse him of hypocrisy. Still others argue that Jefferson's strategy of establishing the country's foundations of domestic stability and power before ending slavery represented a moral failure. Yet others counter that such charges are ahistorical and unfair. For example, as Wilentz contends, "critics fail to recognize that Thomas Jefferson, although a fervent advocate of his principles, never thought he had to live up to some idealized abstraction of 'Jeffersonian Democracy' in the real political world." The debate continues: What some critics call the "grand inconsistencies of Jefferson's presidency" others argue are perhaps better understood not as hypocrisy, but as "flexible responses to contingencies."[67]

In the end, one defense of Jefferson's policies rests on arguments from the realm of grand strategy: what was at stake was building the domestic foundations of national power at a time when both internal and external forces made the nation's future highly uncertain. It is useful to remember that he faced the daunting challenge of dealing with the practical realities of building a new republic in the modern era of grand strategy when rival European states had already developed strong economies and militaries. Jefferson, as much as Washington, succeeded in building a legacy in grand strategy based on strengthening the domestic foundations of American power, which became the enduring basis for U.S. foreign policy for more than fifty years and established principles that endure more than two centuries later.

James Madison – Reasserting Independence

The presidency of James Madison (1809–1817) is included here primarily because of his leadership during the War of 1812.[68] The reasons for the war remain subject to debate. Some argue that the primary cause was the threat of British war policies to American trade with Europe,[69] but an opposing view is that the war started because Britain was attempting to erode the domestic foundations of American power in a bid to reassert the power it lost in North America when it was defeated during the American Revolution.[70]

The argument developed in this study focuses on Madison's contributions to the evolution of American grand strategy.[71] A crucial element of Madison's role relates to the War of 1812 and the extent to which British policies undercut the three principles of grand strategy initiated by Washington: enhance the power and prestige of the federal government, maintain neutrality in European conflicts, and expand the nation's territorial foundations westward.

During Madison's presidency, the British directly sought to undermine all three of these policies. The impressment of U.S. sailors to service in the Royal Navy threatened the power and prestige of the federal government. If Washington could not protect its sailors, it would be viewed as weak domestically and internationally. Britain's policy of impressment also undermined the policies of free trade neutrality, the former because it hurt American shipping interests, the latter because it forced American sailors to fight for the British against Napoleon. Finally, the British threatened territorial expansion westward by encouraging raids by their Indian allies. Madison chose to wage war against Great Britain, but this war changed little in terms of physical control, precisely because he wanted to uphold these core principles in the development of the nation's emerging grand strategy. Without these principles, the nation's first era of grand strategy would have been a complete failure.

The War of 1812

The War of 1812 (also known as the Second War of Independence), which lasted two years and eight months, occurred at the same time that Britain was fighting France in the Napoleonic Wars.[72] Madison's reasoning for proposing war was outlined in his "War Message" to the Congress, dated June 1, 1812. His action was based on "the conduct of [Great Britain's] Government [for] a series of acts hostile to the United States as an independent and neutral nation."[73] As outlined by Madison, the specific causes of the war were "impressments" of formerly British (now American) sailors to rejoin the British navy; the presence of British warships near U.S. ports to intimidate and harass commercial shipping; blockades by British ships; the Orders in Council of 1807, by which Britain declared a blockade of European ports; and London's role in renewing Indian wars in the west.[74]

Notably, Madison did not go to war against Britain simply to help the French. He emphasized the neutral status of the United States, but he also did not express any sympathy for Napoleon's forces. The War of 1812 was an independent war, related in part to the Napoleonic Wars but not governed by the desire to foster better diplomatic alignments. Madison likely believed that the war was necessary to preserve American interests, because these were sufficiently significant to risk fighting a militarily stronger adversary. As the world's most significant military power, Britain possessed a navy with more than 600 ships and an army of nearly 250,000 troops, whereas the United States "could command little more than 6,000 regular troops and a naval force consisting of 16 vessels of all sizes."[75] In this nearly three-year war, American casualties included 2,260 deaths and 4,505 wounded.[76]

Economic Foundations Threatened

British policy at this time was to blockade all European ports that could receive supplies for Napoleon's forces. In addition, they began impressing American sailors into service in the Royal Navy, where service was backbreaking and meant that Americans were forced to fight for their enemy. Finally, the British were harassing outgoing and incoming ships at U.S. ports. All three of these policies combined to threaten the economic foundations of American power.

Madison had seen this as a threat to the federal government since the times when he served as a Virginia congressman. At that time, Madison was concerned about America's financial and commercial dependence on Britain. He believed that "separation from Great Britain, both political and, as much as possible economic, was essential to the internal health and longevity of the republic."[77] Scholars write that Madison "wanted a separation from Great Britain that was 'not only political but economic – above all – moral as well.'"[78]

Although this principle was central to the thinking of Hamilton and other colonial leaders, Madison and Jefferson were wrongly persuaded that the United States could alter British policies by using "trade embargoes."[79] However, this instrument of commercial coercion was not an effective element of U.S. grand strategy against Great Britain prior to the War of 1812. When Madison became president in 1809, as Kagan writes, "Jefferson's hope that 'peaceable coercions' could influence both England and France had been thoroughly discredited."

American Prestige Undermined

Madison was not alone in his view that it was essential to preserve American prestige. For one scholar, the issue for Americans was that their "national character, national honor, and the health and vigor of the republic ... weigh ... more heavily in the calculation of the 'national interests.'" In building the Republic's grand strategy, economic resources and territory were essential, "but American leaders like Henry Clay argued that adopting a passive policy toward Great Britain [forfeited the] 'nation's best treasure, [its] honor.'"[80] The concern for many Americans was that the "failure to respond adequately to British depredations" would further damage "the reputation of republican government both at home and abroad." Madison and others believed that failing to confront Great Britain would seriously, if not fatally, weaken the reputation of the United States – a fragile reputation that had to be protected. As Madison argued, "we must support our rights or lose our character," since America's honor was a "national property of the highest value."[81] Drawing on arguments whose origins trace back to ancient Greece, American politicians and the public worried that as "commercial men they lacked what the ancient Greeks had called *thumos*, a patriotic spiritedness that made men put the honor of their nation ahead of personal comfort and luxury and that made citizens willing to sacrifice for their country."[82]

In addition, the belief in American exceptionalism began to play a prominent role in the nation's politics. During Madison's presidency, the principal objective of American foreign policy shifted from being "not merely to protect the nation and its people but also to preserve and protect its unique institutions and unprecedented liberties." This idea, which evolved into a defining purpose in American foreign policy, "helped distinguish American strategy from that of other eighteenth-century nations [with] different forms of government and political economy."[83] This domestic source of American exceptionalism, though related, is nonetheless different from the concept of American foreign policy exceptionalism examined in this book. The former concerns the uniqueness of American democracy, while the latter concerns the geopolitical benefits and patterns at play in the nation's grand strategy.

This argument prompts the following question: Why did the challenge to America's honor, its virtue, and even its virility seem so much greater to these political leaders in 1812 than it had in the 1790s, when most American leaders had counseled forbearance in the face of similar mistreatment by both France and England? The answer, for Kagan, lies in "Americans' changing perception of themselves and of their place in the international hierarchy." Since "the old tactics of diplomacy, forbearance, and even embargo – the tactics of the weak – could no longer salvage national honor," the republic's grand strategy increasingly encompassed principles that were far greater than commercial or economic interests and involved much more high-minded and noble aspirations.[84]

Territorial Expansion Limited

Yet another impetus for the war was Britain's indirect role in limiting America's territorial expansion through the encouragement of Native American resistance to white settlements along the frontier. The British were suspected of using Native American tribes, particularly those in the Northwest Territory (what is now Ohio and the Great Lakes Region), to harass, attack, and disrupt American frontier settlements as well as kill settlers. The tribes were a very receptive audience to British incitement because the decade before the War of 1812 saw the consolidation of Native American tribes under more militant and prophetic leaders such as the Shawnee brothers, Tecumseh[85] and Tenskwatawa.[86] One U.S. military expedition to curb this rising power of the Northwest tribes culminated in the 1811 Battle of Tippecanoe near the Wabash River in Indiana. After the battle, American soldiers reportedly discovered in the tribe's village new equipment supplied by the British.[87]

The tribal unrest, however, might have had as much to do with unchecked white settlements as it did with British encouragement. It is nonetheless clear that due to these reports and other evidence, British Canada was increasingly seen as a source of supply and support for Native American tribal warriors.[88] And Madison and his advisors soon viewed British Canada as a strategic base of operations for the general prevention and disruption of American expansion into the Louisiana Purchase. Madison saw this problem as worthy of inclusion in his war speech to Congress:

> In reviewing the conduct of Great Britain toward the United States our attention is necessarily drawn to the warfare just renewed by the savages on one of our extensive frontiers – a warfare which is known to spare neither age nor sex and to be distinguished by features peculiarly shocking to humanity. It is difficult to account for the activity and combinations which have for some time been developing themselves among tribes in constant intercourse with British traders and garrisons without connecting their hostility with that influence and without recollecting the authenticated examples of such interpositions heretofore furnished by the officers and agents of that Government.[89]

In sum, not only had the British interfered with America's vital maritime commerce and undermined the prestige of the young republic, it had become an obstacle to one of the fundamental policies for building the domestic foundations of American power: territorial expansion westward.

Consequences of the War

The significance for America of the War of 1812 is not in its military or even political outcome but in the symbolism of a small, young nation asserting its rights by force against a stronger adversary. In fact, the Treaty of Ghent that ended the war – signed on December 24, 1814, but not ratified until February 16, 1815 – essentially enshrined the *status quo ante bellum* and preserved the conditions that existed before the war.[90] Although the war "had generally gone badly for the United States," the "Americans nevertheless emerged from the War of 1812 as if from a great victory." Moreover, the conflict unquestionably changed the British way of thinking about the United States. After the war, Kagan writes, the willingness of the United States to fight against Great Britain may have contributed to stronger relations between Washington and London. In Madison's estimation, this outcome was precisely what the Republic needed as his administration worked to build the domestic foundations of the nation's power.

Domestically, the War of 1812 also proved to be highly effective in rallying public support for a strong central government and in promoting domestic economic and political development.[91] The war helped unify the nation politically as politicians agreed on the strengths and weaknesses of American power that the war revealed. For instance, the Republic's unstable financial condition gave policy makers a sense of "desperation because the federal government did not have sufficient money to fight the war." At the same time, the nation lacked an efficient public transportation system that would enable the government to move military forces around the country. This shortcoming underscored the essential connection in grand strategy between military competitiveness and the development of an economic infrastructure. Before the conflict with Britain, many Republicans "worried about the effects of commerce on republican institutions," but later their thinking changed as they learned that the country's economic health and prosperity derived from having a strong economic basis in manufacturing and global commerce.[92]

Not only did the war trigger a greater consensus on the size and role of the federal government, but it also engendered a renewed sense of American nationalism. As Kagan writes, "The decades after the War of 1812 have rightly been called an 'age of nationalism.'" In shaping the nation's grand strategy, the American people now appeared to "feel and act more as a nation."[93]

Madison's Legacy in American Grand Strategy

The Napoleonic Wars in Europe influenced the evolution of American grand strategy because the Great Powers were too consumed with competition on the Continent to interfere heavily in America's development. Again, the United States benefited from having a long window of opportunity in which to develop the domestic foundations of its power. This did not mean the United States could stand aloof from the European conflagration completely. At first glance, then, the War of 1812 seems a radical departure from America's tradition in grand strategy of staying out of European politics. It was not. In fact, it was a result of Britain's combined assault on the three policies that had consistently guided American grand strategy since Washington: enhance the power of the federal government, preserve neutrality, and expand territory westward. The interplay among those three principles is essential to understanding how the United States went about building the domestic foundations of the nation's power in the earliest decades of its existence as a republic. Madison's decision to go to war was guided by his intention to defend the nation's commerce, prestige, and territory, which persuaded him, like Jefferson, that developing a consolidated, centralized national government was necessary to preserve the Republic.

For these reasons, Madison's legacy is complex. The War of 1812 did not achieve the objectives that had provoked it in the first place, but it set the fledgling republic on a course that helped it become a regional power, which eventually gained it the ability to compete more directly with the European powers.[94] The war directly helped shape American grand strategy, because it reaffirmed the status of the United States as an independent and dominant power in the region, while it demonstrably weakened Great Britain's strength and reputation in the Western Hemisphere and beyond.

James Monroe – Rise to Regional Power Status

President James Monroe's (1817–1825) foreign policy reflects a pivotal moment in the evolution of American grand strategy as the nation began the shift from national to regional power.[95] In his grand strategy, President Monroe not only pursued a strong domestic agenda, but he also aligned it with an equally strong vision for regional security as a way of expanding the influence of the United States in the Western Hemisphere and around the world.[96]

The signature accomplishment of President Monroe was the Monroe Doctrine, which, when articulated in 1823, formed a coherent statement of the central role that was the product of three precedents that continued to endure from the administration of George Washington. First, the Monroe Doctrine was a bold assertion of federal power beyond the borders of the United States. Second, it can be seen as the flip side of the principle of neutrality in European international politics in which Washington asserted that America should stay out of European politics. In effect, the Monroe Doctrine ensured that European politics would stay out of the Americas. Third, the Monroe Doctrine was expansionist, but not in the same sense that it was with the administrations of Washington, Jefferson, and Madison. It did not involve the formal annexation of more territory, but it was expansionist in that it marked the territories that would fall under the American sphere of influence and that would by definition be excluded from the involvement of the European powers in the Western Hemisphere. Finally, Monroe continued the policy of delay and abeyance in the case of slavery; he did not move to end it but instead let it remain as part of the nation's political and economic system. In this sense, Monroe's grand strategy followed the logic that was established by his predecessors.

Expanding the Federal Government's Foreign Policy Influence

The "link" between domestic and foreign policy finds its roots in Monroe's December 1823 message to Congress. Although that speech is now famous primarily if not exclusively for articulating the Monroe Doctrine, most of the address was dedicated to domestic issues. The so-called Monroe Doctrine was limited to "just a few paragraphs" in which Monroe called on the European states to stop their colonizing efforts in the Western Hemisphere because the United States claimed its principal interest in this region. For the rest of the speech, Monroe presented the "republican nationalist agenda."

Here he focused heavily on domestic development, including building roads and canals – as much for transporting troops in times of war as for moving commercial products to market. In formulating his grand strategy, Madison allowed domestic policies to complement his foreign policy, leading one historian to write that "Monroe's confident, progressive, and expansive foreign policy doctrine" aligned nicely "with his confident, progressive, and expansive domestic policies."[97] In practice, Monroe pursued policies that helped build the domestic foundations of American power by expanding federal power at home while projecting it abroad.

The core principle in Monroe's grand strategy was outlined in his now-famous address, which was presented as a response to a proposal by Great Britain's foreign minister George Canning. Canning suggested that the United States and Great Britain – in the face of the crisis sparked by the French invasion of Spain in 1823 – "issue a joint statement declaring that the United States and Great Britain would together oppose any effort by France, or by any other power, to take control of the former Spanish colonies in the Western Hemisphere."[98] President Monroe and nearly all of his advisors initially believed that such an alliance with Great Britain would be sufficiently valuable to make it worthwhile to abandon potential territorial gains. In fact, only Secretary of State John Quincy Adams objected to the proposal, and he ultimately prevailed by persuading President Monroe to reaffirm the United States' strategic interest in freeing the Latin American colonies from European influence. As Gaddis observes, "Americans," for John Quincy Adams, "should accept no binding obligation to align their long-term interests with those of any other state, or to pledge mutual assistance when those interests were challenged."[99]

One factor that contributed to Monroe's grand strategy and his Monroe Doctrine speech to Congress was the Greek war for independence from the Ottomans. Although the Greek cause directly appealed to Americans and their emerging principles of freedom and liberalism, Great Britain took a counterrevolutionary stance in which London viewed the Greeks as belligerent troublemakers. Monroe had a different view, as Kagan explains: "President Monroe himself was a great believer in two mutually reinforcing ideas: that the fate of republicanism in Europe directly affected the safety of republican principles at home, and that the United States, in turn, could and should be an important source of encouragement to liberals and republicans on the European continent." In practice, Monroe was skeptical that the ideological struggle in Europe was distinguishable from the themes in American foreign policy. An initial draft of President Monroe's 1823 message forcefully addressed the issue of Greek independence, the invasion of Spain, and other conflicts throughout Europe. In it, he warned that America's treasured values and republican institutions were under attack and the Americans' "own security was directly implicated in the global ideological struggle."[100]

Despite strong backing from a majority of his cabinet to support defenders of democracy and liberalism in Europe, Secretary of State John Quincy Adams convinced Monroe to soften the ideological position in his speech. However, as the president ultimately declared, "the United States considered European intervention to crush constitutionalism in Spain a threat to its own security." As a result, the United States was forced to take a deeper interest in European affairs. For Monroe, the defense of "republicanism and liberalism abroad as a matter of principle [were seen] as a matter of self-interest and self-defense." Thus, when President Monroe "declared in 1823 that the United States was an 'interested spectator' of the political struggles in Europe," he was implying that Washington had significant interests in Europe.[101]

However, the president used the Monroe Doctrine to establish an ideological and diplomatic barrier between the Old World in Europe and the New World here. The purpose of Monroe's message was less "to draw geographical distinctions [than] to draw ideological distinctions." It was for this reason that Monroe issued warnings "against colonization and acquisition of territory in the Western Hemisphere but also against 'any attempt' by European powers to extend 'their system' to 'any portion of this hemisphere.'"[102] Whereas European states "defined security in a 'traditional and restricted manner, as largely a function of the balance of power,'" a better explanation is that Americans saw security "as a function of the 'internal order maintained by states [and] a favorable ideological balance.'"[103] The speech, then, must be read as a dual grand strategy in which Monroe's domestic policies promoted economic development along with a new and growing sense of American nationalism. In effect, his foreign policy established an ideological sphere of influence that has remained central ever since to how the United States has articulated and implemented its grand strategy.

The Monroe Doctrine: Security through Expansion

Beyond preventing European influence in the Western Hemisphere, the Monroe Doctrine opened the door to American expansionist ambitions. Monroe's grand strategy sought not only to block the rise of European interference in the Americas, but to extend U.S. influence in the hemisphere through establishing "sister republics" and a Pan-American "family of nations." The president's position toward the Western Hemisphere was fueled by a common republican ideology that rested on the presumption that societies in "Latin America were emerging from their long colonial subordination to Spain," often "proclaiming themselves [to be] republics like the United States."[104] Monroe's grand strategy thus established direct linkages to the values and aspirations of states in Latin America that did not want to be subjected to European colonial rule and imperial policies.

By curbing European colonization efforts and establishing friendly relations with neighboring Latin American countries, the United States paved the way for further territorial expansion without European-backed resistance. Kagan, similarly, posits that expansionist ambitions, which are a distinctive element of the American national character, have contributed to the evolution of American grand strategy: "Decades before the phrase 'manifest destiny' entered the foreign policy lexicon, this 'lust for dominion' was an almost unstoppable force in American politics." In practice, Americans saw this as "their right and their destiny to spread across the land," because they represented "the vanguard of human progress."[105]

President Monroe's belief in the idea that the United States was destined to become a continental empire may have instigated or at least contributed to aggression toward the Native Americans, which was related to efforts to take over Spanish provinces and diminish Spain's involvement in North America. For example, in 1818, when General Andrew Jackson "was sent across the Florida boundary to repulse attacks from resisting Seminoles, the real target ... was Florida." To implement this policy of expansion and displacement, "President Monroe wrote [to] Jackson that his pursuit of the Seminoles 'will bring you on a theatre where you may possibly have other services to perform.'"[106]

When the United States pressured Spain to give up the Floridas shortly after acquiring the Louisiana territories, Monroe supported this policy, saying that "'the United States

[is] a rising [power] and Spain a declining power.'"[107] His secretary of state, John Quincy Adams, echoed these sentiments and advanced the belief that, despite America's military and naval weaknesses, "the nation's population, economy, and potential strength could only grow, while the ability of the European powers to control adjoining territories could only diminish."[108]

By this logic, however, John Quincy Adams was not satisfied with merely controlling the Floridas; he also demanded that Spain cede more territory in the Pacific Northwest. Through his role in negotiating the Treaty of Ghent at the end of the War of 1812, and later as secretary of state for President Monroe, John Quincy Adams was crucial in devising a strategy that linked American security to expansion. As Gaddis argues, it was "Adams, more than anyone else, who worked out the methods by which expansion could ... provide the security" that America craved.[109] With the treaty of 1819, Secretary Adams successfully secured the U.S. acquisition of the Floridas in addition to Spain's Oregon Country, which included all Spanish territory north of the forty-second parallel.

The American ideology of expansion, for Kagan, certainly reflected signs of "aggressive behavior on the part of the very young nation." Despite a "haphazard" quality to American expansionism early in the nineteenth century, "Adams and other American leaders had a clear vision of continental empire [but] no specific plans to obtain it." The expansion of the United States was governed neither by "absentmindedness" nor "by careful design." Its origins were more likely a case of "determined opportunism" as the Republic saw and took opportunities to expand its reach just as European powers were gradually withdrawing. One conclusion is that "ambition and opportunism had pro-duced power and security, which in turn produced more ambition and opportunism."[110]

With the Louisiana Purchase, the acquisition of Spanish territories in Florida, and the removal of France, the United States effectively eliminated the imperial challenges to its expansionist goals. However, the nation's newfound confidence and security would not go unchecked as long as the unresolved issue of slavery continued to have devastating consequences for the nation's sense of rightness as well as its grand strategy.

Monroe's Legacy in American Grand Strategy: Rising Tension between Territorial Expansion and Slavery

The building of the domestic foundations hit an inflection point during Monroe's presidency. On the one hand, although the nation had to expand westward to increase its power and security, the result of this territorial expansion meant the formation of new states. Those new states would be either slave states or free states, either of which could disrupt the delicate balance of power fashioned in the Constitution and under increasing strain in the nation. In effect, the tension between two of the principles of grand strategy dating back to Washington – the emphasis on territorial expansion and failures to resolve the slavery issue – were beginning to intensify.

In a dramatic shift from his earlier ambitions in the Spanish Floridas, Monroe decided not to pursue expansion into Texas, because he feared that debates about slavery in the new territory would further inflame passions in the country. The political problem for President Monroe, who was "a Virginia slaveholder," was that the issue of Texas was political "poison," which is consistent with the views of "Andrew Jackson and Martin Van Buren during their presidencies." It was well within American capabilities in the 1820s and 1830s for these administrations to take Texas by military force. The reason, as Monroe told Jefferson, was that "'no European power could prevent' the United States from taking as much Spanish land as it wanted." On the contrary, "the difficulty was 'altogether internal, and [therefore] of the most distressing and dangerous tendency,'" because any further expansion to the "West and South threatened to 'menace the Union itself' [and] open another sectional struggle over slavery."[111]

In this political climate, "Monroe believed, expansion was contrary to the national interest ... because the divided nature of the American polity made it indigestible." Therefore, it was dangerous for the nation to expand until it decided, as he put matters, "what kind of nation it wanted to be."[112] John Quincy Adams shared Monroe's analysis of the implications that slavery presented for the nation and its grand strategy of territorial expansion. As Gaddis observes, "By the end of [Monroe's] life he had come to see that whatever continental expansion might do for national security," it would have the far worse consequence of weakening "domestic tranquility" because it would bring "new slave states into the union." This development in turn would weaken "the delicate balance that had, so far, prevented civil war."[113]

Southern interests coalesced in strong opposition to the Monroe Doctrine in practice if not in theory. The reason was that it was seen as a "potent expression of American international ambition and ideological exuberance," but Southerners saw the implementation of the Doctrine through the lens of slavery: "The danger of slave rebellion demanded ... that the letter and spirit of the Monroe Doctrine had to be applied very selectively in the Western Hemisphere." In terms of implementation, then, "it was one thing to encourage independence in Colombia [but] another thing to stir up revolution in Cuba and Puerto Rico, where the ratio of black slaves to white masters was so great that what began as a revolution could easily become a massive slave rebellion – 'another Haiti.'"[114]

Further, the Monroe Doctrine had significant implications for the size and role of the federal government. At risk was that the Monroe Doctrine, by virtue of the "very boldness of the president's declaration," would be highly "unsettling to southerners" who were deeply concerned that the federal government was becoming far too influential in formulating national policy. For Southerners, the ultimate concern was that "if a president could assume such powers to shape American policy abroad, [then] he could turn those powers against the South."[115]

Facing profound national disagreements over the institution of slavery, the architects of American grand strategy struggled to strike a balance between protecting the interests of the nation abroad and preserving the nation's unity. In the end, these forces shook American politics to its core as the administration of James Monroe endeavored to define a grand strategy in the midst of profound disagreements over equality in American society. And those disagreements would culminate in a civil war that killed hundreds of thousands and put the nation itself at peril.

Andrew Jackson – Departures and Discontinuities in Foreign Policy

The presidency of Andrew Jackson (1829–1837) represents more change than continuity in the formulation and conduct of American policy.[116] Many of these discontinuities in grand strategy are due to the fact that Jackson was much more heavily focused on domestic matters than foreign policy.[117] Unlike his predecessors, he presided over a period of state power retrenchment during which he consistently sought to limit the power of the federal government.

During Jackson's time in office, he opposed building a stronger navy, vetoed the charter for the Second Bank of the United States, and eliminated direct federal funding for infrastructure projects. Also in stark contrast to his predecessor, he did not expand the territory of the United States. Instead, Jackson practiced a policy of ruthless territorial consolidation with his Indian Removal Act. Finally, since Europe was quiescent in terms of overtures toward the United States in the aftermath of the Congress of Vienna in 1815, he did not have to uphold a policy of neutrality and deliberately maintain a geopolitical distance from European politics.

State Power Retrenchment

The political divisions that would lead to civil war deepened when Jackson took office in 1829. One reason was that "Southern politicians who had flirted with progressive nationalism during and after the war with Great Britain now shifted course and adopted an exaggerated version of old republican principles." This translated into a new political order in which Southerners supported a strict interpretation "of the Constitution, jealous guarding of states' rights against the federal government, and retrenchment and parsimony in federal spending."[118]

Jackson was largely aligned with Southerners on the size and role of the federal government. He strongly opposed "the idea of Congress appropriating federal money for local projects," a principle that he put into practice by opposing such projects. He vetoed the National Road project that fit into Henry Clay's American System on the grounds that his veto would protect the rights of the people to enjoy limited government.[119] And in lieu of directly funded federal projects, Jackson proposed that once the national debt that was left over from the War of 1812 was repaid, "the government would make surplus resources available to the states for internal improvements." According to Jackson, any public expenditures beyond "defense and national benefit [were] constitutionally suspect." Jackson was highly suspicious of federal programs that put economic power in the hands of the federal government, because he feared that it could undermine American democracy.[120]

His policy on the Second Bank of the United States was also consistent with his preference for limiting the power of the federal government. During the Jackson administration, the government did not print a national paper currency because the Federal Reserve System was not established until 1913. In practical terms, what this meant for national economic policy, to the extent that there was one, was that "hundreds of small banks (788 of them in 1837) set up under state charters issued their own money." The most powerful of all banks, and the largest lender, was the Philadelphia-based Bank of the United States (BUS). Political opposition to the BUS dated back to debates between Jefferson and Hamilton about the proper role of the government in formulating and supporting economic policies and development. As Gordon Wood explains, the nature of banking remained a largely "mysterious business for many Americans."[121]

There were two principal sources of opposition to the Bank of the United States: the first was "from Southern agrarians like Jefferson who never understood banks and hated them," and the second consisted of the "entrepreneurial interests of the state banks who did not like their paper-issuing abilities restrained in any way."[122] Although the U.S.

Supreme Court had ruled that the BUS was constitutional,"[123] the combination of agrarian and state bank opposition to a strong centralized bank gave Jackson important political cover to institute his reforms. In 1832, Jackson vetoed the charter for the Second Bank of the United States, believing that the BUS had too much power, would give undue favors to the nation's elite, and would send American money to wealthy European financiers. Since Jackson "abhorred this concentration of economic power in what he called a 'hydra-headed monster' that eastern elites would exploit for their own corrupt ends,"[124] his policies departed radically from those of his predecessors, who had concentrated economic power in the federal government.

In another direct move to limit federal power, Jackson opposed building a strong navy to compete with other states. In the late 1820s, the naval buildup that occurred at the same time of the "Jacksonian movement" had many "slaveholders worried about the federal government's expanding powers." In this political climate, a bill in 1827 calling "for the 'gradual improvement of the Navy' was defeated" by the opposition to his policies. In Jackson's first inaugural address, although he said, "'the bulwark of our defense' was the militia," he also declared that there should be an "end to [the] building of large naval ships." As a result, the United States "fell behind European, Asian, and even some Latin American powers both in number and size of ships and in naval architecture."[125]

Territorial Consolidation over Expansion

Like his predecessors, Jackson was committed to the continued westward expansion of the nation, but he was unwilling to annex Texas if it meant heightened domestic tension over slavery. Instead, he implemented the Indian Removal Act to consolidate government control of territory already within American borders.

During the Jackson administration, popular support for westward expansion mingled with doubts about the Union's continued existence. The debate about expansion was inseparable from the debate about slavery. Southern states saw that they were encircled by free states and feared the extinction of their political-economic system. As a result, there was a growing sense in the South "that slavery must continue to expand westward, northward, and, most promisingly, southward toward the tropics of Latin America and the Caribbean."[126] Jackson, therefore, saw the issue of Texas as potentially explosive as he attempted to expand westward with great care. In fact, by the end of this term, he opposed annexation when it became clear that it would damage efforts to build the domestic foundations of American power and would weaken his successor, Martin Van Buren.

Moving quickly after his inauguration, Jackson first attempted, without consulting his cabinet, to buy Texas from Mexico prior to the revolt by Texans.[127]

In August 1829 he directed his minister to Mexico "to offer the Mexican government as much as $5 million cash for Texas with the Rio Grande River as the desirable boundary." Jackson's objective was to "ensure the safety of New Orleans, provide land for Indian removal and a natural boundary with Mexico." He presumably believed that to protect American security, it was necessary for "the rivers and lands adjacent to the Mississippi [to] be placed within American jurisdiction." To move the process along, Jackson told his representative "to urge the Mexicans to sell before it was too late." He likely believed that in the event of a "Texas Revolution ... it would be much more difficult to annex the province," as opposed to simply extending the current territorial boundaries beforehand.[128]

Consequently, once Texas revolted in 1835 and was established as an independent republic in 1836, Jackson changed his position to oppose annexation. Domestically, he feared that the addition of a slave state without a free state to balance it would disrupt the constitutional balance of power. Internationally, he thought that the annexation of Texas would be seen as illegal and could trigger a war with Mexico. Nevertheless, Jackson's reversal on annexation was not a sign of opposition to expansion generally, but this theme in grand strategy continued to have a powerful influence on Jackson's approach to the Texas issue. He was cautious about officially recognizing Texas as a nation, but he did so in the final hours of his presidency, telling "the Texans that the inclusion of California in their boundary claims with Mexico was essential to assure annexation to the United States."[129]

Jackson and the Indian Removal Act

A decisive issue for the Jackson administration was the Indian Removal Act, whose history is illustrative of how the administration struggled with building the foundations of national power.[130] Its origins trace back to the desire to remove various Native American populations from the nation's territories. Although the Cherokees had become "a model of cultural assimilation," contrary to earlier debates about removing the Creek population, the public view now was that Indian populations weakened the ability of the United States to become an independent power. To complicate matters, the Cherokees steadfastly resisted efforts to remove them, which in turn strengthened the resolve of states such as Georgia to do just that. For Jackson's grand strategy to succeed, the demand by tribes for "full tribal sovereignty was [seen as] unconstitutional as well as unrealistic" and hence was opposed.

Scholars debate whether he was uncomfortable with this view, but Jackson "negotiate[d] treaties with the tribes to secure their removal, even though [this] contradicted his rejection of Indian sovereignty." The ends justified the inconsistent means because, for Jackson, "removal was the only way to safeguard both the Indians' future and the Constitution of the United States."[131] He also believed this step was necessary to consolidate the territorial foundations of American power.

The political and psychological consequences of decisions that were taken to support the nation's grand strategy were felt for some time. "Although the worst suffering was inflicted after he left office," Wilentz writes, "Jackson cannot escape responsibility for setting in motion an insidious policy that uprooted tens of thousands of Choctaws and Creeks during his presidency, and would cost upwards of eight thousand Cherokee lives during the long trek west on the 'Trail of Tears.'"[132] When the Indian Removal Bill passed in 1830, Jackson took the step of resettling "nearly forty-six thousand Indians west of the Mississippi," a decision that legitimized subsequent policies by calling for "moving a like number in the future." As a result of this decision, the United States gained "over a hundred million acres of Indian land for white settlement," much of which was located in the cotton-rich regions of Alabama and Mississippi.[133]

Not surprisingly, there was significant public opposition to the Indian Removal Act. When Jackson, in his first annual message to the Congress in December 1829, asked for funds to "remove the remaining southeastern Indians beyond the Mississippi," reformers opposed these policies as a "triumph of crass materialism over respect for humanity and the gospel of Christ." The consensus among reformers was that President Jackson was indifferent to the fate of the Indians, while he remained quite interested in "open[ing] up valuable new lands for white speculators and settlers."[134]

Jackson's Legacy in American Grand Strategy

Andrew Jackson's legacy in the development of American grand strategy is much more focused on domestic populism than foreign policy. As Jackson implemented policies for building the foundations of American power, he did so largely by focusing on the domestic side of grand strategy. One notable achievement was the extent to which Jackson's policies contributed to the rise of a "mass electorate" that changed forever the fabric of American society and its electoral processes.[135]

This new populism had both positive and negative effects on the evolution of American grand strategy. On the positive side, Jackson's policies met the public demand "for cheap or, better, free land in the nineteenth century," which led to the Homestead Act and the possibility for "millions of immigrants and urban workers to start family farms." On the negative side, it contributed to policies that supported what Walter Russell Mead called "systematic and sometimes genocidal removal of Native Americans from their traditional hunting grounds."[136]

What makes this development critical to the Republic's emerging grand strategy is the extent to which the democratic revolution led by Jackson reshaped the conditions under which the United States conducted foreign policy. In effect, Jackson's policies made it both possible and legitimate for public opinion to become a truly decisive force in governing how the Republic conducts its foreign and domestic policies.[137] For this reason alone, Jackson exerted considerable influence on American history and on the ideas that would play a central role in the nation's grand strategy.

For other countries, the ascent of the "Jacksonian sentiment" carries the risk that policies pursued by the United States could "move too far, too fast, and too unilaterally in pursuit of its goals." The converse is equally true: when public opinion strongly opposes a policy, this same Jacksonian sentiment can mean that the United States will "move too slowly or not at all." From this emerges a cardinal principle in American grand strategy: we cannot understand American foreign policy unless we grasp the influence of what Mead calls "Jacksonian beliefs and values."[138] Many observers believe that an enduring challenge for American policy makers is to develop popular support for the nation's grand strategy and the domestic and foreign policies that it pursues in support of that strategy.

James Polk: A Focused, Successful One-Term Grand Strategist

As the last of the strong pre–Civil War presidents, President James Polk (1845–1849) was known for his successes in the field of foreign policy largely in the areas of territorial expansion and economic development.[139] In terms of territory, he dealt effectively with Great Britain over the joint U.S.-British control of the Oregon Territory. After achieving a decisive American victory in the Mexican-American War, he annexed Texas, which dramatically expanded the size of American territory from coast to coast. Economically, he reduced tariffs and reestablished a central bank, which were critical to building the economic foundations of American grand strategy.[140]

After assuming the presidency, which Polk vowed he would occupy for only one term, he privately stated that he would devote his administration – as it turned out, quite successfully – to accomplishing four policy goals. At the time of his inauguration, he sat down with George Bancroft, his navy secretary, and articulated the four central policy goals of his presidency: "First, he said, he planned to settle the Oregon question with Great Britain and extend America to the Pacific Ocean. Second, he would acquire California from Mexico and secure for his country an additional broad expanse of coastal territory. Third, he would reduce the Tariff of 1842 and replace its overt protectionism with a pure revenue rationale. Finally, he would revive Martin Van Buren's 'independent treasury,' designed to protect federal monies and ensure currency stability."[141]

The first two of these goals concerned territorial expansion, which continued the work of his predecessors. The last two concerned building the economic foundations of American power, which were also consistent with the policy of strengthening the economic engine of American progress with policies dating back to the era of Washington and Hamilton. All four goals were part of the first principle in the history of American grand strategy, notably to build the domestic foundations of the nation's power.

Final Implementation of "Manifest Destiny"

Polk came to define what historians call the "era of 'manifest destiny.'"[142] The Polk administration is highly consequential in the development of American grand strategy because it represented what we now see as the supremely "expansionist" moment in the history of the United States.

As an architect of American grand strategy in the mid-nineteenth century, Polk likely understood the concept in grand strategy that calls for marshaling the state's resources so that it can pursue its national interests. Territorial expansion was a means of maximizing the nation's resources, because the acquisition of more territory would lead to a greater abundance of natural resources, waterways, ports, and human capital. This was crucial for American grand strategy to be successful in the future; it would help create strong, defensible borders and eliminate territorial threats for the North American continent. It also would free up tremendous economic and infrastructure resources. Although Polk was from Tennessee and owned slaves, his "territorial ambitions [for the United States] were not limited to lands where slavery could spread." When measured in terms of results, his policies immeasurably strengthened the United States and enhanced the credibility of its grand strategy. To put this into perspective, as Kagan writes, "between 1845 and 1848 the United States under Polk's leadership expanded by more than one million square miles and laid claim to every inch of territory from the Atlantic to the Pacific north of the Rio Grande and south of the forty-ninth parallel." These "vast acquisitions" were seen as the product of the "determined will of a growing nation."[143]

Annexing Texas

James Polk likely had a preemptive rationale for his policies that expanded the territory of the United States to the west. According to Gaddis, one of the reasons the Polk administration cited for its decision to annex Texas in 1845 was the president's concern that "the territory might not be able to retain the independence it had won from the Mexicans nine years earlier." The risk, in turn, was "that the British or the French might then take it over." For some historians, Polk could be seen to "welcome [– if not] provoke – the war with Mexico that soon followed." This expansion symbolized Polk's decision to take full advantage of any "opportunity to take California, whose great harbors at San Diego, Monterey, and San Francisco might also be vulnerable to seizure by Europeans." Nor was it only the ports, because the decision to take California extended the sovereign control of the United States "over all the territory – present-day Arizona, New Mexico, Colorado, Utah, and Nevada – that lay in between."[144]

Acquiring the Oregon Territory

Besides Texas, Polk sought to acquire all of the Oregon Territory up to 54°40′ latitude. In pursuit of this goal, however, Polk likely was not willing to go to war with Great Britain. To make this strategy work, he had to balance his end (obtaining the Oregon Territory and California) with the means at his disposal. The U.S. military was dramatically weaker than that of Great Britain, and Polk needed to conserve the military in the event of a war with Mexico. In the end, Polk negotiated successfully with Great Britain to obtain the Oregon Territory up to the forty-ninth parallel.

In dealing with the Oregon Territory, the challenge for Polk was to keep the nation's grand strategy in general alignment with its broader goals. In his inaugural address on March 4, 1845, Polk said, "Our title to the country of the Oregon is 'clear and unquestionable,' and already are our people preparing to perfect that title by occupying it with their wives and children."[145] Polk claimed that the United States sought the entire Oregon Territory, which, since the Convention of 1827, was held jointly by Great Britain and the United States for an indefinite period and was "subject to abrogation by either party within a year's notice." Polk's provocative rhetoric about the Oregon Territory was a case of "audacious diplomacy,"[146] which "set off firestorms of protest throughout America – and in London."

In response, Prime Minister Sir Robert Peel, who said that he wanted to "state his case in language 'the most temperate, but at the same time the most decisive,' declared it was Britain that held 'clear and unquestionable' rights to Oregon." However, as *The Times of London* wrote, the American people "should be warned 'in the most explicit manner that their pretentions amount, if acted upon, to the clearest casus belli which has ever yet arisen between Great Britain and the American Union.'" Since Polk wanted to avoid war with Great Britain, largely because the War of 1812 was still fresh in American minds, he directed Secretary of State Buchanan to engage in "serious negotiations" that were designed to achieve "compromise [over] the 49th parallel." After considerable diplomatic and domestic political wrangling, Congress agreed to allow President Polk to use diplomacy "to settle the simmering dispute at the 49th parallel."[147] In June 1846, the United States and Great Britain signed the Oregon Treaty, which provided the United States territory to the forty-ninth parallel.

Annexation Leads to the Mexican-American War

Following the decision in early 1845 to annex Texas, Polk sent American troops in January 1846 into the disputed zone between the Nueces River and the Rio Grande. When American forces were challenged by Mexican troops, Polk declared war on Mexico in May of 1846.

Mexico was plagued by such pathologies as "social and economic rigidities, governmental despotism, massive illiteracy, and high mortality."[148] The United States was the "first nation to recognize Mexican independence, had befriended its sister republic, [and] had signed treaties of territorial limits and mutual friendship with Mexico." To complicate matters, "Britain also had threatened military assault if Mexico wouldn't pay reparations," which fueled pressures for "settlement." Early U.S. efforts focused on diplomacy, but peaceful means had achieved little progress. Before Polk became president, and clearly by the end of Andrew Jackson's presidency, the reparations issue along with other violations severely strained diplomatic relations between the two countries.

Polk likely understood these problems when he said that acquiring California from Mexico was one of his primary goals as president. He also may have believed that resolving this gnawing problem would strengthen the United States, produce clear domestic political benefits for his administration, and bolster the power and influence of the United States in the hemisphere.[149]

This, however, would not come to pass in peaceful terms. Mexico opposed the policy of Manifest Destiny. In May 1846, saying that "'Mexico has passed the boundary of the United States, has invaded our territory, and shed American blood on American soil,'" Polk asked the Congress for a declaration of war, to which Congress agreed.[150] The Polk administration's strategy was to take California by force before the British navy could plant its flag there.[151] To accomplish this, Polk "used the good old American ploy of maneuvering the enemy into firing the first shot."[152] By late May of 1846, at the outset of the war, Polk's war strategy called for General Zachary Taylor to "capture enough territory in northern Mexico to force a settlement," and this was territory that Polk sought in the first place. If the United States could capture both New Mexico and California, Polk's bargaining power over Great Britain would increase.

Although historians describe Polk as "a neophyte in military matters," he clearly had a decisive effect on the war. For example, Polk directed "contingency orders drafted eight months before the war began" – an early, if not the first, instance of American "prewar strategic planning." Polk's role only increased as the Mexican-American War unfolded. He controlled "tightly" the "diverse reins of war – strategy, military appointments, finances, diplomacy, and federal-state relations."[153] The end of the Mexican-American War marked a "brief but explosive era" of U.S. territorial expansion in the 1840s.[154]

Opposition to the Mexican-American War

Polk's military strategy generated significant domestic opposition. For example, many Whigs in Congress were vehemently opposed to the Mexican-American War, which they perceived as both a war of aggression and a war to expand slavery. Initially, Polk had broad public support, but soon the opposition Whigs began to denounce the war. Abraham Lincoln, a member of the Whig opposition, "accused Polk of seeking 'to avoid the scrutiny of his own conduct . . . by fixing the public eye upon military glory.'"[155] Lincoln incisively critiqued the preemptive rationale for the war: "Allow the President to invade a neighboring nation whenever he shall deem it necessary to repel an invasion, and you will allow him to do so whenever he may choose to say he deems it necessary for such purpose, and you allow him to make war at pleasure."[156] As a prelude to modern debates about intervention, the decision to fight the war against Mexico likely produced "more dissent than any major military conflict in U.S. history through the twentieth century."[157]

The consensus among activists who vehemently opposed the war was that "'Mr. Polk's War' iniquitous and unnecessary, [was] an unprovoked war of imperial conquest." Many political opponents of the war criticized "Manifest Destiny" on the grounds that "Democrats used [this argument] to make an unjust war palatable." Some political opponents feared that "Polk's pro-southern orientation" would lead the country to expand slavery, which many opposed on moral grounds. The general sentiment in the country was that this "issue [was] so explosive that it might rip the Union apart." The war continued to drag on. Even after General Winfield Scott's army captured the Mexican capital in September 1847, "the enemy still refused to negotiate." The president debated whether to expand the war's aims, which further sharpened political opposition, but Polk finally "accepted less than he wanted [because] the war ... sparked domestic dissent" and raised questions about Polk's judgment.[158]

Public opinion imposed limits on the nation's grand strategy and coincided with increasing tensions in domestic politics between territorial expansion and the enduring problem of how to end slavery without tearing the country apart.

Building the Nation's Economic Power

Although such matters as Oregon and Mexico consumed much of Polk's attention during the first year and a half of his time in the presidency, one of his critical strengths was his ability to stay focused on his other priorities, including domestic ones, which included reducing tariffs and developing an independent treasury. In the mid-nineteenth century, public debate centered on whether the federal government or private banks should exercise custodianship of federal monies.

The issue for Polk was that building the economic power of the United States depended to a significant extent on having an independent treasury. This would permit the "president to deposit government monies in treasury vaults until they were disbursed in the course of government business." In a decision that changed the foundations of American economic power, on August 5, 1846, the House of Representatives and the Senate agreed on the terms that would govern the functions of an independent treasury. This gave President Polk the independent treasury he believed was essential to expanding the nation's economic power. Polk's policy initiative signaled that the United States had moved "into a new era" in terms of how the federal government managed money. From this time until the Federal Reserve System was created in 1913, the United States Treasury functioned as the central bank and held the government's deposits.[159]

Polk's other economic policy was to reduce the tariffs that impeded free trade and the overall pace and scale of U.S. economic development. Polk pushed a tariff bill in which he proposed to significantly decrease the tariffs imposed by the 1842 policy, which had gone into effect a few years before he became president. A significant consequence of the tariff reduction was a challenge to the "idea that import taxes should be imposed strictly" as part of a strategy to protect specific industries.[160] Despite some political support for tariffs and protectionist trade policies, Great Britain's decision to support free trade – in part because of the then-booming British-American commerce – progressively undermined the protectionist impulse in the United States.[161]

Polk's Legacy in American Grand Strategy

Even though Polk was a one-term president, an important conclusion is that his policies had significant effects on building the domestic foundations of the nation's power. Despite having only one term in office, he succeeded in achieving the full settlement of the West, which was a significant geopolitical accomplishment because it established for the first time fully secure borders for the United States. Furthermore, it positioned the United States to continue its rise to power without threatening or being threatened by the great European powers. Second, he succeeded in setting America on the path toward free trade, which in the long run helped bolster the economy because American businesses now had access to new export markets and new incentives to be competitive and innovative.

Yet, Polk's legacy also symbolizes the growing tension in American grand strategy between the goals of territorial expansion and ending slavery. In practical terms, Polk acquired "immensely valuable territory for the United States, territory that would eventually serve the nation well and even be the pillar on which its future global power rested" – but it came at the price of significant political costs for the Republic. As more territories entered the Union, the already-heated controversy over distributing those territories between slave states and free states escalated. The goal in American grand strategy of territorial expansion became increasingly incompatible with keeping the slavery issue unresolved. New territories meant new states, and new states meant unavoidable shifts in the domestic balance of power. The resulting tensions accelerated the nation's move toward civil war, which would begin a little more than a decade after Polk left office.

One counterargument, however, is that this narrative overstates Polk's contribution to the origins of the Civil War. Although Polk's expansionist policies likely contributed to the political fracture in the nation, the war likely was inevitable in view of the depth and intensity of the emotions that rightly boiled over slavery.[162] These two forces in grand strategy were headed inexorably toward a nasty, messy political collision that led to more instability and eventually to war.

Abraham Lincoln – Guiding the Nation to a New Birth of Freedom

The principal achievement of President Abraham Lincoln, as the sixteenth president of the United States (1861–1865), in the domain of grand strategy was to preserve the Union *and* end slavery.[163] Perfunctory though this may sound, to Lincoln goes the lion's share of the credit for setting America on stable domestic foundations in the mid-nineteenth century by ending the debate over whether the newly organized Western territories would come into the Union as free states or as slave states. Without the Lincoln presidency, which kept the nation unified, it is conceivable that we might have had no cause to discuss "American" grand strategy.[164]

Deepening Divisions between North and South

To understand the origins of the struggle over slavery and the civil war, it is important to emphasize how the divisions between North and South reinforced each other along political, economic, and social dimensions.[165]

Two Divergent Economic Systems

By the middle of the 1800s, the North had evolved into a rapidly developing industrial economy whose states embodied the virtues of capitalism, industry, upward social mobility, modernity, and dynamism. As the historian McPherson writes, "The capitalist ideology [paramount in New England] was a free-labor ideology," which "held that the internalized self-discipline of the Protestant ethic created more efficient workers than the coercive external discipline of slavery." By contrast, the Southern society and economy grew highly dependent upon the single staple crop of cotton, requiring the institution of slavery to sustain the prevailing economic and social way of life. The problem, as McPherson argues, was that "the Southern economy *grew*, but it did not *develop*" because of its extraordinary dependence on slavery to produce and distribute cotton.[166]

Throughout the early-to-mid 1800s, the Southern economy remained highly specialized and thus extremely vulnerable to market shocks. Even though a surge in demand for cotton and increases in cotton prices in the 1850s enabled the South to maintain its agriculture-based economy and system of slave labor, the North continued to develop a highly diversified industrial economy.[167] Many Southerners increasingly believed that the more progressive Northern society, with its political character and ideology, threatened not only their economic livelihoods but their society and social lifestyle. Content with its prosperity – while deeply fearful of the modernizing forces emerging in the North – the South turned inward against the forces of progressivism as its strategy for preserving its way of life. Citing the words of the social theorist and defender of slavery, George Fitzhugh, who captured the feelings of many Southerners at the time in his *Cannibals All,* "capitalism was a war of each against all [borrowing a phrase from Thomas Hobbes], a form of social cannibalism."[168]

The French political thinker and historian, Alexis de Tocqueville, observed the economic contrast between the North and the South when traveling down the Ohio River in the mid-1800s. On the Kentucky side, de Tocqueville noted, "the population is spare. From time to time, a group of slaves can be seen ambling in their carefree way though half-cleared fields. The virgin forest never disappears for long. Society seems to slumber. Man appears idle, whereas nature is the very image of activity and life." In contrast, de Tocqueville observed that on the Ohio side of the river, "the confused hum emanating from the right bank proclaims from afar the presence of industry. Prosperity is apparent everywhere."[169] When de Tocqueville describes the contrast between economic stagnation in the South and the North's industrial dynamism, he is outlining the forces that continued to undermine the nation's economic power *and* moral authority.

Republican William H. Seward of New York wrote on a similar trip through Virginia about "an exhausted soil . . . old and decaying towns, wretchedly-neglected roads, and, in every respect, an absence of enterprise and improvement."[170] Worse, slavery as an "institution undermined 'intelligence, vigor, and energy,'" which for Seward was clearly "incompatible with all . . . the elements of the security, welfare, and greatness of nations."[171] By the 1850s, it was clear to many observers, including Lincoln, that these competing economic systems were fundamentally incompatible and would, if they continued, threaten the nation's domestic stability, foreign interests, and survival. As the historian John Majewski explains, it was clear why so "many northerners wanted to stop slavery from spreading to the western territories."[172] As MacPherson analyzes the problem, "Just as European capitalism had to liberate itself from the outworn restrictions of feudalism, so a dynamic American capitalism could no longer exist with the outworn institution of slavery." In prophetic language, people in the "antislavery camp regarded the conflict as no less than a contest over the future of America."[173] When viewed in these terms, at stake was not only the grand strategy of the United States, but also the survival of the deeply fractured and polarized nation.

Two Conflicting Political Parties

These two different economic systems underpinned a rigid two-party system that was highly polarized into two factions. In one faction were the Democrats, who "inherited the Jeffersonian commitment to states' rights, limited government, traditional economic arrangements, and religious pluralism." In the second faction, the "Whigs [who were predominant in the North] inherited the Federalist belief in nationalism, a strong government, economic innovation, and cultural homogeneity."[174] The ideological differences between these factions over the development of politics and economics would rip apart the nation in the immensely violent and destructive Civil War, which began in 1861.

As Lincoln moved to deal with the consequences of the collision between these powerful forces, another source of strife was the palpable sense of uncertainty about what would happen in the vast territories the nation had acquired during the first half of the nineteenth century.[175] The central question of whether these new territories would be organized as slave or free states sparked an intense national debate over the political future of the country, including the economic foundations of its power. While both parties wanted the expansion of the nation, the North and South saw this in different ways. The North wanted to expand "to enhance American prestige, or to fulfill America's 'manifest destiny' to control the whole of the North American continent."[176] The South was eager to expand, but the principal motivation behind its expansionist policies was to increase the number of slave states in order to preserve the tenuous balance of power in the federal government and the economic foundations of its power.

The two major political parties in the early-to-mid nineteenth century also split along regional lines over the nature of westward expansion. Whereas the Whigs, such as Lincoln, "favored expansion *over time* by means of economic growth and modernization," the strategy of the Democrats was to support "expansion *over space* by the acquisition of new territory [as a strategy] to replicate the traditional institutions of older states."[177] The tension between internal economic development and external territorial acquisition was seen as a matter of survival to Southerners.[178]

In this highly polarized climate, Southern perceptions of the threat peaked. With the election of 1860, Abraham Lincoln gained the presidency and brought more Republicans into the Congress. With the collapse of the Whig Party, the new Republican Party was formed with Abraham Lincoln as its leader. This election had momentous political consequences, because "Until 1856 no major party had expressed a clear opposition to slavery." But within four years, the electorate in the North had elected a president whose policies seemed destined to bring slavery to an end. MacPherson continues: "Lincoln's election had foreshadowed the end of [the South's disproportionate power in the national government]." What his election signaled was a dramatic shift in the balance of power in American politics that had disastrous consequences for the "Old South." When the South launched its own counterrevolution of independence that was designed "to escape the dreaded consequences" of the North's growing power and influence over the course of events in the United States, the inevitable result was the Civil War.[179]

Lincoln's ideas about preserving the nation and ending slavery shaped his policies and defined American grand strategy as much as it did for his most influential predecessors, notably Washington and Jefferson. One way to understand the evolution in American grand strategy during Lincoln's administration is to examine his years as a presidential candidate, his wartime presidency, and the consequences for the nation after his death.

Lincoln's Early Views on Slavery

One of Lincoln's most extraordinary qualities was in his selection and maintenance of the twin goals in his grand strategy of preserving the Union and ending slavery. Both political ends were evident in the earliest moments of Lincoln's political career, and to his credit he never veered from them.

Lincoln always sought to end slavery, either through a gradual social and economic process or through legislation. The grand strategic issue for him was not whether to end slavery but how, when, and at what cost. In his first presidential campaign speech delivered on June 16, 1858 – often referred to as the "House Divided" address – Lincoln appeared to be ambivalent about the issue of slavery and yet absolutely emphatic that the Union must be preserved. Historian Sean Wilentz describes the momentous event:

> Addressing a jacketless, sweating crowd inside the state Capitol, Lincoln opened with his main point. For five years, he charged, the federal government had followed an avowed policy of ending agitation over slavery, only to stir that agitation even more: 'In *my* opinion, it *will* not cease until a *crisis* shall have been reached, and passed. 'A house divided against itself cannot stand.' I believe this government cannot endure, permanently half *slave* and half *free*. I do not expect the Union to be *dissolved* – I do not expect the house to *fall* – but I do expect it will cease to be divided. It will become *all* one thing, or *all* the other.'"[180]

In this speech, Lincoln clearly made the point that keeping the nation united was the core principle of his campaign and would govern his presidency, if he should win. Importantly, he stated that he did not expect the house to become all slave; rather "he ... expected freedom would prevail against slavery." However, Lincoln deflected accusations from his opponent Stephen Douglas, who argued that the "House Divided" speech was a cover for abolitionist ambitions. To this charge, Lincoln said "that he had no plan for slavery's elimination, only a certainty that it would one day occur."[181] These are very carefully chosen words. He remains certain of the grand strategic end of eliminating slavery, but he does not admit to having a plan for bringing it about. He did not need a plan because slavery was dying as a result of the trends already discussed in this chapter. The North's economy was stronger, its political power was growing, and as long as new slave states would not be admitted, proslavery politicians would cease to have sufficient power in the federal government to promote and protect their interests.

Lincoln's position proceeded from the view that containment of slavery would inevitably lead to its elimination.[182] Thus, in describing a natural course for the extinction of slavery, Lincoln and the Republicans distinguished themselves from Douglas, whom they claimed saw "no end [to] the institution of slavery."[183] Although Lincoln was keenly aware of the immorality of slavery, he was never an abolitionist until late in his presidency when he sought passage of the Thirteenth Amendment. That is, he never advocated the immediate legal termination of slavery.

Lincoln, however, never deviated from his mission of preserving the Union. As president-elect, Lincoln believed that "the Union was older than any of the states, that secession was anarchy, and that in this current crisis hung the fate of constitutional democracy." His inaugural address sheds light on his initial strategy of appealing to Southerners' nationalist principles, as well as what he believed to be their better judgment in the need to preserve the Union.[184] Even though he believed slavery was wrong, "the only legitimate way to settle the matter, Lincoln insisted . . . was through a deliberate democratic decision by the nation's citizenry."[185]

Lincoln's first inaugural address, delivered on March 4, 1861, was neither a war message nor unfriendly to the South. Although the president clearly sought to steer the nation in a positive moral direction toward a free society, he "privately assured Southern friends that his administration would not interfere with slavery in the states or in the District of Columbia, would do nothing against the interstate slave trade, would enforce the Fugitive Slave Law, and would urge Northern states to repeal or modify their personal liberty laws."[186] The problem lay in the fundamental difference of opinion over slavery's extension into the territories. As Lincoln said in his first inaugural address, "One section of our country believes slavery is *right* and ought to be extended, while the other believes it is *wrong* and ought not to be extended."[187]

Lincoln as a Grand Strategist in the Civil War

Lincoln also understood the principle of unity in the nation's strategy for war and its grand strategy. He understood military objectives in their grand strategic context and saw the political necessities of the conduct of the war more clearly than did many of his generals. He understood, for instance, that the strategic (that is, military) aim was the destruction of the South's ability to wage war, but he also understood the importance of who was the initial aggressor in the war.

When he gave his first inaugural address, Lincoln knew that war – as the scholar Eliot Cohen writes in *Supreme Command* – was imminent, but he also knew that he had to extend the hand of reconciliation to possibly forestall war and to highlight the fact that the South was the aggressor, in the event that war began. In fact, soon after he was inaugurated, the crisis escalated with the Southern siege of Fort Sumter, South Carolina. The issue was whether and how to resupply the fort's federal garrison. As Cohen continues, "overruling his senior advisers, Lincoln ordered the nonviolent resupply of Sumter. Understanding as he did that the South would rise to the bait, he would place the onus of firing the first shots in a civil war on the Confederacy.[188] His decision would bring the crisis to a head, generate widespread public support in the Union for using force against the South, and signal the beginning of hostilities in the American Civil War.

Cohen disagrees with the commonly held view that "Lincoln's greatest challenge as commander in chief was finding a competent general to successfully execute the war."[189]

In reality, Cohen finds that "Lincoln exercised a constant oversight of the war effort from beginning to end [and] did not hesitate to overrule his military advisers." Thus he credits Lincoln with the "ability to do much more than pick a general." One of the more troubling difficulties with Lincoln's strategy was that "too many Union commanders refused to believe that the war would be won by defeating the enemy in the field."[190] To undermine the corrosive effects of this line of thought, Lincoln consistently reiterated the idea that the Union's objective was not *Richmond* (because Lincoln insisted that the whole country was already Union soil), but *Lee's army*.

For the scholar Cohen, Lincoln's war strategy had five interrelated propositions that showed he was a grand strategic thinker of the first order. His fundamental war aim was to restore the Union, which did not mean that he had abandoned his aim of ending slavery. It meant he saw preservation of the Union as the logical precondition for ending slavery and preserving American democracy. In contrast, ending slavery would not necessarily lead to the preservation of the Union. Second, the South had to fire first to ensure that the Union's policy was one of response. Third, the South had to be deprived of external sources of support, notably from Europe. Fourth, Union armies would have to crush the Confederate forces. Finally, this war would have to be waged on the offensive.

"As often occurs in war," writes Cohen, "the fundamental objectives changed as a result of the interactions that the fighting brought about."[191] Although "the war was not initially a war to end slavery – 'If I could save the Union without freeing any slave I would do that'[192] – it became such."[193] As events unfolded, Lincoln's grand strategy shifted toward preserving the Union; ending slavery initially took a backseat. In summarizing the situation Lincoln faced,[194] the historian McPherson argues that Lincoln's challenge "was to mold these disparate elements into a government that could win the war."[195] The president needed to project a clearly defined vision of the concept and character of the Union, if it was to prevail.[196] Lincoln described a struggle "not altogether for today," but "for a vast future," because he saw America's exceptionalism as symbolic of a democratic experiment for humankind. The war was not just about the survival of the U.S. government, but was equally about the survival of the idea of democracy. For Lincoln, the concepts of exceptionalism and grand strategy likely were inextricably linked.

What emerges is the conclusion that preserving the Union was the overriding objective in Lincoln's grand strategy. McPherson identified Lincoln's political predicament precisely when he wrote, "The problem with this lofty rhetoric of dying to make men free was that in 1861 the North was fighting for the restoration of a slaveholding Union." The question is this: Why did Lincoln not simply proclaim "the war to be fought for freedom as well as for the Union?" The answer, McPherson argues, lies in the political problems associated with building and sustaining sufficient public support for Lincoln's wartime policies while executing his constitutional obligations as president to maintain the nation as one sovereign entity.[197]

By the spring of 1862, Lincoln was convinced that the war ultimately had to bring slavery to an end. During the ten weeks before Lincoln issued the Emancipation Proclamation on January 1, 1863, his public statements were marked by "caution and indirection." In balancing "the pros and cons of emancipation in his September 13 reply to a group of Chicago clergymen who had borne to Washington a petition for freedom," President Lincoln "agreed that 'slavery is the root of the rebellion, or at least its *sine qua non*.'" He also agreed that "emancipation would help us in Europe and convince them that we are incited by something more than ambition." However, "with Confederate armies on the offensive and Union armies reeling backwards, 'what *good* would a proclamation of emancipation from me do? Would *my* word free the slaves, when I cannot even enforce the Constitution in the rebel states?'"[198]

The turning point in Lincoln's grand strategy occurred when "Lincoln freed the slaves ... [He did so to] win the war and make the goals of the war consistent with the principles of the Declaration that he had stated to be the essence of American nationhood." This decision Lincoln justified "as a 'military necessity,' but in striking at slavery he also knew he was striking at 'the heart of the rebellion,' the underpinning of the southern way of life." Thereafter, "the northern war aim became not merely the defeat of rebellion," but as the "war for the Union became a war of justice [it became] a moral crusade for liberty."[199] This shift in Lincoln's thinking also imposed a profound shift in his grand strategy; a recurring theme in grand strategy is to keep the military strategy in close unity with the nation's grand strategy. In the case of the Civil War, Lincoln's ideological shift was consistent with a strategy of total war. As Kagan explains, "The ideological nature of the conflict, as well as the evolving technology of warfare, helped determine the brutal, horrific manner of the struggle."

When the Civil War became an ideological struggle, it "became a 'total' war waged not only between combatants but between and against peoples." It was evident to Lincoln and his military advisors that the war likely would have to be waged as a total war if it was to successfully achieve its objectives. Although not a vigorous opponent of slavery, General Grant realized "that the South was fighting for a way of life and ... would not surrender until they concluded that the loss of their civilization was preferable to the horrors of war." In effect, Grant's view was that "the North must 'make the war so terrible ... [and] make them so sick of war that the generations would pass away before that would again appeal to it.'"[200] This view represented a dramatic change in the policies of the Lincoln administration, which had started a limited war for the limited means of preserving the Union and leaving slavery untouched in the original slaveholding states.

With the signing of the Emancipation Proclamation on January 1, 1863, Lincoln and his advisors and generals embarked on a new fight to preserve the nation and redefine the nation's character. Facing an existential threat to the country, Lincoln's grand strategy was designed not only to balance means with ends (for example, the shift to total war to achieve a territorial and ideological victory), but also to reshape the political nature and moral course of the nation he was fighting to preserve.

Lincoln's Legacy in American Grand Strategy

The Civil War had the greatest effect on American grand strategy of any event since the founding of the Republic. It was "America's second great moral war, but unlike the Revolution it was a war of conquest." In practical terms, the function of the war was for the North to "liberate ... the oppressed segment of the South's population and subjugate ... the oppressors." Since the Civil War "was America's first experiment in ideological conquest ... [this] was America's first experiment in 'nation-building.'"[201] In the language of grand strategy, Lincoln's policy built the basis for the expectation that the strategies pursued by the United States should be guided by a moral and humane obligation to help the oppressed and the defeated.[202]

In the context of American grand strategy, Kagan writes that "Americans did not embark on a positive 'mission' to change the world after the Civil War." Nor subsequently has American grand strategy focused on "global reform, nor any deliberate policy to remake any specific country in the liberal mold." This principle in grand strategy profoundly influenced U.S. foreign policy, as we saw when Lincoln appealed to higher morality with his rejection of "the doctrine of self-interest as the sole guide to human action and also as the sole guide to national action." Relying on ideas that resonated deeply in American political culture, Lincoln's contribution to American grand strategy was to link the building of the domestic foundations of American power to its moral identity and political and economic development. The Declaration of Independence was not merely a document to recast the relationship with Great Britain, because under Lincoln it became a repository of the values inherent in American grand strategy.[203]

Prominent citizens as well as public officials, including those in the Lincoln administration, understood that the existence of slavery at home had strategic implications for American power and influence abroad. They believed that "the 'stain' of American slavery prevented the United States from fulfilling its role as the exemplar of republican democracy for peoples struggling against despotism the world over."[204] The problem, as expressed by Charles Sumner, a U.S. Senator and staunch opponent of slavery, was that "slavery had degraded 'our country' and prevented 'its example from being all-conquering.'" Lincoln felt that "the mere existence of slavery deprived 'our republican example of its just influence in the world,'" because it allowed "'the enemies of free institutions to taunt us as hypocrites.'"[205]

Lincoln's influence on the principles that defined American grand strategy during his administration is at least as important as that of his predecessors. What Lincoln emphasized in his policies toward the Civil War is best expressed as a sense of "moral responsibility," which means for Kagan that the community has a "duty to further human equality ... [as well as] a more far-reaching implication [of] the United States [as] more than just a beacon of hope." The Declaration of Independence established an existential "commitment to equality, which as Lincoln insisted, subsequent generations of Americans should hold as 'an abstract truth, applicable to all men at all times.'"[206] These deeply powerful concepts in American grand strategy continue to resonate more than a century later.

In the end, the Civil War unquestionably strengthened American grand strategy, because it unified the nation and provided the basis for its political, economic, and military power. Without this unifying force, it is unclear whether the United States would have emerged as a dominant force in international politics.

Conclusions on the First Principle of American Grand Strategy

The main focus of America's early leadership in the administrations from Washington to Lincoln was to build the domestic foundations of the nation's power. Such leaders as Washington and Jefferson sought to shape America into a state that could strike a balance between its democratic ideals and the need for central authority if it was to survive and thrive. The decentralization of the colonies, coupled with debt from the Revolutionary War, made it necessary to engage in nation-building at home rather than overseas entanglements. It was the fear of being drawn into unnecessary wars that made the nation's early presidents unwilling to enter alliances with foreign governments.[207]

As Alexander Hamilton explained during Washington's presidency, "If we can avoid War for ten or twelve years more we shall then have acquired a maturity, which ... will authorize us on our national decisions to take a higher & more *imposing* tone."[208] In words that exemplify the proper conduct of grand strategy, a state should build the basis for its power first and only then pursue its foreign policy interests. To reverse that sequence is to put the state in danger, particularly in terms of its ability to manage the balance between means and ends, which remains a central guiding principle of grand strategy.

One key aspect to the articulation and implementation of America's early grand strategy was the process of territorial expansion. The nation's early presidents believed it was critical to expand the nation's borders and territory. Washington's focus was westward as he expanded the nation's borders to the Mississippi, believing that America's future was in the untapped resources to the west, and not across the ocean to Europe. Even Jefferson, a man vociferously opposed to the idea of a strong central government, enthusiastically exploited the opportunity for westward expansion with the Louisiana Purchase. Perhaps the most explicit case of artful balancing in grand strategy was James Polk's dramatic expansion of territory through the annexation of Texas and acquisition of the Oregon Territory. Nonetheless, America's westward expansion did not come without costs. In order to continue its march toward the Pacific, the United States engaged in brutal Indian removal policies that were at deep odds with its own expressed ideals.

Much of America's westward expansion prompted another deeply disturbing ethical question – that of slavery. New states confronted the question plaguing the nation since its inception: How should the United States handle the institution of slavery? This institution was morally at odds with America's political ideals and economically at odds with the ideals of a free market economy. The great contrast between economic stagnation in the South and the North's industrial dynamism was sapping the nation's moral, political, and economic foundations. Although slavery undermined American power and moral authority, the aspiration to maintain the Union trumped the desire to deal with the issue in the seventy years that had passed since the Revolution. Finally, in 1861, the tensions between the objectives of territorial expansion and the eradication of slavery were too great for the nation to bear without a great military cataclysm. Out of the debate over whether newly organized western territories would come into the Union as free states or as slave states, the nation saw this long-simmering political conflict burst into a bloody civil war.

Although slavery was the root cause of the Civil War when the South seceded from the United States, an enduring aspect of the war was the priority President Lincoln placed on preserving the Union. By 1862, Lincoln knew that he must strike at the source of the Southern rebellion by outlawing slavery. With the signing of the Emancipation Proclamation, President Lincoln embarked on a struggle to preserve the nation and redefine the national character of the Union. With his actions and the eventual Union victory, Lincoln linked the moral and *realpolitik* dimensions in American grand strategy to the principle that our power abroad depends on adherence to our values at home.

In reviewing the span of history from the late eighteenth century until the end of the Lincoln administration, one of the most deeply resonant themes to emerge is the lasting impact of the emphasis of the nation's early presidents on expanding the nation, preserving its democratic values, and projecting America's long-term interests. Together they succeeded in establishing the domestic foundations of American power so successfully that by the early twentieth century the United States could confidently enter the ranks of the most powerful and influential states in the world.[209] America's entry into global politics is the legacy of American grand strategy to which we turn next.

8 Restraining Sources of Disorder: Theodore Roosevelt to Franklin Delano Roosevelt

This chapter examines the United States' rise to great power status and how that established the second principle of American grand strategy – the principle of restraining sources of disorder and acting to stabilize the system against revolutionary threats. At the turn of the century, the United States' growing economic capacity combined with a large population and vast natural resources enabled it to become a regional and then global power. Under the leadership of Theodore Roosevelt, America began to wield greater power regionally in the Western Hemisphere through its increasing economic and military capabilities. The chapter then turns to Woodrow Wilson's presidency, distinguished by America's entry into World War I, Wilson's liberal institutionalism, and the Senate's rejection of the League of Nations. After World War I, the United States rose to great power status as the European states fell dramatically from their position at the top of the international system. World War II and its devastation of Europe perpetuated this slow rise of America and accelerated Europe's decline. By the end of World War II, America was the world's strongest democratic nation and the "leader of the free world."

The Second Principle: Restraining the Sources of World Disorder and Serving as the System Stabilizer

This section examines American grand strategy in the revolutionary era, when ideological movements and other forces were seeking to transform the international system. Chapter 6 covered this revolutionary era of grand strategy in theory and practice. As we examine the evolution of American grand strategy against the backdrop of the revolutionary era, we shall see that the United States develops a principle in its grand strategy of restraining sources of disorder and addressing any threats to the overall stability of the international system.

During this time, the United States rises from wealth to power, but it does so in some exceptional ways that contribute to the sense of exceptionalism in American grand strategy.[1] The concept of exceptionalism relates to the unique way in which the United States rose to power and in how it exercised that power in favor of stability and world order once it became a great power.[2]

First, America's rise to power in the late nineteenth and early twentieth centuries was peaceful and reluctant. It was peaceful because the United States was taking over from the like-minded, liberal system under the tutelage of the British Empire. It was simultaneously peaceful because it was not so much an American rise to power as the startling and precipitous fall of a European power. In this period from Theodore Roosevelt through World War I and then Franklin Roosevelt through World War II, the European great powers destroyed their own ability to rule the world. They so exhausted one another in two great wars that the United States in each case emerged much stronger at a time when both victors and vanquished were weakened severely.

The reluctance to become a global power was a holdover from the Washingtonian policies that were committed to neutrality, regional autonomy, and nonentanglement in Europe. This resonates with the more populist-based trend in American grand strategy of staying apart from world politics in general and only entering the fray when it is necessary to defend specific interests. The United States, unlike other European great powers in the history of grand strategy, did not want or seek hegemony. It was and remains a reluctant rising power whose people and leaders twice had to be roused by offensive attacks against it before the nation would move to play a more active role in international relations. Its entries into both world wars were triggered not by a deliberate move to achieve hegemony but in response to surprise attacks: in 1917 it was Germany's surprise attacks on American shipping, and in 1941 it was the Japanese attack on Pearl Harbor. These attacks overcame the fundamental American reluctance to enter European wars; to become so entangled had been close to anathema in America's grand strategy since the administration of George Washington.

But the attacks themselves did not simply rouse the American people to rally around the flag and avenge the unjustified aggression. They also represented attacks on the world order, which contributed to the origins of the principle in American grand strategy that emerged in the twentieth century of organizing the nation to restrain sources of world disorder. The exceptionalism in American foreign policy is defined not only in terms of how it rose to power, but in how and why it defined its priorities once it achieved great power status.

In practice, the United States has never been or seen itself as a revolutionary state in the revisionist tradition. Nor has it been a purely status quo–oriented state. In terms of grand strategy, the United States has tended to operate as a gradualist state, as discussed later. When Henry Kissinger defines a revolutionary state, he does so by emphasizing that "the distinguishing feature of a revolutionary power is not that it feels threatened – such feeling is inherent in the nature of international relations based on sovereign states – but that nothing can reassure it. Only absolute security – the neutralization of the opponent – is considered a sufficient guarantee, and thus the desire of one power for absolute security means absolute insecurity for all the others."[3] American grand strategy has never sought absolute security vis-à-vis others because it has been exceptionally favored with having nearly absolute security because of its geopolitical position.

Since Kissinger gave this definition, international relations scholars have refined the definition of revolutionary power to give it the new term of "revisionist." Broadly speaking, a revisionist state is a state that does not only want to adjust the distribution of power in the system but also seeks to change the "rules of the game" and transform the ideological basis of that system. The "rules of the game" are defined as the institutions and systems of regulation that determine the distribution of economic and political power within the system. Napoleonic France and Nazi Germany are classic examples of revisionist powers.

Does this mean American grand strategy is essentially status quo oriented? The answer is emphatically no, because the United States favors changes to the internal structure of some states, but only when those states threaten the stability of the economic and political system. Revisionist states favor wholesale change or transformation of the system, whereas status quo states essentially do not favor change. Gradualist states, of which the United States is a prominent example among the few such states, tend to favor slow, careful democratic change under limited circumstances. This tradition in American grand strategy emerged in the first half of the twentieth century and endures today.

The counterargument to this view of a gradualist orientation in American grand strategy is the idealistic tradition in American foreign policy that the scholar Walter Russell Mead calls "Wilsonianism." This he defines as the tradition rooted in the belief "that the United States has both a moral obligation and an important national interest in spreading American democratic and social values throughout the world, creating a peaceful international community that accepts the rule of law."[4] Indeed, Wilson, as discussed in this chapter, articulated such a vision of American grand strategy, but Wilson's vision was not then, nor is it now, the American vision. Wilson was an idealist who arguably advanced a revisionist agenda in his foreign policy, but his views have to be placed in historical context. Nor do they serve to establish that American grand strategy became fundamentally revisionist in its orientation. On the contrary, the domestic reaction to Wilson's agenda showed that America's preference in grand strategy was for the status quo and avoiding the ambitious, transformative agendas associated with revisionism. Moreover, even Wilson's Fourteen Points and his linking grand strategy to values and interests should be seen in their proper historical context. His agenda was not as revolutionary as some scholars argue, but represented a gradualist preference for slow, calibrated change rather than a revolutionary belief in rapid, far-reaching transformation.

In sum, this chapter examines the evolution of a second principle of American grand strategy for dealing with political and economic changes to the international system. In the era marked by revolutions and revolutionary ideologies, the United States established itself as a source of restraint to prevent rapid and radical change. Its people and its leaders were skeptical of the possibility of achieving fast transformation of the system and also fearful of the unintended consequences. Thus, the tradition, beginning with Theodore Roosevelt and maintained with extraordinary consistency ever since, rested on a principle of restraining the sources of disorder, even when those sources of disorder had democratic and egalitarian roots. Yet, exercising restraint in dealing with the sources of disorder did not always mean a preference for the status quo. Sometimes it meant a preference for slow, gradual democratic change when it could be managed in a way that contributed to the overall stability of the system.

President Theodore Roosevelt – Making Capitalism Safe for Democracy and Projecting Diplomatic and Military Power Overseas

The twenty-sixth president of the United States, Theodore "Teddy" Roosevelt (1901–1909), TR, dramatically shaped the evolution of American grand strategy in the early years of the twentieth century. He was president at the turn of the century after a series of lackluster presidencies in the post–Civil War era. As the first effective articulator and implementer of American grand strategy since Lincoln, Roosevelt's administration exerted a critical influence on the formation of American grand strategy at a time that some observers describe as "the birth of modern America."[5] This era is also an era marked by great revolutionary turmoil in the system.[6]

The character of the revolutionary era was strikingly evident in how Roosevelt came to the presidency. As vice president when President McKinley was shot and killed by an anarchist assassin on September 14, 1901, Roosevelt was sworn in on the same day. McKinley was only one of several victims of assassination during this time, because this was an era of great upheaval and ideological ferment.[7] Roosevelt's response was not to side with the counterrevolutionaries, monarchists, and nobles of Europe. Nor was his response to concede the need for radical change. Instead, he adopted a two-track gradualist grand strategy that would exert a powerful influence on American presidents over the next century. First, his grand strategy focused on building the domestic foundations of American national power by restraining the excesses of capitalism, accomplished through safety regulations and trust busting. Second, in the conduct of foreign policy, his grand strategy focused on using measured, gradual moves in the projection of American power globally through diplomacy and building a modern blue-water navy. He did not move quickly to establish hegemony, but worked within the system to change it so that it would align with America's long-term interests.

Roosevelt pursued a number of policies – notably in building the Panama Canal and using diplomacy – that were designed to increase the nation's power and influence on the international stage. He called the isthmian canal that connected the Atlantic and Pacific Oceans one of the "future highways of civilization." To build the canal, he supported Panamanian rebels against the Colombian government, but only after the Colombian congress refused to cooperate in building the canal. In parallel with this policy, he greatly increased the size and capabilities of the United States Navy, which raised the international prestige of the United States and dramatically increased the nation's ability to project military power. Finally, Roosevelt balanced his policy of military expansion with diplomatic initiatives. For example, he mediated two great power conflicts – the Russo-Japanese War in 1905 and the Moroccan crisis between France and Germany in 1911. Yet, Roosevelt also strengthened the domestic foundations of American power in enduring ways as he pioneered modern food and drug safety regulations, the land conservation system, and pro-competition trust-busting legislation.

Roosevelt's Domestic Policy: Making Capitalism Safe for Democracy

President Roosevelt's domestic grand strategy focused on two specific priorities. These were to protect the American people from the privations of unrestrained capitalism and to preserve the natural environment from the depredations of industrial growth and expansion. In the case of the former, Roosevelt sought to protect the nation from "bad trusts, which injured the public welfare," and from the consequences of mislabeled medicine and unhealthy food.[8] In terms of the latter, he sought to protect the environment from unrestrained industrial development in order to preserve America's natural resources for future generations. These remain the signature accomplishments of his administration on the domestic front.

Trust Busting

Roosevelt focused on several policies as his administration strengthened the domestic foundations of American power. First, Roosevelt sought a balanced approach to dealing with sizable corporations and, specifically, their economic impact. Against these great "trusts," he undertook "trust-busting" actions that were designed to break up these large companies and increase competition in the market. Monopolies are anticompetitive by definition, and Roosevelt understood that monopolistic trusts would eventually undermine the capitalist system's innovative and progressive elements. There was overwhelming public sentiment that monopolies "stifle economic opportunity for the middle class." When early in his first term Roosevelt attempted to "publicize corporate affairs," he "distinguished between good trusts, which were socially useful, and bad trusts, which injured the public."

Roosevelt was not antibusiness but wanted to restrain capitalism's self-destructive excesses, knowing "that it was no longer enough for a modern nation to promote economic growth alone" because it was essential in political and economic terms to "regulate the excesses and the socially harmful actions of corporations." According to Gould, Roosevelt's policies were designed to develop and later use greater government power to regulate large corporations that were arguably acting against, or at least weakening, the nation's interests. Reflecting on his presidency, Roosevelt said, "one of the vital questions with which as President I had to deal was the attitude of the Nation towards the great corporations." To a large extent, Roosevelt embodied the tension between two contending schools of thought on government-business relations in American history. The first group included "men who understand and practice the deep underlying philosophy of the Lincoln school of American political thought," who were "necessarily Hamiltonian in their belief in a strong and efficient National Government." By contrast, the political center of gravity of the second group resided in those who are "Jeffersonian in their belief in the people as the ultimate authority, and in the welfare of the people as the end of Government."[9]

For Roosevelt, those "who first applied the extreme Democratic theory in American life were, like Jefferson, ultra individualists."[10] In the century since the Jefferson presidency, Roosevelt argued, the "need had been exactly reversed" because individualism became a cloaking ideology for corporate dominance. So in Roosevelt's view, "complete freedom for the individual ... turned out in practice to mean perfect freedom for the strong to wrong the weak."[11] In the absence of government control, the United States had seen momentous "growth in the financial and industrial world both of natural individuals and ... corporations." This development worried Roosevelt because, as he warned, "In no other country in the world had such enormous fortunes been gained."[12]

The challenge for American grand strategy posed by these "enormous fortunes" is that, while adding to the nation's economic power, they would weaken the social harmony on which long-term stability of the nation depended.[13] As Roosevelt observed, "The big reactionaries of the business world and their allies ... among politicians and newspaper editors ... fought to keep matters absolutely unchanged." Predictably, these individuals sought "immunity from governmental control," which, if granted, "would have been as ... foolish as immunity to the barons of the twelfth century."[14] The power of corporate interests had to be checked – balanced with that of the people – or the nation would run the risk that revolutionary ideologies would take hold in American society.

The Roosevelt administration targeted Standard Oil Company when "independent oil men in newly opened fields in Kansas complained that Standard Oil's monopolistic tactics were forcing down prices and injuring their interests."[15] As the head of the Bureau of Corporations (which had jurisdiction to investigate market-dominant businesses) concluded, "Standard Oil 'has habitually received from the railroads, and is now receiving, secret rates and other unjust and illegal discriminations.'"[16] Roosevelt complained of "'monopolistic control' that stretched 'from the well of the producer to the door step of the consumer.'"[17] These positions by the president and his subsequent actions were so highly popular politically that economic populism began to emerge as a powerful force during the Roosevelt administration and remains as such in American politics today.[18]

Pure Food and Drug Act and Meat Inspection

Upton Sinclair's *The Jungle*, published in 1906, fueled a public outcry across the United States in which the public and officials deplored the filth of meat-packing plants. In response, Roosevelt pushed for and Congress passed both the Pure Food and Drug Act and the Federal Meat Inspection Act in 1906. After the furor over *The Jungle*, and to show his administration's concern with public fears, Roosevelt appointed two individuals "to conduct an investigation into the Chicago stockyards." Predictably, the report to President Roosevelt confirmed the public's worst fears, leading Roosevelt to declare that the state of food processing was "unclean" and "dangerous to [one's] health."[19] His efforts to regulate the meat-packing industry were part of his agenda to make capitalism safe for the public and to increase the economic power of the United States by striking the right balance between the functions of a free market and the need for government oversight.

For Roosevelt, these problems posed direct threats to the public health and to the nation's welfare. In his annual message of December 1905, Roosevelt called for Congress to pass legislation that would "regulate interstate commerce in misbranded and adulterated foods, drinks, and drugs" in order "to secure the health and welfare of the consuming public."[20] His policies exemplified his commitment to defending the national interests against the excesses of the private sector.

Roosevelt's Foreign Policy: Restraining Revolution, Mediating Conflicts, and Projecting Naval Power

President Roosevelt was thoroughly and intimately interested and involved in foreign affairs, but the same cannot be said about the American public, which was not so attuned to foreign policy matters. His strategy was to use his speeches and the "bully pulpit" (a term whose origins many attribute to Roosevelt) to implore the populace to work on behalf of their country and take active interest in events beyond America's borders. In one speech prior to his presidency, Roosevelt warned, "We cannot sit huddled within our own borders and avow ourselves merely an assemblage of well-to-do hucksters who care nothing for what happens beyond." As nations come "into closer and closer contact," and "if we are to hold our own in the struggle for naval and commercial supremacy," it was imperative for the nation to "build up our Power."[21] Roosevelt anticipated that the tradition dating from George Washington's administration of spurning nonentangling alliances was becoming untenable in the increasingly interdependent economic and political global system of the early twentieth century.

Nevertheless, the American public remained reluctant to involve the United States deeply in international politics. As the scholar Herring writes, "When the nation was not threatened from abroad . . . the mass public . . . showed little interest in foreign policy." A powerful theme in politics at the time was that Americans strongly and fervently believed "their country should not join alliances or assume commitments that could lead to war."[22] Firmly fixed in Roosevelt's mind was how essential it was for him to "conceal his great-power diplomacy" in view of the state of public opinion in the United States. Roosevelt "downplayed and masked his actions [largely] because his countrymen had so little interest in world politics."[23] What was consistent, however, was how public opinion strongly resonated with the Washingtonian tradition of remaining isolated "from affairs outside the Western Hemisphere, particularly in Europe." In effect, this public attitude "formed a barrier to openly [supporting American] involvement in great power politics." Roosevelt had to deal with this lack of public support, which explains in part the "isolationist tradition in his utterances and publicized actions."[24] He clearly believed that the United States was destined to play an important role in world affairs but, like other presidents, realized that he alone could not push the American people toward a more activist role in the world. However, his administration succeeded in gradually shifting American policy toward a more activist posture, which took the form of his major policy legacy known as the Roosevelt Corollary.

Roosevelt Corollary to the Monroe Doctrine

In 1904, President Roosevelt articulated his corollary to the Monroe Doctrine when it became evident that European nations – notably, Germany – intended to establish footholds in the Caribbean. As part of his strategy for reaffirming American hegemony in the hemisphere and dissuading the European powers from interfering in the Western Hemisphere, Roosevelt initiated his corollary – known as the Roosevelt Corollary to the Monroe Doctrine – calling for greater American involvement in Latin American affairs.[25]

In effect, TR's corollary stipulated that the United States would intervene as a last resort to "ensure that other nations in the Western Hemisphere fulfilled their obligations to international creditors, and did not violate the rights of the United States or invite 'foreign aggression to the detriment of the entire body of American nations.'"[26] One criticism of American grand strategy during this era, and which continues to the present, was Washington's tendency to use military force to establish stability in nations in Latin America.

For some observers, Roosevelt routinely, perhaps even casually, resorted to actions that some interpreted as using American power and influence in a wanton and reckless fashion. The historian John Milton Cooper, however, contests this view, writing, "Roosevelt did not throw America's weight around in Panama and the Caribbean just for fun." Whereas "Roosevelt may have exaggerated European designs in the Western Hemisphere," he was fully aware of the "propensities of weak Latin American regimes [to run] up and then default . . . on debts to foreign bankers."[27] In Cooper's view, Roosevelt believed that this condition "created standing temptations [to engage in] outside intervention." A concern in formulating American grand strategy was, according to Cooper, "the European record of finding excuses to establish colonial beachheads in Africa and Asia," none of which was reassuring to Roosevelt. His corollary to the Monroe Doctrine was designed to prevent a race among the European powers to establish themselves in the Western Hemisphere. It was in this strategic climate that the Dominican Republic faced a possible invasion by European debt collectors, and Roosevelt ordered the invasion of the island, the seizure of its customs houses, and its establishment as a protectorate.

Later on, a canal built through the heart of Central America helped build up American naval power, which Roosevelt wanted to use to strengthen his position in Latin America and bolster the nation's strategic position. In geopolitical terms, the canal was crucial to linking America's bicoastal port systems. The Atlantic and Pacific fleets, thereafter, could function as mutually reinforcing military elements, which is a tradition that continues today. By defending the Roosevelt Corollary, Roosevelt said in his 1904 message to Congress that "it is not merely unwise, it is contemptible, for a nation, as for an individual, to use high-sounding language to proclaim its purposes, or to take positions which are ridiculous if unsupported by potential force, and then to refuse to provide this force." By using the powerfully resonating words "Speak softly and carry a big stick; you will go far," Roosevelt established the origins of what became known as the "big stick" principle in American grand strategy. TR's policy would cast a long shadow on the nation's foreign policy throughout the twentieth century.[28]

The Roosevelt Corollary was critical to the conduct of TR's foreign policy. It was consistent with the imperative in President Roosevelt's grand strategy, which he proclaimed quite regularly in speeches and policy statements: that the United States needed to increase its military capabilities if it was to "protect its interests and uphold justice in the world." By virtue of this policy pronouncement, Roosevelt "hammered away" on two fundamental principles in his grand strategy: "the nation's need for strong arms and [its] active involvement in the world."[29] With America's increased activity in the hemisphere, Roosevelt (at the same time as his close friend, the maritime strategist Alfred Thayer Mahan) called for building a much larger navy, capable of protecting trade routes and dissuading aggressive European actions. This policy fit directly into the emerging grand strategy of building American power so that it could influence events in the hemisphere.

The dilemma for Roosevelt was that if he was not willing to allow "foreign powers to collect [debts] by force, he had a 'moral mandate' to intervene and compel the reluctant republics to pay their bills." In a strange twist of logic, Roosevelt used the Monroe Doctrine, which was designed to prevent "intervention by the European powers" as a strategy "to legitimize American intervention." In effect, the Roosevelt Corollary represented "a completely new policy," which Roosevelt likely understood "would gain readier acceptance if attached to an old dogma bearing" his name.[30] The policy had the intended effect of reinforcing the enduring principle in American grand strategy in which Washington would take steps to dissuade European powers from getting involved in the Western Hemisphere.

Mediator-in-Chief: The Russo-Japanese War and the Algeciras Conference

The principles that governed American grand strategy during the Roosevelt administration derived from Roosevelt's policy of strengthening American power while maintaining the rough balance of power and the international status quo. These elements of his grand strategy would, he believed, benefit American interests abroad. To put his grand strategy into practice, President Roosevelt established a reputation as a skilled negotiator who willingly acted on the world stage to promote peace in conflicts that might not always align with American interests. On two occasions, President Roosevelt undertook high-level diplomatic efforts to resolve wars. First, he mediated the Russo-Japanese War, bringing to an end the conflict that pitted the allies of France and Great Britain – Russia and Japan, respectively – against each other.[31] Second, he mediated the

Algeciras Conference over the First Moroccan Crisis as Germany sought to dissuade France from establishing a protectorate over Morocco. This conflict between Germany and France nearly escalated into war.

What emerged during Roosevelt's administration was his distinctive "style in foreign affairs," which proved to be very successful during his presidency. As a consequence of these events, "Roosevelt's personal success as a legislative leader [built on] his standing as a world figure."[32] Since Roosevelt's mediation of the Russo-Japanese War and the Algeciras Conference of 1906 both occurred during the early months of his second term in office, these "triumphs on the international stage" enhanced the president's domestic power and prestige. America's increasing involvement in international affairs under Roosevelt's leadership began to benefit from broader public support, in part because the costs of the nation's global engagement were so low.[33]

As part of his strategy to maintain the balance of power in East Asia, Roosevelt feared that if Japan defeated Russia, as many observers believed was likely to happen, Tokyo would gain far too much power. We see here a preference for the status quo where American interests would be threatened by a radical shift in the power of other states. Roosevelt also feared that a prolonged conflict between Russia and Japan would weaken the alliance between France and Great Britain. According to the historian Howard Beale, Roosevelt had "interesting motives for undertaking the role of peacemaker," which were dominated by two purposes. "First he wished to stop war between civilized powers that was bad for the world and second he hoped to maintain the rights of all nations in the Far East by stabilizing the balance of power there."[34]

Roosevelt's strategic argument was that if "Russia [had] made peace earlier the balance [of power] would not have been so seriously threatened." But if Russia continued to fight and in the process was defeated in eastern Siberia, there would not have been a "counter-weight left to balance Japan at all."[35] "'I should be sorry,' [Roosevelt] wrote to [Henry Cabot] Lodge, 'to see Russia driven completely off the Pacific coast . . . and yet something like this will surely happen if she refuses to make peace.'" As Roosevelt saw matters, "the interest of Russia is the interest of the entire world."[36] Although Roosevelt was not favorably inclined toward Russia, Beale argues that he "did not want her driven out of East Asia or so weakened that she could not check [the power of] Japan."[37]

From Roosevelt's deliberations on how to balance American policy between Russia and Japan, we see that balance-of-power considerations were a critical aspect of his grand strategy for the United States. One scholar gives us this insight into the president's reliance on balance-of-power arguments: "After great victories Japan had 'a right to ask a good deal,' he admitted," yet Roosevelt "urged Japan to moderate her demands." But "'if . . . [the Japanese] made such terms that Russia would prefer to fight for another year,' he conceded, 'they would without doubt get all Eastern Siberia.'" Following this line of argument, Roosevelt proposed that Siberia would be "'an utterly valueless possession to them, while they would make of Russia an enemy whose hostility would endure as long as the nation herself existed.'"[38] Roosevelt warned the Russians that "I should be sorry to see Russia driven completely off the Pacific coast and driven practically east to Lake Baikal, and yet something like this will surely happen if she refuses to make peace."[39]

These matters were central to the grand strategy that emerged during the Roosevelt administration. In Roosevelt's view, bringing an end to the Russo-Japanese War – whose peace treaty was signed at the Wentworth by the Sea Hotel in Portsmouth, New Hampshire – held the prospect of opening "the trade of Manchuria to American and other merchants," stabilizing "the Far Eastern balance, [and] guarantee[ing] peace." The president's objective, as he explained to Henry Cabot Lodge, was to build a postwar balance of power between Russia and Japan. Roosevelt summarized his views as follows: "While Russia's triumph would have been a blow to civilization, her destruction as an eastern Asiatic power would also in my opinion be unfortunate."[40] Clearly, he "worried ... about the war's wider ramifications, especially for the maturing entente, which he supported, between Britain and France against Germany." With an eye to the effects of the Continental balance of power on American grand strategy, Roosevelt likely feared that if "Britain was allied with Japan and France was allied with Russia, a prolonged conflict might play into the hands of Germany."[41]

The Algeciras Conference grew out of Franco-German rivalry over Morocco, which flared up in 1905. Although Morocco was not a serious factor in the global balance of power, it became the "setting for a confrontation between Paris and Berlin that reflected the more profound differences between the two European powers."[42] When Germany "decided [to] oppose France [in Morocco] and test the cohesion of the entente," Germany apparently hoped to "persuade the U.S. to intervene on its behalf and invited Roosevelt to mediate." The problem was that because President Roosevelt "supported France's position [he] mediated a deal that sided with France and forestalled conflict." As a result of his involvement in the Algeciras Conference of 1906, he established the position of the United States as a critical force in defining the European balance of power in the decade before World War I.

What is significant about Roosevelt's intervention in the Moroccan situation was his decision to hold a conference in which "he aided the French and strengthened their entente with Great Britain." Roosevelt supported the idea of keeping Morocco under the control of France regardless of the German reaction. In the end, Roosevelt's policies reinforced Germany's feeling that it faced a number of hostile states, and his diplomatic efforts had at best temporary consequences for building stability in Europe. Roosevelt's domestic critics, writes historian Thomas Bailey, "charged that Roosevelt's interference in the Old World weakened the Monroe Doctrine in the New World." But the contending argument is that Roosevelt effectively "added another corollary to the Monroe Doctrine." In some cases the risk of "intervention in Europe was justified to prevent Europe's wars from engulfing the United States." In Bailey's view, Roosevelt's decision to become involved in Morocco "marked the sharpest departure from traditional isolationism" in American grand strategy before U.S. involvement in World War I.[43]

Roosevelt and Mahan

In discussing his strategy for building the American fleet, Roosevelt often cited acclaimed naval historian and officer Captain Alfred Thayer Mahan as one of the critical strategists whose ideas influenced his thinking about the role of maritime power. Roosevelt and Mahan developed a working relationship when Roosevelt served in the navy, first as civil service commissioner and subsequently as the assistant secretary of the navy.[44] The two, who met in 1887 at the Naval War College when Roosevelt was a visiting lecturer, worked jointly on a strategy that would secure U.S. prominence in the Western Hemisphere through the development of a strong navy that would be capable of confronting hostile powers in the Atlantic and Pacific.

Mahan wrote two important books, one regarding the naval history of Great Britain during its imperial ascendency entitled *The Influence of Sea Power upon History, 1660–1783*, and the other about France's naval power, *The Influence of Sea Power upon the French Revolution and Empire, 1793–1812*. These works established Mahan as the preeminent thinker on the crucial role of sea power on a nation's ability to fight wars and protect its commerce and interests. Mahan's argument was that "in every phase of the prolonged conflict between France and England, from 1688 to the fall of Napoleon, command of the sea by naval domination, or lack of it, determined the outcome."[45] By late in the nineteenth century and throughout the twentieth, maritime power had an increasingly significant influence on American grand strategy.

In addition, Mahan shared Roosevelt's belief in the importance of an isthmian canal connecting the Atlantic and Pacific, along with the need for the United States to have a strong navy to protect its interests, which he believed would expand along with the canal. In 1893 Mahan published an article in the *Atlantic Monthly* entitled "The Isthmus and Sea Power" in which he argued that an isthmian canal would (in his own words) "enable the Atlantic coast [of the United States] to compete with Europe, on equal terms as to distance, for the markets of eastern Asia." He also warned that since the canal would give European navies easier access to the West Coast of the United States, it was imperative for the United States to build a strong navy if it was to maintain its influence in the Western Hemisphere.

But Mahan's arguments reflected existing policy positions more than they shaped them. As a result of Roosevelt's fascination with, and thorough study of, naval power (he published in 1881 the prodigious *Naval War of 1812*, two years after his Harvard graduation), he was well aware of Mahan's scholarship, using his expertise to bolster his policy argument for expanding the fleet.[46] Prior to his presidency, Roosevelt was already well versed in naval affairs.

Although Roosevelt read, reviewed, and recommended Mahan's work, Mahan did not have primary responsibility for deciding what changes would be made to modernize the United States Navy. Mahan's important influence on the U.S. strategy of naval expansion was due to the fact that his work and intellectual reputation bolstered Roosevelt's legitimacy as an authority in his debates with Congress. In practical terms, Mahan's belief about the importance of sea power aligned closely with President Roosevelt's, which led many to believe the exaggerated claim that "Mahan's philosophy of sea power entered the White House in the person of Theodore Roosevelt." However, as Philip Crowl writes, "Theodore Roosevelt and Henry Cabot Lodge needed no conversion to navalism, but were happy nonetheless to have their opinions buttressed by Mahan's seemingly exhaustive scholarship." Lodge, as Crowl noted, "quoted Mahan frequently on the floor of the Senate."[47]

Increasing American Naval Power: The Panama Canal
and the Great White Fleet

As early as 1899, Roosevelt had developed an abiding interest in creating a maritime passageway between the Atlantic and Pacific Oceans.[48] Providing an oceanic link between the coasts was geopolitically important for the nation to undertake combined strategic action between the growing Atlantic and Pacific fleets and also for reducing the costs of transoceanic seaborne trade. There were two plans available – for going through

Panama (the shorter route), which at that time was part of Colombia, or through Nicaragua (the longer route). When the Colombian government balked at the proposed terms and as a sovereign nation demanded more money, the Panamanians, backed by the United States, revolted in 1903, securing both their independence and an isthmian canal. Roosevelt successfully used the means at his disposal, including the willingness of the Panamanian people to revolt, to achieve his end of an isthmian canal at a lower cost. The details of Roosevelt's handling of this situation are set out in the following paragraphs.

The Panama Canal treaty negotiated with Colombia was quite favorable to American strategic interests, but created difficulties with Colombia. The emergence of opposition from Colombia's Congress antagonized Roosevelt who, in seeking the Republican nomination in 1904, "declared that the situation was 'exactly as if a road agent had tried to hold up a man.'"[49] The political unrest then spread in Panama, reflecting popular "discontent with the rule of Bogotá [as seen] by numerous uprisings – fifty-three in fifty-seven years, according to Roosevelt's count."[50]

Matters came to a head when, on November 3, 1903, the day after the U.S. *Nashville* arrived, "the patriot 'army' of Panama revolted." Acting decisively, American forces prevented Colombian troops from intervening, which fueled a successful uprising.[51] With this success, Roosevelt grew increasingly defiant, saying in a speech he gave in 1911 in Berkeley, California, that "'I am interested in the Panama Canal because I started it. If I had followed traditional, conservative methods I would have submitted a dignified State paper of probably 200 pages to Congress and the debates on it would have been going on yet; but I took the Canal Zone and let Congress debate; and while the debate goes on the Canal does also.'"[52] With these words, Roosevelt emphasized the value of taking decisive military action, which became synonymous with his "big stick" aspect of foreign policy.

In a speech in Chile during a tour of South America after his presidency, Roosevelt said, "I love peace, but it is because I love justice and not because I am afraid of war." In defending his actions against Panama, Roosevelt said, "I took the action I did in Panama because to have acted otherwise would have been both weak and wicked." To firmly state his view about the proper role of force in American grand strategy, he affirmed that "I would have taken that action no matter what power had stood in the way. What I did was in the interest of all the world, and was particularly in the interests of Chile and of certain other South American countries."[53]

Roosevelt's decisiveness was consistent with his belief that a strong naval fleet was necessary to preserve the security interests of the United States and peace. He was adamant that the United States could not have naval forces inferior to those of other nations, particularly in terms of international competition to build dreadnoughts. Roosevelt believed that opening an isthmian canal would require a much larger navy if the United States was to deter European ambitions in the Caribbean and Asian ambitions against the West Coast of the United States. Roosevelt's decision to sail the Great White Fleet around the world served the dual purpose of compelling Congress to appropriate more funds for a larger navy and providing a "show of force" to the international community. About achieving his goal of increasing the size of the fleet, Roosevelt later said that this was his greatest accomplishment as president.

Historian Lewis Gould records that "Roosevelt wanted greater attention paid to and more support for the armed forces." In language reminiscent of his views on American grand strategy, he held that the United States should strengthen its navy "because 'an adequate and highly trained Navy is the best guaranty against war, the cheapest and most effective peace insurance.'" The problem, however, was that since the "U.S. Navy ranked fifth in the world in 1900 in overall strength," Roosevelt's recommendation would dramatically increase "the number of battleships and cruisers, as well as additional supporting vessels." His logic was simple: "'The American people must either build and maintain an adequate Navy,'" or they 'make up their minds definitely to accept a secondary position in international affairs, not merely in political, but in commercial matters.'"[54] As Gould wrote, "Theodore Roosevelt had been a great friend of the navy for seven years." During Roosevelt's time as assistant secretary of the navy, "the number of battleships increased from seventeen to twenty-seven, and the nation stood third behind Great Britain and Germany in that category."[55]

The direct consequence of Roosevelt's policies toward the expansion of the United States. Navy was that it became the second largest naval force in the world. Roosevelt's strategy likely impressed on the "Japanese ... this disagreeable fact," thus reaffirming his commitment to dealing aggressively with challenges to American interests and influence. As a way to persuade Japan that the United States was "prepared for any emergency," Bailey argues that Roosevelt adopted the spectacular plan of sending the entire American battleship "fleet around the world."[56] As Roosevelt wrote to his friend Henry White, "I am exceedingly anxious to impress upon the Japanese that I have nothing but the friendliest possible intentions toward them." However, using words that expressed his view of the balance that should exist in grand strategy between defending one's interests and not pursuing one's interests too enthusiastically, he wanted Japan to know that "I am not afraid of them and that the United States will no more submit to bullying than it will bully."[57]

Theodore Roosevelt's Legacy in American Grand Strategy

From these policies of the Roosevelt administration, we see the evolution of the principles of Roosevelt's grand strategy that affirmed the role of using decisive and aggressive actions to defend the nation's global interests. Although the Roosevelt Corollary focused on the Western Hemisphere, it also provided the intellectual and policy precedent for the increasingly activist grand strategy that Washington would pursue during the twentieth century on a global scale.

One of President Roosevelt's critical contributions to grand strategy was expressed by George Herring, who notes that the United States "took a much more active role in the world after 1901" as Roosevelt "embodied the American spirit of his era." This was a time in the evolution of American grand strategy that was characterized by relative calm and no serious international crises. During his nearly eight years in office, Roosevelt successfully demonstrated that the American president has the "capacity to be a world leader" and affirmed his view that the United States would become a global power. Historians argue that Roosevelt was the first modern president to start the process of transforming the "instruments of U.S. power." It was during this era that Roosevelt embodied, in Herring's view, a "practical idealism [that] helped end a war in East Asia and prevent war in Europe, each of which served U.S. needs."

One of Roosevelt's most enduring successes as president was his ability to complete "what his predecessors had long dreamed of," which was to construct "an isthmian canal, by any standard a huge achievement." This contribution to grand strategy, however, is counterbalanced by what some scholars criticize as his "arrogant" treatment of Colombia and Panama. As a consequence, many historians, such as Herring, argue that Roosevelt's "heavy-handed interventions under the Roosevelt Corollary ... changed forever" how Washington was seen in the Western Hemisphere. In the study of grand strategy, the debate continues between seeing America as a status quo or revisionist state, but here the argument is that it was neither and both. As with a classical revisionist state, the United States sought to change the parts of the system. Yet, those changes were much more in line with maintaining the status quo as the world changed around it.

To be sure, for the nations in the Western Hemisphere, the United States was seen as more revisionist in its behavior. Indeed, Herring contends that this pattern of "reflexive military interventions" unquestionably helped "damage U.S. long-term interests" because it fueled "an enduring and understandable legacy of suspicion among Latin Americans [toward] the 'Colossus of the North.'"[58] In the end, Roosevelt's principal achievement as president was to pursue policies that effectively "disengage[d] the United States – and Latin America – from European domination through diplomacy, not belligerence."[59] In a sense, Roosevelt's policies effectively reordered the balance of power in the Western Hemisphere. When the Nobel Committee recognized his accomplishments in foreign policy by awarding him the Nobel Peace Prize in 1906, it effectively "recognized the role of the United States as the world's essential peacemaker in Roosevelt's presidency."[60]

In conclusion, without the policies pursued by President Theodore Roosevelt, a reasonable question is this: When would the modern emphasis in American grand strategy, with its emphasis on taking decisive actions to protect the nation's interests, have emerged as an abiding principle in American foreign policy? Without Roosevelt's policies, it is conceivable that Washington would have faced the problem of constant European involvement in the politics of the Western Hemisphere.[61]

President Woodrow Wilson – From Isolationism to Idealism ... And Back Again

During the early twentieth century and notably with the outbreak of World War I, the policies of the twenty-eighth president of the United States, Woodrow Wilson (1913–1921), were of decisive importance in the evolution of American grand strategy. Prior to World War I, Wilson firmly established his desire to pursue an "America First" policy, which centered on maintaining the long-standing American policy of refraining from direct intervention in European conflicts. The Wilsonian grand strategy represented a return to the nonentanglement tradition as practiced by the Washington administration during the first era of American grand strategy. His strategy rested on pulling back from the more activist foreign policy of Theodore Roosevelt just as Europe descended into instability and war.[62]

Wilson's resolve, however, gradually eroded as he eventually decided to commit the full resources of the United States to win "the war to end all wars." He did so after recognizing both the immediate threat that German naval attacks posed to U.S. commercial interests and the long-term consequences for U.S. interests if Germany were to dominate the European continent through military success. Governed by these realities, Wilson's grand strategy gradually shifted to the conduct of war, although with a notable degree of hesitation, which reflected the crosscurrents of old traditions and new realities in the conduct of American foreign policy at the time.[63]

Some scholars argue that this was the preeminent era of idealism in American foreign policy.[64] Indeed, Wilson is held up as the progenitor and leading advocate of the idealistic tradition in American foreign policy. Walter Russell Mead defines the Wilsonian element in American diplomatic history as standing for the linking of moral values and national interest in policies that seek to promote democracy abroad.[65] It is true that Wilson stood for ideals that would have reshaped American grand strategy and the world along with it, *if* they had been implemented. But this argument rests on evidence drawn from Wilson's views and downplays the role in shaping American grand strategy played by the Congress and the American people. The historical fact remains that the people and their representatives in Congress resoundingly rejected Wilson's grand strategy. Moreover, though the Europeans supported the League of Nations at least superficially, they never embraced it to the point where they let it govern their strategic decisions.

Thus, even though Roosevelt and Wilson as presidents possessed very different images of American grand strategy, the nation's grand strategy as a whole during the early twentieth century shows more evidence of continuity than of change. In reality, American grand strategy did not change much with the Wilson administration's emphasis on the second principle in grand strategy of restraining forces of disorder and avoiding radical alterations to the rules of the game. The fact that Wilson was unable to build a domestic coalition for his idealism shows that in the revolutionary era, the United States did not use one vision of utopia to counter another. Instead, it countered utopianism with a marked preference for slow change, a continuing focus on the domestic foundations of American power, and an enduring skepticism of European geopolitical machinations and its consequences.

As Germany's threat to U.S. commerce intensified during 1915 and 1916, Wilson shifted from a policy of avowed neutrality to one of "armed neutrality," as discussed in the next section. When the United States entered the war, Wilson insisted that only a peace between equals would be lasting, which is what he termed "peace without victory."[66] Wilson supported the entry of the United States into World War I in April 1917 in order to make "the world safe for democracy." Eventually, Wilson became, as the scholar John Ikenberry writes, "the purest believer in the proposition that democracies maintain more peaceful relations." He goes on to say that "his great optimism about the prospects for democracy around the globe after World War I accounts for his exaggerated hopes for world peace."[67]

Wilson ultimately pursued his grand strategy by promoting democratic peace through an international regime based on the principle of collective security, which itself was based on the principle of liberal internationalism.[68] He envisioned a world in which all states would forfeit their sovereignty, at least in part, to the League of Nations, which would serve as a forum for international dialogue and an institution for enforcing global peace and prosperity. Wilson's grand strategy embraced the concept of using international institutions to foster and sustain a more peaceful world order.

From Isolationism to Armed Neutrality

The design of Wilson's grand strategy early in his first term was decidedly noninterventionist. He called it "America First," which was hugely popular. As he said in one speech, "I am not speaking in a selfish spirit when I say that our whole duty, for the present, at any rate, is summed up in this motto: 'America first.'" His central principle, as he articulated it, was "Let us think of America before we think of Europe, in order that we may be Europe's friend when the day of tested friendship comes." President Wilson believed that "'America must remain neutral because there is something better to do than fight; there is a distinction waiting for this country that no other nation has ever yet got.'" This distinction was meant to signal that the United States would be a beacon of self-restrained democracy and act as a different type of state that eschews embroilment in conflict and competition. By using this language, "Wilson was staking out the position that he would cling to not just for the next two months but for the next two years," from 1913 to 1915.[69]

Wilson was a firm believer in, and placed considerable emphasis on, the power of American democracy to serve as a beacon to the rest of the world. And he would maintain this policy while remaining neutral in the face of war in Europe.[70] As Wilson argued, "The example of America must be the example, not merely of peace because it will not fight, but of peace because peace is the healing and elevating influence of the world, and strife is not." However, Wilson understood the limits of this position when he affirmed that "there is such a thing as a man being too proud to fight." By this same logic, in the case of states, "there is such a thing as a nation being so right that it does not need to convince others by force that it is right."[71] What emerged from Wilson's words was his deeply held belief that American grand strategy should be animated by the desire to right wrongs and promote a more moral order in international politics.

The practice of grand strategy in the Wilson administration, however, was more complex. Although Wilson's administration purportedly pursued a neutral policy, it had in practice been doing the opposite through its policy of supplying the raw materials and finished products to keep the Entente powers (France, Great Britain, and Russia) in the war. By this time, the United States had become the great financer of the European war machines as it accumulated war-related debts from the three major Entente powers. In fact, the United States went from assuming the role of the world's largest borrower before the war to that of being the world's largest creditor.[72]

Despite Wilson's determination to keep the United States out of the war, the policies pursued by his administration eventually led Germany to calculate that it had no option but to disrupt and deny the American provision of supplies and money to its adversaries. As a result, Germany pursued a strategy of unrestricted submarine warfare, which to several high-profile incidents on the open seas, including the sinking, most prominently, of the RMS *Lusitania* (a British ocean liner that was sunk by a German submarine in 1915, with the loss of nearly 1,200 lives). Yet even after the sinking of the *Lusitania*, Wilson still sought "to foster a non-punitive outcome to the dispute and build a better world, [believing that] remaining neutral would put him in a position to achieve those two goals." This principle endured for several months after the sinking of the *Lusitania*, and Wilson pledged in his State of the Union address on December 7, 1915, to "keep the process of peace alive."[73]

The fact that the Wilson administration sought to remain neutral does not mean the nation was unprepared for war. In a speech before Congress, as Wilson stated, "'we stand fast on armed neutrality.'" However, after the American steamship *Algonquin* was sunk a week later in a surprise torpedo attack, followed over the next four days by three additional sinkings, this event was seen as "a further provocation," but it did not produce an American declaration of war.[74] The president promised to hold the German Reich "strictly accountable" for violations of American neutrality at sea but at the same time did not hold Great Britain to the same standards with respect to German shipping. This situation exemplifies the policy of favoritism toward London displayed by Washington.[75] It was clear that "by late September 1914, Wilson had arrived at certain basic conclusions about the war," and these principles "gave him a foundation for a diplomatic strategy toward the belligerents." The narrative to which Wilson "held stubbornly" was that the "United States had nothing to do with the war; it had been shamefully attacked in its rights but did not wish to take revenge; [and] it hoped to remain neutral by arming its merchant ships."[76]

In practice, however, Wilson's views were not unlike Roosevelt's on the Russo-Japanese War. On the one hand, Wilson was concerned that the prospect of Germany defeating Great Britain, France, and Russia would "threaten America's ability to avoid a future of militarism." On the other hand, Wilson reasoned that if the "allies had blunted Germany's western offensive [they] were likely, in the long run, to win the war," whereas "a decisive Allied military victory might lead to a continuation of power politics [that would] threaten ... America's security." Lastly, Wilson hoped that the Allies were committed to the principle of disarmament as a component of international politics. From these principles, Wilson had concluded by the latter part of 1914 that the most likely way to attain peace terms that aligned with his ideas about reforming the international system had to be based on "a policy of limited, informal cooperation with the Allied war effort." In line with these beliefs, Wilson showed a willingness "in late 1914 and early 1915" to support Great Britain's maritime campaign against Germany.[77]

In 1916, Wilson conducted a speaking tour around the country in which he supported a policy of national preparedness for war, seeking to prepare the American public for the possibility of American involvement in the war. This policy, in which Wilson used his speeches "to restate his grand vision of America's role in the world," came to be known as "armed neutrality." As he pledged in a speech in Milwaukee, "America has no reason for being unless her destiny and her duty be ideal."[78] Wilson's strategy was "not only to keep the bad influences of European power politics out of the Western Hemisphere," but also to create a new system that would maintain peace and stability with America's backing. In Wilson's words, "'the peace of society is obtained by force.... And if you say we shall not have any war, you have got to have force to make that "shall" bite.'"[79] Although working to organize and mobilize the Congress and the country for war was in sharp contrast with his moral instincts, Wilson came to accept that American participation in the war the last effective option for bringing the conflict brewing in Europe to an end.[80] In effect, Wilson eventually accepted the principle as a preeminent part of his grand strategy that the United States should enter the war, but he did so by framing the entry as "a war to end all wars."[81]

Events throughout 1916 and 1917 demonstrated that Wilson's policy of armed neutrality would be insufficient to defend U.S. commercial interests. As Wilson reflected on his policy in his 1917 war speech, "When I addressed the Congress on the 26th of February last, I thought that it would suffice to assert our neutral rights with arms, our right to use the seas against unlawful interference, our right to keep our people safe against unlawful violence."[82] As this approach increasingly appeared likely to fail, he argued that "armed neutrality, it now appears, is impracticable." His reason was that "armed neutrality is ineffectual enough at best, in such circumstances and in the face of such pretensions it is worse than ineffectual." Wilson's problem with armed neutrality was that "it is likely only to produce what it was meant to prevent" and is "certain to draw us into the war without either the rights or the effectiveness of belligerents."[83]

Peace without Victory

Once Wilson committed the United States to war, he was determined to achieve what he termed, paradoxically, "peace without victory." Citing the sheer destruction involved in pursuing a policy of unconditional victory, Wilson argued that the cycle of reparations and recriminations likely to follow would create resentment among the defeated powers, which eventually would lead to future hostilities.[84] As Wilson observed, "'We see it abundantly demonstrated in the pages of history that the decisive victories and defeats of wars are seldom the conclusive ones.'" In opposing this principle of military strategy, Wilson proposed that "all nations must recognize the uselessness of this 'mechanical slaughter' and join in eliminating war as a 'means of attaining national ambition.'"[85]

Wilson's argument aligned well with the prevailing view that war was too destructive and costly to be fought for rational reasons, thus bringing into doubt whether such a war would lead to peace. This principle was expressed by the Polish banker Ivan Bloch in his 1898 study of modern industrial warfare, *Is War Now Impossible?*[86] The condition of peace would occur, Wilson believed, when the world was "free to build its new peace structure on the solidest foundations it [had] ever possessed." In the end, Wilson "feared the dangers of a 'non-healing peace' [because] any other kind of peace would leave nations determined to right perceived wrongs."[87] Ironically, the reparations against Germany that Wilson feared and sought to avoid came to pass in the aftermath of World War I and served as a powerful catalyst for the outbreak of World War II.

A fundamental principle in Wilson's grand strategy was the hope that states would move beyond a balance-of-power system in Europe toward a collective security regime based on peace between equals. As Wilson framed the matter, "'The question upon which the whole future peace and policy of the world depends is this: Is the present war a struggle for a just and secure peace, or only for a new balance of power?'" It was plain for Wilson that "the choice must be 'not a balance of power, but a community of power; not organized rivalries, but an organized common peace.' Just one part pointed to that goal: it must be a peace without victory [for] only a peace between equals can last." Wilson also expressed his view that we might see "'a People's War for freedom and self-government amongst all the nations of the world.'" In language that resonates in American grand strategy a century later, Wilson proclaimed that this was "a war to make the world safe for the peoples who live upon it . . . [W]oe be to that man or that group of men that seeks to stand in our way in this day of high resolution.'"[88]

From the beginning of the conflict, Wilson was determined to bring World War I to a successful close on the basis of an enduring peace. Wilson outlined in February 1915 "another equally significant part of that later call for a compromise peace . . . [in which] Wilson spelled out a four-point program for instituting a new world order." The four elements of his strategy were these: "'No nation shall ever again be permitted to acquire an inch of land by conquest.' Second, everyone must recognize 'the reality of equal rights between small nations and great.' Third, the manufacture of munitions must no longer remain in private hands. The final and most important element was: 'There must be an association of nations, all bound together for the protection and integrity of each, so that any one nation breaking from the bond will bring upon herself war; that is to say, punishment, automatically.'" As he defined the American strategy for World War I, Wilson focused on fighting "a limited war, though not in the usual sense of a war fought with limited means and in a limited geographic area." In facing this admittedly "delicate task," Wilson proposed using "all the means at his disposal for limited aims [to achieve] something less than total, crushing victory."[89]

Making the World Safe for Democracy

What were the contours of Wilson's grand strategy? In line with the ideas of many observers in the early twentieth century, Wilson sought to guide "American intervention [using the principles of] ideological significance and purpose." In the end, Wilson likely "had no illusions about leading a worldwide crusade to *impose* democracy." To implement this in his grand strategy, Wilson articulated what the historian John Milton Cooper Jr. wrote was the "the most famous phrase from his speech to Congress in 1917 [when he was] asking for war: 'The world must be made safe for democracy.'" According to Cooper, this was "perhaps the most significant choice of passive voice by any president." To limit the scope of this statement, during the next year Wilson said to foreign journalists, "There isn't any one kind of government which we have the right to impose upon any nation. So that I am not fighting for democracy except for those peoples that want democracy."[90]

Thus, as described by one scholar, Wilson "did not say that Americans must make the world safe for democracy; he did not believe that they could [but that they] could only do their part, join with other like-minded nations, and take steps toward that promised land."[91] With these principles in mind, Wilson entered World War I, "not out of economic interest, not because of the violation of neutral rights of the United States, although these played a part, but in order to bring about genuine peace." Comparing Wilson's decision to and contrasting it with Madison's decision to go to war against Great Britain in 1812 is useful here. Unlike Wilson, Madison explicitly started the war to protect American economic interests and its neutral rights. But both went to war reluctantly in efforts to keep the United States from being engaged long term in European power politics. In another sign of continuity in American grand strategy, Wilson likely believed that "mediation through participation would be more effective than neutrality,"[92] which echoes Roosevelt's desire to protect U.S. interests by brokering deals between great powers.

Wilson's Military Strategy in World War I

While initially reluctant to go to war in Europe, once the decision was made to fight, Wilson used all the resources at his disposal.[93] In line with the classic American approach to war, the American strategy was to commit the full material resources of the United States to the war.[94] Wilson, as with many presidents before him, "intended to plunge in fully and decisively." In what became a fundamental element of American grand strategy, Wilson "meant to wage war with every resource at his command, and he meant to do it his way."[95]

To make this strategy work, Wilson had to "field [U.S.] forces ... on the Western Front," which "would require recruiting, training, and equipping more men than the nation had ever put under arms." Implementing this strategy would require mobilization on an unparalleled scale, including "harnessing agriculture, manufacturing, and transportation on an unprecedented scale – [that would go well beyond] meeting mounting demands from the Allies for food, machines, and munitions." Wilson emphasized the domestic side of his grand strategy when he "urged farmers to grow bigger crops, and he asked farmers in the South to grow foodstuffs rather than cotton." As Wilson said, "'The supreme test of the nation has come,' [when] 'We must all speak, act, and serve together.'"[96] With this language, Wilson introduces the concept, which would be severely tested on many occasions during the twentieth century, that an effective grand strategy must enjoy a significant degree of unanimity among the American people.

Clashing Ideologies: Wilsonian Idealism vs. European Realpolitik

The scale of American participation and the extent of resources that were brought to bear by the United States was a decisive factor in bringing World War I to an end on the Entente's terms. Several months before the war's end, Wilson was thinking ahead to what a settlement should look like and what state of peace eventually would prevail. With words that signaled the tone of his grand strategy, on January 8, 1918, in an address to the U.S. Congress, President Wilson "set out a peace programme for Europe based upon fourteen separate points, [all of which were] essentially democratic and liberal in outlook." Critically, for Wilson, "diplomacy and treaty-making would proceed 'frankly and in the public view,'" to ensure the transparency that was essential to international security.[97]

Wilson's final address in support of the League of Nations affirmed that his belief in "peace without victory" had redefined the basis on which the United States would conduct its grand strategy. Yet this "peace" exacted a serious price from Germany in terms of the costs of reparations, which Wilson wrongly believed it could sustain economically. As he warned, "Do not think of this treaty of peace as merely a settlement with Germany. It is that. It is a very severe settlement with Germany, but there is not anything in it that she did not earn."[98] Although his reasoning was much more conciliatory than that of the Allied leadership, he believed that this scale of punishment "is absolutely necessary [to guarantee] that no other nation may ever plot such a thing against humanity and civilization."[99]

However, as Wilson's desire for "peace without victory" slowly unraveled, its undoing thoroughly undermined Wilson's grand strategy that was based on supporting international institutions and the principle of openness. One of the problems lay with America's own government. In July 1919, Wilson addressed the Senate, stating that "a new role and a new responsibility have come to this great nation that we honor and which we would all wish to lift to yet higher levels of service and achievement."[100] In contrast with Wilson's vision for American grand strategy, support from the Republicans in Congress was minimal, particularly on the part of Henry Cabot Lodge and William Borah, whose opposition guaranteed that the United States would not ratify the League of Nations. The American foreign policy establishment was skeptical of utopian projects, resisting this initiative both directly and indirectly, thus highlighting the status quo–oriented nature of American grand strategy. Republicans in Congress directly blocked Wilson's agenda. One reason they succeeded and Wilson failed is that they adhered more consistently to the tradition of gradualism within American grand strategy, which holds that a better way to operate is to act aggressively to restrain the most threatening sources of disorder and also seek to change the system in positive, incremental ways.

Another problem was the insistence of the Entente powers on imposing a crippling and humiliating program of reparations on Germany, which effectively devastated the nation's economy and provided fertile ground for the rise of Adolf Hitler's Nazi party. As Cooper wrote, "The Armistice of November 11 would be [Wilson's] cruelest irony of fate in foreign affairs." Less than "a quarter century later, roughly the same coalition of Allies – augmented by a more powerful Russia – would fight under the banner of 'unconditional surrender,' which itself would be a reaction against alleged flaws in the ending of the war."[101]

In hindsight, many historians and public officials rightly criticized Woodrow Wilson's adherence to the concept of the League of Nations as idealistic and impractical. In his criticism of the economic clauses of the Treaty of Versailles, Winston Churchill joined the debate when he described "the anger of the victors, and the failure of their peoples to understand that no defeated nation or community can ever pay tribute on a scale, which would meet the cost of modern war."[102]

In evaluating Wilson's grand strategy, historians have questioned why he thought such a grand plan was practical. The source of Wilson's conviction that war could be outlawed was found, for the historian Cooper, in "an optimistic attitude toward human nature akin to secular notions of innate human goodness and worth." To understand Wilson's worldview, Cooper holds that "people left to themselves, safeguarded against predatory elements and pursuing their own interests, would produce both a good society and a vital, self-renewing nation."[103] Although this grand strategy ultimately failed to produce the peace that Wilson hoped would emerge, his ideals reemerged after World War II, when Franklin D. Roosevelt and Winston S. Churchill worked to establish the United Nations. But, crucially, the United Nations reflected the power realities of the international system of the time, in which the five victors in the war were the veto-holding powers on the Security Council. The UN has been much more relevant to world politics than the concept of the League of Nations precisely because it reflects the power of the great states and did not seek to alter radically the international system that is based on the power of sovereign states.

Wilson's Legacy in American Grand Strategy

President Wilson's legacy in grand strategy is the product of several themes. To begin, Wilson established the principle of pursuing an "America First" policy, by which he reaffirmed the historic American commitment to avoiding direct involvement in European politics and wars. Wilson was a strong proponent of placing considerable emphasis on the power of the American example, but he sought to remain neutral in the face of the war in Europe and what many Americans saw as the European tendency to be constantly engaged in struggles and wars. This policy, however, gradually changed as Wilson decided to involve the full resources of the United States in the "the war to end all wars." President Wilson believed that the purpose of World War I should be to achieve a lasting peace between equals, producing what he called "peace without victory."[104]

Wilson may not have believed that American grand strategy during his administration and for the duration of the twentieth century should rest essentially on imposing democracy on the defeated powers, but a preeminent principle in his grand strategy nonetheless was "making the world safe for democracy." His grand strategy ultimately sought to build a democratic peace through a collective security regime based on the principles of liberal internationalism.[105] In Wilson's view, the strategy was to build a world in which U.S. policy would be guided by the principle that state actions should be designed to right wrongs and Washington should aspire to build an enduring moral order in international politics.

In the end, Wilson's grand strategy sought to eliminate war as a "means of attaining national ambition." He envisioned a move beyond the balance-of-power system in Europe to a collective security regime based on peace between equals. A core principle in Wilson's grand strategy was to find a way to "end [the war] ... and bring far reaching reform to international affairs." To implement this grand strategy, Wilson outlined a four-element program for building a new world order, the core principle of which rested on making the world "safe for democracy."[106] With this grand strategy, Wilson sought to transform the system, but his ambition was scaled back because it was contrary to the foreign policy tradition dating back to Washington and continuing through Theodore Roosevelt that preferred stability to more revisionist agendas. Nearly one century later, the core principles in Wilson's grand strategy remain central to the ambitions and ethos of American foreign policy.

President Franklin Delano Roosevelt – From Domestic Recovery to Leadership of the Free World

As the thirty-second president of the United States, Franklin Delano Roosevelt (1933–1945) was the steward of American foreign policy in the 1930s and during the conduct of World War II (1941–1945) until his death in April 1945. His immediate predecessors were not grand strategists but political tacticians who did not influence American grand strategy in any decisive sense. They were products of grand strategic inertia that allowed America to become myopically and reflexively isolationist. President Franklin Roosevelt changed that by seeking to bring America out of its isolation only when it was ready and to steer the course of American policy during the Second World War in ways that directly supported American interests. The essential architecture of American grand strategy today owes considerable credit to Roosevelt's contributions.[107]

To put Franklin Delano Roosevelt's (FDR) contributions in perspective, his administration confronted two of the most devastating and defining threats in American history: the Great Depression and World War II. In response to these two events, we see the emergence of two distinct policies that defined American grand strategy during the 1930s and 1940s. The first was the goal of promoting economic recovery and development during and after the Depression. The second was to mobilize the nation's resources along with a global coalition to defeat the Axis powers and set up a postwar peace based on U.S. alliances and partnerships. This period represents one of the most dynamic and innovative phases in the evolution of American grand strategy, perhaps on a par with the events that would lead to the origins of the Cold War.

Rebuilding the Domestic Foundations of American Power

With his inauguration on March 4, 1933, President Roosevelt assumed office clearly motivated by the goal of renewing the American spirit from the despair of the economic collapse in 1929 that plunged the country into the Great Depression. During the presidential campaign, FDR distinguished himself from incumbent President Herbert Hoover by promoting a grand strategy (though not using that term) whose overall purpose was to rebuild the domestic foundations of American economic power and the nation's political confidence. Whereas Hoover looked abroad to policies that sought to cure the Depression, notably by seeking to negotiate free trade agreements and debt settlements with Europe that were left over from World War I, Roosevelt made it clear that he would seek to rebuild the domestic strength of the United States in economic and industrial terms.

In truth, we cannot be sure that FDR saw his dealing with the Great Depression as a component of a broad, unified grand strategy. Any president coming into office during the Depression obviously would have the policy imperative of economic recovery foremost in mind. The historian Robert Dallek describes the events after the election: "On November 12, four days after his defeat, Hoover invited FDR to discuss war debts, disarmament, and preparations for a world economic conference scheduled for early 1933."[108] Here we see the basic components of FDR's economic strategy of renewal with its powerful emphasis on domestic policies.

Roosevelt agreed in broad terms with Hoover that it was important to cooperate with Britain and France, particularly as Germany was moving to adopt an increasingly hostile stance. FDR's philosophical approach to grand strategy was evident when he "told an English journalist in the summer of 1932, [that] if Britain and the United States could achieve 'a complete identity of political and economic interests,' they would . . . 'acquire the true leadership of the world.'"[109] As matters evolved, this strategic relationship was fully developed by late 1940 when the U.S. Congress passed the 1941 Lend-Lease Act to assist Great Britain in its efforts to fight back against the attack by Germany.

Despite Roosevelt's hope to form a stronger relationship with Europe, he was clear as to the priorities of the United States. His highest priority was to stabilize the American domestic economy as the first step in restoring the deeply weakened economy and national morale. Despite Hoover's urging, Roosevelt and his administration refused to enter into any joint decision making with Hoover before they took office.[110] Historians hold that Roosevelt "believed that a close association with Hoover would jeopardize the first goal of his presidential term," which was to restore the "hope that America's economic and governmental machinery could work." The risk for FDR was that since the public saw "Hoover as a prime contributor to the country's mood of gloom," Roosevelt had no choice but to prevent the credibility of his administration from being mortgaged "to the image of helplessness associated with the old [Hoover administration]."[111]

However, in the spirit of promoting national unity, FDR accepted Hoover's request that he should consider his predecessor's international economic policy recommendations. Hoover's strategy was to use free trade agreements and resolving debt settlements with Europe from World War I to help large businesses and corporations weather the economic downturn, whereas FDR's strategy was to use direct infusions of capital to the public as a way to turn the economy around.[112]

President Roosevelt's priorities were outlined quite clearly in his first inaugural address, delivered on March 4, 1933, when he said that "our international trade relations, though vastly important, are in point of time and necessity secondary to the establishment of a sound national economy." In the context of America's economic crisis, FDR said that he would "favor as a practical policy [putting] first things first." As he worked to balance domestic and foreign policy concerns, "starvation, unemployment, business and financial collapse" reduced foreign policy to at best a "secondary concern."[113] FDR's emphasis on first building the domestic foundations of national power echoes Wilson's America First program at the beginning of his first term.

Hoover failed to connect with the emotions gripping the American people in the early 1930s; Roosevelt, in contrast, clearly was sensitive to the situation, as seen by how powerfully he understood the public's sentiment about the urgent need to focus first and foremost on domestic economic priorities.[114] As part of his domestic economic recovery program, Roosevelt promised to "start public works programs to give people jobs, offer low-interest loans to stop home foreclosures, and fix the banking system so people's savings would remain safe."[115] These priorities not only defined Roosevelt's New Deal policies but also dominated the public debate, despite the rise of fascism in Germany and authoritarianism in Japan.

FDR's strategy consisted of a calculated ordering of priorities in which domestic relief for the Depression was his first and highest priority in a long list of actions he believed had to be taken to restore the American economy. Although foreign policy matters remained at best a matter of secondary importance, the risk was to ensure that neither Americans nor international audiences would believe he was ignoring foreign policy.

By 1940, FDR's focus on the domestic economy had shifted to deal with emerging problems in the field of foreign policy, which were reaching a point where the nation's vital interests would be imperiled. Roosevelt had kept an eye on the foreign sphere, but he remained steadfast in his commitment to pursuing the nation's long-term interests, which in his view meant dealing with domestic issues first and foremost. FDR's policies were designed to promote free trade, while he continued to support "domestic legislation that aimed to revive America's economy strictly from within."[116] An enduring principle of FDR's strategy was to reduce the public's feelings of despair and build the basis for hope in the value of international cooperation to solve common problems.

FDR's First Hundred Days: The New Deal

FDR's first hundred days in office was a whirlwind of activity – most of which was directed toward banking and construction programs to energize the domestic economy and restore the optimism inherent in the American national character.[117] As one historian noted, "In a three-month period he had put more major legislation through the Congress than any other President had during a similar period." Since manufacturing and farm price indices were up in June 1933, the press gave FDR some credit for bringing the Depression to an end. As part of his domestic rebuilding agenda, Roosevelt created two new agencies to deal with the recovery – the National Recovery Administration (NRA) and the Agricultural Adjustment Administration (AAA) – whose singular purpose was to develop policies that were designed to provide domestic relief. FDR spent almost the entire summer of 1933 negotiating with major industries on NRA agreements.

The centerpiece of FDR's domestic programs was the New Deal, which involved a series of economic programs enacted from 1933 to 1936. In many ways, the focal point of Roosevelt's grand strategy in domestic terms derived from these programs, which were designed to rejuvenate the American economy after the economic collapse of the Great Depression. For many observers, the expression that describes these programs was the "3 Rs" – which emphasized relief, recovery, and reform.

One notable feature of the American economy was what it did not include, which today we call a social safety net, consisting of programs that are designed to protect

Americans, especially the elderly, from the ravages of economic and social collapse that we saw graphically during the Great Depression. In this economic climate, President Roosevelt focused his domestic programs on establishing what he promised would be a "new deal for the American people." The signature programs of the New Deal included Social Security and unemployment insurance as well as programs that were designed to modernize the infrastructure of American society.

In practice, the New Deal rested on two series of programs that spanned a period of five years: the First New Deal (1933–1934) and the Second New Deal (1935–1938). The first of these New Deal programs focused on rebuilding the infrastructure of the American economy, notably railroads, industry, and farming. In particular, the New Deal created the Public Works Administration (PWA), which guided how the United States invested in major efforts to rebuild the nation's public infrastructure. Using millions of the unemployed, this program funded and managed major projects that helped build the airports, schools, roads, dams, and bridges as well as hospitals and government buildings that would be essential to positioning the United States as a global leader in economics and innovation.

It also addressed macroeconomic policy and reforms of the banking sector – the latter in response to banking problems in the economic collapse that devastated the nation between 1929 and 1933. The First New Deal's fiscal and monetary policies included efforts to balance the budget and institute monetary reform policies and securities regulations.

With an emphasis on the role in its grand strategy of guiding how the nation rebuilt the domestic foundations of American power during the Great Depression, the Roosevelt administration promoted several policies that were integral to developing the economic, industrial, and transportation sources of power that would prepare the nation, unknowably then, for the leadership role it would assume in the decades after World War II.

In the two-year period from 1933 to 1935, the PWA spent more than $3 billion (in 1930s dollars) on literally tens of thousands of projects. A critical part of this program was to put millions of the unemployed back to work building and modernizing the infrastructure – notably, bridges, airports, and thousands of miles of roads – that made American society into a modern power and provided the nation with the foundation it needed to be the preeminent power in the half century after World War II. The modernization of American society, which began in the decades before World War II as a result of programs that rebuilt the domestic foundations of American power, was so well established that when the war ended, the United States had, in contrast with much of the rest of the world that was in shambles, a first-class economy and infrastructure.

The Second New Deal built upon these programs to include what we now know as the signature programs of the 1930s that remade American society. Many observers believe that the most important program in the Second New Deal was the Social Security Act, which was passed on August 14, 1935. The act created, for the first time in American society, a system of universal retirement pensions, unemployment insurance, and welfare benefits for the poor. This program, along with many others like it, established a social safety net that is as central to grand strategy as the issues that classically arise in national security and foreign policy. Without these new programs that helped modernize American society, both in terms of the nation's infrastructure and a social safety net, the United States would not be the global power that it is today.

Slowly Accepting Leadership of the Free World

President Roosevelt's focus on domestic programs, however, did not preclude his administration from seeking to build enduring relationships at the international level. On the contrary, the significant lack of public interest in this arena effectively gave him greater flexibility to engage in foreign affairs and do so with relatively few domestic consequences. In fact, the 1930s were not, contrary to popular belief, "a time of unrelieved isolationism in the United States." As Dallek writes, "During the first two years of his presidency, Roosevelt met not intense isolationism in the country, but a general indifference to outside events which left him relatively free to seek expanded American ties abroad." For this historian, during the early 1930s, "Roosevelt's policies of economic self-protection and political detachment from other nations represented only one side of his foreign policy." By focusing so intently on the domestic economic foundations of grand strategy, FDR was able to "chart ... a separate economic and political course for the United States [while moving] toward greater cooperation abroad."[118]

Domestic Recovery Becomes War Preparation and Supply

The extensive negotiations on the National Recovery Administration (NRA) and FDR's hard work to restore American production proved critical to the war effort that moved into high gear after 1941. The belief that the NRA efforts were undertaken in order to prepare the United States for the war is misleading. The foremost reason for the NRA was Roosevelt's need to pursue economic recovery, apart from what was going on in the rest of the world. Economic recovery efforts had separate goals that began well before war seemed imminent but, because the economic recovery efforts and the later war efforts were mutually beneficial, they were necessarily intertwined in FDR's grand strategy. In fact, these efforts were integral to the rapid acceleration of American war production, even though the effects of the new programs on U.S. economic recovery were modest until the United States began full-scale war production.

America's renewed capacity for production paved the way for the Lend-Lease Act of 1941.[119] This act was a clear departure from the noninterventionist principle in grand strategy that had dominated American foreign policy since the days of President Wilson's administration. FDR devised the Lend-Lease Act to "make it seem as if the United States was simply 'lending' weapons and supplies to Britain (there was never much chance they would be returned or paid for)." In using this strategy, "FDR beat back [the] 'America First' opposition and rescued England and Europe," which he accomplished with "the explicit approval of Congress."[120] In 1941, with Britain deeply involved in the war and struggling desperately to hold back the German attack, FDR was under enormous pressure from Winston Churchill to provide the cash and war materials without which Great Britain could not survive.[121]

In practice, what the British wanted in 1941 was for the United States to provide sufficient military equipment to arm "ten divisions and to increase airplane deliveries from 14,000 to 26,000." To put this level of production in perspective, the decision to accept orders for military equipment on this scale was equivalent to placing the "American economy on a full war footing, [to which] Roosevelt readily agreed and revealed the British request to the public." Interestingly, Roosevelt framed the policy in terms of the recovery. "These purchases," he claimed, would fuel the U.S. economy "in every part of the country" and, in a nod to America's security, would create the economic and production capability for the military hardware that would be necessary to "'serve the needs of the United States in any emergency.'" The latter words were a thinly veiled reference to the possibility that the United States could find itself at war. But this policy also dovetailed with FDR's "determination to give Britain all possible aid short of war."[122]

A study of the evolution of American grand strategy during FDR's administration reveals that the Lend-Lease Act (which was later expanded to include other Allied nations as well) represented the marriage of FDR's resolve to pursue domestic development with his desire to forge cooperative international relationships for the purpose of strengthening America's security. In this way, the Lend-Lease Act is a quintessential example of grand strategy outlining a policy for marshaling the nation's resources to defend the nation and its interests.[123]

The War Production Board (WPB) served as the chief strategic command center for implementing Roosevelt's new policy of domestic development. Created in 1942, the WPB sought to "rationalize and systematize the production and distribution of raw materials" to ensure that the critical needs of the nation's major industrial producers were satisfied.[124] By having "an overall view of the war effort and direct[ing] its strategy," the WPB effectively served as the chief of staff to the production industry in the same capacity as if it were the armed forces. This board, as with many others, reported directly to President Roosevelt and represented a bold new role for the government that would accelerate the production of wartime materials and significantly improve the readiness of the American economy for war. As Historian Tami Davis Biddle writes, "The war created 17 million new jobs. Industrial production increased by 96 percent and corporate profits after taxes more than doubled."[125]

For the United States to produce the large amounts of goods and materials on the short order necessary to support the Allies, Roosevelt leveraged American enterprise. This is another way of saying that the elements of FDR's grand strategy of rebuilding the domestic foundations of American economic power dovetailed with a foreign policy that sought to restrain and then defeat the fascist forces. By creating "a partnership with private industry that resulted in a unique economic structure," the government under President Roosevelt gained an extraordinary "role in funding, supporting, and regulating war production," while leaving "the control of individual enterprises in the hands of industrialists and business men." As Roosevelt said about the emergency mobilization of the American economy for war, "energy was more efficient than efficiency,... speed as important as quality ... and costs mattered less than results."[126] Guided by this political view and massive government funding, American industry and the economy thrived with a momentum that carried domestic prosperity into the decades after World War II.

From Isolationist Neutral to Postwar Superpower

At the beginning of Roosevelt's second term in 1937, the American people were still emphatically opposed to foreign entanglements. The nation had a decidedly isolationist sentiment, in part because the hangover from World War I still remained, which contributed to the profound hesitation in public opinion about whether to enter another war. As one scholar writes about the state of public opinion in the 1930s, "To the 1937 Gallup poll question of whether it had been a mistake for the United States to enter World War I, 70 per cent of those queried answered yes."[127]

The idea of "immediate defense," which was a central element of Roosevelt's grand strategy, resonated powerfully with American public sentiment. Facing strong public opposition to anything other than a strong policy of isolationism, President Roosevelt's grand strategy faced a reality in which the United States soon would face the rise of totalitarianism in both the Atlantic and the Pacific. Roosevelt clearly grasped the danger posed by the Axis powers, knowing that these states would need to be confronted and defeated if Western civilization was to be preserved. However, in the face of significant public opposition to intervention, he could not move as fast as perhaps he wished. In the interim, Roosevelt implemented during the 1930s a grand strategy based on gradually seeking to develop American power, slowly building a coalition of forces to resist totalitarianism, and seeking to restrain the rise of Germany's and Japan's political and military power.[128]

Facing the fervent isolationist sentiment in American society, Congress tied the hands of the Roosevelt administration through passage of neutrality laws that prevented the nation from taking sides in any international conflict. Although later repealed, in 1941, the four Neutrality Acts were designed to prevent the United States from being drawn into foreign wars. The First Neutrality Act, signed into law on August 31, 1935, reflected the deeply entrenched isolationist feelings in the nation in the aftermath of World War I and during the Great Depression. The act, which was designed to keep the United States out of war, called "on the President, whenever he proclaimed a state of war to exist, to declare an arms embargo against all belligerents without distinction between them." The four acts, which ended with the Fourth Neutrality Act in 1939, were designed, as one scholar argues, to prevent "the country from being drawn into a foreign war on the issues of neutral rights and wartime trade and loans."[129] Roosevelt was critical of the acts, fearing that they would limit his administration's options to help and support allies. Despite his opposition, he signed the Neutrality Acts into law because he faced reelection in the midst of growing isolationism in public opinion.

Although the neutrality laws effectively prevented Roosevelt from taking sides in foreign conflicts, his strategy was to help U.S. allies in their struggles against Germany and Italy. Roosevelt wanted to loosen the restrictions in these acts because he believed that it was "impossible for any nation completely to isolate itself from economic and political upheavals in the rest of the world."[130] However, once Roosevelt won his third campaign for the presidency in 1940, he took a more aggressive stance toward combating the two rising foreign aggressors, Germany and Japan. In March 1941, FDR successfully passed the previously mentioned Lend-Lease Act through the Congress, which permitted him to dramatically increase American aid to the Allies, particularly to Great Britain. As one scholar notes, "Although not yet fighting, the United States had taken measures that placed it unofficially at war with the Axis powers."[131]

Roosevelt's foreign policy shifted toward increasing the economic aid provided to the Allies to help them defeat the European Axis powers. He also moved to deny Japan access to the raw materials that were critical to its conquest of East Asia by cutting off the "machine tools, chemicals, and various raw materials [that are] essential to war production." The U.S. strategy was to impose "economic sanctions piecemeal" as part of efforts to cumulatively "deter further Japanese expansion but ... not provoke immediate retaliation" or war.[132] As the United States enacted economic sanctions against Japan, the longstanding frictions with Washington, when combined with the newly imposed sanctions, persuaded many in the Japanese government that their best course of action was to launch a military strike against U.S. naval forces at Pearl Harbor.

As tensions heightened, public attention began to shift to foreign policy. By the mid-1930s, the emerging threat of war in Europe "made the American people [so] aware of foreign events [that it] evoked an isolationist response." The consensus is that it became clear to Roosevelt and the State Department that the mood of the country was slowly beginning to shift to a point where foreign policy matters increasingly "dominated national thinking."[133] The isolationist attitude reversed itself after Japan's attack on Pearl Harbor and Germany's decision to declare war against the United States.[134]

When Roosevelt gained the public support needed to declare war against the Axis powers, he moved swiftly to form a coalition with Britain, France, and the Soviet Union whose singular purpose was to destroy the Axis enemies. The United States eventually adopted a Europe First military strategy. It agreed with its allies to first focus on defeating the Axis powers in Europe and then turn its full attention and resources to the campaign in the Pacific against Japan.[135]

The agreement on Europe first, however, came only after strident debate between FDR and Churchill. In the end, as they agreed, "Germany had to be the main foe ... because she controlled the manpower and technological resources superior to Japan's and hence was the more dangerous enemy." To put this broad strategy into practice, a series of meetings were held between President Roosevelt and Prime Minister Churchill from December 22, 1941, to January 14, 1942, in Washington. It was at the First Washington Conference, which was known by "the code name of ARCADIA," that Churchill strongly pushed "the principle of concentrating the primary war effort in Europe."[136]

This debate over wartime strategy serves as a prime example of how Roosevelt worked to strike a balance between the means at his disposal and the ends he sought to achieve. In fact, Roosevelt followed this policy on wartime priorities when he made the decision to align with Josef Stalin, the leader of the Soviet Union. In a meeting on New Year's Day in 1942 at the White House, "Roosevelt and Churchill, Ambassador Maxim Litvinov from the Soviet Union, and the representatives of twenty-three other nations at war with the Axis powers, brought the grand coalition into formal existence by signing the Declaration of the United Nations." The result of this agreement was that "all signatory governments [joined] an alliance against the Axis ... and [agreed] not to make a separate peace." The problem, however, was that the "Russians were highly suspicious of the Allied failure to establish a genuine second front [because they feared that] the Allies might make a separate peace with Hitler."[137]

Part of the process for aligning American and British policies with those of the Soviet Union involved Roosevelt's call in January 1943 for a policy of unconditional surrender. At the time, the rationale for a policy of unconditional surrender was highly credible and "persuasive." Despite considerable political pressure by Moscow, writes Bailey, "Unconditional surrender appeased them to some degree, and possibly counteracted any impulse on their part to come to terms with Germany."[138] In Roosevelt's own words, unconditional surrender "does not mean the destruction of the population of Germany, Italy, or Japan, but it does mean the destruction of the philosophies in those countries which are based on conquest and the subjugation of other peoples."[139]

As the fight against the Axis powers in Europe centered on Russia's incredible efforts on the Eastern Front, the United States increasingly focused on the strategy and resources necessary for victory in the Pacific. In deliberations that took place in Cairo in November 1943, Roosevelt met with Churchill and Chiang Kai-shek of China to discuss the wartime strategy in the East. At this meeting, the three leaders agreed to the Declaration of Cairo, which pledged that they would fight until Japan unconditionally surrendered. They also agreed that Japan would be "deprived of all Pacific islands acquired since 1914, whether by capture or mandate from the League of Nations [and] Japan would also be forced to return former Chinese territory, notably Manchuria, Formosa, and the Pescadores." Following the conference at Cairo, Roosevelt met with Churchill and Stalin in Tehran between November 28 and December 2, 1943. At this conference, "Churchill and Roosevelt assured Stalin that the cross-channel invasion he so ardently desired would take place in May or soon after." In response, "Stalin again promised he would take Russia into the war against Japan after Germany's defeat."[140]

In formulating the terms of the Allied war strategy, these leaders "deliberated over the future of Germany, apparently at this time favoring dismemberment" or some form of the Morgenthau Plan. The original post–World War II Morgenthau Plan called for returning Germany to a "preindustrial, pastoral state by taking away its industrial capacity" and preventing it from becoming a military threat.[141] This plan fell out of favor, to be was replaced by the partition of Germany and its reconstruction under the Marshall Plan.

Lessons Learned in World War I

Roosevelt looked beyond the American military strategy in World War II to create a grand strategy that spanned the war and the postwar period. He understood that grand strategy must be practiced on the war-peace continuum, using all elements of national power. Here, he used both diplomacy and economic policy. Roosevelt's diplomacy, which sought to promote greater postwar security cooperation, was motivated in part by his view that the absence of such cooperation among states and international institutions contributed to the outbreak of World War I and, subsequently, to that of World War II. He also learned from the mistakes of Wilson, whose League of Nations initiative failed due to the lack of American public support. Roosevelt was determined not to miss a similar opportunity when World War II ended.

Roosevelt's ability to shore up domestic political support for a postwar collective security system was instrumental in the design of what eventually became the United Nations, its architecture developed at the 1945 San Francisco Conference. A critical element of Roosevelt's grand strategy was to use the principle of collective security to build a more secure and peaceful international order among states. In practical terms, this principle was a significant step toward creating the United Nations, a body quite different from the League of Nations in many important respects. Most importantly, it recognized the realities of power and set up a separate, smaller Security Council that gave the five most powerful states at the time a veto over binding resolutions. They would be the only permanent members, and only Security Council resolutions would be binding under international law.[142]

Understanding the necessity of getting early domestic support for his policies, Roosevelt "carefully cultivated Congressional support, among Republicans as well as Democrats." In August, 1943, the senior leadership of the "Republican Party adopted a resolution known as the Mackinac Charter that announced Republican support for participation in a postwar international organization." This concept gained support, as "even isolationists ... praised the concept of collective security at that time." As a result of this domestic support, the United States signed the 1943 Declaration of the Four Nations on General Security among the United States, Great Britain, Russia, and China. These states "agreed to establish 'a general international organization' for the maintenance of 'peace and security,'" known as the Moscow Declaration, which became "the first international commitment for a postwar system of collective security."[143]

In terms of postwar economic policy, Roosevelt's centerpiece program was the Bretton Woods Conference, which took place in July 1944 at the Bretton Woods Resort in New Hampshire. At the conference, "representatives of forty-four nations agreed upon a plan for an International Monetary Fund designed to promote stability in international currencies and to encourage the expansion of world trade." An important theme in the economic dimension of FDR's grand strategy was to create an International Bank for Reconstruction and Development, which "would help finance the rebuilding of devastated areas" and "facilitate the flow of capital into foreign trade and into countries needing it for productive purposes." This international financial institution is known as the World Bank. Just as the United Nations was designed to improve on the League of Nations, the Bretton Woods Conference contrasted sharply with the flawed economic nationalism that dominated economic thinking in the 1920s and early 1930s and relied on sounder, stabilizing macroeconomic policies.[144]

Yalta: Roosevelt's Final Conference

The Yalta Conference, which was held from February 4 to 11, 1945, was the last conference in which Roosevelt took part before his death on April 12, 1945.[145] Its purposes were twofold. The first was to obtain a Soviet commitment to fight against Japan after the defeat of Germany was secured, and the second was to determine how postwar Europe and Asia should be divided between American and Soviet interests. Considerable criticism has been leveled at Roosevelt and Churchill for conceding too much to Stalin. The central criticism is that the Yalta Conference agreed to democracies and free elections in Europe, as outlined in the Atlantic Charter in 1941, but Washington and London agreed to a Soviet sphere of influence in Eastern Europe, which made the Atlantic Charter a dead letter.[146]

Stalin arrived at the conference with the intention of negotiating a larger sphere of Soviet political influence in Eastern and Central Europe, which he deemed was a core element of the USSR's grand strategy. One part of this strategy was to keep as much of Poland under Soviet rule as possible. Stalin stipulated that the Soviet Union would keep the territory of eastern Poland, and as compensation, Poland could extend its western borders at the expense of Germany. Stalin also promised free elections in Poland, despite having already installed a Soviet-sponsored provisional government. Additionally, Stalin declared that in order for the Soviets to enter the Pacific War with the Allies, the United States had to recognize Mongolia's independence from China as well as Soviet interests in the Manchurian railways and in Port Arthur. Roosevelt agreed to both demands, without Chinese representation or consent. As it turned out, the Soviet role in defeating Japan was inconsequential. The USSR declared war on Japan on August 9, 1945, after an atomic bomb destroyed Nagasaki, the second city to be annihilated by such weapons.

The reality of Yalta was that the Soviet Union emerged as one of the most significant states – one whose resources and influence permitted it to shape the postwar world order.

From the perspective of American grand strategy, one argument is that the United States had to adjust American policies to fit the reality of the new balance of power. As Alexander Deconde noted, "Careful analysis of Yalta's diplomacy has pointed out that the concessions were not an abject surrender" but "reflected the great strength of Russia in Europe and her potential power in Asia." Nevertheless, the diplomatic wrangling at Yalta signaled that the world was seeing the emergence of a "new balance of power [in which] the Soviet Union [had] a decisive weight in that balance."[147]

Additionally, Roosevelt negotiated agreements at Yalta about the structure and membership of the future United Nations Organization. With the San Francisco Conference only months away, Roosevelt negotiated with Stalin over the matter of the Soviet Union's membership in the United Nations. Throughout the San Francisco Conference there were intense debates between the United States and the Soviet Union about how to design the United Nations. Critical points of contention included Stalin's insistence that there be veto rights in the Security Council and that any alterations in the UN Charter would require unanimous approval by the five permanent members.[148]

Franklin Roosevelt's Legacy in American Grand Strategy

To express the legacy of FDR's influence on American grand strategy during the Great Depression, it is useful to focus on his central contribution, which was how to balance the needs of foreign policy with rebuilding the American economy and the nation's confidence. Quite separate from Roosevelt's economic recovery policies were his policies during World War II, which were governed by the principle that it was right and proper for the United States to play a leadership role in world affairs if it meant the successful restraint or defeat of forces that threatened the stability of democracy and capitalism. This was seen, for instance, in the case of mobilizing the coalition to defeat totalitarianism in Germany and authoritarianism in Japan and Italy. The policies pursued during the Roosevelt administration aligned quite well with the post–World War II American grand strategy, derived from the principle that the nation should play a leading role in the world when operating in the context of alliances and partnerships with other democracies. The United States assumed precisely this role for the remainder of the twentieth century.

At a time when the United States was threatened by a domestic economic and political crisis, FDR's foremost objective was to rebuild the foundations of the nation's economic power. As the threat from Germany and Japan gradually materialized, FDR shifted his foreign policy to demonstrate that the United States had the political, economic, and military "capacity to be a world leader." By any standard, his grand strategy set the stage for the United States to emerge as the dominant global power for the remainder of the twentieth century. As with his predecessor Teddy Roosevelt, FDR moved in a determined fashion to modernize the United States economically and militarily, at the same time working to globalize the economic, military, and technological mechanisms of American power.[149]

FDR's influence on American grand strategy was evident from his ability to integrate critical economic and foreign considerations into a coherent strategy. This theme in American foreign policy, which endures to the present, proceeds from the overarching principle that rebuilding the national sources of American power – notably, its economic infrastructure – is a necessary condition if the United States is to be successful in foreign policy. In conclusion, with the policies pursued by President Franklin D. Roosevelt and his administration, we see the elements of an American grand strategy that rests on both a global role for the United States and rebuilding the domestic foundations of economic power that are necessary to the nation for defending and promoting its interests. Next we turn to the Cold War, when U.S. grand strategy was forced to grapple with the problems posed by the emergence of nuclear weapons and the Soviet Union as significant threats to U.S. interests.

Conclusions on America's Rise to Great Power Status

This chapter has explored America's rise to great power status over the course of the revolutionary era, and specifically how American grand strategy developed an exceptional ability to restrain sources of disorder that threaten U.S. interests and international stability. Under the leadership of Presidents Theodore Roosevelt, Woodrow Wilson, and Franklin Roosevelt, America grew to become a regional and then a global power with increased economic and military prowess. And yet this rise to global predominance was accompanied by a sense of reluctance. The American people and their leaders were pushed to act boldly by outside forces and direct attacks, causing the nation to play a more active role in international affairs than national sentiment called for at the time. America's reluctance to enter into European entanglements was a trend in American foreign policy first espoused by George Washington as part of his strong belief in American neutrality. When the United States was ultimately roused to action, it moved forward to defend a world order, to restrain sources of disorder, and to promote peace and security.

When Theodore Roosevelt assumed the presidency in 1901, America was beginning to wield greater power, regionally, in the Western Hemisphere, through its increasing economic and military capabilities. Roosevelt had a strong influence on the formation of American grand strategy at the time, as his administration pursued a two-track gradualist grand strategy that focused on both domestic and foreign policy progressions. Domestically, Roosevelt strengthened the foundations of American national power by restraining the excesses of capitalism through safety regulations and trust busting. In foreign policy, Roosevelt's grand strategy focused on gradual moves in the projection of American power through both military and diplomatic means.

Militarily, Roosevelt greatly increased the size and capabilities of the U.S. blue-water navy, which enhanced the nation's ability to project military power. This trend is exemplified in building the Panama Canal, which Roosevelt saw as a path to increase the power and influence of the United States on the international stage. In order to achieve this goal, Roosevelt supported Panamanian rebels against the Colombian government once the Colombian congress refused to cooperate in building the canal. Concurrently, Roosevelt balanced military expansion with diplomatic initiatives by mediating the Russo-Japanese War in 1905 and the Moroccan crisis between France and Germany in 1911, showing the world that America could maintain the stability of the international system through both neutral and peaceful means. As previously emphasized, Roosevelt did not move quickly to seize hegemony, but worked within the system to change it so that it would align with America's long-term interests. Yet, Roosevelt also strived to build the domestic foundations of power through modern food and drug safety regulations, the land conservation system, and pro-capitalism trust-busting legislation.

These remain the signature accomplishments of his administration on the domestic policy front.

President Woodrow Wilson initially aimed to move the United States back toward the long-standing American policy of refraining from direct intervention in European conflicts. As the early twentieth century was consumed by the outbreak of World War I, Wilson's policies had a decisive effect on the evolution of grand strategy. Inevitably, Wilson moved from a more isolationist approach to committing the full resources of the United States to win "the war to end all wars." America's emphasis on the second principle in grand strategy of restraining forces of disorder and avoiding radical alterations to the rules of the game prevailed. An Allied victory was followed by the rise of Wilson's idealism and liberal institutionalism. Some scholars see this period as representing the pinnacle in the preeminent era of idealism in American foreign policy.

Indeed, following World War II, Wilson stood for ideals that have reshaped American grand strategy to inextricably link moral values and national interest in promoting democracy abroad. Wilson ultimately pursued his grand strategy based on promoting democratic peace through a regime based on collective security, which itself was based on the principle of liberal internationalism.[150] Wilson's grand strategy embraced the concept of using international institutions to foster and sustain a more peaceful world order. Yet Congress and the American people rejected the League of Nations and Wilson's worldview, leading the nation's broad grand strategy under Roosevelt and Wilson to represent more continuity than change. After World War I, the United States rose to great power status as the European states fell dramatically from their position at the top of the international system.

As the thirty-second president of the United States, Franklin Delano Roosevelt (1933–1945) was the steward of American foreign policy in the 1930s and during the conduct of World War II, until his death in April 1945. He sought to bring America out of its isolation only when it was ready, and to steer the course of World War II in ways that directly supported American interests. The essential architecture of American grand strategy today owes much to Roosevelt's contributions. FDR's strategy consisted of a calculated ordering of priorities in which domestic relief for the Depression was his first and highest goal in a long list of actions he believed had to be taken to restore the American economy. Foreign policy matters remained, at best, of secondary importance, and by 1940, FDR's focus on the domestic economy shifted to emerging problems in the field of foreign policy. These were reaching a point at which the nation's vital interests would be imperiled.

FDR's administration confronted two of the greatest threats in American history – the Great Depression and World War II. Throughout this chapter, we have seen how FDR successfully implemented two policies that would go on to define grand strategy during the 1930s and 1940s. The first, domestic in nature, was to promote economic recovery and development during and after the Depression. The second, pertaining to America's global leadership role, was to mobilize the nation's resources and public support to join the Allied coalition for defeating Axis power. Thus, FDR's administration contributed elements of an American grand strategy that recognized an inherent need to balance a strong global leadership role for the United States with rebuilding the domestic foundations of economic power. As he developed a grand strategy that spanned the war and the postwar period, Roosevelt understood that grand strategy is practiced on the war-peace continuum using all elements of national power. By the end of World War II, America was the strongest democratic nation in the world and stood on the podium of global superpowers as "leader of the free world."

International relations scholars have defined revisionist states as those that do not only want to adjust the distribution of power in the system, but also seek to change the "rules of the game" and transform the ideological basis of that system. The "rules of the game" are defined as the institutions and systems of regulation that determine the distribution of economic and political power within the system. Although American grand strategy may not be strictly "revisionist," it is not essentially status quo–oriented either. Throughout the nineteenth and twentieth centuries, the United States favored changes to the internal structure of some states, but only when those states threatened the stability of the economic and political system of the current world order. Revisionist states favor wholesale change and transformation of the system, whereas status quo states essentially favor little to no change.

As discussed, gradualist states exemplify both revisionist and status quo characteristics and tend to favor slow, careful democratic change under limited circumstances. In practice, American grand strategy has been capable of gradualist tendencies and has never sought absolute security vis-à-vis others, in part because of its exceptional geopolitical position. Using this advantage, as well as its growing economic and political prowess, the United States rose to power over the course of the administrations discussed here and increased its global leadership role in restraining sources of disorder and strengthening stability in unique and exceptional ways.

Overall, this chapter has examined the evolution of a second principle of American grand strategy that focuses on how to deal with political and economic changes to the international system. In an era marked by revolutions and revolutionary ideologies, the United States established itself as a source of restraint to prevent rapid and radical change. Its people and its leaders were skeptical of the possibility of achieving a rapid transformation of the system while running the risk of becoming entangled in European conflicts. America was moved to take action only when provoked by direct attacks and threats against the current world order and stability. Thus, the tradition, beginning with Theodore Roosevelt and maintained with extraordinary consistency ever since, rested on the principle of restraining the sources of disorder and threats to the international system.

9 Reinforcing Alliances and Partnerships: Truman to Reagan

This chapter focuses on the United States as a great power during the Cold War. Following World War II, America proved itself to be the world's strongest democratic nation and the "leader of the free world." By the middle of the twentieth century, the United States had established itself as a political, economic, and military superpower whose grand strategy was devoted to containing the Soviet Union and the geostrategic challenges that it posed to the United States and the West. As the Cold War progressed, America's grand strategy moved from strictly containing the USSR to efforts to outspend the USSR and ultimately weaken its economic and military sources of power. This era also marks the beginning of America's dialogue with states such as China.

The Cold War is often used as an example of the highest standard in the conduct of American grand strategy. The strategy of containment was articulated clearly, its conceptual basis was readily understandable to both the American people and foreign policy experts, and it was based on intimate knowledge of the adversary. Furthermore, its initial articulation was by one person, George Kennan, who crafted an argument that had the virtues of internal consistency and unity. As for its implementation, the grand strategy of containment experienced several minor doctrinal changes, but the overall strategic concept remained remarkably consistent over the course of seven presidential administrations.

The genius of containment, and something that is true of most successful grand strategies, is that it was specific enough to provide a consistent set of priorities and policy objectives while it remained flexible enough to adapt to the variations in international and domestic circumstances. For instance, containment proved itself able to include seemingly contradictory policies such as détente under the Nixon administration and the principled confrontation policies of the Reagan administration. Finally, it is obvious – but still worth emphasizing – that containment worked just as Kennan and other experts predicted. The containment of the Soviet Union prevented it from expanding its territorial, political, and economic base. This situation was created so that the internal contradictions of Soviet ideology – viz., that its economic system was unsustainable and based on illusion rather than the facts of human nature and the principles of economics – would eventually make it self-destruct. Without outlets for expansion, the system defeated itself. In retrospect, Kennan was exactly right when he argued in his Long Telegram that our goal then should be to prevent the Soviet Union from destroying capitalist strongpoints and lock its own development onto a course of self-induced collapse.[1]

These are the common plaudits for containment, which are well worth noting, but they are, nonetheless, only a part of the story. In this chapter, the goal is to establish three important characteristics of containment that often are overlooked. First, containment was an anomaly in grand strategy in general and, more specifically, in the evolution of American grand strategy, for several reasons. In terms of articulation, it was an anomaly because of the unusual process by which it unfolded. Kennan's Long Telegram was actually a cable from the U.S. Embassy in Moscow, which was not expected to detail an entire grand strategy that would govern American policy for decades. And yet, the fact that it was the product of the mind of one individual meant that it had a logical consistency and unity often lacking in committee-led documents on grand strategy so prominent in later years or in the implicit statements about grand strategy of previous years. Grand strategy, as we have seen in the previous chapters, is rarely articulated succinctly, clearly, and logically in one document. It evolves and changes as many interest groups and elites have ideas and make changes reflecting their own biases and agendas. But here, the strategy of containment came fully articulated, like Aphrodite being born from the head of Zeus. In short, the birth of the strategy of containment was atypically smooth, linear, and without confusion.

Second, containment took place during the nuclear era of grand strategy. This was unprecedented not only because the technology itself was revolutionary but because the United States did not use its nuclear monopoly from 1945 to 1949 to coerce the Soviet Union into political submission. John Lewis Gaddis expresses this historical condition quite well:

> [H]ere the actions the United States took failed to fit traditional patterns of government power behavior. To see this point, assume counterfactually that a hypothetical Country X had gained exclusive control over what seemed, at first glance, to be an "absolute" weapon. Would one not expect X, as a matter of highest national priority and at all costs to try to keep its rival Y and other potential rivals from ever getting the device? Would not one anticipate that X would use its monopoly while it existed, to pressure and if necessary coerce other nations into following its wishes? Would one not predict that X would undertake the immediate mass production of its new weapon, with a view to ensuring continuing superiority even if monopoly were no longer possible? And would one not regard X as very likely, if it should ever get into another military conflict at whatever level, to use its new instrument of warfare to ensure victory as long as there was no realistic prospect of retaliation by Y or someone else? Abstraction suggests that all of those things should have happened during the period in which the United States enjoyed an effective nuclear monopoly. The fact that in reality none of them did requires explanation.[2]

Furthermore, after the United States lost its nuclear monopoly, the threat of nuclear war provided a powerful measure of stability to the strategies pursued by both sides. The threat of mutually assured destruction gave containment a natural solidity because this threat provided a constant disincentive to escalate from containment to a rollback strategy. Offensive war against the Soviet Union was deterred, and the Soviet Union's expansionist policies were similarly limited. Nuclear weapons, in short, gave both sides of the Cold War a strong, overriding preference for the status quo and instilled great fear of the risks of making radical alterations to that status quo. This favored the tradition of gradualism that emerged in American grand strategy in the first part of the twentieth century, as discussed in Chapter 8. The strategy of gradualism was a distinct disadvantage to the Soviet Union, which saw itself as a revolutionary power destined to change the face of global politics one communist uprising at a time. In this environment marked by a strong preference for the status quo with gradual change, the U.S. government thrived, while the Soviet Union slowly withered away and died.

The third reason why containment is anomalous will seem contradictory at first glance. It is that containment was not an American grand strategy so much as a Western grand strategy, especially in terms of its implementation. Kennan, it is true, was an American diplomat who articulated the grand strategy, but in terms of implementation, containment was undeniably, inescapably, and inalterably nested within a multilateral framework of partnerships and alliances. The grand strategy of containment relied, again and again, on the role and support of U.S. allies and multilateral institutions. Much is made of the United States and the Soviet Union operating as the lone superpowers in a bipolar system. In part, this derives from the neorealist emphasis on the essential structure of the international system based on the most basic indicators of the distribution of power, notably the size of a state's military and economy. For analyzing the world structure, these are useful indicators, but they discount the importance of local partners or the lack thereof (e.g., the United States and the USSR both lacked a viable, competent local partner in Vietnam and Afghanistan, respectively) and the necessity of using international institutions to provide a place for efficient information sharing, coordination, and the building and maintaining of diplomatic relationships. In sum, the United States could not have implemented containment alone. It necessitated building a network of pro-American, anti-Soviet allies all over the world who were willing to take enormous risks for this grand strategy.

This brings us to the third principle of American grand strategy: the reinforcement of alliances and partnerships – both old and new – to confront global challenges with a sense of shared responsibility across states and societies. When the United States assumed the mantle of the global hegemon of the West, it built around itself a set of international institutions that gave it a "nested" hegemony.[3] By this, I mean that the United States was *primus inter pares*, first among equals, unlike many of the hegemons we see in the history of European and Asian grand strategy. Indeed, looking at the Cold War, the greatest successes of the United States occurred when it had strong, close alliances and partnerships and used international institutions to their fullest (e.g., the Marshall Plan, the Korean War, the Cuban Missile Crisis, and diplomatic moves toward China), while its worst failures were associated with a lack of allies or local partners (e.g., Vietnam).

Neorealist theorists would counter with the argument that allies, partners, and institutions simply reflect the distribution of power in the system. According to this logic, the U.S. successes in forging alliances and finding local partners depended primarily on whether American power was viewed as likely to prevail and whether it served the interests of those allies and partners. There was nothing "nested" about U.S. hegemony, because it acted as it saw fit and was not constrained by institutions. Allies and partners were available in cases where "bandwagoning" was rational and were not available when balancing against the United States was preferred.[4] Nor did those institutions have any significant effect on political outcomes. In short, neorealists would see alliances and partners as secondary to overall U.S. power.

If this were the case, then, why do we see a proliferation of multilateral institutions in the Cold War? The list is long and consistently builds through the 1940s and 1950s: the United Nations (1945),[5] GATT (1947), Organization of American States (1948), NATO (1949), SEATO (1954), CENTO/Baghdad Pact (1955), and the European Economic Community (1958). What we see in the Cold War is an American reliance on these institutions and the allies within them. The United States invested time, political capital, and financial support to establish these relationships, many of which held for the most part throughout the Cold War regardless of fluctuations in the relative balance of power between the superpowers. We turn next to analyses of the administrations that played critical roles in the articulation and implementation of American grand strategy during the Cold War.

President Harry S. Truman: The Pragmatic Pioneer of Containment

Born in Independence, Missouri, in the late nineteenth century, Harry S. Truman embodied a midwestern pragmatism forged from his upbringing and in the context of America's rise to global power in the aftermath of World War II. His political and intellectual roots originated from a time before the nuclear era of grand strategy, but he succeeded in taking the first and most decisive steps in the articulation and implementation of containment. As the thirty-third president of the United States, Truman (1945–1953) was the pioneer who set the overall direction of the grand strategy of containment that dominated American foreign policy for essentially the rest of the twentieth century.

Following FDR's death, the Allies' victory over the Axis, and a period of rapid demobilization after the war, President Truman and his advisors gradually came to perceive the Soviets as a threat. Although Churchill warned Roosevelt as early as 1943 that the Soviet Union would pose the next great strategic challenge to the West, American policy makers, notably FDR and subsequently Truman, put their emphasis on winning World War II and holding together the Allied coalition, which included Moscow. On several occasions, Churchill warned both Roosevelt and Truman of the prospect of a permanently hostile relationship between the West and Moscow.[6] Toward the end of the war, there were emerging signs of strategic hostility. By 1946, it was increasingly apparent to President Truman that the United States had reached the point where it had to reorient its grand strategy to prepare the nation to deal with the ideological and military threat posed by Moscow.

Because this was one of the most decisive and consequential periods in American foreign policy, scholars and presidential historians have studied Truman's grand strategy with greater attention than those of many other presidents in modern history. As Colin Gray notes, "Because, historically, the Truman years were so significant a strategic moment, they have attracted exceptionally forceful pendulum swings in interpretation." To put the scale of the challenge for American grand strategy into perspective, Gray observes that by the end of World War II, the Truman administration had to deal with "all too familiar conditions of postwar uncertainty, chaos, and the need to comprehend a cluster of contexts substantially different in detail and broad in character from those either experienced before or recently predicted by most observer-participants."[7] These remain precisely the kinds of challenges with which any contemporary grand strategy must contend.

As with many of his predecessors who lived during times of great political and economic change, the broad outlines of President Truman's grand strategy formed relatively quickly during his presidency. By the time of Dwight D. Eisenhower's inauguration on January 20, 1953, the United States was unquestionably the preeminent "global power with global interests" and was "committed to playing a central and abiding role in international affairs."[8] This transformation of the United States to the most powerful Western country in the post–World War II era remains the central accomplishment of Truman's grand strategy.

George Kennan and the Articulation of Containment

When President Truman became president in April 1945, he faced intense debates over the architecture of American national security policy. There were four main positions as to how to respond to the Soviets. First, for many Americans, including policy makers, the overwhelming imperative was to demobilize the U.S. military, return the nation to peacetime conditions, and focus the country on building the American economy for an era in which peace and increased demand for domestic consumer products would lead to economic prosperity. These neo-isolationists harkened back to the long-lived first tradition, which lasted from Washington's "no foreign entanglements" policy in the 1790s to Wilson's "America First" policy up to 1915.

A second option for responding to the Soviet threat was to cooperate with it. This was a minority view of the extreme left whose most vocal proponent was Henry A. Wallace.[9] The third proposal was to roll back the Soviet Union's imperial reach, most prominently advocated by John Foster Dulles. The fourth option was containment as articulated by Kennan, but this view was not articulated in the Long Telegram, which was not published until two years after FDR's death. As for the other three options, FDR kept his views on this matter ambiguous in part because he liked to foster debate among his subordinates. However, this ambiguity led to a deeper problem in which FDR's grand strategy "neither captured the true state of the relationships among the major powers nor hinted at the issues over which they differed."[10]

However, one distinguishing feature of FDR on foreign policy was his view of Stalin as an ally, which was a fundamental of point difference between Roosevelt and Truman. At the time of the Yalta Conference in 1945, "when Roosevelt looked across the meeting table at Stalin, he did not see a brutal and ambitious tyrant but his crucial, if sometimes difficult, wartime ally and the man he deemed his major partner in the postwar world."[11] In contrast, when Truman considered how to work with Stalin, he wrote that "in our dealings with the Russians we had learned that we had to lead from strength and that any show of weakness was fatal."[12]

Domestically, the American people did not want to contemplate another global conflict, especially after the years spent fighting Germany and Japan. Over the course of two years, however, the perceptions of American leaders and the public about Soviet postwar intentions changed as American "concerns about [Soviet] international behavior and ambitions deepened."[13]

Thus, policy makers scrambled to rearticulate the nation's grand strategy and reach a basic consensus that would receive bipartisan support and become the basis of the U.S. Cold War strategy for the better part of the twentieth century. It involved key multilateral initiatives such as the Marshall Plan to reconstruct war-ravaged Western Europe and the establishment of NATO to create a political-military bulwark against Soviet expansion westward. In addition, the Truman Doctrine would rely on bolstering local partners to resist communist subversion and revolution.

The consensus upon which these policies were based emerged despite a wide "range of opinion on what to do about the Soviet Union," because it was clear that the Soviet

Union and its revolutionary ideology posed the primary threat to the stability of postwar democracies and to capitalism's survival.[14] This focus on a singular threat, which remained the defining principle in American grand strategy during the postwar era, contrasts sharply with the history of American grand strategy.

Kennan's Crucial Analysis: The Long Telegram and X Article

The foundation of Truman's grand strategy, which centered on containing the Soviet Union, emerged from an 8,000-word cable drafted in 1946 by George F. Kennan, a diplomat in the U.S. Embassy in Moscow. What became known as the "Long Telegram" first gained prominence within the foreign policy institutions and then reached a national audience with its publication in *Foreign Affairs* in 1947 as the "X Article." These two documents catapulted Kennan's ideas to prominence across a wide cross-section of experts and policy makers who were debating the nature of American grand strategy.

Kennan's analysis rested on the principle that the Kremlin's "neurotic view of the world [reflected] an age-old Russian sense of insecurity." He argued that "the Soviet regime was committed fanatically to the idea that in the long run there could be no peaceful coexistence with the United States, and further that it is desirable and necessary that the internal harmony of [American] society be disrupted, our traditional way of life destroyed, the international authority of our state broken."[15] With these words, Kennan reinforced the growing view and public anxieties that Moscow posed a significant threat to the United States. President Truman described how he "was not altogether disillusioned by finding now that the Russians were not in earnest about peace."[16]

Kennan framed the conflict as primarily political and ideological, rather than military. Because Marxism was predicated on the assumption that capitalism would inevitably collapse upon itself, Kennan argued, "Soviet power, unlike that of Hitlerite Germany, is neither schematic nor adventuristic. It does not work by fixed plans. It does not take unnecessary risks."[17] He argued that Moscow would pursue a flexible policy, which by its very nature would pose a challenge to the United States. Contrary to the views of many policy makers and officials in Washington at the time, Kennan viewed the Soviets as "by far the weaker force" when compared to the West. Kennan saw more than most the internal weaknesses and contradictions within communism, noting that the West's "success will really depend on the degree of cohesion, firmness and vigor which [the] Western World can muster. And this is [a] factor which it is within our power to influence."[18]

For Kennan, the key to *containing* communism was found in two interlocking principles. First, Soviet power was "impervious to the logic of reason, and it is highly sensitive to the logic of force. For this reason it can easily withdraw – and usually does when strong resistance is encountered at any point." This logic was later simplified and distorted into the view that "force is the only thing the Russians understand."[19] Kennan never argued that force was the only means of strategic interaction that would change Soviet behavior. His argument was that it was necessary, but it had to be part of a larger grand strategy to prevent expansion. Territorial expansion would allow the Soviets to ameliorate internal contradictions of their system, but without expansion, the contradictions would grow and corrode the state. Thus, containment was predicated on the "long-term, patient but firm and vigilant containment of Russian expansive tendencies."[20]

This principle of meeting communist expansion with force or the threat of force became one of the guiding concepts in the logic of containment. Second, Kennan believed that the United States had to promote a positive vision for the world. "Much depends," argued Kennan, "on the health and vigor of our own society. World communism is like a malignant parasite which feeds only on diseased tissue." With this principle in mind, Kennan argued that "this is the point at which domestic and foreign policies meet." The United States will need to avail itself of "every courageous and incisive measure to solve internal problems of our own society, to improve self-confidence, discipline, morale and community spirit of our own people."[21]

Kennan's telegram immediately gained the attention of Secretary of State George Marshall, who installed Kennan as the first head of what is now called the Policy Planning Staff, a position that gave Kennan considerable influence over the design and implementation of American grand strategy from the period between 1947 and 1950. In these early, formative stages of developing the grand strategy of containment, Kennan was a major architect of the Marshall Plan, which was the first significant policy initiative designed to contain the growing economic, political, and military influence of the Soviet Union and prevent its spread throughout Europe. It is historically rare, seeing how much Kennan was involved in both the articulation and implementation of grand strategy, for one person to be so central to both stages of grand strategy.

Within several years, however, Kennan would leave the scene, though his ideas very much defined the essence of the Cold War grand strategy. As Secretary Marshall's health failed and Dean Acheson took over at Foggy Bottom, the new secretary brought with him a number of prominent hawks that saw the Soviet threat in predominantly military terms. Acheson soon replaced Kennan with the more confrontational Paul Nitze, who oversaw the drafting of NSC-68, a memo that shifted the emphasis to using U.S. military power to prevent Soviet expansion.[22] It would have the practical effect of dramatically increasing national security spending throughout the Cold War.[23] The influence of Kennan's ideas on American grand strategy was, according to Colin Gray, without parallel.[24] As a result, many people have tried to be the next Kennan in the post–Cold War era, which is a fool's errand, as this discussion shows. The reason is that his prominence was a product not only of the quality of his ideas but more so because of the anomalous contextual factors at play during his time. However, it remains a useful endeavor to articulate ideas that lend overall coherence to the state's grand strategy, especially in an era marked by strategic confusion.

Alliances, Partners, and Institutions: Building the Multilateral Wall of Containment

The Truman Doctrine

In the aftermath of World War II, the emergence of a communist-led guerrilla movement in Greece and Soviet designs on Turkey were the catalysts within the Truman administration for the United States to undertake a military assistance program for local, anti-communist partners. By the spring of 1946, Truman had set in motion a plan for military aid programs throughout Europe, Latin America, and Asia that were designed to combat the spread of communist insurgencies and revolutionary movements. Here, the legacy of the Lend-Lease program of providing military aid during World War II loomed large. As one scholar writes, "After [Lend-Lease], military aid, for many Washington officials, was no longer an unfamiliar or unusual device but a tested instrument for securing American objectives overseas." Truman asked Congress to "approve long-term arms aid [packages for] the Philippines, China, and Latin America." More broadly, Truman "requested authority to send military advisers to any foreign country whenever he thought that such help would advance the national interest." These programs were historically significant because the United States "never before, except in time of war, had ... used military assistance as a *major, continuing* instrument of national policy."[25]

In struggling to build the security architecture of America's emerging grand strategy, officials in the Truman administration believed that communist pressure against Greece and Turkey was part of a larger movement pushed by the Kremlin, whose objective was to inspire "wars of national liberation."[26] Many officials increasingly saw military aid programs as an integral instrument of American foreign policy. Truman articulated his doctrine in an address to Congress on March 12, 1947, in which he said, "I believe it must be the policy of the United States to support free peoples who are resisting attempted subjugation by armed minorities or by outside pressures." He continued, "I recommend that the authority also be provided for the instruction and training of selected Greek and Turkish personnel."[27] Finally, to highlight the urgency of the threat and the magnitude of the responsibility thrust upon the United States and its allies, Truman warned that "the free peoples of the world look to us for support in maintaining their freedoms." The danger was that "if we falter in our leadership, we may endanger the peace of the world – and we shall surely endanger the welfare of our own nation."[28]

American military aid and advisors that were sent to both Greece and Turkey helped, in time, to stem the tide of Soviet influence. The Truman Doctrine ensured that military assistance efforts would not be piecemeal and would henceforth be part of coordinated policies whose objective was to strengthen allies and prevent future communist expansion. For a nation that prior to World Wars I and II had been largely relegated to the sidelines in global affairs, the Truman Doctrine was a bold redefinition of America's more activist role, but it was a role defined by relationships with allies and partners who wanted to prevent communism's expansion. It depended for success on local partners that were willing and potentially able to resist communist expansion. Greece and Turkey had those reliable local partners. Importantly, both these countries would be incorporated into NATO during its first expansion in 1952. The United States, therefore, implemented containment successfully by nesting its hegemonic influence with strong local partner relationships and later within an institutionalized security alliance.

The Marshall Plan

The Marshall Plan was also a policy that sought to implement containment through allies. Truman regarded it as one of his greatest achievements. He wrote in his memoirs that "the Marshall Plan will go down in history as one of America's greatest contributions to the peace of the world."[29] Spearheaded by Secretary of State General George C. Marshall, perhaps the most trusted man in America at the time, the massive aid program underwrote European recovery and allowed Europe to achieve economic self-sustainability by the end of the decade.[30] From 1947 until its termination at the end of 1951, the Marshall Plan provided approximately $13 billion to finance European economic recovery, a figure that represented nearly 5 percent of the U.S. gross domestic product at the time.[31] Describing his reasoning behind the Marshall Plan, Truman stated, "I think the world now realizes that without the Marshall Plan it would have been difficult for Western Europe to remain free from the tyranny of Communism."[32]

For Truman, the Plan's broad objective "was to keep Western Europe free and democratic and secure from Soviet" influence or takeover.[33] A cardinal principle of containment was that strong and prosperous European allies were critical to the success of the prolonged American political, ideological, and military struggle against the Soviet Union. The premise of the Plan was, in addition to preventing a humanitarian disaster of overwhelming proportions, to send aid to states in Western Europe to restore them to their earlier positions of economic power and global influence so that they would act as counterweights to Moscow. "The objective of the Marshall Plan was not to provide relief," writes Marshall Plan historian Greg Behrman, but "to bring Europe to self-sustainability – 'a spark which can fire the engine.'"[34] That engine was Western European capitalism, which had to reconstruct itself after the devastation of two world wars. Truman and Marshall understood that without a strong Western Europe, containment would fail because Europe was its center of gravity. Central Europe in particular was perceived as the most dangerous geostrategic flashpoint. Indeed, many American grand strategists saw conflicts in the periphery in terms of their implications for the confrontation in Europe.[35]

Paul Nitze and NSC-68: Rearticulating the Soviet Threat in Military Terms

By 1949, a number of events made it more urgent for Washington to develop a coherent grand strategy for guiding American policies during the Cold War. In that year, the Soviet Union ended the American nuclear monopoly with its own detonation of an atomic bomb; the Chinese revolution was successful as Mao's forces consolidated control over China and forced the nationalists off the mainland; and, lastly, Ho Chi Minh's Viet Minh was putting much greater pressure on the French throughout Indochina. Moreover, American policy makers were looking for ways to better integrate the Marshall Plan and the Truman Doctrine into a coherent grand strategy for containing Moscow and dealing with its overtures. These events created the opportunity for Paul Nitze, in his capacity as the new director of the Policy Planning Staff at the State Department, to propose a fundamental overhaul of American national security policy.

The authors of the report known as NSC-68, including most notably Paul Nitze, argued that the Soviet Union was an inherently expansionist empire whose leaders in Moscow had the desire and capability to dominate the international system.[36] The NSC-68 recommended marshaling all the resources of American national power through a "more rapid build-up of political, economic, and military strength and thereby of confidence in the free world than is now contemplated." Its authors framed the struggle with the Soviet Union as a matter of national survival for the United States. As Truman biographer David McCullough writes, NSC-68 "was intended to shock [by using an] apocalyptic theme at its core." In retrospect, it used quite dramatic language: "'This republic and its citizens, in the ascendency of their strength, stand in their deepest peril.'" As McCullough continues, "The American colossus, the report said in effect, was sadly wanting in real military might." It was a direct attack against the "policy of 'containment,' as advanced by George Kennan, [which] was no better than a policy of bluff without the 'superior aggregate military strength' – the conventional forces – to back it up." As the authors of NSC-68 declared, "Nuclear weapons were insufficient and, in any event, the Soviets would probably achieve nuclear equity by 1954." Its purpose, as Secretary of State Dean Acheson noted, was to "bludgeon the mass mind of top government."[37]

The NSC-68's claim that the United States needed to take immediate action directly contrasted with the strategic patience urged by Kennan in his Long Telegram. Consequently, NSC-68 paved the way for a massive conventional and nuclear arms buildup over the next decade. Its purpose was "to put forward a strategy not just to contain the Soviets in the hope that their system would eventually wither and die." Under the guidance provided by NSC-68, annual U.S. defense spending grew "from $14.3 billion to $50 billion, a fourfold increase from 5 percent to 20 percent of gross national product."[38] The NSC-68's main conclusion, which held that the Soviet Union represented an imminent threat to American vital interests, was confirmed nearly two months after it was presented to President Truman. On June 25, 1950, North Korean forces stormed over the thirty-eighth parallel to begin the Korean War.

Korean War: Unity of the United Nations and United States

The American entry into the Korean War must be viewed in light of what many in the Truman administration viewed as the relentless and coherent expansionist policies pursued by Moscow and Beijing. The United States, according to (later) Secretary of State Dean Rusk, "had occupied South Korea for five years and had therefore a particular responsibility for South Korea, which, if absorbed by the Communists, would be 'a dagger pointed at the heart of Japan.'"[39] As Truman writes in his memoirs, many in the administration, including General Omar Bradley, "said we would have to draw the line somewhere. Russia, he thought, was not yet ready for war, but in Korea they were obviously testing us, and the line ought to be drawn now."[40] Truman pressed for and received United Nations approval to support military intervention in Korea, which established an important precedent in the early history of this new international organization. Equally important, it reaffirmed that the American grand strategy of containment would be backed by the use of military force with support from international institutions and cooperation with allies. Besides the United States and South Korea, fifteen other nations contributed a total of 150,000 personnel. The highest contributions came from the United Kingdom (60,000), Canada (27,000), Australia (17,000), and Turkey (15,000).[41]

The war had the potential to draw both the Soviets and the Chinese into a nuclear conflict with the United States, a fact that persuaded Truman to avoid steps that would escalate the war. "'There was no doubt in my mind,' Truman wrote, 'that we should not allow the action in Korea to extend to a general war. All-out military action against China had to be avoided, if for no other reason than because it was a gigantic booby trap.'"[42] In fact, when General MacArthur advised the Truman administration to expand the war effort against China, including the possibility of employing tactical nuclear weapons, Truman flatly rejected the notion – and eventually fired MacArthur over matters pertaining to the primacy of civilian control over the military.[43] The Korean War is an example of the United States purposefully restraining itself during the nuclear era while working closely with allied militaries to contain communist expansion.

Truman's Legacy in American Grand Strategy

The most enduring legacy of Truman on American grand strategy in the aftermath of World War II was his decision to direct American power toward containing the growth of Soviet power. In the early years of the Cold War and facing increasing Soviet pressure on Western and Eastern Europe, Truman guided the United States to adopt a more activist role in foreign policy – despite the public's overwhelming desire to refocus the nation's attention on rebuilding the economy in the aftermath of World War II. Without American power, it is almost certain that a coalition would not have emerged to confront and contain Soviet totalitarianism, but it is also true that without America's allies and partners, containment would have failed. The Truman Doctrine, the Marshall Plan, and the NSC-68, among other strategies, developed the outlines of a grand strategy premised on close ties with anti-communist allies, which formed the basis for containment's implementation during the next several decades.

From the triumphant yet hesitant years immediately following the victory against Germany and Japan in 1945, Truman slowly and deliberately, and with prodding from Churchill, shifted American grand strategy to successfully demonstrate that Washington possessed the political will and economic and military capacity to lead the rest of world in a struggle against communism and totalitarianism. Without doubt, Truman's grand strategy provided the intellectual and political vision that directed the United States' emergence as the preeminent world power for the remainder of the twentieth century. As with his predecessor FDR, Truman dramatically altered American power as he redefined Washington's involvement in international affairs.[44]

Another legacy of Truman's influence on American grand strategy was his ability to balance the political values of freedom and economic might along with U.S. military and technological power into policies for containing the influence created by Soviet political and economic ideology. A critical theme in American grand strategy that endures to the present is the belief, adhered to somewhat grudgingly, that the United States has exceptional power and the judgment to play a central role in defending democracy, free markets, and human rights. One cannot escape this legacy, given the imperatives outlined in the Truman Doctrine, because the United States provided the economic and military assistance that kept states from falling into the Soviet sphere of influence.

Once the fundamental architecture of American grand strategy was articulated by President Truman's administration, the next series of presidential administrations organized their foreign policies along these conceptual and institutional lines. In the end, Truman's legacy in grand strategy is among the most significant and enduring of modern American presidents largely because it provided the basis for American foreign policy during the Cold War, which lasted until the formal demise of the Soviet Union in 1991.

President Dwight D. Eisenhower: Containing the Costs of Containment

As the thirty-fourth president of the United States, Dwight D. Eisenhower (1953–1961) was the second of the principal architects of American foreign policy in the years after World War II and during the first years of the Cold War (1947–1991). Eisenhower's time in office coincided with a period of great international hostility and a dramatic American economic resurgence after the Depression and World War II. The hallmarks of the Eisenhower administration's influence on grand strategy were dealing with the Soviet

Union during the Cold War, guiding the United States during a period of great economic prosperity, and defining the role of the United States as the leading nation in the struggle against Soviet totalitarianism.

A prominent feature of President Eisenhower's grand strategy was its emphasis on the necessity of striking the proper balance between the political, economic, and military requirements in formulating and conducting American grand strategy, especially during a time of great international hostility.[45] This emphasis on balancing among resources in the conduct of foreign and domestic policy emerges historically as a defining characteristic of American grand strategy, which we can see during its evolution from George Washington's administration to the present. Eisenhower's concern for effectively managing the country's resources was evident even in the early stages of his presidential campaign. According to the scholar John Lewis Gaddis, a concern for the sustainability of the government and its long-term national security policies helped build the relationship between Eisenhower and his future secretary of state John Foster Dulles. As Gaddis writes, "Dulles's promises of greater effectiveness at less cost appealed to Eisenhower, who had long nursed a vague sense of uneasiness about the country's ability to sustain indefinitely large military expenditures." This sentiment was evident in Eisenhower's famous farewell address to the nation, as discussed later.

Eisenhower, however, was not fully in agreement with Dulles's theory of asymmetrical strategic deterrence or what also was known as the doctrine of retaliation.[46] As a presidential hopeful, Eisenhower warned Dulles that the "exclusive reliance upon a mere power of retaliation is not a complete answer to the broad Soviet threat." The solution in Eisenhower's view was to "be successful in developing collective security measures." Gaddis explains the logic in the campaign: "[Eisenhower] reluctantly accepted language in the Republican platform condemning the 'negative, futile and immoral policy of 'containment.'"[47] Dulles was his principal foreign policy advisor during the campaign and publically condemned containment in favor of moving to a more aggressive rollback strategy. Eisenhower tolerated this new belligerence during the campaign but maintained strong doubts about whether liberating peoples from the Soviet sphere of influence was feasible and wise.[48]

Toward this end, the Eisenhower Doctrine, which was articulated in 1957, held that the United States would be "prepared to use armed force . . . [to counter] aggression from any country controlled by international communism."[49] Eisenhower also authorized the use of U.S. forces "to secure and protect the territorial integrity and political independence of such nations, requesting such aid against overt armed aggression from any nation controlled by international communism."[50] The Eisenhower Doctrine, then, increased the level of commitment to anticommunist allies from the military aid and advice contemplated in the Truman Doctrine to the actual deployment of U.S. forces to defend these nations.

Coming on the heels of the Truman administration's definitive strategy paper, NSC-68, Eisenhower's primary national security concern when he entered office was how to preserve the fragile balance of power as the countries in Western Europe and Asia were rebuilding themselves. His wanted to prevent, in the midst of rebuilding societies that were wrecked by war, a power shift toward the Soviet Union. As Eisenhower warned in his inaugural address on January 20, 1953, "As there is no weapon too small, no arena too remote, to be ignored, there is no free nation too humble to be forgotten."[51]

However, this policy did not mean that Eisenhower thought that absolute security would only come with a mandate for global hegemony. To the contrary, Dulles qualified this policy when he said: "We do not assume that we have any mandate to run the world.... Nothing indeed would be less in keeping with our traditions and our ideals."[52] As Eisenhower explained in a letter to a friend, "We are [so] proud of our guarantees of freedom in thought and speech and worship, that unconsciously, we are guilty of one of the greatest errors that ignorance can make – we assume that our standard of values is shared by all other humans in the world."[53]

In proceeding toward a cautiously proactive but not overbearing foreign policy, Eisenhower sought to overcome barriers within his own party. Sensing that dissension within the administration over the meaning and implementation of containment would undermine the government's effectiveness in foreign policy, he ordered a formal reassessment in what was known as Project Solarium.

Project Solarium and Eisenhower's "New Look" Strategy

In contrast with some administrations that find themselves arriving at a particular grand strategy almost as if by default and reaction, President Eisenhower made an explicit effort to develop a coherent grand strategy at a time when the United States faced a significant threat. To help the United States develop a strategy that aligned with its interests and threats, in the summer of 1953 the Eisenhower administration conducted a planning exercise know as "Operation Solarium." Its purpose was to evaluate all options for dealing with the Soviet threat and then choose the best course of action for the United States.[54]

To articulate his grand strategy, the president tasked three separate study groups at the National War College to outline the case for three alternative, but not mutually exclusive, policy options: first, a continuation of the Truman strategy of containment; second, a strategy of deterrence (with the implied threat of nuclear retaliation); and third, a liberation strategy that was designed to "roll back" areas in which the Soviet Union had gained influence.

The result of these meetings, which took place in the White House solarium (thus the project's name), was to produce a strategic concept that came to be known as the "New Look." Rather than deciding on one path put forth by the War College study groups, the Eisenhower administration's New Look strategy was designed to align the nation's political and military commitments during the Cold War with the resources that Eisenhower believed the United States could reasonably allocate to national security.[55] The New Look strategy also increased the nation's reliance on using nuclear weapons to deter war in the face of the massive conventional and growing nuclear forces of the Soviet Union. To develop a comprehensive strategy, the administration worked on the basis of "a common threat" to integrate "nuclear deterrence, alliances, psychological warfare, covert action, and negotiations." In the president's view, this approach had the merit of being less expensive than the strategy envisioned in NSC-68, which did not call for departing from the grand strategy of containment.[56] As a fiscal conservative, Eisenhower was concerned that NSC-68 would require enormous expenditures that would run the risk of bankrupting the nation. Certain that the Cold War would last for many years, Eisenhower feared that runaway defense spending could destroy the nation economically from within. Nor had he any enthusiasm for further Korea-like military entanglements in peripheral areas. Given how the Eisenhower administration saw U.S. interests and the threats facing the nation, his New Look strategy was designed to be an affordable way to balance means and ends in national security.[57]

The organizing principle of Eisenhower's grand strategy was to "regain … the initiative while lowering costs."[58] Eisenhower believed that because the Cold War would be a protracted conflict and because there would be no quick victory, "the United States had to hoard its resources, limit its efforts and spread its burdens, or else exhaust itself in the long haul." But as Eisenhower warned in 1954, "We can't afford to let the negative actions of the Communists force us into world-wide deployment [because] we need to be free to decide where we can strike most effectively." As Michael Sherry explains, the New Look was "an effort to limit defense spending by relying on enhanced nuclear forces, as well as alliances and covert action, rather than on costly conventional forces to counter enemy initiatives."[59]

In order to explain to the public how the nation's strategic initiative could be compatible with our limited resources and how we might more efficiently expend those, Secretary of State Dulles called anew for a strategy based on asymmetry, which sought to combine the principles of regaining the strategic initiative with a greater sense of "budgetary restraint."[60] According to Dulles, the "deterrent of massive retaliatory power" would discourage potential aggressors and assure that the United States possessed sufficiently great power to control the terms of international engagement. With the New Look strategy in place, Dulles argued that "the Department of Defense and the Joint Chiefs of Staff can shape our military establishment to fit what is *our* policy, instead of having to try to be ready to meet the enemy's many choices."[61] The strategy was for American policy to be more selective and hence less reactive in choosing whether and how to respond to Soviet actions. In a speech to the Council on Foreign Relations in 1954, Dulles recognized the role of allies and institutions in reducing costs. "We need allies and collective security. Our purpose is to make these relations more effective and less costly."[62]

The practical goal, then, was for the United States to gain more security and spend less, in part because its allies would spend more on defense. This was one of the many indirect benefits of the Marshall Plan. It enabled Western European governments to spend more on containment. It also facilitated the move toward European economic integration. United States allies formed the European Coal and Steel Community in 1952 and then broadened and deepened the economic cooperation with the formation of the European Economic Community in 1957. Allies and institutions were therefore a key component of making containment a viable grand strategy in terms of implementation.

Providing "more security at less cost" became a central and enduring objective during Eisenhower's tenure.[63] The argument was that American strategy should carefully balance its policies with available resources so that the nation would not bankrupt itself as its policy makers dealt with a complex mix of challenges. The central idea was to develop the concept of "asymmetrical response – of reacting to adversary challenges in ways calculated to apply one's strengths against the other side's weaknesses, even if this meant shifting the nature and location of the confrontation." If this strategy (consisting of nuclear weapons, alliances, covert action, negotiations, and so forth) were successful, it would help the United States use its economic power more wisely. The study of grand strategy conducted during the Eisenhower administration considered all of these factors, including alliances and negotiations; it articulated a comprehensive strategy for responding to the Soviet threat. Since nuclear weapons were so central to this process, it is useful to examine how that issue evolved during the Eisenhower administration.

The Doctrine of Massive Retaliation

As the first administration to deal with atomic weapons, President Truman and his administration started the process of developing a clear strategy for deriving political benefits from those weapons. Truman described in his memoirs how he was briefed about the existence of the Manhattan Project almost immediately after being sworn in as president.[64] Yet it took nearly eight years before U.S. policy under Eisenhower deliberately emphasized its nuclear capabilities and willingness to use nuclear weapons as part of American grand strategy during the 1950s.

The role of nuclear weapons in grand strategy was evident from the earliest days of the Eisenhower administration, particularly as it related to the balance between nuclear and conventional forces in U.S. defense planning and strategy. In a November 1953 meeting with administration officials, Eisenhower recognized that "the dependence that we are placing on new weapons would justify completely some reduction in conventional forces – that is, both ground troops and certain parts of the Navy."[65] Just as importantly, however, the reliance on nuclear weapons had to reflect an actual willingness to use those weapons. The challenge for the United States was to rely on the "absolute weapon" without crippling its conventional forces or putting itself in the position in which adversaries or allies might doubt Washington's commitment to using nuclear weapons. Dulles proposed a solution in a 1954 *Foreign Affairs* article, when he argued that "the free world must have the means for responding effectively on a selective basis when it chooses. It must not put itself in the position where the only response ... is general war."[66]

The Truman administration emphasized relying on symmetrical strategic responses to promote a deterrence strategy in which the United States "would counter, but not exceed the initial provocation."[67] But for Dulles, who favored asymmetrical responses and deterrence, "the way to maximize U.S. deterrence was by linking the certainty of retaliation with the uncertainty of timing, place, and means of retaliation."[68] Eisenhower returned to this principle in his farewell address when he said, "Our arms must be mighty, ready for instant action, so that no potential aggressor may be tempted to risk his own destruction."[69] Although this logic appealed to the Eisenhower administration, it held the view that the threat to use nuclear weapons would be credible only if its ability to deter aggression were economically tolerable in contrast with the dramatically more expensive ground forces that would be needed to achieve the same deterrent effect.

With this idea playing a central role to his strategy, Eisenhower was an early and strong proponent of the idea that eventually would "become known as the doctrine of 'sufficiency,'" which asserted that beyond some finite point, building more nuclear weapons did not materially strengthen U.S. security.[70] As an early and strong proponent of the idea of sufficiency, rather than superiority, in nuclear weapons, Eisenhower said that when he became president the Joint Chiefs of Staff (JCS) told him that if they could hit seventy targets in the Soviet Union with atomic weapons, the Red Army could not carry on an aggressive war. By the end of his eight years in office, the JCS raised that number to seven hundred targets, which forced Eisenhower to ask, "How many times do we need to kill each Russian?"[71] The assessments undermined the concept of "sufficiency," because the change in the required number of targets suggested that sufficiency is a malleable concept. The doctrine of sufficiency related directly to Eisenhower's support for "strategic asymmetry." It also implied that American grand strategy would adhere to the principle that it was prudent for American policy makers to choose where and how we would engage in a global struggle with Moscow.

The number of nuclear weapons in the U.S. arsenal increased significantly during Eisenhower's tenure in office, but the president was not interested in building an unnecessarily large nuclear stockpile. In keeping with his goal of striking an appropriate relationship between ends and means, Eisenhower was keenly aware of the need for picking his battles wisely. His strategic concept was to identify the activities most essential to undermining the Soviet Union's ability to threaten the United States and thereby alter the balance of world power.

Assessing the New Look

An enduring dilemma in grand strategy is judging whether the strategy is effective in balancing ends and means while accomplishing its purposes. Although the Eisenhower administration resisted pressures to engage in "large-scale overseas military activity" after the Korean War, U.S. grand strategy was judged favorably by the fact that "only [two] countries [were] 'lost' to communism" during the Eisenhower administration: "North Vietnam, already largely under Ho Chi Minh's control when Eisenhower entered the White House, and Cuba, whose communist orientation did not become clear until he was about to leave it."[72] Of equal significance in his grand strategy to balancing foreign and domestic factors, Eisenhower successfully decreased defense spending as a percentage of gross domestic product and as a percentage of the total federal budget, and did so during a time of great hostility and tension.

For critics, however, Eisenhower's strategy had a number of weaknesses. A few are that it relied far too heavily on nuclear weapons, foundered in numerous cases of "third world" revolutions through covert operations, failed miserably in allowing a missile gap to develop, and missed opportunities to negotiate ways to ease Cold War tensions. Furthermore, as Gaddis writes, "It is also difficult to square Eisenhower's assurances that nuclear war could be kept limited with his profound skepticism regarding the utility of advanced planning in war."[73] To reinforce this belief, Eisenhower said in a press conference in 1954 that "there is one thing I can tell you about war, and almost one only, and it is this: no war ever shows the characteristics that were expected; it is always different."[74]

In his defense, Eisenhower's goal was to avoid war in general, including nuclear ones. His conclusion was that "the best way to avoid an all-out nuclear war was *to make that the only military option available to the United States.*" From this argument, Eisenhower's "reasoning was [likely and principally] Clausewitzian, the great Prussian strategist, who in his classic work, *On War* had coupled a vision of total and hence irrational violence with a demonstration of how difficult – and how foolish – it would be to attempt it."[75] However, while Clausewitz's concept of absolute war was viewed as an abstraction at the time, the possibility of using nuclear weapons never disappeared as a serious option during the Eisenhower administration as Cold War hostilities increased. In the final analysis, Eisenhower's New Look strategy was a coherent and prudent study of how to relate ends and means. Scholars may assert that this represents a "modest claim" about Eisenhower's grand strategy, but it is on the whole "a more favorable one than one can reasonably make about either the strategy that preceded, or the one that followed."[76]

For some, Eisenhower's Solarium project and its expression in the New Look strategy are significant examples of how the United States developed a coherent grand strategy in an era of enormous strategic uncertainties and risks. It also demonstrates the value of Eisenhower's dedication to strategic planning, which provides a model for how modern policy makers ought to develop the state's grand strategy.[77] For example, in 2006 Michele Flournoy, who served as the undersecretary of defense for policy in the Obama administration, argued that "the Eisenhower administration offers perhaps the best example of long-term strategic planning in the history of the American Presidency." Her reasoning is that Project Solarium is "directly attributed" to President Eisenhower's ability to "preserve and nurture long-term strategic planning," which she holds is "a basic prerequisite of an effective and responsible foreign policy."[78]

By implication, Eisenhower saw grand strategy in the context of building the moral foundations of American power in the hope that war would be unnecessary. Importantly, this principle endowed American grand strategy with a strong moral overtone as the nation sought to protect the human values of freedom, democracy, and free markets from the ravages of totalitarianism and authoritarianism.[79]

Although Eisenhower agreed that morality was a critical component of the American character and of its grand strategy, when he was asked what the "irreducible American interests in the world" were, the answer for Eisenhower was to stress the role of economics as a fundamental strength of the nation and its policies.[80] As Eisenhower instructed Dulles in 1952, U.S. policies should emphasize free trade, access to raw materials, and America's "natural capabilities for leadership."[81] He believed that if a nation's grand strategy is based on pursuing the national interest, which requires the nation to have healthy political and commercial relationships around the globe, then a country's foreign policy must emphasize the economic foundations of power. Nor can it afford to ignore the moral component by being belligerent or showing disregard for other states.[82]

Still, Eisenhower worried whether the American people shared his enthusiasm for international engagement, particularly after the human and economic tolls exacted by World War II. Of great concern was that the United States would confront the prolonged, inconclusive, and limited wars that only make things worse. Eisenhower believed that "people grow weary of war, particularly when they see no decisive and victorious end to it."[83] When explaining the necessity of bringing an end to the Korean War, he argued that "victory would require such an expansion of the present conflict as to demand practically a general mobilization." The question for Eisenhower was how long the United States "could endure regimentation without losing part of our free system."[84] One danger with containment as a guiding force in American grand strategy was precisely that the United States faced an era, which could have lasted indefinitely, in which it was called on to engage in a constant and unending struggle without a decisive end or victory in sight.[85]

Eisenhower, however, was a realist who recognized that the United States does not have the power or will to be able to fight every fight in every corner of the world.[86] He was famously concerned about how to effectively manage the country's resources and focused his attention on ensuring that military spending was worth the corresponding investments that the nation otherwise would spend on the domestic economy and its infrastructure. Often quoted today in the context of the debate surrounding defense cuts, in April 1953 Eisenhower warned about the opportunity costs that apply to every military expenditure made during peacetime:

> Every gun that is made, every warship launched, every rocket fired signifies, in the final sense, a theft from those who hunger and are not fed, those who are cold and are not clothed.... The cost of one modern heavy bomber is this: a modern brick school in more than 30 cities. It is two electric power plants, each serving a town of 60,000 population. It is two fine, fully equipped hospitals. It is some 50 miles of concrete highway. We pay for a single fighter plane with a half million bushels of wheat. We pay for a single destroyer with new homes that could have housed more than 8,000 people.[87]

As Eisenhower said in a November 1954 address, "let us be strong, but don't let us be strong only in tanks, guns, and planes and ships. There is no lasting peace there. The most they can do is to protect you in what you have for the moment."[88] In perhaps the most surprising argument coming from a career military officer, Eisenhower believed that buying weapons and paying for armies was inherently detrimental to the nation's security. His rationale was that investing in national security will "deplete, rather than enhance, a nation's strength."[89] As Eisenhower said in a press conference, "I have always firmly believed that there is a great logic in the conduct of military affairs. There is an equally great logic in economic affairs." The key for him was that "if these two logical disciplines can be wedded, it is then possible to create a situation of maximum military strength within economic capacities." He reaffirmed the need to balance the two; otherwise the state puts its "military position [in] constant jeopardy."[90] With Eisenhower, we see the direct linkage to grand strategy in the nexus between the domestic foundations of power and foreign policy.

Eisenhower's understanding of the German strategist Clausewitz, which emerged during his years of military training and experience, decisively shaped his views on how ends should relate to means in strategy. Gaddis frames the matter quite directly, writing that what Eisenhower "retained from reading the Prussian strategist was that in politics as well as in war, means had to be subordinated to ends." More broadly, as scholars write, a critical principle for Eisenhower was to understand that "effort expended without purpose served no purpose."[91] This point was particularly significant for Eisenhower in his approach to grand strategy when he declared during his administration that the "cold war must have some objective, otherwise it would be senseless. It is conducted in the belief that if there is no war, if two systems of government are allowed to live side by side, that ours because of its greater appeal to men everywhere – to mankind – in the long run will win out."[92] One way to express Eisenhower's ends-means dilemma in the nuclear age is to focus on the ends of grand strategy without allowing the means (conventional and nuclear forces) to destroy the economic well-being of the state.[93] This remained a central dilemma for Eisenhower as he articulated American grand strategy in an era when diplomacy and strategy were dominated by nuclear weapons.

President Eisenhower also framed the problem for the United States in terms of limiting the costs of containment to the erosion of American values.

> *We must not destroy what we are attempting to defend.* So, just as earnestly as I believe we must all fight communism to the utmost, I believe that we must also fight any truly unjust, un-American way of uprooting them, because in the long run I think we will destroy ourselves if we use that kind of defense.[94]

Building from an awareness that grand strategy must protect America's character as well as its security, policy makers in Eisenhower's National Security Council considered how to preserve U.S. security as defined as its core democratic values and institutions. Unlike

NSC-68, Eisenhower's strategy linked security with defending the nation's permanent values and interests "rather than [repulsing] transitory threats."[95]

This argument reaffirms that domestic politics is an integral, if often dismissed, element in articulating and implementing grand strategy – particularly in the case of democratic societies.[96] Dulles, for one, saw the struggle between the United States and the Soviet Union's ideology of communism as a zero-sum game, very much along the lines of the position adopted by the Truman administration in NSC-68. In Dulles's view, the Soviet strategy was "'to extend its system through the world and establish its 'one world' of state socialism.'"[97] The secretary of state astutely recognized that by emphasizing this threat, he could more much effectively promote anticommunist solidarity at home and abroad. Although the "domestic benefits of crusading against 'communism' were considerable at a time when both McCarthyism and unilateralism still had influence," Dulles worried that "if there's no evident menace from the Soviet blow, our will to maintain unity and strength may weaken." Thus, ". . . in promoting our programs in Congress we have to make evident the international Communist menace." Equally important was the problem that U.S. allies might conclude that "the danger was over and therefore they did not need to continue to spend large sums for defense."[98]

Following this logic, Dulles may have believed that it was "desirable to maintain a certain level of tension between the Soviet Union and the United States, since negotiations (if successful) would tend to lower that tension level, [and thus] Dulles viewed them with little enthusiasm." The risk for Dulles was that "negotiations could lead to détente, and détente – by relaxing tensions – could lead to a lessening of Western [military and moral] strength."[99] Fears about Soviet expansionism decisively shaped the domestic political calculus of grand strategy. A critique, then, is that Secretary of State Dulles too often glossed over internal Soviet vulnerabilities so as to project a menacing, powerful image of the Soviet Union.[100] Dulles pushed the message so relentlessly that it risked losing its political impact. This situation is ironic for developing a grand strategy, because removing or neutralizing the "Soviet challenge" that was "the original goal of containment" now was a "means by which that doctrine's instruments were to be perpetuated as ends in themselves." This development represents a "curious inversion of ends and means," which was the antithesis to Eisenhower's efforts to balance ends and means.[101]

President Eisenhower largely shared Dulles's assessment of the Soviet threat, but rather than focus on fearmongering in American domestic politics, he worried about the economic implications of the Soviet Union's expansionist ambitions. The president believed that the Soviet Union hoped to impose on the United States an "unbearable security burden [that would lead] to economic disaster."[102] In considering Eisenhower's grand strategy, the resource implications of this "unbearable security burden" decisively influenced Eisenhower's efforts to balance the economic and security burdens on the American economy. In Eisenhower's view, any "attempt to match Soviet military capabilities in all respects would be to play into Moscow's hands" and "frighten the West into exhausting itself."[103] The supreme irony here is that, in the end, the Soviet economic system exhausted itself after unsuccessfully trying to compete with capitalism's more efficient resource allocation and the democratic state's ability to fulfill national security requirements without sacrificing domestic economic prosperity.

Eisenhower's Legacy in American Grand Strategy

Eisenhower's influence on the development of U.S. grand strategy in the early years of the Cold War is epitomized by his reliance on nuclear weapons as one instrument for containing Soviet influence and preventing conflict. It was crucial for the president to strike a careful balance between the ends and means of American grand strategy, including serious investments in the nation's infrastructure. As with Truman, Eisenhower believed in an activist role for the United States in foreign policy without sacrificing the society's demand that it rebuild the foundations of American power and prosperity after World War II.

Eisenhower built on the policies developed by President Truman. He saw the United States as the singular state with the power and resources necessary to contain, if not eventually defeat several decades later, the Soviet Union in a global struggle for power. Drawing from his military experience gained during World War II, Eisenhower's judgments undoubtedly were guided by his understanding that only the United States had the power and influence to pursue a grand strategy that could hold back Soviet totalitarianism. It had to do so without bankrupting the United States and its allies, who were recovering from the devastation of World War II.

The framework for American grand strategy during the Eisenhower administration built directly on the policies of the Truman administration, including, as prominent examples, containment, the Truman Doctrine, the Marshall Plan, and the NSC-68. Through Operation Solarium and the New Look strategy, Eisenhower's significant accomplishment was in balancing these policies with an explicit desire to build a cost-effective Cold War strategy for the United States. And although Eisenhower's review of containment's implementation focused very much on domestic budgetary sustainability and economic growth, it nonetheless increased the reliance of the United States on its allies, particularly those in Western Europe, to shoulder the burden of defense against Soviet expansion.

As with Truman, President Eisenhower designed his grand strategy to help the United States mobilize just enough of its economy and society to deter war with Moscow without weakening the American economy with more defense spending than it could reasonably or prudently bear. As the Soviet threat remained acutely dangerous, Eisenhower warned about the dangers to the nation. As he warned in his farewell address to the nation, "We face a hostile ideology global in scope, atheistic in character, ruthless in purpose, and insidious in method." Worse, this "danger . . . promises to be of indefinite duration."[104]

In comparison with the pervasive sense of imminent danger and crisis during the Truman administration, policy makers in the Eisenhower administration understood that they had to organize American grand strategy to ensure that the country's economic and military power were used prudently to prevent the spread of communism. He presided over a strategy that expanded the American role in international affairs with a self-conscious effort to limit American economic expenditures for national security. In the end, Eisenhower emphasized cost-effective strategies for balancing the ends and means that conceptually defined how the nation makes prudent choices to strike a balance between security and economic prosperity.[105] The symbol of Eisenhower's emphasis on "balance" in grand strategy mirrored the language in his famous farewell address. He warned the nation that it needed "to maintain balance in and among national programs – balance between the private and the public economy, balance between the cost and hoped for advantages – balance between the clearly necessary and the comfortably desirable."[106]

Eisenhower's grand strategy sought to maintain the proper balance among American economic might, its commitment to freedom, and the military and technological power necessary to contain Soviet ideological, military, and economic power. A central principle in American foreign policy, which endures to the present, is the belief, adhered to somewhat grudgingly, that the United States was first among equals in its power to defend against totalitarian and authoritarian states.

Lastly, a critical component of Eisenhower's grand strategy was its powerful emphasis on the role of America's values, character, and morals as integral to the nation's grand strategy. With the onset of the Cold War and the struggle between freedom and totalitarianism, the role of America's values lent credibility and power to the nation's grand strategy.

President John F. Kennedy: Expanding the Range of Responses

John F. Kennedy's brief time in office (1961–1963) aligned with a period of hostility with Moscow (including the Cuban Missile Crisis), the rise of Keynesian economics, and such arms-control efforts as the 1963 Partial Test Ban Treaty. A nascent but critical issue in the Kennedy administration was the Vietnam War, which emerged as a defining issue in the grand strategy of the administration of President Johnson, as examined later.

The central theme of Kennedy's foreign policy, which echoed many of the principles of the Truman and Eisenhower administrations, was to assert America's willingness to respond to challenges to freedom and security posed by the Soviet Union. This theme was expressed famously by Kennedy during his inaugural address on January 20, 1961: "Let every nation know, whether it wishes us well or ill, that we shall pay any price, bear any burden, meet any hardship, *support any friend*, oppose any foe, in order to assure the survival and the success of liberty."[107] In Kennedy's audience were U.S. allies and potential allies, and he wanted to show a firm commitment to their safety and keep or induce their participation in the grand strategy of containment.

When President Kennedy came into office, he (like all incoming presidents), sought to distance himself from his predecessor, Dwight Eisenhower.[108] Warning during the campaign of "America's growing weakness, economic decline, [and] failing prestige in the world," Kennedy sought to fine-tune the existing foreign policy in order to better meet the challenges posed by the evolving Soviet threat and Moscow's tactics.[109] As historian Thomas A. Bailey notes, "The Kennedy administration marked no sharp break with the past in foreign affairs." However, Bailey writes that were was an "important reversal [in] the Dulles-Eisenhower concept of 'massive retaliation,' which could well mean nuclear war or nothing, holocaust or humiliation."[110]

The implication is not that the grand strategies of the Truman, Eisenhower, and Kennedy were fundamentally different, because they all pursued essentially similar policies with differences of emphasis in implementation. The Kennedy administration sought to shift away from massive retaliation by adopting a policy known as "flexible response."[111] As discussed later, the policy of flexible response was to "tailor military forces to the challenges posed by states or insurgencies."[112] This policy was central to building alliances in Europe, the Middle East, and Asia. And later, with the administration's initial support, it also served to provide support for the government of South Vietnam, which faced military pressure from North Vietnam, backed by Moscow.

Another shift in the Kennedy administration strategy was its strong emphasis on action. The members of the new administration and their management style reflected Kennedy's youthful vigor and innovative views. Individuals such as Robert McNamara came into the government armed with many new ideas on how to cut through and remake bureaucracy in the mold of the private sector and thus to make the government more efficient in attaining its ends.[113] Included in this new management style was a modern economic outlook, along the lines of policies advocated by the economist John Maynard Keynes, who argued for increased government spending in fiscal policy in order to stimulate demand.

Kennedy believed so much in Keynes's economic theories that Arthur Schlesinger Jr. dubbed JFK as "unquestionably the first Keynesian president."[114] Following Keynesian theory, and in developing a plan to provide the means to support its new strategy for dealing with communist threats, the administration shifted from Eisenhower's focus on a perennially balanced budget. A cardinal belief from the beginning of the Kennedy administration was that "a high rate of economic growth [was] essential if the nation was to maintain its international position." The idea was that a high rate of growth would allow the United States to allocate more resources to national security, and do so "without lowering the high standard of living that made the United States a model for much of the rest of the world." Deficit spending under Keynesian theory would stimulate that high rate of growth.

The "Flexible Response" Strategy

The overarching strategy of the Kennedy administration was one of "flexible response" for dealing with the threats posed by the Soviet Union. Critics of asymmetrical responses, as typified by Dulles's strategy of "massive retaliation," conceived this symmetrical strategy early in the Kennedy administration, using the term "flexible response" from General Maxwell Taylor's book *The Uncertain Trumpet*.[115] Critics were highly skeptical about the strategy of massive retaliation because it presented a set of limited, rigid options bounded by the extremes of acquiescence or nuclear brinkmanship, but failed to articulate a range of options for responding to various Soviet challenges.

Central to Kennedy's strategy was to expand the options at his disposal. As he stated in 1961, "We intend to have a wider choice than humiliation or all out nuclear war."[116] For this defense strategy to succeed, the United States would need the ability to respond to all manner of challenges – from diplomacy to war. But this strategy placed considerable "emphasis ... on calibration, or 'fine tuning'" so that responses to challenges would be "appropriate to the situation" and permit the United States to act in a coherent fashion as it faces a diverse set of political and military challenges to its interests.[117]

In the implementation of Kennedy's strategy of flexible response, scholars argue that its purpose was to calibrate American actions so that they were proportionate to the situation at hand.[118] For example, Gaddis outlines several broad themes in Kennedy's strategy:

> (1) the bolstering of conventional and unconventional military capabilities; (2) the strategic missile build-up, which proceeded even after the myth of the "missile gap" had been exposed; (3) renewed efforts to solidify alliances; (4) a new emphasis on the non-military instruments of containment; (5) attempts to manage more efficiently domestic resources vital to defense; and (6) an expansion of Eisenhower's earlier efforts to open up areas for possible negotiations with the Russians.[119]

Kennedy's strategy of flexible response relied upon the steadily increasing buildup of American conventional and nuclear forces. The rationale for the buildup was to provide another measure of calibration or flexibility so that Kennedy and subsequent American leaders would have the ability to escalate in response to Soviet provocations, specifically in Europe, before being forced to resort to nuclear strikes because no other credible options were available. As a State Department analysis noted in a letter from Secretary of State Dean Rusk to Secretary of Defense Robert McNamara on February 4, 1961, "We attach the greatest importance to 'raising the threshold' beyond which the President might have to decide to initiate the use of nuclear weapons."[120]

To implement his strategy of flexible response, Kennedy knew that it would be necessary to possess the capabilities to counter communist insurgent movements in the face of Khrushchev's assurances that Moscow would lend its active support to "wars of national liberation."[121] As Kennedy said in a 1961 speech at the University of Washington, "We possess weapons of tremendous power – but they are least effective in combating the weapons most often used by freedom's foes: subversion, infiltration, guerrilla warfare, civil disorder."[122] Therefore, his administration greatly increased the number and capabilities of special operations and nontraditional military forces.

Kennedy clearly was aware that the nature of warfare and strategy were changing. In his address to West Point's 1962 graduation class, he said, "This is another type of war, new in its intensity, ancient in its origins – war by guerillas, subversives, insurgents, assassins; war by ambush instead of by combat; by infiltration instead of aggression, seeking victory by eroding and exhausting the enemy instead of engaging him." The conclusion for Kennedy was that these new challenges require "a whole new kind of strategy, a wholly different kind of force, and therefore a new and wholly different kind of military training."[123] Despite resistance from the Department of Defense, who argued that traditional training methods and forces could ably respond to any necessary challenges, special operations forces were quickly expanded and placed into important combat roles. The variety of skills in which these forces were trained was critical to expand the range of options available to the United States.

The growing cadre of special forces units were to be "versed in the techniques of political, social, and economic 'action' as well as irregular warfare" in order to accomplish what Walt Rostow set forth in the "Basic National Security Strategy."[124] As he asserted in this strategy paper, "the U.S. cannot accept in principle an asymmetry which allows Communist probes into the free community without possibility of *riposte*."[125] These irregular soldiers were not only designed to *counter* communist-supported insurgencies, but also to *provide support to nations* so that they did not resort to communism. As Rostow told the Army Special Warfare School in June 1961, "our central task in the underdeveloped areas is to protect the independence of the revolutionary process now going forward."[126] This flexible response strategy was most famously put to the test in the Vietnam War.[127]

Kennedy shifted to the policy of flexible response, from Eisenhower's New Look, based on a different view of the nation's economic capabilities. Kennedy was much less concerned with limiting the costs of containment as he strove to build up conventional forces so that he could "control [the smaller insurgency or] 'brush-fire' wars without reducing the globe to radioactive rubble."[128] The Kennedy administration's new strategy reflected the influence of Keynesian economic theory, which led the administration to increase defense expenditures, reversing the steady decline in defense spending under

Eisenhower.[129] The Kennedy administration assumed that the American economy could handle, and might "even benefit from," greater levels of spending on national security and on programs to strengthen the domestic economy. By 1962, Kennedy's chairman of the Council of Economic Advisers, Arthur Heller, convinced the president that "Eisenhower's persistent efforts to balance the budget had in fact acted as a 'fiscal drag' on the economy," which limited purchasing power and growth and contributed to recession.[130]

Alliances, Negotiations, and Economic Development

In formulating its grand strategy, the Kennedy administration sought to use alliances to counteract the threat posed by the USSR and China. Against China, the United States continued to support the Southwest Asia Treaty Organization (SEATO), even though it had a difficult time operating without significant American support. Against Russia, the United States continued to support NATO in Western Europe, while also using new economic policies to bolster its case for promoting capitalism as a counterweight to communism. According to the historian Bailey, by the late 1950s and early 1960s we saw "the emergence, with American encouragement, of an embryonic United States of Europe." One principle of American grand strategy was to use the industrialized nations in Europe as a bulwark against Soviet power. This became the basis for an economic union, which emerged in 1958 as the European Economic Community that continued to strengthen throughout the 1960s. Policy makers in the Kremlin understood that the economic instrument of American strategy posed a serious counterweight to the policies of Moscow, whose command economy made it more difficult to counteract a market-based strategy.

In terms of negotiations, Kennedy believed that it was important to work with the Russians. As he stated in his inaugural address, "Let us never negotiate out of fear, but let us never fear to negotiate." One element of Eisenhower's grand strategy that "Kennedy did not reject was [seeking] more negotiations with the Russians [as a way] to relax tensions." Kennedy borrowed from Eisenhower's policies because JFK's "impeccably anti-communist [policies]" reduced the domestic political risks of working with the "enemy," making it possible to deal with Moscow without being accused of "appeasement."[131] The strategy of using negotiations with Moscow helped bring about a peaceful resolution to the Cuban Missile Crisis. Dealings with Moscow were based on "almost daily communications with Khrushchev."[132]

Soft Power

Scholars propose that Kennedy's greatest foreign policy legacy in formulating his grand strategy is his role in what we now call "soft power."[133] Such institutions as the Peace Corps and Alliance for Progress in South America, as well as Kennedy's use of uplifting rhetoric – as in the "Ich bin ein Berliner" speech – served as the rhetorical foundations of his foreign policy.[134] Kennedy's plan for a Peace Corps, which was endorsed during the 1960 campaign, was designed to build the basis for promoting democracy and good will around the world.[135] It has remained an example of unconditional success in the annals of public diplomacy.

The Kennedy administration came to understand that political instruments of containment were arguably as important and effective as their military policies. The administration sought to promote progress through indirect means – for example, by "reverting to the approach of the Marshall Plan [of] a decade and a half earlier" – as the United States used its resources to provide substantial economic assistance to other countries as a way to weaken or destroy the "conditions that made communism attractive in the first place."[136] This policy did not promote blanket changes across the globe, but approached each state on a case-by-case basis while seeking ways in which the United States could, as Kennedy adviser Walt Rostow wrote, "protect the frontiers of freedom and induce progress towards peaceful change" and strengthen allies and local partners. Furthermore, its aims were noble: to make "sustained progress towards higher standards of economic welfare, social justice, individual liberties, and popularly based govern- ments throughout the free community."[137] Strictly speaking, the method of communi- cating this principle in American grand strategy permitted the Kennedy administration to rely on the soaring rhetoric that was effective in the 1960 campaign for the presidency and became a central feature of JFK's administration and style of policy making.[138]

Kennedy's Legacy in American Grand Strategy

Following the grand strategies of the Truman and Eisenhower administrations, Kennedy emphasized the obligation of the United States to play an activist leadership role in the world. However, he was acutely aware of the need to pay close attention to society's demand for building and sustaining the domestic foundations of American economic power and prosperity. Kennedy, as well as Truman and Eisenhower, understood that the language of confrontation with Moscow could pose serious political perils in a democ- racy. For this reason, his administration emphasized domestic prosperity in its pro- nouncements about foreign policy.

Toward this end, Kennedy continued using the grand strategy of his predecessors to govern America's role in the world, particularly as he emphasized policies whose purpose was to build the foundations for a cost-effective Cold War strategy through less expensive military engagements and deficit spending. Kennedy, as did his immediate Cold War predecessors, designed his grand strategy to mobilize the American economy for a long, cold war with Moscow without undermining and harming the American economy from excessive levels of defense spending. By emphasizing businesslike strategies for balancing national security with the demands of maintaining domestic economic prosperity, Kennedy, like Eisenhower, helped define U.S. grand strategy so that the nation could make prudent choices for balancing security with prosperity.[139]

Historians tend, rightly, to emphasize the uplifting, ennobling qualities in Kennedy's language about American foreign policy and his underlying grand strategy. With his call for establishing the Peace Corps, for example, Kennedy shifted the emphasis toward positive steps the United States could take as part of his strategy to build a safer interna- tional order through strong alliances and capable local partners, while simultaneously working to diminish the perception that the struggle with the Soviet Union presented an apocalyptic danger to the United States. This strategy was in full play before and during the 1962 Cuban Missile Crisis, when the United States once again faced the reality that resisting the spread of Soviet influence and communism involved serious risks of confrontation.

The rhetoric used by the Kennedy administration imbued American grand strategy with a new missionary zeal to protect freedom and promote democracy, as well as to prevent the spread of communism and Soviet ideology. The more expansive vision of American grand strategy promoted by Kennedy contributed, along with the enduring pressures and fears of confrontation during the Cold War, to deep domestic unrest in American society as thousands died in the ultimate test case of flexible response, Vietnam. Although Johnson deserves the lion's share of the responsibility, Kennedy's grand strategy, after being redefined by President Johnson, renewed American foreign policy with a sense of momentum.

Having built on the architecture of American grand strategy established by the Eisenhower administration, the Kennedy administration and subsequent administrations through that of Ronald Reagan adhered largely to principles and policies developed during the 1950s and early 1960s. In the end, Kennedy's grand strategy legitimized the principle that the United States had an obligation to defend freedom across the world against the depredations that arose from the Soviet expansionist ideology and its totalitarian impulses. In practice, these ideas continued as a part of American foreign policy until the Soviet Union collapsed in 1989 and formally dissolved on December 31, 1991.

President Johnson: Vietnam Leads to the Imbalance of Ends and Means

As the thirty-sixth president of the United States, Lyndon B. Johnson (1963–1969) essentially followed the policies of his Cold War predecessors. Perhaps the most significant event in the evolution of American grand strategy during his administration was President Johnson's decision to fully engage in the Vietnam War. This policy led to domestic unrest, diverted resources away from his domestic vision of building a Great Society, and contributed to his decision in March 1968 not to seek reelection after his one full term in office.[140]

The strategy of flexible response and its principle of calibrated escalation led the nation into a quagmire. Although "Kennedy, Johnson, and their advisers regarded Vietnam as a fair test case of that strategy,"[141] the decision to intervene in Vietnam relates directly to the more expansive and engaged grand strategy that President Kennedy articulated in his inaugural address and implemented during his nearly three years in office. With Kennedy's assassination, President Johnson picked up the mantle of Kennedy's grand strategy with a series of incremental decisions over several years that widened the scope and depth of the U.S. government's defense of South Vietnam.

The principal problem with President Johnson's application of the strategy of flexible response was his administration's inability to balance the nation's means with its desired ends. More seriously, however, when the ends and means are out of balance, it raises questions about the soundness of a nation's grand strategy. Worse, if the rhetoric of the strategy exceeds the nation's actual commitment to its goals, the logical possibility is that the underlying grand strategy is not carefully considered.

Kennedy emphasized the need to balance the ends and means in grand strategy and relied on using uplifting language about America's intent to defend freedom against totalitarianism. Johnson translated Kennedy's activist language into policies that led to massive U.S. involvement in the Vietnam War but that did not have a strategy for producing a successful conclusion. Perhaps more than other considerations, it is the defeat in the Vietnam War and the resulting domestic unrest that explain why historians judge Johnson's grand strategy so harshly. Much like his predecessors, Johnson shaped the grand strategy of containment to support a more activist role for American foreign policy, which in turn contributed to the decision to move the United States toward large-scale involvement in Vietnam. His commitment to Vietnam was consistent with the tenor of Kennedy's grand strategy, although Kennedy did not make the large-scale commitment to Vietnam that Johnson ultimately did.

One element of grand strategy is the reliance on analytical tools to help guide policy makers – in this case, as they allocated resources to wage the Vietnam War and support U.S. national security policies. In that war, "policy makers relied on concepts such as systems analysis – with its emphasis on systematically measuring the cost and effectiveness of military actions – to determine the analytically correct strategy for victory." However, as Robert McNamara, who was secretary of defense in the Kennedy and Johnson administrations, wrote in his memoir, the United States had no choice but to balance the ends and means in policy.[142] Critically, the desire to balance ends and means is not sufficient to produce that balance, since policy makers can make errors of judgment as they assess their strategy and the resources that are required to implement it.

One explanation for the difficulties generated by President Johnson's strategy was an overreliance on statistics, which began early in the Vietnam War as policy makers placed a naïve faith in easily manipulated figures from the South Vietnamese, such as the number of military operations against the Vietcong initiated by Saigon.[143] McNamara admitted to Johnson in 1963 that "[t]he situation has been deteriorating . . . to a far greater extent than we had realized because of our dependence on distorted Vietnamese reporting." Perhaps the most prominent example in Vietnam was to use "enemy 'body counts' as the chief indicator of 'progress' in the ground war."[144] Not only was this a poor statistic to indicate progress in a counterinsurgency fight, but these statistics were often inaccurate. As McNamara explained to Johnson in 1966, "It is possible that our attrition estimates substantially overstate actual VC/NVA losses."[145] Yet, as David Halberstam argues, McNamara was highly inflexible in his decision making. McNamara's numerous trips to Vietnam allowed him to create a "base of knowledge, first-hand, on which he would make his judgments and recommendations [which reflected his] unwillingness to accept civilian assistance in challenging the military reporting [and his] unwillingness to adapt his own standards and criteria."[146]

President Johnson had ample evidence and assessments to prove that his strategy was not working in Vietnam, but he chose to ignore the intelligence in large measure because he and his administration felt they had no other choice. The reason was that the soaring rhetoric of the Kennedy and Johnson administrations about the need to confront Soviet expansionism and protect the freedom of American friends and allies could not be easily dismissed or reversed without calling into question American credibility. By this logic, Vietnam "was important not just in itself, but as a symbol of American resolve throughout the world." In effect, this case of military intervention undermined the credibility of the American grand strategy that rested on defending freedom and allies.[147] The failure of the intervention, however, was due in large part to the lack of a reliable civilian and military local partner in South Vietnam. The French suffered from this same fundamental weakness. Although intervention in Vietnam should have had the opposite effect of showing the world that the United States would come to the aid of allies against communist threats, there was no credible local partner to aid. It became an American war for American interests rather than American assistance in a civil war for Vietnam's future.

Johnson used the similar soaring rhetoric of helping allies in his inaugural address on January 20, 1965: "The American covenant called on us to help show the way for the liberation of man. And that is today our goal." For Johnson, this policy was meant to be expansive: "Thus, if as a nation there is much outside our control, as a people no stranger is outside our hope." In measuring the costs of this strategy, Johnson went on to say that "if American lives must end, and American treasure be spilled, in countries we barely know, that is the price that change has demanded of conviction and of our enduring covenant."[148] In themes reminiscent of Kennedy, President Johnson committed the United States to spend blood and treasure to resist those who might undermine freedom. With these ideas, Johnson emphasized that his grand strategy called for the nation to defend freedom in other countries, despite the efforts of totalitarian governments to weaken the United States.

More worryingly for the implementation of American grand strategy was a gap between the private beliefs of U.S. policy makers and their public pronouncements. In the case of Vietnam, the gap was immense for Johnson. When discussing his strategy for Vietnam with Defense Secretary McNamara on February 26, 1965, the president declared, "I don't think anything is going to be as bad as losing, and I don't see any way of winning."[149] Months later, on June 21st, Johnson reiterated his pessimism about winning, telling McNamara, "I don't see any ... plan for a victory – militarily or diplomatically."[150]

Johnson's fixation upon Vietnam ultimately weakened the position and power of the United States in other regions of the world.[151] As the historian Bailey notes, "The dangers of weakening one's diplomatic hand by military over commitment elsewhere were further driven home in June, 1967, by a frightening explosion in the Middle East."[152] Later, with the 1967 Six-Day War and the 1973 October War, we see signs that the United States may have overextended itself as the grand strategies of the Johnson, Kennedy, Eisenhower, and Truman administrations signaled a commitment to defend friends and allies no matter what the cost. With the political friction over Vietnam, the hostilities and tensions that existed during the Cold War brought extraordinary pressure to meet the commitments outlined in America's evolving grand strategy.

Although Vietnam represented a defeat for the United States, the more serious issue is whether the Vietnam War is an example of what happens when the nation fails to ensure that its grand strategy reflects a careful balance between ends and means.[153] The escalation of the Vietnam War led to an excessive focus by the Johnson administration on Vietnam at the expense of other global initiatives. A particularly scathing critique of the grand strategy that was pursued by both the Kennedy and Johnson administrations is that "the American defeat there ... grew out of assumptions ... that the defense of Southeast Asia was crucial to the maintenance of world order ... and that the effects would be to enhance American power, prestige, and credibility in the world."[154]

Johnson's policies and overall strategy were consistent with Kennedy's belief that American grand strategy should not be constrained by economics when dealing with foreign and domestic challenges to the nation. When Johnson set his sights on domestic reform, he decided to fund simultaneously the Great Society domestic programs and fight a war in Vietnam.[155] Johnson was explicitly mindful of striking a prudent balance between the needs of national security and promoting the nation's domestic economy. As he said, "I was determined to be a leader of war *and* a leader of peace. I refused to let my critics push me into choosing one or the other." His conclusion was that the United States had the ability and obligation to deal with both challenges: "I wanted both, I believed in both, and I believed America had the resources to provide for both."[156] Johnson, ultimately, subscribed to the expansionist and optimistic view of grand strategy that

Kennedy articulated so powerfully in his speeches and policies and that were symbolized in his actions. It sought to defend democracy and extend its reach to other societies and to exude optimism about the American ability to promote democracy as part of the strategy for containing Soviet totalitarianism.

The critics of Johnson's grand strategy argue, however, that both administrations failed to maintain a proper balance between national security and domestic means and ends. In describing the tension between domestic and foreign policy desires, Jeffrey Helsing criticizes President Johnson for misleading the American people into believing that "sacrifices would not be required" and that the nation "could simultaneously fight a limited war in Southeast Asia and create major social programs at home." This happened, as Helsing argues, because "Johnson did not want to have to pay the price for going to war ... [therefore] he opted for a path by which he believed he could avoid the hard policy choices between the war and his domestic agenda."[157]

One observation about the means-ends nexus in grand strategy is that the nation might be better served if its grand strategy is guided deliberately by the prospect of dealing with scarce national resources. Scholars write about the "bracing discipline of stringency," in which the prospect of scarcity or at least limited resources provides more "powerful incentives [to be efficient] than even the most sophisticated management techniques."[158] As Washington faces enormous budget deficits and national debt, it is crucial for policy makers to feel the discipline that exists when they need to promote American security and at the same time prevent the nation's grand strategy from being overcome by excessive confidence, overweening ambition, or reckless spending.[159]

In effect, the Johnson administration failed to maintain a delicate balance between means and ends. The underlying argument is that building the domestic foundations of economic power and prosperity is always a critical aspect of American grand strategy. Johnson, however, did not adhere to this policy with the degree of commitment of the Eisenhower and Kennedy administrations. Instead, he simultaneously pursued significant foreign policy objectives, such as the Vietnam War, and new domestic programs, all of which consumed enormous economic and political resources and eventually contributed to a long bout of inflation and recessions. In a sense, Johnson violated the principle – annunciated by Kennedy and more emphatically by Eisenhower – that American grand strategy must strike a prudent balance between its foreign policy and domestic economic priorities if the United States is to maintain its military security and economic prosperity.

A final element of Johnson's foreign policy was the role of arms control in managing that relationship. Johnson as well as Truman, Eisenhower, and Kennedy before him understood that policies based on tension and the risk of confrontation can undermine the ability and willingness of the public in a democracy to support such policies. To build a more stable relationship with Moscow and to reassure the public, Johnson pursued Kennedy-administration policies such as various arms-control initiatives with Moscow, including the Outer Space Treaty that was signed in 1967 and the Treaty on the Non-Proliferation of Nuclear Weapons in 1968. With these arms-control successes, Johnson built the basis by the late 1960s for a less hostile and hence more stable relationship with the Soviet Union.

In the end, these arms-control initiatives helped reassure the American people that Cold War tensions would not necessarily lead to war and mutual annihilation. Johnson's emphasis on dealing with Moscow helped build some degree of stability and predictability into U.S.-Soviet relations, which would bear fruit in the 1970s during the Nixon administration with various arms-control agreements, notably the SALT and the ABM treaties.

Johnson's Legacy in Grand Strategy

President Johnson's principal legacy in grand strategy was implementing the containment strategy of the Kennedy administration, which in turn aligned quite well with the legacy of the Truman and Eisenhower administrations. In practice, Johnson's grand strategy was a continuation of the existing American grand strategy in place since the late 1940s. The problem for Johnson, however, was that the Vietnam War weakened the United States and its strategy. The three principal elements that define Johnson's legacy in grand strategy remain his conduct of containment, the Vietnam War, and his failure to balance foreign policy and domestic economic priorities.

With his decision to intervene on a large scale in Vietnam, Johnson shifted the emphasis in American grand strategy to active, interventionist policies designed to resist Soviet support for movements that were antithetical to freedom and democracy, of which Vietnam's fate is an enduring example. As Johnson implemented policies designed to resist the efforts of the Soviet Union to spread communism throughout the developing world, he implemented a grand strategy that was designed to defend the U.S. role as a defender of freedom (described by Johnson as an American "covenant"). Unlike Kennedy, Johnson did not base his grand strategy on a self-conscious effort to limit U.S. expenditures for national security and new domestic programs. Instead, he pursued the Great Society, whose programs were by any standard immensely expensive, along with his commitment to Vietnam.

In conclusion, the policies articulated by Kennedy imbued American grand strategy with a degree of enthusiasm for protecting freedom and democracy while also resisting communism and Soviet ideology. By contrast, Johnson attempted to implement lofty policy pronouncements, principally Vietnam, that sapped the will and desire of American society to support containment. Johnson's more activist style of grand strategy contributed, along with the pressures and fears of the Cold War, to domestic unrest in American society as tens of thousands died in Vietnam.

Even though Johnson drew from Kennedy's architecture for American grand strategy as well as that from the Eisenhower administration, subsequent administrations through President Ronald Reagan moved away from Johnson's approach. These administrations established policies that placed stricter limits on the willingness of the American people to devote time, attention, and resources, including blood and treasure, to foreign policy interventions. For the rest of the Cold War, subsequent administrations learned to operate within the limits exposed by President Johnson's failure to balance ends and means in grand strategy. His failure to scale back an expansionist grand strategy weakened this ability to pay careful attention to the domestic limits on foreign policy that exist in all democracies.

President Richard M. Nixon: Foreign Policy Successes and Domestic Disgrace

As the thirty-seventh president of the United States, the grand strategy of Richard M. Nixon (1969–1974) is defined in terms of several narratives: the influence of the

Vietnam War, improving relations with the Soviet Union and China, wars and diplomacy in the Middle East, and the Watergate scandal that forced Nixon to resign.[160] In terms of its effects on grand strategy, the consensus is that Watergate eventually had debilitating consequences for the conduct of American policy because it undermined the president's power at home and abroad.[161]

As policy makers in the Nixon administration viewed the world in 1969, the power and influence of the United States had risen steadily since the beginning of the twentieth century. With the end of World War II, the power of the United States was at its zenith, with the U.S. economy producing half of the world's total goods and services, massive military forces deployed around the globe, and a monopoly on atomic weapons. With the ascent of the Soviet Union's power, however, the uncontested position of the United States began to erode during the 1960s. As European and Asian powers recovered from the devastation of World War II and the United States was engaged in expensive interventions in Korea and Vietnam in terms of lives lost and national treasure spent, these events suggested that the preeminent economic and political standing of the United States was decaying.[162]

This relative decline in the extent of American power, which began to manifest itself in the late 1960s, exerted great influence on the thinking of policy makers in the early days of the Nixon administration. Although the United States continued to enjoy preponderant political, economic, and military influence in the world for many years after the Nixon administration, scholars argue that several factors – "the erosion of American power, the simultaneous ascent of rivals, the truculence of normally loyal allies, and the outbreak of severe international crises . . . in the 1960s and 1970s" – all produced a highly turbulent era in American foreign policy. Facing these geopolitical circumstances, Nixon's national security advisor (and later secretary of state), Henry Kissinger, argued that the country needed to undertake "a major reassessment of American foreign policy" because the United States, though powerful, "was no longer the preeminent state."[163]

It was in the context of a highly dynamic global politics that the Nixon administration focused on building a new balance between the ends of American policy and the means by which it would achieve those ends. During the 1960s, the true cost of President Kennedy's pledge to pay any price and bear any burden to defend freedom and democracy became increasingly apparent. By the time Nixon took office in early 1969, it was clear that Vietnam posed a serious challenge for the United States in terms of how the collapse of domestic harmony would undermine the conduct of American foreign policy.[164] As a way of dealing with the numerous challenges facing the United States, the Nixon administration sought to articulate a grand strategy whose fundamental aim was to "halt the erosion of American power and maintain America's position as one of the world's indisputable superpowers."[165] For some, this strategy was designed to conduct a retrenchment of the American role in the world, whereas for others it was a prudent course of action to help the United States strike a more prudent balance between the ends and the means. One measure of the imbalance was the extraordinary domestic discord in the nation in the late 1960s.

Nixon's grand strategy during his turbulent five and a half years in office centered on three interrelated objectives: first, extricating U.S. forces from Vietnam; second, achieving a rapprochement with China; and third, seeking détente with the Soviet Union.[166] As the architects of the policy, Nixon and Kissinger sought a balance among these objectives in a period of redefinition of American grand strategy. A hallmark of American foreign policy at the time was a concept known as linkage, in which all aspects of foreign policy were linked: "from nuclear weapons to European communism, from relations with China to domestic politics, and from the Vietnam War to Latin America and the Middle East." The decision to emphasize linkage, for Nixon, represented the conclusion that "economic, military, and political revolutions had changed the world irrevocably," in a period of rapid and radical globalization.[167]

The central purpose of Nixon's grand strategy was to build a more stable international system, largely by drawing China and the Soviet Union into the existing international order as counterbalancing forces. "My highest priority in foreign policy," Nixon asserted in 1971, "is to build a structure of international relations that will help to make a more stable and enduring peace in the world."[168] A critical consideration for Nixon was to develop, as the central feature of his grand strategy, a steady relationship with Russia and China – both of which remained the nation's principal geopolitical competitors. For example, President Nixon's decision to visit China in 1972 was designed to "transform" the nation's relationship with China and shift the emphasis from Vietnam to a broad array of other issues in American foreign policy. The process of building a new relationship with China was, for Kissinger, something that "we need [in] our game with the Soviets as well."[169]

With the challenges of Vietnam and dramatic political and economic problems in American foreign policy, the objective of Nixon's grand strategy was to realign the nation's relationships with all states. Influenced heavily by Henry Kissinger, Nixon's policy of engagement derived from a realist approach to balance-of-power politics. Rather than defining American relationships with the hostile language of the Cold War, Nixon's strategy was to rebalance those relationships without "demonizing its adversaries." Thus, the objective of American strategy was to help the nation understand its "own limitations" and accept that the United States could not "seal off its rivals."[170] Nixon explained this logic at a 1969 NATO summit: "We must find ways of living in the real world.... Those who think simply in terms of 'good' nations and 'bad' nations – of a world of staunch allies and sworn enemies – live in a world of their own ... they do not live in the real world."[171]

The sheer enormity of accomplishing these principal objectives in grand strategy consumed much of the intellectual energy of the Nixon presidency. Yet, even Nixon's admirable foreign policy achievements in dealing with Vietnam, China, and the Soviet Union did not save his presidency from the Watergate scandal that led to his resignation on August 9, 1974.

The Nixon Doctrine: New Strategic Relationships

The Nixon Doctrine, as described by President Nixon on November 3, 1969, established three major objectives: "First, the United States will keep all of its treaty commitments; second, we shall provide a shield if a nuclear power threatens the freedom of a nation allied with us or of a nation whose survival we consider vital to our security; third, in cases involving other types of aggression, we shall furnish military and economic assistance when requested in accordance with our treaty commitments. But we shall look to the nation directly threatened to assume the primary responsibility of providing the manpower for its defense."[172]

This doctrine provided the rationale for the withdrawal of troops from Vietnam, while preserving the credibility of the United States. Nixon explained that Americans could not be responsible for Vietnam's future, and that ultimately the Vietnamese people had to assume responsibility for their state and its future. In Nixon's words, "The defense of freedom is everybody's business – not just America's business. And it is particularly the responsibility of the people whose freedom is threatened. In the previous administration, we Americanized the war in Vietnam. In this administration, we are Vietnamizing the search for peace." Following this logic for American grand strategy, Nixon shifted the mission of the U.S. military from fighting to primarily training and advising so that "South Vietnamese forces [will be able] to assume the full responsibility for the security of South Vietnam."[173]

As we saw throughout the Cold War, the perceptions of the United States remained a central concern of the Nixon administration. As early as 1969, Nixon and Kissinger sought to compensate for the perceived abandonment of South Vietnam by pledging large assistance packages. President Nixon's decision to extricate American forces from Vietnam rested on the Nixon Doctrine, which sought to provide political and economic support as a way to end U.S. military intervention.[174]

For historian Robert Dallek, by the late 1960s "it was time for the United States to develop a long-range policy" for dealing with Vietnam. The principle in Nixon's grand strategy was to develop policies that would not encourage states in Asia to be "so dependent upon us that we are dragged into conflicts" such as Vietnam. A core principle for Nixon was to redesign American foreign policy so that the nation would not confront other Vietnam-like cases for intervention. The United States would be willing to help allies fight communist insurgencies. However, as Nixon said, "When you are trying to assist another nation defend its freedom, U.S. policy should be to help them fight the war but not to fight the war for them."[175]

So concerned was the Nixon administration about the potential effects that a withdrawal from Vietnam would have on the credibility of U.S. commitments that Kissinger's *First Annual Report on United States Foreign Policy* emphasized the importance of America's enduring overseas commitments. It was critical for Nixon to be able to reverse the sense that the United States was seeking to scale back its overseas commitments. The logic in Kissinger's report was clear: "The Nixon doctrine rather than being a device to get rid of America's world role is one which is devised to make it possible for us to play a role – and play it better, more effectively than if we continued the policy of the past in which we assumed such a dominant position."[176] This logic reflected a deep change in the American self-image because, as Kissinger commented later, "America went through such a period of self-doubt and self-hatred in the late 1960s."[177]

In a 1970 memo to Kissinger, Nixon wrote that it was necessary to "knock down the assumption that is gaining disturbing currency abroad and in the United States – that this Administration is on an irreversible course of not only getting out of Vietnam but of reducing our commitments around the world." For some, "the United States should reduce its world role and start taking care of the ghettos instead of worrying about Afghanistan." But for Nixon, "for over twenty years, however, I have been saying 'that we can have the best social programs in the world – ones that will end poverty, clean up our air, water and land, provide minimum income, etc., and it isn't going to make a difference if we are not around to enjoy it.'"[178]

Henry Kissinger's Influence on Nixon's Grand Strategy

President Nixon's grand strategy is inseparable from the influence of his national security adviser and secretary of state, Henry Kissinger.[179] From the time Nixon sought to conduct foreign policy from the White House, he moved aggressively during the transition in 1968 to minimize the role of the State Department.[180] According to Kissinger's notes from a meeting with Nixon, the president had "very little confidence in the State Department. Its personnel had no loyalty to him.... He was determined to run foreign policy from the White House."[181] Nixon, for all practical purposes, placed his closest advisor in the top national security post. He supported Kissinger's effort to double "the size of the NSC staff, further enlarging the 'little State Department,' which the NSC staff has in effect become."[182] Such changes in the policy-making apparatus had dramatic consequences for the formulation and conduct of American grand strategy during Kissinger's time in office and in subsequent administrations.[183]

While in academia, Kissinger was heavily influenced by the general principle that "our Founding Fathers were sophisticated statesmen who understood the European balance of power and manipulated it brilliantly to bring about America's independence and then to preserve it."[184] His commitment to creating the conditions that build greater international stability had a profound impact on the Nixon presidency and its grand strategy. As Kissinger succinctly stated, "If I had to choose between justice and disorder, on the one hand, and injustice and order, on the other, I would always choose the latter."[185] As Kissinger's biographer, Walter Isaacson, explains, "Kissinger's conservative realpolitik [reflected] the principle, taught by realists from Karl von Clausewitz to Hans Morgenthau, that diplomacy cannot be divorced from the realities of force and power." In Kissinger's view, "diplomacy should be divorced ... from a moralistic and meddlesome concern with the internal policies of other nations." By his logic, "Stability is the prime goal of diplomacy. It is served when nations accept the legitimacy of the existing world order and when they act based on their national interests; it is threatened when nations embark on ideological or moral crusades."[186] Even though Kissinger saw himself as practicing a European form of diplomacy, these concepts are consistent with the status quo–oriented dimension of the gradualist tradition in American grand strategy.

For American grand strategy, Nixon and Kissinger worked to enhance Washington's influence by using diplomacy and threats rather than fighting wars against states whose alignment with superpowers raised the risk of escalation.[187] This core principle guided Nixon to the policy that called for the United States to negotiate with both the Soviet Union and Mao's China as part of a strategy for building more stable and peaceful relationships – a far cry from his days as vice president and congressman from California as a staunch anticommunist. One of the reasons that it was politically feasible for Nixon to negotiate with communist countries was the very fact that his previous anticommunist credentials insulated him from charges that he was being weak on national security or excessively conciliatory with Moscow and Beijing.

Some scholars and policy makers criticize Kissinger's brand of foreign policy.[188] The first criticism is that the policy of "linkage had not produced the results the administration had promised." Second, observers criticize the fact that during the Nixon and Ford administrations, "the global military balance ... shifted in favor of the Soviet Union." Third, Kissinger, while working for Nixon and Ford, focused excessively "on relations with the USSR and China," which contributed to the administration's tendency to "neglect or distort ... other pressing issues." Lastly, neither the Nixon nor the Ford administration made any serious efforts to promote the "moral principle[s] upon which United States foreign policy had to rest if it was to command support at home and abroad."[189]

First Priority: Ending Vietnam

In articulating the administration's grand strategy, both Nixon and Kissinger believed that finding "an 'honorable' end" to the Vietnam War was the most critical challenge facing the United States. Despite his rhetoric claiming "during the presidential campaign that he had a plan for ending the war," critics argue that this was "nothing more than an election ploy."[190] In fact, once in office, Nixon expanded and escalated the military campaign in Indochina with his authorization to conduct bombing campaigns in Cambodia and limited incursions into Laos. Despite their desire to end the war in Vietnam, both Nixon and Kissinger adhered to the view that the United States "could not simply walk away from an enterprise involving two administrations, five allied countries, and thirty-one thousand dead as if we were switching a television channel."[191]

For this reason, during their first year in office, the strategy for Nixon and Kissinger was to apply military force as a way to persuade North Vietnam to sign an agreement that would protect South Vietnam from tyranny and preserve it as an independent sovereign state.[192] The principle for Nixon and Kissinger was that the United States "had to appear willing to deploy overwhelming force if it wished to forestall the need to use it." This logic relates to the credibility of the threat to retaliate against aggression, which had "under-pinned deterrence of communist aggression, especially in Europe and Asia."[193] Eventually, Nixon's strategy was to persuade Hanoi that the United States would never abandon its ally South Vietnam but that South Vietnam would need to carry the burden of the fight.[194] The constraining factor for Nixon and Kissinger, however, was that the decision to escalate the war would threaten the "comity by which a democratic society must live," seriously damaging the nation and its domestic institutions.[195] Facing public discontent with the policy toward Vietnam, Nixon administration officials operated under historically significant constraints on American strategy.

It is clear from the memoirs of the principal policy makers in the Nixon administration that they spent the bulk of their time in the first term dealing with the Vietnam War.[196] By any standard, there is no serious dispute with the fact that the Nixon administration spent an inordinate amount of time and effort on the Vietnam War, believing, as policy makers from the administration have said, that nothing less than America's international credibility was at stake. To Nixon and Kissinger, "the stakes were not simply South Vietnam's freedom but America's world leadership and the future peace of the world." As Kissinger elucidates, "As the leader of democratic alliances we had to remember that scores of countries and millions of people relied for their security on our willingness to stand by allies, indeed on our confidence in ourselves. No serious policy maker could allow himself to succumb to the fashionable debunking of 'prestige' or 'honor' or 'credibility.'"[197] Relationships with allies were crucial to the implementation of containment as the administration sought to maintain and even strengthen these formal and informal ties across governments and societies.

Ultimately, Nixon believed that withdrawal from Vietnam depended on policies that were heavily influenced by Beijing and Moscow. For this strategy to succeed, Kissinger's approach was to use "military force, multilateral diplomacy [and] compromise among the belligerents."[198] However, this approach changed by the start of Nixon's second term in January 1973, as he moved to end U.S. involvement in Vietnam. Facing intense domestic discord in the United States, the consensus is that ending the war in Vietnam would permit the president to deal with other serious challenges to the United States, including Middle East politics, European relations, and Latin America.

Realpolitik in Asia: Exploiting the Sino-Soviet Split

President Nixon's most revolutionary achievement in the realm of grand strategy was his rapprochement with Beijing.[199] The gradual normalization of relations with the PRC not only undermined the power and status of the Soviet Union, but it also led to an unprecedented level of economic cooperation (and limited political cooperation) between what became in subsequent decades the world's two largest single-state economies.[200] The strategic logic behind the summit with Mao was to help China balance the power of the Soviet Union by building a relationship with Washington. For the Nixon administration, the overture to China would put pressure on Moscow to move arms control forward and end the Vietnam War.[201] Similarly, the U.S. political strategy rested on using China as a strategic counterweight against the Soviet Union in what was known as "triangular diplomacy."[202]

This shift in American foreign policy would create a more stable international order and establish both "Nixon and the Republicans [as] the new leaders in advocating a progressive approach to foreign affairs."[203] At the time, however, Nixon's trip to China was a key feature of a broader policy whose aim was to extricate the United States from Vietnam. Policy makers in the Nixon administration believed that the process of détente or less hostile relationships with Moscow and Beijing would ease tensions in international politics. In effect, this was a version of "Nixon's Wilsonian vision" of a world organized on the basis of principles that would promote peace and prosperity but remain consistent with the principles of realpolitik that promote stability and American national interests. Both were critical elements in American grand strategy during the Nixon administration.

The reason for the shift in the U.S. relationship with China was fear of confrontation with Moscow, which over time would strain the will of the American people to support the nation's foreign policy if tensions never eased. As Mao warned, "The Soviet threat is real and growing," and Moscow's goal "is to occupy both Europe and Asia."[204] Although Nixon and Kissinger emphasized rapprochement as the basis for the U.S.-Sino relationship, their objective was to build a diplomatic bridge to China and pressure Moscow to follow their policy of détente.[205]

Détente with the Soviet Union

Nixon's policy of détente with the Soviet Union was the key to achieving his Wilsonian vision of an end to major wars. As Nixon said during a 1972 address to a joint session of Congress, "Everywhere new hopes are rising for a world no longer shadowed by fear and want and war." Now, the United States could "realize man's oldest dream – a world in which all nations can enjoy the blessings of peace." As a practical step in changing the climate in international politics, the 1972 U.S.-Soviet summit in Moscow signaled the start of "a new era of mutually agreed restraint and arms limitations between the two principal nuclear powers."[206]

But though Nixon and Kissinger sought détente with the Soviet Union for very practical reasons, they also wanted to reset relations with Moscow because they believed that ending the war in Vietnam required the diplomatic support of the Soviet leadership, notably Leonid Brezhnev.[207] The Nixon administration saw détente with Moscow as critical, but Washington and Moscow had limited objectives in pursuing détente – it was "a way to further their own interests within an overall framework of managed competition."[208] In retrospect, it is likely that neither Nixon nor his Soviet interlocutors imagined that they could win the Cold War, envisioning instead that détente established a more peaceful framework for an enduring strategic stalemate.

Strategic Drift in the Middle East and South America

The Nixon administration's grand strategy of seeking to build stability in the Middle East entered a period of drift. As Kissinger admits, "in the Middle East our policy lacked the single-minded sense of direction that Nixon usually demanded and I normally imposed." The problem was that "U.S. policy in the Middle East seemed to be guided by essentially tactical concerns and no signs of being guided by a long-term strategy."[209] From the start of his administration, Nixon was deeply hesitant to become involved in negotiations over the Middle East, which he believed was fraught with perils because there was no clear exit strategy that could lead to success.

The administration's approach to dealing with leftist movements in South America was similarly pragmatic and episodic. The highest priority for the Nixon administration in Latin America was, according to one historian, "not to foster democracy or economic growth but to suppress Soviet-Cuban Communist influence." The reasoning was that transforming states in Latin America "into American style democracies [would] take generations." Thus, the Nixon administration, along with other administrations in the 1960s, believed that "covert activities to block Communist takeovers in Latin America" posed a critical threat to American security.[210] Although the Nixon administration intervened decisively in Chile by indirectly aiding the coup that overthrew Salvador Allende's government, the calculation about the consequences of a left-leaning government in that country led to policies that were ill conceived and ineffective.[211]

Balancing Means and Ends

A critical challenge for the Nixon administration that had dramatic consequences for American foreign policy was drawing back from the sense of overreach that had characterized American grand strategy during the Vietnam War. Dealing with this war and the difficult relationship with Moscow – decisions to rebalance the nation's priorities – marked a significant shift in American grand strategy during the Nixon administration. Nixon and Kissinger made the prudent decision to rebalance the ends and means in American grand strategy. The clear implication was that the United States had become so overextended in Vietnam that this was undermining American foreign policy and the credibility of its grand strategy.

The consequences of the ends-means imbalance during the Johnson administration engendered such deep antagonism in American society that it was increasingly difficult for policy makers to conduct foreign policy. As Kissinger explained in his memoirs, "I was convinced that the deepest cause of our national unease was the realization – as yet dimly perceived – that we were becoming like other nations in the need to recognize that our power, although vast, had limits. Our resources were no longer infinite in relation to our problems; instead we had to set priorities, both intellectual and material."[212]

Nixon expressed the nation's troubles in his first inaugural address with the words "We are caught in war, wanting peace. We are torn by division, wanting unity."[213] The challenge for the Nixon administration was to deescalate the Vietnam War without affirming or legitimizing the principle that the United States was in geopolitical retreat. As Nixon worked to rebalance the ends and means of American grand strategy, his language expressed a desire to build an era of enduring peace and prosperity, which was guided by the precepts of realism that were so ably articulated by Kissinger. The language emanating from the Nixon administration was to balance the demands of global leadership with a better understanding of the physical and psychological limits of American power. This shift had to be accomplished at a time when domestic divisions about Vietnam had reached a breaking point for American society. This experience reaffirms that democracies require public support if their grand strategy is to gain and maintain public support.

Nixon's Legacy in Grand Strategy

President Nixon's principal legacy in grand strategy was implementing policies that built a new strategic relationship with the great communist powers, the Soviet Union and China. The shift was dramatic: in contrast with the more confrontational policies during the Truman, Eisenhower, Kennedy, and Johnson administrations, the Nixon administration deliberately worked to build policies that permitted the United States to contain communism, recognizing that such problems as Vietnam and the Middle East required some degree of coordination with – or at least less overt hostility from – Moscow and Beijing.

As one reviews American grand strategies during the post–World War II era, an enduring element of Nixon's grand strategy was building new relationships that would tone down some of the more strident language and policies that were in fashion during the Cold War. Nixon expressed this sentiment in his first inaugural address, when he extended an invitation: "Those who would be our adversaries, we invite to a peaceful competition – not in conquering territory or extending dominion, but in enriching the life of man."[214] Facing intense domestic divisions over Vietnam and later the Watergate scandal, officials in the Nixon administration understood that policies based on tension and confrontation would eventually lose public support. To build a more stable relationship while reassuring the public, a critical principle of Nixon's grand strategy was to push beyond the arms-control initiatives of the Kennedy and Johnson administrations and achieve dramatic successes with the SALT I Treaty and the Anti-Ballistic Missile Treaty signed with Moscow in 1971 and 1972, respectively.[215] As had his predecessor, Nixon used arms control to establish a better working relationship with Moscow and ultimately to establish the basis for a dramatically less hostile tone in American policy.

In both theory and practice, President Nixon conducted a broad reformulation of American grand strategy that maintained a careful balance between the ends of policy and the means available to support it. Unlike Johnson, who was concerned primarily with promoting his Great Society programs and defending Vietnam, Nixon faced a world in which American public opinion imposed real political and budgetary constraints on the nation's ability and willingness to conduct foreign policy actions. In his first inaugural address, Nixon spoke about the great burdens of domestic spending: "In this past third of a century, government has passed more laws, spent more money, initiated more programs, than in all our previous history."[216] For the first time during the Cold War, the Nixon administration subtly moved beyond Kennedy's "pay any price, bear any burden, meet any hardship, support any friend" principle to articulate its own, more balanced approach to grand strategy that rejected as a matter of course the concept of unlimited commitments. In that same address, Nixon declared his commitment to peace with words that signaled his desire to shift the world's attention away from the tensions of the Cold War: "the chance to help lead the world at last out of the valley of turmoil."[217]

The logic of Nixon's strategy, in contrast with that of Kennedy – whose rhetoric so powerfully expressed the overreach so prominent in the narrative of the 1960s – was increasingly evident as the United States found itself mired in Vietnam, facing great domestic divisions, confronting the great communist states, and dealing with the effects of inflation and economic stagnation. Nixon believed that Johnson had violated one of the central principles in American grand strategy, which holds that the nation must strike a delicate balance between its foreign policy and domestic economic priorities to avoid depleting itself economically and psychologically. In contrast with the acute economic overreach of Johnson's Great Society spending, the Nixon administration rebalanced the means-ends relationship in American grand strategy after nearly a decade of the Great Society programs.

In practical terms, Nixon's grand strategy effectively scaled back the more expansive language and policies of the Kennedy administration to produce a more cautious and restrained approach to foreign policy. Nixon recognized that the grand strategies of his predecessors weakened the will of the American people to support a more activist and interventionist foreign policy. Earlier, these more activist approaches to grand strategy had contributed to the quagmire of Vietnam and the subsequent era of domestic unrest in American society, whose effects included an era of highly polarized politics. Nixon's grand strategy worked to rebalance American foreign policy by imbuing it with a sense of prudent realism. No longer should the United States feel an obligation to defend freedom and its allies at all costs, nor would this role amount to a writ for unlimited interventions.

In practice, Nixon's grand strategy redressed the imbalance between means and ends to manage what Eisenhower warned the nation of in his farewell address about the dangers of an unrestrained foreign policy.[218] Seeing forces that compelled the United States to realign its grand strategy, Nixon scaled back the more expansive visions of earlier administrations. This dramatically altered the conduct of American foreign policy in Vietnam, fostered better relations with the Soviet Union and China, and scaled back American commitments. No nation, including the United States, can possibly conduct an effective grand strategy in the face of domestic discord such as that that enveloped American society in the late 1960s and early 1970s.[219] Subsequent administrations would retool the architecture of American grand strategy to deal with the struggle between freedom and tyranny along with the age-old challenge of balancing the ends and means of strategy.

President Jimmy Carter: Scattered Priorities but Success in Middle East Diplomacy

The thirty-ninth president of the United States, President Jimmy Carter (1977–1981), came into office intent on reversing the policies of the previous administration and restoring America's belief in its enduring values in the wake of Watergate and Nixon's resignation. The core principle that defined Carter's grand strategy was his belief that the strategy of Soviet containment, derived from the elements of realism, had long undermined the core beliefs on which the nation should conduct its foreign policy. In Carter's view, it was time for the United States to pursue a new and more idealistic grand strategy after the policies of Richard Nixon and his successor, Gerald Ford, who did not influence in any significant way the evolution of American grand strategy.[220]

The implication for Carter was that American grand strategy must be based on what he believed were the fundamental and enduring American values of freedom, democracy, and human rights. He powerfully expressed this concept in his inaugural address on January 20, 1977, when he restated America's traditional ideals. In President Carter's words, "I have no new dream to set forth today, but rather urge a fresh faith in the old dream."[221]

Outlining the principles that constituted his new design for American grand strategy, he proclaimed in a speech at Notre Dame in May 1977 that "it is a new world, but America should not fear it. It is a new world, and we should help to shape it." In words that directly signaled the ideas that figured prominently in the articulation and implementation of Carter's grand strategy, he declared that this "new world ... calls for a new American foreign policy." To be true to the ideals of the nation, our foreign has no choice but to reflect a "constant decency in its values and on optimism in our historical vision." For Carter, the cardinal principle in his grand strategy was that human rights should play a guiding role in the design and execution of American foreign policy.[222]

Carter's emphasis on human rights and democracy was expressed in terms of the first principle of building the domestic foundations of American power. As he said in his inaugural address, "the best way to enhance freedom in other lands is to demonstrate here that our democratic system is worthy of emulation."[223] In practice, the grand strategy of the Carter administration rested on the principle that "to be true to ourselves, we must be true to others." To translate this idea into policy, Carter declared that "we will not behave in foreign places so as to violate our rules and standards here at home, for we know that the trust which our Nation earns is essential to our strength."[224]

Carter Articulates His Grand Strategy

The challenge for President Carter was to redefine American grand strategy in the context of geostrategic pressure from the Soviet Union and Iran, both of which undermined his efforts to chart a new foreign policy course. In a move that influenced global politics, Carter developed a new strategic relationship with the Chinese leadership in Beijing, built on the foundations established by the Nixon administration. His efforts to broker the Camp David Accords between Egypt and Israel represented a dramatic accomplishment that changed the conduct of American foreign policy for decades. He also moved to restore the ownership of the Panama Canal to Panama, which was a source of controversy.[225]

Carter's campaign platform and speeches early in his presidency signaled his plan to depart radically from the strategy of containment and the policies followed by the Nixon and Ford administrations. Scholars have written that within three years of taking office, Carter saw "the state of Soviet-American relations as the most critical factor in determining whether the world will live in peace or be engulfed in global conflict." He also "[praised] past efforts at containment, calling for steps toward reconstituting the military draft and lifting 'unwarranted restraints' on intelligence collection capabilities."[226]

During his third State of the Union address, in 1980, in response to the Soviet invasion of Afghanistan, Carter called for a five percent annual increase in defense spending as part of his desire to make the Russians "pay a concrete price for their aggression." In this speech, he proclaimed what became known as the Carter Doctrine, whose most famous statement was that "an attempt by any outside force to gain control of the Persian Gulf region will be regarded as an assault on the vital interests of the United States of America, and such an assault will be repelled by any means necessary, including military force."[227]

The Carter administration, even though it began with a clear architecture based on defending human rights, struggled to define its grand strategy to be both consistent and credible.[228] In the search for such principles, Carter's grand strategy was seen as increasingly ineffective. Although scholars and policy makers differ on the reasons, the consensus is that the problem stemmed principally from Carter's unwillingness to ground his grand strategy on a more skeptical view of the world, his failure to rally domestic support for his policy initiatives, his inability to resolve disagreements among his advisors, and a series of unfortunate world events that were largely beyond Carter's control but had serious consequences for his credibility and policies.

In the evolution of American grand strategy, it probably was premature during the 1976 campaign to call for the end of containment and even riskier to do so once Carter took office in 1977. There are practical and prudent political reasons for a new administration to distance itself from the policies of its predecessor, but Carter's resolve to do so was particularly compelling when we consider the major personalities in the Nixon and Ford administrations that preceded him. In the view of one scholar, Carter's grand strategy related to his desire to move beyond the Nixon-Kissinger nexus, to his discomfort with the tenets of political realism, and to the interplay between realism and idealism in foreign policy. The result was Carter's determination once in office to forge a new vision of America's role in the world.[229]

In public statements and policy declarations, the Carter administration went to considerable effort to distinguish its priorities from those of the two previous administrations. As a consequence, Carter's policies fostered the public impression that his administration would develop a new grand strategy that would be based on "highly visible initiatives designed to make it *seem* as though the American approach to the world had changed." For some, Carter's approach to grand strategy was to "build domestic support for détente" that previous administrations, in his belief, had failed to accomplish. According to one critic, the Carter administration's grand strategy fueled the sense that the administration's "dealings with the Soviet Union [were based on] no strategy at all."[230]

The defining principle in Carter's approach to grand strategy was his emphasis on the role of human rights in the general conduct of foreign policy, including in the specific case of negotiations with the Soviet Union. Carter's personal commitment to human rights was never in question. As he affirmed in his inaugural address, "Our commitment to human rights must be absolute."[231] Not surprisingly, he faced powerful political pressures to make human rights a critical priority in his policies toward the Soviet Union. In terms of domestic politics, pushing a human rights agenda helped Carter win the support of both those on the left who had criticized Kissinger's amorality and those on the right who worried about U.S. weakness and appeasement of authoritarian regimes. As Jody Powell, Carter's press secretary, argued persuasively, "One of the reasons Ford-Kissinger failed ... was because the American people would not support a policy which seemed to abandon our position in support of human rights."[232]

The Carter administration's strategy for building the basis for negotiating with Moscow on arms control and to move beyond the SALT I treaty, signed by Nixon in 1972, was to use Moscow's human rights violations to put pressure on the Soviet leadership.[233] Despite the fact that this strategy weakened his negotiating position on SALT II and antagonized the Soviet leadership, a senior administration official reported that Carter "didn't care whether other folks or other world figures agreed or disagreed."[234] When long-time Soviet Ambassador to the United States Anatoly Dobrynin reflected on Carter's policy, his criticism was that the "policy was based on linking détente to the domestic situation in the Soviet Union." In contrast with the practice of détente in earlier administrations that focused on Moscow's foreign policy actions, the Carter administration focused attention on Soviet domestic policies.[235] As arms-control negotiations were linked to human rights abuses in the Soviet Union, the result was a dramatic deterioration in Washington's relationship with Moscow on many issues.[236]

Explanations for the shift in American grand strategy during the Carter administration vary.[237] Gaddis, for instance, attributes "Carter's simultaneous pursuit of contradictory policies [with seeing] himself as being both a moralist and an engineer." This combination of traits fueled both excessive hubris and a "fascination with technical and ultimate questions that left little room for the realm of strategy that lay in between."[238] One criticism was that Carter's grand strategy "failed to align his moral and domestic political commitment to human rights by defending Soviet dissidents with his geopolitical and . . . humane determination to achieve arms control." Another explanation is that Carter's emphasis on human rights reflected his belief that he could defend Soviet dissidents and continue "business as usual" in arms control.[239] In the end, the rapid deterioration in the relationship between Washington and Moscow, along with a growing sense that Carter's grand strategy was not producing the results promised, contributed to the perception of a grand strategy in drift.

Internal Disarray on Growing Soviet Challenges

A related explanation for the development of Carter's grand strategy is the sense of internal disarray in the White House. The two principal antagonists in foreign policy were Carter's national security advisor, Zbigniew Brzezinski, and Secretary of State Cyrus Vance. Brzezinski's criticism was that Carter pursued "inconsistent objectives: to put the Soviet Union 'ideologically on the defensive' with respect to human rights, to 'promote a more comprehensive and more reciprocal détente,' and to 'move away from what I considered our excessive preoccupation with the U.S.-Soviet relationship.'" Brzezinski's worry was that the Carter administration operated on the assumption that it could simultaneously "reform, negotiate with, and ignore the U.S.S.R., all at the same time."[240]

In contrast with Brzezinski's strategy and the style with which he sought to implement it, Cyrus Vance was an adherent of the classic approach to diplomacy, according to which he directly disavowed linkage. He rejected the idea that each set of negotiations, interests, and threats exist as interconnected issues. The disparate views and the resulting clash between Carter's senior foreign policy advisers over such fundamental principles as the role of linkage in foreign policy likely contributed to the sense of drift in his grand strategy.[241]

Historians have written that the most vivid example of the clash between Brzezinski and Vance involved a June 7, 1978, speech Carter made at the U.S. Naval Academy. This speech was, as Raymond Garthoff described it, "so disjunctive in its combined reaffirmation of détente and articulation of a confrontational strategy that the general reaction was perplexity."[242] As one *Atlantic Monthly* columnist commented, "What he [Carter] did, and this is a literal fact, is staple together the memo from Vance to the one from Brzezinski and that was his speech."[243] But as Robert Strong contends, "the story of the stapled memos has been used by a number of scholars and commentators to illustrate both the inconsistency of the Carter-era policy toward the Soviet Union and the inability of the administration to develop a coherent and effective rhetorical strategy."[244] In broader terms, when seen from the perspective of such Soviet policy makers as Soviet ambassador to the United States Anatoly Dobrynin, the flaw was the lack of "any 'solid and consistent direction.'"[245] The mere sense of confusion in an administration's grand strategy inevitably undermines its broader initiatives and dangerously fosters questions about the effectiveness of its foreign policy. In this case, the result was growing tensions with Moscow.

Sources of Disorder at Home and Abroad

In addition to internal disputes inside the administration, the Carter administration faced challenges from several outside events – including a series of Soviet challenges to the international order, the overthrow of the Shah in Iran, the Sandinista takeover in Nicaragua, increasing dependence on oil as a result of Iran's embargo and the ensuing gas shortage, and the American hostage crisis in Iran – all of which took place toward in the latter years of his administration.

Perhaps the most dramatic event during the Carter administration was the Soviet invasion of Afghanistan, which Carter later wrote caused him to change his thinking about strategy. As Carter told one of his administration officials, the Soviet invasion "is deliberate aggression that calls into question détente and the way we have been doing business with the Soviets for the past decade."[246] In his address to the nation on January 4, 1980, Carter said, "This invasion is an extremely serious threat to peace because of the threat of further Soviet expansion into neighboring countries in Southwest Asia and also because such an aggressive military policy is unsettling to other peoples throughout the world." He called the invasion a "callous violation of international law and the United Nations Charter."[247] One political consequence of the Soviet decision to invade Afghanistan – along with the Iran hostage crisis, Vietnam, and Watergate – was to raise concerns about America's place in the world. These events created doubts about the credibility of the Carter administration, prompted questions about whether American power was in decline, and suggested that America's grand strategy was not effective.

Coming on the heels of the unpopular American involvement in Vietnam and disillusionment with politicians after Watergate, Carter's grand strategy was greatly constrained by a public that, tired of politics, gave limited domestic support for U.S. intervention abroad.[248] Americans, as Kevin Mattson notes, "were jaded and apathetic. Polls showed that the number of citizens who read or worried about public affairs 'hardly at all' jumped upward: 58 percent bothered to vote in the 1976 presidential election, and then 38 percent in the 1978 midterm elections."[249] In practical terms, the public's low interest in both domestic and foreign policy matters effectively reduced Carter's flexibility to act decisively in foreign policy.

A related complication for President Carter in the articulation and implementation of his grand strategy was the economic conditions at home. As the scholar Julian Zelizer frames the problem, "The mood of the country was not good in January 1979." To make matters worse, the economy was in "terrible shape," wracked by high inflation, unemployment, and energy shortages and high prices. To make matters worse, Zelizer reflects, "there was little sense that things would get better."[250] Looking abroad, the Soviet Union seemed to be on the ascent, and the divisive issue of the Vietnam War was still fresh in the public's memory.

Beyond these public sentiments, there were the pressures of securing a second term in office. When the gas crisis hit in 1979 and riots broke out in places such as suburban Levittown, Pennsylvania, Americans asked what the president was "doing in Japan and Korea when all the problems are here at home."[251] As Carter responded to popular demands in an attempt to bolster his presidency, the risk was that day-to-day reelection worries would distort the nation's grand strategy. The scholar Trubowitz writes that Carter's policy challenges worsened when "his party was reluctant to spend vast sums of money on [a] military build-up," which in turn created strong pressures to "find less expensive ways to balance against Soviet power."[252]

Facing these domestic political realities, the 1979 Soviet invasion of Afghanistan cast further doubt on Carter's grand strategy.[253] Any sense of incoherence in the nation's grand strategy has serious and immediate consequences for the nation's foreign policy. In the aftermath of the invasion of Afghanistan, Carter learned how difficult it is to "rally ... support for its new tough line" given "widespread opposition to draft registration, grain and technology embargoes, and even its boycott of the Moscow Olympics." These policy initiatives were burdened by the sense that the Carter administration was experiencing "a crisis of leadership at the top" and "resistance to being led from below." In the depths of the Cold War, Carter's worldview, with his emphasis on human rights and distrust of realist politics, made it more difficult, writes Gaddis, to implement a "coherent grand strategy, much less an effective one."[254]

Although Carter faced many difficulties in articulating and implementing his grand strategy, he still made important and lasting contributions to American foreign policy. By far the most enduring was his effort to accelerate the Middle East peace process by hosting negotiations between Israeli Prime Minister Menachem Begin and Egyptian President Anwar al-Sadat. The Camp David Accords was, in the view of one historian, the result of Carter, in the role of the lead mediator, applying "all of his intelligence, capacity for detail, and moral zeal to achieving an agreement between two men who did not like each other."[255] This peace accord was critical to U.S. policy in the Middle East not only because it helped end thirty years of conflict between the two states and demilitarize the Sinai Peninsula. More importantly, the Camp David Accords served as a model to demonstrated to other Arab states that peace with Israel was possible. The subsequent Oslo Accords, in 1993, and Israel-Jordan Treaty of Peace, in 1994, provide similar examples. It is no exaggeration to say that the most significant contribution of the Carter administration to American grand strategy was to bring the Camp David Accords to fruition.

The other event in the formulation and implementation of American grand strategy that would reshape international politics and slowly alter the foundations of American foreign policy was the visit of China's leader Deng Xiaoping to Washington in 1979. In meetings with President Carter and National Security Advisor Zbigniew Brzezinski, these policy makers outlined in broad terms China's new policies of economic modernization and global engagement that endure to the present. The positive nature of Deng's trip and the resulting normalization of relations led Carter to call the visit "one of the delightful experiences of my Presidency. To me, everything went right, and the Chinese leader seemed equally pleased." As the historian Ezra Vogel explains, "The year 1979 may have marked a reopening of connections that had been cut off for three decades, but within only a few years the scale and scope of the exchanges would far surpass those in the years before 1949."[256]

The achievements of Camp David and the normalization of relations with China highlight Carter's greatest strength as president as he served as mediator and negotiator. These events, though not enough to outline a coherent grand strategy, shape Carter's legacy as president and continue to profoundly influence the conduct of American foreign policy several decades later.

Carter's Legacy in American Grand Strategy

The principal critique of Carter grand strategy was its failure to deal effectively with the problems and challenges to American foreign policy, specifically in terms of the geo-political expansion of Soviet influence. One explanation may be President Carter's deep sense of antipathy to a grand strategy that relied on the exercise of force and other coercive instruments of American power. Having declared symbolically a general philosophical unwillingness to use them, the Carter administration found it increasingly difficult to conduct foreign policy in the face of challenges from Moscow and Iran. Carter's response to the Soviet invasion of Afghanistan, which was seen as less than effective, largely relied on criticisms of Soviet policy and the American boycott of the 1980 Summer Olympics held in Moscow.

As Carter articulated his adherence to human rights as a guide to his foreign policy, he found that it weakened his ability to conduct foreign policy. The result, as the Iran hostage crisis and Soviet invasion of Afghanistan demonstrated, was the impression that Carter was overwhelmed by events in foreign policy. Because he was seen as hesitant to use the more forceful instruments of power to respond to adversaries whose actions undermined American interests, Carter's grand strategy increasingly was perceived as ineffective. Once the Soviets rejected his arms-control initiatives, Iran took Americans hostage, and Moscow launched an invasion of Afghanistan, the Carter grand strategy did not provide avenues or policies for effective responses. Further, in the face of these setbacks, Carter's public persona increasingly communicated a sense of defeat and frustration. To complicate matters, the announcement of the Carter doctrine for dealing with challenges in the Middle East was undermined when the United States failed to resolve the 444-day hostage crisis.[257]

When Carter declared his "absolute" commitment to the defense of human rights, he weakened his grand strategy – or, more precisely, articulated a grand strategy that could not be effective under conditions of duress or hostility in the face of challenges. The difficulty for the Carter administration was how to demonstrate that the United States was willing and able to defend its interests forcefully, and thus signal that the nation was not in retreat. The Iran hostage crisis and the Soviet invasion of Afghanistan, perhaps more than any other factors, seriously weakened the grand strategy of the Carter administration. Scholars, however, continue to evaluate the overall design and merits of Carter's approach to foreign policy.[258]

In conclusion, what began as a reversal of the perceived excesses of the grand strategy pursued by the two preceding administrations did not produce an alternative grand strategy that promoted effectively the principles of human rights, democracy, and self-determination. The values espoused by President Carter, however, returned to influence American grand strategy in the policies pursued by the Clinton and George W. Bush administrations.

President Ronald Reagan: Assertive Containment and Growing Ideological Confrontations

As the fortieth president of the United States (1981–1989), Ronald Reagan engaged in a more assertive form of containment that accelerated the downfall of the Soviet Union. As an architect of policies that sought to roll back the influence of the Soviet Union – a form of containment – Reagan differed sharply from Carter and his policies that emphasized the central role of human rights.[259] As 1980 drew to a close, there were signs that the American people were "skeptical of détente and distressed by American impotence." In the aftermath of the Soviet invasion of Afghanistan in December 1979, a series of international events left the American people feeling "bullied by OPEC, humiliated by the Ayatollah Khomeini, tricked by Castro, out-traded by Japan and out-gunned by the Russians."[260]

When Reagan entered the White House, he did so with a general mandate to restore pride domestically and reassert American strength internationally.[261] As a counterpoint, Reagan's critics often "derided [him] as a telegenic lightweight [who was] too simple-minded to know what containment had been about, much less to have had constructive ideas about how to ensure its success."[262] Yet, while Reagan relied heavily upon his beliefs and instincts to shape his grand strategy, the ends that he articulated were quite clear and the strategy he articulated and implemented was quite consistent and coherent, if controversial.

In practice, Reagan's grand strategy was based on a sustained military, economic, political, and ideological program whose purpose was to target Soviet political and economic weaknesses and ultimately defeat it. More importantly, Reagan's grand strategy was designed to win, rather than to manage, the Cold War. One of Reagan's advisers, Richard Allen, writes that Reagan's strategy for dealing with the Soviet Union was to defeat it. As Allen reported a conversation, Reagan said, "My idea of American policy toward the Soviet Union is simple, and some would say simplistic. It is this: We win and they lose."[263] Indeed, that success would occur within one year after Reagan left office, with the fall of the Berlin Wall in November 1989.

Strategic Beliefs and Assumptions

To better understand the core principles in Reagan's grand strategy, we must first consider some of the beliefs and assumptions under which his policies operated. First, Reagan rejected the basic premise of containment, which evolved into various forms but basically held that "the United States was acting *defensively* against an adversary that was on the offensive, and was likely to continue on that path for the foreseeable future."[264] Reagan believed that the American obligation to advance freedom called on the United States to politically, economically, and technologically challenge the Soviet system rather than hold to a more defensive strategy.

Second, Reagan believed that Soviet aggression was rooted in the nature of its morally and politically inferior political system in comparison with that of the United States and its Western allies.[265] The ideals of democracy and capitalism provided the United States, in Reagan's view, with a "weapon" in the form of money and an "industrial base that meant we had the capacity to maintain a technological edge" over the Soviets.[266] What Reagan outlined was a grand strategy that sought to reverse the status quo of a perpetual struggle between Washington and Moscow and to move toward an American strategy whose ultimate purpose was to defeat the Soviet Union by all means short of war. This view drove Reagan's third belief, which held that political, economic, and military forms of power were essential to ultimately defeat the Soviet Union.[267] In effect, Reagan's grand strategy relied heavily on using both hard and soft power.

Finally, Reagan assumed that the Soviet political and economic system was fundamentally weakened by several crucial structural and ideological weaknesses that could be exploited by Washington. In Reagan's view, those weaknesses included the systemic failure of the Soviet system to show respect for human rights, the utter inferiority of the Soviet economic system, and significant internal dissent.[268] Reagan organized these beliefs and assumptions into a grand strategy whose objective was to remake the international system by defeating the Soviet Union and thereby removing as a serious threat the principal adversary of the United States. Reagan developed a grand strategy in a more coherent way than some of his predecessors, because his grand strategy reflected principles that directly challenged the status quo and sought to radically redefine world politics.

Ideological Confrontations

Reagan's new direction for containment, which was by historical standards a radical departure from earlier administrations, involved far more aggressive rhetoric and policies. President Reagan articulated his administration's strategy in *National Security Decision Directive* 32 (NSDD-32). This directive, which was dated May 20, 1982, stipulated that U.S. national security required the nation to develop and integrate "a set of strategies, including diplomatic, informational, economic/political, and military components" to guide American foreign policy. In NSDD-32, Reagan outlined the "global objectives" that would reflect the core principles of his grand strategy and guide his national security policy. Those objectives fell into several categories, including the ability to "deter military attack" by the Soviet Union against the United States and its allies and "strengthening the influence" of the United States by using alliances and coalitions.[269] This latter objective is worth emphasizing because it shows a consistent prioritization of using alliances even as the American grand strategy of containment became more assertive.

Several principles in NSDD-32 are of particular interest in the evolution of Reagan's grand strategy: "To contain and *reverse* the expansion of Soviet control and military presence throughout the world [and to] *neutralize the efforts of the USSR to increase its influence* through its use of diplomacy, arms transfers, economic pressure, political action, propaganda, and disinformation." To put this grand strategy in practice, the Reagan administration called for the usual policies, including the need for a "well-functioning international economic system," measures to induce "restraint in Soviet military spending," and a desire to "limit Soviet military capabilities," along with preventing nuclear proliferation and maintaining access to space.[270] In effect, Reagan's grand strategy called, quite controversially, for defeating the Soviet Union and ending the Cold War.

Although Reagan adhered to the policy of seeking to "deter military attack by the USSR," the decisive principle in American policy was his decision to "contain and *reverse* the expansion of Soviet control and military presence throughout the world."[271] Reagan's desire to force the leadership in Moscow "to bear the brunt of its economic shortcomings" pointed directly to policies whose economic foundations called for a defense spending strategy of outspending the Soviets.[272] Much of that spending came in efforts to strengthen the U.S. military and simultaneously weaken the Soviet economy by putting pressure on Moscow to increase its own defense spending. Reasonable explanations attribute the end of the Cold War to the U.S. policy of containment or to the cost to Moscow of an arms race, the influence of Mikhail Gorbachev's policies of perestroika and glasnost, and many other factors that led to its general economic collapse.[273] And though the causes remain uncertain, this collapse had clear political, economic, and diplomatic components.[274] A highly plausible explanation is that Reagan's offensive strategy and the USSR's internal economic problems contributed to the success of American grand strategy, which in sharp contrast to that of the president's predecessors sought to defeat rather than contain Moscow while maintaining stability.

The principles that governed the grand strategy of the Reagan administration were fully outlined in two National Security Decision Directives. The first, NSDD-32 (mentioned earlier in this section), was published only two months after Leonid Brezhnev's death (on November 10, 1982). The second, NSDD-75, articulated a combined political-military strategy that guided U.S. relations with the Soviet Union for the duration of the Reagan administration. NSDD-75 (dated January 17, 1983) described the objectives that should govern the broad U.S.-Soviet relationship. These two directives provide the most direct outline of Reagan's grand strategy and show the Reagan administration's resolve to alter U.S. policy toward Moscow.[275]

The basis of Reagan's "carrot and stick" approach was to communicate to the Soviet leadership that unacceptable behavior would elicit costly responses from the United States. The "carrot," however, consisted of opportunities for the Soviet Union to exercise restraint and prudence. For example, Moscow was offered improved relations with the West – in the form of détente, pursued by the Nixon, Ford, and Carter administrations – in exchange for the benefits of greater cooperation. For policy makers in the Reagan administration, this approach was particularly productive because the Soviet Union was distracted by a leadership transition, which presented "a particularly opportune time for external forces to affect the policies of Brezhnev's successors."[276]

Reagan's policy toward the Soviet Union rested on "external resistance to Soviet imperialism; internal pressure on the USSR to weaken the sources of Soviet imperialism; and negotiations to eliminate, on the basis of strict reciprocity, outstanding disagreements." The principle of "arenas of engagement" provided the basis for implementing this policy and shaping Soviet politics and policy.[277] To strengthen the military dimension of U.S. strategy, NSDD-75 called for several critical political objectives, including "steady, long-term growth in U.S. defense spending and capabilities," a "long-term Western consensus for dealing with the Soviet Union," and developing "a strategic relationship with China ... to minimize opportunities" for a rapprochement between Moscow and Beijing. The overall policy called, radically, for promoting "a major ideological/political offensive which … *will be designed to bring about evolutionary change of the Soviet system.*"[278]

This policy directive underscores the radical nature of Reagan's USSR strategy. By moving beyond the well-tested strategy of containment to develop a new approach toward Moscow, Reagan articulated and implemented an unheard-of strategy that called for eventually winning the Cold War. Since Reagan understood that this strategy was unlikely to yield immediate results, the principles outlined in NSDD-75 were designed to reshape U.S. policy for the "long haul." In practice, and quoting from Reagan's NSDD-75, "the U.S. must demonstrate credibly that its policy is not a blueprint for an open-ended, sterile confrontation with Moscow, but a serious search for a stable and constructive long-term basis for U.S.-Soviet relations."[279] Although Reagan's strategy was articulated during his first term, it did not begin to show signs of success until his second term, when Mikhail Gorbachev rose to power in March 1985. The Reagan administration's grand strategy was tested during his first term in office, however.

The Reagan Doctrine

In the conduct of his grand strategy, Reagan's approach was to "shift the U.S. strategy from reacting to challenges and limiting damage to a concerted effort to change Soviet behavior." In practice, this grand strategy required the Soviet leadership to "think differently about Soviet security, the place of the Soviet Union in the world, and the nature of Soviet society."[280]

The challenge of thinking differently about the nature of the Soviet Union and its role in the world would not begin until Reagan's second term in the White House, when the Soviet statesman Mikhail Gorbachev ascended in 1985 to the position of general secretary of the Soviet Communist Party. By then, the roots of Reagan's grand strategy had been planted and were beginning to influence the Soviet Union. In developing his grand strategy, Reagan rebelled against the ideas and strategies that had dominated foreign policy for decades during the Cold War. But as history unfolded, there are several elements of the Reagan Doctrine that unpredictably spurred a radical change in the world order.

From Defending Existing Democracies to Undermining Communist Regimes

The Reagan Doctrine was designed to reverse "the forces of nationalism [within societies] against the gains the Soviet Union had made in recent years in the 'third world,' and eventually against its sphere of influence in Eastern Europe itself."[281] These gains were the product of actions by local partners, such as those in Poland, that actively resisted Soviet expansion. The Reagan administration's grand strategy called for the United States to demonstrate to the world (and later, to the Soviet leadership) that the Soviet empire had become oppressive and contrary to its own founding principles. Reagan described the Soviet Union as the "evil empire" in his now-famous remarks to the National Association of Evangelicals on March 8, 1983. In that same speech, President Reagan stated that he believed that "Communism is another sad, bizarre chapter in human history whose last pages even now are being written." More dramatically, he urged his audience "to speak out against those who would place the United States in a position of military and moral inferiority."[282]

The core principle of the Reagan Doctrine was to provide both overt and covert aid to anticommunist resistance movements. During the Nixon administration, communism made slow inroads into Latin America, Africa, and Southeast Asia; by the end of the Carter administration, the Soviet Union's influence and presence had expanded into parts of Africa, Nicaragua, and Poland.[283] The Soviet invasion of Afghanistan in December 1979 only reinforced this picture. The Carter administration had provided covert assistance to help governments resist these incursions, and Reagan expanded this policy of assistance to the anticommunist rebels in Nicaragua – while selling arms to Iran to finance the program. Known as the Iran-Contra affair, this program produced a political firestorm in Reagan's second term.[284] The intent of Reagan's strategy was, as noted earlier, to "reverse ... the expansion of Soviet control and military presence throughout the world."[285]

In addition to keeping the covert assistance policy veiled from public view, Reagan faced the problem of stopping the advance of communism in Latin America without inadvertently persuading the people in the region that the United States might be a greater imperial threat than communist governments. Having already seen Cuba being lost to communism, Reagan was "determined [that] the Free World was not going to lose Central America or more of the Caribbean to the Communists."[286] With this strategy in mind, President Reagan authorized *Operation Urgent Fury* in October of 1983 to invade Grenada. As background, the Organization of Eastern Caribbean States asked the United States to intervene after a bloody coup by ultra-Marxists left them fearing a Cuban-sponsored military buildup on the island.[287] Understanding that a failure to act would undermine American credibility – particularly in the domestic context of the "post-Vietnam syndrome" – Reagan sent U.S. troops to Grenada to restore the constitutional government. The invasion received widespread public support in the United States. But more importantly, it signaled the U.S. intention to support those societies and governments that defied Soviet-backed aggression, harkening back to the Monroe Doctrine in terms of regional primacy and to the Truman Doctrine in terms of support for anticommunist forces. By January 1985, Reagan openly promised such support.[288] This policy was consistent with Reagan's grand strategy, which called for resisting efforts by Moscow to expand its power and influence.

On the night of August 31, 1983, the Soviets downed a civilian South Korean airliner over the Sea of Japan, killing 269 people.[289] This tragic incident, coming six months after President Reagan's announcement of the U.S. program to develop ballistic missile defenses, put U.S.-Soviet relations at their lowest point in years. More telling, however, was the manner in which the Soviet leadership handled the situation. After denying that the incident had even occurred, the pre-Gorbachev leadership in Moscow accused the United States of causing the tragedy by using the plane to spy as part of a strategy for spoiling relations and setting the stage for an attack. This reaction "illustrated in a microcosm much that hampered normal dealings – even between adversaries – with the Soviet Union."[290] Since he needed a willing counterpart in the Kremlin, observers wrote that Reagan "began to think more seriously about what he could do with a new-style Soviet leadership, should one eventually emerge – and, also, how he might help it understand where real Soviet interests lay."[291] This would not occur until Gorbachev's ascent to power in 1985.

Intensifying Arms Race

One policy shift that generated considerable domestic debate was Reagan's decision to reverse the policy of détente. For reasons discussed earlier, Reagan was skeptical of the fundamental premise on which détente rested. He refused to accept a purely defensive posture for the United States and rejected the policy of mutually assured destruction (MAD) that emerged earlier in the Cold War, calling the policy "the craziest thing I had ever heard of."[292] His strategy for minimizing the risk of nuclear war was to negotiate with the Soviets in order to reduce their nuclear arsenals. At the same time, he knew that before the United States would be ready to take that step, it would first be necessary to improve American military capabilities so that Washington could negotiate from a position of military strength.[293] By declaring that "the fiber of American military muscle was so atrophied that our ability to respond effectively to a Soviet attack was very much in doubt," Reagan sought to change the balance of *military* power when he arrived at the White House in 1981. He did so before implementing a dramatic shift in U.S. policy toward Moscow.[294]

An important principle for Reagan during the 1980 campaign was that U.S. defenses had so deteriorated, particularly since the end of the Vietnam War. Reagan believed that Washington needed to reverse a number of weaknesses and vulnerabilities, because he worried that "an imbalance [in relative military capabilities] could encourage the Soviet leaders to believe that they could use their superior military strength to blackmail the U.S. and split its alliances." Since the Soviets generally insisted upon equal reductions in armaments, Reagan's strategy was to alter the basis for negotiations by substantially increasing U.S. defense spending. He announced his intention to revive the B-1 bomber program, which was previously cancelled by President Carter, and to begin production on a new heavy intercontinental ballistic missile (ICBM) known as the MX.[295] Although Reagan met initial resistance from Congress, both conventional and nuclear programs received additional funding and became important elements of his strategy for improving U.S. military capabilities.

One event that dramatically altered the debate about national security and relations with the Soviet Union was Reagan's address to the American people on March 23, 1983. In that speech, he discussed the significant arms buildup by the Soviet Union that had been in progress during the past decade or so. Most memorably, he announced "a comprehensive and intensive effort to define a long-term research and development program to begin to achieve our ultimate goal of eliminating the threat posed by strategic nuclear missiles."[296] This program became known as the Strategic Defense Initiative (SDI) or, in the public vernacular, "Star Wars."

Once in office, President Reagan was surprised to discover that the United States had no defenses against nuclear attack. As he said on many occasions, he believed it was morally reprehensible for the only available response to nuclear attack to be an act of vengeance that would take the form of mutual annihilation.[297] Reagan saw great strategic value in possessing defenses against ballistic missile attack and in being able to respond to nuclear attack. His view was that defenses, if effective, would contribute to his ultimate goal of abolishing nuclear weapons. However, the proposal generated considerable opposition from among Reagan critics and Soviet commentators. Some viewed the program as a source of instability, but others perceived SDI as an offensive action, and many actively debated whether this system was realistic, feasible, and affordable.[298]

Leaving aside arguments about the technical feasibility of ballistic missile defense, the U.S. missile defense program was consistent with Reagan's strategy of using increased defense spending to pressure Moscow and change the relationship. This initiative also demonstrated that Reagan's grand strategy helped persuade the Soviet leadership to alter its strategy as momentum built for arms-control negotiations. In the language of grand strategy, Reagan's missile defense gambit, while risky, ultimately changed the balance of power between Washington and Moscow because the Soviet leadership increasingly faced the economic consequences of an arms race that it could not win.

Engagement with Gorbachev

Although Reagan referred in a speech in 1983 to the USSR as the "evil empire," he also actively sought to build strong personal relationships with Soviet leadership. Reagan, who was a firm believer in the human element of politics, always saw "Gorbachev in human terms even when they disagreed most profoundly."[299] When Gorbachev became the general secretary of the Soviet Communist Party in March 1985, Reagan found someone with whom, in the words of Margaret Thatcher, the West "could do business." As Reagan reflected in his memoirs, "Gorbachev had the intelligence to admit Communism was not working, the courage to battle for change, and, ultimately, the wisdom to introduce the beginnings of democracy, individual freedom, and free enterprise."[300]

Prior to Gorbachev's rise to power, there was little communication between Reagan and the Soviet leadership. In large measure, the Soviet leadership saw Reagan's position toward the Soviet Union as so belligerent that members were personally unwilling to engage with him. However, as his national security advisor, Robert McFarlane assured Anatoly Dobrynin, Soviet ambassador to the United States, in December 1984, that Reagan "believed that he had fulfilled the basic task of his presidency, which was to restore the potential of the American armed forces." For Reagan, this meant it was now time "to improve relations with the Soviet Union gradually and reach agreements on reducing nuclear arms."[301] As Reagan himself stated prior to his first meeting with Gorbachev in Geneva on November 19, 1985, "preparations for the summit had begun five years earlier, when we began strengthening our economy, restoring our national will, and rebuilding our defenses."[302]

Reagan's strategy for engaging Gorbachev rested on convincing him on three points. The first was that "the United States was sincere in seeking to lower the danger of nuclear war." Second, "a command economy, when coupled with authoritarian politics was a prescription for obsolescence in the modern world." Third, "the Soviet Union had itself become, over the years, what it had originally sought to overthrow – an oppressive empire." To demonstrate that the United States sincerely wanted to reduce the risk of nuclear war, at the first meeting between Gorbachev and Reagan in Geneva, Reagan proposed to eliminate missiles. As Reagan argued, "if there were no nuclear missiles, then there would be no need for defenses against them." Gorbachev took Reagan's ideas quite seriously, so that by January 1986, Gorbachev had "publicly proposed phasing out all nuclear weapons and ballistic missiles by the year 2000."[303]

Reagan continued his personal diplomacy with Gorbachev through written correspondence and joint summits. The personal relationship that Reagan and Gorbachev developed was the key to proving that the desire to eliminate nuclear weapons was not a ploy. As a result of their relationship, Washington and Moscow agreed to the

Intermediate Nuclear Forces Treaty, which was signed "at the third Reagan-Gorbachev summit in Washington in December 1987 [and] led to the dismantling and destruction of an entire category of weapons." As Gorbachev remarked to the Politburo upon his return to Moscow, "In Washington, probably for the first time we clearly realized how much the human factor means in international politics."

In order to persuade Gorbachev of his second point – that "a command economy, when coupled with authoritarian politics was a prescription for obsolescence in the modern world" – Reagan put his secretary of state, George Shultz, to work.[304] Shultz, a former economics professor at MIT and the University of Chicago, presented a seminar series for Gorbachev depicting the transformation occurring in "the worlds of finance, manufacturing, politics, scientific research, diplomacy, indeed, everything." The purpose of these seminars was to prove that the Soviet Union eventually "would fall hopelessly and permanently behind the rest of the world in this new era unless it changed its economic and political system."[305] Although Shultz was not responsible for Gorbachev's *perestroika* initiative, he explained why the Soviet economy was in such a poor state and outlined several options for fixing the economy. These seminars likely affected Gorbachev's views about the Soviet system.

Importantly, Reagan's strategy was based on a position of military strength. He spent his first term rebuilding America's military capabilities as a way to counterbalance and ultimately mitigate the only real source of Soviet strength – its military and nuclear capabilities. Reagan knew that the American economy would give Washington the ability to continue outspending the Soviet Union on defense for the foreseeable future, a fact that he did not hesitate to share with Gorbachev. As Reagan wrote, "He must have looked at the economic disaster his country was facing and concluded that it couldn't continue spending so much of its wealth on weapons and an arms race that – as I told him at Geneva – we would never let his country win."[306]

Finally, in order to prove that the Soviet Union was an "oppressive empire," Reagan used the principles outlined in the Reagan Doctrine. He harnessed the power of nationalism in places around the globe where the Soviet Union had made gains to weaken Moscow. Ironically, the Reagan Doctrine's support for nationalist anticommunist forces had its origins in President Carter's policies that "authorize[d] overt and covert aid to anti-Soviet resistance movements."[307] Reagan then expanded upon Truman's and Carter's strategy based on the argument, initially framed by President Truman in 1947, that Soviet influence in Africa, the Marxist government in Nicaragua, and the growing opposition in Poland all demonstrated that Moscow was pursuing imperial policies. The United States also supported the *mujahedeen* resistance fighters in Afghanistan in order to undermine Moscow's policies. As a result of these policies, Reagan developed a dual-track strategy in which he combined vigorous diplomatic efforts with continued support of communist resistance movements worldwide.

Reagan's Legacy in American Grand Strategy

To the surprise of the foreign policy community, Reagan achieved dramatic successes through the implementation of his grand strategy. He was able to defeat the Soviet Union. This, however, is not to argue that other administrations failed, because it was not until the 1980s and the ascent of the Reagan administration that the conditions in the Soviet Union were ripe for collapse. By that time, the dismal political and economic realities of

Soviet society were apparent to the Soviet leadership, which likely realized by the mid-1980s that radical change was necessary. Reagan was the first to identify, and more importantly to take advantage of, this unique moment in history. Through a combination of strong resistance to Soviet geopolitical designs, principled diplomacy, and a commitment to personal relationships with the Soviet leadership (most notably Mikhail Gorbachev), Reagan defined a grand strategy whose goals previously seemed unattainable.[308]

The most important aspect of Reagan's grand strategy, for Kissinger, was the president himself. He notes, "Reagan's was an astonishing performance – and, to academic observers, nearly incomprehensible.... When all was said and done, a president with the shallowest academic background was to develop a foreign policy of extraordinary consistency and relevance."[309] Even more remarkable, as Gaddis writes, was that Reagan accomplished this by using several "simple habits":

> ... a focus on details; a willingness to choose among priorities rather than be pulled apart by them; an understanding that priorities can shift as policies achieve their purposes; a refusal to be intimidated by orthodoxies; a realization that power resides as much in ideas as in material capabilities; an ability to combine conviction with the capacity to express it; a belief that no strategy can sustain itself if it fails to advance the principles upon which the society is based.[310]

In the end, Reagan focused on striking a balance between the ends and means of American grand strategy as the basis on which to rebuild the economic and later the military foundations of American power – affirming his commitment to peace throughout. However, the core principle in Reagan's grand strategy, which was his commitment to freedom, resonated powerfully with peoples who were under Soviet domination. Reagan was the first president to give hope to America's Eastern European allies that there might be an end to their struggles. Despite decades when the prevailing narrative was that the Soviet Union's power and influence were on the rise and that the Cold War would last in perpetuity, Reagan's grand strategy reversed American policy in ways that, surprisingly, put the Soviet Union on the defensive in political, economic, and military terms.

Conclusions about the Grand Strategy of Containment

Containment as a grand strategy is a paradox. In terms of articulation, it came from one man, George Kennan, an American diplomat in the Moscow Embassy. But in terms of implementation, it was a success because of a wide array of pro-American, anti-Soviet, and nationalist supporters. It was a grand strategy of the West as much as a grand strategy of the U.S. government. It was also a paradox because the strategy for the Cold War relied upon the nonuse of the most destructive weapons in history – weapons that generated enough heat to incinerate entire cities but were never used. These two paradoxes largely define the grand strategy of containment within the evolution of American grand strategy during the latter part of the twentieth century.

The Truman Doctrine relied on local partners, notably nationalists who were willing to resist communism's advancement, particularly in southeast Europe. Eisenhower, while not as explicit in his reliance on allies, was still adamant that the U.S. economy could not afford to spend unlimited amounts on national security and conventional defense. He saw the linkage and tension between the first and second principles of American grand strategic history. The first principle held that America should build the domestic foundations of American power, the second principle that America should exercise leadership to restrain the sources of disorder that threaten vital American interests. Too much emphasis on the second principle would erode the first, which Eisenhower well understood and so warned the nation on several occasions. He implicitly knew that allies and partners would have to share the burden once they had rebuilt their own economies and societies. In the interim, he argued in favor of a heavy reliance on the threat of massive retaliation with nuclear weapons if the Soviets used their superior conventional might to alter the balance of power.

Kennedy shifted the implementation of containment to a more flexible posture by expanding the range of options available to the United States in the event that it was necessary to respond to Soviet aggression. One of the most important options was the twin establishment of Special Forces to teach local partners the skills of military defense, counterinsurgency, and internal defense, and the founding of the Peace Corps to teach local partners how to develop their economies and societies. These two key institutions played a vital role in the implementation of containment over several decades.

The Johnson administration is a study in what happens when a reliable national ally is lacking, which explains the U.S. failure in Vietnam. Washington attempted to shoulder the full burden of containment but exhausted itself in straining against the geopolitical constraints that it could not uphold. It could not win at the national and global levels simultaneously. If it escalated the war and invaded North Vietnam to win at the national level, it risked a third world war, which could involve a nuclear exchange. On the other hand, if it respected the risks of escalation and did not seek to defeat the North Vietnamese with overwhelming military power, then it would lose at the national level. The only escape from this dilemma would have been a viable, capable, and legitimate South Vietnamese government that could bear the primary costs of the war over the long term. This is exactly why Afghanistan was such a success for the United States. They had two reliable and highly effective allies and partners in the region – Pakistan and the mujahidin – who were the key players in this successful chapter of containment.

Nixon's influence on the evolution of grand strategy was to develop arguably the most important bilateral alliance of the twentieth and twenty-first centuries – the U.S.-China relationship. This was perhaps the biggest political victory of the Cold War, because it isolated the Soviets and stretched their resources even further. They now had to be concerned with two fronts – the west and the east. The move by Nixon and Kissinger brilliantly exploited the Sino-Soviet split by shifting the geographic center of gravity from Central Europe to Central Europe *and* East Asia. This put extraordinary pressure on the Soviet Union's already overly stressed national security apparatus.

The Carter one-term presidency foreshadowed the grand strategic drift that would begin during the Clinton years. Carter's contribution to Middle East peace cannot be overstated, but his influence on the evolution of American grand strategy was to show how a lack of clarity and prioritization in the articulation of grand strategy can confound allies and embolden enemies.

Finally, Reagan brought the strategy of containment back full circle to the primacy of local partners. The Reagan Doctrine evinced a commitment to support nationalist movements against communist regimes. In effect, it was the Truman Doctrine on the offensive because it worked in places where the local partners were reliable and capable (e.g., Grenada) but foundered in places where they were neither (e.g., Nicaragua). The Reagan Doctrine also led to the demise of the Soviet Union and the ending of the Cold War.

The next chapter examines the evolution of American grand strategy in the post–Cold War era. This new era involves a layering of the three previous grand strategic eras – the modern, the revolutionary, and the nuclear – in which all three are operating with equal force simultaneously. This new development in the evolution of grand strategy presents a daunting challenge in terms of how the United States articulates and implements its foreign policy.

10 Drifting between Principles: Bush to Obama

This chapter focuses on the United States as a great power after the Cold War ended with the Soviet Union's collapse in 1991. By the late twentieth century, the United States had established itself as a political, economic, and military superpower and the "leader of the free world" whose grand strategy, however, began to show signs of drift, reactiveness, and overcorrection. As the post–Cold War era unfolds, America's grand strategy moves from strictly containing the USSR to dealing with myriad challenges, ranging from state-based threats, such as China, Russia, and Iran, to complex transnational threats, notably terrorism, nuclear proliferation, and economic instability.

The post–Cold War world presented a double-edged sword. It was a great accomplishment for the West to defeat the Soviet Union and usher in another wave of the spread of democracies. Yet, it was also a period of daunting challenges for the United States. But in the absence of a single, identifiable adversary, American grand strategy entered a period of drift and imbalance, often in the direction of being highly reactive to events. In this period, the three previous eras in the evolution of grand strategy – modern, revolutionary, and nuclear – overlapped to eventually coalesce into a complex mosaic of threats.

First, the modern era continued in the sense that the modern nation-state and the importance of state institutions, military organization, and economic growth did not diminish. At the same time, the modern era changed fundamentally as it entered a stage of globalization that would challenge the best minds, strongest governments, and most capable institutions. The process of globalization caused profound shifts in the nature of capitalism, and in the United States it forced a painful transition from an industrial economy to an information and technology-based economy. The domestic foundations of American power had never been so unstable. The rapidity and intensity of globalized capitalism's creative destruction was remaking the social and the economic face of America and the world as the pace of change accelerated to an unprecedented level. The state, the economy, and the military were still important, but they were no longer insulated from large-scale, rapid changes and the pace of innovation as they were in the early modern era. Now these institutions were facing new economic, social, and political dynamics of interdependence and financial contagion that required novel policies and a greater level of adaptability.

Second, the revolutionary era of the early twentieth century reemerged and shifted to a higher level of virulence with the advent of armed groups empowered by information technology, networked forms of organization, and an ease of movement within a globalized marketplace that is now more interdependent and efficient but also more vulnerable to disruption. The post–Cold War world saw a new breed of revolutionaries that had the means and willingness to cause levels of destruction and self-destruction unknown during the twentieth century. True, some fanatical anarchists and communists in the past had zeal comparable to the terrorists of the twenty-first century, but their visions commanded a narrow audience and their groups lacked the capabilities to inflict great harm. In this era, however, the revolutionaries were much more powerful, and able to contend with states in the use of political violence for grand strategic ends. The attacks on September 11, 2001, demonstrated this disturbing fact vividly, on a global scale. This new breed of groups could reach an audience of billions and disrupt and damage the political and economic systems on which the most powerful states depend for their very existence.

Finally, the nuclear era had continued, but in a different form. It continued in the sense that only a handful of industrialized states possess nuclear weapons, but it had changed because the oligopoly on nuclear weapons was fracturing. The technology was proliferating as such rogue states as North Korea, Iran, Libya, Iraq, and Pakistan pursued and in some cases acquired the technology. Furthermore, the threat of revolutionaries acquiring nuclear weapons is closer to becoming a reality than states would like to see. The technology is no longer obtainable only by the richest, most powerful states, but is now becoming available to a broader set of actors. Consequently, the rules that governed the possession of nuclear weapons remained applicable to the traditional nuclear-armed states, whereas new rules and strategies are now needed to govern how these new actors operate.

Against this backdrop of complex sources of continuity and change in grand strategy, the post–Cold War presidents have attempted to articulate and implement a grand strategy for the United States for an era in which there are powerful consistencies and yet radical discontinuities. Without a clearly defined primary adversary, the articulation and implementation of grand strategy is vastly more difficult than in the past. This chapter covers the attempt to manage U.S. grand strategy, which has largely been a record of failures to date, with several brief glimpses of success. One mistake made by many of the presidents and many thinkers in this area is to assume that the grand strategy of containment was the model and that any new grand strategy must possess similar sweep, elegance, and focus. But containment was an anomaly in the history of American grand strategy. It was the exception rather than the norm, and though it worked within the bipolar system of the nuclear era of grand strategy, the equivalent of the applicable conditions simply do not exist in the post–Cold War era.

The second problem is related. In looking back on the most *recent* grand strategy of containment, many American policy makers and the public in general ignored the *older* traditions of American foreign policy that wisely should have served as our touchstones, or those traditions that the nation can use to form enduring principles to govern its foreign policy. This disengagement from tradition, from history, from what it is that American foreign policy has done so well in the past, is something that scholars such as Walter Russell Mead have observed and criticized.[1]

Mead identifies what he calls the four traditions of American foreign policy. The Hamiltonian tradition seeks a strong alliance between big business, finance, and government, whereas the Jeffersonian tradition prioritizes building democracy at home as an example for the rest of the world. This is the tradition that underpinned the periods of American isolationism. The third tradition is the Jacksonian tradition of meeting the basic desire of the American people for physical safety and economic growth. Finally, Mead recognizes Wilsonianism as the fourth tradition in American foreign policy, representing the moralistic, crusading idealism of American history or the vision of democracy promotion and global transformation.

These four traditions are part of American diplomatic history, but the argument here is that they are not all equally embedded in American institutions and its people. Three of the four traditions do not countenance ambitious foreign policy agendas. Hamiltonians only require a foreign policy that stabilizes the global financial system and markets for free trade. By contrast, Jeffersonians and Jacksonians focus on domestic policy. In practice, Wilsonianism is the only transformative tradition and is arguably the least reflective of the broad trends in American foreign policy. As noted previously, President Wilson shifted from an "America First" policy of isolationism, to a policy of fighting a "war to end all wars," and then to replacing the balance-of-power system in Europe with a collective security institution, the League of Nations. But the American people and the Senate did not agree with this shift and rejected the League of Nations Treaty.

President Wilson represented a tradition, albeit a weak tradition, in American foreign policy. What emerges is the observation that American foreign policy expresses a powerful commitment or adherence to gradualist perspective. By gradualism, I mean that it is neither biased toward the status quo nor seeks to create rapid, revolutionary change. What it seeks is gradual, democratic change and is concerned about any forces that accelerate the process of change in the system. The Wilsonian tradition is not as equally influential as the other three traditions outlined by Mead. It should be ranked as a lesser tradition – one that is present but not as influential and hence not terribly representative of American foreign policy in general.

Thus, the challenge is to identify and then return to the principles that represent the best in American foreign policy. These are the three principles described in detail in the preceding chapters. Mead's Jeffersonian and Hamiltonian traditions correspond to the first principle of building the domestic foundations of American power (as examined in Chapter 7). The Jacksonian tradition is more in keeping with the second principle of exercising American leadership (Chapter 8) to restrain the most immediate and pressing sources of disorder. The third principle of working with allies and partners to address global threats is the newest principle and does not correspond to any core element of Mead's framework. Here, it is termed the "cooperationist principle," dating back to Franklin Delano Roosevelt's close cooperation with allies and partners in defeating the Axis powers in World War II and then being utilized throughout the Cold War.

The best attempts at grand strategy in the post–Cold War era have recognized these three principles and sought a balance between them. The story of a palpable sense of drift in grand strategy and of the reactive quality of American grand strategy in the post–Cold War world is, then, a story of balance and imbalance among these three principles. George H. W. Bush perhaps came closest to striking the right balance in implementation, but he did not articulate and enshrine these principles for his successors. Clinton marks the beginning of a deep imbalance as he focused almost exclusively on domestic policy, somewhat to the detriment of foreign policy. Not only did he fail to articulate a grand strategy that provided a balance among these principles, but Clinton implemented a reactive and minimalist foreign policy. George W. Bush, in contrast, is the first post–Cold War president to articulate a grand strategy in which he may have overcompensated for a predecessor's (Clinton's) mistakes. George W. Bush overemphasized the second principle of restraining sources of disorder and disconnected it from the other two principles of maintaining the domestic foundations of American power and working closely with allies and partners to eliminate the worst global threats. The decline in global support for the United States is one symptom of this overemphasis.

Finally, Barack Obama is seeking to find the right balance between the principles, but the danger is that he will overcompensate for Bush's faults by focusing almost exclusively on domestic policy. These wide swings between principles betray a lack of understanding of the history of American diplomacy and the failure to articulate a vision of grand strategy that derives from our principles. The answer to the question "What grand strategy should replace containment?" will never be the right one, because it poses the wrong question. The right question is "What are America's foreign policy principles that have served the nation so well over two hundred years, and how do we strike the right balance between them?" In Chapter 11, we will turn to this question and seek direct answers to it. But first, here in Chapter 10, we examine the successes and failures of post–Cold War American foreign policy that were due to the degree of balance or imbalance between the three principles as various administrations have sought to articulate and implement grand strategy.

President George H. W. Bush: Striking the Right Balance in Implementation but Failing to Articulate

George H. W. Bush (1989–1993) was the first post–Cold War president.[2] He arguably was the most successful in terms of implementing a grand strategy that helped guide the United States through a period of radical geopolitical transition.[3] This was an era that went from the intense bipolarity and confrontation of the Cold War to a time when the United States was the single surviving superpower in the midst of a spirit of increasing cooperation among the big powers in the early years of the post–Cold War era. Strictly speaking, Bush successfully implemented a grand strategy but failed to articulate that vision in a way that garnered broad and enduring public support.

The breadth and depth of Bush's foreign policy experience enabled him to implement a highly effective grand strategy. He left office without establishing for his successors the guidelines that would permit them to conduct American grand strategy in the decades immediately following the end of the Cold War. His successors, who essentially lacked the same depth of experience, struggled to define grand strategies and were subjected to powerful domestic and international pressures that caused further shifts in the nation's grand strategy.[4]

President Bush identified the momentous changes to the international system in his inaugural address on January 20, 1989, in which he said that "a world refreshed by freedom seems reborn [and] the day of the dictator is over." As he declared, "The totalitarian era is passing," and the "[g]reat nations of the world are moving toward democracy through the door to freedom." As a result, the world was likely to "move toward free markets through the door to prosperity."[5]

The fall of the Berlin Wall and the eventual collapse of the Soviet Union, combined with the emergence of regional instability, marked a period of great uncertainty in which policy makers and scholars were compelled to reevaluate America's role in the world. To put this situation into perspective, "for more than four decades, world politics and American grand strategy centered on the U.S.-Soviet confrontation." But facing "the disintegration of the Eastern bloc, the struggle over liberalization of the regimes of the right and the left, and the military victory over Iraq in the Gulf War," the United States entered "a dramatically restructured foreign policy environment."[6]

The response of President Bush and his national security team, in the beginning, was to propose that we were dealing with nothing less than a new world order – indeed, one that would call on the United States to articulate a new grand strategy. According to Bush's national security advisor, Brent Scowcroft, "the easing of Cold War tensions threw open the fundamental assumptions on which the entire postwar security structures ... and our own strategic planning, were based: a Soviet threat and a divided [European] continent."

The strategy that eventually emerged during the Bush administration rested on several objectives: promote global stability, strengthen the law-based international system, and integrate world powers (particularly the Soviet Union and its satellite states) into that system. A central theme in this grand strategy was to recognize how fundamental it was to make the post-Soviet transition peaceful. Although this grand strategy was coherent, the Bush administration struggled during its tenure with the perception that it had failed to articulate an effective replacement to containment.

As the Bush administration adjusted to the reality of a post-Soviet world, Saddam Hussein's invasion and occupation of Kuwait presented the United States with a significant threat to its economic and security interests. In what would be a major foreign policy success for the Bush administration, the United States confronted Saddam within a broad coalition of partners backed by a United Nations authorization. This policy reflected a balance between the second (leadership role for the United States) and third principles (working with allies and partners) to deal with challenges.

As for building the domestic foundations of American power (the first principle), Bush worked to reduce the Reagan deficits. Many Republicans criticized his decision to agree to raise taxes, and he lost support among congressional Republicans for reneging on his promise not to have new taxes. But his determination to bring the budget onto a sustainable course was indispensable in paving the way for the balanced budget that emerged during the Clinton years. In short, George H. W. Bush's implicit grand strategy balanced among the three principles and left America stronger than when he took office.

First Principle: Building Domestic Foundations of American Power through Promoting Capitalism and Fiscal Reform

A core principle in Bush's grand strategy was its emphasis on the economic foundations of American power. In stressing the role of economics in grand strategy, the Bush administration's second National Security Strategy (NSS), published in 1991, explicitly cited how important the expansion of free markets is to the spread of open, democratic societies. The argument in Bush's NSS was that America's support for "an international economic system as open and inclusive as possible, is the best way to strengthen global economic development, political stability and the growth of free societies."[7] In effect, Bush's ideas trace back to President Washington and Secretary of the Treasury Hamilton's emphasis on building the economic foundations of American power.

With these principles, President Bush elevated the role of economic free markets and global free trade to central planks in his grand strategy. "America," he said, "has championed liberal trade to enhance world prosperity as well as to reduce political friction among nations." Bush held that "my administration is committed to working with all nations to promote the prosperity of the free market system and to reduce barriers that unfairly inhibit international commerce."[8] The United States won the Cold War because it had built a formidable economy and a global system of trading partners, which it used to defeat a totalitarian society whose command economy slowly condemned it to economic failure.

Second Principles: Exercising American Leadership to Peacefully Integrate the Former Soviet Union into the World System

The central principle that animated American grand strategy during the Bush administration was how to manage the decline of the Soviet Union while simultaneously building peace and stability in Europe. President Bush's administration spent its early years formulating a soft landing for the Soviet Union following its economic and political decline that began in 1989 with the fall of the Berlin Wall. Facing a climate of strategic uncertainty, Bush and his cabinet spent considerable time and energy constructing a "long-run framework" whose principles were designed to be "deliberate [by] encouraging, guiding, and managing change without provoking backlash and crackdown."[9]

The dramatic and radical nature of how quickly and broadly the Soviet demise occurred during the late 1980s and early 1990s created within the West and the U.S. government a "heightened . . . sense of euphoria." The challenge for the president was "to guard against crossing the line from championing the quest for freedom and self-determination to portraying the changes as victories in the Cold War struggle – thus provoking confrontation." The Bush administration found that operating on this delicate line posed a challenge for the United States. Bush and Scowcroft realized that the dilemma for U.S. policy was to "evolve . . . perhaps even unconsciously, from quietly supporting the transformations to cultivating Soviet acquiescence, even collaboration, in them."[10] This constraint limited the Bush administration's ability to articulate a successor to the grand strategy of containment, because the emphasis on positive principles that ought to dominate grand strategy was overwhelmed by the imperative of avoiding chaos as a nuclear-armed superpower disintegrated in relatively short order.

This transition in world politics occurred remarkably quickly as the Bush administration moved "beyond containment" to building a strategy that was designed to "[integrate] the Soviet Union into the international system as a constructive partner." In formulating principles that immediately dominated American grand strategy, Washington sought "to engage the USSR in a relationship that [was] increasingly cooperative." As Bush continued, "Moscow [would find] a willing partner in creating the conditions that [would] permit the Soviet Union to join, and be welcome[d] in, a peaceful, free and prosperous international community."[11]

Bush's decision to manage the decline of the Soviet Union without subjecting the Soviet leadership, principally Gorbachev, to the humiliations of defeat constituted a departure from the tone of previous American policies during the Cold War – and it remains a significant aspect of American diplomacy during the Soviet collapse. From the earliest days of the Cold War, American grand strategy relied reflexively on direct opposition to and hostile criticism of Soviet policies. As an example of remarkable diplomacy and geopolitical judgment, Bush did not challenge Moscow or humiliate its leadership during its collapse. Rather, he sought to build a peaceful and cooperative relationship with the Soviet Union.

In effect, the Bush administration moved beyond the grand strategy that had held sway since the Truman administration in 1947. It did so by taking advantage of an opportunity to redefine American grand strategy by transcending the ideological, military, and geopolitical struggle that had dominated American strategy for decades. However, the pressures of dealing with Moscow's decline diverted Washington's attention at precisely the moment when it had the opportunity to articulate a new grand strategy whose principles would be relevant well beyond the Soviet collapse.

The failure to redefine American grand strategy was not due to a lack of effort. Facing constant media attention, the Bush administration emphasized the continual search for new concepts, which included such phrases as "status quo plus," "Beyond Containment," and "Post Containment," among several others. The administration's intent was to outline the principles or ideas that symbolized the end of the Cold War, while expressing the American hope for "a new era of international stability."[12] Although this search was dominated by the more mechanical aspects of winding down the Cold War in a peaceful and orderly fashion, it appears that Bush had a coherent and successful grand strategy for navigating America's role in the post–Cold War world. The specific elements of his grand strategy – building the economic foundations of power, balancing ends and means, and promoting democracy and freedom (in the Persian Gulf War) – produced, in effect, a successor grand strategy, which sought to integrate the post-Soviet countries into the international order. By adhering to these principles, the Bush administration ultimately made a significant contribution to the evolution of American grand strategy at the end of the Cold War.

The unraveling of the Soviet Union took place amidst instability in other authoritarian countries, most notably China. Several months after President Bush took office, in April 1989, students and residents of Beijing conducted massive demonstrations in Tiananmen Square. These demonstrations represented the most significant challenge to the authority and legitimacy of China's communist government since its founding in 1949.

The Bush administration responded cautiously at first, fearful of taking a stance that would undermine the independence of the demonstrators and weaken America's relationship with the leaders in Beijing. Eventually, the United States and other European powers implemented an arms embargo to signal their displeasure with the violent crackdown against the demonstrators in Tiananmen Square on June 4, 1989. President Bush said he "deeply deplored the use of force," and UK Prime Minister Margaret Thatcher said she was "shocked and appalled by the shootings."[13] President Bush, however, was hesitant to cut off the emerging commercial and strategic relationship between the United States and China. The Bush administration's policy of promoting free trade and open markets as a way to advance the president's democratic agenda explains in part why the administration refrained from taking more significant steps.

President Bush said that he "believed that the commercial contacts between our countries had helped lead to the quest for more freedom." Bush continued, "If people have commercial incentives, whether it's in China or in other totalitarian systems, the move to democracy becomes inexorable."[14] In formulating ideas that continued to guide policy during the Clinton administration, Bush reaffirmed in his 1990 National Security Strategy that if "the world economic system remains an open and expanding one, we ourselves will benefit from the growth of others." As Bush warned, however, "American leadership will remain pivotal." His reasoning was that unless the United States has a "robust" economy, it cannot "sustain that leadership role,… foster global economic development and ease dangerous pressures for unilateralism, regionalism, and protectionism."[15]

Third Principle: Working with Allies to Eliminate Saddam Hussein's Threat to Regional Stability and Global Economic Growth

History likely will judge that Saddam Hussein's invasion and occupation of Kuwait presented a threat to U.S. vital interests and to the emerging global economic order. It also offered an opportunity for the Bush administration to use American power and resolve to establish this "new world order." In a speech on January 16, 1991, announcing the start of the Persian Gulf War, Bush said precisely this: "We have before us the opportunity to forge for ourselves and for future generations a new world order."[16]

As Bush's 1991 National Security Strategy later noted, "as the war in the Gulf made clear, the easing of the Soviet threat [did] not mean an end to all hazards." The Bush administration likely understood that the United States would face challenges that would call for it to have a coherent grand strategy. Drawing from Bush's 1991 National Security Strategy, the administration's plan was "to build a new world order in the aftermath of the Cold War [in which] we will likely discover that the enemy we face is less an expansionist communism than it is instability itself." As he articulated the principles that guided the post–Cold War American grand strategy, Bush developed a coherent strategy that sought to counter precisely the types of instability that Saddam's invasion represented. To build a united international front against Iraq, the administration operated under the assumption that, with the end of the Cold War, "regional disputes [were] less likely automatically to be perceived as part of a permanent ... global competition," which would encourage "broader international cooperation in their resolution."[17]

To rally the country and the Congress behind his plan to remove Saddam from Kuwait, President Bush made a speech to both chambers of Congress on September 11, 1990. Its purpose, according to Bush, "was to 'defend civilized values around the world,' among them our willingness to 'support the rule of law,' 'stand up to aggression,' and 'defend common vital interests.'"[18] Bush highlighted the widespread rejection of Saddam's actions and the emerging coalition as evidence of the rise of a new but uncertain world order. Not only did the Bush administration seek to evict Saddam from Kuwait and bolster regional confidence in the United States, but it also sought to showcase the principle in American grand strategy that U.S. policy would act when possible as part of an international consensus. In an address before Congress, Bush described Saddam's invasion of Kuwait as "the first assault on the new world that we seek, the first test of our mettle [that affirms that] America and the world must defend [our] common vital interests."[19]

One principle in Bush's grand strategy was to promote the role of a "new partnership of nations." Facing Iraq's invasion of Kuwait, the Bush administration had an "opportunity" to build a new basis for international cooperation.[20] In formulating his grand strategy and contemplating the challenge that Iraq's invasion of Kuwait posed to the international community, Bush drew valuable lessons from Europe's failed efforts to appease Hitler at the 1938 Munich Peace Conference. Although President Bush was criticized for publicly comparing Saddam Hussein to Hitler, what was instructive was Bush's determination not to repeat the mistakes of the late 1930s. He set out to make an example of Saddam's blatant act of aggression through his reliance on a resolute coalition of states that was committed to international cooperation.[21]

The manner in which the United States handled the first major, post–Cold War challenge to international security highlighted the role of the third principle of

American foreign policy. Bush worked within UN institutional norms and relied heavily on allies and partners to implement the military operation. As Bush explained, "we had started self-consciously to view our actions as setting a precedent for the approaching post–Cold War world [and] to operate in a manner that would help establish a pattern for the future." He wrote in his memoirs that the "foundation" of his policy "was a premise that the United States henceforth would be obligated to lead the world community to an unprecedented degree." Of even greater significance, Bush defined U.S. policy as the product of a "framework in concert with our friends in the international community."[22]

In terms of implementation, Bush and his national security team were determined to see the United Nations fulfill its mandate and act unencumbered by Cold War rivalries. "We are now in sight," Bush argued after the passage of UN Security Council Resolution 661, "of a United Nations that performs as envisioned by its founders.... The Security Council has imposed mandatory economic sanctions on Iraq [that are] designed to force Iraq to relinquish the spoils of its illegal conquest."[23] By contrast, Bush said that for decades "political differences, bloc politics and demagogic rhetoric have kept the UN from reaching the full potential envisioned by its founders." Bush now saw "the UN beginning to act as it was designed, freed from the superpower antagonisms that often frustrated consensus."[24]

The goal of the Bush administration was to make the United Nations Security Council "the main instrument for confronting Iraq's aggression, and all future acts of aggression." As Bush wrote in his memoirs, "I wanted the United Nations involved as part of our first response, starting with a strong condemnation of Iraq's attack on a fellow member." To make this strategy effective, Bush and Scowcroft wrote that "decisive UN action would be important in rallying international opposition to the invasion and reversing it."[25] Bush's new order implied a world "in which the United States goes beyond its own national interests," in which it would commit itself "to defending international interests including peace, stability, and the rule of law." This system would be guided and "protected by the United States ... with the support of our international partners – including the Soviet Union."[26]

Weinberger-Powell Doctrine in the First Gulf War

The adoption of the Weinberger-Powell doctrine, which was a significant element of the Bush administration's military strategy in the Gulf War, was entirely consistent with Bush's grand strategy. Bearing in mind the lessons of Vietnam and the 1982–1983 Lebanon intervention, the secretary of defense in the Reagan administration, Casper Weinberger, and his then-senior military assistant, General Colin Powell, articulated a series of "tests" to be passed before the United States would commit its forces abroad.[27] Among other guidelines, it held that the United States should not commit forces to *combat* overseas unless the particular engagement or occasion is deemed vital to our national interests or that of our allies.[28]

This doctrine influenced the planning and execution of the Gulf War. As William Schneider noted, "the Republican [Bush] administration was sensitive to another lesson of Vietnam: Americans don't like limited wars." In a press conference on November 30, 1990, President Bush reiterated the lesson of the Vietnam War when he said, "If there must be war, we will not permit our troops to have their hands tied behind their backs. If one American soldier has to go into battle, that soldier will have enough force behind him to win and then get out as soon as possible.... I will never, ever agree to a halfway effort."[29] Bush's thinking about military intervention related to his mindset on Vietnam. As he wrote, "In this war [Persian Gulf War] – unlike Vietnam – we had a defined mission, and we carried it out."[30]

Military action against Iraq took place just before the onset of an economic recession in the United States and a growing budget crisis debate in Congress. Recognizing that he had no choice but to deal with these constraints on U.S. action, President Bush chose a multilateral approach for building international security and stability during the last years of the Cold War. Mindful of the direct linkage between economic and military power, Bush acknowledged that "our wealth and our strength are not without limits." A central principle of his grand strategy, as the NSS stated, was that "we must balance our commitments with our means and, above all, we must wisely choose now which elements of our strength will best serve our needs in the future." As he noted, "This is the challenge of strategy."[31] This point not only speaks well about how a successful grand strategy should be devised, but reaffirms that Bush did in fact have a grand strategy that attempted to guide America's role in the world after the fall of its main competitor and threat.

Aware of the fact that the United States was not willing to take on the role of an international police power alone, Bush noted that American leadership in the 1990s and beyond will "require strategic vision – a clear perception of our goals, our interests, and the means available to achieve and protect them." With language reminiscent of the grand strategies that were ascendant during the Eisenhower administration and governed the policies of his predecessors during the Cold War, Bush argued, "The essence of strategy is determining priorities. We will make the hard choices."[32]

Being mindful of the public's willingness to support American grand strategy was central to the policies of the Bush administration. President Bush stressed that "at home, the material cost of our leadership can be steep." But he also warned that, although "we are prepared to do our share and more to help carry that load[,] we insist that others do their share as well."[33] By enlisting a broad coalition of international partners, the United States offset the direct financial cost of the war. Efforts to build a broad coalition remained a significant feature of American grand strategy during the Bush administration.[34]

In presenting his case to the American people, President Bush linked the effectiveness of American grand strategy to the nation's economic vitality. Beginning with arguments similar to what Eisenhower proposed, Bush said that "our ability to function effectively as a great power abroad depends on how we conduct ourselves at home." A crucial point in Bush's grand strategy was the direct linkage between economics and national strategy: "Our economy, our Armed Forces, our energy dependence, and our cohesion all determine whether we can help our friends and stand up to our foes." As the president made clear, U.S. national power "ultimately rests on the strength and resilience of our economy, and our security would be badly served if we allowed fiscal irresponsibility at home to erode our ability to protect our interests abroad, to aid new democracies or to help find solutions to other global problems."[35]

At a time when Paul Kennedy published his best-selling book, *The Rise and Fall of Great Powers* (1989), scholars and policy makers debated whether the United States faced decline as a result of the exertions that it undertook during the Cold War. Policy makers in the Bush administration were aware of the perils of overreach if the United States failed to link its grand strategy with economic realities. Kenneth Oye and other scholars argued (writing in 1992) that "the United States has the financial strength to sustain *individual* strands of a unilateralist and activist foreign policy." The United States, however, "cannot afford to implement an activist policy in multiple regions on multiple issues." Put more directly, the United States had to be highly attentive to the risks of formulating a grand strategy that went, in effect, "beyond the means of the United States."[36]

George H. W. Bush's Legacy in American Grand Strategy

Bush's policies successfully stressed domestic economic realities, which have figured prominently at the core of American grand strategy for centuries and constitute a powerful check on the nation's grand strategy. As a consequence, Bush paid careful attention to striking a balance between the ends and means in U.S. grand strategy and between the three principles of domestic strength, global leadership, and alliance building.

A fundamental principle in Bush's grand strategy, as outlined in his inaugural address, was to shift American foreign policy from containing totalitarianism to building an order in which more states could embrace freedom, democracy, and free markets – especially states of the former Soviet Union and in Eastern Europe – while managing the declining power and influence of the Soviet Union. In effect, Bush implemented a grand strategy that marked the transition from an era of confrontational politics to one of greater cooperation in which Washington sought to infuse American policy with the principles of freedom and peace without facing the geopolitical pressures of a totalitarian adversary. However, although the Bush administration pursued a coherent grand strategy that promoted American international leadership, confronted instability and second-tier threats, advanced democracy, and sought to build economic prosperity at home and abroad, its grand strategy did not translate into guidance that would endure across subsequent administrations.

President William J. Clinton: An Emphasis on Principle 1, Domestic Policy

William J. (Bill) Clinton (1993–2001) was almost exclusively a domestic policy president.[37] His grand strategy balanced dealing with the first principle of building the domestic foundations of American power, which was pursued more strongly than the second and third principles.[38] He faced multiple sources of disorder (Northern Ireland, Kosovo) and failures (Somalia, Rwanda, and the Israeli-Palestinian peace process). In the end, these sources of disorder continued to grow, especially in the case of international terrorist organizations.

Clinton's desire to build an international order in which multilateral institutions play a much more dominant role, as the United States balanced its interests with its economic power and political responsibilities, played a decisive role in his foreign policy. Clinton's logic was impeccable: After more than four decades of active American involvement in international affairs under the rubric of containment, the American public was not enthusiastic about seeing the nation embrace an activist foreign policy. For this reason, the role of the United States as a leading force in foreign policy declined somewhat during this period.

Clinton's preference for emphasizing the first principle in grand strategy was articulated in his inaugural address on January 20, 1993, when he signaled the importance of rebuilding the foundations of the American economy. Acknowledging the problems with a struggling economy and recession, he said in his address, "Raised in unrivaled prosperity, we inherit an economy that is still the world's strongest, but is weakened by business failures, stagnant wages, increasing inequality, and deep divisions among our people." Clinton underscored the principle that the nation's domestic economy remained the foundation on which all American power rested.

Referring to such domestic challenges as the high cost of health care and lack of investment in the nation's youth, he then outlined his strategy for ending America's drift. He "pledge[d] an end to the era of deadlock and drift – a new season of American renewal has begun." In his first inaugural address, he said he wanted to rebuild the American economy by eliminating, for instance, "the massive debt,"[39] but his vision for domestic regeneration centered on a grand strategy that put less emphasis on the other two principles. It successfully rested on a domestic policy program to move the Democratic Party to the center on economic issues and to capture widespread electoral support from a center-left coalition.

First-Principle Dominancy: Elevating Domestic Policy

President Clinton took advantage of the increasingly favorable position of the United States in the world as his campaign focused on domestic policies. In the 1992 presidential campaign when the nation was mired in a recession, "Clinton promised to use the peace dividend and 'focus like a laser beam' on the economy."[40]

The "peace dividend," a term also used in the George H. W. Bush presidency, refers to increasing domestic and social spending as defense budgets decline. After the Cold War and Operation Desert Storm, both Bush and Clinton justified reduced military spending to the lack of U.S. engagement in any major wars, hot or cold. In effect, Clinton signaled that in his administration's foreign policy would take a backseat to the domestic economy. In a political climate marked by the end of the Cold War and an economic recession, observers believed that for Clinton, "foreign policy goals were at most an afterthought."[41] As the newly elected Clinton told House Foreign Relations Committee Chair Lee Hamilton, the only people who talked about foreign policy during the entire campaign were a few members of the press corps.[42]

Clinton's grand strategy principally focused on the development of the American economy and its relationship to domestic policies. This, however, should not be interpreted to mean that Clinton was an isolationist president or that he was disinterested in foreign policy. It is true, however, that Clinton exemplified a presidency whose center of gravity rested on domestic politics – in direct contrast with George H. W. Bush's presidency that overwhelmingly focused on foreign policy.[43] According to one scholar, Clinton's grand strategy fits much less neatly into the patterns of previous American leaders, largely because Clinton "kept his campaign promise [of] devoting the lion's share of his presidency to domestic policy." In practice, although "Clinton eschewed costly international commitments . . . he did not favor wholesale retrenchment."[44]

The arc of grand strategy that Clinton followed was, in the view of some scholars, quite predictable for a Democratic president whose strong preferences were for investing in "butter over guns (domestic consumption over military spending)." Clinton placed his highest priority on social programs that were popular with his Democratic constituencies, such as education, while simultaneously decreasing defense spending to take advantage of the "peace dividend."

Clinton's foreign policy, however, remained consistent with many policies that emerged during the Cold War. For example, "he deepened America's commitment to free trade and helped expand the NATO alliance by pushing for the incorporation of former Soviet allies," despite domestic political opposition to such policies. Unlike many of his predecessors since the late 1940s, Clinton did not have the luxury of using a common enemy to help organize American political will and public support for policies that deemphasized the international dimension of his overall policies. With his emphasis on domestic politics, Clinton "had strong domestic incentives not to diverge too much, or too quickly, from past strategic practices [in grand strategy]." The fact that Clinton won in 1992 with only 43 percent of the popular vote meant that he clearly did not possess a mandate in foreign or domestic policy.[45] The broad message in Clinton's grand strategy was that foreign policy would be a less significant aspect of his administration's policies.

The Clinton Doctrine: National Security Strategy of Engagement and Enlargement

The signature policy of the Clinton administration's foreign policy – which defined American grand strategy during his time in office – was known as "Engagement and Enlargement," as expressed in his National Security Strategy document. Published in 1995, A National Strategy of Engagement and Enlargement outlined a grand strategy that rested on two principles: "bolster America's economic revitalization" and "promote democracy abroad."[46] The principle enunciated by President Clinton was that the United States must "exercise global leadership," but he warned that "we are not the world's policeman."[47] In Clinton's view, it was essential for the United States to remain engaged in world affairs, while not assuming primary responsibility for solving all problems.

In effect, these ideas coalesced into what is generally known as the Clinton Doctrine, whose ideas were outlined in a speech on February 26, 1999.[48] The Clinton Doctrine emphasized the dangerous nature of international politics, the desire to promote and enlarge the number of democracies, and the intention of intervening to defend human rights and prevent human rights abuses, including that of genocide.[49]

One principle that represented a signature element of American grand strategy during the Clinton administration was the concept of "enlargement," which called for expanding or enlarging the ranks of democratic states. As Clinton's national security strategy defined the policy, "All of America's strategic interests – from promoting prosperity at home to checking global threats abroad before they threaten our territory – are served by enlarging the community of democratic and free market nations."

The key to this strategy was for the United States to "work ... with new democratic states to help preserve them as democracies committed to free markets and respect for human rights." Even though Clinton's strategy promoted the merit of "help[ing] democracy and markets expand and survive," he warned that this should not be seen as a "democratic crusade." By contrast, he saw it as a "pragmatic commitment to see freedom take hold where that will help us most."[50] The decision to pursue policies that uphold "respect for human rights" was a critical component of Clinton's grand strategy. As expressed in his National Security Strategy, "we must also redouble our efforts to guarantee basic human rights on a global basis."

With the collapse of the Soviet Union, the United States had an opportunity to help states in the former Soviet Union and in Eastern Europe develop democratic institutions and free market economies. Because the Cold War ended successfully on American terms, the core principle in American grand strategy during the Clinton administration was expressed by the following simple yet powerful idea: "Our long-term goal is a world in which each of the major powers is democratic, with many other nations joining the community of market democracies as well."[51]

Borrowing language from Clinton's National Security Strategy, scholars and policy makers often used the concept of "selective engagement" to characterize President Clinton's grand strategy. Quoting from this document, American engagement "must be selective, focusing on the challenges that are most relevant to our own interests and focusing our resources where we can make the most difference."[52] His policy of more selective engagement was a result of the geopolitical reality in which the United States found that it was the most powerful state. This logic was compelling because the demise of the Soviet Union "left America unrivaled militarily, economically, and politically." With the overwhelming power of the United States, Clinton gained an unprecedented "degree of political latitude in making foreign policy that American leaders did not experience during the long Cold War with the Soviet Union."[53] This shift in power was remarkable and historically unique in the annals of American foreign policy, even when compared to the extent of America's power immediately after World War II.[54]

In what emerged as a prominent theme in American grand strategy during his administration, Clinton suggested in his first inaugural address that he would consider using military force to intervene in cases that affected American vital interests and involved humanitarian disasters and abuses. His language was specific: "When our vital interests are challenged, or the will and conscience of the international community is defied, we will act – with peaceful diplomacy whenever possible, with force when necessary."[55] The phrase "will and conscience" is a direct reference to the humanitarian crises – Somalia, Haiti, Rwanda, Bosnia – that contributed to intense foreign policy deliberations within the Clinton administration.

Domestic political incentives had a disproportionate effect on Clinton's foreign policies as he sought to solidify and expand his domestic support. For example, many Democratic constituencies opposed "the expansion of NATO into Poland, Hungary, and the Czech Republic [because this] was unnecessary geopolitically and ... needlessly threatened Moscow's interests." The countervailing view was that Clinton likely interpreted the "expansion of NATO [as] an opportunity to demonstrate that Democrats could be tough on national security." His concern with keeping a hold on his fragile mandate (compounded by the challenges of operating with a divided government – Republicans controlled both houses of Congress for six of Clinton's eight years as president), as well as a personal worry of "being perceived as a second Jimmy Carter," all contributed, according to Trubowitz, to inconsistencies between the articulation and implementation of his grand strategy.

Clinton's grand strategy emphasized the decline of unilateralism and the rise of policies that espoused multilateralism, but this multilateralism seemed to be reactive and drifting rather than focused on building and sustaining coordination against specific threats. Scholars write that Clinton was "rhetorically invested in an 'assertive multi-lateralism' that would reduce the nation's reliance on 'guns' and military power (and freed up a peace dividend for investment in the 'butter' of social spending)." However, in implementation, Clinton was "less ready to abandon the instruments of Cold War balancing – military alliances, forward deployment of U.S. forces, and the direct use of military power ... than his campaign promises or the changed international circum- stances (end of the Cold War) would have predicted."[56] The influence of minimalist pragmatism was a hallmark of Clinton's grand strategy.

Somalia and Rwanda: Consequences of Grand Strategic Flux

The Somalia operation persuaded the Clinton administration to avoid unilateral action and to opt instead for multilateral action. Although U.S. troops were in Somalia under a UN peacekeeping operation, intervention in the Mogadishu operation was a unilateral U.S. initiative that spanned the Bush and Clinton administrations. The previous presi- dent, George H. W. Bush, provided humanitarian assistance under a UN peacekeeping operation to deal with the famine in Somalia, but the infamous "Black Hawk Down" incident on October 3–4, 1993 – which played out on the streets of Mogadishu and in the full glare of media coverage – left eighteen American soldiers dead. The event not only caused public support for international intervention to decline dramatically, but it also significantly decreased Clinton's enthusiasm for peacekeeping operations.

For one scholar, as "the level of domestic political risk for Clinton went up, the *intensity* of his support for multilateralism went down." In effect, without a clear and present threat to vital U.S. national interests, Clinton listened carefully when the public expressed disinterest in unilateral American involvement in foreign policy and supported some withdrawal from international affairs. As he often reminded his advisers, "Americans are basically isolationist. Right now the average American doesn't see our interest threatened to the point where we should sacrifice an American life." In a world in which there were "few geopolitical constraints" on the United States, Clinton's problem was that military intervention had no serious "*international* or *domestic* risks."[57] Selling Congress on the argument that military intervention was both low risk and low cost, Clinton employed a brand of power projection that relied on multilateral intervention in Bosnia, Iraq, and Kosovo.

Yet, after Somalia, the Clinton administration was more risk-averse about using force in complex security emergencies. Moreover, in promoting a less American-centric view of international politics, he fostered a sense that Washington was unwilling to take actions that might involve *any* risks, domestic or international. The Rwanda genocide is a tragic case in point. After the Somalia debacle, Clinton's national security team was overly cautious about military intervention. Clinton candidly describes in his memoirs the reasons behind the lack of response to Rwanda's genocide:

> Within one hundred days, more than 800,000 people in a country of only 8 million would be murdered, most of them by machetes. We were so preoccupied with Bosnia, with the memory of Somalia just six months old, and with opposition in Congress to military deployments in faraway places not vital to our national interests that neither I nor anyone on my foreign policy team adequately focused on sending troops to stop the slaughter. With a few thousand troops and help from our allies, even making allowances for the time it would have taken to deploy them, we could have saved lives.[58]

Another example was the debate, which raged over several years, about whether the United States and NATO should intervene to end the policies of genocide in Bosnia practiced by Serbia's Slobodan Milosevic. As the debate continued for years in Washington and in Europe, the emerging impression was that leaders on both sides of the Atlantic were unwilling to intervene.

Clinton's Legacy in American Grand Strategy

From the onset, with President Clinton's focus on the domestic economy, he presided over a period of dramatic economic growth and prosperity. In effect, Clinton's grand strategy emphasized the economic foundations of American power at the expense of the second and third principles of grand strategy. In this regard, his grand strategy was immensely successful, because it coincided with a period of remarkable domestic and economic prosperity.

In view of the overwhelming focus on domestic politics, his grand strategy often appeared to be ad hoc, often lacking on overall vision. In contrast with the coherence of containment, the policies of the Clinton administration were less compelling, which explains why some observers describe Clinton as an "underachiever" in grand strategy. The countervailing view held that "Clinton presided over a fluid and novel Democratic coalition" when there was considerable "attention [on] whether the United States faced new international dangers."

For some scholars, Clinton's grand strategy entered a period of retrenchment and did so without profoundly altering or redefining the nation's policies. By emphasizing domestic politics, however, the Clinton administration effectively implemented a dramatic redesign of American grand strategy whose policies endure to the present.[59] Nevertheless, the historian Garry Wills writes that "Clinton was a foreign policy minimalist."[60] As Bush before him, President Clinton sought to shape an international order in which other states and institutions assume a greater role in building a more peaceful era. But unlike Bush, he did not give this goal the priority of a grand strategy, though the Clinton administration developed policies that promoted some degree of cooperation among allies. This was the essence of the Clinton Doctrine that formed the administration's grand strategy, and its principles will be revisited by the Obama administration.

President George W. Bush: New Imbalance among Principles – Emphasizing American Leadership to Restrain Sources of Disorder

As the forty-third president of the United States, George W. Bush (2001–2009) led the nation at the time of the most deadly attack on American soil in U.S. history.[61] The events on 9/11 immediately transformed the Bush administration by turning its focus from domestic issues to dealing primarily with international terrorism and foreign policy, which had significant consequences for American grand strategy.[62] The grand strategy rapidly shifted to dealing with the second principle of exercising leadership – to restrain the sources of disorder – and was tested after the terrorist attack.

The period during the 1990s was a largely tranquil and prosperous decade for the United States, as discussed in the section on the Clinton administration. The issues of foreign policy and grand strategy were at best background issues during the 2000 presidential campaign; both candidates made little mention of foreign policy. By far, the topics that dominated the 2000 campaign included such domestic issues as taxes,

Social Security, education reform, increased defense spending, and the character of the candidate – a subtle reference to Bill Clinton.[63] The 2000 campaign affirmed that Bush had relatively little interest in foreign policy for reasons that included the modestly benign nature of international politics in the post–Cold War world, the American public's declining interest in foreign policy, and its much greater interest in domestic issues.

When George W. Bush was sworn in, he – unlike most U.S. presidents since World War II – had little in the way of serious foreign policy experience, having previously been a successful businessman and having served as the twice-elected governor of Texas.[64] However, the events of 9/11 and the subsequent wars in Afghanistan and Iraq quickly changed that focus, serving in effect as the impetus for a new and ambitious grand strategy whose scale of change was unrivaled since the administration of Franklin D. Roosevelt.

Much attention has been devoted to Bush's grand strategy after 9/11 and what became known as the Bush doctrine, as examined later. Admittedly, the events of that September morning dramatically altered how the United States viewed the world and the nature of its foreign policy. In response, the Bush administration articulated and implemented a radically new grand strategy, which commenced more than a decade of war and foreign entanglements in both Afghanistan and Iraq and the global war on terror.[65] To understand the grand strategy behind the foreign policy of the Bush administration, the first step is to examine the vision and policies that George W. Bush brought with him to the White House.

Pre-9/11: Focusing on the Domestic Foundations of American Power

President Bush's experience in business and Texas politics as well as comments he made during the 2000 campaign offer insights into his approach to foreign policy. His general approach to leadership was "that a leader should establish a broad vision for policy, solicit information from a strong and loyal team of advisors, and then make decisive and firm decisions."[66] It also means taking responsibility when problems arise.[67] This style was evident in Bush's primary campaign and would continue throughout his two terms in the White House. Often described as someone who relied on his "gut instinct" and a desire to be decisive, Bush was known to articulate policies in which he sought to make transformative decisions – famously not playing "small ball," as he called it – in domestic and foreign policies.[68] In a style central to the grand strategy that emerged after the 9/11 attacks, Bush "believed that the president should be the dominant player not only within the executive branch, but in the overall policy-making system."[69] This view of foreign policy, his leadership style, and the role of presidential power all influenced Bush's grand strategy.

After his election to the presidency – following the legal challenges during the six weeks after November 7, 2000 – Bush "gave every indication that he, like his father before him, was a conventional 'realist' in foreign affairs," who was firmly "committed to a grand strategy of selective engagement." Although this approach follows Clinton, Bush was critical of the "open-ended nature of the Clinton doctrine and its indiscriminate use of military force in instances that did not put at risk the vital national interests of the United States."[70] The peace operations and missions of the Clinton administration were strongly criticized by Bush during the campaign as futile efforts at nation building.[71] In practice,

President Bush hoped to articulate a grand strategy emphasizing more clearly defined objectives, foreign policy retrenchment, and a military transformation.[72] This strategy was outlined in a campaign speech given at the Citadel on September 23, 1999, when then-governor Bush outlined three defense-related goals that he pledged to follow. "If elected," he said, "I will renew the bond of trust between the American president and the American military. I will defend the American people against missiles and terror. And I will begin creating the military of the next century."[73]

Bush's remarks at the Citadel acknowledged the presence of terrorism and the threat it posed to the United States. After mentioning his mandate to defend the American people against terrorism, Bush cautioned groups or nations that sponsor such attacks that the United States would respond in a "swift and devastating" fashion. Later in the same speech, he stated that "the best defense can be a strong and swift offense." Bush said that "there is more to be done preparing here at home," and emphasized that he "will put a high priority on detecting and responding to terrorism on our soil." Although not the focus of that speech, Bush's comments on terrorism provided a glimpse into his mindset and ideas central to his post-9/11 grand strategy.[74]

Bush opposed continuing Clinton-era peacekeeping operations and rejected an interventionist ideology but did not advocate isolationism. In describing his beliefs about foreign policy, Bush argued, "a president must mix clear-eyed realism with American ideals of spreading freedom and dignity." He reiterated this theme during a speech at the Reagan Presidential Library on November 19, 1999, when he affirmed that the United States, with its unprecedented power and position within the international community, must "turn this time of American influence into generations of democratic peace." In this same speech, Bush outlined several principles that would influence foreign policy during his administration.[75]

During the presidential campaign and from the earliest days of his administration, a central theme in President Bush's grand strategy was his staunch support of building and deploying national missile defenses. Although the Soviet Union no longer posed a serious nuclear threat to the United States and its allies, the proliferation of nuclear weapons – particularly among such states as Iran, Iraq, and North Korea – remained of concern. The principle annunciated by Bush was that "this is still a dangerous world, a less certain, a less predictable one." As "more nations have nuclear weapons and still more have nuclear aspiration," it is "most troubling" that "the list of these countries includes some of the world's least-responsible states."[76]

As both candidate and president, Bush supported a broad strategy of active nonproliferation, counterproliferation, and defenses against ballistic missiles. The logic, though contested, was that missile defenses could strengthen the foundations of strategic deterrence that had previously rested on nuclear retaliation or what was known as mutually assured destruction. In this vein, Bush viewed the 1972 Anti-Ballistic Missile (ABM) Treaty signed with the Soviet Union as a relic of the past and, more worryingly, a hindrance to protecting the United States and its allies against the current generation of plausible nuclear threats.[77] President Bush later cited the events of 9/11 as concrete justification for his views about the danger posed by the proliferation of nuclear weapons (albeit not necessarily on ballistic missiles) and the possible nexus with extremist groups. Bush gave formal withdrawal notice to Russia on December 13, 2001, and in accordance with treaty provisions, the United States unilaterally withdrew (abrogated) from the ABM Treaty six months later.[78]

September 11, 2001: The Revolutionary Era's Violent Reemergence

On Tuesday September 11, 2001, the world and America's role in it changed in historic terms. Of central importance to this study is how the events of 9/11 influenced President Bush's grand strategy for the rest of his time in office. The deaths of three thousand people in New York, Washington, and Pennsylvania vividly established that violent non-state actors with a revolutionary agenda – viz., radical Islamists and Al-Qaeda – were now a first-tier threat to American national security.[79]

In an address to the nation on the evening of the attacks, Bush told the American people, "We're at war.... We will make no distinction between the terrorists who committed these acts and those who harbor them."[80] In explicitly excluding Muslim and Arab friends from among the nation's enemies, President Bush declared a war on terrorism that would involve targeting Islamic extremists wherever they were. As he characterized the forthcoming struggle as "civilization's fight," Bush appealed to every nation that espoused "progress and pluralism, tolerance and freedom" to fight in what became known as the global war on terrorism.[81]

This series of remarks during the months following 9/11 began the gradual formulation of Bush's post-9/11 grand strategy, which was codified in the administration's 2002 National Security Strategy. The events of 9/11 motivated the Bush administration to undertake a radical redefinition of American grand strategy as it rallied public support and international cooperation for the global war on terrorism.

George W. Bush's Articulation of American Grand Strategy

The Axis of Evil Speech: An Invocation and Misinterpretation
of Grand Strategy in World War II

On January 29, 2002, President Bush delivered his first State of the Union address, whose content was so drastically different that few could have anticipated the shift from when Bush was inaugurated earlier that year. The contrast with Bush's first inaugural address, in which he outlined policies that placed considerable emphasis on domestic policy initiatives, could not be starker as the administration moved foreign policy to top priority.

The president, who was elected despite limited foreign policy credentials after a campaign in which foreign policy issues were far less prominent than domestic issues, was now the commander in chief of a wartime nation. For a comparable shift in American grand strategy, we must look back to President Franklin D. Roosevelt's efforts to redefine American policy in the aftermath of the attack on Pearl Harbor. In his speech, Bush drew an implicit parallel between himself and the World War II generation of Allied leaders. The word *axis* invoked the Axis Powers of Germany, Italy, and Japan, and using the word *evil* cast the conflict in clear-cut moral terms – again similar to the memory of World War II as a noble crusade against fascism and immorality. But Bush failed to understand Franklin Delano Roosevelt and Harry Truman's emphasis on working with allies and partners to accomplish this great task of defeating fascism.

Indeed, the United States was a latecomer to the struggle against the Axis, and even after it entered the war, its role in the European theater was secondary to that of the Soviets. FDR and Truman worked consistently and diligently to maintain a united alliance against the Axis, even if this meant making difficult compromises. The

"Europe First" policy, for instance, was a significant compromise for the U.S. government because it had been attacked by Japan, not Germany. To prioritize the German threat over that of Japan required a willingness to work with allies, which expressed the essence of the third principle of grand strategy. Bush let the third principle fall by the wayside as he invoked the second principle using language that was both expansive and moral.

Although the destruction of Al-Qaeda and the apprehension of Osama Bin Laden were the primary goals in American policy in the wake of 9/11, Bush articulated a far more expansive grand strategy whose objective was to eliminate tyranny and terrorism. These are ideas, not physical enemies, and cannot be defeated by military power alone. However, the Bush administration was concerned about regimes with potential access to weapons of mass destruction that could share that technology with extremist groups. As Bush stated in his 2002 State of the Union address, "States like these, and their terrorist allies, constitute an axis of evil, arming to threaten the peace of the world" and posing "a grave and growing danger."[82] By focusing public attention on the regimes in North Korea, Iran, and Iraq, Bush expanded the war on terror and warned "evil" regimes that this would be a central principle of his grand strategy.

2002 West Point Speech

President Bush gave one of the more important speeches of his presidency on June 1, 2002, at the commencement ceremonies for the United States Military Academy at West Point. On that morning, Bush told the graduates that they were about to take their place in history as part of America's new calling to defend itself and foster a broader international concept of peace. Just as previous generations had fought in Europe and the Pacific and in Korea and Vietnam, Bush emphasized that this generation was charged with carrying the American flag wherever necessary to ensure justice and protect freedom. Bush used the language of a just cause in his grand strategy: "We fight, as we always fight, for a just peace – a peace that favors human liberty."[83]

The theme of the West Point speech was that American grand strategy would emphasize the second principle of exercising leadership to restrain the sources of disorder as an ambitious agenda for democratic transformation. This shifted the principle from gradually restraining the sources of disorder to totally eliminating them and elevated the second principle to a level that was not balanced by the other two principles.

Bush's reasoning, however, rested on the principle that these new threats did not lend themselves to a grand strategy of caution and patience that had effectively served the United States and its allies in the past. He made two important arguments. First, the type of enemy threatening the world could not be deterred because suicide terrorists bent on self-destruction are not amenable to deterrence. Second, the amount of warning between threat emergence and actual attack would be too short to act: "We must take the battle to the enemy, disrupt his plans, and confront the worst threats before they *emerge*."[84]

The imperative for the United States to act preemptively emerged as a cornerstone of Bush's grand strategy. It also provoked intense and polarizing debates in the United States about the wisdom of this strategy and the administration's policies.[85] The counterargument to Bush's policy is that preemptive war (recognized as legal under international law as long as the threat is imminent such that it is a form of self-defense) can easily become preventive war, which is illegal under international law because without an imminent threat to limit the scope of self-defense, there is always a potential threat on the nation. The Bush administration then embarked on a more hostile and aggressive grand strategy that caused dissension in the United States and overseas. Whether it restrained those sources of disorder is debated.

2002 U.S. National Security Strategy

The National Security Strategy document published in September 2002 provides a comprehensive articulation of President Bush's post-9/11 grand strategy. It codified the elements of administration thinking into a formal grand strategy that provided both structure and clarity to U.S. actions and policies. In effect, Bush's grand strategy sought to defend the United States in a world threatened by extremist groups, while providing other states with assistance to help defend against terror. A central principle in Bush's grand strategy for fighting the global war on terror was the doctrine of preemption. Whereas the United States relied during the Cold War on a grand strategy centered on containment and deterrence, the 2002 National Security Strategy emphasized that "the United States has long maintained the option of preemptive actions to counter a sufficient threat to our national security."[86] However, these strategies relied on the ability to identify a threat along with an identifiable leader and an identifiable territory. As outlined in the NSS document, the problem was that "rogue states and terrorists do not seek to attack us using conventional means."[87] Or, as one scholar posed the problem, "How do you contain a shadow? How do you deter someone who's prepared to commit suicide?"[88]

Bush's grand strategy relied on more forceful language in line with the second principle of destroying enemies preemptively. He defined the means comprehensively: "We must make use of every tool in our arsenal – military power, better homeland defenses, law enforcement, intelligence, and vigorous efforts to cut off terrorist financing."[89] In effect, the 2002 NSS outlined a grand strategy whose goal was to make the nation and the world more secure.

It was based on two principles. The first principle is that the United States "is fighting a war against terrorists of global reach."[90] This phrase begins the section that discusses the need to strengthen alliances as part of a strategy to "defeat global terrorism." It holds that the United States is engaged in a war, unlike others in modern history, against an unconventional enemy that operates on a global scale. The "Global War on Terrorism (GWOT)" construct established the framework for other key tenets of Bush's strategy. In short, the strategy behind the GWOT was to disrupt and destroy terrorist organizations, but in view of the secretive nature of the enemy, Bush's strategy expressly made no distinction between terrorists and those who knowingly harbored or aided them. The objective of solving the historical problem of how to defeat non-state actors was a distinctive and highly controversial component of Bush's grand strategy.

The new security environment, having evolved radically since the Cold War, now focused on dealing with rogue states and terrorists rather than a nuclear-armed superpower. As stated in the 2002 NSS, "In the Cold War, weapons of mass destruction were considered weapons of last resort whose use risked the destruction of those who used them." The problem today, however, is that "our enemies see weapons of mass destruction as weapons of choice."[91] Bush saw the new enemy as more complex and in many respects more dangerous to the United States and its allies. The greatest danger was that weapons of mass destruction, if placed in the hands of states that support terrorism, might find their way into the hands of extremists. This risk, as cited in the 2002 NSS, undermined classic "concepts of deterrence," which "will not work against a terrorist enemy whose avowed tactics are wanton destruction and the targeting of innocents."

For the Bush grand strategy, these threats required the United States to adapt "the concept of imminent threat to [match] the capabilities and objectives of today's adversaries." If 9/11 was the standard scenario, the state had to respond to terrorist attacks before it engaged in economic and military mobilization – and do so without warning and in a highly effective fashion. Persuaded that the risks of inaction were too great, the United States moved, as outlined in Bush's 2002 NSS, to protect its interests "by identifying and destroying the threat before it reaches our borders." The second principle of American grand strategy was applied through acting "preemptively against such terrorists, to prevent them from doing harm against our people and our country."[92]

The Bush Doctrine

The 2002 NSS has been described variously as proactive, coherent, informed, "Wilsonian," and candid.[93] The foreign policy principles outlined in that document evolved to become the Bush Doctrine, which scholars and policy makers alike have strongly criticized.[94] In his memoirs, Bush wrote, "I developed a strategy to protect the country that came to be known as the Bush Doctrine," which consisted of four prongs, three practical and one idealistic: "Make no distinction between terrorists and the nations that harbor them – and hold both to account. Take the fight to the enemy overseas before they can attack us again here at home. Confront threats before they fully materialize. Advance liberty and hope as an alternative to the enemy's ideology of repression and fear."[95] This articulation, however, is not the Bush Doctrine as he originally articulated it in 2002, which then rested on three ideas: preemption, unilateralism, and democracy promotion. Although he clearly articulated a grand strategy using these three ideas, implementing them in Iraq and Afghanistan would prove to be difficult.

Implementation Unbound

The Afghanistan War: 2001

The impact of the Afghanistan War on American grand strategy is still debated today and will continue well into the future, but several lessons for American grand strategy are relevant for this inquiry. The principal objective was to remove the Taliban regime – perceived as the only serious option for destroying the base of operations from which Al-Qaeda had operated with impunity since the mid-1990s.

The U.S. strategy was to destroy the Taliban regime, reorganize the country's political and economic system, nullify Al-Qaeda's ability to operate terrorist camps there, and develop the foundations of democratic governance.[96] In political terms, the strategy was to rebuild the government and restore civil authority while diminishing the influence of the same warlords that the U.S. coalition empowered through their military partnership to topple the Taliban in 2001.[97] To support this policy, U.S. policy makers declared their willingness to work with the UN to create post-Taliban governance in Afghanistan.[98]

Policy makers assumed that victory was inevitable after the initial military successes but failed to consider – or simply underestimated – the following questions: Who would rule Afghanistan if the Taliban were deposed? Would that rule be weakened by corruption, and could corruption undermine the counterinsurgency? What if it takes decades to translate success into stability? Is the Afghan government fundamentally precarious? What is the prospect for democracy in Afghanistan?[99] Although President Bush expressed concern that "there's been too much discussion of post-conflict Afghanistan,"[100] there were failures of analysis during the initial phase of intervention.

The Iraq War: 2003

The decision to invade Iraq was based on arguments about the intersection of terrorism and weapons of mass destruction (WMD). Early planning for an invasion of Iraq began in the fall of 2001 at approximately the same time that the United States was involved in the invasion of Afghanistan.[101] The Bush administration's stated reason for the war was to eliminate Iraq's WMD and destroy Saddam Hussein's regime in order to end his continued sponsorship of terrorism.

The record clearly establishes that although American policy makers wrongly concluded that Saddam Hussein's regime in Baghdad might possess WMD, this erroneous reasoning remains central to the decision to invade. By as early as October 11, 2001, President Bush declared that Saddam Hussein was actively developing biological and chemical WMD and seeking to acquire nuclear weapons.[102] Reportedly by July 2002, President Bush had decided that it might require the use of military force to remove Saddam Hussein from power.[103] However, the premise about the existence of WMD was rejected by the Robb-Silberman commission (i.e., the Commission on the Intelligence Capabilities of the United States Regarding Weapons of Mass Destruction), which presented serious criticisms about the reason to invade Iraq.[104]

In any case, policy makers declared that the United States must be "prepared to stop rogue states and their terrorist clients," to "prevent the terrorists and regimes who seek chemical, biological or nuclear weapons" from using WMD against the United States or its allies.[105] In a speech delivered in late August 2002, Vice President Dick Cheney accused Saddam Hussein of seeking to acquire chemical and biological WMD as part of a strategy for dominating the Middle East.[106] In the buildup to war in late 2002 and early 2003, American officials warned that Saddam Hussein must comply with all relevant UN Security Council Resolutions (UNSCRs), which mandated that Iraq must fully reveal and dismantle those programs, under UN supervision.[107] On November 8, 2002, the UN Security Council, acting at U.S. urging, adopted UNSCR 1441, declaring that Iraq had one last opportunity to comply with its existing obligations to disarm or face serious consequences.[108] In a speech on March 17, 2003, President Bush declared that with the unanimous passage of UNSCR 1441, the UN Security Council had found "Iraq in material breach of its obligations [and vowed] serious consequences if Iraq did not fully and immediately disarm."[109]

The invasion was designed "to disarm Iraq, to free its people, and to defend the world from grave danger," as well as to destroy those "selected" military targets whose destruction would "undermine Saddam Hussein's ability to wage war."[110] From the beginning, senior American officials explicitly linked the decision to invade Iraq with American grand strategy during the Bush administration to use military force to attack and destroy regimes that support terrorism, to destroy (for reasons long since discredited) Iraqi WMD, and to encourage the development of democratic governance in the Middle East.

The principal U.S. objectives in Operation Iraqi Freedom were outlined in the top-secret National Security Presidential Directive (NSPD) "Iraq: Goals, Objectives and Strategy," which gave guidance to military commanders to "Free Iraq in order to eliminate Iraqi weapons of mass destruction.... End Iraqi threats to its neighbors.... And liberate the Iraqi people from tyranny, and assist them in creating a society based on moderation, pluralism and democracy."[111]

A principal objective was to democratize Iraq and transform the region. In a speech on February 26, 2003, President Bush emphasized that overthrowing Saddam Hussein would promote democracy and stability in the Middle East.[112] In his March 19th address announcing the U.S. invasion, he said that one objective was to "restore control of that country to its own people"; three days later, he reaffirmed that American policy was partly "to free the Iraqi people."[113] The Bush policy of regime change in Iraq was not new, but dated from 1998 when President Clinton signed a law providing $97 million to opposition forces in Iraq "to remove the regime headed by Saddam Hussein" and "to promote the emergence of a democratic government."[114] In terms of implementation, the fears of a civil war in post-conflict Iraq were noted but not prioritized and given the due weight they deserved.[115]

Another objective was to protect the vast oil fields in the Middle East, principally those in Iraq and Saudi Arabia. American policy makers were determined to preserve the flow of oil from the region, maintain stable oil prices, and prevent Iraq from damaging its oil fields.[116] Some claim that the ulterior motive for the U.S.-led invasion was to secure the oil for the U.S. government and/or corporate interests. Despite this critique, U.S. policy makers did not see the invasion of Iraq as an opportunity to seize Iraq's reserves for the government or as a way of ensuring the profits of American energy companies. The strategic concern was to ensure that oil from the Middle East continued to flow to market so that oil prices would remain stable in the medium to long term. In short, stability of the oil supply rather than control of it was a central imperative in American grand strategy.[117]

Distorting the Second Principle: Shifting from Restraining Sources of Disorder to Eliminating Them through Democratization

In contrast with his first inaugural address in which foreign policy matters were mentioned only briefly, Bush's second inaugural address on January 20, 2005, largely focused on national security and how Washington would conduct its policies in the war on terror now that the wars against Afghanistan and Iraq were several years old.

In addressing the nation from the Capitol on January 20, 2005, Bush detailed the consequences of what had emerged from that "day of fire." He described what he called "our vulnerability ... as whole regions of the world simmer in resentment and tyranny – prone to ideologies that feed hatred and excuse murder – [and warned that] violence will gather, and multiply in destructive power, and cross the most defended borders, and raise a mortal threat." In this address, Bush reaffirmed the outward-looking focus of a nation at war, concluding that "the survival of liberty in our land increasingly depends on the success of liberty in other lands." The defining concept in Bush's grand strategy was that "it is the policy of the United States to seek and support the growth of democratic movements and institutions in every nation and culture with the ultimate goal of ending tyranny in our world."[118]

During his second term, Bush's grand strategy emphasized promoting democracy. His remarks were particularly provocative because many observers interpreted this language as a significant shift in his grand strategy to promoting democracy, which to some appeared as a crusade in American policy whose aim was to win in the fight against terrorism.[119] Bush advisers, nonetheless, maintained that the speech represented "no significant shift in U.S. policy" because the implementation of the Bush Doctrine "reflected the president's deepest convictions about the purposes behind his foreign policy."[120]

2006 U.S. National Security Strategy

Released in March 2006, the second National Security Strategy of the Bush presidency rested on two pillars. The first was "promoting freedom, justice, and human dignity – working to end tyranny, to promote effective democracies, and to extend prosperity through free and fair trade and wise development policies." The second called for dealing with modern "challenges . . . by leading a growing community of democracies."[121] These pillars set the tone for a grand strategy that was strikingly similar to Bush's 2002 National Security Strategy. In defining the intent of the strategy, Bush said that "our national security strategy is idealistic about goals, and realistic about means."[122]

Scholars and policy makers continue to debate President Bush's decision to develop and pursue an aggressive response to the attacks of 9/11, which constituted a historically significant shift in the evolution of American grand strategy.[123] Drawing on the geopolitics of the post–Cold War world of emerging democracies, fragile states, and globalization, 9/11 provided the political impetus for a dramatic shift in the nation's grand strategy. The key concept for understanding Bush's grand strategy is found in the first sentence of the 2006 National Security Strategy of the United States, which begins with the premise that "America is at war," in a struggle against "an aggressive ideology of hatred and murder."[124]

The central feature of Bush's grand strategy called for the United States to confront extremism by going on the offensive to defeat it, while promoting freedom and democracy. Drawing on the language in the 2006 NSS, the "inseparable priorities" in American strategy were "fighting and winning the war on terror and promoting freedom as the alternative to tyranny and despair."

With the nation involved in military interventions in Afghanistan and Iraq, American grand strategy emphasized the desire to build democratic societies. For decades, American grand strategy had promoted democracy and freedom, but bounded by the realities of balancing power during the Cold War. After the Cold War, when the United States had no peer competitor to check its foreign policy ambitions, it could articulate and implement policies whose loftier ideals were not centrally embedded in American foreign policy principles. To succeed, this strategy would require coalitions of like-minded states that were organized to resist extremist groups. However, one criticism of Bush's grand strategy was that Washington's heavy reliance on largely unilateral policies undermined the multilateral tradition that had been so prevalent in American policy since World War II.[125]

Unlike his predecessors, however, Bush paid less attention to the domestic foundations of American grand strategy. The prevailing view in the Bush administration was that protecting the safety and security of the United States trumped other considerations.

When measured by the dramatic increases in U.S. spending on defense, intelligence, law enforcement, and homeland security, concerns about the balance between the foreign and domestic elements of U.S. grand strategy were subordinated to preventing future terror attacks. The worst-case scenario that dominated the thinking of policy makers was that terrorists might gain access to nuclear weapons and use them against the United States.[126] In sharp contrast with earlier shifts in American grand strategy, this transformation initially received strong public support in the aftermath of 9/11.[127]

Bush's Legacy in American Grand Strategy

The domestic focus of the Bush administration was shattered by the terror attacks on 9/11. By October 2001, the United States was using military force to remove the Taliban from power in Afghanistan. By the end of his first term, Bush had responded to an attack, revamped the nation's security strategy, and gone on the offensive in the fight against terrorism in both Afghanistan and Iraq. In his next four years, Bush's grand strategy was interpreted as a continuation of the policies developed during the first term. Despite the polarizing political effects of his policies that will be debated for generations, the Bush administration articulated a grand strategy whose outlines remain largely intact more than a decade later.

In the annals of grand strategy, other than President Roosevelt's shift to a wartime footing after Pearl Harbor, no shift in policy has been as dramatic. In historical terms, Bush redefined American grand strategy for the first time in decades to help the nation deal with an adversary that is committed to conducting terror attacks against civilians. In the 2006 National Security Strategy, Bush declared that the "great ideological conflict" is the "struggle against militant Islamic radicalism . . . of the early years of the 21st century."[128] In effect, Bush defined a grand strategy that marked the transition from an era of relatively benign post–Cold War politics to an era in which American policy was designed to defeat extremism by using the values of freedom and democracy as instruments in war.

How will scholars and policy makers judge President Bush's legacy in grand strategy?[129] His grand strategy will be measured in terms of the ability to prevent further attacks against the United States, and secondarily by its success in destroying extremists and the forces that animate them. The Bush administration's grand strategy, which reflected the decision to organize the United States to defeat this threat, represents a significant and controversial shift in the formulation and implementation of American grand strategy whose legacy remains unclear.

President Barack Obama: Searching for the Right Balance

Barack Obama (2009–) assumed the presidency at a time when the United States was embroiled in two wars – in Afghanistan since 2001 and in Iraq since 2003.[130] He also inherited the worst economic crisis since the Great Depression. Despite serious foreign policy issues, including winding down American commitments in Afghanistan and Iraq, the enduring debate over Iran's nuclear program, geopolitical struggles with Russia and China, and the European debt crisis, the most pressing problems facing the Obama administration have been the recession whose high unemployment and weak recovery affect the nation's domestic foundations of power. Consequently, his first priority in grand strategy was to rebuild the domestic foundations of American power.[131]

In his inaugural address on January 20, 2009, President Obama framed his approach to grand strategy largely in terms of dealing with the nation's domestic economic problems. As he warned in that speech, "The state of our economy calls for action, bold and swift, and we will act – not only to create new jobs, but to lay a new foundation for growth."[132] He also warned that "our economy is badly weakened." Later in his inaugural address, Obama invoked the principles of American policy: "Our power grows through its prudent use; our security emanates from the justness of our cause, the force of our example, the tempering qualities of humility and restraint." To put these principles into practice, President Obama pledged that "we can meet those new threats that demand even greater effort – even greater cooperation and understanding between nations."[133]

The Obama administration's 2010 National Security Strategy echoed these views on the primacy of domestic economic issues over foreign policy. For President Obama, "at the center of our efforts is a commitment to renew our economy, which serves as the wellspring of American power." Beyond his discussion of the central role of economic factors in American power, Obama focused on the fact that "the American people are now emerging from the most devastating recession that we have faced since the Great Depression."[134]

Despite the powerful pull of domestic economic matters, the Obama administration was involved from the start in several critical foreign policy initiatives that helped shape and define his grand strategy. Beginning in February 2009, the Obama administration began a several-months-long review of policy toward Afghanistan and then considered whether to withdraw U.S. forces from Iraq. One issue that continues to dominate the Obama administration's foreign policy is how to deal with Iran's nuclear program. In perhaps its greatest accomplishment in the conduct of its global war on terror, the administration launched a raid in Abbottabad, Pakistan, on May 1, 2011, that killed Osama Bin Laden, the head of Al-Qaeda.

When President Obama entered office, the American public was concerned with the threat of terrorist attacks. But there were signs of a war fatigue as public support for intervention in Afghanistan declined. In public opinion polling data published in March 2012, the public showed signs of war weariness and skepticism toward military intervention: 53 percent favored the immediate withdrawal of American troops from Afghanistan, and 67 percent favored ending the American combat role by 2013.[135] With this shift in public opinion, the American public was returning to its principles and eschewing Bush's more active, interventionist role.

The Obama administration's grand strategy shifted to a policy of retrenchment, a priority in the first principle, based on "scaling back foreign commitments or military capabilities, or both."[136] Early signs that President Obama had broadly redefined American grand strategy was outlined in his December 1, 2009, West Point speech. He defined the principles that would govern U.S. policy toward Afghanistan. As the president declared, he refused "to set goals that go beyond our responsibility, our means, or our interests," all of which are direct references to the domestic side of grand strategy. In adhering to this policy, as Obama continued, "That's why our troop commitment in Afghanistan cannot be open-ended – because the nation that I'm most interested in building is our own."[137] Ultimately, the administration conducted a short-term surge in forces and planned to withdraw U.S. forces by 2016.[138]

In effect, President Obama's policies were guided by overlapping priorities, which suggests that "the Obama administration has actually had not just one grand strategy so far but two." The first strategy, known as "multilateral retrenchment," was designed "to curtail the United States' overseas commitments, restore its standing in the world, and shift burdens onto global partners." Some observers argued that this strategy has "delivered underwhelming policy results," but the parallel grand strategy was designed for "counterpunching."[139] Its principle of engaging selectively in foreign policy problems was designed to signal that "the Obama administration has been willing to assert its influence and ideas across the globe when challenged by other countries, reassuring allies, and signaling resolve to rivals." In practice, this element of the Obama grand strategy has "performed better but has been poorly articulated," though some observers have used highly critical language to characterize the strategy as "leading from behind."[140]

One official in the Obama administration, when describing the prevailing principles governing American grand strategy, used the following language: "Wind down these two wars, reestablish American standing and leadership in the world, and focus on a broader set of priorities, from Asia and the global economy to a nuclear-nonproliferation regime."[141] With the wars in Iraq and Afghanistan slowly winding down, the challenge for the Obama administration was to withdraw U.S. forces from these conflicts without destabilizing either state, calling into question the willingness of the United States to intervene, or strengthening fears that the United States is diminishing its leadership role in the world.

In mid-2012, after a dramatic spike in violence in Iraq and Afghanistan with U.S. deaths in Afghanistan reaching two thousand,[142] questions about whether American influence is declining is a central theme in debates about the Obama administration's grand strategy. Observers wonder whether the United States has the political will and economic desire to maintain a globally engaged foreign policy as the nation struggles with a recession and slow recovery.[143] The success of Obama's grand strategy hinges in large measure on what happens in Afghanistan and Iraq, particularly whether these societies achieve some degree of stability or descend into sectarian violence and renewed civil war. The Obama administration's grand strategy also will be judged by whether Iran acquires nuclear weapons and the state of currently hostile relations with Russia, China, Egypt, and Syria. A central challenge is President Obama's ability to retrench without undermining the confidence of U.S. allies or encouraging adversaries to believe that the United States is unwilling to exercise its power.

Iraq and Afghanistan

When Barack Obama campaigned in 2007 and 2008, he emphasized that the war in Iraq was a considerable source of distraction for the United States. His argument was that Iraq diverted Washington from focusing sufficient political attention and economic resources on the central mission, which is defeating Al-Qaeda in Afghanistan. His central argument was that Afghanistan was the origin of the 9/11 attacks that were planned and conducted by Al-Qaeda. This organization was not destroyed by the invasion in 2001, but simply moved its headquarters to neighboring Pakistan, from which it planned and conducted attacks, albeit on a greatly reduced scale since 9/11.[144] It was Pakistan, after all, where Osama bin Laden lived for the last several years until U.S. forces killed him on May 1, 2011.

During the 2008 campaign, as Obama said, "It is unacceptable that almost seven years after nearly 3,000 Americans were killed on our soil, the terrorists who attacked us on 9/11 are still at large." The central problem for the Obama administration is that "the Taliban controls parts of Afghanistan [while] Al Qaeda has an expanding base in Pakistan that is probably no farther from their old Afghan sanctuary than a train ride from Washington to Philadelphia."[145] This condition called into question for the Obama administration the precept of Bush's grand strategy. Although it privileged the second principle over the other two, Obama's grand strategy arguably sought to right the balance.

The danger for American grand strategy was that "this war distracts us from every threat that we face and [from] so many opportunities we could seize." In Obama's view, the war in Iraq "diminishes our security, our standing in the world, our military, our economy, and the resources that we need to confront the challenges of the 21st century." The central principle for the Obama administration was to articulate a policy that prevented "our single-minded and open-ended focus on Iraq [from undermining] a sound strategy for keeping America safe."[146] This debate showed awareness that the second principle had taken too much prominence because it contributed to an imbalance in the implementation of American grand strategy.

President Obama's approach as he entered office was to place greater emphasis in American grand strategy on Afghanistan, the domestic economy, and correspondingly less attention on Iraq. The Obama administration's plan was to increase troops and funding for the war in Afghanistan, while simultaneously drawing down forces and reducing the overall U.S. commitment to Iraq.[147] In fact, Obama's strategy was made possible by the overwhelming success of the 2007 Iraq Surge. With its increased U.S. military presence and resources, the United States engaged in a more precipitous withdrawal of U.S. forces after it stabilized Iraq and restrained the insurgency. Although President Bush signed the Status of Forces Agreement in November 2008, which declared that "all the United States Forces shall withdraw from all Iraqi territory no later than December 31, 2011,"[148] no subsequent status of forces agreement was signed between the United States and Iraq.

Third Principle Restored: Working with Local Partners in Iraq and European Allies in Libya

As a result of this dramatic drawdown and withdrawal of U.S. forces from Iraq, President Obama gained greater flexibility for increasing the number of troops in Afghanistan. After a lengthy review that was outlined in his December 2009 speech at West Point, President Obama declared that he would send an additional 30,000 troops to Afghanistan.[149] In outlining his reasoning for eventually withdrawing U.S. forces from Afghanistan, President Obama declared that the American commitment would not be open-ended. Therefore, the United States would begin to withdraw its forces "after 18 months," arguing that "the absence of a time frame for transition would deny us any sense of urgency in working with the Afghan government."[150]

Consistent with the third principle of relying on local partners, President Obama declared that his policy was designed to make it "clear that Afghans will have to take responsibility for their security, and that America has no interest in fighting an endless war in Afghanistan."[151] This principle is critical to understanding President Obama's grand strategy. It has been the subject of considerable debate precisely because it focuses on whether the United States should reduce its role in international politics as part of a deliberate strategy of disengagement in comparison with American involvement since 9/11.

During the 2008 campaign and after his inauguration, President Obama was highly critical of President Bush's emphasis on unilateralism. In a move that sought to shift the security burden from the United States toward other states and improve the tenor in international politics, President Obama emphasized the role of multilateral diplomatic initiatives in dealing with Iran and North Korea, pursued a policy of "reset" in relations with Russia, revived American commitments to international institutions, and relied on diplomacy rather than coercion to resolve disputes in the political upheavals in Libya and Syria.[152] A prominent feature of President Obama's grand strategy is his emphasis on multilateralism, or what some observers call "leading from behind." This phrase was first used in an essay published in the *New Yorker* on May 2, 2011, in which an adviser "described the President's actions in Libya as 'leading from behind.'" This approach to American leadership is based on two principles: "the relative power of the U.S. is declining, as rivals like China rise," and "the U.S. is reviled in many parts of the world."[153]

The Libya intervention is a classic example of Obama's increased emphasis on multilateralism.[154] Although many of Obama's political opponents criticized the "leading from behind" strategy, it helped produce a UN resolution in support of the no-fly zone and bombing campaign. It was through such multilateral efforts that President Obama differentiated himself from President Bush. Obama employed a strategy of urging other nations to share a greater share of the responsibility for maintaining international security. However, considerable credit goes to the leaders of France and Italy, who aggressively pushed the strategy of using military force against the government of Libya, often, it seemed, against the wishes of the Obama administration. Secretary of State Hillary Clinton affirmed the decision of the Obama administration to refrain from taking a leading role in Libya when she said, during the buildup to the Libya intervention, "If you really parse all the messages that were being sent over the last several weeks on Libya, they were all over the place: 'Somebody needs to do something, but the United States shouldn't do it unilaterally.'"[155]

Relying on a combination of diplomacy and waiting, the administration worked with France and Italy to persuade the Arab League to take the leading role in calling for a UN resolution. In a departure from Bush policies, Obama, instead of unilaterally pushing forward, encouraged others to take the lead in diplomacy. As Secretary Clinton argued in an interview, we will "see whether the Security Council will support *the Arab League*. Not support the *United States*! Support the *Arab League*."[156] According to one senior administration official, "the toppling of Muammar al-Qaddafi was the prime example of the success of their more focused, multilateral approach to the use of force." Noting that this intervention came at "a cost of zero American lives and $1 billion in U.S. funding, the Libya intervention removed an autocrat from power in five months" and saved hundreds of thousands of lives. By contrast, and mindful of the obvious disparities between Libya and Iraq, one observer noted that "the occupation of Iraq claimed 4,484 American lives, cost at least $700 billion, and lasted nearly nine years."[157]

The Obama administration's strategy was expressed by Ben Rhodes, who is the deputy national security advisor for strategic communications: "The light U.S. footprint had benefits beyond less U.S. lives and resources." The benefit flowed from the Obama administration's renewed emphasis on multilateralism in American grand strategy. According to Rhodes, "We believe the Libyan revolution is viewed as more legitimate." Furthermore, "The U.S. is more welcome. And there is less potential for an insurgency because there aren't foreign forces present."[158] This intervention succeeded essentially because European states combined their military capabilities with America's, especially its airpower.[159] Among criticisms of the Obama administration's Libya policy, it revealed indecisiveness in American policy as European states pushed for intervention.[160]

Reemergence of the Second Principle: Drones and Special Operations Forces

The Obama administration, while greatly increasing the emphasis on multilateralism in American grand strategy, continues to rely on unilateral action, when necessary, in the fight against Al-Qaeda. In Obama's first term, the administration relied heavily on using Special Operations Forces (SOF) and unmanned aerial vehicles (UAVs) to kill members of Al-Qaeda's leadership. During the presidential debates, Obama signaled his determination to hunt down Al-Qaeda, in particular Osama bin Laden, regardless of where extremists are located. His decision to pursue Al-Qaeda across sovereign borders highlighted his policy of using Special Operations Forces more frequently than did his predecessor.

As background, then-candidate Obama argued in 2008 that "if Pakistan is unable or unwilling to hunt down bin Laden and take him out, then we should."[161] This statement became a reality when on May 1, 2011, President Obama ordered a special operations force (SOF) mission – which consisted of the Naval Special Warfare Development Group (DEVGRU), better known as SEAL Team 6, and the Army's 160th Special Operations Aviation Regiment – to eliminate Osama bin Laden in Abbottabad, Pakistan.[162]

This policy follows from the second principle of exercising American leadership to restrain the sources of disorder. Obama does not claim the objective of defeating tyranny and terrorism, because his policy is more modest and gradualist. The combined policies of drawing down U.S. forces in Iraq, setting a timetable for U.S. withdrawal from Afghanistan, and continuing to utilize SOF and drones to target extremists all permit the Obama administration to develop and implement a more focused counterterrorism policy. In April 2012, the United States announced that it had reached an agreement with Afghanistan that will preserve U.S. aid for Afghanistan until at least 2024.[163]

The Obama administration's grand strategy has relied extensively on using drone strikes to kill as many of the extremists as possible, despite the friction this policy causes with Pakistan's government.[164] It has increased the use of drones in the U.S. fight against extremism and "dramatically expanded the executive branch's ability to wage high-tech clandestine war." In what may come as a surprise to many observers, "Obama has embraced the CIA, expanded its powers, and approved more targeted killings than any modern president." In terms of strikes against extremists during the past three years, the Obama administration conducted "at least 329 covert drone strikes [which is] more than five times the 44 approved under George W. Bush." In the first year of the Obama administration, the number of drone strikes more than doubled from 23 in 2008 to 53 in 2009, and the strikes more than doubled again – to 118 – in 2010.[165] The primary focus of drone strikes has been in the Federally Administered Tribal Areas (FATA) in Pakistan, but strikes have occurred in Yemen against Al-Qaeda in the Arabian Peninsula (AQAP).

Although President Obama promised "to make counterterrorism operations more transparent and rein in executive power," his policies have moved in the opposite direction, "maintaining secrecy and expanding presidential authority."[166] In mid-2013, reports suggest that the pace of drone strikes had declined during the previous year, while still remaining quite high relative to the Bush administration.

Pivot to the Pacific Rim

A critical theme in the evolution of the Obama administration's grand strategy has been the shift in American policy toward the Asia-Pacific region. While scaling down troop commitments in the Middle East and Central Asia, senior administration officials outlined a "pivot" to the Asia-Pacific region as critically important to American interests.[167] To implement this strategy, President Obama said he would not allow military spending cuts to undermine the emerging "pivot" to Asia. His reasoning is that the United States needs to increase its political, military, and economic role in the Pacific region. Therefore, Obama affirmed in January 2012 that since the United States is committed to "strengthening our presence in the Asia Pacific region," cuts in government spending "will not come at the expense of that critical region."[168] In addition to deploying 2,500 Marines in northern Australia,[169] the Obama administration declared that it views the Asia-Pacific region as a critical area in which the United States should have a strong naval presence.[170]

In the words of Secretary of State Hillary Clinton, "As those wars wind down, we will need to accelerate efforts to pivot to new global realities." It was Clinton's belief that the United States should not "pull back from the world," but must "press forward and renew our leadership." Building on the argument that the United States faces serious economic problems and limited national resources, Washington's challenge in the conduct of grand strategy is to invest "wisely [in areas that] will yield the biggest returns, which is why the Asia-Pacific represents such a real 21st-century opportunity for us."[171] The shift to Asia-Pacific is central to maintaining the proper balance in grand strategy between domestic economic strength and prosperity on the one hand, and the national security and foreign policy interests of the United States on the other.[172]

The motivation for the pivot toward the Pacific stems largely from China's rise, politically, economically, and militarily, and its emergence as a regional rival of the United States. The policy review for this shift began in the fall of 2010, when, according to a March 2012 *Congressional Research Service* report, "the Obama Administration issued a series of announcements indicating that the United States would be expanding and intensifying its already significant role in the Asia-Pacific." The Obama administration's goal is to preserve U.S. power and influence in the region and to develop and shape "Asia-Pacific's norms and rules." Its related purpose, which observers call a "pivot" or "rebalancing" toward the Asia-Pacific region "is to deepen U.S. credibility in the region at a time of fiscal constraint."[173]

Obama's Legacy in American Grand Strategy: To Be Determined

At this writing, President Obama is in the sixth year of his presidency, and many elements of his grand strategy continue to unfold. Although the results remain open to debate and will be the subject of study for future generations, some early conclusions about his administration's grand strategy are possible.

President Obama's decision to move toward less American involvement in global affairs – placing greater emphasis on involvement through multilateralism and the concept of "leading from behind" – constitutes a significant return to or a rebalancing among the principles of American grand strategy.[174] Its origins are found in the deep recession, which began in late 2007 and accelerated dramatically with the market collapse in September 2008. This economic downturn continues to influence both the American and global economies. It also contributes to weariness in the United States with the burdens of global leadership, particularly in an age of protracted overseas interventions.[175] As the Obama administration builds a grand strategy that provides a more balanced approach to using American power, a cardinal principle is its desire to further emphasize the third principle of relying on allies and partners. In effect, the shift in American grand strategy during the Obama administration emphasizes building a "just and sustainable international order."

A prominent feature of Obama's grand strategy has been its demand that the United States develop a less unilateral, and hence more multilateral, approach to managing problems in foreign policy.[176] In contrast with the realignment of U.S. grand strategy during the Bush administration toward a wartime footing, the central theme in President Obama's grand strategy revolves around his strong commitment to renewing American leadership in the world in part by seeking to "forge [greater] international cooperation." The Obama administration has stressed that American grand strategy must rest on policies of "engagement," which are designed to reaffirm "our commitment to an international order based upon rights and responsibilities."[177]

President Obama's grand strategy sought to continue the fight against extremism in Afghanistan and Iraq, but his policies also demonstrated that a priority in American policy was gradually disengaging from these wars. A principle in Obama's grand strategy is the need for the nation to refocus its policies on reinvigorating the economy. However, the United States under President Obama has continued to emphasize building coalitions of states that work together with American leadership to resist extremism.

In direct contrast to the Bush administration, the Obama administration places much greater emphasis on rebuilding the domestic foundations of grand strategy. In his 2010 National Security Strategy, President Obama declared that the United States has "not adequately advanced priorities like education, energy, science and technology, and health care – all of which are essential to U.S. competitiveness, long-term prosperity, and strength."[178] In practice, the prevailing view in the Obama administration is that the United States previously failed to maintain the delicate balance between ends and means in U.S. grand strategy – in large measure because of the Bush administration's focus on defeating extremism.

A principle in Obama's grand strategy, as expressed in his 2010 National Security Strategy, was to shift American foreign policy from simply defeating extremists to doing so while building more lasting foundations of peace and security. In one particular area, notably in relations with Russia, the hallmark of the Obama administration's policy was defined by the "reset." Its purpose, while subject to difficulties, was "to deepen our cooperation with other 21st century centers of influence – including China, India, and Russia – on the basis of mutual interests and mutual respect."[179]

In the end, President Obama's legacy in grand strategy will be determined by whether his efforts to rebalance American foreign policy on a more collaborative and multilateral basis are successful. The outcome of relations with Russia and China and Iran's efforts to acquire nuclear weapons will be the standard against which observers will judge the Obama administration's grand strategy. At this writing, it is too soon to tell whether

President Obama's grand strategy will successfully balance between the three principles. To be fair, one risk is that the desire to reemphasize the domestic foundations of American power could be interpreted by some as an American desire to disengage from the burdens of global affairs. For example, we see reports about the dangers of America's withdrawal from Iraq and Afghanistan, with suggestions that the grand strategy of the Obama administration in the cases of Russia, Iran, and Syria is showing signs of serious difficulties.[180] There are warnings from former secretary of state Hillary Clinton about the risks of an American disengagement.[181] Nevertheless, the shift in American grand strategy will take time to unfold, and this will give scholars and policy makers opportunities to evaluate it.

Conclusions about American Grand Strategy in the Post–Cold War World

Each post–Cold War presidential administration, from George H. W. Bush to Barack Obama, attempted to articulate and implement a new grand strategy to replace containment to better realign American policy with the world they confronted. Although the contours of American grand strategy remain unclear, an analysis of grand strategy during this period reveals several important themes among the three principles in American foreign policy that merit further consideration.

George H. W. Bush came the closest to setting the right balance between the three principles, especially in terms of implementation. The central accomplishment of the George H. W. Bush administration was bringing the Cold War to a peaceful conclusion. Understanding that the Soviet collapse would produce a radical shift in the balance of power, Bush's challenge was to realign American foreign policy to fit a world in which the United States did not have a strategic competitor. Importantly, he sought to build a world that rests on economic prosperity at home and abroad. A defining principle of Bush's grand strategy was to build an international order, or a "new world order," that relied on coalitions to enforce the principles articulated by the United Nations Charter.

The grand strategy of the Bush administration also called for building coalitions of like-minded states to resist actions that contravened the principles in the UN Charter, as seen in the case of the 1991 Persian Gulf War. At other times, however, the Bush administration acted unilaterally, as seen in the 1989 invasion of Panama. In reality, the Bush administration articulated a grand strategy that provided considerable coherence to American foreign policy during a time when the nation faced enormous strategic shifts overseas. Perhaps the most important contribution of the Bush administration's grand strategy was to smooth the transition from the post–Cold War era to a more peaceful and less confrontational era, while avoiding an outbreak of violence in Europe as the Soviet empire collapsed.

Along with his many foreign policy achievements, Bush also made politically difficult and ultimately dangerous choices to end the Reagan-era deficits and position the U.S. government to achieve a budget surplus under Clinton. To do this, he raised taxes, which cost him a second term, but it was a courageous decision that helped rebuild the domestic foundations of American power and arguably laid the fiscal groundwork for economic growth and prosperity in the 1990s.

President Clinton sought to give American priorities and policies a more pronounced domestic focus. Clinton's grand strategy built an order in which multilateral institutions exerted a greater influence on American policy, largely by balancing national security interests with rejuvenating the country's economic power and reorienting its political responsibilities. He strove to build an order that diminished the role of the superpowers, while working more closely with other states and institutions. Thus, the Clinton administration developed policies based on greater cooperation among allies rather than relying solely upon U.S. power and influence to manage problems. Such policies redefined American grand strategy at a time when the nation put much greater emphasis on cooperation and less on unilateral action and strength.

Although Clinton's domestic approach successfully emphasized the economic foundations of American power, it paid too little attention to the second principle, allowing sources of disorder, especially international terrorism, to become more powerful. Clinton entered office without a grand strategy and left with the Clinton Doctrine, which for many observers represents a mix of successes and failures. When Al-Qaeda attacked on 9/11, the George W. Bush administration overcorrected as it elevated the second principle in grand strategy over all other considerations.

President George W. Bush's grand strategy of aggressively pursuing extremists after the 9/11 attacks represented a dramatic shift in American foreign policy.[182] Bush's grand strategy initially placed considerable focus on domestic programs, including education and crime, but his domestic focus was upended by the events of 9/11. This attack provided the impetus for a shift in American grand strategy at a scale unseen since President Roosevelt's declaration of war in 1941. Yet a crucial difference between FDR and Bush is that Bush defined the nation's grand strategy and the means without significant input from allies and partners. When he declared war on the "ideology of hatred and murder" – not on a state and its leaders as did FDR and the Allies – it demonstrated a commitment to rely on an offensive strategy to defeat extremism, while drawing on the language of promoting freedom and democracy.[183] In promoting those values, American grand strategy sought to build democracies in Afghanistan and Iraq. In effect, U.S. policy increasingly aligned with movements designed to support democracy and self-determination, as seen with the Arab Spring movements in Tunisia, Egypt, and Libya.[184]

Unlike its predecessors, the Bush administration after 9/11 placed less emphasis on the first principle of building the domestic foundations of American power. Bush feared above all a nuclear terrorist attack against the United States.[185] Despite such rational fears, the focus on combating terrorism demonstrated how a nation can see its policies shift spasmodically from one priority to the next, from one threat to the next, and from long-term thinking to policies driven by fear and short-term thinking. Bush's strategy prevented another major terrorist attack on American soil during his administration and alienated allies and partners in the international community. The shift in grand strategy ushered in by Bush after 9/11 focused to the exclusion of other principles on destroying, not restraining, extremists and preventing attacks against the United States.

It is still too early to write definitively about the legacy of President Obama's grand strategy; his administration has begun a rebalancing of American foreign policy whose effects are yet to be judged. A relevant observation, however, is that President Obama's decision to reduce overt American leadership on issues and to increase the role of multilateralism – what some call the strategy of retrenchment or "leading from behind" – signals a dramatic shift in American grand strategy.[186]

The origins of Obama's grand strategy reside in the economic collapse that occurred with the market crash in September 2008 as well as the growing unpopularity of the wars in Iraq and Afghanistan during the 2008 presidential campaign. In Obama's view, the American strategy rests on using "our military might, economic competitiveness, moral leadership, global engagement, and efforts to shape an international system that serves the mutual interests of nations and peoples."[187] A crucial theme in his grand strategy is to develop a less unilateral and activist role for the United States, while building an international order in which the United States works with allies and partners. His decision to follow the lead of France and an international coalition during the Libyan intervention demonstrated the nature of this new role.[188] For Obama, one imperative in U.S. grand strategy is to develop a more shared approach between the United States and its allies, so that American policies are consistent with building collaboratively a "just and sustainable international order."[189]

Despite the dramatic change in tone, in policy and practice the Obama administration's emphasis on defeating extremism and promoting freedom and democracy aligns with major principles in the grand strategies of prior administrations. However, in order for the United States to be a positive force in global affairs, the Obama administration has emphasized that the nation's grand strategy must rest on policies of "engagement," which demonstrate "our commitment to an international order based upon rights and responsibilities."[190]

When viewed broadly, the period of American history following the Cold War has failed to produce what American society understands to be a coherent, long-term grand strategy. Nevertheless, as each administration has put its distinctive imprimatur on the nation's grand strategy, this evolution in grand strategy raises several major points of note. First, in the absence of a peer competitor, American grand strategy has proven episodic in nature. As policy makers have struggled with establishing a coherent long-term approach that expresses succinctly what the United States wants to accomplish in foreign policy.

Second, the grand strategy of the United States since the end of the Cold War has generally been reactive as new threats emerged. With the rise of extremism after 9/11, the United States pivoted toward a grand strategy that focused on defeating non-state actors and gradually to dealing with the emergence of China as a potential competitor. The reactive nature of American grand strategy relates to the nature of democracies, which may be better at responding to threats than anticipating them.[191] This also raises the eternal issue of how well a democracy organizes its grand strategy in the absence of a clear threat.

Third, the domestic foundations of American power that encompass the nation's economic power have increasingly gained attention as external challenges seem to be less significant. Foreign policy observers refer to the need to rebuild the nation's economic foundations of power as the Obama administration winds down the wars in Afghanistan and Iraq.[192] On the other hand, the nuclear challenge posed by Iran and the geopolitical resurgence of Russia raise questions about whether the world remains benign.

Fourth, the emerging geopolitical landscape – which is dominated by great powers, some of which have authoritarian impulses – is altering how American society views, articulates, and implements its grand strategy.[193] Each of these arguments provides a piece of the puzzle as to why the United States has struggled with articulating a grand strategy in the wake of the Cold War that resonates with the American people and our allies. We examine these issues in the final chapter.

Part III

The shifts in American foreign policy across four presidential administrations since the late 1980s illustrate dramatic changes in the nature and conduct of the nation's grand strategy. As discussed in Chapter 10, the George H. W. Bush administration emphasized such concepts as "status quo plus," "Beyond Containment," and "Post Containment" – among others – to describe the nature of American grand strategy at the end of the Cold War and hoped for "a new era of international stability."[194] The Clinton administration focused on political engagement and enlargement of the number of democratic, free-market states – essentially abandoning efforts to articulate a successor grand strategy.[195] After 9/11, the George W. Bush administration embraced policies of unilateralism and preemption to prevent terrorist attacks.[196] Most recently, the Obama administration embraced a policy of diminished engagement, based in part on a rejection of many of the principles that animated the Bush administration's foreign policy.[197] In effect, during the span of two decades, American foreign policy has swung between the extremes of a defense of the status quo and unilateral revision of the system. If we ask why there have been such dramatic shifts in policy, one answer is the failure to develop a new national strategy for relating fundamental changes in the international system to a grand strategy for governing the conduct of American foreign policy. We conclude this study with an inquiry into the subject of how to strike a prudent balance among the three principles that govern American grand strategy.

PART III

Conclusion

11 The Making of Future American Grand Strategy

The purpose of this book is to provide a framework that helps guide scholars and policy makers as they articulate and implement a grand strategy. A coherent grand strategy that plays a fundamental role in guiding the state's foreign and domestic policies is key in both times of peace and war because only it provides the broad sense of direction, clarity, and vision that policy makers operating at the highest levels of government need as they make difficult and consequential decisions. Fundamentally, grand strategy describes a broad consensus on the state's goals and the means by which to put them into practice.

This book has explored analytically the evolution of grand strategy and used a number of historical case studies to understand the practice of grand strategy. In so doing, it has examined grand strategies pursued by various states and empires, some of which have been highly successful, and others less so. Whereas many studies of grand strategy have a discrete historical focus, this book also examines grand strategy in analytic terms by using a breadth of case studies. By covering the evolving nature of grand strategy from ancient Greece and China and throughout American history to the present administration, this study deliberately seeks to examine the crucial patterns and themes that have shaped the historical evolution and implementation of grand strategy.

To this end, Part I of this book examined analytically the evolution of the *concept* of grand strategy. It described grand strategy as a concept in theory and practice as states, ancient and modern, conducted their foreign policy. It defined grand strategy as the state's highest, overarching strategy that considers the long-term consequences of using all instruments of national power, including its military, economic, diplomatic, and informational capabilities. When scholars describe a "hierarchy of strategies" – which in ascending order evolve from tactics, operations, and military strategy to, ultimately, grand strategy – what emerges is the observation that grand strategy operates at the broadest and most conclusive level for the state.[1] Definitional precision is essential, because, for example, when the state conducts policies, including when it uses military force, its ability to succeed depends in part on whether those policies link directly to and are consistent with the state's overarching grand strategy. In all cases, grand strategy should govern all the decisions that operate at the lower levels of strategy, and it should likewise be the case that the lower levels never determine or directly influence the state's grand strategy.

Thus, grand strategy provides guidance to the affairs of the state in the broadest conceptual sense. In the hierarchy of interests and principles that guide a nation's overall approach to foreign policy, grand strategy provides the central organizing framework or consensus that guides how policy makers articulate and implement their policies. It is precisely because grand strategy, when properly defined and practiced, exerts the greatest influence on foreign policy that it deserves considerable attention and study. Yet policy makers also find that it is difficult to articulate and implement grand strategy effectively, for reasons that are discussed in more detail in this chapter.

Fundamental Attributes of Grand Strategy

The first and perhaps most challenging attribute relates to the confusion that surrounds *defining* the term *grand strategy* clearly. Whereas earlier thought about grand strategy centered on military strategy and how to handle serious if not existential threats to the polity, the current problem with grand strategy runs much deeper. At present, we need to define grand strategy in ways that help policy makers more effectively incorporate domestic economic priorities along with diplomatic and military considerations into the nation's broader strategy.

As mentioned at the beginning of this book, one reason for the failure to deal properly with grand strategy relates directly to debates about the relationship between strategy, grand strategy, and foreign policy – and the failure to properly distinguish among these concepts. Whereas foreign policy tells us what politics to pursue and strategy tells us how to do so, grand strategy deals with the broader questions of *why* the state pursues particular policies. Essentially, the unalloyed purpose of grand strategy is, first and foremost, to define for policy makers the goals that they want the state to achieve and its role in the international system. In this sense, grand strategy provides a framework for outlining what kind of world the state seeks to build.

The second attribute of grand strategy is that it should encompass all dimensions of policy and doctrine, including the domains of operations and tactics. In every sense of the word, *grand strategy* implies an integrated and inclusive approach to the policies that the state pursues in order to achieve its desired ends. Less-than-successful grand strategies often fail precisely because they do not base the nation's policies on a coherent and agreed-upon set of the nation's foreign and domestic policy goals. Put another way, the success of a grand strategy derives from its ability to completely integrate the military and nonmilitary elements of the state's policies in a coherent, consistent, and effective manner.

The third attribute examined in this book is that articulating and implementing grand strategy is a never-ending process. Formulating grand strategy should not begin when a crisis grips the state or end during periods of relative peace and calm. Policy makers and scholars should be constantly reassessing the strategy, its relevance, and utility as it shapes and is reshaped by domestic and international influences. The conduct of grand strategy is as relevant to the conduct of policy in peacetime as it is during periods of war. It is a failure for the state if discussions about grand strategy occur only after the nation finds itself facing an imminent risk or crisis. If policy makers ignore grand strategy until the moment of a crisis, which unfortunately is a recurring pattern for democracies, the nation will experience unnecessary risks, confusion among allies and adversaries, and polarizing domestic debates.[2] One premise in this book is that although grand strategy often evolves in response to significant, even if not necessarily existential, threats, it should not disappear from the public debate simply because the state does not face an obvious enemy or adversary. On the contrary, grand strategy should always be foremost in the minds of policy makers as they strive to ensure that the state's policies align with its overall strategy.

The fourth attribute is that grand strategy should guide the state as it marshals all of its resources – human, political, economic, technological, and military, among others – to defend and promote its long-term interests. Often ignored or misused, this attribute has been a prominent feature in the study of grand strategy as far back as the writings of Thucydides, then Machiavelli, and more recently as the United States mobilized itself to fight World Wars I and II and later the Cold War. This attribute first emerged prominently in the strategies pursued by the antagonists during the Peloponnesian Wars, to the struggles among Italian city-states during the Renaissance, and to the wars of the Napoleonic age when states learned how to mobilize their entire society for the conduct of foreign policy, including war. By the late nineteenth and early twentieth centuries, the challenge for grand strategy was how to mobilize society for the conduct of foreign policy by marshaling all of its resources but without bankrupting the state.

The fifth defining attribute is the concept of balancing ends and means in grand strategy. From Thucydides's writings, to the ideas articulated by so many of the classic theorists, to the rise and decline of the Ottoman and Soviet Empires, to the economic resources that the United States devotes to foreign policy, no issue has played a more prominent role in the articulation, implementation, and eventual success (or failure) of grand strategy than the ability to balance means and ends. This classic means-ends balance is of fundamental prominence as policy makers struggle with how to articulate and implement the state's grand strategy in the face of perpetually evolving economic and political constraints. This challenge presents a lesson in the perils of overreach, which is all-too-common when states miscalculate what level of resources and public support their grand strategy calls for.[3] As first discussed in Chapter 3 and subsequently throughout the book, the relationship between means and ends is an intellectual centerpiece of grand strategy.[4]

The sixth attribute relates to the idea that an effective grand strategy must reflect a fundamental political, philosophical, and ideological unity among the state's goals and policies. Since its purpose is to defend and promote the state's interests, the central function of grand strategy is to ensure that the means by which those objectives are pursued closely align with the state's national character and political tradition and culture. This critical element has been revisited time and again throughout the development of grand strategy. Notably, this attribute was evident during the American Civil War when President Lincoln was reluctant to engage in total war because he feared it would lead to the destruction of the country that he so desperately sought to protect. In modern times, various U.S. presidential administrations have struggled with how to develop the grand strategy of containment during the Cold War, the credibility of which derived in part from the threat to use nuclear weapons without having to destroy the nation and civilization itself.

Part I also demonstrated the extent to which grand strategy has evolved through different historical eras, notably the modern, the revolutionary, and the nuclear. Grand strategy in each era was the product of the central role played by nation-states, the existence of opposing political ideologies, and the military technologies available. In a study of grand strategy that is conducted across millennia, an inquiry that examines different societies, regions, political ideologies, and systems will reveal distinct patterns and principles, all of which offer important and relevant principles to contemporary scholars and policy makers.

These attributes, of course, emerged in the early chapters of this study as it examined the influences from ancient to modern times that shaped the evolution of grand strategy. In the ancient era of grand strategy, such ancient strategists as Sun Tzu and Thucydides, who made significant contributions to thinking about the conduct of war and diplomacy, provide early glimpses of intentional and systematic efforts to articulate grand strategy as an instrument for balancing the state's aspirations with its means and ends. We should note, however, that many of these ideas and principles were largely, if not entirely, derived from the study of military strategy. Although we can extrapolate many lessons from the wisdom of Thucydides and Sun Tzu, their emphasis on strategy as a product of the nature and conduct of war clearly only scratches the surface of grand strategy.

The nonmilitary dimensions of grand strategy emerged in the modern era, beginning with the Renaissance and later with the Enlightenment. In the wake of Machiavelli's insights, political philosophers rapidly developed ideas that contributed to the formation of grand strategy as a distinct and separate field, which exists in conjunction with the disciplines of philosophy, military strategy, economics, and social science. A number of seminal thinkers brought about a renewed focus on using a coordinated political, military, and economic strategy to enhance and preserve the state's interests. Clausewitz significantly advanced the state of the art with his study of strategy, because his ideas expanded its definition to establish, along with contributions by many other thinkers, the foundations of what we now know as grand strategy. The role of political objectives in military strategy was the product of his famous maxim "War is a continuation of policy by other means." These developments, when combined with later contributions on the economic foundations of strategy that derive from the deliberations of Adam Smith and Alexander Hamilton, defined the modern era of grand strategy. Together, these ideas help develop an integrated military, political, and economic approach to achieving the state's objectives.

Thus, the modern era of grand strategy was defined in terms of a bureaucratized state, which is based on a nationalist identity that relied primarily on conventional military means to provide internal and external security and pursue the ends of its grand strategy. These ends typically involved territorial expansion and internal political consolidation. In this modern era, systematic thinking about grand strategy continued to develop, but it changed with the advent of the revolutionary era. The hallmarks of this era in the late nineteenth century and early twentieth century were the decline of European empires, the emergence of violent international groups that proclaimed adherence to the counter-nationalist ideologies of anarchism, and the ideologies of communism and nationalism that often took on the mantle of anti-imperialism and fascism. Military technology in this era – which included handguns, rifles, and explosives – proliferated dramatically, and the period of assassinations and the first manifestations of modern terrorism began to emerge. Finally, the nuclear era, which began with the end of World War II, was defined by global superpowers that created a worldwide bipolar system based on the opposing ideologies of capitalism and communism. The grand strategies of these states were stabilized by the concept of mutual deterrence that emerged from the threat of nuclear war.

Part II in the study shifted the focus to the evolution of American grand strategy, which shared both similarities with and differences from the traditional development of grand strategy. It was similar in the sense that American grand strategy continued to evolve during these three eras of grand strategy. During the course of the modern era, the United

States became a modern, industrialized nation-state that had to deal with the fall of the European empires and the emergence of revolutionaries in the revolutionary era. But it was different in the sense that grand strategy during the nuclear era was dominated by two superpowers whose concepts of politics were based on radically opposing ideological systems of thought. During these periods, the evolution and content of American grand strategy was marked by the formation of three core traditions that dominated American foreign policy.

Three Unique Traditions of American Foreign Policy

First, a unique tradition of American foreign policy stems from the fact that the United States benefits from distance to other significant powers. It has never faced the constant threat of naval or land invasion since its Continental neighbors were generally too weak to mount a land invasion. And the distance across two oceans made it a nearly impossible target for a naval assault or amphibious invasion. In short, the United States had the luxury of time to develop the domestic foundations of its power. This first tradition rests on the ability to stand aloof from world politics to strengthen the American economy, achieve enduring prosperity and growth, and maintain internal political stability. Rooted in the American ethos of self-reliance and entrepreneurship, it shuns activist foreign policy agendas and prioritizes economic and trade policy. At its worst, this tradition can evolve into isolationism, whereas at its best it can produce a tradition of humility – but not ignorance – when it comes to engagement in world politics.

What makes this stage in the evolution of grand strategy unique to the United States is that most states did not have the luxury of pursuing this option. European states, by contrast, could not afford to remain disengaged from their nearby competitors, who were too close and often ambitious. This reality was evident in their foreign policies. To paraphrase John Quincy Adams, Europeans lacked the option of going abroad in search of monsters to destroy because the monsters came to them.

The second tradition also has a uniquely American character. In this tradition, the United States is a gradualist power that seeks democratic change but not at the expense of systemic disorder. Most European states have had either a status quo or revolutionary tradition. Britain, for example, has generally had a strong preference for a stable status quo based on a balance of power on the Continent. Napoleonic France, however, was a revolutionary power whose policies sought to transform the European state system. This was true of Nazi Germany and, to a lesser extent, Soviet Russia. But the United States does not fit neatly into these categories. This second tradition is best described as a gradualism that highlights the principle of restraining, while rarely totally eliminating, the sources of disorder and encouraging gradual change toward democracy and capitalism. This tradition is a reflection of America's own revolutionary tradition, which was based on a largely conservative revolution that did not seek to destroy the old ways so much as to reform and tailor them to suit a new set of political and economic imperatives. American revolutionaries were not fanatical or ideological, but some of the Founders did have a deep suspicion of democracy.

Finally, the third tradition of American foreign policy arose during the nuclear era. This tradition, as examined in Chapter 9, reflects the reinforcing value of using alliances and partnerships – both old and new – to confront global challenges with a sense of shared responsibility across states and societies. Containment is often held in high regard as an ideal grand strategy because it was clear, was global in scale, operated on a long-term time horizon, and marshaled all the instruments of national power across the private and public sectors. What is rarely underscored is the fact that containment worked not only because of American leadership and power, but more importantly because of close diplomatic ties between U.S. allies and partners.

What also was unique about the evolution of American grand strategy in the nuclear era was the extent to which the weapons altered the logic by which states conducted foreign policy. Critically, the United States did not use its nuclear monopoly in the late 1940s to coerce its enemies and prevent them from acquiring similar technology. The United States never sought to use its hegemony to radically and rapidly alter the system and its constituent states during the interval when it alone possessed atomic weapons.[5]

The last chapter of Part II (Chapter 10) concerned the evolution of post–Cold War grand strategy, or what might more accurately be termed a regressive *de*-evolution of grand strategy. This recent history reveals two critical factors. First, the United States has become unmoored from the traditions in its grand strategy and thus is struggling to define core principles to guide its foreign and domestic policies. Second, the absence of guiding principles has led to policies that lurch from one priority to another, often based primarily upon urgent, short-term concerns rather than on a coherent, long-term strategy of what best serves the nation's overall interests. The absence of guiding principles in the face of current challenges provides the ingredients for a series of risky moves.

The Clinton administration was the first to project this imbalance as it focused heavily on domestic policy (i.e., the first principle), with minimal cases of action guided by the second principle of restraining sources of disorder. Clinton's administration arguably was more successful with the third principle of building strong alliances (e.g., NATO expansion), but this policy saw multilateralism used as a catchphrase more than as an essential instrument for articulating and implementing a shared grand strategy, as we saw in the West during the Cold War. After 9/11, President Bush shifted to the second principle of confronting sources of disorder (i.e., terrorism). With his policies, he elevated the second principle of restraining sources of disorder above the other two principles – building foundations of power and sharing burdens with other states and institutions – while simultaneously calling for a crusade against the ideology of terrorism and tyranny rather than simply fighting against a specific enemy, Al-Qaeda, and its direct sponsors. President Obama is once again shifting this balance, but the question is Can he avoid the problem of over-correction? Will he swing back to the first principle by implementing a foreign policy that largely deemphasizes the necessity of the second and third principles?[6] A central argument in this study is that presidential administrations must balance these principles but cannot run the risk of overemphasizing one principle over the others. The world is too complex and the relationship between domestic and foreign policy too close for one principle to dominate to the exclusion of the others.

Moving from Traditions to Principles

These traditions in American grand strategy served the nation well in the past and should form the basis for principles that will help guide the next generation of U.S. policy makers.[7] Indeed, one challenge in the twenty-first century is how to build on these traditions in ways that make sense for the world that we confront today. We cannot throw out these traditions because they are too deeply embedded in our political culture, people, and institutions. Nor can we blindly follow them because they arose out of a different time. One question is how we should take what is best from these traditions so that they become an asset in American foreign policy decision making, and another is how we should discard what is outdated or reactionary.

These three traditions are embedded in what scholars define as American political culture, yet American grand strategists rarely articulate them explicitly.[8] This is the case for several reasons. First, the tracing of the evolution of American grand strategy in Part II outlines the extent to which American grand strategy is not something created by a few select foreign policy elites behind closed doors. In American diplomatic history, we see that the nation's grand strategy has been formed as much through, by, and for the people as it has been by Washington politicians. American grand strategy is a collective endeavor, a constant process of articulation and rearticulation as the American public senses what is consistent with its own values and traditions. Grand strategy is governed by the nation's prevailing political culture, particularly in a democracy.

The second reason is that these traditions operate across multiple presidential administrations. No one president can articulate and implement a grand strategy. Containment, for example, was not solely a Truman, Eisenhower, or Johnson grand strategy, but it was a grand strategy that guided the deliberations of the eight Cold War presidents, from Truman to Reagan. One of its greatest strengths was providing specific and consistent guidance to inform the foreign policy of successive administrations, and also providing the flexibility to compensate for varying problems and shifting emphases that occurred across those administrations. Eisenhower emphasized the limits imposed by economic costs on national security policy, Kennedy expanded the range of strategic tools available to respond to Soviet expansion, and Nixon moved to exploit the Sino-Soviet split. Each president had a different angle, but they all worked toward the same goal. Grand strategy, then, is not something that can be found in one document drafted under one president, but it is, so to speak, a living document that is constantly evolving in response to events and personalities.

Lastly, the third reason these traditions are more implicit and unstated is historical in nature. The United States is still so young relative to many other great powers. Unlike states whose institutions and traditions trace back for centuries if not millennia, the United States is still in the throes of forming the traditions that will govern its grand strategy.

In practice, these implicit traditions should become conscious and explicit principles of American foreign policy because they are invaluable in forming the basis of a coherent grand strategy. For American policy makers to convert these traditions into principles, they must become more aware of and heed the lessons of American diplomatic history. They also must be willing to leave behind the ideal of emulating containment, which was a grand strategy that remains, as a product of the revolutionary nuclear era, largely a historical anomaly. At present, the structure of the international system is no longer bipolar as long as the threats do not connect in a pervasive or systematic sense to one adversary. In the history of American grand strategy, the threats are more often myriad in a largely multipolar world. The better model on which to guide the articulation and implementation of grand strategy may be to draw from the period between the founding of the Republic in the late eighteenth century and the early twentieth century.

As the United States looks to the future, a reevaluation of its grand strategy is in order. As the shifts in the global order continue to cascade upon each other, there are many questions that society and its policy makers can no longer avoid. How should the United States move to articulate a grand strategy for managing a world that shows signs of increasing disorder? What choices should this society make in order to create order out of the emerging chaos? Answering these and other questions is the central challenge if today's policy makers want to ensure peace, freedom, and security. Today, the United States lacks a strategic framework within which to answer these critical questions that, to cut to the heart of the matter, define its role in world, what the nation seeks to achieve, and how to bring that role into balance with the nation's resources and public will. Above all else, American society needs to answer some basic questions: What principles should govern U.S. policy in an increasingly unstable world? What, in effect, should America's grand strategy be today?

But before turning to these questions, the next section discusses the evolution of grand strategy as America emerged from the Cold War, the very different world we confront today, and the lack of solid principles with which to address effectively current threats to international peace and security. Although the current void in American grand strategy is palpable, how to move forward with a new vision is an area marked by contending ideas among scholars and policy makers.

Consensus on the Problem, Disagreement on the Solution

Demise of Containment

Although grand strategy has undoubtedly required a makeover since the end of the Cold War, American grand strategy since the dissolution of the Soviet Union (as examined in earlier chapters) is dramatically less coherent than it has been. The strategy of containment was replaced by a series of episodic and reactionary grand strategies as successive administrations attempted to develop compelling principles to guide American foreign policy. The Cold War period, as examined in this study, was atypical as to the deep consensus in American society and among its allies on the overall direction of the nation's grand strategy. Consequently, a defining feature of the Cold War was that the United States and its allies debated less about the ultimate ends of grand strategy and more about the details of implementation.

In the absence of clear and decisive threats along the lines that societies faced during the Cold War, the once-solid organizing principles of grand strategy simply are no longer relevant or useful. Policy makers now face a world characterized by vastly greater unpredictability, often giving rise to the false belief that the risks are so low and dispersed among so many global actors that the world is somehow less dangerous.

The inescapable conclusion, however, is that the old grand strategy of containment no longer fits our world. Where it once worked, containment no longer aligns with how the modern world is organized politically and economically. Simply put, it no longer offers practical guidance in a highly interconnected global economy in which states do not face a singular ideological threat. What has replaced the clear-cut nuclear deterrence balance between countries is a wide range of inchoate and uncertain risks that emanate from both unstable states and non-state actors alike.

Despite the need for organized and coherent principles for confronting a rapidly changing world, there is no consensus within the United States on the importance of thinking about grand strategy.[9] This is a dangerous development, given the sources of disorder in the world. The United States has adopted policies that rely on the residue of containment or on piecemeal and halfhearted responses to challenges, and the nation on occasion has a propensity to ignore challenges altogether. Take the war currently raging in Syria or the rapidly evolving chaos of the Arab Spring movements as prime examples. Now more than ever, if the nation is going to act decisively and effectively, American policy makers must develop coherent principles that provide guidance and consensus on the challenges posed by the modern world and how the nation should conduct its foreign policy.

In direct contrast with the opposite viewpoint to which many policy makers have adhered since the end of the Cold War, a number of developments point to an increasingly unstable world. One source of the problem is systemic shifts in the geopolitical, social, and economic status quo, all of which defy comprehension but require policy makers to adapt intellectually to the challenges. Part of the problem is the unwillingness of policy makers to adopt new forms of strategic thinking – a result, perhaps, of clinging stubbornly to familiar approaches despite overwhelming evidence that the world is gripped by profound uncertainties and growing disorder.

Current Sources of Disorder

Although by no means a panacea, grand strategy will help the United States understand what threats are inevitable, which ones really matter, and how to deal with them. Where states once faced singular ideological, political, or military threats, today's problems flow from complex and overlapping sources of disorder. Furthermore, modern threats and challenges, ranging from rising great powers to unpredictable non-state actors, do not lend themselves to the simple guidance offered by earlier grand strategies. The function of grand strategy, as studied in this book, is to organize foreign policy issues in a useful way for policy makers and their society. Facing global disorder, the United States has moved well beyond the point at which policy makers can rely on old solutions to new problems. Rather than using the tired approaches of focusing on states, issues, and regions that threaten U.S. interests, this chapter outlines an alternative approach. The first step in articulating a grand strategy is to categorize the fragmented, fragile, and unstable world into "sources of disorder."

The United States faces multiple sources of disorder, which fall into several categories. The foremost sources are challenges posed by resurgent great powers, destabilizing middle powers, a rising authoritarian axis, and less predictable non-state actors. Throughout America's history, threats have emanated from these sources of disorder with varying degrees of frequency and emphasis on certain sources over the others. For example, the first half of the twentieth century witnessed a time of intense and protracted conflict that embroiled the great powers in two deadly and costly world wars. The second half of the twentieth century was characterized by an enduring cold war between the Soviet Union and the United States.

In today's time, the United States faces challenges brought about by all of these sources of disorder, but by different methods and degrees than in the past. Therefore, America must develop a new strategy that incorporates action and engagement with each of them in order to maintain peace and security. The following section includes descriptions of each source of disorder and examples that illustrate their current state of play. Although the specific states and actors representing these sources of disorder may change over time, this categorization is a useful tool for policy makers and students who are thinking critically about and developing a new American grand strategy.

The first category includes the challenges posed to American interests and security by resurgent great powers. The rise of China is a prominent example. Beijing's growing economy, increasingly competent military, and assertive foreign policy signal China's desire and ability to play a larger role in regional and global affairs. Engaging with China's stronger regional presence requires America to reinforce both principles two and three of the grand strategy outlined here. These include reinforcing American leadership in the region and working closely with alliances and partners such as the ASEAN nations, Australia, Japan, and South Korea. If the United States strengthens its commitment to developing these principles, both America and its allies can effectively engage and cooperate with a stronger and more active China. However, if China's resurgence continues in the face of American strategic drift, states in Asia will rightly worry about the territorial and security consequences of China's rise.

Russia is another dominant example of a resurgent great power playing a more increased role in global affairs. Today, the world witnesses the Russian government's inexorable creep toward what many see as a rebirth of authoritarianism. This shift under President Vladimir Putin, with his "cult of personality," has come to dominate Russian society and politics. Putin's increasingly strident rhetoric toward the United States, past predatory energy policies toward Europe, and support for authoritarian governments in Iran and Syria are reasons for growing concern for the United States and many of its allies in Eurasia. This source of disorder requires America to strengthen all three principles of grand strategy. Effective engagement with Russia requires strong American leadership to pressure Russia to refrain from using its oil and natural gas as a weapon against its neighbors, including Ukraine and Georgia. Forming and bolstering alliances and partnerships with states along Russia's border signals to Moscow that Washington will exercise leadership when Russia employs aggressive and intimidating tactics through its energy markets. Lastly, another way to effectively pressure Russia is to explore potential export markets in the United States and Eastern Europe as America's develops its own increasing domestic sources of energy.

The second category or sources of disorder includes the expected but nonetheless demanding challenge of destabilizing middle powers. Hardly a new problem, these smaller states are not simply proxies for larger adversaries, but represent powerful sources of disorder on their own that threaten to undermine peace and security. A prominent case today is Iran. Tehran's nuclear weapon and missile programs and strident rhetoric pose – while softened by the recently elected President Hassan Rouhani – a threat to Israel and the United States. Worse, other states in the Middle East could be persuaded to develop their own nuclear deterrent. America now faces the delicate task of balancing the West's desire to maintain stability in the Middle East with preventing Iran from possessing nuclear weapons.

North Korea is the perpetually difficult case whose isolated and insular regime, inexperienced leader Kim Jong-un, active ballistic missile and nuclear weapon tests, moribund domestic economy, prolific international trade in illicit goods, and demonstrated aptitude for winning diplomatic concessions from the international community all underscore Pyongyang's ability to create disorder. In addition, the destabilizing middle powers include Afghanistan, which is slowly unraveling in the face of the withdrawal of U.S. and NATO forces, and Pakistan, which remains an immensely dangerous and nuclear source of disorder. The current worries include Pakistan's instability, active support for extremist groups such as the Taliban in Afghanistan, and its nuclear arsenal falling into the hands of extremists. Lastly, the civil war in Syria, which increasingly threatens regional chaos involving Turkey, Iraq, and Iran, remains a powerful source of disorder. At this point, more than a hundred thousand civilians have died, Syria's government likely ordered the use of chemical weapons, and Russia protects President Bashar al-Assad's government from U.S. military pressure and international diplomatic pressure. Despite a rapidly evolving situation, one enduring characteristic is that Syria sits astride a region with the potential to become a flashpoint for a broader war.

A third source of disorder for American grand strategy is the rising "authoritarian axis." This axis, or bloc, describes an imperfect but still tangible coordination between such great powers as China and Russia, and destabilizing middle powers including Iran, North Korea, and Syria. Its foremost members, China and Russia, continue to forge stronger bonds that strengthen their strategic partnership, while their support of nations such as Iran and Syria constitutes a dangerous source of disorder. Iran is a state that receives significant support from the axis powers and remains a worrisome source of disorder and a potential flashpoint. As it moves closer to acquiring nuclear weapons, Iran's enduring interest in acquiring such weapons remains a subject of contentious debates in the West, especially given earlier threats to annihilate Israel.

North Korea, under its leader Kim Jung-un, is a worrisome, if only slightly less dangerous, element of the authoritarian axis. It routinely threatens its neighbors with careless and reckless language, while its military and elite consume most of the nation's scarce resources. North Korea's principal benefactor is China, which provides significant economic support but remains unwilling to rein in its provocative behavior. Pyongyang's long-range ballistic missiles and nuclear weapons make it clear that the "hermit kingdom," with its past behavior of sharing such dangerous technologies with Syria and Iran, remains a source of instability in Asia.

The fourth category of sources of disorder is the eternally difficult problem of managing the less predictable non-state actors. Within this category exist several flashpoints for conflict that require increased American attention and engagement. Foremost is the resurgence of extremists in Afghanistan. With U.S. forces withdrawing and the Taliban's power growing, Afghanistan risks sliding back into violence and repression. Accelerating its deterioration was the U.S. announcement that its forces would leave no later than 2014. Where once the Taliban believed they were losing, their resurgence is a stark reminder that they are seemingly biding their time until the U.S./NATO withdrawal. This is an illustrative example of the long-term objectives and methods employed by non-state actors who are driven by ideology. To effectively counter this source of disorder, America must continually reevaluate and redefine new objectives and tactics in its overarching grand strategy.

Second, despite hopes for democracy in the Middle East, another source of concern in this fourth category is that the once promising Arab Spring shows signs of chaos and violence. Egypt continues to struggle through the transition to democracy as it witnesses once again the dominating control of the military. Continuing political confrontation will likely keep the country on the edge of civil war. Meanwhile, Libya is a breeding ground for extremists, while events in Yemen point to the rise of Al-Qaeda. The civil war in Syria and the rise of the Islamic state in 2014, including the use of chemical weapons, shows no signs of abating. Although U.S. policy once rightly encouraged the democratic "spring," Washington's strategy remains unclear.

The solution includes strengthening American leadership in the region in order to maintain stability, safeguarding national interests, and reinforcing our alliances with moderate nations and forces.

Global trade and rapid technological change continue to alter relationships among individuals, firms, and states. With globalization altering the nature and distribution of power, American policy makers need a grand strategy, using soft and hard power, to help them manage unexpected developments in the public and private sectors. American grand strategy must contend with the rise of new and unforeseen non-state actors whose ideologies mobilize followers such as ISIS. Beyond its military and economic might, America's soft power permits it to help shape a global community based on shared interests, universal values, and ideals. In working with nongovernmental and civil-society actors, the United States must effectively communicate what values shape its foreign policy.

Policy makers also face the truly modern challenge of cyber warfare in the hands of non-state actors. Never before have non-state actors, groups, and movements possessed an instrument capable of inflicting such immense harm. One element of American grand strategy must consider how to deal with groups that could attack the physical and economic infrastructure of American society. Policy makers worry that cyber hackers from an extremist organization might be able to cut off U.S. electric power during the winter or hack into the safety controls of a nuclear reactor. The old grand strategy of containment has become passé in the face of modern foreign and domestic challenges represented by these new and unpredictable sources of disorder.

Lastly, policy makers also must contemplate self-generated sources of disorder. The United States, whose current grand strategy is seen as adrift and disengaging, remains deeply divided politically. It faces the additional burden of operating without a positive, reassuring, and bipartisan strategy to guide its foreign policy. How can policy makers expend resources – the nation's blood and treasure – when it is unclear why they are doing so and for what purposes? How can policy makers ask the public to support policies when people rightly wonder about the purpose and objectives of American foreign policy? Why should we, much less others, make sacrifices when the goals of American foreign policy are unknown? These are the fundamental questions that a new American grand strategy, when developed and implemented effectively, seeks to answer.

A decaying grand strategy or one that may be seen as disengaging despite powerful sources of global disorder presents a serious problem. The United States will struggle to manage challenges from resurgent great powers, destabilizing middle powers, a rising authoritarian axis, and less predictable non-state actors as long as the nation lacks a coherent, positive, and compelling vision for its grand strategy. Ultimately, the sources of disorder and the inevitable crises will compel the United States to formulate a new grand strategy – one better aligned and more precisely attuned to the risks and opportunities we face. As this book strongly proposes, it is far better to do so now than to wait until a crisis strikes. In the end, grand strategy is about much more than responding to problems. To be effective, it must embrace the fundamental reasons and motivations that shape how, why, and to what ends the United States engages in foreign policy.

Establishing the broad outlines of the problems with which American grand strategy must deal will help policy makers overcome the current confusion. Policy makers must ensure that grand strategy deals with complexities *and* provides clear guidance that helps them articulate policies for dealing with the sources of disorder. Such disorder has disoriented our vision of policy and demoralized the present generation of policy makers, whose failure to define a coherent grand strategy for helping the state deal with the expected ebbs and flows in world politics remains an enduring problem. While such strategic shifts are routine, these have destabilizing consequences when policy makers do not remain mindful of the critical sources of disorder facing the nation.

The Current Void in American Grand Strategy

By the beginning of the twentieth century, with its resource-rich territory now stretching from coast to coast and its thriving industrial economy, the United States was poised to become a great power. Until then, American grand strategy had been focused inward, driven largely by the desire to build the nation's territorial and economic foundations of power, and subsequently, in the early twentieth century, by a bout of isolationism. However, the outbreak of two world wars forced the United States off the sidelines and toward a more robust foreign policy. At the end of World War II, the United States claimed a new position of global leadership, and President Truman enjoyed the political license of articulating the more activist grand strategy of containment that was implemented through such policies as the Marshall Plan and documents as NSC-68.

More than four decades later, the end of the Cold War left America without a grand strategy to guide its foreign and domestic policies. Whereas American leaders during the Cold War successfully marshaled the nation's resources for the purpose of containing and perhaps defeating the Soviet Union, the United States today lacks a coherent and unified grand strategy. A nation without such a grand strategy is vulnerable to having policies that are shifting, erratic, and ineffective. This is an urgent issue; with signs of drift in American foreign policy, scholars are paying more attention to this void in grand strategy.[10] The increasing volume of literature devoted to U.S. grand strategy will be useful if it helps policy makers deal with the most enduring problems, rather than simply the most urgent priorities.

Ultimately, only grand strategy provides the broad vision that helps policy makers conduct foreign policy. Grand strategy encompasses the totality of the concepts upon which a state builds its policies, allowing it to guide its foreign, domestic, and economic policies toward agreed-upon and unified ends. In effect, no state can articulate and implement coherent and effective foreign and domestic policies unless these derive from a consistent set of principles. Without such principles, the state's foreign policy will show signs of chaos and confusion. Scholars and policy makers must understand that they cannot articulate a coherent grand strategy without first achieving a consensus on the political goals that shape the state's policies and allowing policy makers to garner broad public support for that goal. For the United States, achieving this working consensus is more important than ever, and yet so illusive.

When the state lacks a central adversary, its ability to prioritize interests is extremely difficult, particularly at a time when the nation confronts a complex mix of transnational problems. This includes, inter alia, terrorism, global economic crises, uncontrolled migration, world food shortages, narcotics trafficking, pollution, and climate change. The challenge for American grand strategy is to balance foreign and domestic priorities so that the nation can marshal the economic, military, and diplomatic clout necessary to maintain a world that contributes to peace, democracy, prosperity, and free markets. Failing to balance ends and means in the context of the principles governing American grand strategy puts at risk the nation's substantial economic, military, and political advantages.

Although it is rare for a grand strategy to come to a formal end, this can occur when a major adversary is defeated or collapses. For example, what passes for American grand strategy today is influenced by the country's experiences during the Cold War.[11] What shifted was the consensus following the 9/11 attacks about the nature of the threat posed by non-state armed groups. The United States now finds itself at another critical junction as the wars in Iraq and Afghanistan come to an end and as the nation pivots east to Asia despite chaos in the Middle East and elsewhere.

One area of consensus in the current literature holds that grand strategy emerges when the state faces a period of great struggle or new threats. One consequence is that grand strategy, albeit misleadingly, can become too reactive. When societies must conduct foreign policy in the midst of disorder, taking actions without a coherent grand strategy, they naturally fall prey to difficulties and anxieties. How could citizens of states that face an increasingly disordered world, and yet lack a grand strategy to guide their actions, feel or act otherwise? Disorder without strategy is a recipe for confusion and failure.

To start with, Americans generally want to exercise leadership, but it is unclear whether the United States is willing and able to provide that leadership. Worse, it is difficult to articulate a grand strategy when policy makers do not have a coherent framework that relates the arc of problems to core principles in that strategy. The United States will remain in intellectual limbo until policy makers come to grips with building a grand strategy that deals effectively with the sources of disorder. Beyond the usual domestic political differences, one source of political polarization in Washington is profound uncertainty about what really matters in foreign policy. Americans are especially vulnerable to weariness from the daily grind of foreign policy, particularly when their actions are not guided by a positive vision of foreign policy. Grand strategy, then, is essential for establishing a consensus on goals and maintaining domestic support for long-term foreign policies.

Yet, the United States has been dangerously adrift for more than two decades, operating without a positive and reassuring vision of its grand strategy. How can policy makers expend resources – "blood and treasure" – when it is not clear why they are doing so and for what purposes? Without clear objectives and goals in foreign policy – the Holy Grail of grand strategy – it is a virtual law of nature that societies will lose the sense of focus and purpose that give foreign policy strategic direction and momentum. What follows like an inexorable law of nature is perpetual drift, as a nation's foreign policy swings from strong public support for fighting wars (Afghanistan and Iraq) to public opposition and then to indifference. For example, the level of domestic support for the initial invasion of Afghanistan in 2001 was 90 percent,[12] but a decade later 56 percent support the withdrawal of most U.S. forces from Afghanistan by 2016.[13]

Lastly, the failure to develop a grand strategy contributes to debates about America's relative decline in power. The United States faces grinding wars without end, a deep economic crisis, the emergence of authoritarian powers such as China and Russia (perhaps as the leaders of an emerging authoritarian axis with Iran, Syria, North Korea, and Venezuela), deep worries about the future, and no clear sense of purpose. How could the society not worry about decline?

Faint Outlines of a Solution

As for a solution to this problem, it is useful to recognize where scholars and practitioners agree and disagree. Differences exist in the various approaches to organizing a coherent set of principles around foreign policy. For some, the solution lies in organizing our thinking by focusing on the states that pose the greatest challenges. For others, however, the preferred approach entails thinking in terms of what we often call transnational issues – challenges such as proliferation or extremism that transcend individual states and regions. For still others, the best approach is to focus on regions, such as Asia and the Middle East.

There is broad agreement that grand strategy is more art than science. Although each type of study of grand strategy – historical, social scientific, policy oriented, and military strategic – has its strengths and weaknesses, they all either implicitly or explicitly recognize that grand strategy is a highly subjective undertaking. It does not offer an objective, scientific, precise, or linear formula for determining what the state should do or what policies it should pursue. Furthermore, it is difficult to predict the "results" of a given grand strategy, because those often are based upon judgments about future trends and a complex array of political, economic, and social variables. However, for grand strategy to be effective, it is imperative for the state to clearly articulate the goals it intends to accomplish and how these will be achieved.

What is equally clear is that grand strategy is a never-ending process that must be constantly updated and adapted by scholars and policy makers to ensure that its ends and means are closely aligned. By articulating the goals for the world it seeks to build, the state addresses the real purpose of grand strategy, which is to express the principles that provide order to its beliefs and expectations about the world it wants to create and the domestic and foreign policies that it will pursue to accomplish that objective.

In essence, grand strategy is not governed by strict scientific laws but by rules of thumb or rough guidelines that allow policy makers to practice the art of making informed judgments about long-term trends and trade-offs. Finding the right balance between the three principles, then, is always going to have an irreducible degree of subjectivity and uncertainty. There will never be one right answer to what a state's grand strategy should be. Rather, it is a matter of choosing between grand strategies that are better than others across a range of options. The issue of trade-offs is crucial, as George H. W. Bush wisely observed: "The essence of strategy is determining priorities" and then making "the hard choices."[14] It is the trade-offs that make the choices "hard." In effect, prioritizing one policy necessarily means deprioritizing another, while emphasizing one principle necessarily means deemphasizing another. The question is how to weigh these trade-offs in grand strategy over time, especially when they are complex and likely to occur and reoccur over decades. The rules of thumb outlined here offer broad guidance.

Three Rules of Thumb

Up to this point, our discussion has focused largely on the historical and analytical underpinnings that have shaped the evolution of grand strategy and the principles to guide foreign policy. For this book to remain relevant and contribute advice and strategic direction on America's evolving role in the world, we must now look forward. The discussion since the end of the Cold War has proven particularly interesting, as both scholars and policy makers have struggled with developing a coherent American grand strategy that helps the nation deal with the modern world and offers recommendations for achieving such an objective. The remainder of this chapter is written as a contribution to the development of a more clear, confident, and optimistic trajectory for American grand strategy.

The first rule of thumb is that the U.S. cannot afford to have "domestic policy" or "foreign policy" presidents in the post–Cold War era. Bill Clinton's agenda was heavily domestic policy oriented, whereas George W. Bush's was heavily foreign policy oriented. Both left the United States vulnerable in the areas they neglected when they left office. Looking forward, the president's policy agenda has to strike a careful balance among the three principles of grand strategy. So the first rule of thumb for balancing between the principles is to strike a delicate balance between the nation's foreign and domestic policy agendas. The reality is that neither should dominate and neither should be neglected. The United States cannot afford to get this balance wrong for long.

In an earlier era, the United States could afford to disregard foreign problems; it no longer has this option. States in Asia, for example, are deeply troubled at the thought of America's withdrawal from the Pacific, particularly with China's increasingly assertive and aggressive actions in its near abroad.[15] A domestically oriented United States would signal to the world that Washington is less interested in foreign policy, which Beijing, Moscow, Tehran, and Pyongyang likely would interpret as an invitation to operate more aggressively, while expanding their reach. However, if the United States fails to devote significant political and economic attention and resources to rebuilding the domestic foundations of its national power, it will be increasingly difficult to compete in the world. The consequence will be the greater risk of an erosion of the American people's willingness to support a leadership role for the United States. The nation may be experiencing weariness in terms of supporting the costs and burdens of global leadership.

The second rule of thumb is that a president has to lead the American people but also respect their role as a check on idealism. Most American voters do not gravitate to Wilsonian or neoconservative ideals, but they have an innate sense of optimism about life in America, matched by a healthy skepticism about efforts to remake the world in America's image. To be sure, there are numerous examples in which democratic societies have been incited toward exuberance for war and the prospect for radical political change, but they have a sense of costs and benefits that should be respected.[16] This does not mean that the president should conduct foreign policy by poll, but it points strongly toward the principle that policy makers should show respect for the preference for gradualism that runs deeply in American politics. As Mead points out, the American people are woefully ignorant about foreign policy, world history, and basic geography.[17] It is equally true, however, that American grand strategy derives largely from the people. The public has good instincts when they see a severe imbalance in foreign policy, and they can be instrumental in helping policy makers find exactly the right balance that accords with public sentiments.

The third rule of thumb is to have and put into practice policies that show a preference for gradualism. As discussed earlier, gradualism is the aspect of American foreign policy exceptionalism that sets America apart from both status quo and revolutionary powers. It rests on the idea that the United States has the power to change the world for the better, while noting that such change usually happens slowly and incrementally rather than as a product of sudden and dramatic shifts. Grand strategies that call for defeating tyranny, terrorism, illegal drugs, state failure, or poverty, or fighting a "war to end all wars" are largely inconsistent with American foreign policy principles and are likely to fail. This is not to argue that we should acquiesce to these terrible conditions, but a prudent grand strategy, if practiced wisely, must reflect some self-awareness that we cannot solve problems quickly or solve them alone. Eras of great success in the conduct of American grand strategy were all marked by the combination of modest ambitions and the slow, incremental successes often produced by diplomacy and other instruments of policy. A crucial exception is the case of World War II, but that victory was won as a result of strong alliances and close partnerships, and thus it remains the exception that proves the rule.

These three rules of thumb provide the basis for determining new principles to guide American grand strategy moving forward.

Three Guiding Principles for American Grand Strategy

If we are to stipulate that the United States has failed to develop a coherent and modern grand strategy, the first step in righting this problem is to reapply and reassert the three critical organizing principles that provide the foundations for a positive strategy to guide American foreign policy.

The First Principle: Rebuilding Domestic Foundations of Power

First, the United States can no longer postpone the moment when it must devote greater time, attention, and resources to rebuilding the domestic foundations of its national power. Beginning with World War II, the United States used its national power to engage globally on an unprecedented scale. Completing work begun in the 1930s, we built our world-class infrastructure – industry, roads, bridges, schools, energy, and so forth – during the decades after World War II.

Many observers, unfortunately, believe wrongly that grand strategy is largely about foreign and defense policy. But a cardinal principle of grand strategy is to rebuild the domestic foundations of America's national power. This practice, dating back to the administration of George Washington, has been central to the deliberations that have governed the decisions of virtually every administration since then. Grand strategy rests on much more than foreign policy because its influence derives directly from the free-market economic foundations of the nation's power.

In determining if this principle is given due regard, one indicator is the state of the nation's infrastructure. To be a global player, the United States must have world-class roads, bridges, electric power grids, national broadband, and mass transit systems, among other elements of domestic power. To compete economically, these elements of infra-structure will be as important for national power as are armies, navies, and air forces for defending our interests. Nor can we forget the importance of education, health care, and retirement systems as instruments for ensuring broad opportunities for every American. Our grand strategy cannot be effective until we restore the infrastructure and social safety nets that assure all Americans of their opportunity to compete and succeed. All of this is as central to the successful conduct of foreign policy as anything the nation does.

Another indicator for determining if this principle is best served concerns the state and pace of innovation. The hallmarks of the U.S. economy's strength are not only its size and growth rate but, for future prosperity, the level of innovation. If the United States is not leading in venture capital per person or number of NASDAQ corporations, for example, then its grand strategy will fail and its standing in the world will decline. Finally, growing numbers of jobs and a strong middle class are enduring indicators of the strength of the domestic foundations of American power.[18]

Just as U.S. grand strategy needs to look outward, it also must look inward to address the problems facing American society. For too long, scholars and policy makers have preoccupied themselves with the foreign policy and national security elements of grand strategy. Sadly, most current thinking about foreign policy operates almost exclusively through the lens of security and military affairs. However, at this moment the "grand strategy imperative" calls for policy makers to define America's roles and responsibilities in a less hegemonic, and perhaps more humble, demeanor. To reinforce American leadership abroad, the United States must demonstrate that its grand strategy is as much about devoting attention and resources to reinforcing the domestic foundations of power as it is to conducting foreign policy. Unfortunately, modern policy makers often forget this most basic of principles.

Policy makers and scholars must remember that grand strategy embraces vastly more than foreign policy. American influence derives precisely from the free-market economic underpinnings that give the nation such immense influence – often permitting it to marshal tremendous power when it is necessary to do so. If America is to remain a global leader, as many Americans and others globally believe it should, then it must recommit itself first to reinforcing the domestic foundations of America's national power. Let me express this another way: When the nation ignores the domestic foundations of power, it courts disasters, which often unfold in slow motion as the will of American society lags behind its commitments.

With global powers in ruins after World War II, the United States used its national power as the leading actor on an unprecedented scale to rebuild many who are its closest allies today. Throughout the twentieth century, America also built its own world-class infrastructure – a national network of industries, roads, bridges, schools, and energy infrastructure, including electric power grids. Without that investment and the national consensus it symbolized, the United States could not have been such an effective force on the world stage.

Nor can policy makers and scholars forget the critical role of education, health care, and social safety systems for ensuring broad opportunities for all Americans. U.S. grand strategy cannot be effective until we restore the infrastructure and social safety nets that assure all Americans of the opportunity to compete and succeed. America's global role derives from the strength of its people, its ability to be innovative, and the entrepreneurial spirit that Americans harness to solve the most daunting challenges. This, however, is not a prescription for throwing "more money than god" at problems. Simply spending money is unlikely to reinforce the foundations of the nation's power. For that, the nation needs a political consensus, largely absent from the national debate, *and* resources. To restore the nation's grand strategy, it is time to rebuild the American spirit of innovation, hard work, ingenuity, and collective action.

Such considerations, while often subordinated or ignored altogether in the national debate, often fall by the wayside as debates about foreign policy and national security compete for policy makers' time and attention. For the public, the daily onslaught of media reports – problems with ISIS, Iran, Syria, Egypt, North Korea, Russia, China, the

European Union, energy, or the crisis of the moment – shift vital attention away from the domestic sources of power that define American influence and are central to its grand strategy. Rebuilding the national foundations of American power on which grand strategy rests is essential to dealing with a world whose innumerable risks and opportunities demand American leadership.

To be direct, emphasizing the domestic foundations of power is not a veiled call for the United States to withdraw from the world or see its leadership decline. On the contrary, it is a call for realigning the nation's grand strategy to meet the challenges of the world as it is. With this realignment, American policy makers and the public once again can, strategically and effectively, rebalance how the nation allocates resources and attention to meet the demands imposed by foreign and domestic challenges and opportunities. This is the right time, as friends and allies urge the United States to maintain an active leadership role, for the American people and their policy makers to realign the nation's policies with its interests and priorities.

The Second Principle: Exercising American Leadership to Restrain Sources of Disorder That Present Direct Threats to U.S. Vital Interests

The palpable sense of drift in American foreign policy, which relates directly to the failure to define a grand strategy to guide the nation, is occurring at precisely the moment when the world faces increasingly dangerous sources of disorder. The rise of great powers, middle powers, authoritarianism, and unexpected sources of disorder undermine the peaceful and secure world that the United States historically seeks to build. These sources of disorder pose a direct challenge to American leadership.

The United States must define its grand strategy to actively restrain the sources of disorder that contribute to insecurity and chaos in a world, which remains more dangerous and unstable than many observers anticipated.[19] Despite being mired in a painfully slow recovery from the "Great Recession," the time has come for the United States to exercise world leadership instead of exercising the options of retrenching and withdrawing from the international arena. The problems generated by China, Russia, Iran, and Syria, among others, especially in the highly unstable Middle East, call for more active and assertive leadership from Washington. As discussed, with no evident shortage of serious risks and problems, the United States can no longer afford the luxury of defining its foreign policy in terms of containment. This "old think," as we have discovered, is worse than ineffectual. In this climate, the central imperative for Washington is to define its strategy not in terms of containing problems, but of restraining the forces that contribute to instability, chaos, and war.

One question that arises from the review of the evolution of American grand strategy is How can we distinguish a Hitler from a Saddam? The Axis Powers were a threat that required American leadership as well as its military and economic power. It was worth a debt-to-GDP ratio that reached 118 percent by 1945. Hitler in Europe and Japan in Asia were sources of disorder that required making them the highest priority and using military force on a global scale. Saddam Hussein in 2003 was likened to Hitler, but he did not reach the same level of threat because he lacked the capability to invade and occupy other countries. His military was weak by comparison to the militaries of Germany and Japan, and his economy was in shambles.

The Bush administration argued, however, that none of these indicators mattered. Saddam's potential to cause unimaginable disorder stemmed from his potential to develop and use weapons of mass destruction. Yet, this was a speculative and later disproven basis for perceiving him as a threat. Moreover, the decision to invade Iraq in 2003 caused disorder itself because it created a power vacuum in Iraq that led to a civil war and insurgency. It alienated the international community and showed contempt for the United Nations and international law. Although it might have eliminated a potential source of disorder, in practice it actually created greater disorder.

American grand strategy in the post–Cold War era has to show a strong commitment to international order and stability. This is not to argue that Washington should tolerate injustice, tyranny, and human rights atrocities, but that the exercise of American power should generally be governed by the desire to maintain order rather than live with disorder. This remains the fundamental difference between Hitler and Saddam. Hitler sought to destroy the old European order and remake it as the Third Reich, while the Allies stood for the idea of stopping this radical, violent change to the system. Saddam, by contrast, sought to stay in power but lacked the means to remake any significant political or economic aspect of the system. He was not a source of disorder because he preferred to maintain the status quo.

This leads us to the issue of authoritarian great powers. Iraq under Saddam Hussein was a middle-tier regional power, which could pose a threat only if it possessed WMD, notably nuclear weapons. Russia and China, and to some extent Iran, are first-tier regional authoritarian powers that have the capability to become major sources of disorder in their regions, if not the world. One indicator of whether the second principle is being applied is whether the authoritarian great powers are rising in power. Are their spheres of influence expanding or contracting? Are their militaries deploying farther afield and overseas? Are they coercing smaller, weaker neighbors or supporting such states in ways that undermine security? If the answer to most or all of these questions is yes, then American grand strategy has to rebalance in favor of the second principle.

Building on the second principle, policy makers must contemplate defining American grand strategy in terms of actively *restraining* the forces, actions, and ideas that contribute to instability, insecurity, and chaos. Since the world remains dangerous and unpredictable, it is strategically necessary for the United States to remain engaged – to lead on occasion, so to speak, "from the front." This principle of American grand strategy must rest on more than simple rhetoric. Its purpose should be to make the world safer, freer and more prosperous, and secure as Washington exudes strength, purpose, and commitment. By "strength," I do not mean in the classic military sense, but strength in the depth and extent of using all the nation's tools – political, economic, technological, and diplomatic – to help defend the nation's interest in building a peaceful and free world. For its grand strategy to succeed, the United States must demonstrate *in word and deed* a sense of vision as well as the judgment and power to use its strength to promote a just and peaceful world.

Simply put, America needs to stand for and defend principles that promote human rights and dignity, equality for all peoples – men and women – freedom of expression, free enterprise, and fair elections. These values are consistent with the historical principles that existed in American foreign policy well before the Cold War and will endure well beyond this and subsequent generations. This principle of America's leadership role emphasizes just how essential it is to discourage states or actors from taking actions that harm the interests of the United States or other free societies. In promoting these values, American grand strategy has many tools at its disposal. It can withhold political or economic support from, use military power against, or build alliances to confront actors whose behaviors undermine peace, security, and prosperity.

The Third Principle: Forging Alliances and Partnerships to Confront the Most Pressing Threats to Global Stability

For political and economic reasons, this is precisely the moment when the United States faces a new imperative in its grand strategy. Its challenge is to articulate a grand strategy that reinforces the nation's influence and ability to exercise a leadership role, but without going so far in the opposite direction that the nation effectively disengages from the world – or creates the impression that it is doing so. If its inaction creates a leadership vacuum, the United States will face all manner of risks, challenges, and dangerous outcomes. While some argue that the United States is in decline and must scale back its involvement, my own view is that an enduring element of American grand strategy must be to reinforce the role of alliances and partnerships. This powerful and enduringly positive principle should be central to and wholly enshrined in every facet of the nation's grand strategy. The failure to do so encourages others to believe that the nation is in decline or that it is simply disinterested. Both conclusions will contribute to a more dangerous world.

A new American grand strategy must reinforce alliances and partnerships – both old and new – in order to confront global challenges with a sense of shared responsibility among nations. The nation's grand strategy must proceed from the realization that Americans do not have unlimited power; the nation cannot do everything and cannot be everywhere all of the time for the rest of the world. Americans willingly carried the mantle of global leadership for decades – from winning in World War II and the Cold War to strengthening security against extremism after 9/11. But they may be reluctant to carry that burden once again, especially considering the nation's current economic difficulties. The baby boom generation has been as active as its predecessor – and as generous in spirit when asked to help.

The two extremes – where America engages less as expressed by "leading from behind" or where America takes the lead on all issues – are unacceptable.[20] Now is the time for other states in the West to rise to the occasion and to share the burden of leadership rather than criticizing from the sidelines. We can hope for a new bipartisan consensus on foreign policy, but if Washington fails to lead, then it must be prepared for the consequences if other states, whose interests may be radically at odds with its own, take the lead. Consider the case of Syria's use of chemical weapons in August 2013, when the United States threatened to use military force, Britain voted against using force, and Russia sided with Syria in proposing a deal for Syria to give up its chemical weapons.[21]

The United States must also commit itself to building a world in which other states contribute to regional leadership, while working collaboratively toward common goals. These principles of reinforcing the domestic foundations of power, exercising strong leadership, and practicing greater collaboration often exist in tension. However, it is vital for the nation to develop a framework that guides how it deals with competing challenges at home and abroad. Neither the public nor their policy makers should assume that America's supposed preeminence is guaranteed to exist in perpetuity. In the end, the

United States needs a strategy that encourages positive American leadership and maintains security, while balancing the need for all states to work together to rebuild and reinforce the foundations of peace, security, and prosperity. It did so before, and it can do so again.

Thus, one indicator of the strength of the third principle is whether the United States shares the burden with allies and partners. In Afghanistan, how much of the work of nation building is done by Afghans themselves? In principle, it should always be proportionally more than what America is doing, because the United States cannot shoulder the full burden of developing a state economically, politically, and socially. Such an approach is both unrealistic and unwise. As for allies, the question is how capable they are of acting alongside the United States. The demilitarization of Europe is deeply problematic for U.S. grand strategy because this translates into a fundamentally weaker NATO. It also implies that the United States will have to pay the costs of military interventions. Over the long term, this will lead to a decline in relative power, which suggests that it might be useful to consider a new Marshall Plan for the European global security capabilities. A similar proposal for a Marshall Plan for states in the Middle East has been raised.[22]

A second indicator of the health of the third principle is America's diplomatic standing. By diplomatic standing, I mean its ability to interact with key interlocutors in other states and societies and its ability to mediate conflicts. In the past, especially under Presidents Theodore Roosevelt and Jimmy Carter, America had the diplomatic standing to mediate great conflicts. Now, it seems to have lost that ability and image, while American embassies and consulates seem to be fortresses rather than places for the conduct of diplomacy. Dangerously, this practice continues to isolate the United States.

In practice, Washington's credibility and influence increase when it willingly demonstrates its support and encouragement for other states to exercise leadership. Washington only gains when it shows greater support for multilateralism. It must learn to use existing international institutions, while building new ones, as part of its strategy for encouraging states and actors to work together to restrain the dangers to international security. One corollary to the principle of greater multilateralism in American grand strategy is that Washington should no longer view challenges as essentially "American problems." The new lens through which to view American grand strategy is to strengthen alliances and partnerships so that more nations are helping to solve the world's problems.

Policy makers know, if occasionally ignore, that American power is limited. Policy makers in Washington will learn that they can accomplish vastly more once they enshrine American grand strategy with the value of collaborating with states and institutions who share a commitment to building a peaceful, stable, and secure world. Whether diminishing nuclear proliferation, preventing genocide, providing humanitarian assistance, restraining extremism, or confronting economic policies that threaten the global economy, the United States and its allies will be better able to build a more secure and prosperous world when they work together. Policy makers and the public should not forget the eminently practical and straightforward reason for building stronger alliances and partnerships. In practice, it is no longer necessary or appropriate for Washington's grand strategy to rely on diplomatic domination or to play the role of referee of last resort.

In reality, the United States cannot afford to exempt itself from global leadership. The time has come, despite being mired in an anemic and slow recovery from the "Great Recession," for the United States to exercise greater world leadership. This is crucial when one looks at the challenges posed by China, Russia, Iran, North Korea, and Venezuela – and increasingly Egypt and Syria in the highly unstable Middle East. However, the counterpoint to this principle of leadership is that the United States does not have unlimited power – as mentioned previously, everywhere, all of the time, for the rest of the world. Attempts to "do everything" only further erode the American public's support, as the public asks why the nation is carrying the burden while other states apparently get a "free ride."

The two extremes – one where America engages less and retrenches, or one where America takes the lead on all issues – are equally unacceptable and impractical. This is the right time, after nearly seven decades, for America to reinforce its alliances and partnerships – new and old – so that other states and institutions can rise to the occasion to share the responsibility and burden of leadership. The United States rebuilt states and regions after World War II and protected them for fifty years, so now is the time for those states to join in efforts to resolve global problems. The practical challenge for U.S. grand strategy is how to balance working in concert with others in the international community, while keeping options open in those crucial moments when the United States might decide that it is necessary to act alone. Grand strategy, if it is to be effective, must use principles such as these to help build a world in which states are permitted and encouraged to pursue peace and prosperity.

Balancing among Principles

To be successful, American grand strategy must embody positive principles that match the circumstances of the moment, build a world based on peace and security, and be guided broadly by the consent of the people. But simply having the right principles is only part of the equation. As most observers would expect, society and its policy makers must carefully balance how they put those principles into practice.

This balance applies with equal force to the principle of reinforcing the leadership role of the United States abroad. To build a secure and peaceful world, it is essential for the United States to play a leadership role. No other state can fill this role; a world without American leadership is fraught with perils. Getting this principle right requires a particularly delicate balancing act. If the United States pursues a leadership role based on too much involvement, it will antagonize other states, which rightly would believe that America does not have the right or authority to dominate the globe. If it recedes into a foreign policy of minimalism, the sources of disorder will metastasize and grow – and create an unending series of foreign policy difficulties and challenges.

The principle of American grand strategy that calls for working more cooperatively and collaboratively with other states and institutions raises similar challenges. To ignore or merely pay lip service to this principle will suggest that the United States wants to "go it alone." States will respond by isolating the United States or limiting their support for solving problems that require coordinated action among several nations.

What emerges is a cautionary note about American grand strategy. The unbalanced application of any one of these principles alone will inflict significant harm on U.S. priorities and those of its friends and allies. Worse, to put too much emphasis on any two principles also will undermine America's grand strategy. For example, policies that emphasize rebuilding the domestic foundations of power and relying heavily on the role of cooperation will reinforce the impression that the United States is unwilling to lead in the current and future international system. States will see this as a strategy for gradually disengaging from the world – until the next crisis occurs.

A strategy that deemphasizes American global leadership and promotes cooperation will weaken the nation's ability to promote global stability. Strictly speaking, this describes the state of American policy today. The inherent trap with grand strategy lies in how effectively it is implemented. Policy makers cannot simply pursue any or several principles to the exclusion of the others. To do so will be completely self-defeating. The only path to success is to implement these principles of grand strategy in a balanced and purposeful fashion. Any other approach will weaken the United States, embolden its adversaries, demoralize friends and allies, and eviscerate the world order that America seeks to build.

This survey of the areas of consensus and disagreement among the valuable contributions to the study of grand strategy returns us to the question of how America articulates and implements a grand strategy for this post–Cold War era. How can we think more systematically and rigorously about American grand strategy so we can evaluate these arguments and use them to improve American foreign policy over the long term?

Ultimately, the central question is toward what ends the United States should rebuild the domestic foundations of its power, exercise stronger leadership, and collaborate with alliances and partnerships. Put another way, what is the fundamental goal for American grand strategy? When reflecting on American history, my strongest inclination is that the primary goals of American foreign policy are and always have been to build the foundations of peace and security. Such a world is the greatest legacy that the United States can aspire to achieve. This logic holds today more than ever. At the moment, however, the nation does not have the economic resources or domestic support to build democracy and freedom in other nations. This is especially true as America pivots away from the entangling nation-building episodes in Iraq and Afghanistan.

Since World War II, America has taken the lead in creating a more peaceful world order. One reason is selfish: a peaceful international system that keeps threats and sources of disorder to a minimum permits the United States to pursue its vital national interest in seeing democracies grow, prosper, and build a vibrant global order. Let us remember the world that FDR envisioned when he outlined his iconic four freedoms: freedom of speech, freedom of worship, freedom from want, and freedom from fear. In declaring freedom from fear to be a human right, FDR positioned the United States *to lead in efforts* to reduce armaments and dissuade aggressive nations from threatening and bringing harm to peaceful states. American political and economic power and diplomatic and military might are essential instruments in building the peace and security that must prevail if Americans and all states strive to live in a world, as FDR envisioned, free from fear.

For America, an Optimistic Grand Strategy

First, American policy makers must express, in words and actions, that they are (and they truly should be) supremely confident in America's abilities and policies – largely because the force of history is on our side. Is anyone willing to argue that the repression of freedom, civil rights, and expression – all values that the United States has resisted with rhetoric, policies, and force of arms – represents anything other than a failed past? America's grand strategy should build from an inner sense of confidence – sadly somewhat lacking at the moment – that free societies and free markets are the wave of the future. While the West faces a stalled and anemic economic recovery with most of the European Union in recession, the cyclical nature of economics suggests that the West and its confidence will rebound. Eventually, the West will organize itself to exercise effective leadership in direct opposition to states that promote authoritarian values and predatory policies.

Second, America is the symbol in foreign policy of three powerful concepts, which historically have dominated its grand strategy. One is the role of freedom as a central organizing principle in the formation and conduct of civil society. Another is the role of free markets that embrace the importance of the private sector in the development of market-based societies. The last is the role of promoting the value of peace in the actions of the public sector. The confluence of these principles helps to endow the United States with a sense of confidence. The contrast with the authoritarian states could not be starker, as these states are unlikely to marshal the political and economic values that provide the wherewithal to be proponents of a peaceful, prosperous, and free international order.

Third, the West should not feel, much less show, any sense of weakness, indecision, or dithering. America's grand strategy rests on freedom, while authoritarian states adhere slavishly to the failed logic of controlling all facets of life in their societies – as seen in North Korea and Syria as well as Russia and China. Put directly, the greatest risk for the future of America's role in the world is a self-inflicted failure to adapt and to lead. Failing to articulate and implement a coherent and positive grand strategy is a sure way to undermine the foundations on which international security rests.

Policy makers must bear in mind, however, that the United States is advised to guard against the twin dangers of under- and over-reaction. There will always be authoritarian states and rogue non-state actors willing to use provocative language and actions to threaten the current world order. Although threats to American security should be taken seriously, such provocative language does not mean that Washington should always reciprocate. However, failing to respond forcefully and patiently only emboldens those seeking to upend the status quo. In the end, the United States must marshal its self-confidence into a coherent strategy that empowers it to deal with current threats, anticipate new challenges, and embrace arising opportunities in a direct, measured, and leader-like fashion.

When policy makers step back from the details of their language and policies, the case for the United States to think carefully about its grand strategy is fundamentally simple. It is designed to meet serious threats while creating and taking advantage of strategic opportunities. To continue on the present course of "drifting" from crisis to crisis effectively invites powers to believe that America is in decline. Worse, Americans too might believe wrongly that the nation's decline is inevitable, which in turn will make matters more difficult and dangerous for the West, at least for now.

A strategic weakness with American foreign policy is the deep and enduring political polarization in Washington that complicates, and often paralyzes, U.S. policy making. While the United States once conducted its foreign policy on a largely bipartisan basis, we now see divisions in Washington on virtually all issues. The failure of policy makers in Washington to move beyond this polarized environment puts at risk the nation's ability to act with one voice on foreign policy. Essentially, it puts at risk the entire enterprise of grand strategy, because a deeply divided nation cannot implement policies to defend its interests that call for using its resources effectively and in a coordinated fashion.

By definition, American grand strategy demands that policy makers and politicians take the long view. While it is an eternal challenge for policy makers in Washington to look beyond the next election, the nation simply has no choice. It must build a grand strategy that addresses how the United States deals with the future that extends beyond coming months or years. Abroad, the nation must work with other states and institutions to shape the secure international order that all states desperately need. The alternative of a world marked by uncertainty, fear, and strife is one that no American policy maker can willingly countenance.

An enduring grand strategy must evoke a positive vision of the peace, security, and prosperity to which American policy makers should aspire and which the public will energetically endorse. It should express, perhaps more than any other idea, the principles that Americans are more likely to embrace, and these historically have rested on democratic and shared values that are not unique to the United States.

To be successful, America's grand strategy should demonstrate a sense of optimism that this state, while working with others, can build a more secure, peaceful, and prosperous world. This optimism is based on the simple yet powerful principle that all states need to work together to confront dangers in this world. These dangers call for reinforcing the foundations of American power, strengthening American leadership, and building strong and lasting alliances that can work cooperatively in promoting a better world.

A grand strategy must cultivate the resources, ingenuity, and tools of an irrepressibly innovative and dynamic society. As importantly, it gives policy makers and the public a positive notion of what American foreign policy seeks to accomplish. Lastly, it articulates a vision of the world that America wants to build and the risks it confronts, while reassuring the people that their nation's foreign policy is organized on the basis of principles that call for the prudent exercise of power. With such principles, the nation can avoid the dual perils of drift and overreach or fixating on tired arguments about the nation's inevitable decline.

If America is to assure its future security and prosperity, we need a new grand strategy that harnesses its peoples' spirit, sense of optimism, and perseverance to help the nation meet the challenges and grasp the opportunities of this era. This remains the greatest challenge for contemporary scholars and policy makers, and it is one that we cannot lose sight of if we are to build a stronger and enduring vision for American global leadership.

Notes

1 Introduction

1. George F. Kennan, as Deputy Chief of Mission in Moscow, first articulated the strategy (known as the Long Telegram) in response to an inquiry from the U.S. Department of the Treasury inquiry in February 1946. See George Kennan, "Sources of Soviet Conduct," *Foreign Affairs*, July 1947, pp. 556–582. Also, George F. Kennan, "On American Principles," *Foreign Affairs* (1995), pp. 116–126.

2. See, as examples, Bernard Brodie, *War and Politics* (New York: Pearson, 1974); B. H. Liddell Hart, "Fundamentals of Strategy and Grand Strategy," in *Strategy*, 2nd ed. (New York: Faber & Faber, 1967); Henry Antony Sargeaunt and Geoffrey West, *Grand Strategy* (New York: Thomas Y. Crowell Company, 1941).

3. See, e.g., Walter Russell Mead, *Power, Terror, Peace, and War: America's Grand Strategy in a World at Risk* (New York: Alfred A. Knopf, 2004); Paul Kennedy, *Grand Strategies in War and Peace* (New Haven, CT: Yale University Press, 1991); Edward Luttwak, *The Grand Strategy of the Roman Empire from the First Century A.D. to the Third* (Baltimore: Johns Hopkins University Press, 1979).

4. *The American Heritage Dictionary of the English Language*, 4th ed., 2000.

5. See William C. Martel, *Victory in War: Foundations of Modern Strategy* (New York: Cambridge University Press, 2011), pp. 20–21. Also, Azar Gat, *Origins of Military Thought*, pp. 41–42: "The conduct of operations was the second branch of the art of war. [Paul Gideon Joly de] Maizeroy [1719–1780] gave this branch a new technical term, 'strategy', whose origins in modern military theory also seem to have been lost.... Strategy belongs to the most sublime faculty of mind, to reason.... Strategy ... is dependent upon innumerable circumstances – physical, political, and moral. These rules of strategy (also called the 'military dialectic' by Maizeroy) are: not to do what one's enemy appears to desire; to identify the enemy's principal objective in order not to be misled by his diversions ..."

6. See Hal Brands, *The Promise and Pitfalls of Grand Strategy* (U.S. Army War College, Strategic Studies Institute, August 2012).

7. See William C. Martel, "R.I.P. Containment," *The Diplomat*, September 24, 2013, at www.thediplomat.com/2012/09/24/r-i-p-containment/.

8. See Gideon Rachman, "Think Again: American Decline," *Foreign Policy*, January/February 2011, at www.foreignpolicy.com/articles/2011/01/02/think_again_american_decline. Cf. John Pomfret, "Defense Secretary Gates: U.S. Underestimated Parts of China's Military Modernization," *Washington Post*,

January 9, 2011, at www.washingtonpost.com/wp-dyn/content/article/2011/01/09/ AR2011010901068.html: "Gates rejected the theory – popular in some circles in China – that the United States is in an unstoppable decline. 'History's dustbin,' he said, 'is filled with countries that underestimated the resilience of the United States.'"

2 Contemporary Classics in American Grand Strategy

1. Another critical thinker at Yale whose ideas are examined subsequently is Charles Hill, *Grand Strategies: Literature, Statecraft, and World Order* (New Haven, CT: Yale University Press, 2010).
2. This is a paraphrase of a quotation attributed to Mark Twain, though scholars have not been able to identify where and when he first wrote or said it: "History doesn't repeat itself, but it does rhyme."
3. Paul Kennedy, *The Rise and Fall of the Great Powers*, 1st ed. (New York: Vintage Books, 1989), p. 515.
4. Kennedy, *The Rise and Fall of the Great Powers*, 1st ed. (New York: Vintage Books, 1989), p. 533.
5. On empires, see Arnold J. Toynbee, *A Study of History* (New York: Dell, 1965).
6. However, Kennedy is not exact about the threshold for decline-inducing defense spending.
7. Fareed Zakaria, *The Post-American World* (New York: W.W. Norton, 2008), p. 199. See also Charles A. Kupchan, "Empire, Military Power, and Economic Decline," *International Security* 13, No. 4 (April 1, 1989), pp. 36–53.
8. Contrary to Kennedy's thesis, in the U.S. states the signs of budgetary "overstretch" are not arising from security-related spending but from entitlements. See, e.g., the Congressional Budget Office report, *The Budget and Economic Outlook: Fiscal Years 2013 to 2023*, pp. 22–24.
9. See, e.g., John Lewis Gaddis, *Surprise, Security, and the American Experience* (Cambridge, MA; London: Harvard University Press, 2005).
10. John Lewis Gaddis, "A Grand Strategy of Transformation," *Foreign Policy* (November 2002), pp. 50–57.
11. John Lewis Gaddis, *Surprise, Security, and the American Experience* (Cambridge, MA; London: Harvard University Press, 2005).
12. John Lewis Gaddis, "A Grand Strategy of Transformation," *Foreign Policy* (November 2002), pp. 50–57.
13. See Chapter 8 on the reluctant rise of the United States to the ranks of a global power.
14. His two best books on American grand strategy are: Walter Russell Mead, *Special Providence: American Foreign Policy and How It Changed the World*, 1st ed. (Routledge, 2002); Walter Russell Mead, *Power, Terror, Peace, and War: America's Grand Strategy in a World at Risk* (New York: Vintage Books, 2005).
15. Mead, *Special Providence: American Foreign Policy and How It Changed the World*, 1st ed. (Routledge, 2002), pp. 34–51.
16. Mead, *Special Providence: American Foreign Policy and How It Changed the World*, 1st ed. (Routledge, 2002), identifies, defines, and tracks the influence of these four traditions.

17. However, Mead does track the entry of a new school of foreign policy when the neoconservatives rose to power under George W. Bush. See Walter Russell Mead, *Special Providence: American Foreign Policy and How It Changed the World*, 1st ed. (Routledge, 2002); Walter Russell Mead, *Power, Terror, Peace, and War: America's Grand Strategy in a World at Risk* (New York: Vintage Books, 2005), pp. 84–94.

18. See Williamson Murray, *War, Strategy, and Military Effectiveness* (New York: Cambridge University Press, 2011); Williamson Murray, ed., *The Shaping of Grand Strategy: Policy, Diplomacy, and War* (New York: Cambridge University Press, 2011); Williamson Murray, MacGregor Knox, and Alvin Bernstein, eds., *The Making of Strategy: Rulers, States, and War* (New York: Cambridge University Press, 1994).

19. Williamson Murray, "Thoughts on Grand Strategy," in Williamson Murray, Richard Hart Sinnreich, and James Lacey (eds.), *The Shaping of Grand Strategy: Policy, Diplomacy, and War* (New York: Cambridge University Press, 2011), p. 1.

20. Murray, "Thoughts on Grand Strategy," in Williamson Murray, Richard Hart Sinnreich, and James Lacey (eds.), *The Shaping of Grand Strategy: Policy, Diplomacy, and War* (New York: Cambridge University Press, 2011), p. 1.

21. Murray, "Thoughts on Grand Strategy," in Williamson Murray, Richard Hart Sinnreich, and James Lacey (eds.), *The Shaping of Grand Strategy: Policy, Diplomacy, and War* (New York: Cambridge University Press, 2011), pp. 1–2.

22. Murray, "Thoughts on Grand Strategy," in Williamson Murray, Richard Hart Sinnreich, and James Lacey (eds.), *The Shaping of Grand Strategy: Policy, Diplomacy, and War* (New York: Cambridge University Press, 2011), p. 2.

23. Joseph S. Nye, *Soft Power: The Means to Success in World Politics* (New York: Public Affairs, 2004), pp. x–xiii.

24. Nye, *Soft Power: The Means to Success in World Politics* (New York: Public Affairs, 2004), pp. x–xiii.

25. Joseph S. Nye, *The Future of Power* (New York: Public Affairs, 2011), pp. 177–186.

26. For his seminal work on offensive realism, see John J. Mearsheimer, *The Tragedy of Great Power Politics* (New York: Norton, 2001).

27. John J. Mearsheimer, "Better to Be Godzilla Than Bambi," *Foreign Policy*, No. 146 (January 1, 2005), pp. 47–48; John J. Mearsheimer, "The False Promise of International Institutions," *International Security* 19, No. 3 (Winter 1994–1995), pp. 5–49.

28. Lawrence Summers, "The United States and the Global Adjustment Process." Speech presented at the Third Annual Stavros S. Niarchos Lecture (Washington, DC: Institute for International Economics, 2004).

29. Mearsheimer, "Better to Be Godzilla Than Bambi," *Foreign Policy*, No. 146 (January 1, 2005), pp. 47–48.

30. Robert Gilpin, *War and Change in World Politics* (Cambridge: Cambridge University Press, 1981); Robert Gilpin and Jean M. Gilpin, *Global Political Economy: Understanding the International Economic Order* (Princeton, NJ: Princeton University Press, 2001).

31. Gilpin, *War and Change in World Politics* (Cambridge: Cambridge University Press, 1981), pp. 10–14.

32. Gilpin, *War and Change in World Politics* (Cambridge: Cambridge University Press, 1981), pp. 170–190.

33. Gilpin, *War and Change in World Politics* (Cambridge: Cambridge University Press, 1981), pp. 240–244.

34. Henry Kissinger, *Nuclear Weapons and Foreign Policy* (New York: W.W. Norton, 1969); Henry Kissinger, *The World Restored* (London: V. Gollancz, 1974); Henry Kissinger, *Does America Need a Foreign Policy? Toward a Diplomacy for the 21st Century* (New York: Simon & Schuster, 2002); Henry Kissinger, *Diplomacy* (New York: Simon & Schuster, 1994).

35. Kissinger, *Diplomacy* (New York: Simon & Schuster, 1994), pp. 25–29.

36. Kissinger, *Diplomacy* (New York: Simon & Schuster, 1994), pp. 17–29.

37. See Michael Howard, "The World According to Henry: From Metternich to Me," *Foreign Affairs* 73, No. 3 (May 1, 1994), pp. 132–140.

38. Niall Ferguson, *The Pity of War: Explaining World War I* (New York: Basic Books, 2000), pp. 161–168. The scholarship on the origins of World War I is dauntingly extensive and cross-disciplinary, but Keir A. Lieber provides an excellent overview of the main causal arguments in "The New History of World War I and What It Means for International Relations Theory," *International Security* 32, No. 2 (October 1, 2007), pp. 155–191.

39. Then foreign secretary Sir Edward Grey perhaps best articulated the reasons for British intervention: a German victory could not be risked because it would have made Germany "supreme over all the Continent of Europe and Asia Minor." Ferguson also attributes British intervention to the Liberal government's need to stay ahead of the Conservative and Unionist opposition. Cf. Michael Howard, "The World According to Henry: From Metternich to Me," *Foreign Affairs* 73, No. 3 (May 1, 1994), p. 139, who argues that the motivation was more to fulfill treaty obligations to defend Belgian neutrality and to uphold the rule of law in the international system more generally.

40. For an excellent article that uses survey and experimental data to argue that there is actually a realist tradition in the American electorate's views, see Daniel W. Drezner, "The Realist Tradition in American Public Opinion," *Perspectives on Politics* 6, No. 1 (March 2008), pp. 51–70. The arguments in this book are more in line with Drezner than Kissinger on this score, the difference being that "realism" is not the most accurate term for describing the tradition in American foreign policy. It is defined by a preference for "gradualism" – for nondisruptive, positive changes to the status quo, as this concept is developed in Chapters 7–10.

41. For an excellent review of Kissinger's book *Diplomacy* and a cogent critique of its argument, see Michael Howard, "The World According to Henry: From Metternich to Me," *Foreign Affairs* 73, No. 3 (May 1, 1994), pp. 132–140.

42. Zbigniew Brzezinski, *Strategic Vision: America and the Crisis of Global Power* (New York: Basic Books, 2012); Zbigniew Brzezinski, *The Grand Chessboard: American Primacy and Its Geostrategic Imperatives* (New York: Basic Books, 1997).

43. Brzezinski, *The Grand Chessboard: American Primacy and Its Geostrategic Imperatives* (New York: Basic Books, 1997), pp. 30–56.

44. For the classic statement of the Heartland Theory, see H.J. Mackinder, "The Geographical Pivot of History," *Geographical Journal* 23, No. 4 (April 1, 1904), pp. 421–437.

45. Zbigniew Brzezinski, *Strategic Vision: America and the Crisis of Global Power* (New York: Basic Books, 2012), pp. 7–36.

46. Zbigniew Brzezinski, *Second Chance: Three Presidents and the Crisis of American Superpower* (New York: Basic Books, 2007).

47. Zbigniew Brzezinski, *Strategic Vision: America and the Crisis of Global Power* (New York: Basic Books, 2012), pp. 132–154.

48. Walter Russell Mead agrees, as discussed in *Special Providence*, p. 7.

49. Zbigniew Brzezinski, *Strategic Vision: America and the Crisis of Global Power* (New York: Basic Books, 2012).

50. Richard Haass, *War of Necessity, War of Choice: A Memoir of Two Iraq Wars* (New York: Simon & Schuster, 2010).

51. Richard Haass, *Foreign Policy Begins at Home: The Case for Putting America's House in Order* (New York: Basic Books, 2013).

52. Haass, *Foreign Policy Begins at Home: The Case for Putting America's House in Order* (New York: Basic Books, 2013).

53. Haass, *Foreign Policy Begins at Home: The Case for Putting America's House in Order* (New York: Basic Books, 2013), pp. 267–278.

54. Although the U.S. government conquered and displaced the territories of Native American tribes, this was never regarded as bearing on the legitimacy of the state system, which offers one reason, arguably, why this conquest was accepted.

55. Richard Haass, *Foreign Policy Begins at Home: The Case for Putting America's House in Order* (New York: Basic Books, 2013); Richard Haass, *War of Necessity: War of Choice: A Memoir of Two Iraq Wars* (New York: Simon & Schuster, 2010).

56. See Colin S. Gray, *War, Peace and International Relations: An Introduction to Strategic History* (New York: Routledge, 2011); Colin S. Gray, *Modern Strategy* (Oxford: Oxford University Press, 1999); Colin S. Gray, *Strategic Studies and Public Policy: The American Experience* (Lexington: University Press of Kentucky, 1982).

57. Colin S. Gray, *The Sheriff: America's Defense of the New World Order* (Lexington: University Press of Kentucky, 2009).

58. Colin S. Gray, *Weapons Don't Make War: Policy, Strategy, and Military Technology* (Lawrence: University Press of Kansas, 1993).

59. Colin S. Gray, *War, Peace and International Relations: An Introduction to Strategic History* (New York: Routledge, 2011).

60. Colin S. Gray, *Modern Strategy* (Oxford: Oxford University Press, 1999), p. 29.

61. Colin S. Gray, *Weapons Don't Make War: Policy, Strategy, and Military Technology* (Lawrence: University Press of Kansas, 1993).

62. Stephen Peter Rosen, *Winning the Next War: Innovation and the Modern Military* (Ithaca: Cornell University Press, 1991).

63. Rosen, *Winning the Next War: Innovation and the Modern Military* (Ithaca: Cornell University Press, 1991), pp. 5–54.

64. Rosen, *Winning the Next War: Innovation and the Modern Military* (Ithaca: Cornell University Press, 1991), pp. 251–262.

65. See Stephen Peter Rosen, "Military Effectiveness: Why Society Matters," *International Security* 19, No. 4 (April 1, 1995), pp. 5–31, who contends that the degree of internal political division within a society determines whether a state can translate economic power into military effectiveness.

3 Foundations of Grand Strategy

1. Kimberly Kagan, "Redefining Roman Grand Strategy," *Journal of Military History* 70, No. 2 (April 2006), pp. 333–362; Edward Luttwak, *The Grand Strategy of the Roman Empire from the First Century A.D. to the Third* (Baltimore: Johns Hopkins University Press, 1979).

2. Edward Mead Earle, *Makers of Modern Strategy* (Princeton, NJ: Princeton University Press, 1971), p. viii.

3. For critical works on strategy, see Williamson Murray and Mark Grimsley, "Introduction: On Strategy," in Williamson Murray, MacGregor Knox, and Alvin Bernstein (eds.), *The Making of Strategy: Rulers, States, and War* (New York: Cambridge University Press, 1994), pp. 1–23; Colin S. Gray, "Why Strategy Is Difficult," *Joint Forces Quarterly* 20 (1997), pp. 6–12; Michael I. Handel, *Masters of War: Classical Strategic Thought*, 3rd ed. (London: Frank Cass, 2001); Peter Paret, ed., with Gordon A. Craig and Felix Gilbert, *Makers of Modern Strategy: From Machiavelli to the Nuclear Age* (Princeton, NJ: Princeton University Press, 1986); B. H. Liddell Hart, *Strategy: The Indirect Approach* (New York: Praeger, 1954).

4. See Henry Antony Sargeaunt and Geoffrey West, *Grand Strategy* (New York: Thomas Y. Crowell Company, 1941); also, book review: Sargeaunt, West, *Grand Strategy* (New York: Thomas Y. Crowell, 1941), in *Annals of the American Academy of Political and Social Science* 221, No. 1 (May 1942), pp. 207–208. Cf. Edward Mead Earle, *Makers of Modern Strategy* (Princeton, NJ: Princeton University Press, 1971).

5. Sargeaunt and West, *Grand Strategy* (New York: Thomas Y. Crowell Company, 1941), pp. 21–25.

6. For further assessment of Edward Mead Earle's *Makers of Modern Strategy*, see David Ekbladh, "Present at the Creation: Edward Mead Earle and the Depression Era Origins of Security Studies," *International Security* 36 (Winter 2011/2012), p. 107–141.

7. Edward Mead Earle, *Makers of Modern Strategy* (Princeton, NJ: Princeton University Press, 1971), p. viii.

8. B. H. Liddell Hart, *Strategy: The Indirect Approach* (New York: Praeger, 1954), p. 333.

9. B. H. Liddell Hart, *The Classic Book on Military Strategy*, 2nd rev. ed. (London: Faber & Faber Ltd., 1967), p. 349.

10. Robert Art, *A Grand Strategy for America* (Ithaca, NY: Cornell University Press, 2004), p. 10.

11. See Terry L. Deibel, *Foreign Affairs Strategy: Logic for American Statecraft* (New York: Cambridge University Press, 2007), pp. 4–6.

12. Edward Luttwak, *Strategy: The Logic of War and Peace* (Cambridge, MA: Belknap Press of Harvard University Press, 2001), p. 70.

13. See P. Gove, ed., *Webster's Third New International Dictionary* (Springfield, MA: Merriam-Webster Inc., 1981), p. 2348.

14. Edward Luttwak, *Strategy: The Logic of War and Peace* (Cambridge, MA: Belknap Press of Harvard University Press, 2001), p. 70.

15. Luttwak, *Strategy: The Logic of War and Peace* (Cambridge, MA: Belknap Press of Harvard University Press, 2001), p. 70, who argues that technical effects are

relevant when they have "tactical consequences," while in turn, tactical-level actions depend on "technical performance to some extent."

16. Luttwak, *Strategy: The Logic of War and Peace* (Cambridge, MA: Belknap Press of Harvard University Press, 2001), p. 76.

17. Luttwak, *Strategy: The Logic of War and Peace* (Cambridge, MA: Belknap Press of Harvard University Press, 2001), p. 76, who uses the example of "the perfect" infantry rifle made to such high specifications that the cost of mass producing it is prohibitive. He argues that it would be better to have a higher quantity of rifles that are simply "very good" (p. 78).

18. Remarks by Defense Secretary Robert M. Gates, United States Department of Defense, January 27, 2009, at www.defense.gov/news/newsarticle.aspx?id=52838. Cf. Alain C. Enthoven and Wayne K. Smith, *How Much Is Enough? Shaping the Defense Program, 1961–1969* (New York: Harper & Row, 1971).

19. Edward Luttwak, *Strategy: The Logic of War and Peace* (Cambridge, MA: Belknap Press of Harvard University Press, 2001), p. 81, who frames the problem using a maritime analogy: "Politicians are still the captains of the ship of the state, and soldiers operate its gundeck, but now there are technicians in charge of the engine room, whose doings propel the ship on uncharted routes toward an unknown destination."

20. For a definition of *tactical*, see P. Gove, ed., *Webster's Third New International Dictionary* (Springfield, MA: Merriam-Webster Inc., 1981), p. 2327.

21. See P. Gove, ed., *Webster's Third New International Dictionary* (Springfield, MA: Merriam-Webster Inc., 1981), p. 2327.

22. For a detailed analysis of how military theorists and strategists have used the term *tactical* in strategy, see "Historical Origins of Victory," pp. 15–51, and "Modern Origins of Victory," pp. 52–82, in William C. Martel, *Victory in War: Foundations of Modern Strategy* (New York: Cambridge University Press, 2011). Cf. Brian Bond, *The Pursuit of Victory: From Napoleon to Saddam Hussein* (New York: Oxford University Press, 1996); Colin S. Gray, *Defining and Achieving Decisive Victory* (Carlisle Barracks, PA: Strategic Studies Institute, U.S. Army War College, April 2002), p. 19; Russell F. Weigley, *The Age of Battles: The Quest for Decisive Warfare from Breitenfeld to Waterloo* (Bloomington: Indiana University Press, 1991), p. 34; Russell F. Weigley, *American Way of War: A History of United States Military Strategy and Policy* (New York: Macmillan, 1973), pp. 32–34.

23. See Robert L. Helmbold, *Decision in Battle: Breakpoint Hypotheses and Engagement Termination Data, R-772-PR* (Santa Monica, CA: RAND Corporation, June 1971), pp. 1–2.

24. See Helen J. Nicholson, "The Practice of Land Warfare," *Medieval Warfare: Theory and Practice of War in Europe, 300–1500* (New York: Palgrave Macmillan, 2004), p. 141: "The war could end when one side withdrew to their territory, with the surrender of one side and acceptance of the other's authority, or with a peace treaty as if between equals. Sometimes the defeated side would pay the victor to go away: forcing an enemy to make a treaty or to pay tribute was in itself a sign of victory" (p. 143).

25. In an earlier study (Martel, *Victory in War*, 2011), the category of tactical matters focuses on the outcome and effects of battles between opposing forces,

which is often but not exclusively used to describe the result of interactions between armies or military forces on the battlefield. For military historian John Keegan, the prominence placed by strategists on battles is natural because military history is "in the last resort about battle." See John Keegan, *The Face of Battle: A Study of Agincourt, Waterloo and the Somme* (New York: Penguin Books, 1984), p. 18: "Complex manoeuvres and the size of the army were less important."

26. Edward Luttwak, *Strategy: The Logic of War and Peace* (Cambridge, MA: Belknap Press of Harvard University Press, 2001), pp. 83–84: "... military-balance estimates formed at the technical level alone are so systematically misleading: in presenting lists of weapons side by side, they offer comparisons of attractive precision that exclude the greater part of the whole."

27. Luttwak, *Strategy: The Logic of War and Peace* (Cambridge, MA: Belknap Press of Harvard University Press, 2001), p. 88: "Particular forces are not independent agents pursuing their own goals. Their entire existence at the time is merely a fragment of the larger scheme of things for the successive layers of command of the respective armies and national authorities."

28. Luttwak, *Strategy: The Logic of War and Peace* (Cambridge, MA: Belknap Press of Harvard University Press, 2001), pp. 89–90.

29. Luttwak, *Strategy: The Logic of War and Peace* (Cambridge, MA: Belknap Press of Harvard University Press, 2001), p. 91.

30. Luttwak, *Strategy: The Logic of War and Peace* (Cambridge, MA: Belknap Press of Harvard University Press, 2001), p. 108.

31. Luttwak, *Strategy: The Logic of War and Peace* (Cambridge, MA: Belknap Press of Harvard University Press, 2001), p. 69.

32. Luttwak also includes the theater level of strategic interaction, but for the purposes of this study it is unnecessary to include since the operational and theater levels are roughly synonymous, as a chart at the end of this section clarifies.

33. P. Gove, ed., *Webster's Third New International Dictionary* (Springfield, MA: Merriam-Webster, 1981), p. 2256. Also, Scott A. Boorman, "Fundamentals of Strategy: The Legacy of Henry Eccles," *Naval War College Review* 62, No. 2 (Spring 2009), pp. 91–115.

34. See Quincy Wright, *A Study of War*, abr. Louise Leonard Wright (Chicago: University of Chicago Press, 1964), p. 18, for a reference to the "expectation of victory through the use of mutually recognized procedures." Also, there are potential economic gains from victory (pp. 427–428). See T. N. Dupuy, *Understanding Defeat: How to Recover from Loss in Battle to Gain Victory in War* (New York: Paragon House, 1990), on the concept of defeat.

35. According to *Air Force Basic Doctrine: Air Force Doctrine Document 1* (Maxwell AFB, AL: Air University Press, 1997), p. 86, *strategy* is defined as "the art and science of developing and using political, economic, psychological, and military forces as necessary during peace and war, to afford the maximum support to policies, in order to increase the probabilities and favorable consequences of victory and to lessen the chances of defeat."

36. See Terry L. Deibel, *Foreign Affairs Strategy: Logic for American Statecraft* (New York: Cambridge University Press, 2007), p. 3.

37. Edward Luttwak, *Strategy: The Logic of War and Peace* (Cambridge, MA: Belknap Press of Harvard University Press, 2001), p. 155: "At the level of theater strategy the consequences of single operations are felt in the overall conduct of offense and defense – those overriding military purposes that scarcely figure at the operational level ... in which an attack can serve to better defend a front while holding operations on some sectors often figure in offensive war." For instance, the question of whether it is prudent for the state to use battlefield nuclear weapons "cannot be answered within the scope of theater strategy," since it "transcends the considerations that arise from the organization of military power" (pp. 69–70).

38. According to *Air Force Basic Doctrine: Air Force Doctrine Document 1* (Maxwell AFB, AL: Air University Press, 1997), *strategy* is "the art and science of developing and using political, economic, psychological, and military forces as necessary during peace and war, to afford the maximum support to policies, in order to increase the probabilities and favorable consequences of victory and to lessen the chances of defeat" (p. 86), whereas *doctrine* is "fundamental principles by which the military forces or elements thereof guide their actions in support of national objectives" (p. 81). Cf. Harald Hoiback, "What Is Doctrine?" *Journal of Strategic Studies* 34, No. 6 (December 2011), pp. 879–900.

39. Edward Luttwak, *Strategy: The Logic of War and Peace* (Cambridge, MA: Belknap Press of Harvard University Press, 2001), p. 70. Cf. Richard N. Rosecrance and Arthur A. Stein, eds., *The Domestic Base of Grand Strategy* (Ithaca, NY: Cornell University Press, 1993).

40. See Richard Hart Sinnreich, "Patterns of Grand Strategy," in Williamson Murray, Richard Hart Sinnreich, and James Lacey (eds.), *The Shaping of Grand Strategy: Policy, Diplomacy, and War* (New York: Cambridge University Press, 2011), p. 254. In successfully developing grand strategies, he quotes Williamson Murray: "Those who have developed successful grand strategies in the past have been very much the exception ... [A] strategic framework, much less a grand strategy, has rarely guided those responsible for the long-term survival of the state."

41. Sinnreich, "Patterns of Grand Strategy," in Williamson Murray, Richard Hart Sinnreich, and James Lacey (eds.), *The Shaping of Grand Strategy: Policy, Diplomacy, and War* (New York: Cambridge University Press, 2011), p. 256.

42. See Stephen D. Krasner, "An Orienting Principle for Foreign Policy: The Deficiencies of Grand Strategy," *Policy Review*, Hoover Institution, No. 163 (October 1, 2010), at www.hoover.org/publications/policy-review/article/49786.

43. See Walter A. McDougall, "Can the United States Do Grand Strategy?" FPRI-Temple University Consortium on Grand Strategy, *The Telegram*, No. 3 (April 2010), at www.fpri.org/telegram/201004.mcdougall.usgrandstrategy.html.

44. See Terry L. Deibel, *Foreign Affairs Strategy: Logic for American Statecraft* (New York: Cambridge University Press, 2007), p. 3.

45. Hans J. Morgenthau, *Politics among Nations: The Struggle for Power and Peace*, 5th ed. (New York: Alfred A. Knopf, 1973), p. 141.

46. John Lewis Gaddis, "What Is Grand Strategy?" keynote address, "American Grand Strategy after War," sponsored by the Triangle Institute for Security Studies and the Duke University Program in American Grand Strategy, February 26, 2009.

47. John Lewis Gaddis, "Containment and the Logic of Strategy," *National Interest*, No. 10 (Winter 1987–1988), p. 19.

48. Paul Kennedy, ed., *Grand Strategies in War and Peace* (New Haven, CT: Yale University Press, 1991), pp. ix–xx.

49. See Stephen D. Biddle, *Military Power: Explaining Victory and Defeat in Modern Battle* (Princeton, NJ: Princeton University Press, 2004), pp. 252–53, who discusses strategy in the context of the concept of levels of war.

50. See Stephen D. Biddle, *American Grand Strategy after 9/11: An Assessment* (Carlisle Barracks, PA: Strategic Studies Institute, U.S. Army War College, April 2005), p. 1, who cites Paul Kennedy, ed., *Grand Strategies in War and Peace* (New Haven, CT: Yale University Press, 1991), pp. 1–7; B. H. Liddell Hart, *Strategy* (New York: Penguin, 1991 ed. of 1954 orig.), pp. 353–360, xvii–xxi, 319–337.

51. Peter Feaver, "What Is Grand Strategy and Why Do We Need It?" *Foreign Policy*, April 8, 2009; Peter Feaver, "Debating American Grand Strategy after Major War," *Orbis* (Fall 2009), pp. 547–552.

52. See William C. Martel, "American Grand Strategy after November 2012," *Society* 49, No. 5 (2012), pp. 433–438; William C. Martel, "Why America Needs a Grand Strategy," *The Diplomat*, June 18, 2012, at www.thediplomat.com/2012/06/18/why-america-needs-a-grand-strategy/.

53. Edward Luttwak, *Strategy: The Logic of War and Peace* (Cambridge, MA: Belknap Press of Harvard University Press, 2001), p. 181.

54. Luttwak, *Strategy: The Logic of War and Peace* (Cambridge, MA: Belknap Press of Harvard University Press, 2001), p. 179, in the category of "further interaction with the nonmilitary transactions of states."

55. See Stephen Biddle, *Military Power: Explaining Victory and Defeat in Modern Battle* (Princeton, NJ: Princeton University Press, 2004), p. 26. As a consequence, "many of the effects of grand strategy or institutional structure can best be understood via the effects on preponderance, technology, and operational/tactical force employment."

56. Biddle, *Military Power: Explaining Victory and Defeat in Modern Battle* (Princeton, NJ: Princeton University Press, 2004), p. 26.

57. Biddle, *Military Power: Explaining Victory and Defeat in Modern Battle* (Princeton, NJ: Princeton University Press, 2004), p. 26.

58. Biddle, *Military Power: Explaining Victory and Defeat in Modern Battle* (Princeton, NJ: Princeton University Press, 2004), pp. 26–27. How one knows that these considerations matter is the extent to which the "effects are ultimately felt as changes in the balance of forces engaged."

59. Sherle R. Schwenninger, "Revamping American Grand Strategy," *World Policy Journal* 20 (Fall 2003), pp. 20–21.

60. Schwenninger, "Revamping American Grand Strategy," *World Policy Journal* 20 (Fall 2003), pp. 20–21.

61. John Lewis Gaddis, "Toward the Post-Cold War World," *Foreign Affairs* 70, No. 2 (Spring 1991), p. 102.

62. See Colin S. Gray, "Harry S. Truman and the Forming of American Grand Strategy in the Cold War, 1945–1953," in Williamson Murray, Richard Hart Sinnreich, and James Lacey (eds.), *The Shaping of Grand Strategy: Policy,*

Diplomacy, and War (New York: Cambridge University Press, 2011), pp. 210–253. Drawing on concepts consistent with Gaddis's language of "geopolitical cartography," Gray writes, "In short, in 1945, Truman confronted the historically all too familiar conditions of postwar uncertainty, chaos, and the need to comprehend a cluster of contexts substantially different in detail and broad character from those either experienced before or recently predicted by most observer-participants."

63. John Lewis Gaddis, "Toward the Post-Cold War World," *Foreign Affairs* 70, No. 2 (Spring 1991), p. 103.

64. Peter Paret, ed., with Gordon A. Craig and Felix Gilbert, *Makers of Modern Strategy: From Machiavelli to the Nuclear Age* (Princeton, NJ: Princeton University Press, 1986), pp. 870–871.

65. Paret, ed., with Gordon A. Craig and Felix Gilbert, *Makers of Modern Strategy: From Machiavelli to the Nuclear Age* (Princeton, NJ: Princeton University Press, 1986), p. 871. When "hostilities broke out in Korea … [this] exercise in strategy … would almost certainly have won Clausewitz' approbation." Furthermore, it was implemented with "a realistic assessment of the current state of affairs in international politics," because it reflected "an accurate view of the capabilities and proclivities of potential opponents."

66. B. H. Liddell Hart, *The Classic Book on Military Strategy*, 2nd rev. ed. (London: Faber & Faber Ltd., 1967), p. 349. Note that in this context *policy* and *grand strategy* are synonymous.

67. A. J. P. Taylor, *The Origins of the Second World War* (New York: Atheneum, 1962), pp. 18–39, 61–86, who states (p. 19) that "the first war explains the second and, in fact, caused it, in so far as one event causes another."

68. B. H. Liddell Hart, *The Classic Book on Military Strategy*, 2nd rev. ed. (London: Faber & Faber Ltd., 1967), p. 345: "It became evident that there was something wrong with the theory, or at least its application … [T]he appalling losses suffered in pursuit of the 'ideal' objective, and the post-war exhaustion of nominal victors, showed that a thorough re-examination of the whole problem of the object and aim was needed."

69. Liddell Hart, *The Classic Book on Military Strategy*, 2nd rev. ed. (London: Faber & Faber Ltd., 1967), p. 358.

70. Liddell Hart, *The Classic Book on Military Strategy*, 2nd rev. ed. (London: Faber & Faber Ltd., 1967), p. 357.

71. Liddell Hart, *The Classic Book on Military Strategy*, 2nd rev. ed. (London: Faber & Faber Ltd., 1967), p. 357: "1) While fighting is a physical act, its direction is a mental process. The better your strategy, the easier you will gain the upper hand, and the less it will cost you; 2) The more strength you waste, the greater your risk for defeat. Even if you succeed, the less strength you will have to profit by the peace; 3) The more brutal your methods, the more you harden the resistance and consolidate the enemy's troops and people behind their leaders; 4) The more determined you appear to impose your version of peace, the greater the resistance you will face; and 5) If and when you reach your military goal, the more you ask of the defeated side, the more trouble you will have and the more cause you will provide for an attempt to reverse the settlement achieved by war."

72. Liddell Hart, *The Classic Book on Military Strategy*, 2nd rev. ed. (London: Faber & Faber Ltd., 1967), p. 357. His reasoning is that "force is a vicious cycle – or rather, a

spiral – unless its application is controlled by the most carefully reasoned calculation." This leads to the observation that "war, which begins by denying reason,
comes to vindicate it – throughout all the phases of the struggle."

73. Cf. Paul Kennedy, *The Rise and Fall of the Great Powers* (New York: Random
    House, 1987).

74. Paul Kennedy, ed., *Grand Strategies in War and Peace* (New Haven, CT: Yale
    University Press, 1991), p. 2.

75. B. H. Liddell Hart, *The Classic Book on Military Strategy*, 2nd rev. ed. (London:
    Faber & Faber Ltd., 1967), p. 349.

76. Liddell Hart, *The Classic Book on Military Strategy*, 2nd rev. ed. (London: Faber &
    Faber Ltd., 1967), p. 345: "It became evident that there was something wrong with
    the theory, or at least its application ... [T]he appalling losses suffered in pursuit of
    the 'ideal' objective, and the post-war exhaustion of nominal victors, showed that a
    thorough re-examination of the whole problem of the object and aim was needed."
    Cf. A. J. P. Taylor, *The Origins of the Second World War* (New York: Atheneum,
    1962), p. 19.

77. Bernard Brodie, *War and Politics* (New York: Macmillan, 1973), p. 446.

78. Brodie, *War and Politics* (New York: Macmillan, 1973), p. 492.

79. Brodie, *War and Politics* (New York: Macmillan, 1973), p. 492.

80. Brodie, *War and Politics* (New York: Macmillan, 1973), p. 492. As a partial counter
    argument, at least in the case of the United States, senior military leaders spend
    considerable time during their careers in graduate programs and war colleges
    precisely to remedy this concern.

81. On ideology, cf. Daniel Bell, *The End of Ideology: On the Exhaustion of Political
    Ideas in the Fifties* (New York: Free Press, 1962); Hannah Arendt, "Ideology and
    Terror: A Novel Form of Government," *The Review of Politics* 15, No. 3 (July
    1953), pp. 303–327; Hannah Arendt, *The Origins of Totalitarianism* (New York:
    Houghton Mifflin, 1948).

82. Bernard Brodie, *War and Politics* (New York: Macmillan, 1973), p. 452.

83. Brodie, *War and Politics* (New York: Macmillan, 1973), p. 452.

84. Brodie, *War and Politics* (New York: Macmillan, 1973), p. 462. Systems
    analysis, however, "is likely to be more effective if it is done under an
    authority who has no difficulty subordinating service interests to other inter-
    ests of the nation" (p. 471).

85. Brodie, *War and Politics* (New York: Macmillan, 1973), p. 451.

86. Brodie, *War and Politics* (New York: Macmillan, 1973), p. 447–448. For Brodie,
    "... every war [or choice in the field of strategy] is rich in individual phenomena."

87. Brodie, *War and Politics* (New York: Macmillan, 1973), p. 448.

88. Paul Kennedy, ed., *Grand Strategies in War and Peace* (New Haven, CT: Yale
    University Press, 1991), p. 171, who discusses "a constant regard to the peace you
    desire," which implies that policy makers must "conduct peace with constant
    regard to the war."

89. Kennedy, ed., *Grand Strategies in War and Peace* (New Haven, CT: Yale
    University Press, 1991), p. 171.

90. Robert Art, *A Grand Strategy for America* (Ithaca, NY: Cornell University Press,
    2004), p. 10.

91. Art, *A Grand Strategy for America* (Ithaca, NY: Cornell University Press, 2004), p. 10.

92. David Baldwin, *Economic Statecraft* (Princeton, NJ: Princeton University Press, 1985), pp. 8–9; Felix E. Oppenheim, "Power Revisited," *Journal of Politics* 40, No. 3 (August 1978), pp. 589–608.

93. Sherle R. Schwenninger, "Revamping American Grand Strategy," *World Policy Journal* 20 (Fall 2003), p. 25.

94. Schwenninger, "Revamping American Grand Strategy," *World Policy Journal* 20 (Fall 2003), p. 25.

95. Edward Luttwak, *Strategy: The Logic of War and Peace* (Cambridge, MA: Belknap Press of Harvard University Press, 2001), p. 190, who argues that grand strategy often is "changed by the reactions [that it] induce[s]."

96. This has profound implications for the so-called "global war on terrorism," a type of war that has the potential to lack the decisive ending like other wars in the past. While terrorism can never be completely defeated, specific terrorist organizations can be defeated, but even their defeat will not be recognized and sanctified as was typical in interstate and intrastate wars.

97. See William C. Martel, "Grand Strategy of the Authoritarian Axis," *The Diplomat*, July 24, 2012, at www.thediplomat.com/2012/07/24/grand-strategy-of-the-authoritarian-axis/; William C. Martel, "Containment R.I.P.," *The Diplomat*, September 24, 2012, at www.thediplomat.com/2012/09/24/r-i-p-containment/.

98. Edward Luttwak, *Strategy: The Logic of War and Peace* (Cambridge, MA: Belknap Press of Harvard University Press, 2001), p. 190. Finality occurs "when all other external transactions have had their impact on the military levels."

99. Luttwak, *Strategy: The Logic of War and Peace* (Cambridge, MA: Belknap Press of Harvard University Press, 2001), p. 182.

100. See Paul Kennedy, ed., *Grand Strategies in War and Peace* (New Haven, CT: Yale University Press, 1991). Also, B. H. Liddell Hart, "The Theory of Strategy," in his *Strategy*, 2nd rev. ed. (New York: Frederick A. Praeger, 1967).

101. Edward Luttwak, *Strategy: The Logic of War and Peace* (Cambridge, MA: Belknap Press of Harvard University Press, 2001), p. 177.

102. Peter Feaver, "Debating American Grand Strategy after Major War," *Orbis* 53, No. 4 (Fall 2009), p. 552.

103. Feaver, "Debating American Grand Strategy after Major War," *Orbis* 53, No. 4 (Fall 2009), pp. 551–52: "Bipartisanship is honed more in the breach than in the observance, more in retrospect than in prospect." Also, William C. Martel, "Polarized Politics and America Paralyzed?" *Providence Journal*, December 22, 2007.

104. See Edwin Mead Earle, "Introduction," *Makers of Modern Strategy* (Princeton, NJ: Princeton University Press, 1971), p. viii.

105. Earle, *Makers of Modern Strategy* (Princeton, NJ: Princeton University Press, 1971), p. viii: "But as war and society have become more complicated – and war, it must be remembered, is an inherent part of society – strategy has of necessity required increasing consideration of nonmilitary factors, economic, psychological, moral, political, and technological."

106. Earle, "Introduction," *Makers of Modern Strategy* (Princeton, NJ: Princeton University Press, 1971), p. viii: "It is in this broader sense that the word strategy is used in this volume."

107. Earle, "Haushofer: The Geopoliticians," *Makers of Modern Strategy* (Princeton, NJ: Princeton University Press, 1971), pp. 388–411, note 18, p. 393: "If all the resources of the nation are to be directed toward the making of war, they must be controlled by the overall *political* authority of the country, rather than exclusively by its *military agent*; hence the term used here, 'political strategy.'" The term also appears in a study of modern warfare from the viewpoint of political science by Edward Mead Earle, "Political and Military Strategy of the United States," an address before the Academy of Political Science at its annual meeting on "The Defense of the United States," New York, November 13, 1940: *Proceedings of the Academy of Political Science*, Vol. XIS (1941), pp. 2–9.

108. J. H. Elliott, "Managing Decline: Olivares and the Grand Strategy of Imperial Spain," in Paul Kennedy (ed.), *Grand Strategies in War and Peace* (New Haven, CT: Yale University Press, 1991), pp. 87–104. Cf. Geoffrey Parker, *The Grand Strategy of Philip II* (New Haven, CT: Yale University Press, 1998); Geoffrey Parker, "The Place of Tudor England in the Messianic Vision of Philip II of Spain," *Transactions of the Royal Historical Society*, 6th ser., No. 12 (2002); David Kaiser, *Politics and War: European Conflict from Philip II to Hitler*, (Cambridge, MA: Harvard University Press, 2000).

109. See Paul Kennedy, *The Rise and Fall of Great Powers* (New York: Random House, 1987).

110. J. H. Elliott, "Managing Decline: Olivares and the Grand Strategy of Imperial Spain," in Paul Kennedy (ed.), *Grand Strategies in War and Peace* (New Haven, CT: Yale University Press, 1991), p. 102. Cf. Parker, *The Grand Strategy of Philip II* (New Haven, CT: Yale University Press, 1998); Parker, "The Place of Tudor England in the Messianic Vision of Philip II of Spain," *Transactions of the Royal Historical Society*, 6th ser., No. 12 (2002), p. 12.

111. John B. Hattendorf, "Alliance, Encirclement, and Attrition: British Grand Strategy in the War of the Spanish Succession, 1702–1713," in Paul Kennedy (ed.), *Grand Strategies in War and Peace* (New Haven, CT: Yale University Press, 1991), pp. 11–29.

112. Cf. William C. Martel, *Victory in War: Foundations of Modern Strategy*, revised and expanded edition (New York: Cambridge University Press, 2011), pp. 139–142.

113. On *policy*, see P. Gove, ed., *Webster's Third New International Dictionary* (Springfield, MA: Merriam-Webster Inc., 1981), p. 1754.

114. On *doctrine*, see P. Gove, ed., *Webster's Third New International Dictionary* (Springfield, MA: Merriam-Webster Inc., 1981), p. 666; Harald Hoiback, "What Is Doctrine?" *Journal of Strategic Studies* 34, No. 6, pp. 879–900; Cecil V. Crabb Jr., *The Doctrines of American Foreign Policy: Their Meaning, Role, and Future* (Baton Rouge: Louisiana State University Press, 1982). *Doctrine* also describes "something that is held, put forth as true."

115. Henry A. Kissinger, *Nuclear Weapons and Foreign Policy* (New York: Harper & Brothers, 1957), p. 404: "By explaining the significance of events in advance of their occurrence, it enables society to deal with most problems as a matter of routine and reserves creative thought for unusual or unexpected situations."

116. For an analysis of doctrine in foreign policy, see Cecil V. Crabb Jr., *The Doctrines of American Foreign Policy: Their Meaning, Role, and Future* (Baton Rouge:

Louisiana State University Press, 1982). Also, Henry A. Kissinger, *Nuclear Weapons and Foreign Policy* (New York: Harper & Brothers, 1957), pp. 403–404.

117. Paul Kennedy, ed., *Grand Strategies in War and Peace* (New Haven, CT: Yale University Press, 1991), pp. 5–6.

118. Kennedy, ed., *Grand Strategies in War and Peace* (New Haven, CT: Yale University Press, 1991), p. 171. Is there any other kind of "reassessment" that is not "intelligent"? or that "conducts peace with constant regard to the war."

119. Kennedy, ed., *Grand Strategies in War and Peace* (New Haven, CT: Yale University Press, 1991), passim.

120. Dennis E. Showalter, "Total War for Limited Objectives: An Interpretation of German Grand Strategy," in Paul Kennedy (ed.), *Grand Strategies in War and Peace* (New Haven, CT: Yale University Press, 1991), pp. 105–123.

121. Showalter, "Total War for Limited Objectives: An Interpretation of German Grand Strategy," in Paul Kennedy (ed.), *Grand Strategies in War and Peace* (New Haven, CT: Yale University Press, 1991), p. 106.

122. Condoleezza Rice, "The Evolution of Soviet Grand Strategy," in Paul Kennedy (ed.), *Grand Strategies in War and Peace* (New Haven, CT: Yale University Press, 1991), pp. 145–164. Cf. George Kennan, "Sources of Soviet Conduct," *Foreign Affairs*, July 1947, pp. 556–582.

123. See Karl Marx and Friedrich Engels, "Communist Manifesto," in Robert C. Tucker (ed.), *The Marx-Engels Reader* (New York: W. W. Norton, 1972), pp. 331–362, at p. 362. Also, Sigmund Neumann and Mark Von Hagen, "Engels and Marx on Revolution, War, and the Army in Society," in Peter Paret (ed.) with Gordon A. Craig and Felix Gilbert, *Makers of Modern Strategy: From Machiavelli to the Nuclear Age* (Princeton, NJ: Princeton University Press, 1986), pp. 262–280, at p. 263.

124. See Richard K. Betts, "Is Strategy an Illusion?" *International Security* 25, No. 2 (Autumn 2000), pp. 5–50, p. 9.

125. As examples, see Glenn A. Kent and David Thaler, *A New Concept for Streamlining Up-Front Planning* (Santa Monica, CA: RAND Corporation, 1993); David E. Thaler, *Strategies to Tasks: A Framework for Linking Means and Ends* (Santa Monica, CA: RAND Corporation, 1993).

126. John Lewis Gaddis, "Containment and the Logic of Strategy," *National Interest* 10 (Winter 1987–1988), p. 29. Also, Terry L. Deibel, "Strategies before Containment: Patterns for the Future," *International Security* 16, No. 4 (Spring 1992), pp. 79–108; David Mayers, "Containment and the Primacy of Diplomacy: George Kennan's Views, 1947–1948," *International Security* 11, No. 1 (Summer 1986), pp. 124–162.

127. Michael Howard, "The Forgotten Dimensions of Strategy," *Foreign Affairs* 57, No. 5 (Summer 1979), pp. 975–986.

128. On how states mobilize their economy to support the logistics of war, see Thomas J. Christensen, *Useful Adversaries, Grand Strategy, Domestic Mobilization, and Sino-American Conflict, 1947–1955* (Princeton, NJ: Princeton University Press, 1996), p. 13; Stephen Van Evera, *Causes of War: Power and the Roots of Conflict* (Ithaca, NY: Cornell University Press, 1999); Stephen Van Evera, "The Cult of the Offensive and the Origins of the First World War," *International Security* 9.1

(Summer 1984), pp. 58–107; Mark Harrison, "Resource Mobilization for World War II: The U.S.A., U.K., U.S.S.R., and Germany, 1938–1945," *Economic History Review*, New Series, 41, No. 2 (May 1988), pp. 171–192; R. J. Overy, *War and Economy in the Third Reich* (New York: Oxford University Press, 1995); Mark Harrison, ed., *The Economics of World War II: Six Great Powers in International Comparison* (New York: Cambridge University Press, 1998); Roger Chickering and Stig Forster, eds., *Great War, Total War: Combat and Mobilization on the Western Front, 1914–1918* (New York: Cambridge University Press, 2000); Theda Skocpol, "Social Revolutions and Mass Military Mobilization," *World Politics* 40, No. 2 (January 1988), pp. 147–168; Michael I. Handel, *Masters of War: Classical Strategic Thought*, 3rd ed. (London: Frank Cass, 2001); R. J. Overy, "Mobilization for Total War in Germany, 1939–1941," *English Historical Review* 103, No. 408 (July 1988), pp. 613–639; Dan Reiter and Allan C. Stam, "Winning Wars on Factory Floors: The Myth of Democratic Arsenals of Victory," in *Democracies at War* (Princeton, NJ: Princeton University Press, 2002), pp. 114–143; also, Reiter and Stam, "Democracy, Technology, and Victory," *Democracies at War* (Princeton, NJ: Princeton University Press, 2002), pp. 134–135; Richard J. Overy, *The Air War, 1939–1945* (Virginia: Potomac Books, 2005); Richard Bean, "War and the Birth of the Nation State," *Journal of Economic History* 33, No. 1, "The Tasks of Economic History" (March 1973), pp. 203–221.

129. Consider Napoleon's disastrous invasion of Russia in 1812 and the need for logistics in a war in which he "found conditions with which he was unfamiliar – a vast country with few good roads and without supplies." See [Bernard Law Montgomery] Viscount Montgomery of Alamein, *A History of Warfare* (New York: William Morrow, 1983), p. 365.

130. Michael Howard, "The Forgotten Dimensions of Strategy," *Foreign Affairs* 57, No. 5 (Summer 1979), pp. 975–986.

131. For an analysis of Douhet's ideas and influence, see Bernard Brodie, "The Heritage of Douhet," in his *Strategy in the Missile Age* (Princeton, NJ: Princeton University Press, 1959), pp. 71–106, at p. 88. Cf. Edward Warner, "Douhet, Mitchell, Seversky: Theories of Air Warfare," in Edward Mead Earle (ed.), *Makers of Modern Strategy: Military Thought from Machiavelli to Hitler* (Princeton, NJ: Princeton University Press, 1943), pp. 485–503, at p. 488.

132. Edward Warner, "Douhet, Mitchell, Seversky: Theories of Air Warfare," in Edward Mead Earle (ed.), *Makers of Modern Strategy: Military Thought*, pp. 485–503, at p. 488.

133. For a detailed analysis of Douhet's ideas about air power and its influence on strategy, see Brodie, "Heritage of Douhet." His argument was that "to be defeated in the air ... is finally to be defeated and at the mercy of the enemy, with no chance at all of defending oneself, compelled to accept whatever terms he sees fit to dictate" (23).

134. Cf. Stephen Peter Rosen, *Winning the Next War: Innovation and the Modern Military* (Ithaca, NY: Cornell University Press, 1991).

135. Michael Howard, "The Forgotten Dimensions of Strategy," *Foreign Affairs* 57, No. 5 (Summer 1979), pp. 975–986.

136. Peter Paret, ed., with Gordon A. Craig and Felix Gilbert, *Makers of Modern Strategy: From Machiavelli to the Nuclear Age* (Princeton, NJ: Princeton University Press, 1986), p. 703.

137. Paret, ed., with Gordon A. Craig and Felix Gilbert, *Makers of Modern Strategy: From Machiavelli to the Nuclear Age* (Princeton, NJ: Princeton University Press, 1986), p. 869.

138. Paret, ed., with Gordon A. Craig and Felix Gilbert, *Makers of Modern Strategy: From Machiavelli to the Nuclear Age* (Princeton, NJ: Princeton University Press, 1986), p. 871. When "hostilities broke out in Korea ... [this] exercise in strategy ... would almost certainly have won Clausewitz' approbation." Furthermore, it was implemented with "a realistic assessment of the current state of affairs in international politics," because it reflected "an accurate view of the capabilities and proclivities of potential opponents."

139. John Lewis Gaddis, "Toward the Post-Cold War World," *Foreign Affairs* 70, No. 2 (Spring 1991), p. 102.

140. Joseph S. Nye Jr., *Power in a Global Information Age: From Realism to Globalization* (New York: Routledge, 2004).

141. John Lewis Gaddis, "Toward the Post-Cold War World," *Foreign Affairs* 70, No. 2 (Spring 1991), p. 107. Also, William C. Martel, "An Authoritarian Axis Rising?" *The Diplomat*, June 29, 2012, at www.thediplomat.com/2012/06/29/an-authoritarian-axis-rising/.

142. John Lewis Gaddis, *The United States and the End of the Cold War: Implications, Reconsiderations, Provocations* (New York: Oxford University Press, 1992), p. 196.

143. John Lewis Gaddis, "Toward the Post-Cold War World," *Foreign Affairs* 70, No. 2 (Spring 1991), p. 113.

144. See Dwight D. Eisenhower, Farewell Address, January 17, 1961, at www.american rhetoric.com/speeches/dwightdeisenhowerfarewell.html: "We cannot mortgage the material assets of our grandchildren without risking the loss also of their political and spiritual heritage."

145. John Lewis Gaddis, "Toward the Post-Cold War World," *Foreign Affairs* 70, No. 2 (Spring 1991), p. 113.

146. See Dennis Drew and Donald Snow, "Grand Strategy" in *Making Strategy: An Introduction to National Security Process and Problems* (Maxwell AFB, AL: Air University Press, 1988).

147. Donald E. Nuechterlein, *America Overcommitted: United States National Interests in the 1980s* (Lexington: University of Kentucky Press, 1985), p. 15.

148. Nuechterlein, *America Overcommitted: United States National Interests in the 1980s* (Lexington: University of Kentucky Press, 1985).

149. Cf. William C. Martel, *Victory in War: Foundations of Modern Strategy*, revised and expanded edition (New York: Cambridge University Press, 2011), pp. 145–148.

150. See Dennis Drew and Donald Snow, "Grand Strategy" in *Making Strategy: An Introduction to National Security Process and Problems* (Maxwell AFB, AL: Air University Press, 1988).

151. George Washington, Farewell Address, September 19, 1796, at http://www.presidency.ucsb.edu/ws/index.php?pid=65539&st=&st1=, asked a fundamental

question about American grand strategy: "Why, by interweaving our destiny with that of any part of Europe, entangle our peace and prosperity in the toils of European ambition, rivalship, interest, humor or caprice?" And Washington continued: "It must be unwise in us to implicate ourselves by artificial ties in the ordinary vicissitudes of her politics, or the ordinary combinations and collisions of her friendships or enmities."

152. Joseph S. Nye, *The Future of Power* (New York: Public Affairs, 2011), pp. 20–21.

153. Nye, *The Future of Power* (New York: Public Affairs, 2011), p. 123.

154. Joseph S. Nye Jr., *Power in a Global Information Age: From Realism to Globalization* (New York: Routledge, 2004), p. 82.

155. Cf. Joseph S. Nye Jr., "Get Smart: Combining Hard and Soft Power," *Foreign Affairs* 88, No. 4, (2009), pp. 160–163.

156. See Edward Mead Earle, ed., with Gordon A. Craig and Felix Gilbert, *Makers of Modern Strategy: Military Thought from Machiavelli to Hitler* (Princeton, NJ: Princeton University Press, 1973).

157. Earle, ed., with Gordon A. Craig and Felix Gilbert, *Makers of Modern Strategy: Military Thought from Machiavelli to Hitler* (Princeton, NJ: Princeton University Press, 1973), p. viii.

158. Earle, ed., with Gordon A. Craig and Felix Gilbert, *Makers of Modern Strategy: Military Thought from Machiavelli to Hitler* (Princeton, NJ: Princeton University Press, 1973), p. vii.

159. Earle, ed., with Gordon A. Craig and Felix Gilbert, *Makers of Modern Strategy: Military Thought from Machiavelli to Hitler* (Princeton, NJ: Princeton University Press, 1973), p. vii.

160. See Eliot A. Cohen, *Supreme Command: Soldiers, Statesmen, and Leadership in Wartime* (New York: The Free Press, 2002), passim.

161. Edward Mead Earle, ed., with Gordon A. Craig and Felix Gilbert, *Makers of Modern Strategy: Military Thought from Machiavelli to Hitler* (Princeton, NJ: Princeton University Press, 1973), p. viii.

162. Earle, ed., with Gordon A. Craig and Felix Gilbert, *Makers of Modern Strategy: Military Thought from Machiavelli to Hitler* (Princeton, NJ: Princeton University Press, 1973), p. x.

163. Samuel Huntington, "The Erosion of American National Interests," *Foreign Affairs* 76, No. 5 (September–October, 1997), pp. 28–49.

164. Huntington, "The Erosion of American National Interests," *Foreign Affairs* 76, No. 5 (September–October, 1997), pp. 28–29.

165. Huntington, "The Erosion of American National Interests," *Foreign Affairs* 76, No. 5 (September–October, 1997), pp. 33–34: "They deny the existence of a common culture in the United States, denounce assimilation, and promote the primacy of racial, ethnic, and other subnational cultural identities and groupings."

166. Huntington, "The Erosion of American National Interests," *Foreign Affairs* 76, No. 5 (September–October, 1997), pp. 33–34.

167. Huntington, "The Erosion of American National Interests," *Foreign Affairs* 76, No. 5 (September–October, 1997), p. 35.

168. Huntington, "The Erosion of American National Interests," *Foreign Affairs* 76, No. 5 (September–October, 1997), pp. 36.

169. See William C. Martel, "Why America Needs a Grand Strategy," *The Diplomat*, June 18, 2012, at www.thediplomat.com/2012/06/18/why-america-needs-a-grand -strategy/.

170. Condoleezza Rice, "Promoting the National Interest," *Foreign Affairs* 79, No. 1 (January–February 2000), pp. 45–62.

171. Rice, "Promoting the National Interest," *Foreign Affairs* 79, No. 1 (January–February 2000), p. 46, who argues that the nation's critical priorities are to (1) ensure the U.S. military can deter war, project power, and fight in defense of the national interests, if deterrence fails; (2) promote economic growth and political openness through free trade and stable international monetary system; (3) renew relationships with allies who share American values and will share the burden of promoting peace, prosperity and freedom; (4) focus energy on comprehensive relationships with big powers (Russia and China) to shape the character of international political system; and (5) deal decisively with rogue regimes and hostile powers (terrorism and the development of weapons of mass destruction).

172. Rice, "Promoting the National Interest," *Foreign Affairs* 79, No. 1 (January–February 2000), p. 47: "The belief that the U.S. is exercising power legitimately only when doing so on behalf of someone or something else is deeply rooted in Wilsonian thought."

173. Rice, "Promoting the National Interest," *Foreign Affairs* 79, No. 1 (January–February 2000), p. 47.

174. Rice, "Promoting the National Interest," *Foreign Affairs* 79, No. 1 (January–February 2000), p. 54.

175. Rice, "Promoting the National Interest," *Foreign Affairs* 79, No. 1 (January–February 2000), p. 60.

176. Rice, "Promoting the National Interest," *Foreign Affairs* 79, No. 1 (January–February 2000), p. 62: "In the absence of a compelling vision," societies will find that "parochial interests [fill] the void."

177. Rice, "Promoting the National Interest," *Foreign Affairs* 79, No. 1 (January–February 2000), p. 62.

178. Jim Lacy, "Toward a Strategy: Creating an American Strategy for Global War, 1940–1943," in Williamson Murray (ed.), *The Shaping of Grand Strategy: Policy, Diplomacy, and War* (New York: Cambridge University Press, 2011), p. 183.

179. Lacy, "Toward a Strategy: Creating an American Strategy for Global War, 1940–1943," in Williamson Murray (ed.), *The Shaping of Grand Strategy: Policy, Diplomacy, and War* (New York: Cambridge University Press, 2011), p. 187: "The president also directed the services that these numbers be sufficiently firm so that industrial planners could accurately estimate how much industrial capacity the war effort would require from the American economy."

180. Stephen D. Krasner, "An Orienting Principle for Foreign Policy: The Deficiencies of Grand Strategy," *Policy Review*, Hoover Institution, No. 163 (October 1, 2010), p. 2, at www.hoover.org/publications/policy-review/article/49786: "Some fail because they envision a world that cannot be realized [while] [o]thers fail because resources cannot be aligned with policies because of institutional constraints or a lack of domestic or international political support."

181. Douglas Porch, "Arms and Alliances: French Grand Strategy and Policy in 1914 and 1940," in Paul Kennedy (ed.), *Grand Strategies in War and Peace* (New Haven, CT: Yale University Press, 1991), pp. 71–85.

182. Porch, "Arms and Alliances: French Grand Strategy and Policy in 1914 and 1940," in Paul Kennedy (ed.), *Grand Strategies in War and Peace* (New Haven, CT: Yale University Press, 1991), pp. 71–85.

183. Porch, "Arms and Alliances: French Grand Strategy and Policy in 1914 and 1940," in Paul Kennedy (ed.), *Grand Strategies in War and Peace* (New Haven, CT: Yale University Press, 1991), pp. 141–142.

184. Paul Kennedy, *The Rise and Fall of the Great Powers: Economic Change and Military Conflict from 1500 to 2000* (New York, NY: Random House, 1987).

185. B. H. Liddell Hart, *The Classic Book on Military Strategy*, 2nd rev. ed. (London: Faber & Faber Ltd., 1967), p. 357. His reasoning is that "force is a vicious cycle – or rather, a spiral – unless its application is controlled by the most carefully reasoned calculation." This leads to the observation that "war, which begins by denying reason, comes to vindicate it – throughout all the phases of the struggle."

186. Paul Kennedy, *The Rise and Fall of the Great Powers: Economic Change and Military Conflict from 1500 to 2000* (New York: Random House, 1987).

187. Paul Kennedy, ed., *Grand Strategies in War and Peace* (New Haven, CT: Yale University Press, 1991), p. 2.

188. Christopher Layne, "Rethinking American Grand Strategy: Hegemony or Balance of Power in the Twenty-First Century," *World Policy Journal* 15, No. 2 (Summer 1998), p. 8.

189. John Lewis Gaddis, "Containment and the Logic of Strategy," *National Interest* 10 (Winter 1987–1988), p. 29.

190. Arther Ferrill, "The Grand Strategy of the Roman Empire," in Paul Kennedy (ed.), *Grand Strategies in War and Peace* (New Haven, CT: Yale University Press, 1991), pp. 71–85.

191. Ferrill, "The Grand Strategy of the Roman Empire," in Paul Kennedy (ed.), *Grand Strategies in War and Peace* (New Haven, CT: Yale University Press, 1991), p. 74. Also, Kimberly Kagan, "Redefining Roman Grand Strategy," *Journal of Military History* 70, No. 2 (April 2006), pp. 333–362; Thomas R. Phillips et al., "The Military Institutions of the Romans (De Re Militari)," *Roots of Strategy; A Collection of Military Classics* (Harrisburg, PA: Military Service Publishing Company, 1940).

4 Ancient and Modern Eras of Grand Strategy

1. On Sun Tzu, see Roger T. Ames, trans., "Introduction," *Sun-Tzu: The Art of Warfare* (New York: Ballantine Books, 1993). Also, Robert Cowley and Geoffrey Parker, eds., *The Reader's Companion to Military History* (New York: Houghton Mifflin Harcourt Publishing Company, 1996); Arthur Waldron, "Chinese Strategy from the Fourteenth to the Seventeenth Centuries," in Williamson Murray, MacGregor Knox, and Alvin Bernstein (eds.), *The Making of Strategy: Rulers, States, and War* (New York: Cambridge University Press, 1996), pp. 85–114; Edward O'Dowd and Arthur Waldron, "Sun Tzu for Strategists,"

Comparative Strategy 10 (1991), pp. 25–36; Douglas M. McCready, "Learning from Sun Tzu," *Military Review* 83, No. 3 (May/June 2003), pp. 85–88.

2. Sun Tzu, *The Art of War*, trans. and intro. Samuel B. Griffith (New York: Oxford University Press, 1971), pp. 142–143. Cf. Hans J. Morgenthau, *Politics among Nations: The Struggle for Power and Peace* (New York: Alfred A. Knopf, 1973), p. 7: "It stands to reason that not all foreign policies have always followed so rational, objective, and unemotional a course.... Especially where foreign policy is conducted under the conditions of democratic control, the need to marshal popular emotions to the support of foreign policy cannot fail to impair the rationality of foreign policy itself."

3. Cf. Hans J. Morgenthau, *Politics among Nations: The Struggle for Power and Peace* (New York: Alfred A. Knopf, 1973), p. 8: "... political realism considers a rational foreign policy to be a good foreign policy; for only a rational foreign policy *minimizes risks* and maximizes benefits ..." (emphasis added).

4. Sun Tzu, *The Art of War*, trans. and intro. Samuel B. Griffith (New York: Oxford University Press, 1971), pp. 77–78.

5. Sun Tzu, *The Art of War*, trans. and intro. Samuel B. Griffith (New York: Oxford University Press, 1971), p. 138.

6. Sun Tzu, *The Art of War*, trans. and intro. Samuel B. Griffith (New York: Oxford University Press, 1971), p. 140: and do so "with a date secretly fixed."

7. Sun Tzu, *The Art of War*, trans. and intro. Samuel B. Griffith (New York: Oxford University Press, 1971), p. 77. For the principle of damage limitation in strategy, which relates to prudence, see Hans J. Morgenthau, *Politics among Nations: The Struggle for Power and Peace*, 5th ed. (New York: Alfred A. Knopf, 1973), p. 11: "Realism, then, considers prudence – the weighing of the consequences of alternative political actions – to be the supreme virtue in politics." As Morgenthau continues, "Moderation in policy cannot fail to reflect the moderation of moral judgment."

8. Sun Tzu, *The Art of War*, trans. and intro. Samuel B. Griffith (New York: Oxford University Press, 1971), pp. 70–73.

9. Compare B. H. Liddell Hart, *Strategy: The Indirect Approach* (New York: Praeger, 1954), p. 370: "Victory in the true sense implies that the state of peace, and of one's own people, is better after the war than before.... Victory in this sense is only possible if a quick result can be gained or if a long effort can be economically proportioned to the national resources. The end must be adjusted to the means."

10. Sun Tzu, *The Art of War*, trans. and intro. Samuel B. Griffith (New York: Oxford University Press, 1971), p. 77.

11. Michael I. Handel, *Masters of War: Classical Strategic Thought* (London: Frank Cass Publishers, 2001), p. 57.

12. Sun Tzu, *The Art of War*, trans. and intro. Samuel B. Griffith (New York: Oxford University Press, 1971), pp. 87, 138.

13. Sun Tzu, *The Art of War*, trans. and intro. Samuel B. Griffith (New York: Oxford University Press, 1971), p. 65.

14. Sun Tzu, *The Art of War*, trans. and intro. Samuel B. Griffith (New York: Oxford University Press, 1971), p. 65.

15. Sun Tzu, *The Art of War*, trans. and intro. Samuel B. Griffith (New York: Oxford University Press, 1971), p. 70.

16. Sun Tzu, *The Art of War*, trans. and intro. Samuel B. Griffith (New York: Oxford University Press, 1971), p. 139.

17. Michael I. Handel, *Masters of War: Classical Strategic Thought* (London: Frank Cass Publishers, 2001), pp. 1–2.

18. See John Lewis Gaddis, *Strategies of Containment* (Oxford, New York: 2005), esp. p. 386.

19. On Thucydides, see Robert B. Strassler, ed., *The Landmark Thucydides: A Comprehensive Guide to the Peloponnesian War* (New York: Simon & Schuster, 1996); and Thucydides, *History of the Peloponnesian War*, trans. Rex Warner (Hammondsworth, UK: Penguin Books, 1972). See also Donald Kagan, *The Outbreak of the Peloponnesian War* (Ithaca, NY: Cornell University Press, 1969), esp. chapters 19 ("The Causes of the War") and 20 ("Thucydides and the Inevitability of the War"). Also, Donald Kagan, "Athenian Strategy in the Peloponnesian War," in Williamson Murray, MacGregor Knox, and Alvin Bernstein (eds.), *The Making of Strategy: Rulers, States, and War* (New York: Cambridge University Press, 1996), pp. 24–55; Athanassios G. Platias and Constantinos Koliopoulos, *Thucydides on Strategy: Athenian and Spartan Grand Strategies in the Peloponnesian War and their Relevance Today* (New York: Columbia University Press, 2010); Laurie Bagby, "The Use and Abuse of Thucydides," *International Organization* 48, No. 1 (Winter 1994), pp. 131–153.

20. Thucydides, *History of the Peloponnesian War*, trans. Rex Warner (Hammondsworth, UK: Penguin Books, 1972), p. 113.

21. Thucydides, *History of the Peloponnesian War*, trans. Rex Warner (Hammondsworth, UK: Penguin Books, 1972), p. 179.

22. Thucydides, *History of the Peloponnesian War*, trans. Rex Warner (Hammondsworth, UK: Penguin Books, 1972), p. 83.

23. Thucydides, *History of the Peloponnesian War*, trans. Rex Warner (Hammondsworth, UK: Penguin Books, 1972), pp. 367–368: "In this very convention there are many points that are still disputed. Again, some of the most powerful states have never yet accepted the arrangement at all. Some of these are at open war with us; others (as the Spartans do not yet move) are restrained by truces renewed every ten days, and it is only too probable that if they found our power divided, as we are hurrying to divide it, they would attack us vigorously with the Siceliots." Further, "Our struggle therefore, if we are wise, will not be for the barbarian Egestaens in Sicily, but to defend ourselves most efficiently against the oligarchic machinations of Sparta."

24. Thucydides, *History of the Peloponnesian War*, trans. Rex Warner (Hammondsworth, UK: Penguin Books, 1972), p. 127.

25. Thucydides, *History of the Peloponnesian War*, trans. Rex Warner (Hammondsworth, UK: Penguin Books, 1972), p. 85.

26. Thucydides, *History of the Peloponnesian War*, trans. Rex Warner (Hammondsworth, UK: Penguin Books, 1972), p. 113. "If we turn to our military policy, there also we differ from our antagonists. We throw open our city to the world, and never by alien acts exclude foreigners from any opportunity of learning or observing . . ."

27. Thucydides, *History of the Peloponnesian War*, trans. Rex Warner (Hammondsworth, UK: Penguin Books, 1972), p. 179.

28. Thucydides, *History of the Peloponnesian War*, trans. Rex Warner (Hammondsworth, UK: Penguin Books, 1972), pp. 181–182. Citing Diodotus, we must "see how by moderate chastisements we may be enabled to benefit in the future by the revenue-producing powers of our dependencies; and we must make up our minds to look for our protection not to legal terrors but to careful administration."

29. Thucydides, *History of the Peloponnesian War*, trans. Rex Warner (Hammondsworth, UK: Penguin Books, 1972), p. 43.

30. Thucydides, *History of the Peloponnesian War*, trans. Rex Warner (Hammondsworth, UK: Penguin Books, 1972), p. 67.

31. Thucydides, *History of the Peloponnesian War*, trans. Rex Warner (Hammondsworth, UK: Penguin Books, 1972), pp. 40, 45–46. Also, Chester G. Starr, *The Influence of Sea Power on Ancient History* (New York: Oxford University Press, 1989).

32. Thucydides, *History of the Peloponnesian War*, trans. Rex Warner (Hammondsworth, UK: Penguin Books, 1972), p. 67.

33. Thucydides, *History of the Peloponnesian War*, trans. Rex Warner (Hammondsworth, UK: Penguin Books, 1972), p. 478.

34. Thucydides, *History of the Peloponnesian War*, trans. Rex Warner (Hammondsworth, UK: Penguin Books, 1972), p. 165: "You will free yourselves from the accusation made against you of not supporting insurrection." As the Mytilenians noted to the Spartans, "But if you will frankly support us, you will add to your side a state that has a large navy, which is your great want; you will smooth the way to the overthrow of the Athenians by depriving them of their allies, who will be greatly encouraged to come over."

35. Thucydides, *History of the Peloponnesian War*, trans. Rex Warner (Hammondsworth, UK: Penguin Books, 1972), p. 379: "Indeed, the greater it is the better, with regard to the rest of the Sicilians, whom dismay will make more ready to join us."

36. Thucydides, *History of the Peloponnesian War*, trans. Rex Warner (Hammondsworth, UK: Penguin Books, 1972), p. 182.

37. Thucydides, *History of the Peloponnesian War*, trans. Rex Warner (Hammondsworth, UK: Penguin Books, 1972), p. 352.

38. Thucydides, *History of the Peloponnesian War*, pp. 352–356.

39. Thucydides, *History of the Peloponnesian War*, trans. Rex Warner (Hammondsworth, UK: Penguin Books, 1972), p. 443: "The heavy charges that fell upon them . . . produced their financial distress; and it was at this time that they imposed upon their subjects, instead of tribute, the tax of a twentieth upon all imports and exports by sea, which they thought would raise more money for them; their expenditure being now not the same as at first, but having grown with the war while their revenues decayed."

40. Thucydides, *History of the Peloponnesian War*, trans. Rex Warner (Hammondsworth, UK: Penguin Books, 1972), p. 233. Quoting the Spartan envoy, "Indeed if great enmities are ever to be really settled, we think it will be, not by the system of revenge and military success, and by forcing an opponent to swear to a treaty to his disadvantage; but when the more fortunate combatant waives his privileges."

41. Thucydides, *History of the Peloponnesian War*, trans. Rex Warner (Hammondsworth, UK: Penguin Books, 1972), p. 372: "It is thus that empire has been won, both by us and by all others that have held it, by a constant readiness to support all . . . that invite assistance."

42. Thucydides, *History of the Peloponnesian War*, trans. Rex Warner (Hammondsworth, UK: Penguin Books, 1972), p. 375.

43. Thucydides, *History of the Peloponnesian War*, trans. Rex Warner (Hammondsworth, UK: Penguin Books, 1972), esp., pp. 512–517.

44. For analyses of Machiavelli, see Felix Gilbert, "Machiavelli: The Renaissance of the Art of War," in Paret (ed.), *Makers of Modern Strategy*, pp. 11–31; and Azar Gat, *The Origins of Military Thought: From the Enlightenment to Clausewitz* (Oxford: Clarendon Press, 1991). pp. 1–9; William C. Martel, *Victory in War: Foundations of Modern Strategy* (New York: Cambridge University Press, 2011), pp. 66–69. Alger, *Quest for Victory*, pp. 6–7, observed that "Machiavelli's writings marked the beginning of nearly three centuries of military thought that was strongly influenced by classical thought, that reflected an interest in the search for principles, fundamentals, general rules, or any of the variety of synonyms used to define such basic concepts" of war. See also Isaiah Berlin, "The Originality of Machiavelli," in *The Proper Study of Mankind* (New York: Farrar, Straus and Giroux, 1997), pp. 269–325, for an analysis of the Machiavelli's writings and their philosophical foundation as it relates to grand strategy. Cf. Harvey C. Mansfield, *Machiavelli's Virtue* (Chicago: University of Chicago Press, 1996).

45. See Gat, *Origins of Military Thought*, p. 6: "*The Art of War* is Machiavelli's positive and complete scheme for the building of armies, and reflects the full scope of his military outlook."

46. Felix Gilbert, "Machiavelli: The Renaissance of the Art of War," in Edward Mead Earle (ed.), *Makers of Modern Strategy: Military Thought from Machiavelli to Hitler* (Princeton, NJ: Princeton University Press, 1943), p. 7. Also, See Garrett Mattingly, *Renaissance Diplomacy* (Baltimore: Penguin Books, 1964), for a review of politics and diplomacy during this era, esp. pp. 140–146.

47. See Garrett Mattingly, *Renaissance Diplomacy* (Baltimore: Penguin Books, 1964), for a review of politics and diplomacy during this era, esp. pp. 140–146.

48. Niccolò Machiavelli, *The Prince*, trans. W. K. Marriott (New York: Random House, 1992), p. 104.

49. Felix Gilbert, "Machiavelli: The Renaissance of the Art of War," in Edward Mead Earle (ed.), *Makers of Modern Strategy: Military Thought from Machiavelli to Hitler* (Princeton, NJ: Princeton University Press, 1943), pp. 13–14. As Machiavelli wrote, "That cannot be called war where men do not kill each other, cities are not sacked, nor territories laid waste."

50. Gilbert, "Machiavelli: The Renaissance of the Art of War," in Edward Mead Earle (ed.), *Makers of Modern Strategy: Military Thought from Machiavelli to Hitler* (Princeton, NJ: Princeton University Press, 1943), p. 8.

51. Gilbert, "Machiavelli: The Renaissance of the Art of War," in Edward Mead Earle (ed.), *Makers of Modern Strategy: Military Thought from Machiavelli to Hitler* (Princeton, NJ: Princeton University Press, 1943), p. 13.

52. Gilbert, "Machiavelli: The Renaissance of the Art of War," in Edward Mead Earle (ed.), *Makers of Modern Strategy: Military Thought from Machiavelli to Hitler* (Princeton, NJ: Princeton University Press, 1943), p. 15.

53. Gilbert, "Machiavelli: The Renaissance of the Art of War," in Edward Mead Earle (ed.), *Makers of Modern Strategy: Military Thought from Machiavelli to Hitler* (Princeton, NJ: Princeton University Press, 1943), p. 22: "To him political life was a struggle for survival between growing and expanding organisms. War was natural and necessary, [as] it would establish which country would survive and determine between annihilation and expansion."

54. Gilbert, "Machiavelli: The Renaissance of the Art of War," in Edward Mead Earle (ed.), *Makers of Modern Strategy: Military Thought from Machiavelli to Hitler* (Princeton, NJ: Princeton University Press, 1943), p. 22.

55. See Charles R. Schrader, "The Influence of Vegetius' *De re militari*," *Military Affairs* 45.4 (December 1981), pp. 167–172, at p. 167.

56. Niccolò Machiavelli, *The Prince*, trans. W. K. Marriott, (New York: Random House, 1992), p. 66.

57. Niccolo' Machiavelli, *Discourses on the First Decade of Titus Livius*, in *Machiavelli: Chief Works and Others*, Vol. I, 3 vols., trans. Allan Gilbert (Durham, NC: Duke University Press, 1965), p. 380.

58. For an analysis of pyrrhic (or "hollow") victory, see Thomas E. Phipps Jr., "Strategy of War Limitation," *Journal of Conflict Resolution* 7, No. 3, *Weapons Management in World Politics: Proceedings of the International Arms Control Symposium, December 1962* (September 1963), pp. 215–227: "Victory becomes hollow when the gain is small compared to the losses mutually sustained. We can afford, if need be, to grant our opponent any reasonable number of hollow victories and still accomplish our basic objective of conditioning him to refrain from wanton aggression. For, as he begins to count the cost of repeated Pyrrhic victories, he should notice that he is suffering net losses just as surely as if he had sustained stalemate in each engagement" (p. 219CR).

59. Sheldon S. Wolin, "The Economy of Violence," in Niccolò Machiavelli, *The Prince: A New Translation, Backgrounds, Interpretations*, trans. and ed. Robert M. Adams (New York: W. W. Norton, 1977), p. 187.

60. For more analyses of these philosophers, see William T. Bluhm, *Theories of the Political System: Classics of Political Thought & Modern Political Analysis* (Englewood Cliffs, NJ: Prentice Hall, 1965); George Holland Sabine and Thomas Landon Thorson, *A History of Political Theory* (Hinsdale, IL: Dryden Press, 1973).

61. Charles Hill, *Grand Strategies: Literature, Statecraft, and World Order* (New Haven, CT: Yale University Press, 2010).

62. Hill, *Grand Strategies: Literature, Statecraft, and World Order* (New Haven, CT: Yale University Press, 2010), p. 88.

63. For critical scholarship on Thomas Hobbes, see William T. Bluhm, "Naturalistic Political Science and Mathematics: Hobbes, Downs, and Riker," *Theories of the Political System: Classics of Political Thought & Modern Political Analysis* (Englewood Cliffs, NJ: Prentice Hall, 1971), pp. 285–326; Perez Zagorin, "Hobbes on Our Mind," *Journal of the History of Ideas* 51, No. 2 (1990);

Perez Zagorin, *Hobbes and the Law of Nature* (Princeton, NJ: Princeton University Press, 2009); Patricia Springborg, ed., *The Cambridge Companion to Hobbes' Leviathan* (New York: Cambridge University Press, 2007); Thomas Ertman, *Birth of the Leviathan: Building States and Regimes in Medieval and Early Modern Europe* (New York: Cambridge University Press, 1997); George Holland Sabine and Thomas Landon Thorson, *A History of Political Theory* (Hinsdale, IL: Dryden Press, 1973), pp. 442–440; Leo Strauss, *The Political Philosophy of Hobbes: Its Basis and Its Genesis* (1936), trans. Elsa M. Sinclair (Chicago: University of Chicago Press, 1952).

64. Charles Hill, *Grand Strategies: Literature, Statecraft, and World Order* (New Haven, CT: Yale University Press, 2010), p. 89. Also, William T. Bluhm, "Naturalistic Political Science and Mathematics: Hobbes, Downs, and Riker," *Theories of the Political System: Classics of Political Thought & Modern Political Analysis* (Englewood Cliffs, NJ: Prentice Hall, 1971), pp. 285–326.

65. Hill, *Grand Strategies: Literature, Statecraft, and World Order* (New Haven, CT: Yale University Press, 2010), p. 89: "Hobbes's theory of the state derived less from revelation or reason than from his sense of human psychological drives and passions. To Hobbes, a person's regard for safety and well-being come first, and generate a constant striving for power and rank as protection from a dangerous world. Monarchy imposes order on the human maelstrom. The most chaotic form of polity, and thus the worst, is democracy."

66. Hill, *Grand Strategies: Literature, Statecraft, and World Order* (New Haven, CT: Yale University Press, 2010), p. 90.

67. For example, Hill, *Grand Strategies: Literature, Statecraft, and World Order* (New Haven, CT: Yale University Press, 2010), p. 92: "The only way to save your skin in the international 'state of nature' is to grab as much power as you can." And for this reason, Hill believes "Hobbes is the anti-Grotius; there is no 'international community.'"

68. See *Leviathan*, "Chapter XXX: Of the Office of the Sovereign Representative." As Hobbes wrote, "the law of nations and the law of nature is the same thing . . . and every sovereign hath the same right, in procuring the safety of his people, that any particular man can have, in procuring the safety of his own body."

69. See Hobbes's more complete quote: "In such condition, there is no place for industry; because the fruit thereof is uncertain: and consequently no culture of the earth; no navigation, nor use of the commodities that may be imported by sea; no commodious building; no instruments of moving, and removing, such things are require much force; no knowledge of the face of the earth; no account of time; no arts; no letters; no society; and which is worst of all, continual fear, and dangers of violent death; and life of man, solitary, poor, nasty, brutish, and short." See *Leviathan III*, "Chapter XIII: Of the Natural Condition of Mankind as Concerning Their Felicity, and Misery."

70. See William T. Bluhm, "Lockean Theory: Naturalism as Tradition," *Theories of the Political System: Classics of Political Thought & Modern Political Analysis* (Englewood Cliffs, NJ: Prentice Hall, 1971), pp. 327–357. Also, Hans J. Morgenthau, *Politics among Nations: The Struggle for Power and Peace*, 5th ed. (New York: Alfred A. Knopf, 1973).

71. See George Holland Sabine and Thomas Landon Thorson, *A History of Political Theory* (Hinsdale, IL: Dryden Press, 1973), pp. 483–499.

72. Charles Hill, *Grand Strategies: Literature, Statecraft, and World Order* (New Haven, CT: Yale University Press, 2010), p. 19, who summarizes these elements to include "the right to own property and to increase it through the free market; the individual's ownership of property in himself; the corollary that slavery is impermissible; the establishment of government by consent of the governed; and – in contrast to Hobbes's Anglo-European social contract – the inalienability of the rights of life, liberty, property, and freedom from absolute, arbitrary power." Hill emphasizes that Locke believed "the rights that individuals cede to the state are revocable if the government fails to perform the responsibilities entrusted to it. But the right to punish under law is not revocable, but 'wholly given up.'"

73. George Mace, *Locke, Hobbes, and the Federalist Papers: An Essay on the Genesis of the American Political Heritage* (Carbondale: Southern Illinois University Press, 1979), p. 30.

74. Mace, *Locke, Hobbes, and the Federalist Papers: An Essay on the Genesis of the American Political Heritage* (Carbondale: Southern Illinois University Press, 1979), p. 17.

75. For an excellent discussion of the Hobbes-Locke debate within the context of the modern debate about the grand strategy of trade, see Theodore H. Moran, "Grand Strategy: The Pursuit of Power and the Pursuit of Plenty," *International Organization* 50, No. 1 (January 1, 1996), pp. 175–205.

76. Charles Hill, *Grand Strategies: Literature, Statecraft, and World Order* (New Haven, CT: Yale University Press, 2010), p. 144: "The astonishing fact about America is that the state would be designed to protect the individual's 'metaphysical' rights of life, freedom and property."

77. Hill, *Grand Strategies: Literature, Statecraft, and World Order* (New Haven, CT: Yale University Press, 2010), p. 118.

78. Hill, *Grand Strategies: Literature, Statecraft, and World Order* (New Haven, CT: Yale University Press, 2010), pp. 118–119. The questions for the new "modern" world, asks Hill, are these: "Would diplomacy be taken seriously as the legitimate mechanism for managing international disputes?... Is peace the overarching goal which the international system approaches, however imperfectly?... What, if anything, would be the role of religion in the international state system?" For analyses of Kant's impact on the development grand strategy, see Francis A. Boyle, *Foundations of World Order: The Legalist Approach to International Relations, 1898–1922* (Durham, NC: Duke University Press, 1999); Dorothy V. Jones, *Code of Peace: Ethics and Security in the World of the Warlord States* (Chicago: University of Chicago Press, 1989); and Daniel George Lang, *Foreign Policy in the Early Republic: The Law of Nations and the Balance of Power* (Baton Rouge: Louisiana State University Press, 1985).

79. Hill, *Grand Strategies: Literature, Statecraft, and World Order* (New Haven, CT: Yale University Press, 2010), p. 123: "a thinking-through of what might qualify as rightful human action without reference to outside authority."

80. Immanuel Kant, "Section I: Containing the Definitive Articles for Perpetual Peace among States," *Perpetual Peace: A Philosophical Sketch* (1795), at www.mtholyoke.edu/acad/intrel/kant/kant1.htm.

81. Charles Hill, *Grand Strategies: Literature, Statecraft, and World Order* (New Haven, CT: Yale University Press, 2010), p. 123: "The vast external realm was anarchic and could be survived only through the accumulation and wielding of power."

82. Hill, *Grand Strategies: Literature, Statecraft, and World Order* (New Haven, CT: Yale University Press, 2010), p. 124: He "thinks through the questions of international order without any reference to the Treaty of Westphalia or any other supposedly foundational principle supplied by the past ..."

83. Immanuel Kant, "Section I: Containing the Preliminary Articles for Perpetual Peace among States," *Perpetual Peace: A Philosophical Sketch* (1795), at www.mtholyoke.edu/acad/intrel/kant/kant1.htm.

84. Immanuel Kant, "First Definitive Article for Perpetual Peace," *Perpetual Peace: A Philosophical Sketch* (1795), at www.mtholyoke.edu/acad/intrel/kant/kant1.htm.

85. Kant, "First Definitive Article for Perpetual Peace," *Perpetual Peace: A Philosophical Sketch* (1795), at www.mtholyoke.edu/acad/intrel/kant/kant1.htm.

86. Immanuel Kant, "Second Definitive Article for Perpetual Peace," *Perpetual Peace: A Philosophical Sketch* (1795), at www.mtholyoke.edu/acad/intrel/kant/kant1.htm.

87. Immanuel Kant, "First Definitive Article for Perpetual Peace," *Perpetual Peace: A Philosophical Sketch* (1795), at www.mtholyoke.edu/acad/intrel/kant/kant1.htm.

88. Michael E. Brown, Sean M. Lynn-Jones, and Steven Miller, eds., *Debating the Democratic Peace* (Cambridge, MA, The MIT Press, 1996), p. 25–26. For further discussion of this argument, see Michael C. Desch, "Democracy and Victory: Why Regime Type Hardly Matters," *International Security* 27, No. 2 (Fall 2002), p. 5–47, esp. the section "Do Democracies Really Win Wars More Often?" (pp. 9–25). See also these consecutive articles in *International Security* 28, No. 1 (Summer 2003): Agin Choi, "The Power of Democratic Cooperation," p. 142–153; David A. Lake, "Fair Fights? Evaluating Theories of Democracy and Victory," p. 154–179; and Michael C. Desch, "Democracy and Victory: Fair Fights or Food Fights?" p. 136.

89. See Immanuel Kant, "First Definitive Article for Perpetual Peace," *Perpetual Peace: A Philosophical Sketch* (1795), at www.mtholyoke.edu/acad/intrel/kant/kant1.htm.

90. Charles Hill, *Grand Strategies: Literature, Statecraft, and World Order* (New Haven, CT: Yale University Press, 2010), p. 125–126.

91. Hill, *Grand Strategies: Literature, Statecraft, and World Order* (New Haven, CT: Yale University Press, 2010), p. 143.

92. Immanuel Kant, "Section II: Containing the Preliminary Articles for Perpetual Peace among States," *Perpetual Peace: A Philosophical Sketch* (1795), at www.mtholyoke.edu/acad/intrel/kant/kant1.htm.

93. For analyses of the consequences for strategy, see William C. Martel, *Victory in War: Foundations of Modern Strategy* (New York: Cambridge University Press, 2011), pp. 76–83.

94. Crane Brinton, Gordon A. Craig, and Felix Gilbert, "Jomini," in Edward Mead Earle (ed.), *Makers of Modern Strategy: Military Thought from Machiavelli to Hitler* (Princeton, NJ: Princeton University Press, 1943), pp. 77–92, at p. 77.

95. Brinton, Craig, and Gilbert, "Jomini," in Edward Mead Earle (ed.), *Makers of Modern Strategy: Military Thought from Machiavelli to Hitler* (Princeton, NJ: Princeton University Press, 1943), p. 92.

96. Bernard Brodie, *Strategy in the Missile Age* (Princeton, NJ: Princeton University Press, 1959), p. 78, quoted Mahan, who said of Jomini that his "methods change but principles are unchanging." See Alger, *Quest for Victory*, pp. 17–50; and Brinton et al., "Jomini," in Edward Mead Earle (ed.), *Makers of Modern Strategy: Military Thought from Machiavelli to Hitler* (Princeton, NJ: Princeton University Press, 1943), pp. 84–85.

97. Azar Gat, *The Origins of Military Thought: From the Enlightenment to Clausewitz* (Oxford: Clarendon Press, 1991), p. 139.

98. Brinton et al., "Jomini," in Edward Mead Earle (ed.), *Makers of Modern Strategy: Military Thought from Machiavelli to Hitler* (Princeton, NJ: Princeton University Press, 1943), pp. 87–88: "Jomini believed that the practice of warfare could be reduced to a set of general rules which could be learned and applied in all situations."

99. Baron de Jomini, *The Art of War: A New Edition, with Appendices and Maps*, trans. G. H. Mendell and W. P. Craighill (Westport, CT: Greenwood Press, 1971), p. 182. Subsequent citations are given in the text. See "Jomini's *Art of War*," in *Roots of Strategy, Book 2: 3 Military Classics* (Harrisburg, PA: Stackpole Books, 1987), pp. 389–557, at p. 498. In wars of all types, Jomini held that strategy depends on "activity, boldness, and skill," (28) while also noting that in "every battlefield [there is] a decisive point the possession of which ... helps to secure the victory." He also wrote that "war is always to be conducted according to the great principles of the art," which embrace the field of strategy as the ideas that guide the state in war. In terms of strategy, Jomini saw the ability to seize territory as a central postulate in his theory, whose objectives were "the secession of the territory by the enemy, and the means to threaten him in the heart of his own country."

100. Gat, *Origins of Military Thought*, p. 110: "Jomini gave theoretical expression to the new military reality and ideal raised to prominence by Napoleonic warfare: concentration of forces."

101. As Brinton et al., "Jomini," in Edward Mead Earle (ed.), *Makers of Modern Strategy: Military Thought from Machiavelli to Hitler* (Princeton, NJ: Princeton University Press, 1943), observed (p. 89), for Jomini the "purpose of warfare is to occupy all or part of the enemy's territory." The principle of occupying territory was of such critical importance in Jomini's strategy that in "national wars, the country should be occupied and subjugated, the fortified places besieged and reduced, and the armies destroyed."

102. Gat, *Origins of Military Thought*, p. 115: "The destruction of the enemy's field armies was the new military aim."

103. To understand Jomini's influence on modern strategy, Brinton et al., "Jomini," in Edward Mead Earle (ed.), *Makers of Modern Strategy: Military Thought from*

Machiavelli to Hitler (Princeton, NJ: Princeton University Press, 1943), p. 92, argued that the "progressive totalitarianism of warfare has effectually destroyed the validity of purely geographical campaigns and has made limited war impossible." The matter of the relationship between conquering territory and victory is of contemporary interest. See "Chapter 3: The Army in Military Operations," *FM-1 The Army* (Washington, DC: Headquarters, Department of the Army, June 14, 2001), which cites Army doctrine: "The primary functions of The Army, as outlined in Department of Defense Directive 5100.1, are to organize, equip, and train forces for the conduct of prompt and sustained combat operations on land. Accordingly, The Army must possess the capability to *defeat enemy land forces and seize, occupy, and defend land areas*" (at chrishaase.com/aa/FM1/ch3.htm; emphasis added).

104. Azar Gat, *The Origins of Military Thought: From the Enlightenment to Clausewitz* (Oxford: Clarendon Press, 1991), pp. 128, 130–131: "Jomini always stressed that he did not believe in a military 'system', certainly not in a complete geometrical system such as that of Bülow. Instead, he believed in 'principles', or, in other words, in a much more flexible and less pretentious theoretical framework."

105. Baron de Jomini, *Art of War: New Edition*, trans. G. H. Mendell and W. P. Craighill (Westport, CT: Greenwood Press, 1971), p. 282. In terms of the meaning of strategy, he argued that "victory does not always depend upon the superiority of the arm, but upon a thousand other things"; for instance, the "courage of troops, the presence of mind of the commanders, the opportuneness of maneuvers, the effect of artillery and musketry fire, rain, – mud, even – have been the causes of repulses or of victories." See William C. Martel, *Victory in War: Foundations of Modern Strategy* (New York: Cambridge University Press, 2011), pp. 76–78.

106. For an analysis of Jomini, see Gat, *Origins of Military Thought*, pp. 106–131. As Gat explained (p. 123), "Jomini's abstract principles," for Clausewitz, "ignored the living reality of war, the operation of moral forces, and the unique conditions of every particular case."

107. Carl von Clausewitz, *On War*, ed. and intro. Anatol Rapoport (Baltimore: Penguin Books, 1971), p. 119.

108. Carl von Clausewitz, *On War*, eds. and trans. Michael Howard and Peter Paret (Princeton, NJ: Princeton University Press, 1976), p. 75, 81: "Sometimes the political object and military object is the same.... In other cases, the political object will not provide a suitable military objective. In that event, another military objective must be adopted that will serve the political purpose and symbolize it in the peace negotiations." In addition, when he differentiated between the political and military objectives of war, he gave the former priority.

109. Recalling the levels of strategic interaction chart in Chapter 3, the "accumulationist" view would argue that success at one level flows from success at the lower levels. This was the view of grand strategy until the advent of sophisticated modern irregular war – e.g., North Vietnamese forces lost every single battle against the American forces. At the tactical, operational level they were defeated, but at the strategic and grand strategic levels they prevailed. See William C. Martel, "Victory in Strategy on Scholarship and War," *Cambridge Review of International Affairs* 24, No. 3, pp. 513–536, at pp. 519, 530.

110. Hans Rothfels, "Clausewitz," in Edward Mead Earle (ed.), *Makers of Modern Strategy: Military Thought from Machiavelli to Hitler* (Princeton, NJ: Princeton University Press, 1943), pp. 93–113, at p. 102.

111. Michael I. Handel, *Masters of War: Sun Tzu, Clausewitz and Jomini* (London: Frank Cass, 1992), p. 24. See Raymond Aron, "Introduction," in Herman Kahn, *Thinking about the Unthinkable* (New York: Avon Books, 1962), pp. 1–15, at p. 14. As French philosopher and political scientist Raymond Aron noted, in the nuclear era, "it [disarmament] is no longer necessary to take away all the enemy's weapons from him; it will suffice to take away his means of retaliation to hold him at your mercy." For Aron, Clausewitz "defines absolute victory in terms of the disarmament of the enemy."

112. Of the vast literature on Clausewitz, see Carl von Clausewitz, *On War*, eds. and trans. Michael Howard and Peter Paret (Princeton, NJ: Princeton University Press, 1976); Peter Paret, *Clausewitz and the State: The Man, His Theories, and His Times* (Princeton, NJ: Princeton University Press, 1976); Paret, "Clausewitz," in Paret (ed.), *Makers of Modern Strategy: Military Thought from Machiavelli to Hitler* (Princeton, NJ: Princeton University Press, 1943), pp. 186–213; Paret, "Clausewitz: A Bibliographical Survey," *World Politics* 17.2 (January 1965), pp. 272–285; Gat, *Origins of Military Thought*, esp. pp. 156–254; Christopher Bassford, *Clausewitz in English: The Reception of Clausewitz in Britain and America* (New York: Oxford University Press, 1994); Alan D. Beyerchen, "Clausewitz, Nonlinearity, and the Unpredictability of War," *International Security* 17.3 (Winter 1992–1993), pp. 59–90; Michael I. Handel, *Clausewitz and Modern Strategy* (London: Frank Cass, 1986); Handel, *Masters of War*; and Michael Howard, *Clausewitz* (Oxford: Oxford University Press, 1983); Hew Strachan, *Carl von Clausewitz's on War: A Biography* (London: Atlantic, 2007). See Rothfels, "Clausewitz," p. 94, who notes that *On War* was divided into eight books, which focused on the nature of war, the theory of war, strategy, combat, military forces, defense, the attack, and the plan of war. Also, Jon Tetsuro Sumida, "The Relationship of History and Theory in *On War*: The Clausewitzian Ideal and Its Implications," *Journal of Military History* 65 (April, 2001), pp. 333–354.

113. Gat, *Origins of Military Thought*, p. 123: "That the conduct of war could not be reduced to universal principles was the general message of *On War*."

114. Gat, *Origins of Military Thought*, p. 198: "Clausewitz argued for the feasibility of a universal theory of war, citing a long list of propositions." As quoted in Gat, *Origins of Military Thought*, p. 189, "Our purpose was not to assign, in passing, a handful of principles of warfare to each period.... Each period, therefore, would have held to its own theory of war, even if the urge had always and universally existed to work things out on scientific principles."

115. Gat, *Origins of Military Thought*, p. 205. As Gat wrote, for Clausewitz, "the aims in the conduct of war are (a) to conquer and destroy the armed forces of the enemy; (b) to take possession of the resources of his army; and (c) to win public opinion. These aims ... are intended to secure the complete defeat of the enemy."

116. Raymond Aron, *Clausewitz: Philosopher of War* (Englewood Cliffs, NJ: Prentice Hall, 1985), pp. 97, 100. In Clausewitz's words, "By the medium of victory, strategy

attains the end which it has devised for the combat.... A victory which aims to weaken the armed forces of the enemy is something other than a victory which only enables us to occupy a position" (pp. 97, 101). See also James M. McPherson, "Lincoln and the Strategy of Unconditional Surrender," in Gabor S. Boritt (ed.), *Lincoln, the War President* (New York: Oxford University Press, 1992), pp. 29–62, at p. 38: "The first usually means a limited war ended by a negotiated peace. The second usually means a total war ending in unconditional surrender by the loser."

117. Hans Rothfels, "Clausewitz," in Edward Mead Earle (ed.), *Makers of Modern Strategy: Military Thought from Machiavelli to Hitler* (Princeton, NJ: Princeton University Press, 1943), p. 96, argued that wars "involved the very existence of the nations concerned and, as in the religious wars of the sixteenth century, they involved opposing principles, opposing philosophies of life."

118. Carl von Clausewitz, *On War*, eds. and trans. Michael Howard and Peter Paret (Princeton, NJ: Princeton University Press, 1976), p. 227.

119. Brodie, *Strategy in the Missile Age*, p. 53. Also, Clausewitz, *On War*, eds. Howard and Paret, p. 596. However, as Clausewitz asked, "What constitutes defeat? The conquest of his whole territory is not always necessary, and total occupation of his territory may not be enough."

120. Carl von Clausewitz, *On War*, eds. and trans. Michael Howard and Peter Paret (Princeton, NJ: Princeton University Press, 1976), pp. 90–91.

121. Clausewitz, *On War*, eds. Howard and Paret, p. 93.

122. See Rothfels, "Clausewitz," p. 99, in which war is "an affair of the whole nation."

123. Clausewitz, *On War*, eds. Howard and Paret, pp. 617–637, for a discussion of the conduct of "total war."

124. For Clausewitz's analysis of the concept of "major victory," see Clausewitz, *On War*, eds. Howard and Paret, pp. 253–270.

125. Rothfels, "Clausewitz," p. 107.

126. Clausewitz, *On War*, eds. Howard and Paret, p. 128.

127. Clausewitz, *On War*, eds. Howard and Paret, p. 92: "To discover how much of our resources must be mobilized for war, we must first examine our own political aim and that of the enemy ... [S]ince war is not an act of senseless passion but is controlled by the political object, the value of this object must determine the sacrifices made for it in magnitude and duration."

128. Clausewitz, *On War*, eds. Howard and Paret: "Once the expenditure of efforts exceeds the value of the political object, the object must be renounced and peace must follow."

129. Gat, *Origins of Military Thought*, pp. 123–124.

130. For a discussion of German military thinkers, see Antulio J. Echevarria II, *After Clausewitz: German Military Thinkers before the Great War* (Lawrence: University Press of Kansas, 2000).

131. Hans Rothfels, "Clausewitz," in Edward Mead Earle (ed.), *Makers of Modern Strategy: Military Thought from Machiavelli to Hitler* (Princeton, NJ: Princeton University Press, 1943), p. 96: "These new tensions were intertwined with fundamental changes in the political and social structure of Europe."

132. Rothfels, "Clausewitz," in Edward Mead Earle (ed.), *Makers of Modern Strategy: Military Thought from Machiavelli to Hitler* (Princeton, NJ: Princeton University Press, 1943), p. 99.

133. Rothfels, "Clausewitz," in Edward Mead Earle (ed.), *Makers of Modern Strategy: Military Thought from Machiavelli to Hitler* (Princeton, NJ: Princeton University Press, 1943), p. 108.

134. Rothfels, "Clausewitz," in Edward Mead Earle (ed.), *Makers of Modern Strategy: Military Thought from Machiavelli to Hitler* (Princeton, NJ: Princeton University Press, 1943), p. 105–106: "How could it be otherwise? Do the political relations between different peoples and governments ever cease when the exchange of diplomatic notes has ceased?"

135. Rothfels, "Clausewitz," in Edward Mead Earle (ed.), *Makers of Modern Strategy: Military Thought from Machiavelli to Hitler* (Princeton, NJ: Princeton University Press, 1943), p. 105–106.

136. Rothfels, "Clausewitz," in Edward Mead Earle (ed.), *Makers of Modern Strategy: Military Thought from Machiavelli to Hitler* (Princeton, NJ: Princeton University Press, 1943), p. 106. For Clausewitz, "the greater and more powerful the motives of a war, the more it affects the whole existence of the nations concerned, the more violent the tension which precedes the war – by so much the nearer will the war approach its abstract form, so much the more purely military and less political will war appear to be."

137. Rothfels, "Clausewitz," in Edward Mead Earle (ed.), *Makers of Modern Strategy: Military Thought from Machiavelli to Hitler* (Princeton, NJ: Princeton University Press, 1943), p. 107: "According to a variety of circumstances the 'center of gravity' may be differently placed. In most cases it lies in the armed force of the enemy. This was true not only of the Napoleonic Wars but also of those of Alexander, Gustavus Adolphus, Charles XII, and Frederick the Great. If the enemy country is divided by civil dissension, however, the 'center of gravity' may lie in the capital. In wars of coalition, the 'center' lies in the army of the strongest of the allies or in the community of interest between the allies. In national wars 'public opinion' is an important center of gravity, a vital military objective." Also, "He points out further that, whatever the decision, the state must regard the bond uniting the enemy alliance as a legitimate military objective."

138. Rothfels, "Clausewitz," in Edward Mead Earle (ed.), *Makers of Modern Strategy: Military Thought from Machiavelli to Hitler* (Princeton, NJ: Princeton University Press, 1943), p. 112.

139. See Garrett Mattingly, *Renaissance Diplomacy* (Baltimore: Penguin Books, 1964), for a review of politics and diplomacy during this era, esp. pp. 140–146.

140. For background on total war, see Raymond Aron, *Century of Total War*; and Paul Kecskemeti, *Strategic Surrender: The Politics of Victory and Defeat* (Stanford, CA: Stanford University Press, 1958), pp. 13–27; Alger, *Quest for Victory*, pp. 97–119. See also Arthur Marwick and Clive Emsley, "Introduction," in Arthur Marwick, Clive Emsley, and Wendy Simpson (eds.), *Total War and Historical Change: Europe 1914–1955* (Philadelphia: Open University Press, 2001), pp. 1–12; Hew Strachan, "Total War in the Twentieth Century," pp. 255–283, in Arthur Marwick, Clive Emsley, and Wendy Simpson (eds.),

Total War and Historical Change: Europe 1914–1955 (Philadelphia: Open University Press, 2001), pp. 255–283; Arthur Marwick, *Britain in the Century of Total War* (Boston: Little, Brown, 1968); and Manfred F. Boemeke, Roger Chickering, and Stig Forster, eds., *Anticipating Total War: The German and American Experiences* (Cambridge, MA: Cambridge University Press, 1999).

141. William C. Martel, *Victory in War: Foundations of Modern Strategy* (New York: Cambridge University Press, 2011), pp. 72–73. Cf. Dennis Showalter, *The Wars of Frederick the Great* (New York: Longman Group, 1996), pp. 356–357. The purpose of armies during Frederick's time was to "win victories, then to demonstrate the state's readiness and capacity to defend its interests."

142. John J. Mearsheimer, *Conventional Deterrence* (Ithaca, NY: Cornell University Press, 1983), p. 30. See R. R. Palmer, "Frederick the Great, Guibert, Bülow: From Dynastic to National War," in Earle (ed.), *Makers of Modern Strategy: Military Thought from Machiavelli to Hitler* (Princeton, NJ: Princeton University Press, 1943), p. 49, who argues that since the French Revolution, war "has become increasingly a clash between peoples, and hence has become increasingly 'total.'"

143. See Rothfels, "Clausewitz," p. 99, in which war is "an affair of the whole nation."

144. Edward Mead Earle, "Adam Smith, Alexander Hamilton, Friedrich List: The Economic Foundations of Military Power," in Earle (ed.), *Makers of Modern Strategy: Military Thought from Machiavelli to Hitler* (Princeton, NJ: Princeton University Press, 1943), p. 117: "This interrelationship is one of the most critical and absorbing problems of statesmanship. It involves the security of the nation and, in large measure, determines the extent to which the individual may enjoy life, liberty, and happiness."

145. Earle, "Adam Smith, Alexander Hamilton, Friedrich List: The Economic Foundations of Military Power," in Earle (ed.), *Makers of Modern Strategy: Military Thought from Machiavelli to Hitler* (Princeton, NJ: Princeton University Press, 1943), p. 117.

146. Earle, "Adam Smith, Alexander Hamilton, Friedrich List: The Economic Foundations of Military Power," in Earle (ed.), *Makers of Modern Strategy: Military Thought from Machiavelli to Hitler* (Princeton, NJ: Princeton University Press, 1943), p. 107.

147. Earle, "Adam Smith, Alexander Hamilton, Friedrich List: The Economic Foundations of Military Power," in Earle (ed.), *Makers of Modern Strategy: Military Thought from Machiavelli to Hitler* (Princeton, NJ: Princeton University Press, 1943), p. 117.

148. See Robert Gilpin, *The Political Economy of International Relations* (Princeton, NJ: Princeton University Press, 1987); Stephen D. Krasner, "State Power and the Structure of International Trade," *World Politics* 28.3 (April 1976), pp. 317–348.

149. See Edward Mead Earle, "Adam Smith, Alexander Hamilton, Friedrich List: The Economic Foundations of Military Power," in Earle (ed.), *Makers of Modern Strategy: Military Thought*, pp. 117–154, at p. 122.

150. A late twentieth-century form of this argument, the *democratic peace theory*, suggested that the rise of democratic governments would decrease the chance of war. For a discussion of these arguments, see Michael C. Desch, "Democracy and Victory: Why Regime Type Hardly Matters," *International Security* 27.2 (Fall

2002), pp. 5–47, esp. the section "Do Democracies Really Win Wars More Often?" (pp. 9–25). See also these consecutive articles in *International Security* 28.1 (Summer 2003): Ajin Choi, "The Power of Democratic Cooperation," pp. 142–153; David A. Lake, "Fair Fights? Evaluating Theories of Democracy and Victory," pp. 154–179; and Michael C. Desch, "Democracy and Victory: Fair Fights or Food Fights?" pp. 180–194.

151. See Viscount Montgomery of Alamein (Bernard Law Montgomery), "European War in the Seventeenth Century," *A History of Warfare* (New York: William Morrow, 1983), pp. 263–289.

152. See Edward Mead Earle, "Adam Smith, Alexander Hamilton, Friedrich List," p. 143, who argued that the "greater the productive power, the greater the strength of the nation ... and the greater its independence in time of war." This often translates into the notion that the "ability of a nation to wage war is measured in terms of its power to produce wealth."

153. Adam Smith, *An Inquiry into the Nature and Causes of the Wealth of Nations*, (London, 1904), pp. 460–461, in Edward Mead Earle (ed.), *Makers of Modern Strategy: Military Thought from Machiavelli to Hitler* (Princeton, NJ: Princeton University Press, 1943), p. 120.

154. Smith, *An Inquiry into the Nature and Causes of the Wealth of Nations* (London, 1904), pp. 460–461, in Edward Mead Earle (ed.), *Makers of Modern Strategy: Military Thought from Machiavelli to Hitler* (Princeton, NJ: Princeton University Press, 1943), p. 120.

155. Adam Smith *Wealth of Nations*, pp. 878–879, in *Makers of Modern Strategy*, p. 121: "The nation which, from the annual produce of its domestic industry, from the annual revenue arising out of its lands, labour, and consumable stocks, has wherewithal to purchase those consumable goods in distant countries, can maintain foreign wars there."

156. G. S. Graham, "Sea Power and British North America" (Cambridge, MA, 1941), p. 15, in Edward Mead Earle (ed.), *Makers of Modern Strategy: Military Thought from Machiavelli to Hitler* (Princeton, NJ: Princeton University Press, 1943), p. 122: "Your trade is the mother and nurse of your seamen: your seamen are the life of your fleet: and your fleet is the security and protection of your trade ..."

157. Adam Smith, *An Inquiry into the Nature and Causes of the Wealth of Nations*, Book IV (London, 1904), p. 204.

158. Smith, *The Wealth of Nations*, pp. 430–431, in Edward Mead Earle, *Makers of Modern Strategy*, p. 123–124.

159. G. S. Graham, "Sea Power and British North America" (Cambridge, MA, 1941), p. 15, in Edward Mead Earle (ed.), *Makers of Modern Strategy: Military Thought from Machiavelli to Hitler* (Princeton, NJ: Princeton University Press, 1943), p. 125.

160. Francis Hutcheson, *A Short Introduction to Moral Philosophy* (2 vols., Glasgow, 1764), II, pp. 348–349, in Edward Mead Earle (ed.), *Makers of Modern Strategy: Military Thought from Machiavelli to Hitler* (Princeton, NJ: Princeton University Press, 1943), pp. 126–127: "The state of the mechanical, as well as some of the other arts, with which it is necessarily connected, determines the degree of perfection to which it is capable of being carried out at any particular time ..."

161. See Edward Mead Earle, "Adam Smith, Alexander Hamilton, Friedrich List," p. 136.

162. Earle, "Adam Smith, Alexander Hamilton, Friedrich List," p. 129.

163. Alexander Hamilton, *The Works of Alexander Hamilton*, IV, ed. Henry Cabot Lodge (New York: G. P. Putnam's Sons, 1904), p. 70, in Edward Mead Earle (ed.), *Makers of Modern Strategy: Military Thought from Machiavelli to Hitler* (Princeton, NJ: Princeton University Press, 1943), p. 130.

164. Hamilton, *The Works of Alexander Hamilton*, IV, 105–106, in *Makers of Modern Strategy*, p. 131.

165. Alexander Hamilton, "The Federalist No. 11," para. 5, at www.constitution.org/fed/federal1.htm: "There can be no doubt that the continuance of the Union under an efficient government would put it in our power, at a period not very distant, to create a navy which, if it could not vie with those of the great maritime powers, would at least be of respectable weight if thrown into the scale of either of two contending parties. This would be more peculiarly the case in relation to operations in the West Indies. A few ships of the line, sent opportunely to the reinforcement of either side, would often be sufficient to decide the fate of a campaign, on the event of which interests of the greatest magnitude were suspended. Our position is, in this respect, a most commanding one. And if to this consideration we add that of the usefulness of supplies from this country, in the prosecution of military operations in the West Indies, it will readily be perceived that a situation so favorable would enable us to bargain with great advantage for commercial privileges. A price would be set not only upon our friendship, but upon our neutrality."

166. See Edward Mead Earle, "Adam Smith, Alexander Hamilton, Friedrich List," p. 132. Also, Alexander Hamilton, "The Federalist No. 11," para. 12, at www.constitution.org/fed/federal1.htm. Citing Federalist Paper No. 11, Hamilton argues that "an unrestrained intercourse between the States themselves will advance the trade of each by an interchange of their respective productions, not only for the supply of reciprocal wants at home, but for exportation to foreign markets . . ."

167. See Earle, "Adam Smith, Alexander Hamilton, Friedrich List," p. 132.

168. Alexander Hamilton, "The Federalist No. 25," para. 7, at www.constitution.org/fed/federa25.htm: "We must expose our property and liberty to the mercy of foreign invaders, and invite them by our weakness to seize the naked and defenseless prey, because we are afraid that rulers, created by our choice, dependent on our will, might endanger that liberty, by an abuse of the means necessary to its preservation."

169. *Writings of Thomas Jefferson* (Memorial Edition), V, 94, in Edward Mead Earle (ed.), *Makers of Modern Strategy: Military Thought from Machiavelli to Hitler* (Princeton, NJ: Princeton University Press, 1943), p. 137.

170. *Writings of Thomas Jefferson* (Memorial Edition), V, 94, in Edward Mead Earle (ed.), *Makers of Modern Strategy: Military Thought from Machiavelli to Hitler* (Princeton, NJ: Princeton University Press, 1943), p. 137: "When forced into war, the interception of exchanges which must be made across a wide ocean, becomes a powerful weapon in the hands of an enemy domineering over that element."

171. See Edward Mead Earle, "Adam Smith, Alexander Hamilton, Friedrich List: The Economic Foundations of Military Power," in Earle (ed.), *Makers of Modern Strategy: Military Thought*, pp. 117–154, at p. 143. As List put it, "all warlike operations depend so much on the condition of the national revenue."

172. Earle, "Adam Smith, Alexander Hamilton, Friedrich List: The Economic Foundations of Military Power," in Earle (ed.), *Makers of Modern Strategy: Military Thought*, p. 149: "List foresaw that the network of railway lines … would enable the army of a unified Germany, in the event of an invasion, to move troops from any point in the country to the frontiers in such a way as to multiply many fold its defensive potential."

173. See Robert Gilpin, *The Political Economy of International Relations* (Princeton, NJ: Princeton University Press, 1987); Stephen D. Krasner, "State Power and the Structure of International Trade," *World Politics* 28.3 (April 1976), pp. 317–348. Also, see Edward Mead Earle, "Adam Smith, Alexander Hamilton, Friedrich List: The Economic Foundations of Military Power," in Earle (ed.), *Makers of Modern Strategy: Military Thought*, p. 142. As List stated, "The object of the economy of this body is not only wealth as in individual and cosmopolitical economy, but power and wealth, because national wealth is increased and secured by national power, as national power is increased and secured by national wealth."

174. See Edward Mead Earle, "Adam Smith, Alexander Hamilton, Friedrich List: The Economic Foundations of Military Power," in Earle (ed.), *Makers of Modern Strategy: Military Thought*, p. 145. For List, a nation should "posses the power of beneficially affecting the civilisation of less advanced nations, and by means of its own surplus population and of its mental and material capital to found colonies and beget new nations."

175. Earle, "Adam Smith, Alexander Hamilton, Friedrich List: The Economic Foundations of Military Power," in Earle (ed.), *Makers of Modern Strategy: Military Thought*, p. 151.

176. Earle, "Adam Smith, Alexander Hamilton, Friedrich List: The Economic Foundations of Military Power," in Earle (ed.), *Makers of Modern Strategy: Military Thought*, p. 148–149. According to Earle, "The single greatest contribution which List made to modern strategy was his elaborate discussion on the influence of railways upon the shifting balance of military power."

177. Earle, "Adam Smith, Alexander Hamilton, Friedrich List: The Economic Foundations of Military Power," in Earle (ed.), *Makers of Modern Strategy: Military Thought*, p. 152: "Only with the aid of a German railway system is it possible for the social economy of the Germans to rise to national greatness, and only through such national greatness can a system of railways realize its full potentialities."

5 Grand Strategies of Empire in the Modern Era: Sixteenth to Twentieth Centuries

1. On Philip II's grand strategy, see J. H. Elliott, "Managing Decline: Olivares and the Grand Strategy of Imperial Spain," in Paul Kennedy (ed.), *Grand Strategies in War and Peace* (New Haven, CT: Yale University Press, 1991), pp. 87–104;

Geoffrey Parker, "The Making of Strategy in Habsburg Spain: Philip II's 'Bid for Master,' 1556–1598," in Williamson Murray, MacGregor Knox, and Alvin Bernstein (eds.), *The Making of Strategy: Rulers, States, and War* (New York: Cambridge University Press, 1996), pp. 115–150; Geoffrey Parker, "Conclusion: Agent and Structure," *The Grand Strategy of Philip II* (New Haven, CT: Yale University Press, 1998), pp. 281–296.

2. On the divine right of kings, see George Holland Sabine and Thomas Landon Thorson, *A History of Political Theory* (Hinsdale, IL: Dryden Press, 1973), pp. 364–369.

3. Paul M. Kennedy, *The Rise and Fall of the Great Powers: Economic Change and Military Conflict from 1500 to 2000* (New York: Random House, 1987), p. 35. For more analyses of Philip II, see also J. H. Elliott, "Managing Decline: Olivares and the Grand Strategy of Imperial Spain," in Paul Kennedy (ed.), *Grand Strategies in War and Peace* (New Haven, CT: Yale University Press, 1991), pp. 87–104; David Kaiser, *Politics and War: European Conflict From Philip II to Hitler* (Cambridge, MA: Harvard University Press, 2000); and Geoffrey Parker, "The Making of Strategy in Habsburg Spain: Philip II's 'Bid for Master,' 1556–1598," in Williamson Murray, MacGregor Knox, and Alvin Bernstein (eds.), *The Making of Strategy: Rulers, States, and War* (New York: Cambridge University Press, 1996), pp. 115–150.

4. Geoffrey Parker, *The Grand Strategy of Philip II* (New Haven, CT: Yale University Press, 1998), p. 3.

5. Parker, *The Grand Strategy of Philip II* (New Haven, CT: Yale University Press, 1998), p. 22, notes, "The conciliar system of government created by Charles V and his advisors in the 1520s served Philip well. Despite the relentless expansion of matters with which he and the central bureaucracy had to deal, he found it necessary to create only three new institutions.... Each organ, however, met for ever longer as the reign advanced, and the quantity of paperwork generated increased alarmingly."

6. See Gianfranco Poggi, "The Formation of the Modern State and the Institutionalization of Rule," in Gerard Delanty and Engin F. Isin (eds.), *Handbook of Historical Sociology* (Thousand Oaks, CA: Sage Publications, 2003), pp. 250–260.

7. Geoffrey Parker, *The Grand Strategy of Philip II* (New Haven, CT: Yale University Press, 1998), p. 28.

8. Parker, *The Grand Strategy of Philip II* (New Haven, CT: Yale University Press, 1998), p. 73: "Philip's strategic planning did not suffer because he, like the statesmen of 1914, accumulated more knowledge than could be assimilated, sorted and absorbed in time." Further, "he ruled over a monarchy composed of many different and dispersed territories, each with its own separate identity and independent sentiments ..."

9. Parker, *The Grand Strategy of Philip II* (New Haven, CT: Yale University Press, 1998), p. 67: "In taking them when we lack time, money and opportunity, in making savings that cost three times more than is saved, starting in haste because we are late, and in starting badly because we are in haste."

10. Paul M. Kennedy, *The Rise and Fall of the Great Powers: Economic Change and Military Conflict from 1500 to 2000* (New York: Random House, 1987), p. 48.

11. Kennedy, *The Rise and Fall of the Great Powers: Economic Change and Military Conflict from 1500 to 2000* (New York: Random House, 1987), p. 48.

12. Geoffrey Parker, *The Grand Strategy of Philip II* (New Haven, CT: Yale University Press, 1998), p. 41: "In 1588 the shortage of funds became so acute that the king began to receive a special statement every Saturday from his treasury advisers to show how much cash they had in hand – the grand total was often less than 30,000 ducats, the cost of the Armada for just one day – and how many obligations remained outstanding." Furthermore, he notes that "Castile served as the financial motor of the entire Monarchy." Parker also observes that "its periodic fiscal collapses had serious repercussions on the king's Grand Strategy ... he occasionally boasted that he would never compromise simply because of lack of funds." However, "bankruptcy eventually induced him at least to open talks – in 1558–59 with Turks and French; in 1576–77 with the Turks and Dutch; and in 1597–98 with French, English, and Dutch" (p. 88).

13. J. H. Elliott, "Managing Decline," in *Grand Strategies in War and Peace*, by Paul M. Kennedy (New Haven, CT: Yale University Press, 1991), p. 89. These resources "depended essentially on the willingness and ability of the international banking community (especially the Genoese) to continue making loans to the Spanish crown."

14. David Kaiser, *Politics and War: European Conflict from Philip II to Hitler* (Cambridge, MA: Harvard University Press, 2000), p. 33.

15. J. H. Elliott, "Managing Decline," in *Grand Strategies in War and Peace*, by Paul M. Kennedy (New Haven, CT: Yale University Press, 1991), p. 89: "The payments of the Army of Flanders were already enormous by the 1570s, and nearly always overdue: this in turn provoking the revolts of the troops, particularly after Philip's 1575 suspension of payments to his Genovese bankers."

16. Paul M. Kennedy, *The Rise and Fall of the Great Powers: Economic Change and Military Conflict from 1500 to 2000* (New York: Random House, 1987), p. 47.

17. Kennedy, *The Rise and Fall of the Great Powers: Economic Change and Military Conflict from 1500 to 2000* (New York: Random House, 1987), p. 47.

18. Andrew Pettegree, *Europe in the Sixteenth Century* (Oxford: Blackwell, 2002), p. 214.

19. Geoffrey Parker, *The Grand Strategy of Philip II* (New Haven, CT: Yale University Press, 1998), p. 113.

20. Parker, *The Grand Strategy of Philip II* (New Haven, CT: Yale University Press, 1998), p. 113: "At the public level, Philip's unqualified commitment to advancing the Catholic cause deprived him of potential friends and made him unnecessary enemies: he broke with England, Spain's ally for almost two centuries, essentially over religious differences. At the private level, it set up a tension between principle and practice that caused severe problems. Philip firmly believed – and his many devout advisers frequently reminded him – that he served as God's lieutenant on earth and therefore had an obligation to pursue at all times policies consistent with the needs of the Catholic church." For example, "several rebellions against Philip ... and some international crises stemmed from his desire to stamp out Protestantism." But these "confessional goals ... often conflicted with other interests."

21. Geoffrey Parker, "The Place of Tudor England in the Messianic Vision of Philip II of Spain," *Transactions of the Royal Historical Society*, 6th ser., No. 12 (2002), p. 180.

22. David Kaiser, *Politics and War: European Conflict from Philip II to Hitler* (Cambridge, MA: Harvard University Press, 2000), p. 32.

23. See Sebastien le Prestre de Vauban, *A Manual of Siegecraft and Fortification*, trans. and intro. George A. Rothrock (Ann Arbor: University of Michigan Press, 1968). For an excellent analysis of Vauban's influence on military strategy, see Henry Guerlac, "Vauban: The Impact of Science on War," in Edward Mead Earle (ed.), *Makers of Modern Strategy: Military Thought from Machiavelli to Hitler* (Princeton, NJ: Princeton University Press, 1943), pp. 26–48, who advances the notion that Vauban had a decisive effect on strategic thinking.

24. R. R. Palmer, "Frederick the Great, Guibert, Bülow: From Dynastic to National War," in Edward Mead Earle (ed.), *Makers of Modern Strategy: Military Thought from Machiavelli to Hitler* (Princeton, NJ: Princeton University Press, 1943), p. 59: "He could not make Prussia a wealthy state; he could not like the governments of the French Revolution, let his armies live on occupied countries, although he recommended this procedure." In practice, Frederick's strategy rested on the principle that "his armies would melt away if dispersed to seek subsistence, and lose morale if they were not regularly supplied." Nor could he "communicate moral enthusiasm to his troops without changing his whole system and view of life."

25. Palmer, "Frederick the Great, Guibert, Bülow: From Dynastic to National War," in Edward Mead Earle (ed.), *Makers of Modern Strategy: Military Thought from Machiavelli to Hitler* (Princeton, NJ: Princeton University Press, 1943), p. 58. *Blitzkrieg* translates to "lightning war."

26. Cf. Dennis Showalter, *The Wars of Frederick the Great* (New York: Longman Group, 1996), pp. 356–357. The purpose of armies during Frederick's time was to "win victories, then to demonstrate the state's readiness and capacity to defend its interests." This was "an age when battles were decided by the firepower of linear formations and victory was completed by cavalry charges." Furthermore, "victory offers at least the promise of cutting the Gordian knot of agreements, expectations, and premises that sustain any system involving sovereign powers."

27. This and the following quotations in this paragraph are all from Frederick the Great, "Article XXII, Of Combats and Battles," in "Military Instructions, The King of Prussia's Military Instruction to His Generals." The present quotation continues: "It is the custom to allow fifteen yards of interval between squadrons in a difficult, intersected country, but where the ground is good and even, they form in a line entire."

28. T. R. Phillips, ed., *Roots of Strategy*, pp. 301–400, at p. 391. Frederick's emphasis on the role of surprise in military operations made an important contribution to the debate in the eighteenth century about how the tactical foundations of strategy relate to the theory of war.

29. R. R. Palmer, "Frederick the Great, Guibert, Bülow: From Dynastic to National War," in Edward Mead Earle (ed.), *Makers of Modern Strategy: Military Thought*

from *Machiavelli to Hitler* (Princeton, NJ: Princeton University Press, 1943), pp. 54–55. According to Palmer, "A king of Prussia, in Frederick's view, must, to have an army, hold a firm balance between classes in the state, and between economic production and military power."

30. Palmer, "Frederick the Great, Guibert, Bülow: From Dynastic to National War," in Edward Mead Earle (ed.), *Makers of Modern Strategy: Military Thought from Machiavelli to Hitler* (Princeton, NJ: Princeton University Press, 1943), p. 54.

31. Michael Howard, "Jomini and the Classical Tradition in Military Thought," in Michael Howard (ed.), *The Theory and Practice of War: Essays Presented to B. H. Liddell Hart on His Seventieth Birthday* (New York: Praeger Publishers, 1966), pp. 3–20; Baron de Jomini, *The Art of War* (New York: G. P. Putnam, 1854), passim; Archer Jones, "Jomini and the Strategy of the American Civil War: A Reinterpretation," *Military Affairs* 34 (December 1970), pp. 127–131; and Crane Brinton, Gordon A. Craig, and Felix Gilbert, "Jomini," in Edward Mead Earle (ed.), *Makers of Modern Strategy: Military Thought*, pp. 77–92.

32. Quoted in John I. Alger, "Napoleon and the Birth of Modern Military Thought," in his *Quest for Victory*, pp. 17–50, at p. 17. Napoleon articulated the fundamental principles of war, such as "unity of forces, urgency, and a firm resolution to perish with glory." Thus, he argued, "to keep one's forces together, to bear speedily on any point, to be nowhere vulnerable – such are the principles that assure victory."

33. See Marshal Ferdinand Foch, *The Principles of War*, trans. Hilaire Belloc (New York: Henry Holt, 1920), p. 294. Cf. "The Military Maxims of Napoleon," in T. R. Phillips (ed.), *Roots of Strategy*, pp. 389–557, p. 410: "A rapid march exerts a beneficial moral influence on the army and increases its means of victory." For Napoleon, human and psychological dimensions comprised an important component of the state's strategy: "Never despair while there remain brave men around the colors. This is the conduct which wins, and deserves to win, the victory" (p. 412).

34. Brian Bond, *The Pursuit of Victory: From Napoleon to Saddam Hussein* (New York: Oxford University Press, 1996), p. 2. This is what Napoleon called "rapid, decisive victories."

35. John J. Mearsheimer, *Conventional Deterrence* (Ithaca, NY: Cornell University Press, 1983), p. 30. See Palmer, "Frederick the Great, Guibert, Bülow," p. 49, who argues that because of the French Revolution, war "has become increasingly a clash between peoples, and hence has become increasingly 'total.'"

36. See Holger H. Herwig, "Strategic Uncertainties of a Nation-State: Prussia-Germany, 1871–1918," in Williamson Murray, MacGregor Knox, and Alvin Bernstein (eds.), *The Making of Strategy: Rulers, States, and War* (New York: Cambridge University Press, 1996), pp. 242–277.

37. Henry A. Kissinger, *A World Restored* (Boston: Houghton Mifflin Company, 1957).

38. Kissinger, *A World Restored* (Boston: Houghton Mifflin Company, 1957), p. 1.

39. Kissinger, *A World Restored* (Boston: Houghton Mifflin Company, 1957), p. 2.

40. Kissinger, *A World Restored* (Boston: Houghton Mifflin Company, 1957), p. 2: "That Europe rescued stability from seeming chaos was primarily the result of the work of two great men: of Castlereagh, the British Foreign Secretary, who negotiated the international settlement, and of Austria's minister, Metternich, who legitimized it."

41. Kissinger, *A World Restored* (Boston: Houghton Mifflin Company, 1957), p. 5.

42. Kissinger, *A World Restored* (Boston: Houghton Mifflin Company, 1957), p. 5.

43. Kissinger, *A World Restored* (Boston: Houghton Mifflin Company, 1957), p. 6.

44. Kissinger, *A World Restored* (Boston: Houghton Mifflin Company, 1957), p. 30.

45. Kissinger, *A World Restored* (Boston: Houghton Mifflin Company, 1957), p. 43: "A nation situated in the center of Europe cannot find security save in a world in which negotiation is the normal pattern of relation."

46. Michael V. Leggiere, *The Fall of Napoleon: The Allied Invasion of France 1813–1814* (New York: Cambridge University Press, 2007), p. 42: "Before the battle of Leipzig, the general objective of the Alliance was to liberate central Europe from French control." However, "the attainment of this goal would provide only *one* essential component of each power's complex and unique grand strategy ... no serious dissension in Coalition politics could be perceived while the three continental powers cooperated to complete this core task."

47. Henry A. Kissinger, *A World Restored* (Boston: Houghton Mifflin Company, 1957), p. 58.

48. Kissinger, *A World Restored* (Boston: Houghton Mifflin Company, 1957), p. 316.

49. Kissinger, *A World Restored* (Boston: Houghton Mifflin Company, 1957), p. 321.

50. Quoted from Clemens Metternich, *Aus Metternich's Nachgelassenen Paperen*, Vol. 1, edited by Alfons von Klinkowström (Vienna, 1880), p. 13: "Isolated states exist only as the abstractions of so-called philosophers. In the society of states each state has interests ... which connect it with the others. The great axioms of political science derive from the recognition of the true interests of *all* states; it is in the general interests that the guarantee of existence is to be found, while particular interests – the cultivation of which is considered political wisdom by restless and short-sighted men – have only a secondary importance.... Modern history demonstrates the application of the principle of solidarity and equilibrium ... and of the united efforts of states against the supremacy of one power in order to force a return to the common law."

51. Henry A. Kissinger, *A World Restored* (Boston: Houghton Mifflin Company, 1957), p. 20.

52. Kissinger, *A World Restored* (Boston: Houghton Mifflin Company, 1957), p. 20: "To show one's purpose is to court disaster; ... the traitor and the statesman are distinguished, not by their acts, but by their motives." However, Kissinger argues that such a policy "places particular strain on the domestic principles of obligation [which] can never be legitimized by its real motives."

53. See Paul W. Schroeder, "The Congress of Vienna, 1814–1815," in *The Transformation of European Politics, 1763–1848* (New York: Oxford University Press, 1994), pp. 517–582; Paul W. Schroeder, "Did the Vienna Settlement Rest on a Balance of Power?" *American Historical Review* 97, No. 3 (June 1992), 683–706.

54. Michael V. Leggiere, *The Fall of Napoleon: The Allied Invasion of France 1813–1814* (New York: Cambridge University Press, 2007), p. 42: "Liberating Germany provided only one step, albeit a monumental step, toward the achievement of greater national security objectives." As military historian Michael V. Leggiere writes, the "Russian – and by extension Prussian – as well as Austrian

grand strategy demanded more than reaching the Rhine could provide, although Metternich perceived he was much closer to realization of his goals than Alexander. As a result, Coalition politics immediately eclipsed both military operations and military cooperation. Naturally, Metternich wanted the Alliance to follow a course that reflected Austria's grand strategy and was conducive to acquiring Austrian national security objectives." But "upon reaching the Rhine, [the Concert] could not agree on their next and ultimate objective: should they continue the war to overthrow Napoleon or should they negotiate a peace with the French emperor?" It was at "this moment" that "the façade of the concert ended," and with it "a grand strategy that would help to provide stability and security in Europe."

55. For background on Bismarck, see Otto Pflanze, *Bismarck and the Development of Germany, The Period of Unification, 1815–1871* (Princeton, NJ: Princeton University Press, 1963); Henry A. Kissinger, "The White Revolutionary: Reflections on Bismarck," *Daedalus* 97, No. 3, *Philosophers and Kings: Studies in Leadership* (Summer, 1968), p. 902; Marcus Jones, "Strategy as Character: Bismarck and the Prusso-German Question, 1862–1878," pp. 79–110, in Williamson Murray (ed.), *The Shaping of Grand Strategy* (New York: Cambridge University Press, 2011), at pp. 80–81.

56. Williamson Murray, *War, Strategy, and Military Effectiveness* (New York: Cambridge University Press, 2011), p. 116. Also, Holger H. Herwig, "Strategic Uncertainties of a Nation-State: Prussia-Germany, 1871–1918," in Williamson Murray, MacGregor Knox, and Alvin Bernstein (eds.), *The Making of Strategy: Rulers, States, and War* (New York: Cambridge University Press, 1996), pp. 242–277; Josef Joffe, "'Bismarck' or 'Britain': Toward an American Grand Strategy after Bipolarity," *International Security* 19, No. 4 (Spring 1995), pp. 94–117.

57. Henry A. Kissinger, "The White Revolutionary: Reflections on Bismarck," *Daedalus* 97, No. 3, *Philosophers and Kings: Studies in Leadership* (Summer, 1968), p. 902.

58. Williamson Murray, *The Shaping of Grand Strategy: Policy, Diplomacy, and War* (New York: Cambridge University Press, 2011), p. 9.

59. Henry A. Kissinger, "The White Revolutionary: Reflections on Bismarck," *Daedalus* 97, No. 3, *Philosophers and Kings: Studies in Leadership* (Summer, 1968), pp. 902–903.

60. Kissinger, "The White Revolutionary: Reflections on Bismarck," *Daedalus* 97, No. 3, *Philosophers and Kings: Studies in Leadership* (Summer, 1968), p. 905: "For four decades Prussian policy had been stymied by the paradox that it could achieve hegemony in Germany only by allying itself with forces believed to be contrary to its domestic structure. Bismarck showed that the paradox was only apparent. Prussia's sense of cohesion was sufficiently strong for it to combine a repressive policy at home with revolutionary activity abroad."

61. Otto von Bismarck, *Die gesammelten Werke* 14, No. 1 (3rd ed.; Berlin, 1924), November 14, 1833, p. 3.

62. Henry A. Kissinger, "The White Revolutionary: Reflections on Bismarck," *Daedalus* 97, No. 3, *Philosophers and Kings: Studies in Leadership* (Summer, 1968), pp. 906–907.

63. Kissinger, "The White Revolutionary: Reflections on Bismarck," *Daedalus* 97, No. 3, *Philosophers and Kings: Studies in Leadership* (Summer, 1968), p. 911.

64. Kissinger, "The White Revolutionary: Reflections on Bismarck," *Daedalus* 97, No. 3, *Philosophers and Kings: Studies in Leadership* (Summer, 1968), p. 909.

65. On realism, see Hans J. Morgenthau, "A Realist Theory of International Politics," *Politics among Nations: The Struggle for Power and Peace*, 5th ed. (New York: Alfred A. Knopf, 1973), pp. 3–15.

66. Henry A. Kissinger, "The White Revolutionary: Reflections on Bismarck," *Daedalus* 97, No. 3, *Philosophers and Kings: Studies in Leadership* (Summer, 1968), pp. 920–921.

67. Kissinger, "The White Revolutionary: Reflections on Bismarck," *Daedalus* 97, No. 3, *Philosophers and Kings: Studies in Leadership* (Summer, 1968), pp. 920–921.

68. Otto Pflanze, *Bismarck and the Development of Germany, The Period of Unification, 1815–1871* (Princeton, NJ: Princeton University Press, 1963).

69. Pflanze, *Bismarck and the Development of Germany, The Period of Unification, 1815–1871* (Princeton, NJ: Princeton University Press, 1963), p. 9.

70. Pflanze, *Bismarck and the Development of Germany, The Period of Unification, 1815–1871* (Princeton, NJ: Princeton University Press, 1963), pp. 10–11, 14.

71. Pflanze, *Bismarck and the Development of Germany, The Period of Unification, 1815–1871* (Princeton, NJ: Princeton University Press, 1963), pp. 88.

72. Pflanze, *Bismarck and the Development of Germany, The Period of Unification, 1815–1871* (Princeton, NJ: Princeton University Press, 1963), pp. 89.

73. Cf. Hans J. Morgenthau, *Politics among Nations: The Struggle for Power and Peace* (New York: Alfred A. Knopf, 1973), p. 8: ". . . political realism considers a rational foreign policy to be a good foreign policy; for only a rational foreign policy *minimizes risks* and maximizes benefits . . ." (emphasis added).

74. Otto Pflanze, *Bismarck and the Development of Germany, The Period of Unification, 1815–1871* (Princeton, NJ: Princeton University Press, 1963), pp. 91–92.

75. Pflanze, *Bismarck and the Development of Germany, The Period of Unification, 1815–1871* (Princeton, NJ: Princeton University Press, 1963), p. 79. In reference to France, which had mobilized 40,000 troops on the Rhine frontier, for Bismarck, "it is not worthy of a large state to fight for a thing which is not in its own interest. Just show me an objective worth a war, gentlemen, and I will agree with you."

76. Marcus Jones, "Strategy as Character: Bismarck and the Prusso-German Question, 1862–1878," pp. 79–110, in Williamson Murray (ed.), *The Shaping of Grand Strategy* (New York: Cambridge University Press, 2011), pp. 80–81.

77. Jones, "Strategy as Character: Bismarck and the Prusso-German Question, 1862–1878," pp. 79–110, in Williamson Murray (ed.), *The Shaping of Grand Strategy* (New York: Cambridge University Press, 2011), pp. 82–83, who writes that "his success was inseparable from his broad knowledge of European cultures and societies, linguistic talents, and diplomatic conventions and his exceptional gift for analysis and prose." Furthermore, Bismarck's success was "reflective of a cast of mind born of a deeply and intuitively humanistic understanding of political affairs, a cautious patience, and humility about the extent of one's own knowledge and influence, the hallmark of his much-touted realism."

78. Jones, "Strategy as Character: Bismarck and the Prusso-German Question, 1862–1878," pp. 79–110, in Williamson Murray (ed.), *The Shaping of Grand Strategy* (New York: Cambridge University Press, 2011), p. 83.

79. Jones, "Strategy as Character: Bismarck and the Prusso-German Question, 1862–1878," pp. 79–110, in Williamson Murray (ed.), *The Shaping of Grand Strategy* (New York: Cambridge University Press, 2011), p. 84–85.

80. Jones, "Strategy as Character: Bismarck and the Prusso-German Question, 1862–1878," pp. 79–110, in Williamson Murray (ed.), *The Shaping of Grand Strategy* (New York: Cambridge University Press, 2011), p. 86: "What stands out in Bismarck's formulation is his emphasis on a conscious flexibility in achieving his ends, and quite possibly flexibility in framing the ends themselves – in short, a coldly unsentimental understanding of the state's interests and how to pursue them."

81. Jones, "Strategy as Character: Bismarck and the Prusso-German Question, 1862–1878," pp. 79–110, in Williamson Murray (ed.), *The Shaping of Grand Strategy* (New York: Cambridge University Press, 2011), p. 109: Bismarck's "long experience as a diplomat and deep understanding of the cultural and historical identities of the other major European states permitted him to make good assumptions about their own principles and interests."

82. For background, see Duncan Bell, *The Idea of Greater Britain: Empire and the Future of World Order, 1860–1900* (Princeton, NJ: Princeton University Press, 2007), pp. 92–119; John Gallagher and Ronald Robinson, "The Imperialism of Free Trade," *Economic History Review* 4, No. 1 (1953), pp. 1–15; Andrew S. Thompson, *Imperial Britain: The Empire in British Politics, c. 1880–1932* (New York: Routledge, 2000). Also, J. A. Hobson, *Imperialism: A Study* (London: James Pott and Co., 1902).

83. Paul M. Kennedy, *The Realities behind Diplomacy: Background Influences on British External Policy, 1865–1980* (London: George Allen & Unwin, 1981), pp. 19–20: "The navy's decisive victories gave its merchants the lion's share in maritime trade, which itself helped to stimulate the Industrial Revolution." Cf. William S. Maltby, "The Origins of a Global Strategy: England to 1713," in Williamson Murray, MacGregor Knox, and Alvin Bernstein (eds.), *The Making of Strategy: Rulers, States, and War* (New York: Cambridge University Press, 1996), pp. 151–177. Also, John Gooch, "The Weary Titan: Strategy and Policy in Great Britain, 1890–1918," in Williamson Murray, MacGregor Knox, and Alvin Bernstein (eds.), *The Making of Strategy: Rulers, States, and War* (New York: Cambridge University Press, 1996), pp. 278–306.

84. Kennedy, *The Realities behind Diplomacy: Background Influences on British External Policy, 1865–1980* (London: George Allen & Unwin, 1981), pp. 19–20.

85. Kennedy, *The Realities behind Diplomacy: Background Influences on British External Policy, 1865–1980* (London: George Allen & Unwin, 1981), p. 20: "Moreover, 36 per cent of the total exports of all other countries went to Britain in the 1840s, making it by far the largest market for raw materials the world had ever known."

86. Kennedy, *The Realities behind Diplomacy: Background Influences on British External Policy, 1865–1980* (London: George Allen & Unwin, 1981), p. 19.

87. Kennedy, *The Realities behind Diplomacy: Background Influences on British External Policy, 1865–1980* (London: George Allen & Unwin, 1981), p. 19.

88. Alfred T. Mahan, *The Influence of Sea Power Upon History, 1660–1783* (Boston: Little, Brown and Company, 1890), p. 28 (emphasis added).

89. Paul M. Kennedy, *The Realities behind Diplomacy: Background Influences on British External Policy, 1865–1980* (London: George Allen & Unwin, 1981), pp. 32–33: "When they were exposed, as in the Crimean War or in the mistaken attempt of Palmerston and Russell to interfere in the Schleswig-Holstein affair in 1864, the country's leaders drew the conclusion that their interventions in Europe should be even more restricted."

90. Kennedy, *The Realities behind Diplomacy: Background Influences on British External Policy, 1865–1980* (London: George Allen & Unwin, 1981), pp. 32–33.

91. Kennedy, *The Realities behind Diplomacy: Background Influences on British External Policy, 1865–1980* (London: George Allen & Unwin, 1981), pp. 32–33.

92. Michael Howard, *The Lessons of History* (New Haven, CT: Yale University Press, 1991), p. 69.

93. On the origins of social Darwinism, see George Holland Sabine and Thomas Landon Thorson, *A History of Political Theory* (Hinsdale, IL: Dryden Press, 1973), p. 687: "... after the publication of Darwin's Origin of Species, Marx sometimes claimed for his theory of social development an affinity with organic evolution, and there is in fact a superficial similarity between the class struggle and natural selection."

94. Michael Howard, *The Lessons of History* (New Haven, CT: Yale University Press, 1991), p. 68.

95. Howard, *The Lessons of History* (New Haven, CT: Yale University Press, 1991), p. 73.

96. Howard, *The Lessons of History* (New Haven, CT: Yale University Press, 1991), p. 66.

97. Howard, *The Lessons of History* (New Haven, CT: Yale University Press, 1991), p. 73: "As Roman imperialism laid the foundations of modern civilisation and led the wild barbarians of these islands along the path of progress, so in Africa today we are repaying the debt, and bringing dark places of the earth, the abode of barbarism and cruelty, the torch of culture and progress, while ministering the needs of our own civilisation. We hold these countries because it is the genius of our race to colonise, to trade, and to govern."

98. Howard, *The Lessons of History* (New Haven, CT: Yale University Press, 1991), p. 66.

99. Howard, *The Lessons of History* (New Haven, CT: Yale University Press, 1991), p. 68: "There must be great new spaces which to settle.... Instead of a restive proletariat remaining bottled up in the stinking cities of late-Victorian England ... let there be massive emigration to the new lands of white settlement, where emigrants could rediscover the good life, establish healthy pastoral communities, and provide secure markets for their brethren who remained at home."

100. Alfred T. Mahan, *The Influence of Sea Power Upon History, 1660–1783* (Boston: Little, Brown and Company, 1890), pp. 29–59.

101. "The Heartland Theory" as proposed by Sir Halford (1904) in his "The Geographical Pivot of History" provides the argument that Russia was in the

most strategically important area of the world. See H. J. Mackinder, "The Geographical Pivot of History," *Geographical Journal* 23, No. 4 (April 1, 1904), pp. 421–437.

102. Paul M. Kennedy, *The Realities behind Diplomacy: Background Influences on British External Policy, 1865–1980* (London: George Allen & Unwin, 1981), p. 34: "The 'Columbian Era' inaugurated by those early Iberian adventures had given the west European maritime states an influence in world affairs out of all proportion to their actual size and population." This was especially true "with industrialization, with railways, with investment, with new agricultural and mining techniques."

103. Kennedy, *The Realities behind Diplomacy: Background Influences on British External Policy, 1865–1980* (London: George Allen & Unwin, 1981), p. 22.

104. Kennedy, *The Realities behind Diplomacy: Background Influences on British External Policy, 1865–1980* (London: George Allen & Unwin, 1981), p. 30: "Seeley, whose book *The Expansion of England* (1884) was probably the most influential of all these tracts, pointed to the immense changes which 'steam and electricity' were bringing to the United States and Russia, against whose consolidated resources the British would be unable to compete unless they drew upon the white settlers living in the self-governing colonies. Extrapolating from economic and population trends, these writers (and the politicians who joined them to campaign for 'imperial federation') argued on the one hand that the days of the traditional European powers were drawing to a close; and on the other, that Britain could escape their fate by merging with Canada, Australia, New Zealand (and later, the Union of South Africa) into a trans-global but organic power unit."

105. Michael Howard, *The Lessons of History* (New Haven, CT: Yale University Press, 1991), p. 68.

106. J. A. S. Grenville, *Lord Salisbury and Foreign Policy: The Close of the Nineteenth Century* (London: University of London, Athlone Press, 1964), p. 19. To translate this policy into action, the "means he adopted to attain this end, however, were flexible, while his outlook was intensely practical."

107. Salisbury was prime minister from 1885 to January 1886, July 1886 to 1892, and 1895 to 1902. J. A. S. Grenville, *Lord Salisbury and Foreign Policy: The Close of the Nineteenth Century* (London: University of London, Athlone Press, 1964), p. 21: "As an imperialist Salisbury looked beyond the phase of conquest to the future. He was second to none in his defence of Britain's imperial interests and in pursuing a policy which aimed at forestalling rival powers."

108. Grenville, *Lord Salisbury and Foreign Policy: The Close of the Nineteenth Century* (London: University of London, Athlone Press, 1964), p. 21.

109. Peter Clarke, *The Last Thousand Days of the British Empire* (Bloomsbury Press, 2008).

110. J. A. S. Grenville, *Lord Salisbury and Foreign Policy: The Close of the Nineteenth Century* (London: University of London, Athlone Press, 1964), p. 22.

111. Lord Rosebery was the British prime minister from March 1892 to June 1895.

112. Paul M. Kennedy, *The Realities behind Diplomacy: Background Influences on British External Policy, 1865–1980* (London: George Allen & Unwin, 1981), p. 105.

113. Kennedy, *The Realities behind Diplomacy: Background Influences on British External Policy, 1865–1980* (London: George Allen & Unwin, 1981), p. 116.

114. Kennedy, *The Realities behind Diplomacy: Background Influences on British External Policy, 1865–1980* (London: George Allen & Unwin, 1981), pp. 116–117.

115. Kennedy, *The Realities behind Diplomacy: Background Influences on British External Policy, 1865–1980* (London: George Allen & Unwin, 1981), p. 122.

116. Kennedy, *The Realities behind Diplomacy: Background Influences on British External Policy, 1865–1980* (London: George Allen & Unwin, 1981), p. 127.

117. Michael Howard, *The Lessons of History* (New Haven, CT: Yale University Press, 1991), pp. 85–86.

118. Paul M. Kennedy, *The Realities behind Diplomacy: Background Influences on British External Policy, 1865–1980* (London: George Allen & Unwin, 1981), p. 128.

119. Kennedy, *The Realities behind Diplomacy: Background Influences on British External Policy, 1865–1980* (London: George Allen & Unwin, 1981), pp. 138–139: "Yet Grey, too, for all his Liberal scruples, had been haunted by the idea that Germany would overrun France one day." In British politics, "Conservatives in general, and the Chamberlainites in particular, who had worried about Britain's long-term decline and feared Germany's advance, were convinced that Britain should not stay out of war."

120. On such power dynamics, see Christopher Layne, "From Preponderance to Offshore Balancing: America's Future Grand Strategy," *International Security* 22.1 (1997), pp. 86–124.

121. See Williamson Murray, "The Collapse of Empire: British Strategy, 1919–1945," in Williamson Murray, MacGregor Knox, and Alvin Bernstein (eds.), *The Making of Strategy: Rulers, States, and War* (New York: Cambridge University Press, 1996), pp. 393–427.

122. For background on the Ottoman Empire, see Leila T. Fawaz, *An Occasion for War: Civil Conflict in Lebanon and Damascus in 1860* (Los Angeles: University of California Press, 1994); William L. Cleveland and Martin Bunton, *A History of the Modern Middle East* (Boulder, CO: Westview Press, 2009); Sevket Pamuk, "Institutional Change and the Longevity of the Ottoman Empire, 1500–1800," *Journal of Interdisciplinary History*, MIT Press, 25, No. 2 (Autumn, 2004), pp. 225–247; William Hale, *Turkish Foreign Policy 1774–2000* (London: Frank Cass, 2002); Roger Owen, *The Middle East in the World Economy 1900–1914* (London: Methuen & Co., 2002); Stanford J. Shaw, *History of the Ottoman Empire and Modern Turkey: Volume 1, Empire of the Gazis, 1280–1808* (New York: Cambridge University Press, 1976); Caroline Finkel, *Osman's Dream: The History of the Ottoman Empire* (New York: Basic Books, 2006); Halil İnalcık, Donald Quataert, *An Economic and Social History of the Ottoman Empire, Volume 1* (New York: Cambridge University Press, 1994); M. Sükrü Hanioglu, *A Brief History of the Late Ottoman Empire* (Princeton, NJ: Princeton University Press, 2008); Stanford J. Shaw, *Between Old and New: The Ottoman Empire under Sultan Selim III, 1789–1807* (Cambridge, MA: Harvard University Press, 1971); Michael Reynolds, *Shattering Empires: The Clash and Collapse of the Ottoman and Russian Empires 1908–1918* (London: Cambridge University Press, 2011).

123. Cf. Leila T. Fawaz, *An Occasion for War: Civil Conflict in Lebanon and Damascus in 1860* (Los Angeles: University of California Press, 1994), esp. pp. 1–7; Youssef

M. Choueiri, *Arab History and the Nation-State: A Study in Modern Arab Historiography, 1820–1980* (New York: Routledge, 1989); Sevket Pamuk, "Institutional Change and the Longevity of the Ottoman Empire, 1500–1800," *The Journal of Interdisciplinary History*, MIT Press, 25, No. 2 (Autumn, 2004), pp. 225–247; William L. Cleveland and Martin Bunton, *A History of the Modern Middle East* (Boulder, CO: Westview Press, 2009).

124. Sevket Pamuk, "Institutional Change and the Longevity of the Ottoman Empire, 1500–1800," *Journal of Interdisciplinary History*, MIT Press, 25, No. 2 (Autumn 2004), p. 230: "The areas most closely administered by the capitol had institutions nearly identical to those in the Istanbul region. As distance from the capital increased, institutions and administrative practices reflected the power balances between the capital and the local structures and forces." Cf. Albert H. Hourani, "Ottoman Reform and the Politics of the Notables," in William R. Polk, and Richard L. Chambers (eds.), *The Beginnings of Modernization in the Middle East* (Chicago: University of Chicago Press, 1968), pp. 41–68.

125. Pamuk, "Institutional Change and the Longevity of the Ottoman Empire, 1500–1800," *Journal of Interdisciplinary History*, MIT Press, 25, No. 2 (Autumn 2004), p. 238, pp. 233–234. As Pamuk discusses, "states did not pursue public interest in some abstract sense. Instead, both the goals and design of economic policies, as well as institutions related to their implementation, were shaped by social structure."

126. Pamuk, "Institutional Change and the Longevity of the Ottoman Empire, 1500–1800," *Journal of Interdisciplinary History*, MIT Press, 25, No. 2 (Autumn 2004), p. 226.

127. Pamuk, "Institutional Change and the Longevity of the Ottoman Empire, 1500–1800," *Journal of Interdisciplinary History*, MIT Press, 25, No. 2 (Autumn 2004), p. 226.

128. Pamuk, "Institutional Change and the Longevity of the Ottoman Empire, 1500–1800," *Journal of Interdisciplinary History*, MIT Press, 25, No. 2 (Autumn 2004), p. 226. Cf. Giancarlo Gasale, "The Ottoman Administration of the Spice Trade in the Sixteenth-Century Red Sea and Persian Gulf," *Journal of the Economic and Social History of the Orient* 49, No. 2 (2006), pp. 170–198.

129. See Leila T. Fawaz, *An Occasion for War: Civil Conflict in Lebanon and Damascus in 1860* (Los Angeles: University of California Press, 1994), pp. 14–15. Cf. Donald C. Blaisdell, *European Financial Control in the Ottoman Empire* (New York: Columbia University Press, 1929).

130. William L. Cleveland and Martin Bunton, *A History of the Modern Middle East* (Boulder, CO: Westview Press, 2009), p. 50: "The penetration of European manufactured goods into the empire and the eventual domination of Ottoman commerce by Europeans and their protégés were facilitated by a series of commercial treaties, known as the Capitulations." Cf. Donald C. Blaisdell, *European Financial Control in the Ottoman Empire* (New York: Columbia University Press, 1929); Bruce Masters, *The Origins of Western Economic Dominance in the Middle East: Mercantilism and the Islamic Economy in Aleppo, 1600–1750* (New York: New York University Press, 1988).

131. See Albert H. Hourani, "Ottoman Reform and the Politics of the Notables," in William R. Polk and Richard L. Chambers (eds.), *The Beginnings of Modernization in the Middle East* (Chicago: University of Chicago Press, 1968), pp. 41–68.

132. See Donald C. Blaisdell, *European Financial Control in the Ottoman Empire* (New York: Columbia University Press, 1929).

133. William Hale, *Turkish Foreign Policy 1774–2000* (London: Frank Cass, 2002), p. 16: "Until the nineteenth century, this diversity did not pose too serious a challenge to the empire's territorial integrity.... However, modern ideas of ethnic nationalism began to affect the Greeks and Serbs in the early nineteenth century, and later spread to the Romanians, Bulgarian and Macedonian Slavs, and Armenians."

134. Giancarlo Gasale, "The Ottoman Administration of the Spice Trade in the Sixteenth-Century Red Sea and Persian Gulf," *Journal of the Economic and Social History of the Orient* 49, No. 2 (2006), p. 172: "This era of active state intervention and support became progressively more sophisticated over time, until by the end of the 1560's, a comprehensive infrastructure was in place, including a rationalized empire-wide tax regime for regulating private trade."

135. Roger Owen, *The Middle East in the World Economy 1900–1914* (London: Methuen & Co., 2002), p. 93; Donald C. Blaisdell, *European Financial Control in the Ottoman Empire* (New York: Columbia University Press, 1929).

136. William L. Cleveland and Martin Bunton, *A History of the Modern Middle East* (Boulder, CO: Westview Press, 2009), p. 49.

137. Roger Owen, *The Middle East in the World Economy 1900–1914* (London: Methuen & Co., 2002), p. 107.

138. See Youssef M. Choueiri, *Arab History and the Nation-State: A Study in Modern Arab Historiography, 1820–1980* (New York: Routledge, 1989); William L. Cleveland and Martin Bunton, *A History of the Modern Middle East* (Boulder, CO: Westview Press, 2009), p. 50: "The shortage of revenue and the rise of inflation had a devastating effect on the large numbers of state employees on fixed salaries and created an atmosphere that fostered bribery and other forms of corruption."

139. William L. Cleveland and Martin Bunton, *A History of the Modern Middle East* (Boulder, CO: Westview Press, 2009), p. 50.

140. Cleveland and Bunton, *A History of the Modern Middle East* (Boulder, CO: Westview Press, 2009), p. 75.

141. William Hale, *Turkish Foreign Policy 1774–2000* (London: Frank Cass, 2002), p. 16.

142. William L. Cleveland and Martin Bunton, *A History of the Modern Middle East* (Boulder, CO: Westview Press, 2009), p. 75, who attribute this to a "resurgence of Greek literature and a new awareness of the classical Greek past."

143. Cleveland and Bunton, *A History of the Modern Middle East* (Boulder, CO: Westview Press, 2009), p. 75.

144. See Gabor Agoston, "Information, Ideology, and the Limits of Imperial Policy: Ottoman Grand Strategy in the Context of Ottoman-Habsburg Rivalry," in Virginia Aksan and Daniel Goffman (eds.), *The Early Modern Ottomans: Remapping the Empire* (New York: Cambridge University Press, 2007), p. 77.

145. Youssef M. Choueiri, *Arab History and the Nation-State: A Study in Modern Arab Historiography, 1820–1980* (New York: Routledge, 1989); William L. Cleveland and Martin Bunton, *A History of the Modern Middle East* (Boulder, CO: Westview Press, 2009), p. 62.

146. William L. Cleveland and Martin Bunton, *A History of the Modern Middle East* (Boulder, CO: Westview Press, 2009), p. 62.

147. Stanford J. Shaw, *Between Old and New: The Ottoman Empire under Sultan Selim III, 1789–1807* (Cambridge, MA: Harvard University Press, 1971); William Hale, *Turkish Foreign Policy 1774–2000* (London: Frank Cass, 2002), p. 18.

148. William L. Cleveland and Martin Bunton, *A History of the Modern Middle East* (Boulder, CO: Westview Press, 2009), p. 63: "Convinced of the superiority of their system, [the Ottomans] had not deemed it necessary to round out an exchange." As Stanford J. Shaw, *Between Old and New: The Ottoman Empire under Sultan Selim III, 1789–1807* (Cambridge, MA: Harvard University Press, 1971), p. 185, writes, "Throughout the centuries of Ottoman greatness and decay, no permanent Ottoman embassies were established in Europe since it was felt that nothing could be learned from the infidels of the West and that it was for the inferior monarchs of Europe to petition for the Sultan's favor through their representatives at the Porte."

149. Cleveland and Bunton, *A History of the Modern Middle East* (Boulder, CO: Westview Press, 2009), p. 63.

150. Stanford J. Shaw, *Between Old and New: The Ottoman Empire under Sultan Selim III, 1789–1807* (Cambridge, MA: Harvard University Press, 1971), p. 180.

151. William L. Cleveland and Martin Bunton, *A History of the Modern Middle East* (Boulder, CO: Westview Press, 2009), p. 63: "The powerful *derbeys* were alarmed by the way in which the sultan financed his forces – he confiscated *timars* and directed the revenue toward the *nizam-i jedid*. Further opposition came from the ulama and other members of the ruling elite who objected to the European models on which Selim based his military reforms."

152. Jeremy Black, *The Great Power Quest for Hegemony: The World Order Since 1500* (New York: Routledge, 2008), p. 32: "The Ottoman Empire, with its major naval presence in the Mediterranean, made no efforts to project its power into the Atlantic. This was not necessarily some proof of defective strategic judgment and culture, anachronistic elite values and redundancy, but a response to the marginal nature of such concerns for the Ottoman Empire."

153. Stanford J. Shaw, *Between Old and New: The Ottoman Empire under Sultan Selim III, 1789–1807* (Cambridge, MA: Harvard University Press, 1971), p. 383.

154. William L. Cleveland and Martin Bunton, *A History of the Modern Middle East* (Boulder, CO: Westview Press, 2009), p. 64.

155. Cleveland and Bunton, *A History of the Modern Middle East* (Boulder, CO: Westview Press, 2009), pp. 78–79.

156. Cleveland and Bunton, *A History of the Modern Middle East* (Boulder, CO: Westview Press, 2009), p. 78.

157. Caroline Finkel, *Osman's Dream: The Story of the Ottoman Empire 1300–1923* (New York: Basic Books, 2005), p. 480: "His ambitions, unlike those of his predecessors, were not limited to the military sphere alone: it was evident to him

that no piecemeal enhancement of military effectiveness was of itself sufficient to maintain Ottoman integrity and sustain an active role for the Ottoman Empire in international decision-making. His aim, therefore, was nothing less than a transformation of society."

158. William L. Cleveland and Martin Bunton, *A History of the Modern Middle East* (Boulder, CO: Westview Press, 2009), pp. 78–79: "In the 1830s Mahmud II moved to fill this void by reestablishing the Ottoman embassies in Europe by opening a translation office to deal with state correspondence and train Ottoman officials in European languages."

159. Roger Owen, *The Middle East in the World Economy 1900–1914* (London: Methuen & Co., 2002), pp. 108–109. Cf. David Fromkin, *A Peace to End All Peace* (New York: Holt, 1989), p. 47. "Because the Porte had defaulted on a public debt of more than a thousand million dollars in 1875, the Sultan was obliged to issue a decree in 1881 that placed administration of the Ottoman public debt in European hands."

160. Owen, *The Middle East in the World Economy 1900–1914* (London: Methuen & Co., 2002), pp. 108–109. Cf. David Fromkin, *A Peace to End All Peace* (New York: Holt, 1989), p. 47. Cf. Donald C. Blaisdell, *European Financial Control in the Ottoman Empire* (New York: Columbia University Press, 1929).

161. William L. Cleveland and Martin Bunton, *A History of the Modern Middle East* (Boulder, CO: Westview Press, 2009), pp. 86–87; Donald C. Blaisdell, *European Financial Control in the Ottoman Empire* (New York: Columbia University Press, 1929).

162. David Fromkin, *A Peace to End All Peace* (New York: Holt, 1989), p. 47.

163. William Hale, *Turkish Foreign Policy 1774–2000* (London: Frank Cass, 2002), p. 20.

164. William L. Cleveland and Martin Bunton, *A History of the Modern Middle East* (Boulder, CO: Westview Press, 2009), p. 87.

165. William Hale, *Turkish Foreign Policy 1774–2000* (London: Frank Cass, 2002), p. 29.

166. William L. Cleveland and Martin Bunton, *A History of the Modern Middle East* (Boulder, CO: Westview Press, 2009), pp. 89, 133: "Serbia, Montenegro, Romania, and part of Bulgaria were recognized as independent states; Russia gained Kars and Batum in eastern Anatolia; and Austria was granted the right to administer the province of Bosnia."

167. Cleveland and Bunton, *A History of the Modern Middle East* (Boulder, CO: Westview Press, 2009), pp. 133–137.

168. David Fromkin, *A Peace to End All Peace* (New York: Holt, 1989), p. 48.

169. Fromkin, *A Peace to End All Peace* (New York: Holt, 1989), p. 48.

170. William L. Cleveland and Martin Bunton, *A History of the Modern Middle East* (Boulder, CO: Westview Press, 2009), p. 138. Also, Youssef M. Choueiri, *Arab History and the Nation-State: A Study in Modern Arab Historiography, 1820–1980* (New York: Routledge, 1989).

171. David Fromkin, *A Peace to End All Peace* (New York: Holt, 1989), p. 49.

172. See Donald C. Blaisdell, *European Financial Control in the Ottoman Empire* (New York: Columbia University Press, 1929). Also, David Fromkin, *A Peace to End All Peace* (New York: Holt, 1989), pp. 64–67, 69.

173. William L. Cleveland and Martin Bunton, *A History of the Modern Middle East* (Boulder, CO: Westview Press, 2009), p. 134.

174. Cleveland and Bunton, *A History of the Modern Middle East* (Boulder, CO: Westview Press, 2009), pp. 150–151: "In early 1914 the German general Liman von Sanders arrived in Istanbul.... The CUP granted the mission extensive powers, and its efforts, combined with the government's willingness to introduce far-reaching military reforms, had begun to produce notable results by the outbreak of the war."

175. Cleveland and Bunton, *A History of the Modern Middle East* (Boulder, CO: Westview Press, 2009), p. 157.

176. Cleveland and Bunton, *A History of the Modern Middle East* (Boulder, CO: Westview Press, 2009), p. 160.

177. Cleveland and Bunton, *A History of the Modern Middle East* (Boulder, CO: Westview Press, 2009), p. 153.

178. David Fromkin, *A Peace to End All Peace* (New York: Holt, 1989), p. 534.

179. Fromkin, *A Peace to End All Peace* (New York: Holt, 1989), p. 534.

180. Cf. William Hale, *Turkish Foreign Policy 1774–2000* (London: Frank Cass, 2002); Roger Owen, *The Middle East in the World Economy 1900–1914* (London: Methuen & Co., 2002); Stanford J. Shaw, *History of the Ottoman Empire and Modern Turkey: Volume 1, Empire of the Gazis, 1280–1808* (New York: Cambridge University Press, 1976). Also, William L. Cleveland and Martin Bunton, *A History of the Modern Middle East* (Boulder, CO: Westview Press, 2009), p. 167.

181. See Youssef M. Choueiri, *Arab History and the Nation-State: A Study in Modern Arab Historiography, 1820–1980* (New York: Routledge, 1989).

6 *Revolutionary and Nuclear Eras of Grand Strategy*

1. For a discussion of insurgency warfare, see John Shy and Thomas W. Collier, "Revolutionary War," in Peter Paret (ed.), *Makers of Modern Strategy: From Machiavelli to the Nuclear Age* (Princeton, NJ: Princeton University Press, 1986), pp. 815–862. For a review of how technological forces have changed the conduct of guerrilla wars, see Martin van Creveld, "Real War," chap. 20 in *Technology and War: From 2000 B.C. to the Present* (New York: The Free Press, 1991), pp. 297–310. On revolutionary wars, see Charles A. Joiner, "The Organization Theory of Revolutionary Warfare: A Review Article," *Vietnam Perspectives* 2, No. 3 (February 1967), pp. 15–34; Seth G. Jones, "The Rise of Afghanistan's Insurgency: State Failure and Jihad," *International Security* 32, No. 4 (Spring 2008), pp. 7–40, at p. 7.

2. For a discussion of revolutions, see John Shy and Thomas W. Collier, "Revolutionary War," in Paret (ed.), *Makers of Modern Strategy*, pp. 815–862; John Foran, *Theorizing Revolutions* (New York: Routledge, 1997); Stephen M. Walt, *Revolution and War* (Ithaca, NY: Cornell University Press, 1996); Lawrence Kaplan, *Revolutions: A Comparative Study* (New York: Random House, 1973); Hannah Arendt, *On Revolution* (New York: Penguin, 1965).

3. Henry A. Kissinger, *White House Years* (Boston: Little, Brown, 1979), pp. 195–225.

4. Harry S. Truman, *Memoirs by Harry S. Truman*, Vol. 2: *Years of Trial and Hope* (New York: Doubleday, 1955), p. 345: "Every decision I made in connection with the Korean conflict had this one aim in mind: to prevent a third world war and the terrible destruction that it would bring to the civilized world."

5. For insights into their contributions to understanding strategy in the context of politics, see William C. Martel, *Victory in War: Foundations of Modern Strategy*, revised and expanded edition (New York: Cambridge University Press, 2011), pp. 85–87.

6. Since, ultimately, Marx and Engels defined a stateless world, we will address grand strategy as a class-based and stateless phenomenon in this chapter.

7. See Sigmund Neumann and Mark Von Hagen, "Engels and Marx on Revolution, War, and the Army in Society," in Paret (ed.), *Makers of Modern Strategy*, pp. 262–280, at p. 263.

8. Karl Marx and Friedrich Engels, *The Communist Manifesto*, in Robert C. Tucker (ed.), *The Marx-Engels Reader* (New York: W. W. Norton, 1972), p. 58.

9. Marx and Engels, *The Communist Manifesto*, p. 62.

10. Marx and Engels, *The Communist Manifesto*, p. 66.

11. Karl Marx, "Address to the Communist League," in *The Marx-Engels Reader*, 2nd ed. (New York: W. W. Norton & Company, 1972), p. 505 (emphasis added): "It is our interest and our task to make the revolution permanent, until all more or less possessing classes have been forced out of their position of dominance, *until* the proletariat has conquered state power, and the association of proletarians, not only in one country but in all dominant countries of the world, has advanced so far that competition among the proletarians of these countries has ceased and that at least the decisive productive forces are concentrated in the hands of the proletarians."

12. Karl Marx, *The Communist Manifesto*, p. 61. Cf. Karl Marx, *The Communist Manifesto*, p. 66: "The development of Modern Industry, therefore, cuts from under its feet the very foundation on which the bourgeoisie produces and appropriates products. What the bourgeoisie, therefore, produces, above all, is its own grave-diggers. Its fall and the victory of the proletariat are equally inevitable."

13. Frederick Bender, "Foreword," *The Communist Manifesto*, p. 33. The reason is that, while "changes in the material forces of production create the conditions that make revolution possible, [this is not the same as arguing that they] automatically create [a] successful revolution itself."

14. Karl Marx and Friedrich Engels, "The German Ideology, Part I," in Robert C. Tucker (ed.), *Marx-Engels Reader*, pp. 110–164, at pp. 115–116. As Marx and Engels wrote in their "Communist Manifesto" in 1888, "Thus, the whole historical movement is concentrated in the hands of the bourgeoisie; every victory so obtained is a victory for the bourgeoisie" (p. 342).

15. See Sigmund Neumann, "Engels and Marx: Military Concepts of the Social Revolutionaries," in Earle (ed.), *Makers of Modern Strategy: Military Thought*, pp. 155–171, who noted that "Engels regarded ["movements of armed mobs"] as a 'drama without parallel in the annals of military history.'" (p. 66).

16. See James Noren, "CIA's Analysis of the Soviet Economy," in Gerald K. Haines and Robert E. Leggett (eds.), *Watching the Bear: Essays on CIA's Analysis of the Soviet Union: 1947–1991* (Washington, DC: Center for the Study of Intelligence, Central Intelligence Agency, 2001).

17. Karl Marx and Friedrich Engels, *The Communist Manifesto*, p. 63: As industry develops, "the proletariat not only increases in number; it becomes concentrated in greater masses, its strength grows ... Thereupon the workers begin to form combinations (Trade Unions) against the bourgeoisie."

18. Marx and Engels, *The Communist Manifesto*, p. 67.

19. Frederick Bender, "Foreword," *The Communist Manifesto*, p. 9.

20. See V. I. Lenin, *State and Revolution (1918)*, at http://www.fordham.edu/halsall/mod/lenin-staterev.asp: "By educating the workers' party, Marxism educates the *vanguard of the proletariat*, capable of assuming power and leading the whole people to socialism, of directing and organizing the new system, of being the teacher, the guide, the leader of all the working and exploited people in organizing their social life without the bourgeoisie and against the bourgeoisie" (emphasis added).

21. Karl Marx and Friedrich Engels, *The Communist Manifesto*, p. 86.

22. Karl Marx, "The Upcoming Upheaval," in *The Marx-Engels Reader*, 2nd ed. (New York: W. W. Norton & Company, 1972), p. 218: "An oppressed class is the vital condition for every society founded on the antagonism of classes. The emancipation of the oppressed class thus implies necessarily the creation of a new society. For the oppressed class to be able to emancipate itself it is necessary that the productive powers already acquired and the existing social relations should no longer be capable of existing side by side."

23. Karl Marx, "Address to the Communist League," in *The Marx-Engels Reader*, 2nd ed. (New York: W. W. Norton & Company, 1972), p. 506.

24. Karl Marx, "The Upcoming Upheaval," in *The Marx-Engels Reader*, 2nd ed. (New York: W. W. Norton & Company, 1972), p. 219: "Do not say that social movement excludes political movement. There is never a political movement which is not at the same time social." Also, "Indeed, is it at all surprising that a society founded on the opposition of classes should culminate in brutal 'contradiction,' the shock of body against body, as its final denouement?"

25. Karl Marx and Friedrich Engels, *The Communist Manifesto*, p. 74: "and to increase the total of productive forces as rapidly as possible."

26. For an excellent analysis of the influence of Soviet thinkers on war, see Edward Mead Earle, "Lenin, Trotsky, Stalin: Soviet Concepts of War," in Earle (ed.), *Makers of Modern Strategy: Military Thought*, pp. 322–364.

27. The central themes that define Lenin's grand strategy derive from two volumes of selected works (*The Lenin Reader*, 1966; and *Selected Works Vol. 1*, 1967). Also, Karel Kara, "On the Marxist Theory of War and Peace," *Journal of Peace Research* 5, No. 1, 1968, pp. 1–27: "The conclusion Lenin drew from his analysis of the existing world conditions was that socialist revolution could be achieved [if] he considered the possibility of victory of then almost only by violent means, and the socialist revolution by peaceful evolution, as he wrote after the February Revolution in Russia, 'as an extremely rare possibility in the history of revolutions'" (pp. 14–15).

28. On political theory, see William T. Bluhm, "Political Theory and Political Ideology," *Theories of the Political System: Classics of Political Thought & Modern Political Analysis* (Englewood Cliffs, NJ: Prentice Hall, 1965), pp. 6–8; George Sabine, "What Is Political Theory," *Journal of Politics* 1 (1939), p. 3.

29. "The Urgent Tasks of Our Movement," V. I. Lenin, *Selected Works, Vol. 1*, International Publishers, 1967, p. 93.

30. Stefan T. Possony, ed., "The Tasks of the Russian Social Democracy," *The Lenin Reader* (Henry Regnery Co., 1966), p. 372. Cf. "The Urgent Tasks of Our Movement," V. I. Lenin, *Selected Works, Vol. 1*, International Publishers, 1967, p. 91: "Russian Social-Democracy has repeatedly declared the immediate political task of a Russian working-class party to be the overthrow of the autocracy, the achievement of political liberty."

31. "The Urgent Tasks of Our Movement," V. I. Lenin, *Selected Works, Vol. 1*, International Publishers, 1967, p. 94.

32. Stefan T. Possony, ed., "A Protest by Russian Social Democrats," *The Lenin Reader* (Henry Regnery Co., 1966), p. 385.

33. "The Urgent Tasks of Our Movement," V. I. Lenin, *Selected Works, Vol. 1*, International Publishers, 1967, p. 92: "In waging only economic struggle, the working class loses its political independence; it becomes the tail of other parties and betrays the great principle: 'The emancipation of the working classes must be the act of the working classes themselves.'"

34. Stefan T. Possony, ed., "The Stages, Trends and Prospects of the Revolution," *The Lenin Reader* (Henry Regnery Co., 1966), pp. 394–395.

35. Stefan T. Possony, ed., "The Revolutionary Army and the Revolutionary Government," *The Lenin Reader* (Henry Regnery Co., 1966), p. 351. Arguing somewhat disingenuously given the totalitarianism that emerged in the Soviet Union as a result of his efforts, Lenin wrote, "Only an armed people can serve as a real bulwark of popular liberty." Cf. Stefan T. Possony, ed., "The Beginning of the Revolution in Russia," V. I. Lenin, *The Lenin Reader* (Henry Regnery Co., 1966), p. 344. For Lenin, "a revolutionary government is as essential and necessary at the present stage of the popular uprising as a revolutionary army."

36. Possony, ed., "The Revolutionary Army and the Revolutionary Government," *The Lenin Reader* (Henry Regnery Co., 1966), p. 351.

37. Stefan T. Possony, ed., "Explanation of the Program of the Social Democratic Party," *The Lenin Reader* (Henry Regnery Co., 1966), p. 370.

38. Stefan T. Possony, ed., "The Tasks of the Russian Social Democracy," *The Lenin Reader* (Henry Regnery Co., 1966), p. 375.

39. Stefan T. Possony, ed., "The Two Tactics of Social Democracy in the Democratic Revolution," *The Lenin Reader* (Henry Regnery Co., 1966), pp. 345–346: "The deeper the indignation of the people becomes, the less reliable become the troops and the more government officials begin to waver."

40. Stefan T. Possony, ed., "A Protest by Russian Social Democrats," *The Lenin Reader* (Henry Regnery Co., 1966), p. 384.

41. Edward Mead Earle, "Lenin, Trotsky, Stalin: Soviet Concepts of War," in Edward Mead Earle, with Gordon A. Craig and Felix Gilbert (eds.), *Makers of Modern Strategy: Military Thought from Machiavelli to Hitler* (1941; reprint, Princeton, NJ: Princeton University Press, 1960), p. 326.

42. Earle, "Lenin, Trotsky, Stalin: Soviet Concepts of War," in Edward Mead Earle, with Gordon A. Craig and Felix Gilbert (eds.), *Makers of Modern Strategy: Military Thought from Machiavelli to Hitler* (1941; reprint, Princeton, NJ: Princeton

University Press, 1960), p. 327. For an analysis of Clausewitz's ideas, see William C. Martel, *Victory in War: Foundations of Modern Strategy*, revised and expanded edition (New York: Cambridge University Press, 2011), pp. 78–83.

43. Stefan T. Possony, ed., "What Is to Be Done? Burning Questions of Our Movement," *The Lenin Reader* (Henry Regnery Co., 1966), p. 393: "For that reason, the principal content of the activity of our party organization, the focus of this activity should be, to carry on work that is possible and necessary in the period of the most powerful outbreaks as well as the period of complete calm."

44. Stefan T. Possony, ed., "Explanation of the Program of the Social Democratic Party," *The Lenin Reader* (Henry Regnery Co., 1966), p. 370.

45. Stefan T. Possony, ed., "'Left Wing' Communism, an Infantile Disorder: A Popular Essay in Marxian Strategy and Tactics," *The Lenin Reader* (Henry Regnery Co., 1966), p. 430.

46. Stefan T. Possony, ed., "Explanation of the Program of the Social Democratic Party," *The Lenin Reader* (Henry Regnery Co., 1966), p. 369. See, for example, "What do we mean when we say that the struggle of the working class is a political struggle? We mean that the workers cannot wage the struggle for their emancipation without striving to influence affairs of state, to influence the administration of the state, the passing of laws."

47. Edward Mead Earle, "Lenin, Trotsky, Stalin: Soviet Concepts of War," in Edward Mead Earle, with Gordon A. Craig and Felix Gilbert (eds.), *Makers of Modern Strategy: Military Thought from Machiavelli to Hitler* (1941; reprint, Princeton, NJ: Princeton University Press, 1960), pp. 322–364, at p. 323.

48. Earle, "Lenin, Trotsky, Stalin: Soviet Concepts of War," in Edward Mead Earle, with Gordon A. Craig and Felix Gilbert (eds.), *Makers of Modern Strategy: Military Thought from Machiavelli to Hitler* (1941; reprint, Princeton, NJ: Princeton University Press, 1960), p. 323.

49. Earle, "Lenin, Trotsky, Stalin: Soviet Concepts of War," in Edward Mead Earle, with Gordon A. Craig and Felix Gilbert (eds.), *Makers of Modern Strategy: Military Thought from Machiavelli to Hitler* (1941; reprint, Princeton, NJ: Princeton University Press, 1960), p. 328.

50. Earle, "Lenin, Trotsky, Stalin: Soviet Concepts of War," in Edward Mead Earle, with Gordon A. Craig and Felix Gilbert (eds.), *Makers of Modern Strategy: Military Thought from Machiavelli to Hitler* (1941; reprint, Princeton, NJ: Princeton University Press, 1960), p. 329: "'The Bolshevist Revolution has proved to every honest communist the absolute necessity of the armament of the proletariat' ... and the duty of every citizen of the Soviet Union, as 'a warrior for socialism consists of making all the necessary preparations for such a war – political, economic, and military; of strengthening the Red Army, the power weapon of the proletariat, and of training the working masses at large in military science.'"

51. Stefan T. Possony, ed., "'Left Wing' Communism, an Infantile Disorder: A Popular Essay in Marxian Strategy and Tactics," *The Lenin Reader* (Henry Regnery Co., 1966), p. 424: "when it is able, during and after the seizure of power, to obtain adequate support from adequately broad strata of the working class and of the non-proletarian toiling masses, and when it is able thereafter to maintain, consolidate and extend its rule by educating, training and attracting ever broader masses of the toilers."

52. Possony, ed., "'Left Wing' Communism, an Infantile Disorder: A Popular Essay in Marxian Strategy and Tactics," *The Lenin Reader* (Henry Regnery Co., 1966), p. 436: "Only when the *'lower classes' do not want* the old way and when the 'upper classes' *cannot carry on in the old way* can revolution win."

53. Possony, ed., "'Left Wing' Communism, an Infantile Disorder: A Popular Essay in Marxian Strategy and Tactics," *The Lenin Reader* (Henry Regnery Co., 1966), p. 437: "To throw the vanguard alone into the decisive battle, before the whole class before the broad masses have taken up a position either of direct support of the vanguard or at least of benevolent neutrality toward it and one in which they cannot possibly support the enemy, would be not merely folly but a crime."

54. Irving Howe, "Introduction," *Basic Writings of Trotsky* (Random House, 1963), p. 38.

55. Trotsky's original quote "You may not be interested in the dialectic, but the dialectic is interested in you" has included "war" and "strategy" instead of "the dialectic." See Michael Walzer, *Just and Unjust Wars: A Moral Argument with Historical Illustrations* (New York: Basic Books, 2006), p. 29.

56. See Edward Mead Earle, "Lenin, Trotsky, Stalin: Soviet Concepts of War," in Edward Mead Earle, with Gordon A. Craig and Felix Gilbert (eds.), *Makers of Modern Strategy: Military Thought from Machiavelli to Hitler* (1941; reprint, Princeton, NJ: Princeton University Press, 1960), p. 336.

57. Irving Howe, "Introduction," *Basic Writings of Trotsky* (Random House, 1963), p. 25.

58. Irving Howe, "Three Concepts of the Russian Revolution," by Leon Trotsky, *Basic Writings of Trotsky* (Random House, 1963), p. 138.

59. Irving Howe, "Introduction," *Basic Writings of Trotsky* (Random House, 1963), p. 15: "For that, there would be neither a sufficiently secure economic base nor a working class sufficiently strong and conscious."

60. Irving Howe, "Three Concepts of the Russian Revolution," by Leon Trotsky, *Basic Writings of Trotsky* (Random House, 1963), p. 139: "The Eastern revolution will infect the Western proletariat with revolutionary idealism and arouse in it the desire to start talking 'Russian' with its enemy ..."

61. Irving Howe, "Introduction," *Basic Writings of Trotsky* (Random House, 1963), p. 15: This means for Trotsky, "more particularly, only under the leadership of the revolutionary party speaking for the working class. But the workers, having gained power, will not be able to stop short before the problems of the bourgeois revolution."

62. Howe, "Introduction," *Basic Writings of Trotsky* (Random House, 1963), p. 15.

63. Quote of V. I. Lenin, *History of the Russian Revolution*, Leon Trotsky (translated by Max Eastman), University of Michigan Press, 1961, p. 909: "When we began at the time we did the international revolution ... [o]ur thought was either the international revolution will come to our aid, and in that case our victories are wholly assured, or we will do our modest revolutionary work in the consciousness that in case of defeat we have nevertheless served the cause of the revolution, and our experiment will be of help to other revolutions."

64. Irving Howe, "Five Year Plan in Four Years," Leon Trotsky, *Basic Writings of Trotsky* (Random House, 1963), p. 181.

65. Irving Howe, "Introduction," *Basic Writings of Trotsky* (Random House, 1963), p. 27: "In a bitterly ironic turn of events, [Trotsky] was suffering from the vindication of his own theory of permanent revolution, by means of which he had predicted that a proletarian revolution in a backward country would, if it continued to suffer isolation, find itself in an historical limbo."

66. Ernest Mandel, *Trotsky as Alternative* (London: Verso, 1995), pp. 14–15: "It was impossible, either in Russia or in the 'socialist camp', to achieve a higher average productivity of labour than the leading industrial nations of the world.... The theory and strategy of permanent revolution thus had a sound economic basis."

67. Mandel, *Trotsky as Alternative* (London: Verso, 1995), p. 60. Also, Richard D. Day, *Leon Trotsky and the Politics of Economic Isolation* (New York: Cambridge University Press, 1973), p. 137: "We must not ... forget for a moment the great mutual dependence which existed between the economies of tsarist Russia and world capital. We must just bring to mind the fact that nearly two-thirds of the technical equipment of our works and factories used to be imported from abroad. This dependence has hardly decreased in our time, which means that it will scarcely be economically profitable for us in the next few years to produce at home the machinery we require, at any rate, more than two fifths of the quantity, or at best more than half of it."

68. Harold W. Nelson, *Leon Trotsky and the Art of Insurrection 1905–1917* (Frank Cass and Company Limited, 1988), p. 58, who cites this paragraph as follows: "Definitions of 'strategy' are numerous." Those used here are derived from the "Introduction," Edward Mead Earle, ed., *Makers of Modern Strategy* (New York: Atheneum, 1967), p. viii.

69. Ernest Mandel, *Trotsky as Alternative* (Verso, 1995), p. 1.

70. "Three Concepts of the Russian Revolution," by Leon Trotsky, *Basic Writings of Trotsky*, Irving Howe, Random House, 1963, p. 129.

71. *Leon Trotsky and the Art of Insurrection 1905–1917*, Harold W. Nelson, Frank Cass and Company Limited, 1988, p. 58.

72. "Dual Power," by Leon Trotsky, *Basic Writings of Trotsky*, Irving Howe, Random House, 1963, p. 104.

73. Edward Mead Earle, "Lenin, Trotsky, Stalin: Soviet Concepts of War," in Edward Mead Earle, with Gordon A. Craig and Felix Gilbert (eds.), *Makers of Modern Strategy: Military Thought from Machiavelli to Hitler* (1941; reprint, Princeton, NJ: Princeton University Press, 1960), pp. 331–332: "It was like a living model of war.... The small war was a big school."

74. Irving Howe, "The USSR in War," by Leon Trotsky, *Basic Writings of Trotsky* (Random House, 1963), pp. 36–37. As he writes, "If, however, it is conceded that the present war will provoke not revolution but a decline of the proletariat, then there remains another alternative: the further decay of monopoly capitalism, its further fusion with the state and the replacement of democracy wherever it still remained by a totalitarian regime."

75. Edward Mead Earle, "Lenin, Trotsky, Stalin: Soviet Concepts of War," in Edward Mead Earle, with Gordon A. Craig and Felix Gilbert (eds.), *Makers of Modern Strategy: Military Thought from Machiavelli to Hitler* (1941; reprint, Princeton, NJ: Princeton University Press, 1960), p. 337.

76. Earle, "Lenin, Trotsky, Stalin: Soviet Concepts of War," in Edward Mead Earle, with Gordon A. Craig and Felix Gilbert (eds.), *Makers of Modern Strategy: Military Thought from Machiavelli to Hitler* (1941; reprint, Princeton, NJ: Princeton University Press, 1960), p. 339: "With us, the problem was to make a clean sweep of the remains of the old army, and in its place to build, under fire, a new army whose plan was not to be discovered in any book."

77. Earle, "Lenin, Trotsky, Stalin: Soviet Concepts of War," in Edward Mead Earle, with Gordon A. Craig and Felix Gilbert (eds.), *Makers of Modern Strategy: Military Thought from Machiavelli to Hitler* (1941; reprint, Princeton, NJ: Princeton University Press, 1960), p. 341.

78. Earle, "Lenin, Trotsky, Stalin: Soviet Concepts of War," in Edward Mead Earle, with Gordon A. Craig and Felix Gilbert (eds.), *Makers of Modern Strategy: Military Thought from Machiavelli to Hitler* (1941; reprint, Princeton, NJ: Princeton University Press, 1960), p. 341.

79. Quoted from L. Trotsky, *My Life* (English translation, New York, 1930), p. 438. Also, Edward Mead Earle, "Lenin, Trotsky, Stalin: Soviet Concepts of War," in Edward Mead Earle, with Gordon A. Craig and Felix Gilbert (eds.), *Makers of Modern Strategy: Military Thought from Machiavelli to Hitler* (1941; reprint, Princeton, NJ: Princeton University Press, 1960), p. 342: However, "Trotsky believed that the doctrine of his opponents was 'really nothing but an idealization of our weakness.'"

80. Earle, "Lenin, Trotsky, Stalin: Soviet Concepts of War," in Edward Mead Earle, with Gordon A. Craig and Felix Gilbert (eds.), *Makers of Modern Strategy: Military Thought from Machiavelli to Hitler* (1941; reprint, Princeton, NJ: Princeton University Press, 1960), p. 343.

81. For Mao and his writings and pronouncements, see Mao Tse-tung, *Selected Military Writings of Mao Tse-tung* (Peking: Foreign Languages Press, 1966); Stuart R. Schram, *The Political Thought of Mao Tse-tung* (New York: Frederick A. Praeger, 1966); and Mao, *The Writings of Mao Zedong, 1949–1976*, eds. Michael Y. M. Kau and John K. Leung (New York: M. E. Sharpe, 1986). Also, see Alexander Pantsov, *The Bolsheviks and the Chinese Revolution, 1919–1927* (Honolulu: University of Hawaii Press, 2000); Lucien Bianco, *Origins of the Chinese Revolution, 1915–1949* (Stanford, CA: Stanford University Press, 1971); Alexander V. Pantsov and Steven I. Levine, *Mao: The Real Story* (New York: Simon & Schuster, 2012).

82. Chen Jian, *Mao's China and the Cold War* (Chapel Hill: University of North Carolina Press, 2001). Also, Lorenz M. Luthi, *The Sino-Soviet Split: Cold War in the Communist World* (Princeton, NJ: Princeton University Press, 2008).

83. Ralph Thaxton, "On Peasant Revolution and National Resistance: Toward a Theory of Peasant Mobilization and Revolutionary War with Special Reference to Modern China," *World Politics* 30, No. 1, October, 1977, pp. 24–57. Mao, *Selected Military Writings of Mao Tse-tung*, p. 88: However, he wrote that "victory or defeat in war is determined mainly by the military, political, economic, and natural conditions on both sides." Also, Schram, *Political Thought of Mao Tse-tung*, p. 207: Whether the state actually achieves victory or defeat "is not decided by these [conditions] alone [because] these alone constitute only the possibility of victory or defeat."

84. Mao Tse-tung, *Selected Military Writings of Mao Tse-tung* (Peking: Foreign Languages Press, 1966), p. 78.

85. Stuart Schram, *Political Thought of Mao Tse-tung*, p. 257: "This is the historical epoch in which world capitalism and imperialism are going down to their doom and world socialism and democracy are marching toward victory" (p. 281). As Mao also observed, "it is possible for China's revolutionary war to develop and attain victory" (p. 203).

86. Mao, *The Writings of Mao Zedong, 1949–1976*, eds. Michael Y. M. Kau and John K. Leung (New York: M. E. Sharpe, 1986), p. 220: "I hope that the people of our country will solidly unite among themselves as well as with our ally the Soviet Union, solidly unite with all the People's Democracies, with all the nations and people of the world that sympathize with us, and continue to march forward in the direction of victory in the struggle against aggression, victory in constructing our great country, and victory in the defense of lasting peace in the world. Comrades, if we do this, I believe our victory is assured."

87. Mao, *Selected Military Writings of Mao Tse-tung*, p. 78.

88. Mao, *Selected Military Writings of Mao Tse-tung*, p. 130.

89. Mao, *Selected Military Writings of Mao Tse-tung*, pp. 194–195. Later (p. 328), Mao argued, "Unless we reduce the enemy to extreme fatigue and complete starvation, we cannot win final victory." Also, "Only through such a war of total resistance can final victory be won."

90. Stuart Schram, *Political Thought of Mao Tse-tung*, p. 207. Mao, *Selected Military Writings of Mao Tse-tung*, p. 129: "Victory or defeat in the first battle has a tremendous effect upon the entire situation, all the way to the final engagement." Subsequent citations are given in the text.

91. For critical works on the strategy of revolutionary warfare, see Carleton Beals, *The Nature of Revolution* (New York: Thomas W. Crowell, 1970); Bernard Fall, "Theory and Practice of Insurgency and Counter-insurgency," *History of Revolutionary Warfare, Vol. VI* (West Point, New York: United States Military Academy, 1983), pp. 9–1 to 10–1; Peter Paret, *French Revolutionary Warfare from Indochina to Algeria* (New York: Frederick A. Praeger, 1964); John Shy and Thomas W. Collier, "Revolutionary War," in Peter Paret (ed.) with Gordon A. Craig and Felix Gilbert, *Makers of Modern Strategy: From Machiavelli to the Nuclear Age* (Princeton, NJ: Princeton University Press, 1986), pp. 815–862.

92. Mao, *Selected Military Writings of Mao Tse-tung*, pp. 228–229, p. 261.

93. Mao, *Selected Military Writings of Mao Tse-tung*, pp. 194–195. "Strategy for the Second Year of the War of Liberation," September 1, 1947 (p. 329): Mao expressed his view of the role of strategy: "It dealt the enemy a heavy blow, created profound defeatism in the whole enemy camp, elated the people throughout the country-side, and laid the foundation for the complete annihilation of the enemy by our army and for final victory."

94. Stuart Schram, *The Thought of Mao Tse-tung* (New York: Cambridge University Press, 1989), p. 44.

95. Stuart Schram, *Mao Tse-tung* (Simon & Schuster, 1966), p. 224.

96. Stuart Schram, *The Thought of Mao Tse-tung* (New York: Cambridge University Press, 1989), p. 83.

97. Richard Solomon, *Mao's Revolution and the Chinese Political Culture* (University of California Press, 1971), p. 186.

98. Mao Tse-tung, *On Guerrilla Warfare*, chapter 1: "We consider guerrilla operations as but one aspect of our total or mass war because they, lacking the quality of independence, are of themselves incapable of providing a solution to the struggle."

99. Mao, *Selected Military Writings of Mao Tse-tung*, p. 69.

100. Mao, *Selected Military Writings of Mao Tse-tung*, p. 87.

101. Mao, *Selected Military Writings of Mao Tse-tung*, p. 72.

102. Mao, *Selected Military Writings of Mao Tse-tung*, p. 72: "These tactics are just like casting a net; at any moment we should be able to cast it or draw it in. We cast it wide to win over the masses and draw it in to a deal with the enemy."

103. Mao, *On Guerrilla Warfare*, chapter 6: "Many people think it impossible for guerrillas to exist for long in the enemy's rear. Such belief reveals lack of comprehension of the relationship that should exist between the people and the troops. The former may be likened to water the latter to the fish who inhabit it. How may it be said that these two cannot exist together? It is only undisciplined troops who make the people their enemies and who, like the fish out of its native element cannot live."

104. Mao, *Selected Military Writings of Mao Tse-tung*, p. 81. "Wherever there is war, there is a war situation as a whole ..."

105. Mao, *Selected Military Writings of Mao Tse-tung*, p. 155.

106. Tang Tsou and Morton Halperin, "Mao Tse-tung's Revolutionary Strategy and Peking's International Behavior," *American Political Science Review* 59, No. 1 (March 1965), p. 80.

107. Mao Tse-tung, *Selected Military Writings of Mao Tse-tung*, pp. 88–89: "Unquestionably, victory or defeat in war is determined mainly by the military, political, economic, and natural conditions on both sides ... Therefore, given the objective material foundations, *i.e.*, the military, political, economic, and natural conditions, our Red Army commanders must display their prowess and marshal all their forces to crush the national and class enemies and to transform this evil world."

108. Mao, *Selected Military Writings of Mao Tse-tung*, pp. 277–279.

109. Mao, *Selected Military Writings of Mao Tse-tung*, p. 279.

110. John M. Collins, *Military Strategy: Principles, Practices, and Historical Perspective* (Brassey's, Inc., 2002), p. 172.

111. Mao Tse-tung, *Selected Military Writings of Mao Tse-tung*, p. 282.

112. Mao, *Selected Military Writings of Mao Tse-tung*, pp. 78–79, who cites "differences in their time, place, and nature."

113. Edward Mead Earle, "Hitler: The Nazi Concept of War," in Edward Mead Earle, with Gordon A. Craig and Felix Gilbert (eds.), *Makers of Modern Strategy: Military Thought from Machiavelli to Hitler* (1941; reprint, Princeton, NJ: Princeton University Press, 1960), p. 511. Cf. Alan Bullock, *A Study in Tyranny* (New York: Harper & Row, 1971); Wilhelm Deist, "The Road to Ideological War: Germany, 1918–1945," in Williamson Murray, MacGregor Knox, and Alvin Bernstein (eds.), *The Making of Strategy: Rulers, States, and War* (New York: Cambridge University Press, 1996), pp. 352–392.

114. Randall Schweller, *Deadly Imbalances: Tripolarity and Hitler's Strategy of World Conquest* (New York: Columbia University Press, 1998). Edward Mead Earle, "Hitler: The Nazi Concept of War," in Edward Mead Earle, with Gordon A. Craig and Felix Gilbert (eds.), *Makers of Modern Strategy: Military Thought from Machiavelli to Hitler* (1941; reprint, Princeton, NJ: Princeton University Press, 1960), p. 504.

115. Edward Mead Earle, "Hitler: The Nazi Concept of War," in Edward Mead Earle, with Gordon A. Craig and Felix Gilbert (eds.), *Makers of Modern Strategy: Military Thought from Machiavelli to Hitler* (1941; reprint, Princeton, NJ: Princeton University Press, 1960), pp. 504–505: "... which crushed the defenses of Western Europe almost as easily as Joshua razed the walls of Jericho."

116. Earle, "Hitler: The Nazi Concept of War," in Edward Mead Earle, with Gordon A. Craig and Felix Gilbert (eds.), *Makers of Modern Strategy: Military Thought from Machiavelli to Hitler* (1941; reprint, Princeton, NJ: Princeton University Press, 1960), p. 505. Hitler's development of Germany's motor industry is also an important element of the next theme: marshaling all of society's resources.

117. Earle, "Hitler: The Nazi Concept of War," in Edward Mead Earle, with Gordon A. Craig and Felix Gilbert (eds.), *Makers of Modern Strategy: Military Thought from Machiavelli to Hitler* (1941; reprint, Princeton, NJ: Princeton University Press, 1960), p. 510.

118. Earle, "Hitler: The Nazi Concept of War," in Edward Mead Earle, with Gordon A. Craig and Felix Gilbert (eds.), *Makers of Modern Strategy: Military Thought from Machiavelli to Hitler* (1941; reprint, Princeton, NJ: Princeton University Press, 1960), p. 510.

119. Adolf Hitler, *Mein Kampf* (New York: Houghton Mifflin Company, 1998), pp. 459–460 and p. 624. Edward Mead Earle, "Hitler: The Nazi Concept of War," in Edward Mead Earle, with Gordon A. Craig and Felix Gilbert (eds.), *Makers of Modern Strategy: Military Thought from Machiavelli to Hitler* (1941; reprint, Princeton, NJ: Princeton University Press, 1960), pp. 510–511.

120. On the effects on civilian morale during strategic bombing campaign against Germany during World War II, see *The United States Strategic Bombing Survey [USSBS], Summary Report, Pacific War*, July 1, 1946 (Washington, DC: U.S. GPO; rpt., Maxwell AFB, AL: Air University Press, 1987).

121. For an analysis of total war, cf. William C. Martel, *Victory in War: Foundations of Modern Strategy* (New York: Cambridge University Press, 2011), pp. 101–104.

122. Edward Mead Earle, "Hitler: The Nazi Concept of War," in Edward Mead Earle, with Gordon A. Craig and Felix Gilbert (eds.), *Makers of Modern Strategy: Military Thought from Machiavelli to Hitler* (1941; reprint, Princeton, NJ: Princeton University Press, 1960), p. 511: The story Earle considers "has been told too often to need repetition here."

123. Earle, "Hitler: The Nazi Concept of War," in Edward Mead Earle, with Gordon A. Craig and Felix Gilbert (eds.), *Makers of Modern Strategy: Military Thought from Machiavelli to Hitler* (1941; reprint, Princeton, NJ: Princeton University Press, 1960), p. 511: "... adequate measures – such as the development of synthetic raw materials and the building up of stock piles of critical minerals – must be taken against blockade ..."

124. On the economic dimensions of strategy, see William C. Martel, *Victory in War: Foundations of Modern Strategy* (New York: Cambridge University Press, 2011), pp. 84–85.

125. Edward Mead Earle, "Hitler: The Nazi Concept of War," in Edward Mead Earle, with Gordon A. Craig and Felix Gilbert (eds.), *Makers of Modern Strategy: Military Thought from Machiavelli to Hitler* (1941; reprint, Princeton, NJ: Princeton University Press, 1960), p. 512.

126. Earle, "Hitler: The Nazi Concept of War," in Edward Mead Earle, with Gordon A. Craig and Felix Gilbert (eds.), *Makers of Modern Strategy: Military Thought from Machiavelli to Hitler* (1941; reprint, Princeton, NJ: Princeton University Press, 1960), p. 513: "Political warfare was constantly carried on, writes a former member of Hitler's entourage, 'not only to render the tactical situation favorable to a succession of bloodless victories, but also to determine the particular issues which the general political situation may make ripe for settlement in accordance with the aims of National Socialism."

127. Earle, "Hitler: The Nazi Concept of War," in Edward Mead Earle, with Gordon A. Craig and Felix Gilbert (eds.), *Makers of Modern Strategy: Military Thought from Machiavelli to Hitler* (1941; reprint, Princeton, NJ: Princeton University Press, 1960), p. 514.

128. For in-depth analysis on the German economy during the Nazi era, as well as a comprehensive account of Hitler's attempts to achieve his ideological aims without the necessary means, see Adam Tooze, *The Wages of Destruction: The Making and the Breaking of the Nazi Economy* (London: Penguin Books, 2008).

129. Edward Mead Earle, "Hitler: The Nazi Concept of War," in Edward Mead Earle, with Gordon A. Craig and Felix Gilbert (eds.), *Makers of Modern Strategy: Military Thought from Machiavelli to Hitler* (1941; reprint, Princeton, NJ: Princeton University Press, 1960), pp. 505–506. For a grim portrayal of the ideological aims and consequences of Stalin's Soviet Union and Hitler's Nazi Germany between the years 1933 and 1945, see Timothy Snyder, *Bloodlands: Europe between Hitler and Stalin* (New York: Basic Books, 2010).

130. Earle, "Hitler: The Nazi Concept of War," in Edward Mead Earle, with Gordon A. Craig and Felix Gilbert (eds.), *Makers of Modern Strategy: Military Thought from Machiavelli to Hitler* (1941; reprint, Princeton, NJ: Princeton University Press, 1960), p. 507: In 1887, Bismarck wrote, "France's continued existence as a great power is just as needful to us as that of any other of the great powers." He continued, "If we should be attacked by France and emerge victorious, we would nevertheless not even consider it a possibility to annihilate a nation of forty million Europeans so highly endowed and sensitive as the French." However, as Earle notes, "the Nazis think otherwise and have been determined almost from the beginning to reduce France to the status of a German colony" (p. 510).

131. In a message congratulating senior military officers for the success of the air campaign against Germany on October 11, 1943, Churchill emphasized the nature of Allied policy as one of "beating the life out of Germany." See "Beating the Life Out of Germany, October 11, 1943," *The War Speeches of the Rt. Hon. Winston S. Churchill*, 6 vols., comp. Charles Eade (Boston: Houghton Mifflin, 1953), Vol. 3: *The End of the Beginning*, pp. 41–42. When the three leaders of the

Allied coalition – President Franklin D. Roosevelt, Prime Minister Winston S. Churchill, and General Secretary Josef Stalin – met in southeastern Ukraine on the Black Sea at the Yalta Conference in February 1945, they reiterated that Allied policy was to prosecute the war until Germany and Japan accepted unconditional surrender. See "Results of the Yalta Conference: A Speech to the House of Commons," February 27, 1945," pp. 376–398. This strategy was rooted in the stark language of the Atlantic Charter (signed by Allied leaders on August 14, 1941), in which Roosevelt and Churchill cited as their fifth objective the "final destruction of the Nazi tyranny" or, as Churchill said, "until victory is won." (See "Atlantic Charter," at http://avalon.law.yale.edu/subject_menus/wwii.asp; see also "Until Victory Is Won: A Speech to a Conference of Dominion High Commissioners and Allied Countries' Ministers, at St. James's Palace, London, June 12, 1941," *War Speeches of Winston S. Churchill*, Vol. 3, p. 444.) Moreover, when Churchill was asked at an Oval Office press conference with Roosevelt in December 1941 whether he had "any doubt of the ultimate victory," his answer was unequivocal: "I have no doubt whatsoever." Jon Meacham, *Franklin and Winston: An Intimate Portrait of an Epic Friendship* (New York: Random House, 2003), p. 144.

132. Edward Mead Earle, "Hitler: The Nazi Concept of War," in Edward Mead Earle, with Gordon A. Craig and Felix Gilbert (eds.), *Makers of Modern Strategy: Military Thought from Machiavelli to Hitler* (1941; reprint, Princeton, NJ: Princeton University Press, 1960), p. 508.

133. "Visit to Cyprus: A Speech to a Representative Gathering of the Islanders," February 1, 1943, *War Speeches of Winston S. Churchill*, p. 397.

134. Edward Mead Earle, "Hitler: The Nazi Concept of War," in Edward Mead Earle, with Gordon A. Craig and Felix Gilbert (eds.), *Makers of Modern Strategy: Military Thought from Machiavelli to Hitler* (1941; reprint, Princeton, NJ: Princeton University Press, 1960), p. 509.

135. For background on Ho Chi Minh, see Pierre Brocheux, *Ho Chi Minh: A Biography* (New York: Cambridge University Press, 2007); William J. Duiker, *Ho Chi Minh: A Life* (New York: Hyperion, 2000); Sophie Quinn-Judge, *Ho Chi Minh: The Missing Years, 1919–1941* (Berkeley and Los Angeles: University of California Press, 2002); Tin Bui, *Following Ho Chi Minh: The Memoirs of a North Vietnamese Colonel* (Honolulu: University of Hawaii Press, 1995); Peter Anthony DeCaro, *Rhetoric of Revolt: Ho Chi Minh's Discourse for Revolution* (Westport, CT: Praeger, 2003).

136. See Herman Kahn, "On the Possibilities for Victory or Defeat," in Frank E. Armbruster, Raymond D. Gastil, Herman Kahn, William Pfaff, and Edmund Stillman, *Can We Win in Vietnam?* (New York: Frederick A. Praeger, 1969), pp. 178–204. Also, Guenter Lewy, *America in Vietnam* (New York: Oxford University Press, 1978), esp. "Could the United States Have Won in Vietnam?" pp. 430–441.

137. William C. Martel, *Victory in War: Foundations of Modern Strategy*, revised and expanded edition (New York: Cambridge University Press, 2011), pp. 161–166.

138. For background on the Vietnam War, see Daniel Ellsberg, *Papers on the War* (New York: Simon & Schuster, 1972); Leslie H. Gelb with Richard K. Betts, *The Irony of Vietnam: The System Worked* (Washington, DC: The Brookings Institution, 1979);

Marc J. Gilbert, *Why the North Won the Vietnam War* (New York: Palgrave, 2002); David Halberstam, *The Best and the Brightest* (New York: Random House, 1972); George C. Herring, *America's Longest War: The United States and Vietnam, 1950–1975* (New York: John Wiley & Sons, 1979); David Kaiser, *American Tragedy: Kennedy, Johnson, and the Origins of the Vietnam War* (Cambridge, MA: Belknap, 2000); Stanley Karnow, *Vietnam: A History* (New York: Viking, 1983); David W. Levy, *The Debate over Vietnam* (Baltimore: Johns Hopkins University Press, 1995); Lewy, *America in Vietnam*; Robert E. Osgood, "The Lessons of Vietnam" and "Post-Vietnam Refinements of Limited War Strategy," in *Limited War Revisited*, pp. 33–51 and 52–66, respectively; Lewis Sorley, *A Better War: The Unexamined Victories and Final Tragedy of America's Last Years in Vietnam* (New York: Harcourt Brace, 1999); Harry G. Summers Jr., *On Strategy: A Critical Analysis of the Vietnam War* (Novato, CA: Presidio Press, 1982); Robert Thompson, *No Exit from Vietnam* (New York: David McKay, 1969); Stanley Hoffmann, Samuel P. Huntington, Ernest R. May, Richard N. Neustadt, and Thomas C. Schelling, "Vietnam Reappraised," *International Security* 6, No. 1 (Summer 1981), pp. 3–26; Richard K. Betts, "Misadventure Revisited," *Wilson Quarterly* (1976–) 7, No. 3 (Summer 1983), pp. 94–113.

139. Nguyen Van Hieu, "We Are Confident of Final Victory," *International Affairs* 18, No. 10 (1962), pp. 65–66; William C. Martel, *Victory in War: Foundations of Modern Strategy*, revised and expanded edition (New York: Cambridge University Press, 2011), pp. 162.

140. Jeffrey Record, "Vietnam in Retrospect: Could We Have Won?" *Parameters* 26.4 (Winter 1996–1997), pp. 51–65, at p. 61: ". . . a failure to appreciate the fundamental civil dimensions of the war, and preoccupation with the measurable indices of military power and attendant disdain for the ultimately decisive intangibles."

141. Pierre Brocheux, *Ho Chi Minh: A Biography* (New York: Cambridge University Press, 2007), p. 28.

142. The Comintern international, which was established by Moscow in March 1919, sought to fight "by all available means, including armed force, for the overthrow of the international bourgeoisie and for the creation of an international Soviet republic as a transition stage to the complete abolition of the State." As Brocheux, *Ho Chi Minh: A Biography*, notes, the Comintern "did indeed denounce Great Russian or Greater Han nationalism and generally considered national struggle to be contradictory to class action . . ." p. 28.

143. Brocheux, *Ho Chi Minh: A Biography* (New York: Cambridge University Press, 2007), pp. 74–75.

144. Brocheux, *Ho Chi Minh: A Biography* (New York: Cambridge University Press, 2007), p. 17.

145. Foreword by William J. Duiker, in Pierre Brocheux, *Ho Chi Minh: A Biography* (New York: Cambridge University Press, 2007), p. x: "Ho Chi Minh was equally adept at disguising his true ideological convictions. Having begun his political career as a fervent Vietnamese patriot, he embraced communism shortly after settling in Paris at the end of World War I."

146. Foreword by Duiker, in Brocheux, *Ho Chi Minh: A Biography* (New York: Cambridge University Press, 2007), p. x.

147. Quote of Ho Chin Minh, Brocheux, *Ho Chi Minh: A Biography* (New York: Cambridge University Press, 2007), p. 18: "As for the Second International, it is not concerned about the colonial question."

148. Brocheux, *Ho Chi Minh: A Biography* (New York: Cambridge University Press, 2007), p. 41. These conclusions about Ho are somewhat inferential, since "he left us no records of his impressions ..." Also, "the contradictory advice given by the envoys of the International; and the confusion that ensued."

149. Brocheux, *Ho Chi Minh: A Biography* (New York: Cambridge University Press, 2007), p. 41.

150. Brocheux, *Ho Chi Minh: A Biography* (New York: Cambridge University Press, 2007), p. 72.

151. William J. Duiker, *Ho Chi Minh: A Life* (New York: Hyperion, 2000), p. 156: "Joseph Stalin forced the delegates at the party congress to abandon the broad united front strategy that had been originally initiated at the Second Congress eight years earlier."

152. Pierre Brocheux, *Ho Chi Minh: A Biography* (New York: Cambridge University Press, 2007), p. 42: "[Ho Chi Minh] claimed that the peasantry['s] cohesion and political clairvoyance were never acknowledged by Marx ..."

153. Brocheux, *Ho Chi Minh: A Biography* (New York: Cambridge University Press, 2007), pp. 73–74. "They would confiscate only the land of 'colonialists and landlords who are traitors to our country' and distribute it to the poor peasants and landless laborers." For Ho, the movement would have "to throw open their ranks to as many people as possible, meaning that they would have to abandon their plans for a radical agrarian revolution."

154. William J. Duiker, *Ho Chi Minh: A Life* (New York: Hyperion, 2000), p. 166: "A strategy document approved at the conference called for efforts to win the support of intellectuals, middle peasants (a Party term for farmers who had enough land to live on, but not to hire laborers), the petty bourgeoisie, as well as nationalist groups ..."

155. Duiker, *Ho Chi Minh: A Life* (New York: Hyperion, 2000), p. 133.

156. Pierre Brocheux, *Ho Chi Minh: A Biography* (New York: Cambridge University Press, 2007), p. 41.

157. William J. Duiker, *Ho Chi Minh: A Life* (New York: Hyperion, 2000), p. 552. "To colleagues who expressed a sense of urgency about winning the final victory, Ho compared the situation to preparing rice for a meal. If you remove the rice from the fire too soon, it is inadequately cooked; if removed too late, it will be burned."

158. Duiker, *Ho Chi Minh: A Life* (New York: Hyperion, 2000), p. 255.

159. For this argument, see Lawrence Freedman, "The First Two Generations of Nuclear Strategists," in Paret (ed.), *Makers of Modern Strategy*, pp. 735–778, at pp. 736–738. See also Freedman, *Evolution of Nuclear Strategy* (London: Oxford University Press, 1981). Cf. Henry A. Kissinger, *Nuclear Weapons and Foreign Policy*, abridged edition (New York: W. W. Norton, 1969), p. 7. As Kissinger observed (abr., p. 12), "we saw it [the atomic bomb] merely as another tool in a concept of warfare which knew no goal save total victory, and no mode of war except all-out war."

160. Bernard Brodie, *Absolute Weapon: Atomic Power and World Order* (New York: Harcourt, Brace, 1946), p. 212.

161. Bernard Brodie, "War in the Atomic Age," in Brodie (ed.), *Absolute Weapon*, pp. 21–69, at p. 47. For an analysis of deterrence, see Brodie, "The Anatomy of Deterrence," in his *Strategy in the Missile Age* (Princeton: Princeton University Press, 1959) pp. 264–304.

162. Bernard Brodie, *War and Politics* (New York: Macmillan, 1973), pp. 425–426: "and thus lesser wars … might too easily lead up to the large-scale thermonuclear variety." This reasoning was outlined in a chapter entitled "On Nuclear Weapons: Utility in Nonuse," pp. 375–432.

163. Brodie, "Implications for Military Policy," in Brodie (ed.), *Absolute Weapon*, p. 76: "It [our military establishment] can have almost no other useful purpose."

164. Herman Kahn, *On Thermonuclear War: Three Lectures and Several Suggestions* (Princeton, NJ: Princeton University Press, 1961), p. 11, which he described as an outcome that represents a "plausible conviction."

165. Kahn, *On Thermonuclear War: Three Lectures and Several Suggestions* (Princeton, NJ: Princeton University Press, 1961), p. 24, in which he referred to the "old-fashioned concept of victory, as denoting the one who writes the peace treaty, while at the same time making explicit that victory can be costly."

166. Thomas C. Schelling, *Arms and Influence* (New Haven, CT: Yale University Press, 1966), p. 22: "There was a time when the assurance of victory – false or genuine assurance – could make national leaders not just willing but sometimes enthusiastic about war. Not now."

167. Paul Kecskemeti, *Strategic Surrender: The Politics of Victory and Defeat* (Stanford: Stanford University Press, 1958), p. 5. Subsequent citations are given in the text.

168. Kecskemeti, *Strategic Surrender*, p. 249. Later (p. 254), he argues that "such wars cannot reasonably be expected to result in complete victory in the political sense. What the winner can reasonably expect is only a relatively modest gain, not departing significantly from the status quo." Kecskemeti also refers to "low-stake" nuclear wars, which "can end in complete victory in the political sense: if the stake is low, the military loser will give it up entirely without much difficulty" (p. 256).

169. See the discussion of unconditional surrender in "The Allies' Policy in World War II," chap. 7 of Paul Kecskemeti, *Strategic Surrender*, pp. 215–241.

170. Raymond Aron, *Century of Total War*, pp. 37, 158. Also, Benedict J. Kerkvliet, "A Critique of Raymond Aron's Theory of War and Prescriptions," *International Studies Quarterly* 12, No. 4 (December 1968), pp. 419–442.

171. Raymond Aron, *The Great Debate: Theories of Nuclear Strategy*, trans. Ernst Pawel (New York: Doubleday, 1965), pp. 198–199.

172. Vasily D. Sokolovskii, ed., *Soviet Military Strategy*, trans. and annot. Herbert S. Dinerstein, Leon Gouré, and Thomas W. Wolfe (Englewood Cliffs, NJ: Prentice–Hall, 1963), p. 281.

173. Sokolovskii, ed., *Soviet Military Strategy*, pp. 312–313. "N. S. Khrushchev has pointed out that 'under present conditions, the most probable wars are not likely to be between capitalist, imperialist countries, although the possibility is not to be excluded. The imperialists are preparing wars mainly against the socialist countries and primarily against the Soviet Union as the most powerful of the socialist states'" (pp. 355–356). See N. S. Khrushchev, "Toward New Victories of the World

Communist Movement," *Kommunist* 1 (1961), pp. 17–18, as cited in *Soviet Military Strategy*, p. 356.

174. From the first edition (May 1924) of Stalin's pamphlet *Foundations of Leninism*, quoted in Leon Trotsky, *Challenge of the Left Opposition (1926–1927)* (New York: Pathfinder, 1980), p. 157: "Can the final victory of socialism be attained in a single country without the joint efforts of the proletariat in several advanced countries?" he asked. "No, it cannot."

175. Vasily D. Sokolovskii, ed., *Soviet Military Strategy*, p. 231. Subsequent citations are given in the text.

176. For interpretations of the Soviet Union's collapse, see Daniel Deudney and G. John Ikenberry, "Soviet Reform and the End of the Cold War: Explaining Large-Scale Historical Change," *Review of International Studies* 17, No. 3 (July 1991), pp. 225–250; John Blaney and Mike Gfoeller, "Lessons from the Failure of Perestroika," *Political Science Quarterly* 108, No. 3 (Autumn 1993), pp. 481–496; Francois Furet, *The Passing of an Illusion: The Idea of Communism in the Twentieth Century*, translated by Deborah Furet (Chicago: University of Chicago Press, 1999); Andrew Gamble, "Marxism after Communism: Beyond Realism and Historicism," *Review of International Studies* 25, *The Interregnum: Controversies in World Politics 1989–1999* (December 1999), pp. 127–144; Brad Rose and George Ross, "Socialism's Past, New Social Democracy, and Socialism's Futures," *Social Science History* 18, No. 3 (Autumn 1994), pp. 439–469. See also Richard Pipes, "The Soviet Union Adrift," *Foreign Affairs* 70, No. 1 (1990–1991), pp. 70–87; Seweryn Bialer, "The Death of Soviet Communism," *Foreign Affairs* 70, No. 5 (Winter 1991), pp. 166–181; Alexander J. Motyl, "Empire or Stability? The Case for Soviet Dissolution," *World Policy Journal* 8, No. 3 (Summer 1991), pp. 499–524; Michael Mandelbaum, "Coup de Grace: The End of the Soviet Union," *Foreign Affairs* 71, No. 1 (1991–1992), pp. 164–183; Daniel Deudney and G. John Ikenberry, "The International Sources of Soviet Change," *International Security* 16, No. 3 (Winter 1991–1992), pp. 74–118; Rey Koslowski and Friedrich V. Kratochwil, "Understanding Change in International Politics: The Soviet Empire's Demise and the International System," *International Organization* 48, No. 2 (Spring 1994), pp. 215–247; Nancy Bernkopf Tucker, "China as a Factor in the Collapse of the Soviet Empire," *Political Science Quarterly* 110, No. 4 (Winter 1995–1996), pp. 501–518; Z, "To the Stalin Mausoleum," *Daedalus* 119, No. 1 (*Eastern Europe … Central Europe … Europe*, Winter 1990), pp. 295–344.

177. For a discussion on industrial potential and victory, see Kissinger, *Nuclear Weapons and Foreign Policy* (New York: Harper & Brothers, 1957), (unabridged), pp. 88–94.

178. Paul Kecskemeti, *Strategic Surrender*, p. 246.

179. Kecskemeti, *Strategic Surrender*, p. 128.

180. Richard Rhodes, "The General and World War III," *New Yorker* 71.15 (June 19, 1995), pp. 47–59, at p. 54.

181. Richard Rhodes, "The General and World War III," *New Yorker* 71.15 (June 19, 1995), p. 55.

182. Thomas Schelling, *Arms and Influence*, p. 23, who noted, "Deterrence rests today on the threat of pain and extinction, not just on the threat of military defeat."

183. See, for example, Bernard Brodie, "Limited War," in his *Strategy in the Missile Age*, pp. 305–357, who notes (p. 305) that the word "'victorious' ... is put in quotation marks only to remind ourselves that it has lost its former meaning and needs redefining."

184. Robert E. Osgood, *Limited War*, p. 29. Kissinger, *Nuclear Weapons* (unabridged), pp. 86–131, made the same argument.

185. Osgood, *Limited War*, p. 25; Robert E. Osgood, *Limited War Revisited* (Boulder, CO: Westview, 1979); Osgood, *The Nuclear Dilemma in American Strategic Thought* (Boulder, CO: Westview Press, 1988). For a discussion of limited victory, see John J. Mearsheimer, *Conventional Deterrence* (Ithaca, NY: Cornell University Press, 1983), p. 57, who observed that "modern nation-states invariably prefer [decisive victory] to limited victories." Mearsheimer argued that decisive victory was produced by the "natural preference of military officers, the rise of the mass army, the effect of industrialization on warfare, the increasing democratization of societies, and the impact of nationalism" (p. 61).

186. Osgood, *Limited War*, p. 44; also, Benjamin O. Fordham, *Building the Cold War Consensus: The Political Economy of U.S. Security Policy, 1949–51* (Ann Arbor: University of Michigan Press, 1998).

187. For this argument, see Lawrence Freedman, "The First Two Generations of Nuclear Strategists," in Paret (ed.), *Makers of Modern Strategy*, pp. 735–778, at pp. 736–738. See also Freedman, *Evolution of Nuclear Strategy* (London: Oxford University Press, 1981).

188. Michael Howard, "The Influence of Clausewitz," in Carl von Clausewitz, *On War*, ed. and trans. Michael Howard and Peter Paret (Princeton, NJ: Princeton University Press, 1976), pp. 27–44, at p. 43, which continues: "The development of atomic weapons by both sides already made it likely that the kind of military solution advocated by General MacArthur might involve a quite unacceptable degree of reciprocal destruction, which the advent of thermonuclear weapons would soon raise to an inconceivable order of magnitude."

189. See Colin S. Gray and Keith B. Payne, "Victory Is Possible," *Foreign Policy* 39 (Summer 1980), pp. 14–27.

190. See Colin S. Gray, *Defining and Achieving Decisive Victory* (Carlisle Barracks, PA: Strategic Studies Institute, U.S. Army War College, April 2002), p. v: "The idea of victory, let alone decisive victory, was very much out of style during the Cold War."

191. See Lawrence Freedman, *Evolution of Nuclear Strategy* (London: Oxford University Press, 1981), pp. 213–242.

192. For a discussion of conventional weapons during the Cold War, see Freedman, *Evolution of Nuclear Strategy*, pp. 269–314; Michael Carver, "Conventional Warfare in the Nuclear Age," in Paret (ed.), *Makers of Modern Strategy*, pp. 779–814.

193. John Mearsheimer, *Conventional Deterrence* (Ithaca, NY: Cornell University Press, 1983).

194. B. H. Liddell Hart, *Defence of the West* (London: Cassell, 1950).

195. B. H. Liddell Hart, *Thoughts on War*, p. 42. Subsequent citations are given in the text.

196. See Dmitri Volkogonov, *Stalin: Triumph and Tragedy*, trans. Harold Shukman (London: Wiedenfield and Nicolson, 1991); Richard Pipes, "Building the One-Party State," in *A Concise History of the Russian Revolution* (New York: Vintage Books, 1995), pp. 150–165; Richard Overy, *Russia's War: A History of the Soviet War Effort, 1941–1945* (New York: Penguin Books, 1997), pp. 1–72.

197. On Marxist-Leninist ideology, see Sigmund Neumann and Mark Von Hagen, "Engels and Marx on Revolution, War, and the Army in Society," in Paret (ed.), *Makers of Modern Strategy*, pp. 262–80; Karl Marx and Friedrich Engels, "Communist Manifesto," in Robert C. Tucker (ed.), *The Marx-Engels Reader* (New York: W. W. Norton, 1972), pp. 331–362; Edward Mead Earle, "Lenin, Trotsky, Stalin: Soviet Concepts of War," in Earle (ed.), *Makers of Modern Strategy: Military Thought*, pp. 322–364; Earl F. Ziemke, "Strategy for Class War: the Soviet Union, 1917–1941," in Williamson Murray, MacGregor Knox, and Alvin Bernstein (eds.), *The Making of Strategy: Rulers, States, and War* (New York: Cambridge University Press, 1996), pp. 498–533.

198. See "Task Force on Russia and U.S. National Interests Report," *Russia and U.S. National Interests: Why Should Americans Care?* (Cambridge, MA: Harvard University, Belfer Center for Science and International Affairs, 2011); Andrei P. Tsygankov, *Russia's Foreign Policy: Change and Continuity in National Identity* (New York: Rowman & Littlefield, 2006); Edward Luttwak, *The Grand Strategy of the Soviet Union* (New York: St. Martin's Press, 1983).

199. Edward Mead Earle, "Lenin, Trotsky, Stalin: Soviet Concepts of War," in Edward Mead Earle, with Gordon A. Craig and Felix Gilbert (eds.), *Makers of Modern Strategy: Military Thought from Machiavelli to Hitler* (1941; reprint, Princeton, NJ: Princeton University Press, 1960), p. 350: As Earle observed, "these objectives could be attained only by the offensive."

200. Earle, "Lenin, Trotsky, Stalin: Soviet Concepts of War," in Edward Mead Earle, with Gordon A. Craig and Felix Gilbert (eds.), *Makers of Modern Strategy: Military Thought from Machiavelli to Hitler* (1941; reprint, Princeton, NJ: Princeton University Press, 1960), p. 350: "Stalin's regime prepared for total war on a scale which few persons in the outside world even remotely suspected or comprehended."

201. Williamson Murray, "Thoughts on Grand Strategy," in Williamson Murray, Richard Hart Sinnreich, and James Lacey (eds.), *The Shaping of Grand Strategy: Policy, Diplomacy, and War* (New York: Cambridge University Press, 2011), p. 18, who notes that this "must be counted as one of the most disastrous strategic mistakes in history . . ."

202. Murray, "Thoughts on Grand Strategy," in Williamson Murray, Richard Hart Sinnreich, and James Lacey (eds.), *The Shaping of Grand Strategy: Policy, Diplomacy, and War* (New York: Cambridge University Press, 2011), p. 18.

203. Colin S. Gray, "Harry S. Truman and the Forming of American Grand Strategy in the Cold War, 1945–1953," in Williamson Murray, Richard Hart Sinnreich, and James Lacey (eds.), *The Shaping of Grand Strategy: Policy, Diplomacy, and War* (New York: Cambridge University Press, 2011), p. 249. "[Stalin] knew that he and his personal and ideological vehicle-state, Lenin's monstrous creation, the USSR," were at war with the West. Furthermore, "The detailed implications of this

profound belief for Soviet policy, strategy, and tactics would have to vary oppor-
tunistically with evolving circumstances and events."

204. Albert L. Weeks, quote of Josef Stalin in *Stalin's Other War: Soviet Grand Strategy 1939–1941* (New York: Rowman and Littlefield, Inc., 2002), p. vii: "On our part we will maneuver while pitting one country against the other so that they can fight each other all the better. The nonaggression pact to a degree helps Germany. But in the next moment, it batters the other side." Furthermore, "We're not opposed to the idea of their fighting among themselves very well. Nor would it be bad if by the hands of Germany the position of the richest capitalist countries were shattered (in particular that of England)."

205. Henri Lefebvre, *Dialectical Materialism* (Minneapolis: University of Minnesota Press, 2009), pp. xiv–xv: "Based on a narrow and schematic reading of Engels's *Dialectics of Nature* and *Anti-Dühring*, Stalin's dialectical materialism combined a nominally dialectical philosophy of nature with a mechanical conception of materialism, complete with a reflection of theory of consciousness. Diamat was meant to furnish a 'science of the history of society' akin to the natural sciences (historical materialism) that could provide party leaders with an unerring approach to policy."

206. Richard Rosecrance and Arthur A. Stein (eds.), *The Domestic Bases of Grand Strategy* (Ithaca, NY: Cornell University Press, 1993), p. 49.

207. Albert L. Weeks, *Stalin's Other War: Soviet Grand Strategy 1939–1941* (New York: Rowman and Littlefield, Inc., 2002), p. 9: "Victory in revolution never comes of itself. It must be prepared for and won."

208. Richard Rosecrance and Arthur A. Stein, eds., *The Domestic Bases of Grand Strategy* (Ithaca, NY: Cornell University Press, 1993), p. 244.

209. Edward Luttwak, *The Grand Strategy of the Soviet Union* (New York: St. Martin's Press, 1983), pp. 23–43: ". . . peace was a function of international politics, which were beyond the exclusive control of the Kremlin leader who otherwise controlled so much; but Stalin did what he could. A major war would inevitably interrupt the Soviet Union's steady ascent to the centrally planned millennium – the key to its eventual worldwide political victory."

210. George F. Kennan "Telegram: The Charge in the Soviet Union to the Secretary of State," at http://www2.gwu.edu/~nsarchiv/coldwar/documents/episode-1/kennan .htm: The Kremlin "is dealing in ideological concepts which are of long-term validity, and it can afford to be patient. It has no right to risk the existing achievements of the revolution for the sake of vain baubles of the future."

211. Edward Luttwak, *The Grand Strategy of the Soviet Union* (New York: St. Martin's Press, 1983), pp. 1–2.

212. Albert L. Weeks, *Stalin's Other War: Soviet Grand Strategy 1939–1941* (New York: Rowman and Littlefield, Inc., 2002), pp. 4–5: "This second, secret – or 'other' – war was to be waged after the capitalist countries had mutually destructed each other in a 'big war,' as Stalin called it."

213. Weeks, *Stalin's Other War: Soviet Grand Strategy 1939–1941* (New York: Rowman and Littlefield, Inc., 2002), pp. 16–17. Citations on realism: Morgenthau, Kissinger.

214. Weeks, *Stalin's Other War: Soviet Grand Strategy 1939–1941* (New York: Rowman and Littlefield, Inc., 2002), p. 16.

215. Robert Gellately, *Stalin's Curse: Battling for Communism in War and Cold War* (New York: Knopf, 2013), p. 162. Cf. Harry S. Truman, *Memoirs by Harry S. Truman*, 2 vols. (New York: Doubleday, 1955), Vol. 1: *Year of Decisions*, p. 87: Stimson "explained that he thought it necessary for him to share his thoughts with me about the revolutionary changes in warfare that might result from the atomic bomb *and the possible effects of such a weapon on our civilization.*" Further, "If expectations were to be realized, he told me, the *atomic bomb would be certain to have a decisive influence on our relations with other countries*" (emphasis added).

216. David Holloway, "Nuclear Weapons and the Escalation of the Cold War, 1945–1962," *Cambridge History of the Cold War: Origins*, Vol. 1 (New York: Cambridge University Press, 2010), pp. 376–377.

217. John Lewis Gaddis, *We Now Know: Rethinking the Cold War* (New York: Oxford University Press, 1997), pp. 95–96.

218. Gaddis, *We Now Know: Rethinking the Cold War* (New York: Oxford University Press, 1997), p. 89.

219. David Holloway, "Nuclear Weapons and the Escalation of the Cold War, 1945–1962," *Cambridge History of the Cold War: Origins*, Vol. 1 (New York: Cambridge University Press, 2010), pp. 379–380.

220. John Lewis Gaddis, *We Now Know: Rethinking the Cold War* (New York: Oxford University Press, 1997), p. 98.

221. David Holloway, "Nuclear Weapons and the Escalation of the Cold War, 1945–1962," *Cambridge History of the Cold War: Origins*, Vol. 1 (New York: Cambridge University Press, 2010), p. 379.

222. Robert Gellately, *Stalin's Curse: Battling for Communism in War and Cold War* (New York: Knopf, 2013), p. 163.

223. John Lewis Gaddis, *We Now Know: Rethinking the Cold War* (New York: Oxford University Press, 1997), pp. 94, 99.

224. Robert Service, *Stalin: A Biography* (Cambridge, MA: Harvard University Press, 2006), p. 492: "The question was not whether Stalin would rule moderately or fiercely, but how fiercely he would rule."

225. Albert L. Weeks, *Stalin's Other War: Soviet Grand Strategy 1939–1941* (New York: Rowman and Littlefield, Inc., 2002), p. 18.

226. Weeks, *Stalin's Other War: Soviet Grand Strategy 1939–1941* (New York: Rowman and Littlefield, Inc., 2002), p. 18.

227. Andreas Hillgruber, *Germany and the Two World Wars* (Cambridge, MA: Harvard University Press, 1981), p. 82.

228. Albert L. Weeks, *Stalin's Other War: Soviet Grand Strategy 1939–1941* (New York: Rowman and Littlefield, Inc., 2002), p. 18.

229. See Colin S. Gray, "Harry S. Truman and the Forming of American Grand Strategy in the Cold War, 1945–1953," in Williamson Murray, Richard Hart Sinnreich, and James Lacey (eds.), *The Shaping of Grand Strategy: Policy, Diplomacy, and War* (New York: Cambridge University Press, 2011), p. 249.

230. Edward Luttwak, *The Grand Strategy of the Soviet Union* (New York: St. Martin's Press, 1983), p. 62.

231. Henry A. Kissinger, *Nuclear Weapons and Foreign Policy* (New York: Harper & Brothers, 1957), p. 86.

232. Kissinger, *Nuclear Weapons and Foreign Policy* (New York: Harper & Brothers, 1957), p. 233. See also p. 15: "Going all-out to defeat the enemy may lead to paralysis when total war augurs social disintegration even for the victor."

233. Kissinger, *Nuclear Weapons and Foreign Policy*, abridged edition (New York: W. W. Norton, 1969), p. 7. As Kissinger observed (abr., p. 12), "we saw it [the atomic bomb] merely as another tool in a concept of warfare which knew no goal save total victory, and no mode of war except all-out war." Subsequent citations given in this subsection's text are to the abridged edition.

234. Kissinger, *Nuclear Weapons*, p. 20.

235. Kissinger, *Nuclear Weapons*, pp. xi–xii. See also Henry A. Kissinger, "Force and Diplomacy in the Nuclear Age," *Foreign Affairs* 34, No. 3 (April 1956), pp. 349–366.

236. President Truman outlined the Truman Doctrine in an address to a joint session of Congress on March 12, 1947, when he urged an appropriation of $400 million, plus unspecified civilian and military personnel, to assist Greece and Turkey. Although the short-term goal in Greece was rebuilding after World War II, the stated goal was to prevent the communist takeover of either country. See Dennis Merrill, "The Truman Doctrine: Containing Communism and Modernity," *Presidential Studies Quarterly* 36, No. 1, *Presidential Doctrines* (March 2006), pp. 27–37; the text of the speech is at http://avalon.law.yale.edu/20th_century/trudoc.asp.

237. See Bernard Brodie, "The Weapon," in Brodie (ed.), *The Absolute Weapon: Atomic Power and World Order* (New York: Harcourt Brace, 1946), pp. 21–69.

238. See Lawrence Freedman, *The Evolution of Nuclear Strategy* (New York: St. Martin's Press, 1989), pp. 60–61.

239. Kissinger, *Nuclear Weapons*, p. vi, wrote that, given "a fear that any strong action on the part of the United States anywhere in the world may ignite a full-scale nuclear war, we find ourselves more and more reluctant to frame a strong foreign policy or implement it so as to preserve the vital interests of the free world."

240. Cf. Lawrence Freedman, *The Evolution of Nuclear Strategy* (New York: St. Martin's Press, 1989); Colin S. Gray, "Strategy in the Nuclear Age," in Williamson Murray, MacGregor Knox, and Alvin Bernstein (eds.), *The Making of Strategy: Rulers, States, and War* (New York: Cambridge University Press, 1996), pp. 579–613.

241. For arguments about this conclusion, see, See Colin S. Gray and Keith B. Payne, "Victory Is Possible," *Foreign Policy* 39 (Summer 1980), pp. 14–27.

242. Kissinger, *Nuclear Weapons*, p. 3.

243. Avi Shlaim, *The Iron Wall: Israel and the Arab World* (New York: W. W. Norton and Co., 2001), pp. 318–321.

244. See Henry A. Kissinger, *Years of Upheaval* (Boston: Little, Brown, 1982), pp. 475–511, passim.

245. Avi Shlaim, *The Iron Wall: Israel and the Arab World* (New York: W. W. Norton and Co., 2001), 321–324.

246. For the argument that it was a strategic victory (while noting that grand strategic victory was not discussed), see Zbigniew Brzezinski, "The Cold War and Its Aftermath," *Foreign Affairs* 71, No. 4 (Fall 1992), pp. 31–49.

247. Kissinger, *Nuclear Weapons*, pp. 196–198, for a discussion of catalytic nuclear war.

248. Felix Gilbert, "Machiavelli: The Renaissance of the Art of War," in Edward Mead Earle (ed.), *Makers of Modern Strategy: Military Thought from Machiavelli to Hitler* (Princeton: Princeton University Press, 1943), p. 17.

249. As a way of saying the annihilation of the enemy's military forces, this principle would be re-expressed in the twentieth century – using remarkably consistent wording – in the *Soviet Field Service Regulations* of 1936, which held that the "principal objectives of the Soviet Union" in war were "decisive victory and the complete crushing of the enemy." As quoted in Alger, *Quest for Victory*, p. 134: "In order to gain victory, it is necessary to concentrate decidedly superior forces for the main effort by a regrouping of forces and combat means."

250. See Dennis Merrill, "The Truman Doctrine: Containing Communism and Modernity," *Presidential Studies Quarterly*, Special issue *Presidential Doctrines* 36, No. 1 (March, 2006), pp. 27–37.

251. For greater detail on the historical evolution and theoretical foundations of American exceptionalism, see Torrey Taussig, *From Liberty to Liberation: The Theory and Practice of American Exceptionalism* (Thesis: the Fletcher School of Law and Diplomacy, Tufts University, 2014).

252. P. Gove, ed., *Webster's Third New International Dictionary* (Springfield, MA: Merriam-Webster Inc.), at http://www.merriam-webster.com/dictionary/ exceptionalism. Also, Ian Tyrrell, "What Is American Exceptionalism?" at www .iantyrrell.wordpress.com/papers-and-comments/. Also, Ian Tyrrell, "American Exceptionalism and Anti-Americanism," in Brendon O'Connor (ed.), *Anti-Americanism: History, Causes, and Themes*, Vol. 2: *Historical Perspectives* (Oxford: Greenwood World Publishing, 2007), pp. 99–117.

253. Ian Tyrrell, "Exceptionalism in an Age of International History," *American Historical Review* 96, No. 4 (October 1991), pp. 1031–1055, at p. 1034.

254. Chinese grand strategists speak of China's peaceful rise in the early twenty-first century, but it was America that set the precedent in the early twentieth century for rising to power without making a deliberate and calculated bid for hegemony.

7 Building Domestic Foundations of American Power: Washington to Lincoln

1. See John Charmley, *Splendid Isolation? Britain, the Balance of Power and the Origins of the First World War* (London: Faber & Faber, 2009).

2. For background on Washington, see Washington Irving, *Life of George Washington*, Vol. 1 (London: Henry G. Bohn, 1855); Joseph Ellis, *His Excellency: George Washington* (New York: Knopf, 2004); Ron Chernow, *Washington: A Life* (New York: Penguin Books, 2010); James Thomas Flexner, *Washington: The Indispensable Man* (New York: Back Bay Books, 1994).

3. Cf. Robert J. Art, *A Grand Strategy for America* (Ithaca, NY: Cornell University Press, 2004), p. 174; Felix Gilbert, *To the Farewell Address: Ideas of Early American Foreign Policy* (Princeton, NJ: Princeton University Press, 1961); Christopher Layne and Bradley A. Thayer, *American Empire: A Debate* (New York: Routledge Publishing, 2006); George F. Kennan, "On American Principles," *Foreign Affairs* 74, No. 2 (March–April, 1995), pp. 116–126.

4. Joseph Ellis, *His Excellency: George Washington* (New York: Knopf, 2004), pp. 189–190, 170; Felix Gilbert, *To the Farewell Address: Ideas of Early American Foreign Policy* (Princeton, NJ: Princeton University Press, 1961).

5. Don Higginbotham, *George Washington: Uniting a Nation* (Oxford: Rowman & Littlefield Publishers, 2004), pp. 53.

6. Joseph Ellis, *His Excellency: George Washington* (New York: Knopf, 2004), pp. 237, 140 (emphasis added).

7. Ellis, *His Excellency: George Washington* (New York: Knopf, 2004), p. 169; George Washington, *The Writings of George Washington*, Vol. 4 (New York: G. P. Putnam's Sons, 1889).

8. Williamson Murray, MacGregor Knox, and Alvin H. Bernstein, eds., *The Making of Strategy: Rulers, States, and War* (New York: Cambridge University Press, 1994), p. 208.

9. Murray, Knox, and Bernstein, eds., *The Making of Strategy: Rulers, States, and War* (New York: Cambridge University Press, 1994), p. 210. Thus, Washington truly thought in grand strategic terms about distance, time, and geography.

10. Joseph Ellis, *His Excellency: George Washington* (New York: Knopf, 2004), p. 170.

11. Ellis, *His Excellency: George Washington* (New York: Knopf, 2004), pp. 169–170.

12. James MacGregor Burns and Susan Dunn, *George Washington* (New York: Times Books, 2004), p. 79.

13. Burns and Dunn, *George Washington* (New York: Times Books, 2004), pp. 79, 82, 86.

14. Burns and Dunn *George Washington* (New York: Times Books, 2004), p. 153.

15. Walter Isaacson, ed., *Profiles in Leadership: Historians on the Elusive Quality of Greatness Profiles in Leadership* (W. W. Norton & Co Inc., 2011), p. 22.

16. Gordon S. Wood, *Empire of Liberty: A History of the Early Republic, 1789–1815* (New York; Oxford: Oxford University Press, 2011), p. 111.

17. George C. Herring, *From Colony to Superpower: U.S. Foreign Relations Since 1776* (New York: Oxford University Press, 2011), p. 57.

18. Herring, *From Colony to Superpower: U.S. Foreign Relations Since 1776* (New York: Oxford University Press, 2011), p. 50.

19. Herring, *From Colony to Superpower: U.S. Foreign Relations Since 1776* (New York: Oxford University Press, 2011), p. 57.

20. Gordon S. Wood, *Empire of Liberty: A History of the Early Republic, 1789–1815* (New York; Oxford: Oxford University Press, 2011), p. 137.

21. Wood, *Empire of Liberty: A History of the Early Republic, 1789–1815* (New York; Oxford: Oxford University Press, 2011), p. 138.

22. Wood, *Empire of Liberty: A History of the Early Republic, 1789–1815* (New York; Oxford: Oxford University Press, 2011), p. 203.

23. Quote of George Washington, in Joseph Ellis, *His Excellency: George Washington* (New York: Knopf, 2004), p. 235.

24. Ellis, *His Excellency: George Washington* (New York: Knopf, 2004), p. 223.

25. James MacGregor Burns and Susan Dunn, *George Washington* (New York: Times Books, 2004), p. 153: "To be sure, Europe was the cockpit of international affairs and the central theater in the ongoing Anglo-French struggle for global supremacy."

26. Joseph Ellis, *His Excellency: George Washington* (New York: Knopf, 2004), p. 209: "Washington regarded Europe as only a sideshow that must not divert attention from the enduring strategic interests of the United States."

27. Ellis, *His Excellency: George Washington* (New York: Knopf, 2004), p. 58: "the British government was determined to block that expansion and stifle that growth."

28. Don Higginbotham, *George Washington: Uniting a Nation* (Oxford: Rowman & Littlefield Publishers, 2004), pp. 63–64.

29. Joseph Ellis, *His Excellency: George Washington* (New York: Knopf, 2004), p. 223. Scholars write that "there is no evidence that he struggled over the decision." Cf. Edmund S. Morgan, "Slavery and Freedom: The American Paradox," *Journal of American History* 59, No. 1 (June 1972), pp. 5–29.

30. Ellis, *His Excellency: George Washington* (New York: Knopf, 2004), p. 202.

31. James MacGregor Burns and Susan Dunn, *George Washington* (New York: Times Books, 2004), p. 156. The explanation is his belief "that a public stand in favor of abolition would endanger the value he prized above all," which was a national "unity grounded in order, the stability and survival of the nation." Further, "in public Washington was silent about slavery.... Not because he was any kind of racist ... as some critics claimed."

32. For background on federalist political thought, see Jennifer Nedelsky, "Confining Democratic Politics: Anti-Federalists, Federalists, and the Constitution," *Harvard Law Review* 96, No. 1 (November 1982), pp. 340–360; Roger H. Brown, *Redeeming the Republic: Federalists, Taxation, and the Origins of the Constitution* (Baltimore: Johns Hopkins University Press, 1993); Richard A. Kohn, *Eagle and Sword: The Federalists and the Creation of the Military Establishment in America, 1783–1802* (New York: The Free Press, 1975); Dauer J. Manning, *The Adams Federalists* (Baltimore: Johns Hopkins University Press, 1968). On anti-federalist political thought, see Herbert J. Storing, *What the Anti-Federalists Were For: The Political Thought of the Opponents of the Constitution* (Chicago: University of Chicago Press, 1981); Cecelia M. Kenyon, "Men of Little Faith: The Anti-Federalists on the Nature of Representative Government," *The William and Mary Quarterly*, Third Series, 12, No. 1 (January 1955), pp. 3–43.

33. For background on Jefferson, see Sean Wilentz, *The Rise of American Democracy: Jefferson to Lincoln* (New York: W. W. Norton, 2005); Gordon S. Wood, *Empire of Liberty: A History of the Early Republic 1789–1815* (New York: Oxford University Press, 2009); Gilbert Chinard, *Thomas Jefferson: The Apostle of Americanism* (The Floating Press, 2011); E. M. Halliday, *Understanding Thomas Jefferson* (New York: HarperCollins Publishers, 2001); Fawn M. Brodie, *Thomas Jefferson: An Intimate History* (New York: W. W. Norton, 2010); Stephen E. Ambrose, *Undaunted Courage: Meriwether Lewis, Thomas Jefferson, and the Opening of the American West* (New York: Simon & Schuster, 1996).

34. It was formally the Democratic-Republic Party, but contemporaries referred to its members as "Republicans."

35. Gordon S. Wood, *Empire of Liberty: A History of the Early Republic 1789–1815* (New York: Oxford University Press, 2009), pp. 535, 167.

36. Walter Russell Mead, *Special Providence: American Foreign Policy and How It Changed the World* (New York: Knopf, 2001), pp. 177–178.

37. Gordon S. Wood, *Empire of Liberty: A History of the Early Republic 1789–1815* (New York: Oxford University Press, 2009), p. 172.

38. Wood, *Empire of Liberty: A History of the Early Republic 1789–1815* (New York: Oxford University Press, 2009), p. 298. Debt was "the major means by which nations carried on war, something they [Jefferson and Madison] wished to avoid," and Jefferson routinely "called for further reductions in the debt."

39. For scholarship on the American civil-military relationship, see the seminal work, Samuel P. Huntington, *The Soldier and the State: The Theory and Politics of Civil-Military Relations* (Cambridge, MA: Harvard University Press, 1957). Also, see Eliot Cohen, *Supreme Command: Soldiers, Statesmen, and Leadership in Wartime* (New York: The Free Press, 2002); Richard A. Kohn, *Eagle and Sword: The Federalists and the Creation of the Military Establishment in America, 1783–1802* (New York: The Free Press, 1975); Peter D. Feaver, *Armed Servants: Agency, Oversight, and Civil-Military Relations* (Cambridge, MA: Harvard University Press: 2003).

40. Gordon S. Wood, *Empire of Liberty: A History of the Early Republic 1789–1815* (New York: Oxford University Press, 2009), p. 292: "Because the officer corps of the army was Federalist-dominated, it needed to be radically reformed ..."

41. Sean Wilentz, *The Rise of American Democracy: Jefferson to Lincoln* (New York: W. W. Norton, 2005), p. 129. "The real threat the conspiracy [of Vice President Andrew Burr] posed to American democracy concerned the uncertain political allegiances of the nation's military leadership."

42. Peter Maslowski, "To the Edge of Greatness: The United States, 1783–1865," in Williamson Murray, MacGregor Knox, and Alvin Bernstein (eds.), *The Making of Strategy: Rulers, States, and War* (New York: Cambridge University Press, 1994), p. 221.

43. Robert Kagan, *Dangerous Nation: America's Foreign Policy from Its Earliest Days to the Dawn of the Twentieth Century* (New York: Knopf, 2006), p. 201, or what Kagan called "differing aspirations for the development of America's political economy."

44. Sean Wilentz, *The Rise of American Democracy: Jefferson to Lincoln* (New York: W. W. Norton, 2005), p. 130.

45. Wilentz, *The Rise of American Democracy: Jefferson to Lincoln* (New York: W. W. Norton, 2005), p. 126: "and to avoid replication of the British system that he abhorred."

46. Gordon S. Wood, *Empire of Liberty: A History of the Early Republic 1789–1815* (New York: Oxford University Press, 2009), pp. 176, 179, 181: "That nation, Great Britain, he said in 1789, 'has moved heaven, earth and hell to exterminate us in war, has insulted us in all her councils in peace, shut her doors to us in every port where her interests would admit it, libeled us in foreign nations, [and] endeavored to poison them against the reception of our most precious commodities.'" Further, Great Britain was "the only nation on earth who wished us ill from the bottom of their souls." As Wood, p. 181, notes, some scholars believe "Jefferson seems to have generated his identity as an American from his hatred of England."

47. Sean Wilentz, *The Rise of American Democracy: Jefferson to Lincoln* (New York: W. W. Norton, 2005), p. 131.

48. Gordon S. Wood, *Empire of Liberty: A History of the Early Republic 1789–1815* (New York: Oxford University Press, 2009), p. 654.

49. Sean Wilentz, *The Rise of American Democracy: Jefferson to Lincoln* (New York: W. W. Norton, 2005), pp. 131–132: "The embargo was certainly a role of the dice ..." Also, "By embracing neutrality, Jefferson and Madison thought they could counter the duke of Portland's Tory ministry by influencing British as well as American public opinion ..."

50. Gordon S. Wood, *Empire of Liberty: A History of the Early Republic 1789–1815* (New York: Oxford University Press, 2009), p. 656. As an example of the economic pain from the embargo, in its first year, "the Massachusetts fleet, which comprised nearly 40 percent of the nation's tonnage, lost over $15 million in freight revenues alone, a sum equal to the entire income of the federal government in 1806."

51. Wood, *Empire of Liberty: A History of the Early Republic 1789–1815* (New York: Oxford University Press, 2009), p. 657. Jefferson and Madison saw this as "a great opportunity to teach the world a new way of dealing with international conflicts ..."

52. For background, see Frank Lambert, *The Barbary Wars: American Independence in the Atlantic World* (New York: Hill and Wang, 2005).

53. Robert Kagan, *Dangerous Nation* (New York: Knopf, 2006), p. 97. "Insurance rates for Mediterranean voyages soared; profits disappeared; merchants and sailors were seized, enslaved, and physically abused by their captors."

54. Kagan, *Dangerous Nation* (New York: Knopf, 2006), pp. 99–100.

55. Kagan, *Dangerous Nation* (New York: Knopf, 2006), p. 134.

56. Sean Wilentz, *The Rise of American Democracy: Jefferson to Lincoln* (New York: W. W. Norton, 2005), pp. 109–110: "the Louisiana Purchase was the result of many factors and the work of many people, including the ex-slaves of Saint Domingue. Conquering the island for France and reinstating slavery proved [difficult] in part because of the locals' continued armed resistance and in part because an outbreak of yellow fever began killing off the French invaders by the hundreds ..."

57. Robert Kagan, *Dangerous Nation* (New York: Knopf, 2006), p. 134: "When Napoleon ultimately decided to abandon his plans for a North American empire and to sell Louisiana to the United States, part of the reason was the disastrous conquest of the island of Santo Domingo, where thousands of French soldiers fell to yellow fever." As Kagan writes, Napoleon's "fear that the American people would not long tolerate foreign control of Louisiana influenced his thinking."

58. Gordon S. Wood, *Empire of Liberty: A History of the Early Republic 1789–1815* (New York: Oxford University Press, 2009), p. 369.

59. Wood, *Empire of Liberty: A History of the Early Republic 1789–1815* (New York: Oxford University Press, 2009), p. 357: Jefferson was "a firm believer in what might be called demographic imperialism ... [in order to create] what he referred to more than once as an 'empire of liberty.' In looking to the future, Jefferson arguably believed that expanding toward the West would allow the United States to "redeem ... itself if its Eastern [urban] sections should ever become corrupt."

60. Robert Kagan, *Dangerous Nation* (New York: Knopf, 2006), pp. 131–132: "When Jefferson took office, most of Tennessee was in the hands of the Cherokees and Creeks. Creeks, Choctaws, and Chickasaws occupied nearly all of the future states

of Mississippi and Alabama. What would later become Florida was mostly in the hands of Seminoles. And in the West, Indians occupied substantial portions of what would later be the states of Indiana, Illinois, Arkansas, and Missouri."

61. Gordon S. Wood, *Empire of Liberty: A History of the Early Republic 1789–1815* (New York: Oxford University Press, 2009), p. 397. For Jefferson, the Native American populations "were 'becoming more and more sensible of the superiority of this dependence [on husbandry] for clothing and subsistence over the precarious resources of hunting and fishing.'"

62. Sean Wilentz, *The Rise of American Democracy: Jefferson to Lincoln* (New York: W. W. Norton, 2005), p. 87: "Since the Revolution, when the British had offered freedom to rebellious slaves, the possibility of some sort of slave uprising had loomed as all too real to southern slaveholders. Here and there, after American independence, runaway slaves managed to escape recapture and establish their own maroon communities, a potential threat to local stability." As Wilentz writes, of even greater concern "was the revolutionary example of Saint Domingue (present-day Haiti), where slaves and free blacks overthrew and massacred much of the resident French planter elite in 1791, and then established ... the first black controlled country in the free world."

63. Gordon S. Wood, *Empire of Liberty: A History of the Early Republic 1789–1815* (New York: Oxford University Press, 2009), p. 165: "The Southern states held well over 90 percent of the country's slaves. They served their masters' every need, from making hogshead and horseshoes to caring for gardens and children. The planters' reliance on the labor of their slaves inhibited the growth of large middling groups of white artisans, who were increasingly emerging in the Northern states."

64. Sean Wilentz, *The Rise of American Democracy: Jefferson to Lincoln* (New York: W. W. Norton, 2005), p. 136.

65. Gordon S. Wood, *Empire of Liberty: A History of the Early Republic 1789–1815* (New York: Oxford University Press, 2009), p. 541: "Anyone who talked about emancipating the black slave was confronted with the problem of what to do with the freedmen." For Jefferson, "Deep rooted prejudices entertained by the white; ten thousand recollections, by the blacks, of the injuries they have sustained ... will produce convulsions which will probably never end but in the extermination of the one or the other race."

66. Sean Wilentz, *The Rise of American Democracy: Jefferson to Lincoln* (New York: W. W. Norton, 2005), pp. 136–137: "If he became maddeningly circumspect about slavery, with the fear of black insurrection always in the back of his mind – and, with respect to Saint Domingue, on the front of his mind – Jefferson always considered racial bondage a threat to white liberty and equality, contrary to the growing view among slaveholders that slavery made white equality possible ..."

67. Wilentz, *The Rise of American Democracy: Jefferson to Lincoln* (New York: W. W. Norton, 2005), pp. 135–136: "Historians have accused Jefferson of betraying his principles once he reached office by expanding federal power and outfederalizing the Federalists, chiefly through the Louisiana Purchase and the embargo ..." Further, "Some have contended that Jefferson was a hypocrite who vaunted human equality and at the same time dispossessed Indians, owned slaves (and sired children with one of them), did nothing to benefit free blacks (while himself

benefiting politically from extra representation and electoral votes given the slave South), and held what have become distasteful views about women." For another example of his hypocrisy, see Gordon S. Wood, *Empire of Liberty: A History of the Early Republic 1789–1815* (New York: Oxford University Press, 2009), p. 539: One example of Jefferson's hypocrisy is his belief that "all men are created equal" despite, as Wood writes, his "suspicion only, that the blacks, whether originally a distinct race, or made distinct by time and circumstances, are inferior to the whites in endowments both of body and mind."

68. For background on Madison, see Ralph Louis Ketcham, *James Madison: A Biography* (New York: Macmillan, 1971); Lance Banning, *The Sacred Fire of Liberty: James Madison and the Founding of the Federal Republic* (Ithaca, NY: Cornell University Press, 1995); Alexander Hamilton, James Madison, and John Jay, *The Federalist Papers* (New York: Oxford University Press, 2008); Drew R. McCoy, *The Last of the Fathers: James Madison and the Republican Legacy* (New York: Cambridge University Press, 1989).

69. As Frank A. Updyke, *The Diplomacy of the War of 1812* (Baltimore: Johns Hopkins University Press, 1915), p. 1, observed, "The fundamental cause of the War of 1812 was the irreconcilable conflict of the British navigation acts with the commercial development of the United States."

70. See H. M. Brackenridge, *History of the Late War between the United States and Great Britain* (Philadelphia: James Kay, Jun., & Brother, 1844), p. 13, who argued that, "With the acknowledgement of our independence, Great Britain did not renounce her designs of subjugation. Force had been found unavailing, she next resolved to try what might be done by insidious means." For other sources on the causes of the War of 1812, see J. C. A. Stagg, *Mr. Madison's War: Politics, Diplomacy, and Warfare in the Early American Republic, 1783–1830* (Princeton, NJ: Princeton University Press, 1983), pp. ix–xii, 3–47; Reginald Horsman, *The Causes of The War of 1812* (Philadelphia: University of Pennsylvania Press, 1962), p. 263.

71. For Madison on grand strategy, see James Madison, *The Complete Madison: His Basic Writings* (New York: John Wiley & Sons, 1953); Gaillard Hunt, ed., *The Writings of James Madison: 1769–1783* (New York: G. P. Putnam's Sons, 1900); Donald R. Hickey, *The War of 1812: A Forgotten Conflict* (Urbana: University of Illinois Press, 1989); Bradford Perkins, *Prologue to War: England and the United States, 1805–1812* (Oakland, CA: University of California Press, 1961).

72. See Donald R. Hickey, *The War of 1812: A Forgotten Conflict* (Urbana: University of Illinois Press, 1989), p. 301; Jeremy Black, *America as a Military Power: From the American Revolution to the Civil War* (Westport, CT: Praeger, 2002), pp. 39–74; Bradford Perkins, *Prologue to War: England and the United States, 1805–1812* (Oakland, CA: University of California Press, 1961); Harry L. Coles, *The War of 1812* (Chicago: University of Chicago Press, 1965); Reginald Horsman, *The War of 1812* (New York: Alfred A. Knopf, 1969); J. C. A. Stagg, *Mr. Madison's War: Politics, Diplomacy, and Warfare in the Early American Republic, 1783–1830* (Princeton, NJ: Princeton University Press, 1983). See also Thomas A. Bailey, *A Diplomatic History of the American People*, 9th ed. (Englewood Cliffs, NJ: Prentice Hall, 1974), pp. 131–162.

73. See "Madison's War Message, June 1, 1812, Washington," in Kate Caffrey, *The Twilight's Last Gleaming: Britain vs. America, 1812–1815* (New York: Stein & Day, 1977), pp. 310–313.

74. Harry L. Coles, *The War of 1812* (Chicago: University of Chicago Press, 1965), pp. 23–25.

75. See Stagg, *Mr. Madison's War*, p. 3. "The risks involved in discarding the cautious neutrality pursued by successive American administrations since 1789 were undeniably great. The United States was a barely stable republic, untested by the strains of war."

76. Donald R. Hickey, *The War of 1812: A Forgotten Conflict* (Urbana: University of Illinois Press, 1989), p. 302. In terms of military forces, the number of American troops involved in the war was 130,000, which includes total militia forces of 458,000.

77. *Annals of Congress*, 3rd Cong., 1st sess. (January 14, 1794), quoted in Stanley Elkins and Eric McKitrick, *The Age of Federalism: The Early American Republic, 1788–1800* (New York: Oxford University Press, 1993), p. 375. Excerpt in Robert Kagan, *Dangerous Nation* (New York: Vintage Books, 2007), p. 107.

78. Elkins and McKitrick, *Age of Federalism*, p. 128. Quoted in Robert Kagan, *Dangerous Nation* (New York: Vintage Books, 2007), p. 107.

79. Robert Kagan, *Dangerous Nation* (New York: Vintage Books, 2007), p. 35.

80. Kagan, *Dangerous Nation* (New York: Vintage Books, 2007), p. 143.

81. Quoted in William Earl Weeks, *John Quincy Adams and American Global Empire* (Lexington: University Press of Kentucky, 1992), p. 109. Cf. Robert Kagan, *Dangerous Nation* (New York: Vintage Books, 2007), p. 148.

82. Robert Kagan, *Dangerous Nation* (New York: Vintage Books, 2007), p. 144.

83. Kagan, *Dangerous Nation* (New York: Vintage Books, 2007), p. 72.

84. Kagan, *Dangerous Nation* (New York: Vintage Books, 2007), pp. 144–145.

85. Tecumseh was later commissioned as a British army general. He was killed in the Battle of the Thames, near Detroit, in 1813. See Eric Foner, *Give Me Liberty! An American History*, Vol. 1 (New York: W. W. Norton & Co., 2011), p. 313.

86. Eric Foner, *Give Me Liberty! An American History*, Vol. 1 (New York: W. W. Norton & Co., 2011), pp. 309–310.

87. John K. Mahon, *The War of 1812* (Gainesville, FL: Da Capo Press, 1972), pp. 25–26.

88. Irving Brant, *The Fourth President: A Life of James Madison* (London: Eyre & Spottiswoode, 1969), pp. 473, 500.

89. See "Madison's War Message, June 1, 1812, Washington," in Kate Caffrey, *The Twilight's Last Gleaming: Britain vs. America, 1812–1815* (New York: Stein & Day, 1977), pp. 310–313.

90. Donald R. Hickey, *The War of 1812: A Forgotten Conflict* (Urbana: University of Illinois Press, 1989), p. 303: "Indeed, these issues [failure to achieve 'maritime goals'] were not even mentioned in the peace treaty, which merely provided for restoring all conquered territory and returning to the *status quo ante bellum*." The text of the treaty is available from the Library of Congress at www.memory.loc.gov/cgi-bin/ampage?collId=llsl&fileName=008/llsl008.db&recNum=231.

91. See Robert Kagan, *Dangerous Nation* (New York: Vintage Books, 2007), p. 147: "The requirements of fighting the war expanded the role of the federal government and exposed deficiencies in the operation of federal power under the old Jeffersonian Republican scheme – much as the Revolutionary War had pointed to the deficiencies of the Articles of Confederation." With the end of the war in 1815, there were "calls for augmented national powers even from Republicans." In political terms, James Madison, who was "Jefferson's staunch colleague in the struggle against Hamiltonian policies in the 1790s, now all but embraced the Hamiltonian system." Madison's "Republican administration called for . . . a new national bank, . . . federal monies to encourage the building of roads and canals, and proposed moderate tariff protection for domestic manufactures."

92. Kagan, *Dangerous Nation* (New York: Vintage Books, 2007), pp. 147–148.

93. Quoted in Reginald C. Stuart, *War and American Thought: From the Revolution to the Monroe Doctrine* (Kent, OH: Kent State University Press, 1982), p. 155. Cf. Robert Kagan, *Dangerous Nation* (New York: Vintage Books, 2007), p. 152.

94. Frank A. Updyke, *The Diplomacy of the War of 1812* (Baltimore: Johns Hopkins University Press, 1915) p. 437), argued that this interpretation is "true if one looks to the [Ghent] treaty of peace alone to discover results, for the treaty contains not a word as to the settlement of the avowed causes of the war."

95. For background on Monroe, see Harry Ammon, *James Monroe: The Quest for National Identity* (Virginia: University of Virginia Press, 1990); George Morgan, *The Life of James Monroe* (Kila, MT: Kessinger Publishing, 2006); Fred I. Greenstein, "The Political Competence of James Monroe," *Inventing the Job of President: Leadership Style from George Washington to Andrew Jackson* (Princeton, NJ: Princeton University Press, 2009), pp. 63–74; Harlow G. Unger, *The Last Founding Father: James Monroe and a Nation's Call to Greatness* (Philadelphia: Da Capo Press, 2009).

96. On Monroe's grand strategy, see Kinley J. Brauer, "The United States and British Imperial Expansion, 1815–60," *Diplomatic History* 12, No. 1 (1988), pp. 19–37; Walter Russell Mead, "American Grand Strategy in a World at Risk," *Orbis* 49, No. 4 (Autumn 2005), pp. 589–598; Dexter Perkins, *The Monroe Doctrine, 1867–1907*, Vol. 3 (Baltimore, MD: Johns Hopkins Press, 1937); Albert H. Bowman, "Jefferson, Hamilton and American Foreign Policy," *Political Science Quarterly* 71, No. 1 (March 1956), pp. 18–41; Gaddis Smith, *The Last Years of the Monroe Doctrine, 1945–1993* (New York: Macmillan, 1995); Mark T. Gilderhus, "The Monroe Doctrine: Meanings and Implications," *Presidential Studies Quarterly* 36, No. 1 (March 2006), pp. 5–16; Worthington Chauncey Ford, "John Quincy Adams and the Monroe Doctrine," *American Historical Review* 8, No. 1 (October 1902), pp. 28–52; Charles E. Hughes, "Observations on the Monroe Doctrine," *American Journal of International Law* 17, No. 4 (October 1923), pp. 611–628.

97. Robert Kagan, *Dangerous Nation* (New York: Vintage Books, 2007), p. 154.

98. Kagan, *Dangerous Nation* (New York: Vintage Books, 2007), p. 167. Perhaps his hope was to call "the New World into existence to redress the balance of the Old."

99. John Lewis Gaddis, *Surprise, Security, and the American Experience* (Cambridge, MA: Harvard University Press, 2004), p. 23.

100. Robert Kagan, *Dangerous Nation* (New York: Vintage Books, 2007), p. 172.

101. Kagan, *Dangerous Nation* (New York: Vintage Books, 2007), p. 263.

102. Excerpted in Walter LaFeber, ed., *John Quincy Adams and Continental Empire: Letters, Papers, and Speeches* (Chicago: Quadrangle Books, 1965), p. 112. Quoted in Robert Kagan, *Dangerous Nation* (New York: Vintage Books, 2007), p. 175.

103. Robert W. Tucker, and David C. Hendrickson, *Empire of Liberty: The Statecraft of Thomas Jefferson* (New York: Oxford University Press, 1990), p. 238.

104. Robert Kagan, *Dangerous Nation* (New York: Vintage Books, 2007), pp. 307–308. Also, "In the 1820s Monroe and Clay had set out to establish a Pan-American 'family of nations,' a 'good neighborhood' among the 'sister republics' of the Western Hemisphere."

105. See Kagan, *Dangerous Nation* (New York: Vintage Books, 2007), p. 131. "If possible, they would civilize those who stood in the way. If necessary, they would remove them. But either way the land would be taken and settled." However, "In the end, the 'lust for dominion' . . . doomed Indian civilization on the continent."

106. William Earl Weeks, *John Quincy Adams and American Global Empire* (Lexington: University Press of Kentucky, 1992), p. 109. Quoted in Robert Kagan, *Dangerous Nation* (New York: Vintage Books, 2007), p. 136. What Monroe likely understood was that "Great interests are at issue. . . . This is not a time for repose . . . until our cause is carried triumphantly thro'. Jackson's triumph was swift, and Pensacola fell."

107. Stuart Gerry Brown, ed., *The Autobiography of James Monroe* (Syracuse, NY: Syracuse University Press, 1959), p. 215.

108. John Lewis Gaddis, *Surprise, Security, and the American Experience* (Cambridge, MA: Harvard University Press, 2004), p. 27.

109. Gaddis, *Surprise, Security, and the American Experience* (Cambridge, MA: Harvard University Press, 2004), p. 15, rightly considers John Quincy Adams as perhaps "the most influential American grand strategist of the nineteenth century."

110. Robert Kagan, *Dangerous Nation* (New York: Vintage Books, 2007), pp. 137–139.

111. James Monroe to Jefferson (May 1820), quoted in William Earle Weeks, *John Quincy Adams and American Global Empire* (Lexington: University Press of Kentucky, 1992), pp. 167–168.

112. James Monroe to Jefferson (May 1820), quoted in William Earle Weeks, *John Quincy Adams and American Global Empire* (Lexington: University Press of Kentucky, 1992), pp. 167–168. Excerpt from Robert Kagan, *Dangerous Nation* (New York: Vintage Books, 2007), p. 201.

113. John Lewis Gaddis, *Surprise, Security, and the American Experience* (Cambridge, MA: Harvard University Press, 2004), p. 19.

114. Robert Kagan, *Dangerous Nation* (New York: Vintage Books, 2007), p. 205: "Coming on the heels of the Missouri crisis, Monroe's December 1823 message had struck many southerners as fraught with risks."

115. Kagan, *Dangerous Nation* (New York: Vintage Books, 2007), p. 206.

116. For background on Jackson, see Marquis James, *Andrew Jackson: Portrait of a President* (New York: Grosset & Dunlap, 1937); Robert V. Remini, *The Life of Andrew Jackson* (New York: HarperCollins, 1988); Jon Meacham, *American Lion: Andrew Jackson in the White House* (New York: Random House, 2009);

H. W. Brands, *Andrew Jackson: His Life and Times* (New York: Doubleday, 2005); Andrew Burstein, *The Passions of Andrew Jackson* (New York: Random House, 2007); Fred I. Greenstein, "Andrew Jackson: Force of Nature," *Inventing the Job of President: Leadership Style from George Washington to Andrew Jackson* (Princeton, NJ: Princeton University Press, 2009), pp. 85–95; John C. Yoo, "Andrew Jackson and Presidential Power," *Charleston Law Review* 2 (2008), p. 521.

117. On Jackson's grand strategy, see Anthony Wallace, *The Long, Bitter Trail: Andrew Jackson and the Indians* (New York: Hill & Wang, 1993); Donald B. Cole, *The Presidency of Andrew Jackson* (Lawrence: University Press of Kansas, 1993); Robert Kagan, *Dangerous Nation: America's Foreign Policy from Its Earliest Days to the Dawn of the Twentieth Century* (New York: Knopf, 2006); Walter Russell Mead, *Special Providence: American Foreign Policy and How It Changed the World* (New York: Knopf, 2001), pp. 97–102.

118. Robert Kagan, *Dangerous Nation* (New York: Knopf, 2006), p. 203.

119. Robert W. Merry, *A Country of Vast Designs: James K. Polk, the Mexican War, and the Conquest of the American Continent* (New York: Simon & Schuster, 2009), p. 31. As Jackson forcefully argued, "The people . . . had a right to expect a 'prudent system of expenditure' that would allow the government to 'pay the debts of the union and authorize the reduction of every tax to as low a point as . . . our national safety and independence will allow.'"

120. Merry, *A Country of Vast Designs: James K. Polk, the Mexican War, and the Conquest of the American Continent* (New York: Simon & Schuster, 2009), pp. 31–32: "The president feared that such power in the hands of federal officials would lead inevitably to 'a corrupting influence upon the elections' by giving people a sense that their votes could purchase beneficial governmental actions to 'make navigable their neighboring creek or river, bring commerce to their doors, and increase the value of their property.' This, he said in a series of 'notes' on the issue, would prove 'fatal to just legislation' and the 'purity of public men.'"

121. Gordon S. Wood, *Empire of Liberty: A History of the Early Republic 1789–1815* (New York: Oxford University Press, 2009), p. 294: "The BUS was semi-official, chartered by Congress in 1826. Of its $35 million in capital, one-fifth was put up by the government." Further, "The only real money, of course was specie or gold and silver. But since there was never enough specie and it was unwieldy to carry, the banks issued pieces of paper (that is, made loans) in their own names, promising to pay gold and silver to the bearer on demand. Yet most people, confident that the bank could redeem their notes at any time, did not bother to have them redeemed and instead passed the notes on to one another in commercial exchanges. The banks soon realized they could lend out two, three, four, or five times in paper notes the amount of gold and silver they had in their vaults to cover these notes. Since the banks made money from these loans, they had a vested interest in issuing as many notes as they could."

122. Wood, *Empire of Liberty: A History of the Early Republic 1789–1815* (New York: Oxford University Press, 2009), p. 294: "In 1792 Jefferson was so angry at Hamilton that he told Madison that the federal government's chartering of the BUS, which it had no right to do, was 'an act of *treason*' against the states, and anyone who tried to 'act under colour of the authority of a foreign legislature' (that is, the federal

Congress) and issue and pass notes ought to be 'adjudged guilty of high treason and suffer death accordingly, by the judgment of the state courts.'"

123. Harry L. Watson, "Old Hickory's Democracy," *Wilson Quarterly* 9, No. 4 (Autumn 1985), p. 124: "In Jackson's day, the government issued no national paper currency, and there was no Federal Reserve System (it was not created until 1913)."

124. Robert W. Merry, *A Country of Vast Designs: James K. Polk, the Mexican War, and the Conquest of the American Continent* (New York: Simon & Schuster, 2009), p. 36. As Merry argues, "Jackson's veto message portrayed the bank as a government-sponsored monopoly that employed the money of taxpayers to enhance the power, privileges, and wealth of a very few Americans and foreigners – 'chiefly the richest class' – who owned stock in the bank."

125. Robert Kagan, *Dangerous Nation* (New York: Knopf, 2006), p. 341.

126. Kagan, *Dangerous Nation* (New York: Knopf, 2006), p. 213.

127. John M. Belohlavek, "Let the Eagle Soar! Democratic Constraints on the Foreign Policy of Andrew Jackson," *Presidential Studies Quarterly* 10, No. 1 (Winter 1980), p. 45: "The Tennessean long envisioned the Southwest as a part of the United States ..." Further, "For a period of almost seven years, Jackson, through his representatives, attempted the purchase of a Mexican province without consulting his cabinet, Congress or without waging a campaign in the press for its acquisition."

128. Belohlavek, "Let the Eagle Soar! Democratic Constraints on the Foreign Policy of Andrew Jackson." *Presidential Studies Quarterly* 10, No. 1 (Winter 1980), p. 45.

129. Belohlavek, "Let the Eagle Soar! Democratic Constraints on the Foreign Policy of Andrew Jackson," *Presidential Studies Quarterly* 10, No. 1 (Winter 1980), p. 46: "The unpleasant alternative was Texas commercial and financial reliance upon Great Britain ..."

130. On Jackson's policies toward native Americans, see Robert V. Remini, *The Legacy of Andrew Jackson: Essays on Democracy, Indian Removal, and Slavery* (Baton Rouge: Louisiana State University Press, 1988); F. P. Prucha, "Andrew Jackson's Indian Policy: A Reassessment," *Journal of American History* 56, No. 3 (December 1969), pp. 527–539; James M. McClurken, "Ottawa Adaptive Strategies to Indian Removal," *Michigan Historical Review* 12, No. 1 (Spring 1986), pp. 29–55: Alfred A. Cave, "Abuse of Power: Andrew Jackson and the Indian Removal Act of 1830," *Historian* 65, No. 6 (December 2003), pp. 1330–1353; Helen Hunt Jackson, Henry Benjamin Whipple, and Julius Hawley Seelye, *A Century of Dishonor: A Sketch of the United States Government's Dealings with Some of the Indian Tribes* (Boston: Roberts Brothers, 1890).

131. Sean Wilentz, *The Rise of American Democracy: Jefferson to Lincoln* (New York: W. W. Norton, 2005), pp. 323–325. For the United States to accept the claims of the Cherokees would, for Jackson, "violate that clause, giving Congress the illegitimate power to dismember a state while imposing a burden on Georgia and Alabama that other states did not bear." The decision to grant "tribal sovereignty would establish both congressional powers and an Indian *imperium in imperio*, which would threaten the integrity of the nation."

132. Wilentz, *The Rise of American Democracy: Jefferson to Lincoln* (New York: W. W. Norton, 2005), p. 327.

133. Wilentz, *The Rise of American Democracy: Jefferson to Lincoln* (New York: W. W. Norton, 2005), p. 425.

134. Wilentz, *The Rise of American Democracy: Jefferson to Lincoln* (New York: W. W. Norton, 2005), p. 323.

135. Robert W. Merry, *A Country of Vast Designs: James K. Polk, the Mexican War, and the Conquest of the American Continent* (New York: Simon & Schuster, 2009), p. 28: "any candidate who could reach these new voters could blow away the opposition," a political fact that "Jackson understood ... [while] Adams and Clay missed it."

136. Walter Russell Mead, "The Tea Party and American Foreign Policy: What Populism Means for Globalism," *Foreign Affairs* 90, No. 2 (March/April 2011), p. 33: "Antiestablishment populism has been responsible for some of the brightest, as well as some of the darkest, moments in U.S. history."

137. Robert Kagan, *Dangerous Nation* (New York: Knopf, 2006), p. 211.

138. Walter Russell Mead, *Special Providence: American Foreign Policy and How It Changed the World* (New York: Knopf, 2001), pp. 259–260: "... to anticipate the course of American policy it is important to understand the structure of Jacksonian beliefs and values."

139. For background on Polk, see Eugene Irving McCormac, *James K. Polk: A Political Biography* (Berkeley: University of California Press, 1922); Robert W. Merry, *A Country of Vast Designs: James K. Polk, the Mexican War and the Conquest of the American Continent* (New York: Simon & Schuster, 2009); Powell Moore, "James K. Polk: Tennessee Politician," *Journal of Southern History* 17, No. 4 (November 1951), pp. 493–516; Thomas M. Leonard, *James K. Polk: A Clear and Unquestionable Destiny* (Wilmington, DE: Scholarly Resources, 2001); Walter R. Borneman, *Polk: The Man Who Transformed the Presidency and America* (New York: Random House, 2008); John C. Pinheiro, *Manifest Ambition: James K. Polk and Civil-Military Relations during the Mexican War* (Westport, CT: Praeger, 2007); Fred I. Greenstein, "The Policy-Driven Leadership of James K. Polk: Making the Most of a Weak Presidency," *Presidential Studies Quarterly* 40, No. 4 (December 2010), pp. 725–733.

140. On Polk's grand strategy, see Walter Russell Mead, "American Grand Strategy in a World at Risk," *Orbis* 49, No. 4 (2005), pp. 589–598; Robert W. Merry, *A Country of Vast Designs: James K. Polk, the Mexican War and the Conquest of the American Continent* (New York: Simon & Schuster, 2009); John Seigenthaler, *James K. Polk: The American Presidents Series: The 11th President, 1845–1849* (New York: Times Books, 2003); Thomas M. Leonard, *James K. Polk: A Clear and Unquestionable Destiny* (Wilmington, DE: Scholarly Resources, 2001).

141. Robert W. Merry, *A Country of Vast Designs: James K. Polk, the Mexican War, and the Conquest of the American Continent* (New York: Simon & Schuster, 2009), p. 131.

142. Robert Kagan, *Dangerous Nation* (New York: Knopf, 2006), p. 224. Cf. Arthur Schlesinger Jr., "The American Empire? Not So Fast," *World Policy Journal* 22, No. 1 (Spring 2005), pp. 43–46; Thomas M. Leonard, *James K. Polk: A Clear and Unquestionable Destiny* (Wilmington, DE: Scholarly Resources, 2001).

143. Kagan, *Dangerous Nation* (New York: Knopf, 2006), pp. 224–225: "Although a southerner from Tennessee and the owner of more than one hundred slaves . . .," this was seen as "an ambitious continental agenda that appeared to serve national rather than sectional interests."

144. John Lewis Gaddis, *Surprise, Security, and the American Experience* (Cambridge, MA: Harvard University Press, 2004), pp. 18–19: "Now even the prospect of power vacuums invited preemption," and "the doctrine of preemption also came, in time, to justify expansion at the expense of states that might fail."

145. See James Knox Polk, Inaugural Address, March 4, 1845, at www.rohan.sdsu.edu/dept/polsciwb/brianl/docs/1845JamesPolkInauguralAddress.pdf.

146. Robert W. Merry, *A Country of Vast Designs: James K. Polk, the Mexican War, and the Conquest of the American Continent* (New York: Simon & Schuster, 2009), pp. 168–171.

147. Merry, *A Country of Vast Designs: James K. Polk, the Mexican War, and the Conquest of the American Continent* (New York: Simon & Schuster, 2009), p. 171–173, 236: "For good measure, the British government ordered the Admiralty to keep frigates in the vicinity of Oregon and asked the Colonial Office to assess the country's military prospects in Oregon should war break out."

148. Merry, *A Country of Vast Designs: James K. Polk, the Mexican War, and the Conquest of the American Continent* (New York: Simon & Schuster, 2009), pp. 180: "The German scientist Alexander von Humboldt, after travelling through Mexico in 1803, called it 'the country of inequality. Nowhere does there exist such a fearful difference in the distribution of fortune, civilization, cultivation of the soil and population.'" However, "American citizens who had ventured in or near Mexico had experienced abuses at the hands of Mexican officials and citizens . . . U.S. ships were seized in Mexican ports by government officials . . . U.S. businessmen operating in the fledgling republic were abducted and impressed into servitude or thrown into jails without benefit of jurisprudence" (p. 184).

149. Merry, *A Country of Vast Designs: James K. Polk, the Mexican War, and the Conquest of the American Continent* (New York: Simon & Schuster, 2009), pp. 186–187: "No doubt Polk had this in mind when he listed the acquisition of California among his top four presidential goals. A grant of rich Mexican territory could serve as a tidy bit of recompense for those American claims, with the U.S. government then paying off the claimants in cash."

150. Peter Maslowski, "To the Edge of Greatness: The United States, 1783–1865," in Williamson Murray, MacGregor Knox, and Alvin Bernstein (eds.), *The Making of Strategy: Rulers, States, and War* (New York: Cambridge University Press, 1994), p. 230.

151. Walter A. McDougall, "The Constitutional History of U.S. Foreign Policy: 222 Years of Tension in the Twilight Zone," *Foreign Policy Research Institute*, September 2010, p. 13: "President James K. Polk, a Tennessee Jacksonian known as 'Young Hickory,' meant to take California by force lest the British navy plant the Union Jack there first."

152. McDougall, "The Constitutional History of U.S. Foreign Policy: 222 Years of Tension in the Twilight Zone," *Foreign Policy Research Institute*, September 2010,

p. 13: "In 1846, when Mexican soldiers contested General Zachary Taylor's advance to the Rio Grande, Polk had his *casus belli*. Claiming 'American blood has been spilled on American soil,' Democrats closed off debate over a declaration of war, and Whigs dared not protest lest they suffer the fate of the Federalist Party that had opposed war in 1812."

153. Peter Maslowski, "To the Edge of Greatness: The United States, 1783–1865," in Williamson Murray, MacGregor Knox, and Alvin Bernstein (eds.), *The Making of Strategy: Rulers, States, and War* (New York: Cambridge University Press, 1994), p. 230.

154. Robert W. Merry, *A Country of Vast Designs: James K. Polk, the Mexican War, and the Conquest of the American Continent* (New York: Simon & Schuster, 2009), p. 452.

155. Merry, *A Country of Vast Designs: James K. Polk, the Mexican War, and the Conquest of the American Continent* (New York: Simon & Schuster, 2009), p. 411: "that rainbow that rises in showers of blood – that serpent's eye that charms but to destroy."

156. Walter A. McDougall, "The Constitutional History of U.S. Foreign Policy: 222 Years of Tension in the Twilight Zone," *Foreign Policy Research Institute*, September 2010, p. 14. Lincoln continued this line of reasoning in a discussion with his law partner, William Herndon, in 1848: "... If to-day he should choose to say he thinks it necessary to invade Canada to prevent the British from invading us, how could you stop him? You may say to him, 'I see no probability of the British invading us'; but he will say to you, 'Be silent. I see it, if you don't.'"

157. Sean Wilentz, *The Rise of American Democracy: Jefferson to Lincoln* (New York: W. W. Norton, 2005), p. 602: "The doubts and misgivings that turned into repulsion arose not from American setbacks, but from American victories, culminating in the capture of Mexico City in September 1847. The result was a schizophrenic experience on the home front, filled with both exhilarated celebration of our troops and embittered criticism of the war and its goals."

158. Peter Maslowski, "To the Edge of Greatness: The United States, 1783–1865," in Williamson Murray, MacGregor Knox, and Alvin Bernstein, eds., *The Making of Strategy: Rulers, States, and War* (New York: Cambridge University Press, 1994), p. 231: "As the toll in blood and treasure, Polk believed the United States should take as an indemnity more territory than he had originally contemplated. Some expansionists even demanded 'All Mexico' ..." Furthermore, "Since a decision for war is a political act, it involves political judgment, which may or may not be wise or just. Many Americans questioned Polk's judgment."

159. Robert W. Merry, *A Country of Vast Designs: James K. Polk, the Mexican War, and the Conquest of the American Continent* (New York: Simon & Schuster, 2009), p. 276: "Later it was amended to stipulate that only specie was to be received by the government" (p. 273).

160. Merry, *A Country of Vast Designs: James K. Polk, the Mexican War, and the Conquest of the American Continent* (New York: Simon & Schuster, 2009), p. 274: "The tariff bill was not truly a free trade measure. The ad valorem rates [percentage rates that would fluctuate with price] on a few commodities would reach as high as 100 percent, and rates on some products ... actually would increase."

161. Merry, A *Country of Vast Designs: James K. Polk, the Mexican War, and the Conquest of the American Continent* (New York: Simon & Schuster, 2009), p. 277. This policy was particularly important later when the "railroad boom generated huge demand for Pennsylvania iron and steel, and textile manufacturing soon discovered high tariffs only spawned troublesome domestic competitors . . ."

162. Robert Kagan, *Dangerous Nation* (New York: Knopf, 2006), pp. 226–227, who writes that by the 1840s, "the national parties gradually dissolved into sectional parties [and] the specter of sectional conflict doomed all attempts at compromise over the new territorial questions created by Polk's expansionism."

163. For background on Lincoln, see William E. Gienapp, *Abraham Lincoln and Civil War America: A Biography* (Oxford: Oxford University Press, 2002); Ronald C. White Jr., *A. Lincoln: A Biography* (New York: Random House, 2009); Stephen B. Oates, *With Malice toward None: The Life of Abraham Lincoln* (New York: HarperCollins, 2009); Carl Sandburg, edited by Edward C. Goodman, *Abraham Lincoln: The Prairie Years and the War Years* (New York: Sterling Publisher, 2007); David Herbert Donald, *Lincoln Reconsidered: Essays on the Civil War Era* (New York: Vintage Books, 2001); Doris Kearns Goodwin, *Team of Rivals: The PoliticalGenius of Abraham Lincoln* (New York: Simon & Schuster, 2005); David Blight, *Race and Reunion: The Civil War in American Memory* (Cambridge, MA: Harvard University Press, 2002); Sean Wilentz, *The Rise of American Democracy: Jefferson to Lincoln* (New York: W. W. Norton, 2005); Garry Wills, *Lincoln at Gettysburg: The Words that Remade America* (New York: Simon & Schuster, 2006).

164. On Lincoln's grand strategy, see Carl Sandburg, *Abraham Lincoln: The War Years* (New York: Harcourt, Brace & Company, 1939); David Herbert Donald, *Lincoln Reconsidered: Essays on the Civil War Era* (New York: Vintage Books, 2001); Eliot Cohen, *Supreme Command: Soldiers, Statesmen, and Leadership in Wartime*, 1st reprint ed. (New York: Anchor Books, September 2003); Archer Jones, *Civil War Command and Strategy: The Process of Victory and Defeat* (New York: Simon & Schuster, 1992); Russell F. Weigley, *A Great Civil War: A Military and Political History, 1861–1865* (Bloomington: Indiana University Press, 2000); Abraham Lincoln, Second Inaugural Address, March 4, 1865, at www.bartleby.com/124/pres32.html.

165. James McPherson, *Ordeal by Fire: The Civil War and Reconstruction* (New York: Knopf, 1982), p. 1. Both the North and the South "evolved institutions and values based on its labor system. These values in turn generated ideologies that justified each section's institutions and condemned those of the other."

166. See McPherson, *Ordeal by Fire: The Civil War and Reconstruction* (Knopf: New York, 1982), pp. 28–44, passim. "The South failed to develop a substantial urban middle class and skilled-labor population or to generate a diversified economy producing a wide variety of goods and services . . ." Further, "A fundamental reason for the South's failure to modernize and become economically independent was a lack of diversity in its economy – that is, too great a dependence on a single staple crop, cotton."

167. Robert Kagan, *Dangerous Nation* (Knopf: New York, 2006) p. 190. "The rejuvenation of the slave economy in the early decades of the nineteenth century [due to

an increase in the demand for cotton] set the South off on a pattern of economic development different in some significant respects from what the North was experiencing ..." In practice, the South's "economy was a hybrid: capitalist in some respects, but in other respects something different [than the North's market economy]."

168. James McPherson, *Ordeal by Fire: The Civil War and Reconstruction* (Knopf: New York, 1982) p. 111: As Fitzhugh wrote, "We slaveholders say you must recur to domestic slavery, the oldest, the best, and most common form of Socialism." In defense of slavery, Fitzhugh wrote that "slavery, on the other hand, was an ancient institution that guaranteed the employer's paternal interest in his workers ..." To put these differences in perspective, Fitzhugh wrote that "All problems of the North stemmed from its belief in the false doctrine that all men were created equal ..."

169. Alexis De Tocqueville, *Democracy in America*, trans., Arthur Goldhammer, Literary Classics of the United States (New York: Library of America, 2004), p. 399.

170. John D. Majewski, *Modernizing a Slave Economy: The Economic Vision of the Confederate Nation* (Chapel Hill: University of North Carolina Press, 2009), p. 48.

171. Robert Kagan, *Dangerous Nation* (Knopf: New York, 2006), p. 190.

172. John D. Majewski, *Modernizing a Slave Economy: The Economic Vision of the Confederate Nation* (Chapel Hill: University of North Carolina Press, 2009), p. 48.

173. James McPherson, *Ordeal by Fire: The Civil War and Reconstruction* (Knopf: New York, 1982), p. 44.

174. The Whig Party had formed in opposition to the policies of Andrew Jackson and the Democratic Party and, with Lincoln as a member, wanted to end slavery, modernize the nation, and promote protectionist economic policies. Cf. McPherson, *Ordeal by Fire: The Civil War and Reconstruction* (Knopf: New York, 1982), p. 21.

175. McPherson, *Ordeal by Fire: The Civil War and Reconstruction* (Knopf: New York, 1982), p. 1. The enormous "social and political strains produced by [this] rapid growth provoked repeated crises that threatened to destroy the republic." The Louisiana Purchase nearly doubled the size of the United States, and after the Mexican-American War, "the United States had acquired a million and a quarter square miles of new territory" (p. 58).

176. Robert Kagan, *Dangerous Nation* (Knopf: New York, 2006), p. 186.

177. James McPherson, *Ordeal by Fire: The Civil War and Reconstruction* (Knopf: New York, 1982), p. 22. The differences were profound: "To the Whigs, 'progress' meant internal development; to the Democrats, it meant external growth."

178. Robert Kagan, *Dangerous Nation* (Knopf: New York, 2006), p. 187: "... the 'defensive' impulse toward expansion became more urgent, culminating in the 1840s in the southern drive for the annexation of Texas and in the 1850s in the effort to purchase Cuba and build a southern empire in the Caribbean."

179. James McPherson, *Ordeal by Fire: The Civil War and Reconstruction* (Knopf: New York, 1982), pp. 125, 132.

180. Abraham Lincoln, "Speech at Springfield, Illinois, June 26, 1857," in John G. Nicolay and John Hay (eds.), *The Collected Works of Abraham Lincoln*, Vol. 2 (New York: Francis D. Tandy Company, 1905), pp. 461–469. Quoted in

Sean Wilentz, *The Rise of American Democracy: Jefferson to Lincoln* (New York: W. W. Norton, 2005), p. 730.

181. Sean Wilentz, *The Rise of American Democracy: Jefferson to Lincoln* (New York: W. W. Norton, 2005), pp. 730, 741. Cf. Paul M. Angle, ed., *Created Equal? The Complete Lincoln-Douglas Debates of 1858* (Chicago: The University of Chicago Press, 1958), pp. 195–196, 235. Quoted in Sean Wilentz, *The Rise of American Democracy: Jefferson to Lincoln* (New York: W. W. Norton, 2005), p. 741. Lincoln insisted that he had no ambitions to create "a perfect social and political equality between the white and black races" and speculated that the question of slavery's morality would "continue in this country when these poor tongues of Judge Douglas and myself shall be silent. It is the eternal struggle between these two principles – right and wrong – throughout the world. They are the two principles that have stood face to face from the beginning of time; and will ever continue to struggle."

182. However, Robert Kagan, *Dangerous Nation* (New York: Vintage Books, 2007), pp. 228–229, writes, "Although many northerners were indifferent to southern slavery, for Lincoln and many others this northern containment strategy was not intended to be neutral regarding the future of slavery in the United States. In the North as in the South there was a common assumption that slavery 'required expansion to survive, and that confinement to the states where it already existed would kill it.'" James M. McPherson, *Ordeal By Fire: The Civil War and Reconstruction* (New York: Alfred A. Knopf, Inc., 1982), p. 107. For Lincoln, McPherson writes, "the real question was the morality of bondage. If it was right, it should exist everywhere; if wrong, everything possible should be done to restrict and ultimately end it."

183. Roy P. Basler, ed., *The Collected Works of Abraham Lincoln*, 9 vols. (New Brunswick, NJ, 1953–1955), Vol. 3, p. 315. Quoted in James M. McPherson, *Ordeal By Fire: The Civil War and Reconstruction* (New York: Alfred A. Knopf, Inc., 1982), p. 107.

184. The final text of the inaugural address appears in John G. Nicolay and John Hay, eds., *The Collected Works of Abraham Lincoln*, Vol. 4 (New York: Francis D. Tandy Company, 1905), p. 262–271. Quoted in Sean Wilentz, *The Rise of American Democracy: Jefferson to Lincoln* (New York: W. W. Norton, 2005), pp. 782–783: "Lincoln tried to compose a message that would help preserve the Union without abdicating his duty to assert federal authority. At the very last minute, he revised his text on Seward's advice, to emphasize conciliation." Lincoln's strategy arguably was to insist that "as president ... he would refuse 'directly or indirectly, to interfere with the institution of slavery in the States where it exists,' but he would not countenance secession."

185. Sean Wilentz, *The Rise of American Democracy: Jefferson to Lincoln* (New York: W. W. Norton, 2005), p. 783: "'Why should there not be a patient confidence in the ultimate justice of the people? Is there any better, or equal hope, in the world? In our present differences, is either party without faith of being in the right? If the Almighty Ruler of nations, with his eternal truth and justices, be on your side of the North, or on yours of the South, that truth, and that justice will surely prevail, by the judgment of this great tribunal, the American people.'"

186. James M. McPherson, *Ordeal By Fire: The Civil War and Reconstruction* (New York: Alfred A. Knopf, Inc., 1982), p. 136.

187. See Abraham Lincoln, First Inaugural Address, March 4, 1861, at www.bartleby.com/124/pres31.html.

188. Eliot Cohen, *Supreme Command: Soldiers, Statesmen, and Leadership in Wartime*, 1st reprint ed. (New York: Anchor Books, September 2003), pp. 17–18. "He chose an act of military imprudence – refusing to either withdraw or reinforce out-numbered garrisons – to achieve a broader political effect."

189. See, e.g., T. Harry Williams's *Lincoln and His Generals* and Kenneth P. Williams's massive (but unfinished) *Lincoln Finds a General*; cf. Cohen, *Supreme Command: Soldiers, Statesmen, and Leadership in Wartime*, 1st reprint ed. (September 2003), p. 16. For a contrasting view, see James M. McPherson, *Tried by War: Abraham Lincoln as Commander in Chief* (New York: Penguin Books, 2009).

190. Eliot Cohen, *Supreme Command: Soldiers, Statesmen, and Leadership in Wartime*, 1st reprint ed. (New York: Anchor Books, September 2003), p. 17: "The strategic principles that Lincoln had laid out required modification in practice, and their execution required his active monitoring and intervention." In Cohen's view, "Finding the right generals was only a prerequisite for strategy success; directing them proved for Lincoln, as for other war statesman, the critical matter" (p. 38).

191. Cohen, *Supreme Command: Soldiers, Statesmen, and Leadership in Wartime*, 1st reprint ed. (New York: Anchor Books, September 2003), pp. 30–31.

192. "Letter to Horace Greeley," August 22, 1862, in Roy P. Basler (ed.), *The Collected Works of Abraham Lincoln*, 9 vols. (New Brunswick, NJ, 1953–1955), Vol. 5, p. 338. Lincoln's complete quote is worth noting: "If I could save the Union without freeing any slave I would do it, and if I could save it by freeing all the slaves I would do it; and if I could save it by freeing some and leaving others alone I would also do that. What I do about slavery, and the colored race, I do because I believe it helps to save the Union; and what I forbear, I forbear because I do not believe it would help to save the Union."

193. "Letter to Horace Greeley," August 22, 1862, in Roy P. Basler (ed.), *The Collected Works of Abraham Lincoln*, Vol. 5 (New Brunswick, NJ, 1953–1955), p. 338. Quoted in Eliot Cohen, *Supreme Command: Soldiers, Statesmen, and Leadership in Wartime*, 1st reprint ed. (New York: Anchor Books, September 2003), p. 32. In effect, this war "became a revolutionary struggle, against Lincoln's will."

194. James M. McPherson, *Ordeal By Fire: The Civil War and Reconstruction* (New York: Alfred A. Knopf, Inc., 1982), p. 261. "Although a significant amount of internal disaffection existed in the Confederacy, the North suffered more disunity over war aims than the South. The South fought for independence. So long as the North fought simply for restoration of the Union, Northern unity was impressive. But the hard question of what kind of Union was to be restored soon divided the North. Was it to be a Union without slavery, as abolitionists and radical Republicans hoped? Or 'the Union as it was, the Constitution as it is,' as Democrats insisted? Was the South to be *restored* to the Union with its rights and power intact, or *reconstructed* in the image of the free-labor North? Disagreement about ends soon became disagreement about means as well. Was it to be a total war

fought for total victory, or a limited war looking toward an early peace conference to restore the Union through compromise?"

195. McPherson, *Ordeal by Fire: The Civil War and Reconstruction* (New York: Alfred A. Knopf, Inc., 1982), p. 262.

196. Roy P. Basler, ed., *The Collected Works of Abraham Lincoln*, 9 vols. (New Brunswick, NJ, 1953–1955), Vol. 4, p. 438. Quoted in McPherson, *Ordeal By Fire: The Civil War and Reconstruction* (New York: Alfred A. Knopf, Inc., 1982), p. 264: "The central idea pervading this struggle is the necessity . . . of proving that popular government is not an absurdity. We must settle this question now, whether in a free government the minority have the right to break up the government whenever they choose." Early in the conflict, Lincoln argued, "On the side of the Union it is a struggle for maintaining in the world that form and substance of government whose leading object is to elevate the condition of men . . . to afford all an unfettered start, and a fair chance in the race of life."

197. McPherson, *Ordeal by Fire: The Civil War and Reconstruction* (New York: Alfred A. Knopf, Inc., 1982), pp. 265–266: "In his July 4 message to Congress, Lincoln reiterated the inaugural pledge that he had 'no purpose, directly or indirectly, to interfere with slavery in the states where it exists.'" Also, "Because as President of *all* the states, he still considered himself bound by the constitutional guarantee of slavery in the states. The Union government fought the war on the theory that, secession being illegal, the Confederate states were still legally in the Union although temporarily under control of insurrectionists. The need to retain the loyalty of the border slave states was another factor in Lincoln and Congress's assurances on slavery. Beyond that was the desire for bipartisan support of the war. Nearly half of the voters in the free states had cast anti-Lincoln ballots in the 1861 election. The Northern Democrats were a proslavery party. Any signs of an antislavery policy in 1861 might divide the North and alienate most Democrats."

198. Roy P. Basler, ed., *The Collected Works of Abraham Lincoln* (New Brunswick, NJ, 1953–1955), Vol. 5, pp. 388–389. Excerpt from James M. McPherson, *Ordeal by Fire: The Civil War and Reconstruction* (New York: Alfred A. Knopf, Inc., 1982), pp. 278–279: "I do not want to issue a document that the whole world will necessarily see must be inoperative, like the Pope's bull against the comet!"

199. Robert Kagan, *Dangerous Nation* (New York: Vintage Books, 2007), pp. 266–267.

200. Kagan, *Dangerous Nation* (New York: Vintage Books, 2007), pp. 268–269.

201. Kagan, *Dangerous Nation* (New York: Vintage Books, 2007), pp. 269–270: As Kagan writes, "To the North, the defeated South was, in the argot of the twentieth century, an underdeveloped nation. Its underdevelopment, its backwardness, exemplified by the archaic institution of slavery, many northerners believed, had been responsible for the horrendous conflict that had almost destroyed the entire nation." As a consequence, "the North, having subdued the rebellion and punished its leaders, had the task not only of standing the conquered land back on its feet, but of curing it of the evils that had led to war, which in turn meant dragging it forcibly into the modern world."

202. See William C. Martel, *Victory in War: Foundations of Modern Strategy* (New York: Cambridge University Press, 2011), pp. 50–54. Cf. Eliot Cohen, *Supreme*

Command: Soldiers, Statesmen, and Leadership in Wartime, 1st reprint ed. (New York: Anchor Books, September 2003).

203. Robert Kagan, *Dangerous Nation* (New York: Vintage Books, 2007), pp. 261–262. With ideas that altered American grand strategy, Lincoln's principles rested on the belief that, "if the 'central idea' of the American nation was to be found not in the Constitution or in the Union but in the Declaration of Independence's promise of equal rights, this meant that at the core of American nationhood was a set of universal principles that transcended national boundaries."

204. Quoted from Kagan, *Dangerous Nation* (New York: Vintage Books, 2007), p. 262. "As Eric Foner notes, they saw their struggle against the southern slaveholders as but 'one part of a world-wide movement from absolutism to democracy, aristocracy to equality, backwardness to modernity.'" Cf. Eric Foner, *Free Soil, Free Labor, Free Men: The Ideology of the Republican Party before the Civil War* (New York: Oxford University Press, 1995), p. 72.

205. Kagan, *Dangerous Nation* (New York: Vintage Books, 2007), p. 262.

206. Abraham Lincoln, "Letter to Henry L. Pierce and Others," April 6, 1859, quoted in Harry V. Jaffa, *A New Birth of Freedom: Abraham Lincoln and the Coming of the Civil War* (Lanham, MD: Rowman & Littlefield, 2000), p. 73.

207. Cf. Robert Jervis, "Security Regimes," *International Organization* 36, No. 02 (Spring 1982), pp. 357–378. Also, Andrew J. Bacevich, *Washington Rules: America's Path to Permanent War* (New York: Macmillan Books, 2010).

208. Dennis Merrill and Thomas G. Paterson, *Major Problems in American Foreign Relations: To 1920* (Boston: Wadsworth, 2010), p. 72.

209. Cf. Daniel J. Boorstin, *The Americans: The National Experience* (New York: Random House, 2010), esp. part III, pp. 113–168. Also, Robert O. Keohane, Joseph S. Nye Jr., "Power and Independence Revisited," *International Organization* 41, No. 04 (Autumn 1987), pp. 725–753.

8 Restraining Sources of Disorder: Theodore Roosevelt to Franklin Delano Roosevelt

1. See, for example, Fareed Zakaria, *From Wealth to Power: The Unusual Origins of America's World Role* (Princeton, NJ: Princeton University Press, 1999).

2. On exceptionalism, see Seymour Martin Lipset, *American Exceptionalism: A Double-Edged Sword* (New York: W. W. Norton & Company, 1997); Godfrey Hodgson, *The Myth of American Exceptionalism* (New Haven, CT: Yale University Press, 2010); Aaron L. Friedberg, *A Contest for Supremacy: China, America, and the Struggle for Mastery in Asia* (New York: W. W. Norton & Company, 2012); Andrew Bacevich, *The Limits of Power: The End of American Exceptionalism* (New York: Henry Holt, 2008); Jason A. Edwards and David Weiss, eds., *The Rhetoric of American Exceptionalism: Critical Essays* (Jefferson, NC: McFarland & Company, 2011); Thomas R. Hietala, *Manifest Design: American Exceptionalism and Empire* (Ithaca, NY: Cornell University Press, 1985); Charles W. Dunn, ed., *American Exceptionalism: The Origins, History, and Future of the Nation's Greatest Strength* (Lanham, MD: Rowman & Littlefield, 2013).

3. Henry A. Kissinger, *A World Restored* (Boston: Houghton Mifflin Company, 1957), p. 2.
4. Walter Russell Mead, *Special Providence: American Foreign Policy and How It Changed the World* (New York: Knopf, 2001), pp. iv, 88–97.
5. On Roosevelt's influence on grand strategy, see Theodore Roosevelt, *Theodore Roosevelt – An Autobiography* (New York: Charles Scribner's Sons, 1913); James R. Holmes, *Theodore Roosevelt and World Order: Police Power in International Relations* (Washington, DC: Potomac Books, 2006); William N. Tilchin and Charles E. Neu, eds., *Artists of Power: Theodore Roosevelt, Woodrow Wilson, and Their Enduring Impact on U.S. Foreign Policy* (Westport, CT: Praeger, 2006); John Milton Cooper Jr., *The Warrior and the Priest: Woodrow Wilson and Theodore Roosevelt* (Cambridge, MA: Belknap Press of Harvard University, 1983); Lewis L. Gould, *The Presidency of Theodore Roosevelt* (Lawrence: University Press of Kansas, 2011).
6. Clifford Lee Staten, "Theodore Roosevelt: Dual and Cooperative Federalism," *Presidential Studies Quarterly* 23, No. 1 (Winter 1993), p. 131.
7. Barbara W. Tuchman, *The Proud Tower: A Portrait of a World before the War, 1890–1914* (New York: Macmillan Company, 1966).
8. Lewis L. Gould, *The Presidency of Theodore Roosevelt* (Lawrence: University Press of Kansas, 2011), p. 28.
9. Gould, *The Presidency of Theodore Roosevelt* (Lawrence: University Press of Kansas, 2011), p. 29.
10. Theodore Roosevelt, *Theodore Roosevelt – An Autobiography* (New York: Charles Scribner's Sons, 1913), pp. 423–424.
11. Roosevelt, *Theodore Roosevelt – An Autobiography* (New York: Charles Scribner's Sons, 1913), pp. 423–424.
12. Roosevelt, *Theodore Roosevelt – An Autobiography* (New York: Charles Scribner's Sons, 1913), pp. 423–424: "The power of the mighty industrial overlords of the country had increased with giant strides, while the methods of controlling them, or checking abuses by them, on the part of the people, through the Government, remained archaic and therefore practically impotent." As Roosevelt warned, "In no other country in the world was such power held by the men who gained these fortunes ..."
13. Roosevelt, *Theodore Roosevelt – An Autobiography* (New York: Charles Scribner's Sons, 1913), p. 425.
14. Roosevelt, *Theodore Roosevelt – An Autobiography* (New York: Charles Scribner's Sons, 1913), p. 425.
15. Lewis L. Gould, *The Presidency of Theodore Roosevelt* (Lawrence: University Press of Kansas, 2011), p. 215.
16. *Report of the Commissioner of Corporations on the Transportation of Petroleum, May 2, 1906*, House Document 812, 59th Cong., 1st sess. (Washington, DC: Government Printing Office, 1906) pp. xx–xxi, in Lewis L. Gould, *The Presidency of Theodore Roosevelt* (Lawrence: University Press of Kansas, 2011), p. 216.
17. *Report of the Commissioner of Corporations on the Transportation of Petroleum, May 2, 1906*, House Document 812, 59th Cong., 1st sess. (Washington, DC:

Government Printing Office, 1906) pp. xx, xxi, in Lewis L. Gould, *The Presidency of Theodore Roosevelt* (Lawrence: University Press of Kansas, 2011), p. 216.

18. See John Cassidy, "Rationality and Irrationality," *New Yorker*, October 11, 2011; Al Baker, "Overtime, Solidarity and Complaints in Wall St. Protests," *New York Times*, October 13, 2011; Brian Stelter, "A News Story Is Growing with 'Occupy' Protests," *New York Times*, October 13, 2011, p. A20.

19. TR to the Senate and House of Representatives, 4 June 1906, *Conditions in Chicago Stock Yards*, 59th Cong., 1st sess., House Document 873 (Washington, DC: Government Printing Office, 1906), in Lewis L. Gould, *The Presidency of Theodore Roosevelt* (Lawrence: University Press of Kansas, 2011), p. 167: "They reported back to the president, in Roosevelt's words, that 'the stockyards and packing houses are not kept even reasonably clean, and that the method of handling and preparing food products is uncleanly and dangerous to health.'"

20. Lewis L. Gould, *The Presidency of Theodore Roosevelt* (Lawrence: University Press of Kansas, 2011), p. 165: Despite ongoing calls for legislation regarding labeling drugs since the 1890s, there was little action and "up to the end of 1903, legislation on the pure-food problem had been stalled."

21. Theodore Roosevelt, "Address at the Hamilton Club in Chicago, Illinois," April 10, 1899, at www.theodore-roosevelt.com/images/research/speeches/trstrenlife.pdf.

22. George C. Herring, *From Colony to Superpower: U.S. Foreign Relations since 1776* (New York: Oxford University Press, 2008), p. 346.

23. John M. Thompson, *The Impact of Public Opinion on Theodore Roosevelt's Foreign Policy* (Cambridge, UK: University of Cambridge, Dissertation, 2010); John Milton Cooper Jr., *The Warrior and the Priest: Woodrow Wilson and Theodore Roosevelt*, (Cambridge, MA: Belknap Press of Harvard University Press, 1983), pp. 75–76.

24. John Milton Cooper Jr., *The Warrior and the Priest: Woodrow Wilson and Theodore Roosevelt* (Cambridge, MA: Belknap Press of Harvard University Press, 1983), pp. 75–76.

25. On the Roosevelt Corollary to the Monroe Doctrine, see Edward J. Renehan, *The Monroe Doctrine: The Cornerstone of American Foreign Policy* (New York: Chelsea House, 2007); James MacGregor Burns and Susan Dunn, *The Three Roosevelts: Patrician Leaders Who Transformed America* (New York: Grove Press, 2001); Gaddis Smith, *The Last Years of the Monroe Doctrine, 1945–1993* (New York: Macmillan, 1995); Lewis L. Gould, *The Presidency of Theodore Roosevelt* (Lawrence: University Press of Kansas, 2011).

26. See *Roosevelt Corollary to the Monroe Doctrine, 1904*, Office of the Historian (Washington, DC: U.S. Department of State), at www.history.state.gov/milestones/1899-1913/RooseveltandMonroeDoctrine.

27. John Milton Cooper Jr., *The Warrior and the Priest: Woodrow Wilson and Theodore Roosevelt* (Cambridge, MA: Belknap Press of Harvard University Press, 1983), p. 73.

28. Cooper, *The Warrior and the Priest: Woodrow Wilson and Theodore Roosevelt* (Cambridge, MA: Belknap Press of Harvard University Press, 1983), p. 73.

29. T. R. Roosevelt, "Speak Softly ..." (Washington, DC: Library of Congress), at www.loc.gov/exhibits/treasures/trm139.html.

30. Thomas A. Bailey, *A Diplomatic History of the American People* (Englewood Cliffs, NJ: Prentice Hall, 1980), pp. 504–505: "The United States might then have a full-fledged war on its hands. Roosevelt realized that the 'insurrectionary habits' of these 'wretched republics' imposed certain obligations on Washington."

31. For more on the Russo-Japanese War, see Geoffrey Jukes, *The Russo-Japanese War 1904–1904* (Oxford: Osprey Publishing, 2002), pp. 7–13; Denis Warner, Peggy Warner, *The Tide at Sunrise: A History of the Russo-Japanese War, 1904–1905* (New York: Frank Cass, 1974).

32. Lewis L. Gould, *The Presidency of Theodore Roosevelt* (Lawrence: University Press of Kansas, 2011), p. 187: Roosevelt, in Gould's view, "also enjoyed a position as a natural mediator among those involved." As Gould argues, Roosevelt practiced "diplomacy at the highest level … without concern for domestic public opinion."

33. Gould, *The Presidency of Theodore Roosevelt* (Lawrence: University Press of Kansas, 2011), p. 165: "Americans watched with admiration as their president worked for peace among kings and emperors." Also, "As long as their international involvement brought gain to the United States at little cost, Roosevelt's foreign policy enjoyed their support."

34. Howard K. Beale, *Theodore Roosevelt and the Rise of America to World Power* (Baltimore: Johns Hopkins Press, 1956), pp. 312–313.

35. Beale, *Theodore Roosevelt and the Rise of America to World Power* (Baltimore: Johns Hopkins Press, 1956), pp. 312–313.

36. See Theodore Roosevelt, *Theodore Roosevelt and His Time, An Autobiography, Letters to His Children*, 2 vols., at www.archive.org/stream/acl8524.0001.001 .umich.edu/acl8524.0001.001.umich.edu_djvu.txt: "I am entirely sincere when I tell them that I act as I do because I think it in the interest of Russia, and in this crisis I think the interest of Russia is the interest of the entire world."

37. Howard K. Beale, *Theodore Roosevelt and the Rise of America to World Power* (Baltimore: Johns Hopkins Press, 1956), pp. 312–313.

38. Beale, *Theodore Roosevelt and the Rise of America to World Power* (Baltimore: Johns Hopkins Press, 1956), p. 314.

39. See Theodore Roosevelt, *Theodore Roosevelt and His Time, An Autobiography, Letters to His Children*, 2 vols., at www.archive.org/stream/acl8524.0001.001 .umich.edu/acl8524.0001.001.umich.edu_djvu.txt.

40. Howard K. Beale, *Theodore Roosevelt and the Rise of America to World Power* (Baltimore: Johns Hopkins Press, 1956), p. 314: "It is best that she should be left face to face with Japan so that each may have a moderative action on the other."

41. John Milton Cooper Jr., *The Warrior and the Priest: Woodrow Wilson and Theodore Roosevelt* (Cambridge, MA: Belknap Press of Harvard University Press, 1983), p. 74.

42. Lewis L. Gould, *The Presidency of Theodore Roosevelt* (Lawrence: University Press of Kansas, 2011), p. 182.

43. Thomas A. Bailey, *A Diplomatic History of the American People* (Englewood Cliffs, NJ: Prentice Hall, 1980), p. 513.

44. Cf. Richard W. Turk, *The Ambiguous Relationship: Theodore Roosevelt and Alfred Thayer Mahan* (New York: Praeger, 1987); Peter Karsten, "The Nature of 'Influence': Roosevelt, Mahan and the Concept of Sea Power," *American*

Quarterly 23, No. 4 (October 1971), pp. 585–600; J. Simon Rofe, "Under the Influence of Mahan: Theodore and Franklin Roosevelt and Their Understanding of American National Interest," *Diplomacy & Statecraft* 19, No. 4 (2008), pp. 732–745.

45. Philip A. Crowl, "Alfred Thayer Mahan: The Naval Historian," in Peter Paret (ed.), *Makers of Modern Strategy from Machiavelli to the Nuclear Age* (Princeton, NJ: Princeton University Press, 1986), p. 451.

46. See Theodore Roosevelt, *The Naval War of 1812, or The History of the United States Navy during the Last War with Great Britain to Which Is Appended an Account of the Battle of New Orleans* (1881), at www.gutenberg.org/cache/epub/9104/pg9104.html.

47. Philip A. Crowl, "Alfred Thayer Mahan: The Naval Historian," in Peter Paret (ed.), *Makers of Modern Strategy from Machiavelli to the Nuclear Age* (Princeton, NJ: Princeton University Press, 1986), p. 471–472.

48. Theodore Roosevelt, "Address at the Hamilton Club in Chicago, Illinois" (April 10, 1899), at www.theodore-roosevelt.com/images/research/speeches/trstrenlife .pdf: "We must build the isthmian canal, and we must grasp the points of vantage which will enable us to have our say in deciding the destiny of the oceans of the East and the West."

49. Thomas A. Bailey, *A Diplomatic History of the American People* (Englewood Cliffs, NJ: Prentice Hall, 1980), p. 491: "The impatient Roosevelt . . . insisted that the 'cut throats' and 'blackmailers of Bogotá' should not be permitted 'permanently to bar one of the future highways of civilization.'"

50. Bailey, *A Diplomatic History of the American People* (Englewood Cliffs, NJ: Prentice Hall, 1980), p. 492: "Now came the rejection of the Hay-Herran Treaty, from which the people of Panama had expected juicy commercial benefits. Disappointment rapidly gave way to anxiety when the Panamanians realized that Roosevelt might turn to Nicaragua, as contemplated by act of Congress. Plainly the situation was ripe for revolt – another Isthmian revolt."

51. Bailey, *A Diplomatic History of the American People* (Englewood Cliffs, NJ: Prentice Hall, 1980), p. 493: "The American naval forces, acting under orders, kept the Isthmus clear by preventing the Colombian troops from moving . . ."

52. *New York Times*, March 25, 1911, p. 10:3. Quoted in Thomas A. Bailey, *A Diplomatic History of the American People* (Englewood Cliffs, NJ: Prentice Hall, 1980), p. 497.

53. Lewis L. Gould, *The Presidency of Theodore Roosevelt* (Lawrence: University Press of Kansas, 2011), p. 254.

54. Gould, *The Presidency of Theodore Roosevelt* (Lawrence: University Press of Kansas, 2011), pp. 42–43.

55. Gould, *The Presidency of Theodore Roosevelt* (Lawrence: University Press of Kansas, 2011), p. 259: "The navy shot better . . . the morale of the service had improved; and its personnel were better trained."

56. Thomas A. Bailey, *A Diplomatic History of the American People* (Englewood Cliffs, NJ: Prentice Hall, 1980), p. 524.

57. Allan Nevins, *Henry White: Thirty Years of American Diplomacy* (New York: Harper & Brothers, 1930), pp. 292–293 (Roosevelt to White, July 30, 1907), in

Thomas A. Bailey, *A Diplomatic History of the American People* (Englewood Cliffs, NJ: Prentice Hall, 1980), p. 524.

58. George C. Herring, *From Colony to Superpower: U.S. Foreign Relations Since 1776* (New York: Oxford University Press, 2008), pp. 376–377.

59. Richard H. Collin, *Theodore Roosevelt's Caribbean: The Panama Canal, the Monroe Doctrine, and the Latin American Context* (Baton Rouge: Louisiana State University Press, 1990), p. 548.

60. Collin, *Theodore Roosevelt's Caribbean: The Panama Canal, the Monroe Doctrine, and the Latin American Context* (Baton Rouge: Louisiana State University Press, 1990), p. 548.

61. On Roosevelt's influence on American foreign policy, see Walter LaFeber, *American Age: U.S. Foreign Policy at Home and Abroad, From 1750 to the Present*, 2nd ed. (New York: W. W. Norton, 1994). On America's rise to great power status, see Fareed Zakaria, *From Wealth to Power: The Unusual Origins of America's World Role* (Princeton, NJ: Princeton University Press, 1999).

62. On Wilson's foreign policy, see John Milton Cooper Jr., *Woodrow Wilson: A Biography* (Knopf: New York, 2009); Harley A. Notter, *The Origins of the Foreign Policy of Woodrow Wilson* (New York: Russell & Russell, 1965); Thomas J. Knock, *To End All Wars: Woodrow Wilson and the Quest for a New World Order* (Princeton, NJ: Princeton University Press, 1995); Walter LaFeber, *American Age: U.S. Foreign Policy at Home and Abroad, From 1750 to the Present*, 2nd ed. (New York: W. W. Norton, 1994); Frank Ninkovich, *The Wilsonian Century: U.S. Foreign Policy Since 1900* (Chicago: Chicago University Press, 1999).

63. Ross A. Kennedy, *The Will to Believe: Woodrow Wilson, World War I, and America's Strategy for Peace and Security* (Kent, OH: Kent State University Press, 2009), p. xii. Cf. Tony Smith, *America's Mission: The United States and the Worldwide Struggle for Democracy in the Twentieth Century* (Princeton, NJ: Princeton University Press, 2012), pp. 1–76.

64. Henry Kissinger, *Diplomacy* (New York: Simon & Schuster, 1995), pp. 18–19, 29–30.

65. Walter Russell Mead, *Power, Terror, Peace, and War* (New York: Alfred A. Knopf, 2004), pp. 88–97.

66. See William C. Martel, *Victory in War: Foundations of Modern Strategy* (New York: Cambridge University Press, 2011), pp. 148–154, for an analysis of World War I and Wilson's strategy.

67. G. John Ikenberry, "Why Export Democracy? The 'Hidden Grand Strategy' of American Foreign Policy," *Wilson Quarterly* 23, No. 2 (Spring 1999), pp. 56–65.

68. Charles A. Kupchan and Clifford A. Kupchan, "The Promise of Collective Security," *International Security* 20, No. 1 (Summer 1995), pp. 52–61.

69. John Milton Cooper Jr., *Woodrow Wilson: A Biography* (Knopf: New York, 2009), p. 178.

70. See Henry Kissinger, *Diplomacy* (New York: Simon & Schuster, 1995), pp. 17–20, who argues that this idea of being a beacon of democracy, that the best way to promote American values abroad is to strengthen democracy and prosperity at home, is one of the two fundamental traditions of American foreign policy. The

other is the tradition of actively crusading to promote democracy abroad with a missionary's zeal.

71. John Milton Cooper Jr., *Woodrow Wilson: A Biography* (Knopf: New York, 2009), p. 287.

72. This stands in stark contrast to the status of the United States in 2013, which holds the largest public debt in absolute terms at $16.8 trillion dollars. Its debt-to-GDP ratio, another metric for measuring relative levels of debt, is around 106 percent. Historically, the U.S. debt-to-GDP ratio has been roughly on the order of 30 percent, excluding higher levels during wars and the current economic downturn. See Matt Phillips, "The Long Story of U.S. Debt: From 1790 to 2011, in 1 Little Chart," *The Atlantic*, November 13, 2012, at www.theatlantic.com/business/archive/2012/11/the-long-story-of-us-debt-from-1790-to-2011-in-1-little-chart/265185/.

73. John Milton Cooper Jr., *Woodrow Wilson: A Biography* (Knopf: New York, 2009), pp. 300, 305.

74. Martin Gilbert, *The First World War: A Complete History* (Holt: New York, 1994), p. 314.

75. Ross A. Kennedy, *The Will to Believe: Woodrow Wilson, World War I, and America's Strategy for Peace and Security* (Kent, OH: Kent State University Press, 2009), p. 7.

76. Jan Willem Schulte Nordholt, *Woodrow Wilson: A Life for World Peace* (Berkeley: University of California Press, 1991), p. 221.

77. Ross A. Kennedy, *The Will to Believe: Woodrow Wilson, World War I, and America's Strategy for Peace and Security* (Kent, OH: Kent State University Press, 2009), pp. 65, 79: "... embracing peace terms obviously premised on Germany's deciding that it had lost the war."

78. John Milton Cooper Jr., *Woodrow Wilson: A Biography* (Knopf: New York, 2009), p. 309.

79. Cooper, *Woodrow Wilson: A Biography* (Knopf: New York, 2009), p. 326.

80. Jan Willem Schulte Nordholt, *Woodrow Wilson: A Life for World Peace* (Berkeley: University of California Press, 1991), p. 223.

81. See Thomas J. Knock, *To End All Wars: Woodrow Wilson and the Quest for a New World Order* (Princeton, NJ: Princeton University Press, 1995).

82. His concern for American maritime rights and the free flow of oceanic travel and trade was reminiscent of Madison in his decision to begin the War of 1812.

83. Woodrow Wilson, Woodrow Wilson's War Message to Congress, April 2, 1917, at http://wwi.lib.byu.edu/index.php/Wilson's_War_Message_to_Congress.

84. On unconditional surrender, cf. William C. Martel, *Victory in War: Foundations of Modern Strategy* (New York: Cambridge University Press, 2011), pp. 174–198. Also, Anne Armstrong, *Unconditional Surrender: The Impact of the Casablanca Policy upon World War II* (New Brunswick, NJ: Rutgers University Press, 1961); Paul Kecskemeti, *Strategic Surrender: The Politics of Victory and Defeat* (Stanford, CA: Stanford University Press, 1958).

85. John Milton Cooper Jr., *Woodrow Wilson: A Biography* (Knopf: New York, 2009), p. 363.

86. Norman Angell, *The Great Illusion* (New York: Cosimo Books, 2007). Cf. Ivan S. Bloch, *Is War Now Impossible? Being an Abridgement of the War of the Future in*

Its Technical, Economic and Political Relations (Aldershot, Hampshire, UK: Gregg Revivals, 1891), p. 80: "Even supposing … that the allies in operations against fortresses and first lines of defence were always victorious, yet such victories would cost them so dear that the stoppage of further operations would seem inevitable." As by Edwin D. Mead, "Introduction," Is War Now Impossible?, p. iii: "He [Bloch] said that if it came to a great European war, that war could only cease with the annihilation of one combatant and the financial ruin of the other.… The destructiveness of modern warfare, with its frightful new weapons, becomes so appalling that a general European war would bring the universal bankruptcy of nations."

87. John Milton Cooper Jr., *Woodrow Wilson: A Biography* (New York: Knopf, 2009), pp. 363, 442.

88. Cooper, *Woodrow Wilson: A Biography* (New York: Knopf, 2009), pp. 370, 417. Wilson's "only major speech during the nation's first six months at war [was] a Flag Day address on June 14."

89. Cooper, *Woodrow Wilson: A Biography* (New York: Knopf, 2009), p. 276.

90. See Tony Smith, "Making the World Safe for Democracy in the American Century," *Diplomatic History* 23, No. 2, 1999, pp. 173–188; John Milton Cooper Jr., *Woodrow Wilson: A Biography* (New York: Knopf, 2009), pp. 5–6 (emphasis added); Fareed Zakaria, "Rise of Illiberal Democracy," *Foreign Affairs* 76, No. 6 (1997), pp. 22–43; Arthur Schlesinger Jr., "Has Democracy a Future?" *Foreign Affairs* 76, No. 5 (September–October, 1997), pp. 2–12.

91. Cooper, *Woodrow Wilson: A Biography* (New York: Knopf, 2009) p. 387.

92. Jan Willem Schulte Nordholt, *Woodrow Wilson: A Life for World Peace* (Berkeley: University of California Press, 1991), p. 225.

93. William C. Martel, *Victory in War: Foundations of Modern Strategy* (New York: Cambridge University Press, 2011), pp. 148–154; John Milton Cooper Jr., *Woodrow Wilson: A Biography* (New York: Knopf, 2009), p. 385. "Wilson proceeded to outline what belligerency would require: large-scale military and industrial mobilization, to be financed 'by well conceived taxation,' together with continued material aid to the allies."

94. On the American way of war, see Russell F. Weigley, *American Way of War: A History of United States Military Strategy and Policy* (New York: Macmillan, 1973).

95. John Milton Cooper Jr., *Woodrow Wilson: A Biography* (New York: Knopf, 2009), p. 390. On the underlying American logic of victory, cf. William C. Martel, *Victory in War: Foundations of Modern Strategy* (New York: Cambridge University Press, 2011), pp. 174–197.

96. Cooper, *Woodrow Wilson: A Biography* (New York: Knopf, 2009), p. 390–393.

97. Martin Gilbert, *The First World War: A Complete History* (New York: Holt, 1994), pp. 392–394: "Freedom of navigation would be assured on the sea. Economic barriers would be removed and an equality of trade conditions established among all nations. Naval armaments would be reduced. In questions of colonial sovereignty, the interests of populations concerned must have equal weight with the equitable claims of the government whose title is to be determined.… Finally, a general association of nations must be formed to guarantee political independence and territorial integrity to great and small States alike."

98. Woodrow Wilson, "Final Speech in Support of the League of Nations, September 25, 1919," at www.americanrhetoric.com/speeches/wilsonleagueofnations.htm: "Indeed, she earned more than she can ever be able to pay for, and the punishment exacted of her is not a punishment greater than she can bear . . ."

99. Wilson, "Final Speech in Support of the League of Nations, September 25, 1919," at www.americanrhetoric.com/speeches/wilsonleagueofnations.htm.

100. Kendrick A. Clements, *The Presidency of Woodrow Wilson*, 3rd ed. (Lawrence: University Press of Kansas, 1992), p. 189; Walter LaFeber, *American Age: U.S. Foreign Policy at Home and Abroad, From 1750 to the Present*, 2nd ed. (New York: W. W. Norton, 1994).

101. John Milton Cooper Jr., *Woodrow Wilson: A Biography* (New York: Knopf, 2009), p. 452: "It was at once his greatest triumph and his greatest tragedy."

102. William C. Martel, *Victory in War: Foundations of Modern Strategy* (New York: Cambridge University Press, 2011), p. 153: For Churchill, "The economic clauses of the Treaty were malignant and silly to an extent that made them obviously futile."

103. John Milton Cooper Jr., *Woodrow Wilson: A Biography* (New York: Knopf, 2009), p. 178.

104. Cf. Tony Smith, *America's Mission: The United States and the Worldwide Struggle for Democracy in the Twentieth Century* (Princeton, NJ: Princeton University Press, 2012), pp. 1–76; William C. Martel, *Victory in War: Foundations of Modern Strategy* (New York: Cambridge University Press, 2011), pp. 148–154, for an analysis of World War I and Wilson's strategy for victory.

105. Charles A. Kupchan and Clifford A. Kupchan, "The Promise of Collective Security," *International Security* 20, No. 1 (Summer 1995), pp. 52–61. The *democratic peace theory* suggested that the rise of democratic governments would decrease the chance of war. For a discussion of these arguments, see Michael C. Desch, "Democracy and Victory: Why Regime Type Hardly Matters," *International Security* 27, No. 2 (Fall 2002), pp. 5–47, esp. "Do Democracies Really Win Wars More Often?" (pp. 9–25). See also these consecutive articles in *International Security* 28, No. 1 (Summer 2003): Ajin Choi, "The Power of Democratic Cooperation," pp. 142–153; David A. Lake, "Fair Fights? Evaluating Theories of Democracy and Victory," pp. 154–179; and Michael C. Desch, "Democracy and Victory: Fair Fights or Food Fights?" pp. 180–194.

106. John Milton Cooper Jr., *Woodrow Wilson: A Biography* (New York: Knopf, 2009), p. 276.

107. On FDR's grand strategy, see Cecil V. Crabb, Kevin V. Mulcahy, *Presidents and Foreign Policy Making: From FDR to Reagan* (Baton Rouge: Louisiana State University Press, 1986); James Dougherty, *American Foreign Policy: FDR to Reagan* (New York: Harper and Row, 1986); Robert Dallek, *Franklin D. Roosevelt and American Foreign Policy, 1932–1945*, with a new afterword (New York: Oxford University Press, 1995); Walter Russell Mead, *Special Providence: American Foreign Policy and How It Changed the World* (New York: Knopf, 2001); Stephen E. Ambrose and Douglas G. Brinkley, *Rise to Globalism: American Foreign Policy Since 1938*, 9th rev. ed. (New York: Penguin Books, 2011); Walter LaFeber, *American Age: U.S. Foreign Policy at Home and Abroad, From 1750 to the Present*, 2nd ed. (New York: W. W. Norton, 1994).

108. Dallek, *Franklin D. Roosevelt and American Foreign Policy, 1932–1945* (New York: Oxford University Press, 1979), p. 23: "With the war debt moratorium coming to an end and the British asking for a fresh review of their obligations, Hoover saw a last chance to reverse the nation's continuing downward slide." Also, Hoover "wished to tie FDR to international negotiations which neither the British nor Congress would take seriously without Roosevelt's support." Nancy Gibbs and Michael Duffy, *The President's Club: Inside the World's Most Exclusive Fraternity* (New York: Simon & Schuster, 2012), pp. 20–22.

109. Dallek, *Franklin D. Roosevelt and American Foreign Policy, 1932–1945* (New York: Oxford University Press, 1979), p. 23.

110. See Nancy Gibbs and Michael Duffy, *The President's Club: Inside the World's Most Exclusive Fraternity* (New York: Simon & Schuster, 2012), p. 20: "Hoover tried to enlist his successor to act with him, although in ways that would have undercut Roosevelt's own progressive agenda. Roosevelt rejected the overture." Cf. Roy Jenkins, *Franklin Delano Roosevelt* (New York: Times Books, 2003), p. 66.

111. Robert Dallek, *Franklin D. Roosevelt and American Foreign Policy, 1932–1945* (New York: Oxford University Press, 1979), p. 24.

112. Brenda Haugen, *Franklin Delano Roosevelt: The New Deal President* (Minneapolis: Compass Point Books, 2006), p. 68: As Hoover reasoned, "if large companies were healthy, they'd hire more people, who in turn would have more money to put back into the economy and help it grow. Roosevelt, on the other hand, chose to help the most downtrodden first. He knew these people needed assistance to survive and couldn't wait for the economy to improve."

113. Robert Dallek, *Franklin D. Roosevelt and American Foreign Policy, 1932–1945* (New York: Oxford University Press, 1979), p. 23.

114. See Nancy Gibbs and Michael Duffy, *The President's Club: Inside the World's Most Exclusive Fraternity* (New York: Simon & Schuster, 2012), p. 20: "Hoover, Truman said, was handicapped by having arrived at the White House too easily. The only political job he'd ever held was as commerce secretary.... Without a strong attachment to the grass roots, Truman observed, 'he didn't really understand ... the needs of the American people.'"

115. Brenda Haugen, *Franklin Delano Roosevelt: The New Deal President* (Minneapolis: Compass Point Books, 2006), p. 68.

116. Robert Dallek, *Franklin D. Roosevelt and American Foreign Policy, 1932–1945* (New York: Oxford University Press, 1979), p. 38: "The conflict between what he was urging in national affairs and what he was urging in international affairs was clear to his advisers by the second month of his term."

117. Brenda Haugen, *Franklin Delano Roosevelt: The New Deal President* (Minneapolis: Compass Point Books, 2006), p. 69: "An emergency banking bill helped get the banking system back on its feet and protected those who had entrusted their savings there. The Emergency Relief Act brought help to the unemployed, and the Civilian Conservation Corps provided jobs for 2 million young men."

118. Robert Dallek, *Franklin D. Roosevelt and American Foreign Policy, 1932–1945* (New York: Oxford University Press, 1979), p. 78.

119. See Quincy Wright, "The Lend-Lease Bill and International Law," *American Journal of International Law* 35, No. 2 (April 1941), pp. 305–314; George

C. Herring Jr., "The United States and British Bankruptcy, 1944–1945: Responsibilities Deferred," *Political Science Quarterly* 86, No. 2 (June 1971), pp. 260–280; Arthur A. Stein, "Domestic Constraints, Extended Deterrence, and the Incoherence of Grand Strategy: The United States, 1938–1950," in Richard N. Rosecrance and Arthur A. Stein (eds.), *The Domestic Base of Grand Strategy* (Ithaca, NY: Cornell University Press, 1993), pp. 96–123; Richard W. Steele, "The Great Debate: Roosevelt, the Media, and the Coming of the War, 1940–1941," *Journal of American History* 71, No. 1 (June 1984), pp. 69–92.

120. Jonathan Alter, *The Defining Moment: FDR's Hundred Days and the Triumph of Hope* (New York: Simon and Schuster, 2006), p. 333.

121. Brenda Haugen, *Franklin Delano Roosevelt: The New Deal President* (Minneapolis: Compass Point Books, 2006), p. 81.

122. Robert Dallek, *Franklin D. Roosevelt and American Foreign Policy, 1932–1945* (New York: Oxford University Press, 1979), p. 252.

123. See Quincy Wright, "The Lend-Lease Bill and International Law," *American Journal of International Law* 35, No. 2 (April 1941), pp. 305–314; George C. Herring Jr., "The United States and British Bankruptcy, 1944–1945: Responsibilities Deferred," *Political Science Quarterly* 86, No. 2 (June 1971), pp. 260–280; Arthur A. Stein, "Domestic Constraints, Extended Deterrence, and the Incoherence of Grand Strategy: The United States, 1938–1950," in Richard N. Rosecrance and Arthur A. Stein (eds.), *The Domestic Base of Grand Strategy* (Ithaca, NY: Cornell University Press, 1993), pp. 96–123; Richard W. Steele, "The Great Debate: Roosevelt, the Media, and the Coming of the War, 1940–1941," *Journal of American History* 71, No. 1 (June 1984), pp. 69–92.

124. Tami Davis Biddle, "Leveraging Strength: The Pillars of American Grand Strategy in World War II," *Orbis* 55, No. 1 (Winter 2011), pp. 4–29, at p. 11.

125. Biddle, "Leveraging Strength: The Pillars of American Grand Strategy in World War II," *Orbis* 55, No. 1 (Winter 2011), p. 11: In terms of the distribution of national resources, "more than 13 percent of the government's war plant money was spent in the West, chiefly for permanent assets." Furthermore, regions in the "South and West saw extensive growth and industrialization as military training camps and war factories exploited the open space in these regions." Further, "To increase employment and take advantage of skilled workers who lived in and near U.S. cities … war production facilities sprang up near Detroit, Baltimore, Indianapolis, Buffalo, Hartford, St. Louis, Portland, and Seattle."

126. Michael Janeway, *The Fall of the House of Roosevelt: Brokers of Ideas and Power from FDR to LBJ* (New York: Columbia University Press, 2006), p. 11. Cf. Biddle, "Leveraging Strength: The Pillars of American Grand Strategy in World War II," *Orbis* 55, No. 1 (Winter 2011), p. 12.

127. George E. Mowry, *The Urban Nation: 1920–1960* (New York: Hill and Wang, 1965), p. 130: "Both the question and the answer were obviously prompted as much by future possibilities of as by past history, but both also reflected fifteen years in which the American mind had been conditioned against any war save that of immediate defense."

128. See William C. Martel, "Grand Strategy of 'Restrainment,'" *Orbis* 54, No. 3 (Summer 2010), pp. 356–373, p. 362: "The grand strategy of restrainment is

reflected in the policies President Franklin D. Roosevelt pursued in the late 1930s and early 1940s. Roosevelt understood the dangers posed by the Axis powers and attempted to implement policies to stop them. Following this logic, President Roosevelt practiced self-restraint, realizing that America possessed neither the public will nor the means necessary to stop the Axis powers. Facing these constraints, Roosevelt practiced cooperative restrainment as he sought to develop a coalition of like-minded states, including Great Britain, to work with others and to pursue such policies as Lend Lease, embargoes, and sanctions. In a Fireside Chat on September 11, 1941, Roosevelt warned the American people about 'unrestrained seekers of world conquest.'" See President Franklin D. Roosevelt, "Fireside Chat 18: On The Greer Incident (September 11, 1941)," at www.miller center.org/scripps/archive/speeches/detail/3323. In effect, the theory and practice of restrainment (though not referred to in such terms) has been followed more often than not by most U.S. presidents. In fact, it was the dominant practice during the period of America's economic development, particularly before World War II.

129. Alexander Deconde, A History of American Foreign Policy (New York: Charles Scribner's Sons, 1963), p. 567.

130. George E. Mowry, The Urban Nation: 1920–1960 (New York: Hill and Wang, 1965), p. 133.

131. Alexander Deconde, A History of American Foreign Policy (New York: Charles Scribner's Sons, 1963), p. 593.

132. Deconde, A History of American Foreign Policy (New York: Charles Scribner's Sons, 1963), p. 596. Cf. Hossein G. Askari, John Forrer, Hildy Teegen, and Jiawen Yang, eds., Economic Sanctions: Examining Their Philosophy and Efficacy (Westport, CT: Praeger, 2003), pp. 177–185; Michael Barnhart, Japan Prepares Total War: The Search for Economic Security, 1919–1941 (Ithaca, NY: Cornell University Press, Studies in Security Affairs, 1987); Edward S. Miller, Bankrupting the Enemy: The U.S. Financial Siege of Japan before Pearl Harbor (Annapolis, MD: Naval Institute Press, 2007).

133. Robert Dallek, Franklin D. Roosevelt and American Foreign Policy, 1932–1945 (New York: Oxford University Press, 1979), p. 97.

134. For data on the dramatic shift in public opinion from being against war to being for it, see Adam J. Berinsky, Eleanor Neff Powell, Eric Schickler, and Ian Brett Yohai, "Revisiting Public Opinion in the 1930s and 1940s," Political Science, July 2011, pp. 515–520, esp. p. 519.

135. See Ronald H. Spector, Eagle against the Sun (New York: The Free Press, 1985), p. 418; see also Joint Chiefs of Staff, "Strategic Plan for the Defeat of Japan," May 8, 1943, at www.fdrlibrary.marist.edu/psf/box2/a18j01.html. Cf. Thomas B. Allen and Norman Polmar, Code-Name Downfall (New York: Simon & Schuster, 1995), p. 126. See also Unconditional Surrender, Federation of the American Scientists, at www.fas.org/irp/eprint/arens/chap1.htm (through /chap5.html), for a discussion of two subordinate operations: Operation Olympic, which was an invasion of the island of Kyushu in the fall of 1945, and Operation Coronet, which was an invasion of the island of Honshu in the spring of 1946.

136. Alexander Deconde, A History of American Foreign Policy (New York: Charles Scribner's Sons, 1963), p. 615.

137. Deconde, *A History of American Foreign Policy* (New York: Charles Scribner's Sons, 1963), p. 615. Historians argue that "with this executive agreement, never submitted to the Senate, Roosevelt defied the long tradition of nonentanglement" in foreign affairs.

138. Thomas A. Bailey, *A Diplomatic History of the American People* (Englewood Cliffs, NJ: Prentice Hall, 1980), p. 758.

139. Alexander Deconde, *A History of American Foreign Policy* (New York: Charles Scribner's Sons, 1963), p. 621.

140. Thomas A. Bailey, *A Diplomatic History of the American People* (Englewood Cliffs, NJ: Prentice Hall, 1980), p. 760: "The Cairo Declaration was thus a public pledge to squeeze the Japanese genie back into the pre-Perry bottle."

141. See John Gimbel, *The Origins of the Marshall Plan* (Stanford, CA: Stanford University Press, 1976), pp. 1–3, 25, 71–79. Cf. Imanuel Wexler, *The Marshall Plan Revisited: The European Recovery Program in Economic Perspective* (Westport, CT: Greenwood Press, 1983); Michael J. Hogan, *The Marshall Plan: America, Britain, and the Reconstruction of Western Europe, 1947–1952* (New York: Cambridge University Press, 1987); "Germany" and "Japan," chaps. 1 and 2 in James Dobbins et al., *America's Role in Nation-Building* (Santa Monica, CA: RAND Corporation, 2003), pp. 3–23, 25–53; John Meacham, *Franklin and Winston: An Intimate Portrait of an Epic Friendship* (New York: Random House, 2003), p. 301.

142. Gerhard von Glahn, *Law among Nations: An Introduction to Public International Law*, 3rd ed. (New York: Macmillan, 1976).

143. Alexander Deconde, *A History of American Foreign Policy* (New York: Charles Scribner's Sons, 1963), pp. 622–623.

144. Deconde, *A History of American Foreign Policy* (New York: Charles Scribner's Sons, 1963), p. 626.

145. Philip E. Mosely, "Dismemberment of Germany: The Allied Negotiations from Yalta to Potsdam," *Foreign Affairs* 28, No. 3 (April 1950), pp. 487–498. See "The Yalta Conference," at http://avalon.law.yale.edu/wwii/yalta.asp. Cf. Geoffrey Warner, "From Teheran to Yalta: Reflections on F.D.R.'s Foreign Policy," *International Affairs* (Royal Institute of International Affairs, 1944–), 43, No. 3 (July 1967), pp. 530–536; Fraser J. Harbutt, *Yalta 1945: Europe and America at the Crossroads* (New York: Cambridge University Press, 2010).

146. See "Atlantic Charter," at http://avalon.law.yale.edu/wwii/atlantic.asp.

147. Alexander Deconde, *A History of American Foreign Policy* (New York: Charles Scribner's Sons, 1963), p. 633.

148. See *The Formation of the United Nations*, Office of the Historian, U.S. Department of State, at www.history.state.gov/milestones/1937-1945/UN.

149. George C. Herring, *From Colony to Superpower: U.S. Foreign Relations since 1776* (New York: Oxford University Press, 2008), pp. 376–377.

150. Charles A. Kupchan and Clifford A. Kupchan, "The Promise of Collective Security," *International Security* 20, No. 1 (Summer 1995), pp. 52–61.

9 *Reinforcing Alliances and Partnerships: Truman to Reagan*

1. George F. Kennan, "Long Telegram," at www.gwu.edu/~nsarchiv/coldwar/documents/episode-1/kennan.htm; George Kennan, "Sources of Soviet Conduct," *Foreign Affairs*, July 1947, pp. 556–582.

2. John Lewis Gaddis, *We Now Know: Rethinking the Cold War* (New York: Oxford University Press, 1997), p. 88, who provides several explanations, but the one relevant here is that to exploit its nuclear advantage was contrary to American grand strategic tradition and its values.

3. On the concept of "nested" in hegemony, see George Tsebelis, *Nested Games: Rational Choice in Comparative Politics* (Berkeley: University of California Press, 1990), pp. 239–248. Also, Robert O. Keohane and Joseph S. Nye, *Power and Independence: World Politics in Transition* (Boston: Little, Brown, 1977).

4. On the bandwagon effect, see Robert G. Kaufman, "To Balance or to Bandwagon? Alignment Decisions in 1930s Europe," *Security Studies* 1, No. 3 (1992), pp. 417–447; Kevin Sweeney and Paul Fritz, "Jumping on the Bandwagon: An Interest-Based Explanation for Great Power Alliances," *Journal of Politics* 66, No. 2 (2004), pp. 428–449; Avery Goldstein, *From Bandwagon to Balance-of-Power Politics: Structural Constraints and Politics in China, 1949–1978* (Stanford, CA: Stanford University Press, 1991); Eric J. Labs, "Do Weak States Bandwagon?" *Security Studies* 1, No. 3 (1992), pp. 383–416.

5. The year following each institution is the year of its formation.

6. For Churchill's belief that conflict with the Soviet Union was inevitable, see John Colville, *The Fringes of Power: 10 Downing Street Diaries 1939–1955* (New York: W. W. Norton & Company, 1985), p. 479, who reported that in March 1944, "the P.M. ... said that it was now obvious our efforts to forge a Soviet-Polish agreement had failed and that he would soon have to make a cold announcement in Parliament to this effect. It all seems to augur ill for the future of relations between this country and the U.S.S.R." As Colville observed in April 1944, "And over everything hangs the uncertainty of Russia's future policy towards Europe and the world" (p. 484).

7. Colin S. Gray, "Harry S. Truman and the Forming of American Grand Strategy in the Cold War, 1945–1953," in Williamson Murray (ed.), *The Shaping of Grand Strategy: Policy, Diplomacy, and War* (New York: Cambridge University Press, 2011), p. 214.

8. Wilson D. Miscamble, "Roosevelt, Truman and Development of Postwar Grand Strategy," *Orbis* 53, No. 4 (Fall 2009), pp. 553–570.

9. In one of the most consequential contingencies of history, Henry Wallace missed the presidency by a mere 82 days. FDR moved him to secretary of commerce and selected Truman to be his running mate. Truman had only been Vice President for about four months when FDR died in April 1945. Had Wallace succeeded to the presidency, the Cold War might have been more of a Warm Peace, with U.S. acquiescence to the expansion of Soviet power.

10. Wilson D. Miscamble, "Roosevelt, Truman and Development of Postwar Grand Strategy," *Orbis* 53, No. 4 (Fall 2009), pp. 553–570.

11. Miscamble, "Roosevelt, Truman and Development of Postwar Grand Strategy," *Orbis* 53, No. 4 (Fall 2009), pp. 553–570.

12. Harry S. Truman, *Memoirs of Harry S. Truman: Years of Trial and Hope*, Vol. 2 (Garden City, NY: Doubleday & Company, 1956), p. 214. For Truman, "the Russians simply did not understand – or would not – our peaceful intentions and our genuine desire to co-operate through the United Nations toward the

establishment of a climate of peace; that we did not want to force and had no intention of forcing our way of life upon them or anyone else, as we would resist to the utmost any attempt to impose another system upon us; that I wanted to see if we could not understand one another a little better, and we had to do something about our poor communications. Surely our side had tried. The Russians must also try if the future of the world and the very survival of civilization were not to be lost."

13. See Wilson D. Miscamble, "Roosevelt, Truman and Development of Postwar Grand Strategy," *Orbis* 53, No. 4 (Fall 2009), pp. 553–570. Cf. Harry S. Truman, *Memoirs of Harry S. Truman: Years of Trial and Hope*, Vol. 2 (Garden City, NY: Doubleday & Company, 1956), p. 214.

14. Peter Feaver, "Debating American Grand Strategy after Major War," *Orbis* 53, No. 4 (Fall 2009), pp. 547–552.

15. See David McCullough, *Truman* (New York: Simon and Schuster, 1992), p. 587. Cf. Robert Frazier, "Kennan, 'Universalism,' and the Truman Doctrine," *Journal of Cold War Studies* 11, No. 2 (Spring 2009), pp. 3–34. David C. Engerman, "Ideology and the Origins of the Cold War," in Melvyn P. Leffler and Odd Arne Westad (eds.), *The Cambridge History of the Cold War*, Vol. I (New York: Cambridge University Press, 2010), pp. 20–43.

16. Harry S. Truman, *Memoirs of Harry S. Truman: Year of Decisions*, Vol. 1 (Garden City, NY: Doubleday & Company, 1955), pp. 411–412: "It was clear that the Russian foreign policy was based on the conclusion that we were heading for a major depression and they were already planning to take advantage of our setback."

17. George F. Kennan, "Long Telegram," at www.gwu.edu/~nsarchiv/coldwar/documents/episode-1/kennan.htm

18. Kennan, "Long Telegram," at www.gwu.edu/~nsarchiv/coldwar/documents/episode-1/kennan.htm

19. Harry S. Truman, *Memoirs of Harry S. Truman: Year of Decisions*, Vol. 1 (Garden City, NY: Doubleday & Company, 1955), p. 412.

20. See William C. Martel, "The Search for Strategy: Review Essay," *Naval War College Review*, Summer 2007, pp. 123–132, p. 129.

21. George F. Kennan, "Long Telegram," at www.gwu.edu/~nsarchiv/coldwar/documents/episode-1/kennan.htm

22. On NSC-68, see Samuel F. Wells, "Sounding the Tocsin: NSC 68 and the Soviet Threat," *International Security* 4.2 (1979), pp. 116–158; John Lewis Gaddis and Paul Nitze, "NSC 68 and the Soviet Threat Reconsidered," *International Security* 4.4 (1980), pp. 164–176; John Lewis Gaddis, "NSC 68 and the Problem of Ends and Means," *International Security* 4.4 (1980), pp. 164–170.

23. For historical analysis of U.S. military spending, see Dinah Walker, "Trends in U.S. Military Spending," Council on Foreign Relations, August 23, 2012, at www.cfr.org/geoeconomics/trends-us-military-spending/p28855

24. Colin S. Gray, "Harry S. Truman and the Forming of American Grand Strategy in the Cold War, 1945–1953," in Williamson Murray (ed.), *The Shaping of Grand Strategy: Policy, Diplomacy, and War* (New York: Cambridge University Press, 2011), p. 224. Also, Melvyn P. Leffler, "The Emergence of an American Grand Strategy," in Melvyn P. Leffler and Odd Arne Westad (eds.), *The Cambridge History of the Cold War*, Vol. I (New York: Cambridge University Press, 2010), pp. 67–88.

25. Chester J. Pach, *Arming the Free World: The Origins of the United States Military Assistance Program* (Durham: University of North Carolina Press, 1991), p. 7 (emphasis added).

26. See James E. Bond, *The Rules of Riot: Internal Conflict and the Law of War* (Princeton, NJ: University Press, 1974); Lee C. Buchheit, *Secession: The Legitimacy of Self-Determination* (New Haven, C: Yale University Press, 1978; Hedley Bull, ed., *Intervention in World Politics* (Oxford: Clarendon Press, 1984); Richard A. Falk, "Intervention and National Liberation," in Hedley Bull (ed.), *Intervention in World Politics* (Oxford: Clarendon Press, 1984, pp. 119–133; Evan Luard, "Civil Conflicts in Modern International Relations," in Evan Luard (ed.), *The International Regulation of Civil Wars* (London: Thames and Hudson, 1972), pp. 7–25; James N. Rosenau, *International Aspects of Civil Strife* (Princeton, NJ: Princeton University Press, 1964); Heather A. Wilson, *International Law and the Use of Force by National Liberation Movements* (Oxford: Clarendon Press, 1988).

27. Chester J. Pach, *Arming the Free World: The Origins of the United States Military Assistance Program* (Durham: University of North Carolina Press, 1991), p. 88.

28. Harry S. Truman, "Truman Doctrine: President Harry S. Truman's Address before a Joint Session of Congress," March 12, 1947, at http://avalon.law.yale.edu/20th_century/trudoc.asp.

29. Harry S. Truman, *Memoirs of Harry S. Truman, Years of Trial and Hope*, Vol. 2 (Garden City, NY: Doubleday & Company, Inc., 1956), p. 119.

30. Greg Behrman, *The Most Noble Adventure: The Marshall Plan and the Time When America Helped Save Europe* (New York: Free Press, 2007), p. 165. Cf. John Gimbel, *The Origins of the Marshall Plan* (Stanford, CA: Stanford University Press, 1976), pp. 1–3, 25, 71–79; Imanuel Wexler, *The Marshall Plan Revisited: The European Recovery Program in Economic Perspective* (Westport, CT: Greenwood Press, 1983); Michael J. Hogan, *The Marshall Plan: America, Britain, and the Reconstruction of Western Europe, 1947–1952* (New York: Cambridge University Press, 1987); "Germany" and "Japan," chaps. 1 and 2, in "Germany" and "Japan," chaps. 1 and 2 in James Dobbins et al., *The Beginner's Guide to Nation Building* (Santa Monica, CA: RAND Corporation, 2007); Dobbins, et al., *America's Role in Nation-Building*, pp. 3–23, 25–53; John Meacham, *Franklin and Winston: An Intimate Portrait of an Epic Friendship* (New York: Random House, 2003), p. 301.

31. Greg Behrman, *The Most Noble Adventure: The Marshall Plan and the Time When America Helped Save Europe* (New York: Free Press, 2007), p. 4.

32. Harry S. Truman, *Memoirs of Harry S. Truman, Years of Trial and Hope*, Vol. 2 (Garden City, NY: Doubleday & Company, Inc., 1956), p. 119.

33. Greg Behrman, *The Most Noble Adventure: The Marshall Plan and the Time When America Helped Save Europe* (New York: Free Press, 2007), p. 165.

34. Behrman, *The Most Noble Adventure: The Marshall Plan and the Time When America Helped Save Europe* (New York: Free Press, 2007), p. 132.

35. See David L. DiLeo, *George Ball, Vietnam, and the Rethinking of Containment* (Chapel Hill: University of North Carolina Press, 1991), p. 25.

36. For background on the National Security Council, and the NSC-68 in particular, see David Rothkopf, *Running the World: The Inside Story of the National Security Council and the Architects of American Power* (New York: PublicAffairs, 2005), pp. 4–6, 59, 85.

37. David McCullough, *Truman* (New York: Simon and Schuster, 1992), p. 925.

38. Robert Dallek, *Harry S. Truman* (New York: Times Books, 2008), p. 102.

39. Dallek, *Harry S. Truman* (New York: Times Books, 2008), p. 932.

40. Harry S. Truman, *Memoirs of Harry S. Truman, Years of Trial and Hope*, Vol. 2 (Garden City, NY: Doubleday & Company, Inc., 1956), p. 335.

41. Jeffrey Grey, *The Commonwealth Armies and the Korean War* (Manchester, UK: Manchester University Press, 1988).

42. Robert Dallek, *Harry S. Truman* (New York: Times Books, 2008), p. 977. Cf. Harry S. Truman, *Memoirs of Harry S. Truman, Years of Trial and Hope*, Vol. 2 (Garden City, NY: Doubleday & Company, Inc., 1956), p. 337: "The Reds were probing for weaknesses in our armor; we had to meet their thrust *without getting embroiled in a world-wide war*" (emphasis added).

43. See Matthew B. Ridgway, *The Korean War*, 2nd ed. (De Capo Press, 1986), pp. 141–184.

44. George C. Herring, *From Colony to Superpower: U.S. Foreign Relations Since 1776* (New York: Oxford University Press, 2008), pp. 376–377.

45. For background on Eisenhower's grand strategy, see Robert J. Art, "A Defensible Defense: America's Grand Strategy after the Cold War," *International Security* 15.4 (1991), pp. 5–53; John Lewis Gaddis, Strategies *of Containment* (New York: Oxford University Press, 2005); Aaron L. Friedberg, *In the Shadow of the Garrison State: America's Anti-statism and Its Cold War Grand Strategy* (Princeton, NJ: Princeton University Press, 2000); Colin Dueck, *Reluctant Crusaders: Power, Culture, and Change in American Grand Strategy* (Princeton, NJ: Princeton University Press, 2008); Ray Takeyh, *The Origins of the Eisenhower Doctrine: The US, Britain, and Nasser's Egypt, 1953–57* (New York: St. Martin's Press, 2000); Thomas J. Christensen, *Useful Adversaries: Grand Strategy, Domestic Mobilization, and Sino-American Conflict, 1947–1958* (Princeton, NJ: Princeton University Press, 1996); Christopher Layne, "Rethinking American Grand Strategy: Hegemony or Balance of Power in the Twenty-First Century? *World Policy Journal* 15.2 (1998), pp. 8–28; Steven Metz, "Eisenhower and the Planning of American Grand Strategy," *Journal of Strategic Studies* 14.1 (1991), pp. 49–71.

46. John Lewis Gaddis, *Strategies of Containment* (New York: Oxford University Press, 2005), p. 126: "But Eisenhower did have strong initial reservations about Dulles's theory of asymmetrical strategic deterrence (already coming to be known, confusingly, as the doctrine of 'retaliation')." Also, Robert R. Bowie and Richard H. Immerman, *Waging Peace: How Eisenhower Shaped an Enduring Cold War Strategy* (New York: Oxford University Press, 1998), p. 74.

47. Gaddis, *Strategies of Containment* (New York: Oxford University Press, 2005), p. 126: "... which abandons countless human beings to a despotism and godless terrorism, but felt obliged to remind Dulles that liberation [of Soviet satellites] could only come by peaceful means."

48. Martin Walker, *The Cold War* (London: Fourth Estate, Ltd, 1993), p. 83.

49. See Dwight D. Eisenhower, "The Eisenhower Doctrine on the Middle East, A Message to Congress, January 5, 1957" (Washington, DC: The Department of State Bulletin XXXVl, 1957; Ray Takeyh, *The Origins of the Eisenhower Doctrine: The US, Britain, and Nasser's Egypt, 1953–57* (New York: St. Martin's Press, 2000).

50. Eisenhower, "The Eisenhower Doctrine on the Middle East, A Message to Congress, January 5, 1957" (Washington, DC: The Department of State Bulletin XXXVl, 1957; Ray Takeyh, *The Origins of the Eisenhower Doctrine: The US, Britain, and Nasser's Egypt, 1953–57* (New York: St. Martin's Press, 2000).

51. Michael S. Sherry, *In the Shadow of War: The United States Since the 1930s* (New Haven, CT: Yale University Press, 1995), p. 193.

52. John Lewis Gaddis, *Strategies of Containment* (New York: Oxford University Press, 2005), p. 128.

53. Robert Jervis, *American Foreign Policy in a New Era* (New York: Routledge, 2005), p. 81.

54. Aaron L. Friedberg, "Strengthening U.S. Strategic Planning," *Washington Quarterly*, Winter 2007–2008, pp. 47–60. Also, John Lewis Gaddis, *Strategies of Containment* (New York: Oxford University Press, 2005), p. 143.

55. See Bernard Brodie, *Strategy in the Missile Age* (Princeton, NJ: Princeton University Press, 1959), p. 248; Samuel P. Huntington, *The Common Defense* (New York: Columbia University Press, 1961), pp. 67–68; Robert E. Osgood, *Limited War* (Chicago: University of Chicago Press, 1957; Maxwell D. Taylor, *The Uncertain Trumpet* (New York: Harper & Row, 1960).

56. George C. Herring, *From Colony to Superpower: U.S. Foreign Relations since 1776* (New York: Oxford University Press, 2008), p. 659. Cf. Warren I. Cohen, *The Cambridge History of American Foreign Relations: Volume IV, America in the Age of Soviet Power, 1945–1991* (New York: Cambridge University Press, 1993), p. 87: "The historian John Lewis Gaddis has argued that Truman intended a 'symmetrical' response, a policy of meeting Soviet probes with comparable force."

57. John Lewis Gaddis, *Strategies of Containment* (New York: Oxford University Press, 2005), p. 159. This was an "integrated and reasonably efficient adaptation of resources to objectives, of means to ends." This common threat "implied a willingness to shift the nature and location of competition from the site of the original provocation, thereby admittedly risking escalation; but they also promised retention of the initiative, which is the key to minimizing costs." Cf. George C. Herring, *From Colony to Superpower: U.S. Foreign Relations since 1776* (New York: Oxford University Press, 2008), p. 660: "While sticking to established foreign policy goals, Eisenhower's New Look significantly altered the means to achieve them."

58. Gaddis, *Strategies of Containment* (New York: Oxford University Press, 2005), p. 144.

59. Michael S. Sherry, *In the Shadow of War: The United States Since the 1930s* (New Haven, CT: Yale University Press, 1995), p. 192.

60. John Lewis Gaddis, *Strategies of Containment* (New York: Oxford University Press, 2005), p. 145.

61. John Foster Dulles, Department of State Bulletin, Vol. XXX, 017–110, in Gary Donaldson, *Modern America: A Documentary History of the Nation Since 1945* (Armonk, New York: M. E. Sharpe), p. 68: "That permits a selection of military

means instead of a multiplication of means. As a result, it is now possible to get, and share, more basic security at less cost."

62. John Foster Dulles speech, "Documents on American Foreign Relations" (New York: Council on Foreign Relations, 1954), pp. 7–15.

63. See Alain C. Enthoven, Wayne K. Smith, *How Much Is Enough? Shaping the Defense Program, 1961–1969* (New York: Harper & Row, 1971). Also, John Lewis Gaddis, *Strategies of Containment* (New York: Oxford University Press, 2005), p. 145.

64. Harry S. Truman, *Memoirs of Harry S. Truman: Year of Decisions*, Vol. 1 (Garden City, NY: Doubleday & Company, 1955), p. 419.

65. Andreas Wenger, *Living with Peril: Eisenhower, Kennedy, and Nuclear Weapons* (Lanham, MD: Rowman and Littlefield, 1997), p. 44.

66. John Foster Dulles, "Policy for Security and Peace," *Foreign Affairs* 32, No. 3 (April 1954), pp. 353–364: "... local defense is important. But in such areas the main reliance must be on the power of the free community to retaliate with great force by mobile means at places of its own choice.... The essential thing is that a potential aggressor should know in advance that he can and will be made to suffer for his aggression more than he can possibly gain by it."

67. John Lewis Gaddis, *Strategies of Containment* (New York: Oxford University Press, 2005), p. 149.

68. Andreas Wenger, *Living with Peril: Eisenhower, Kennedy, and Nuclear Weapons* (Lanham, MD: Rowman and Littlefield, 1997), p. 46.

69. See Eisenhower's Farewell Address to the Nation, January 17, 1961, at www .speeches-usa.com/Transcripts/031_eisenhower.html

70. See Lawrence Freedman, *Evolution of Nuclear Strategy* (London: Oxford University Press, 1981), p. 147. Also, John Lewis Gaddis, *Strategies of Containment* (New York: Oxford University Press, 2005), p. 186: "The President was an early believer in what would later become known as the doctrine of 'sufficiency.'"

71. Günter Bischof and Stephen E. Ambrose, *Eisenhower: A Centenary Assessment* (Baton Rouge: Louisiana State University Press, 1995), p. 254.

72. John Lewis Gaddis, *Strategies of Containment* (New York: Oxford University Press, 2005), p. 162.

73. For these arguments, see Gaddis, *Strategies of Containment* (New York: Oxford University Press, 2005), p. 163.

74. Dwight D. Eisenhower, "The President's News Conference," March 17, 1954, *The American Presidency Project* at http://www.presidency.ucsb.edu/ws/index.php? pid=10184&st=&st1= "What we are trying to say now is to express a generalization that would apply in an infinite variety of cases, under an infinite variety of provocations, and I just don't believe it is possible."

75. John Lewis Gaddis, *Strategies of Containment* (New York: Oxford University Press, 2005), p. 173.

76. Gaddis, *Strategies of Containment* (New York: Oxford University Press, 2005), p. 196. It was seen to be "coherent, bearing signs of his influence at every level, careful for the most part, in its relation of ends to means, and on the whole, more consistent with than detrimental to the national interest."

77. As David Rothkopf argues in his book, *Running the World* (New York: Public Affairs, 2005), pp. 71–72. "The Solarium Project therefore was not just the work of a good executive or a master bureaucrat or even a canny politician; it was a magisterial illustration of an effective president in action, perhaps one of the signal events of the past sixty years of the American presidency."

78. Michele A. Flournoy and Shawn W. Brimley, "Strategic Planning for National Security," *Joint Forces Quarterly*, No. 41 (2006), pp. xx.

79. See George W. Bush, Second Inaugural Address, on the value of promoting universal human values.

80. John Lewis Gaddis, *Strategies of Containment* (New York: Oxford University Press, 2005), p. 130: "Eisenhower almost always emphasized economic rather than moral considerations."

81. Norman A. Graebner, *The National Security: Its Theory and Practice, 1945–1960* (New York: Oxford University Press, 1986), p. 94. John Lewis Gaddis, *Strategies of Containment* (New York: Oxford University Press, 2005), p. 130: "The minimum requirement is that we are able to trade freely, in spite of anything Russia may do, with those areas from which we obtain the raw materials that are vital to our country. . . . We must state that no foreign power will be allowed to cut us off from those areas of the world that are necessary to the health, strength and development of our country."

82. John Lewis Gaddis, *Strategies of Containment* (New York: Oxford University Press, 2005), p. 130: "Eisenhower and Dulles could agree that the chief American interest in the world was access to the world, and that in turn required a world of at least minimal congeniality."

83. Robert D. Hormats, *The Price of Liberty: Paying for America's Wars* (New York: Times Books, 2007), p. 200.

84. Hormats, *The Price of Liberty: Paying for America's Wars* (New York: Times Books, 2007), p. 200. "This would mean regimentation [the kind of economic controls and sacrifices experienced in World War II]."

85. For an analysis of the American logic of victory, see William C. Martel, *Victory in War: Foundations of Modern Strategy* (New York: Cambridge University Press, 2011), pp. 174–197.

86. John Lewis Gaddis, *Strategies of Containment* (New York: Oxford University Press, 2005), p. 131: The United States "cannot be strong enough to go to every spot in the world, where our enemies may use force or the threat of force, and defend those nations."

87. Dwight D. Eisenhower, "The Chance for Peace" (address delivered before the American Society of Newspaper Editors, April 16, 1953), at www.eisenhower .archives.gov/all_about_ike/speeches/chance_for_peace.pdf

88. Dwight D. Eisenhower, "Remarks at Annual Meeting of the Association of Land-Grant Colleges and Universities," November 16, 1954, The American Presidency Project, at http://www.presidency.ucsb.edu/ws/index.php?pid=10136&st=&st1=

89. Andrew Bacevich, "The Tyranny of Defense Inc.," *The Atlantic*, January/February 2011: "By diverting social capital from productive to destructive purposes, war and the preparation for war deplete, rather than enhance, a nation's strength. And while assertions of military necessity might camouflage the costs entailed, they can never negate them altogether." See also, John Lewis Gaddis, *Strategies of Containment*

(New York: Oxford University Press, 2005), p. 132; Andrew J. Bacevich, *Washington Rules: America's Path to Permanent War* (New York: Macmillan Books, 2010).

90. Dwight D. Eisenhower, "The President's News Conference," April 30, 1953, at The American Presidency Project at http://www.presidency.ucsb.edu/ws/index .php?pid=9832&st=&stl= "It has been the purpose of this administration ever since it took office, finding itself confronted with a crazy quilt of promises, commitments, and contracts, to bring American military logic and American economic logic into joint strong harness."

91. John Lewis Gaddis, *Strategies of Containment* (New York: Oxford University Press, 2005), p. 133.

92. Dwight D. Eisenhower, "Remarks to the Staff of the United States Information Agency," November 10, 1953, at The American Presidency Project at http://www .presidency.ucsb.edu/ws/index.php?pid=9758&st=&stl= John Lewis Gaddis, *Strategies of Containment* (New York: Oxford University Press, 2005), p. 133: the problem was that the "objective had to be more than merely 'victory,' because a victory gained without regard to costs and effects, especially in a nuclear age, could be as devastating as defeat." Cf. William C. Martel, *Victory in War: Foundations of Modern Strategy* (New York: Cambridge University Press, 2011), pp. 126–135, for an analysis of victory in the context of nuclear weapons.

93. Gaddis, *Strategies of Containment* (New York: Oxford University Press, 2005), p. 133: "The whole idea was that 'we must not destroy what we are attempting to defend.' What the United State was defending was a way of life in which the central values are freedom of choice for individuals, democratic procedures for government, and private enterprise for the economy. An unthinking quest for absolute security could undermine all of these."

94. Dwight D. Eisenhower, "The President's News Conference" November 11, 1953, The American Presidency Project, at http://www.presidency.ucsb.edu/ws/index .php?pid=9760&st=&stl=

95. John Lewis Gaddis, *Strategies of Containment* (New York: Oxford University Press, 2005), p. 134: "It implied the existence of interests distinct from threats, as well as a determination not to carry actions intended to counter threats so far that they endangered interests."

96. On how public opinion influences decisions about policy, see John E. Mueller, *War, Presidents and Public Opinion* (New York: John Wiley & Sons, Inc., 1973); Ole R. Holsti, *Public Opinion and American Foreign Policy* (Ann Arbor: University of Michigan Press, 1996); John E. Mueller, *Policy and Opinion in the Gulf War* (Chicago: University of Chicago Press, 1994), pp. 60–67; Richard Sobel, *The Impact of Public Opinion on U.S. Foreign Policy Since Vietnam* (New York: Oxford University Press, 2001); and Matthew A. Baum, "How Public Opinion Constrains the Use of Force: The Case of Operation Restore Hope," *Presidential Studies Quarterly* 34, No. 2 (June 2004), pp. 187–226. Also, Peter Trubowitz, *Politics and Strategy: Partisan Ambition and American Statecraft* (Princeton, NJ: Princeton University Press, 2011).

97. John Lewis Gaddis, *Strategies of Containment* (New York: Oxford University Press, 2005), p. 135.

98. Stanley E. Spangler, *Force and Accommodation in World Politics* (Maxwell Air Force Base, Alabama: Air University Press, 1991), p. 88.

99. Spangler, *Force and Accommodation in World Politics* (Maxwell Air Force Base, AL: Air University Press, 1991), pp. 87–88. As he explained it to a State Department colleague: "If there's no evident menace from the Soviet bloc, our will to maintain unity and strength may weaken. It's a fact, unfortunate though it be, that in promoting our programs in Congress we have to make evident the international Communist menace.... The same situation would probably prevail among our allies [as a result of a détente]. They might feel that the danger was over and therefore they did not need to continue to spend large sums for defense."

100. The notion of internal Soviet political and especially economic weaknesses was a minor part of the debate about how effective the Soviet Union was as a geostrategic competitor of the United States. See Karl W. Deutsch, *The Analysis of International* Relations (Prentice Hall, 1968), pp. 29–31, 174, for the argument that coalition failures can bring down the system.

101. John Lewis Gaddis, *Strategies of Containment* (New York: Oxford University Press, 2005), p. 143.

102. Gaddis, *Strategies of Containment* (New York: Oxford University Press, 2005), p. 137. By implication, the Soviet leadership likely believed "that free people cannot preserve their way of life and at the same time provide enormous military establishments." Cf. Henry A. Kissinger, *Nuclear Weapons and Foreign Policy*, for this argument.

103. Gaddis, *Strategies of Containment* (New York: Oxford University Press, 2005), p. 137: "It further followed that if, as claimed, Soviet intentions were to achieve world revolution by means short of war, then that goals might be thwarted or at least deterred by a willingness on the part of the West to *threaten* war."

104. See Eisenhower's Farewell Address to the Nation, January 17, 1961, at www .speeches-usa.com/Transcripts/031_eisenhower.html.

105. George C. Herring, *From Colony to Superpower: U.S. Foreign Relations Since 1776* (New York: Oxford University Press, 2008), pp. 376–377.

106. See Eisenhower's Farewell Address to the Nation, January 17, 1961, at www .speeches-usa.com/Transcripts/031_eisenhower.html "Good judgment seeks balance and progress; lack of it eventually finds imbalance and frustration." And "... balance between our essential requirements as a nation and the duties imposed by the nation upon the individual; balance between the actions of the moment and the national welfare of the future." Further, "We cannot mortgage the material assets of our grandchildren without asking the loss also of their political and spiritual heritage. We want democracy to survive for all generations to come, not to become the insolvent phantom of tomorrow."

107. See Inaugural Address of President John F. Kennedy, Washington, DC, January 20, 1961, at http://www.presidency.ucsb.edu/ws/index.php?pid=8032&st=&st1= (emphasis added).

108. See Nancy Gibbs and Michael Duffy, *The President's Club: Inside the World's Most Exclusive Fraternity* (New York: Simon & Schuster, 2012), pp. 115–125.

109. See Gibbs and Duffy, *The President's Club: Inside the World's Most Exclusive Fraternity* (New York: Simon & Schuster, 2012), p. 109.

110. Thomas A. Bailey, *A Diplomatic History of the American People* (Englewood Cliffs, NJ: Prentice Hall, 1980), p. 868.

111. See Lawrence Freedman, *The Evolution of Nuclear Strategy* (New York: St. Martin's Press, 1989), pp. 228, 285–286.

112. See William C. Martel, *Victory in War: Foundations of Modern Strategy* (New York: Cambridge University Press, 2011), p. 165. Cf. Lawrence Freedman, *Evolution of Nuclear Strategy* (London: Oxford University Press, 1981), pp. 216, 271–272. Also, Lawrence Freedman, "Vietnam and the Disillusioned Strategist," *International Affairs* (Royal Institute of International Affairs) 72, No. 1 (January 1996), pp. 133–151.

113. For works on McNamara and the problem of resource allocation in defense planning, systems analysis, and PPBS, see E. S. Quade and W. I. Boucher, "Introduction," in *Systems Analysis and Policy Planning* (New York: American Elsevier, 1968), pp. 1–19; Charles J. Hitch and Alain C. Enthoven, "Systems Analysis," in Samuel A. Tucker (ed.), *A Modern Design for Defense Decision* (Washington, DC: Industrial College of the Armed Forces, 1966), pp. 119–195; Charles J. Hitch and Roland N. McKean, *The Economics of Defense in the Nuclear Age* (Cambridge, MA: Harvard University Press, 1961). Cf. Robert S. McNamara, *In Retrospect: The Tragedy and Lessons of Vietnam* (New York: Times Books, 1995); David Halberstam, *The Best and the Brightest* (New York: Random House, 1972).

114. See Nicholas Wapshott, *Keynes Hayek: The Clash that Defined Modern Economics* (New York: W. W. Norton, 2011), pp. 235–239.

115. Maxwell D. Taylor, *The Uncertain Trumpet* (New York: Harper & Brothers, 1960); John Lewis Gaddis, *Strategies of Containment* (New York: Oxford University Press, 1982), p. 214.

116. John Lewis Gaddis, *Strategies of Containment* (New York: Oxford University Press, 1982), pp. 203, 214. Kennedy "placed his emphasis on minimizing risks by giving the United States sufficient flexibility to respond without either escalation or humiliation."

117. Gaddis, *Strategies of Containment* (New York: Oxford University Press, 1982), p. 215.

118. Lawrence Freedman, *The Evolution of Nuclear Strategy* (New York: St. Martin's Press, 1989), pp. 218.

119. John Lewis Gaddis, *Strategies of Containment* (New York: Oxford University Press, 1982), p. 215.

120. See "Letter From Secretary of State Rusk to Secretary of Defense McNamara," February 4, 1961, *Foreign Relations of the United States, 1961–1963, Volume viii, National Security Policy* (Washington, DC: U.S. Department of State, Office of the Historian; Gaddis, *Strategies of Containment* (New York: Oxford University Press, 1982), p. 215.

121. William C. Martel, *Victory in War: Foundations of Modern Strategy* (New York: Cambridge University Press, 2011), pp. 109–112.

122. John F. Kennedy, "University of Washington 100th Anniversary Program, November 16, 1961" (speech), at www.jfklibrary.org/Asset-Viewer/Aw3MwwJMf0631R6JLmAprQ.aspx.

123. Susan L. Marquis, *Unconventional Warfare: Rebuilding U.S. Special Operations Forces* (Washington, DC: The Brookings Institution, 1997), p. 13.

124. John Lewis Gaddis, *Strategies of Containment* (New York: Oxford University Press, 1982), p. 217.

125. Walt W. Rostow, Draft, "Basic National Security Policy," March 26, 1962, p. 25, in John Lewis Gaddis, *Strategies of Containment* (New York: Oxford University Press, 1982), pp. 217–218.

126. Later named the "John F. Kennedy Special Warfare Center and School" due to the president's vital support to special operations forces. Walt W. Rostow, Speech at Fort Bragg, North Carolina, June 28, 1961, *DSB*, XLV (August 7, 1961), in John Lewis Gaddis, *Strategies of Containment* (New York: Oxford University Press, 1982), p. 225.

127. For background on the Vietnam War, see Daniel Ellsberg, *Papers on the War* (New York: Simon & Schuster, 1972); Leslie H. Gelb with Richard K. Betts, *The Irony of Vietnam: The System Worked* (Washington, DC: The Brookings Institution, 1979); David Halberstam, *The Best and the Brightest* (New York: Random House, 1972); Stanley Karnow, *Vietnam: A History* (New York: Viking, 1983); Robert E. Osgood, "The Lessons of Vietnam" and "Post-Vietnam Refinements of Limited War Strategy," in *Limited War Revisited*, pp. 33–51 and 52–66, respectively; Lewis Sorley, *A Better War: The Unexamined Victories and Final Tragedy of America's Last Years in Vietnam* (New York: Harcourt Brace, 1999); Harry G. Summers Jr., *On Strategy: A Critical Analysis of the Vietnam War* (Novato, CA: Presidio Press, 1982); Stanley Hoffmann, Samuel P. Huntington, Ernest R. May, Richard N. Neustadt, and Thomas C. Schelling, "Vietnam Reappraised," *International Security* 6, No. 1 (Summer 1981), pp. 3–26; Richard K. Betts, "Misadventure Revisited," *Wilson Quarterly* 7, No. 3 (Summer 1983), pp. 94–113.

128. Thomas A. Bailey, *A Diplomatic History of the American People* (Englewood Cliffs, NJ: Prentice Hall, 1980), pp. 868–869.

129. Nicholas Wapshott, *Keynes Hayek: The Clash That Defined Modern Economics* (New York: W. W. Norton, 2011), p. 237.

130. John Lewis Gaddis, *Strategies of Containment* (New York: Oxford University Press, 1982), pp. 204, 227. "Kennedy's economic advisers, like Keyserling under Truman, were Keynesian expansionists, committed to full employment and economic growth, less concerned than their Republican counterparts about budget deficits and inflation."

131. Gaddis, *Strategies of Containment* (New York: Oxford University Press, 1982), p. 228. In practice, Kennedy "found it easier than it otherwise might have been to incorporate the patient skills of the diplomat to his arsenal of 'flexible responses.'"

132. Robert F. Kennedy, *Thirteen Days* (New York: W. W. Norton & Company, 1971), p. 57.

133. Joseph S. Nye, *The Powers to Lead* (New York: Oxford University Press, 2010).

134. Joseph S. Nye, "JFK50 Insight Interview – Joseph Nye on JFK's Legacy and Foreign Policy," at www.youtube.com/watch?v=x1CNboaLeoY.

135. Thomas A. Bailey, *A Diplomatic History of the American People* (Englewood Cliffs, NJ: Prentice Hall, 1980), p. 869: "the government send abroad specially trained

men and women who would share their skills with the underprivileged." This was, "in short, a demonstration of democracy at work ... (initially) condemned by critics as too starry-eyed, too expensive, and too much of a temptation to draft-dodgers." In the end, however, "(it) proved so helpful that the host countries soon requested more than could be trained," and would become a hallmark of American foreign policy. By September 1961, "a once-skeptical Congress passed by wide margins a bill to put the Corps on permanent footing."

136. John Lewis Gaddis, *Strategies of Containment* (New York: Oxford University Press, 1982), p. 223.

137. Walt W. Rostow, draft, "Basic National Security Policy," March 26, 1962, p. 25, in John Lewis Gaddis, *Strategies of Containment* (New York: Oxford University Press, 1982), p. 223.

138. See Nancy Gibbs and Michael Duffy, *The President's Club: Inside the World's Most Exclusive Fraternity* (New York: Simon & Schuster, 2012), p. 106: "the campaign was about other things; age and energy and a vision for a new decade. Kennedy would 'get the country moving again.'"

139. George C. Herring, *From Colony to Superpower: U.S. Foreign Relations Since 1776* (New York: Oxford University Press, 2008), pp. 376–377.

140. Lyndon B. Johnson, "President Lyndon B. Johnson's Address to the Nation Announcing Steps to Limit the War in Vietnam and Reporting His Decision Not to Seek Reelection," March 31, 1968," at www.lbjlib.utexas.edu/johnson/archives.hom/speeches.hom/680331.asp.

141. John Lewis Gaddis, *Strategies of Containment* (New York: Oxford University Press, 1982), p. 237.

142. Robert S. McNamara, *In Retrospect: The Tragedy and Lessons of Vietnam* (New York: Times Books, 1995), p. 6: McNamara affirmed this reasoning when he wrote, "I see quantification as a language to add precision to reasoning about the world." Also, William C. Martel, *Victory in War: Foundations of Modern Strategy* (New York: Cambridge University Press, 2011), pp. 163–164: "In this climate, the question was whether there exists some optimal allocation of resources that would increase the probability of victory in the Vietnam War or any war. Quite the opposite proved true because detailed analyses of strategy and operations could not be translated easily into concrete achievements that align with 'victory.'"

143. See Jeffrey Record, "Vietnam in Retrospect: Could We Have Won?," *Parameters* 26, No. 4 (Winter 1996–1997), pp. 51–65, at p. 61: "The key to U.S. defeat was a profound misunderstanding of enemy tenacity and fighting power ... a failure to appreciate the fundamental civil dimensions of the war, and preoccupation with the measurable indices of military power and attendant disdain for the ultimately decisive intangibles."

144. McNamara to Johnson, December 21, 1963, the *Pentagon Papers*, vol. 2, pp. 410–411, in John Lewis Gaddis, *Strategies of Containment* (New York: Oxford University Press, 1982), pp. 256–257.

145. McNamara to Johnson, November 17, 1966, *Pentagon Papers*, vol. 4, pp. 371, in John Lewis Gaddis, *Strategies of Containment* (New York: Oxford University Press, 1982), p. 257: "For example, the VC/NVA apparently lose only about one-sixth as many weapons as people, suggesting the possibility that many of the killed are unarmed porters or bystanders."

146. David Halberstam, *The Best and the Brightest* (New York: Random House, 1972), p. 249.

147. John Lewis Gaddis, *Strategies of Containment* (New York: Oxford University Press, 1982), p. 265: the "narrowing of perspective, this failure to detect the extent to which short-term means can corrupt long-term ends, was … perhaps the most lasting deficiency of 'flexible response' as applied in Vietnam."

148. See Lyndon Baines Johnson, Inaugural Address, Washington, DC, January 20, 1965, at www.bartleby.com/124/pres57.html.

149. Michael Beschloss, *Reaching for Glory: Lyndon's Johnson's Secret White House Tapes, 1964–1965* (New York: Simon & Schuster, 2001), p. 194 (emphasis added). Although Johnson rejected victory, he said (p. 238), "I don't believe I can walk out.… If I did, they'd take Thailand.… They'd take Cambodia.… They'd take Burma.… They'd take Indonesia.… They'd take India.… They'd come right back and take the Philippines.… I'd be another Chamberlain and … we'd have another Munich."

150. See Beschloss, *Reaching for Glory* (2001), p. 343. See Martel, *Victory in War: Foundations of Modern Strategy* (New York: Cambridge University Press, 2011), p. 164: "Furthermore, on July 2, Johnson confided to McNamara that 'We cannot win with our existing commitment,' (p. 382); and on July 25, Presidential Advisor Clark Clifford said in Johnson's tape-recorded diary, '[H]e [Johnson] doubted that America could win the war'" (p. 406).

151. John Lewis Gaddis, *Strategies of Containment* (New York: Oxford University Press, 1982), p. 270: "Relations with Latin America, which Kennedy had emphasized, were for the most part neglected under Johnson.… The Middle East became the focus of attention only during the June 1967 Arab-Israeli War: the administration did little to try to head off that conflict, or to solve the resulting difficulties created by the Israeli occupation of Arab territory and by Moscow's growing influence in the region. The 1968 Soviet invasion of Czechoslovakia also caught the administration off guard, able to do little in response but to postpone (and then only briefly) talks on strategic arms limitations."

152. Thomas A. Bailey, *A Diplomatic History of the American People* (Englewood Cliffs, NJ: Prentice Hall, 1980), p. 907.

153. William C. Martel, *Victory in War: Foundations of Modern Strategy* (New York: Cambridge University Press, 2011), pp. 161–166; Jeffrey Record, "Vietnam in Retrospect: Could We Have Won?" *Parameters* 26, No. 4 (Winter 1996–1997), pp. 51–65, at p. 61. For a discussion of North Vietnam's strategy for victory, see Cecil B. Currey, *Victory at Any Cost: The Genius of Viet Nam's Gen. Vo Nguyen Giap* (Washington, DC: Brassey's, 1997). For arguments about whether the United States could win the Vietnam War, see William Colby, *Lost Victory: A Firsthand Account of America's Sixteen-Year Involvement in Vietnam* (Chicago: Contemporary Books, 1989); Armbruster et al., *Can We Win in Vietnam?*; C. Dale Walton, *The Myth of Inevitable U.S. Defeat in Vietnam* (London: Frank Cass, 2002); Mark W. Woodruff, *Unheralded Victory: The Defeat of the Viet Cong and the North Vietnamese Army 1961–1973* (Arlington, VA: Vandamere, 1999); Jeffrey Record, "Vietnam in Retrospect," who asks (p. 51), "Was the United States in fact defeated?" For a discussion of the dilemmas of fighting guerrilla wars, see John Shy

and Thomas W. Collier, "Revolutionary War," in Peter Paret (ed.), *Makers of Modern Strategy from Machiavelli to the Nuclear Age* (Princeton, NJ: Princeton University Press, 1986), pp. 815–862.

154. John Lewis Gaddis, *Strategies of Containment* (New York: Oxford University Press, 1982), p. 238.

155. See Jeffrey W. Helsing, *Johnson's War/Johnson's Great Society: The Guns and Butter Trap* (Westport, CT: Praeger, 2000).

156. Quoted in Doris Kearns, *Lyndon Johnson and the American Dream* (New York: Harper & Row, 1976), p. 283.

157. Jeffrey W. Helsing, *Johnson's War/Johnson's Great Society: The Guns and Butter Trap* (Westport, CT: Praeger, 2000), p. 2.

158. John Lewis Gaddis, *Strategies of Containment* (New York: Oxford University Press, 1982), p. 273.

159. See Anthony H. Cordesman, Robert Hammond, and Jordan D'Amato, *The Macroeconomics of US Defense Spending* (Washington, DC: Center for Strategic and International Studies, 2010).

160. See Bob Woodward and Carl Bernstein, *All the President's Men* (New York: Warner Books, 1976). As Kissinger wrote in *Years of Upheaval*, p. 124, "With every passing day Watergate was circumscribing our freedom of action." Also, Bob Woodward, *Shadow: Five Presidents and the Legacy of Watergate* (New York: Simon & Schuster, 1999); Fred Emery, *Watergate: The Corruption of American Politics and the Fall of Richard Nixon* (New York: Times Books, 1994).

161. For background on Nixon, see Stephen E. Ambrose, *Nixon: The Education of a Politician, 1913–1962* (New York: Simon & Schuster, 1987); Richard Reeves, *President Nixon: Alone in the White House* (New York: Simon & Schuster, 2001).

162. This debate reemerged during the 1980s with respect to Japan, and in the early twenty-first century is coming around again with respect to China. For the theory of imperial overstretch that leads to relative decline, see Paul Kennedy, *The Rise and Fall of the Great Powers* (New York: Vintage, 1989). For discussions of the U.S. position in the world, see Henry A. Kissinger, *White House Years* (Boston: Little, Brown, 1979); Henry A. Kissinger, *Diplomacy* (New York: Simon & Schuster, 1995).

163. Fredrik Logevall and Andrew Preston, eds., *Nixon in the World: American Foreign Relations, 1969–1977* (New York: Oxford University Press, 2008), p. 4.

164. Robert Dallek, *Nixon and Kissinger* (New York: HarperCollins, 2007), p. 168. In political and strategic terms, "Vietnam stood in the way of renewed national harmony and ... serious consideration of domestic issues like segregation and welfare reform."

165. Fredrik Logevall and Andrew Preston, eds., *Nixon in the World: American Foreign Relations, 1969–1977* (New York: Oxford University Press, 2008), p. 6.

166. See Richard Nixon, *RN: The Memoirs of Richard Nixon* (New York: Grosset & Dunlap, 1978), pp. 363–434, passim.

167. Fredrik Logevall and Andrew Preston, eds., *Nixon in the World: American Foreign Relations, 1969–1977* (New York: Oxford University Press, 2008), p. 7.

168. See quote, President Richard Nixon, "Talking Points on China," July 17, 1971, in Robert Dallek, *Nixon and Kissinger* (New York: HarperCollins, 2007), p. 285.

169. Dallek, *Nixon and Kissinger* (New York: HarperCollins, 2007), p. 288.
170. Fredrik Logevall and Andrew Preston, eds., *Nixon in the World: American Foreign Relations, 1969–1977* (New York: Oxford University Press, 2008), p. 8.
171. David H. Herschler, David S. Patterson, and Louis J. Smith, eds., *Foreign Relations of the United States, 1969–1976, Vol. 1, Foundations of Foreign Policy, 1969–1972* (Washington: US Government Printing Office, 1976), pp. 70–71.
172. Richard Nixon, Nixon Doctrine, press conference, July 25, 1969, at www.princeton. edu/~achaney/tmve/wiki100k/docs/Nixon_Doctrine.html. Cf. Henry Kissinger, *White House Years* (New York: Little, Brown and Company, 1979), pp. 222–225. Also, Richard Nixon, *RN: The Memoirs of Richard Nixon* (New York: Grosset & Dunlap, 1978), pp. 394, 397.
173. See Richard Nixon, "Address to the Nation on the War in Vietnam," November 3, 1969, at www.nixonlibrary.gov/forkids/speechesforkids/silentmajority/silentmajority_transcript.pdf.
174. Fredrik Logevall and Andrew Preston, eds., *Nixon in the World: American Foreign Relations, 1969–1977* (New York: Oxford University Press, 2008), p. 6.
175. Richard Nixon, "Address to the Nation on the War in Vietnam," November 3, 1969, at www.pbs.org/wgbh/americanexperience/features/primary-resources/nixon-vietnam/
176. See Henry A. Kissinger, "Memorandum From President Nixon to His Assistant for National Security Affairs (Kissinger), February 10, 1970, Foreign Relations, 1969–1976, Volume I," *Foundations of Foreign Policy* (Washington, DC: Department of State, Office of the Historian, Documents 54–67, paper prepared in the National Security Council Staff.
177. Henry Kissinger, *White House Years* (New York: Little, Brown and Company, 1979), p. 56.
178. Memorandum from President Nixon to his assistant for national security affairs (Kissinger), in David Goldman, Edward Mahan, and Edward C. Keefer (eds.), *Foreign Relations of the United States, 1969–1976* (Washington, DC: U.S. Government Printing Office, 2010), pp. 186–187.
179. Fredrik Logevall and Andrew Preston, eds., *Nixon in the World: American Foreign Relations, 1969–1977* (New York: Oxford University Press, 2008), p. 3. The better part of the 1970s, "it could be said, [was] the Kissinger Era. Among senior officials, only Henry Kissinger served the entire eight years." Throughout the Nixon and Ford administrations, Kissinger was "at all times ... the very center of decision making, first as national security advisor and then as secretary of state."
180. Robert Dallek, *Nixon and Kissinger* (New York: HarperCollins, 2007), p. 80. Nixon was "determined to run foreign policy from the White House ... he felt it imperative to exclude the CIA [and the State Department] from the formulation of policy."
181. Henry Kissinger, *White House Years* (Boston: Little, Brown and Company, 1979), p. 11. Cf. Duncan L. Clarke, "Why State Can't Lead," *Foreign Policy* 66 (Spring 1987), pp. 128–142.
182. Fredrik Logevall and Andrew Preston, eds., "The Adventurous Journey of Nixon on the World," *Nixon in the World: American Foreign Relations, 1969–1977* (New York: Oxford University Press, 2008), p. 5.

183. David Rothkopf, *Running the World: The Inside Story of the National Security Council and the Architects of American Power* (New York: PublicAffairs, 2005).

184. Henry Kissinger, *White House Years* (Boston: Little, Brown and Company, 1979), p. 58. Cf. Robert Dallek, *Nixon and Kissinger* (New York: HarperCollins, 2007), pp. 45–46: "Kissinger would accept the proposition that once revolutionary states gained enough of 'a stake in the legitimacy of the international order,' they could be persuaded to give up destabilizing attacks on the system."

185. Walter Isaacson, *Kissinger: A Biography* (New York: Simon & Schuster, 2005), p. 76.

186. Isaacson, *Kissinger: A Biography* (New York: Simon & Schuster, 2005), p. 75.

187. Jeremi Suri, "Henry Kissinger and American Grand Strategy," in Fredrik Logevall and Andrew Preston (eds.), *Nixon in the World: American Foreign Relations, 1969–1977* (New York: Oxford University Press, 2008), p. 69: "Washington would exert its influence through diplomatic agreements and threats of force, not extend conflicts like the war in Vietnam."

188. For prominent examples, see William P. Bundy, *A Tangled Web: The Making of Foreign Policy in the Nixon Presidency* (New York: Hill & Wang, 1998); Larry Berman, *No Peace, No Honor: Nixon, Kissinger, and Betrayal in Vietnam* (New York: The Free Press, 2001); Seymour Hersh, *The Price of Power: Kissinger in the Nixon White House* (New York: Summit Books, 1983).

189. John Lewis Gaddis, *Strategies of Containment* (New York: Oxford University Press, 2005), pp. 307–308.

190. Robert Dallek, *Nixon and Kissinger* (New York: HarperCollins, 2007), p. 105.

191. Robert J. McMahon, *The Limits of Empire: The United States and Southeast Asia Since World War II* (New York: Columbia University Press, 1999), p. 156.

192. Henry Kissinger, *White House Years* (New York: Little, Brown and Company, 1979), p. 228; Robert Dallek, *Nixon and Kissinger* (New York: HarperCollins, 2007), p. 253; Jeffrey Record, "Vietnam in Retrospect: Could We Have Won?" *Parameters* 26, No. 4 (Winter 1996–1997), pp. 51–65, at p. 61: known as "peace with honor."

193. Jeremi Suri, "Henry Kissinger and American Grand Strategy," in Fredrik Logevall and Andrew Preston (eds.) *Nixon in the World: American Foreign Relations, 1969–1977* (New York: Oxford University Press, 2008), p. 72: "In order to avoid fighting everywhere, Washington had to frighten its adversaries, convincing them that they faced an overwhelming response if they challenged local American vulnerabilities like West Berlin and South Korea."

194. Richard Nixon, *RN: The Memoirs of Richard Nixon* (New York: Grosset & Dunlap, 1978), p. 349.

195. Henry Kissinger, *White House Years* (New York: Little, Brown and Company, 1979), p. 226.

196. Richard Nixon, *RN: The Memoirs of Richard Nixon* (New York: Grosset & Dunlap, 1978); Henry Kissinger, *White House Years* (New York: Little, Brown and Company, 1979); Robert Dallek, *Nixon and Kissinger* (New York: HarperCollins, 2007), p. 168: "The first fifteen months of the Nixon presidency largely centered on Vietnam – how to continue fighting the war; hold domestic opponents at bay; and pressure Hanoi into a settlement that did not cost Saigon its

independence and saddle the United States with a military defeat that diminished American sacrifices in blood and treasure and undermine its international credibility."

197. Henry Kissinger, *White House Years* (Boston: Little, Brown and Company, 1979), p. 228. Also, Robert J. McMahon, *The Limits of Empire: The United States and Southeast Asia Since World War II* (New York: Columbia University Press, 1999), p. 156.

198. Jeremi Suri, " Henry Kissinger and American Grand Strategy," in Fredrik Logevall and Andrew Preston (eds.), *Nixon in the World: American Foreign Relations, 1969–1977* (New York: Oxford University Press, 2008), p. 71.

199. Cf. Margaret MacMillan, *Nixon and Mao: The Week That Changed the World* (New York: Random House, 2007); K. A. Hamilton, "A 'Week That Changed the World': Britain and Nixon's China Visit of 21–28 February 1972," *Diplomacy & Statecraft* 15, No. 1 (2004), pp. 117–135.

200. The European Union as a single economy is larger than both the United States and China, but it is the aggregate of multiple national economies. See European Commission, *The EU Economy: 2002 Review: Summary and Main Conclusions* (Brussels: Office for Official Publications of the European Communities, 2002).

201. See Henry A. Kissinger, *White House Years*, pp. 163–194.

202. Kissinger, *White House Years* (Boston: Little, Brown and Company, 1979), p. 165: "In a subtle triangle of relations between Washington, Peking, and Moscow, we improve the possibilities of accommodations with each as we increase our options toward both."

203. Robert Dallek, *Nixon and Kissinger* (New York: HarperCollins, 2007), p. 269. This move toward China was a clear "demonstration of how pragmatic [Nixon] could be to achieve something he believed would establish him as a great president."

204. Henry A. Kissinger, *Years of Upheaval* (New York: Little, Brown and Company, 1982), p. 67. Cf. Margaret MacMillan, *Nixon and Mao: The Week That Changed the World* (New York: Random House, 2007); Michael B. Yahuda, "China's New Foreign Policy," *The World Today* 28, No. 1 (January 1972), pp. 14–22.

205. Fredrik Logevall and Andrew Preston, eds., *Nixon in the World: American Foreign Relations, 1969–1977* (New York: Oxford University Press, 2008), p. 12: "Nixon and Kissinger recognized and took advantage of an international balance of power of the kind not seen since before World War II." This confluence of events "gave them the opportunity to improve relations with both Moscow and Beijing and thereby enable the United States to play one communist power against another . . ." In the calculations of grand strategy, "the simple, timeless political art of triangulation, then, would enable America to regain the upper hand."

206. David H. Herschler, David S. Patterson, and Louis J. Smith, eds., *Foreign Relations of the United States, 1969–1976*, Vol. 1, *Foundations of Foreign Policy, 1969–1972* (Washington: U.S. Government Printing Office, 1976), pp. 392–394.

207. Richard Nixon, *RN: The Memoirs of Richard Nixon* (New York: Grosset & Dunlap, 1978), pp. 586–587.

208. Fredrik Logevall and Andrew Preston, eds., *Nixon in the World: American Foreign Relations, 1969–1977* (New York: Oxford University Press, 2008), p. 14: "There was simply no room for both sides to realize this mutually exclusive goal [of

winning the Cold War]." At the limit, "neither side sought an end to the Cold War; rather, détente would enable each side to withstand the uncertainties of a new era and eventually prevail in the Cold War."

209. Henry A. Kissinger, *White House Years* (Boston: Little, Brown and Company, 1979), p. 559.

210. Robert Dallek, *Nixon and Kissinger* (New York: HarperCollins, 2007), pp. 230–231.

211. Cf. Gil Merom, "Democracy, Dependency, and Destabilization: The Shaking of Allende's Regime," *Political Science Quarterly* 105, No. 1 (Spring 1990), pp. 75–95.

212. Henry A. Kissinger, *White House Years* (Boston: Little, Brown and Company, 1979), p. 57: "instead, we had to set priorities, both intellectual and material." Quoted in Robert J. McMahon, *The Limits of Empire: The United States and Southeast Asia Since World War II* (New York: Columbia University Press, 1999), p. 156.

213. See Richard Milhous Nixon, First Inaugural Address, Washington, DC, January 20, 1969, at www.bartleby.com/124/pres58.html

214. See Nixon, First Inaugural Address, Washington, DC, January 20, 1969, at www .bartleby.com/124/pres58.html

215. Cf. Jeffrey W. Knopf, *Domestic Society and International Cooperation: The Impact of Protest on US Arms Control Policy* (New York: Cambridge University Press, 1998).

216. See Richard Milhous Nixon, First Inaugural Address, Washington, DC, January 20, 1969, at www.bartleby.com/124/pres58.html

217. See Nixon, First Inaugural Address, Washington, DC, January 20, 1969, at www. bartleby.com/124/pres58.html "If we succeed, generations to come will say of us now living that we mastered our moment, that we helped make the world safe for mankind."

218. Op. cit., Eisenhower's Farewell Address to the Nation, January 17, 1961, at www .speeches-usa.com/Transcripts/031_eisenhower.html "we have been compelled to create a permanent armaments industry of vast proportions. Added to this, three and a half million men and women are directly engaged in the defense establishment. We annually spend on military security more than the net income of all United States corporations."

219. See Bob Woodward and Carl Bernstein, *All the President's Men* (New York: Warner Books, 1976); Bob Woodward, *Shadow: Five Presidents and the Legacy of Watergate* (New York: Simon & Schuster, 1999).

220. See Jimmy Carter, *Keeping Faith: Memoirs of a President* (New York: Bantam Books, 1982); Tami R. Davis and Sean M. Lynn-Jones, "City Upon a Hill," *Foreign Policy* 66 (Spring 1987), pp. 20–38; Peter G. Bourne, *Jimmy Carter: A Comprehensive Bibliography from Plains to Postpresidency* (New York: Scribner, 1997); Erwin C. Hargrove, *Jimmy Carter as President: Leadership and the Politics of Public Good* (Baton Rouge: Louisiana State University Press, 1988); Robert A. Strong, *Working in the World: Jimmy Carter and the Making of American Foreign Policy* (Baton Rouge: Louisiana State University Press, 2000).

221. Haynes Johnson, "Carter Is Sworn In as President, Asks 'Fresh Faith in Old Dream,'" *Washington Post*, January 21, 1977, at www.washingtonpost.com/wp-srv/national/longterm/inaug/history/stories/carter77.htm: "And the essence of his message was in urging the nation to learn the lessons from 'our recent mistakes.'" Quoting Carter, "We have learned that 'more' is not necessarily 'better' . . . [E]ven our great nation has its recognized limits, and . . . we can neither answer all questions nor solve all problems. We cannot afford to do everything, nor can we afford to lack boldness as we meet the future. So together, in a spirit of individual sacrifice, we must simply do our best." Cf. President Jimmy Carter, Inaugural Address, January 20, 1977, at www.bartleby.com/124/pres60.html

222. Jimmy Carter, "Human Rights and Foreign Policy," University of Notre Dame – Address at Commencement Exercises at the University, May 22, 1977, The American Presidency Project, at www.presidency.ucsb.edu/ws/?pid=7552 Cf. David Schmitz and Vanessa Walker, "Jimmy Carter and the Foreign Policy of Human Rights: The Development of a Post Cold War Foreign Policy," *Diplomatic History* 28 (January 2004), pp. 113–143; William F. Buckley Jr., "Human Rights and Foreign Policy: A Proposal," *Foreign Affairs* 58, No. 4 (Spring 1980), pp. 775–796.

223. President Jimmy Carter, Inaugural Address, January 20, 1977, at www.bartleby .com/124/pres60.html.

224. Carter, Inaugural Address, January 20, 1977, at www.bartleby.com/124/pres60 .html.

225. See Robert A. Strong, "Jimmy Carter and the Panama Canal Treaties," *Presidential Studies Quarterly* 21, No. 2 (*Measures of the Presidents: Hoover to Bush*, Spring 1991), pp. 269–286.

226. John Lewis Gaddis, *Strategies of Containment* (New York: Oxford University Press, 2005), pp. 343–344.

227. Jimmy Carter, "State of the Union Address Delivered at a Joint Session of Congress," January 23, 1980, The American Presidency Project, at www.presi dency.ucsb.edu/ws/index.php?pid=33079

228. John Lewis Gaddis, *Strategies of Containment* (New York: Oxford University Press, 2005), p. 344.

229. Cf. J. L. S. Girling, "Carter's Foreign Policy: Realism or Ideology?" *The World Today* 33, No. 11 (November 1977), pp. 417–424; Zbigniew Brzezinski, "Opinion: The Balance of Power Delusion," *Foreign Policy* 7 (Summer 1972), pp. 54–59.

230. John Lewis Gaddis, *Strategies of Containment* (New York: Oxford University Press, 2005), p. 345, thus leading to references to "surface innovation with subsurface continuity."

231. President Jimmy Carter, Inaugural Address, January 20, 1977, at www.bartleby .com/124/pres60.html

232. Quoted in John Dumbrell, *The Carter Presidency: A Re-Evaluation* (Manchester, UK: University of Manchester Press, 1993), p. 122, in Julian E. Zelizer, *Jimmy Carter* (New York: Henry Holt and Company, 2010), p. 57.

233. See Julian E. Zelizer, *Jimmy Carter* (New York: Henry Holt and Company, 2010), p. 57.

234. Bert Lance, *Truth of the Matter: My Life In and Out of Politics* (New York: Summit, 1991), p. 73, in Julian E. Zelizer, *Jimmy Carter* (New York: Henry Holt and Company, 2010), p. 58. "As far as [Carter] was concerned, anyone who disagreed was simply wrong."

235. On the role of human rights in Carter's grand strategy, see Gebhard Schweigler, "Carter's Détente Policy: Change or Continuity," *The World Today* 34, No. 3 (March 1978), pp. 81–89; Odd Arne Westad, *The Fall of Détente: Soviet-American Relations during the Carter Years* (Oslo: Scandinavian University Press, Nobel Symposium 95, 2009), pp. 3–33; George W. Breslauer, "Do Soviet Leaders Test New Presidents?" *International Security* 8, No. 3 (Winter 1983–1984), pp. 83–107; Raymond L. Garthoff, *Detente and Confrontation: American-Soviet Relations from Nixon to Reagan* (Washington, DC: The Brookings Institution, 1994); John Kane, "American Values or Human Rights? U.S. Foreign Policy and the Fractured Myth of Virtuous Power," *Presidential Studies Quarterly* 33, No. 4 (December 2003), pp. 772–800; David Forsythe, "US Foreign Policy and Human Rights," *Journal of Human Rights* 1, No. 4 (2002), pp. 501–521.

236. Andrew J. Pierre, "The Diplomacy of SALT," *International Security* 5, No. 1 (Summer 1980), pp. 178–197; John Lewis Gaddis, *Strategies of Containment* (New York: Oxford University Press, 2005), p. 345.

237. For example, see David Skidmore, "Carter and the Failure of Foreign Policy Reform," *Political Science Quarterly* 108, No. 4 (Winter 1993–1994), pp. 699–729; David Skidmore, *Reversing Course: Carter's Foreign Policy, Domestic Politics, and the Failure of Reform* (Nashville: Vanderbilt University Press, 1996).

238. John Lewis Gaddis, *Strategies of Containment* (New York: Oxford University Press, 2005), p. 346.

239. Alan Tonelson, "The Real National Interest," *Foreign Policy* 61 (Winter, 1985–1986), pp. 49–72; Gaddis, *Strategies of Containment* (New York: Oxford University Press, 2005), p. 346, which implies "interfering in the internal affairs of that country."

240. Gaddis, *Strategies of Containment* (New York: Oxford University Press, 2005), p. 346.

241. Cf. Cyrus R. Vance, *Hard Choices: Critical Years in America's Foreign Policy* (New York: Simon & Schuster, 1983); Alexander Moens, "President Carter's Advisers and the Fall of the Shah," *Political Science Quarterly* 106, No. 2 (Summer 1991), pp. 211–237. Also, Martin Hollis and Steve Smith, "Roles and Reasons in Foreign Policy Decision Making," *British Journal of Political Science* 16, No. 3 (July 1986), pp. 269–286; Jean A. Garrison, "Framing Foreign Policy Alternatives in the Inner Circle: President Carter, His Advisors, and the Struggle for the Arms Control Agenda," *Political Psychology* 22, No. 4 (December 2001), pp. 775–807; Walter LaFeber, "From Confusion to Cold War: The Memoirs of the Carter Administration," *Diplomatic History* 8, No. 1 (1984), pp. 1–12; Simon Serfaty, "Brzezinski: Play It Again, Zbig," *Foreign Policy* 32 (Autumn 1978), pp. 3–21; Terry L. Diebel, "Teaching Foreign Policy with Memoirs," *International Studies Perspectives* 3, No. 2 (May 2002), pp. 128–138; Robert A. Strong, *Working in the World: Jimmy Carter and the Making of American Foreign Policy* (Baton Rouge: Louisiana State University Press, 2000).

242. Raymond Garthoff, *Détente and Confrontation* (Washington, DC: The Brookings Institution Press, 1994), p. 666.

243. James Fallows, "The Passionless Presidency," *Atlantic Monthly*, May 1979, p. 43, in Robert A. Strong, *Working in the World: Jimmy Carter and the Making of American Foreign Policy* (Baton Rouge: Louisiana State University Press, 2000), p. 99.

244. Robert A. Strong, *Working in the World: Jimmy Carter and the Making of American Foreign Policy* (Baton Rouge: Louisiana State University Press, 2000), p. 99.

245. John Lewis Gaddis, *Strategies of Containment* (New York: Oxford University Press, 2005), p. 347.

246. Hamilton Jordan, *Crisis: The Last Year of the Carter Presidency* (New York: G. P. Putnam's Sons, 1982), p. 90, in Julian E. Zelizer, *Jimmy Carter* (New York: Henry Holt and Company, 2010), p. 103.

247. Jimmy Carter, "Address to the Nation on the Soviet Invasion of Afghanistan" January 4, 1980, The American Presidency Project, at www.presidency.ucsb.edu/ws/index.php?pid=32911

248. Cf. Andrew Z. Katz, "Public Opinion and the Contradictions of Jimmy Carter's Foreign Policy," *Presidential Studies Quarterly* 30, No. 4 (December 2000), pp. 662–687.

249. Kevin Mattson, *What the Heck Are You Up To, Mr. President? Jimmy Carter, America's "Malaise," and the Speech That Should Have Changed the Country* (New York: Bloomsbury, 2009), p. 14.

250. Julian E. Zelizer, *Jimmy Carter* (New York: Henry Holt and Company, 2010), p. 88.

251. Kevin Mattson, *What the Heck Are You Up To, Mr. President? Jimmy Carter, America's "Malaise," and the Speech That Should Have Changed the Country* (New York: Bloomsbury, 2009), pp. 3, 119. The riots in Levittown, just after the Camp David Accords, led the *Wall Street Journal* to editorialize that "the social fabric of this society is stretched tauter than anytime in a decade.... Meanwhile, our president look inscrutable as he goes about his sightseeing and partying in Japan."

252. Peter Trubowitz, *Politics and Strategy: Partisan Ambition and American Statecraft* (Princeton, NJ: Princeton University Press, 2011), pp. 131–132.

253. John Lewis Gaddis, *Strategies of Containment* (New York: Oxford University Press, 2005), p. 349, who succinctly outlines the glum predicament for grand strategy in 1980: "Those who listened to the President's forceful 'Carter doctrine' speech on January 23, 1980 ... might well have concluded that Afghanistan had shocked his administration into embracing the undifferentiated view of interests and threats that was characteristic of symmetrical response."

254. Gaddis, *Strategies of Containment* (New York: Oxford University Press, 2005), p. 349: "even in [the case of] a more disciplined administration than Carter's."

255. Erwin C. Hargrove, *Jimmy Carter as President: Leadership and the Politics of the Public Good* (Baton Rouge: Louisiana State University Press, 1988), p. 128.

256. Ezra F. Vogel, *Deng Xiaoping and the Transformation of China* (Cambridge, MA: The Belknap Press of Harvard University Press, 2011), pp. 345–346. Nixon's visit to China in 1972 undoubtedly contributed to developing political and economic relationships between the United States and China.

257. President Jimmy Carter, State of the Union Address 1980, January 23, 1980, at http://www.presidency.ucsb.edu/ws/index.php?pid=33079&st=&st1=; and Bob Woodward, *The Commanders* (New York: Simon & Schuster, 1991), p. 230.

258. Cf. Douglas Brinkley, "The Rising Stock of Jimmy Carter: The 'Hands On' Legacy of Our Thirty-Ninth President," *Diplomatic History* 20, No. 4, 1996, pp. 505–530; Gary W. Reichard, "Early Returns: Assessing Jimmy Carter," *Presidential Studies Quarterly* 20, No. 3 (*The Constitution, Progressivism and Reform*, Summer 1990), pp. 603–620; Gaddis Smith, *Morality, Reason and Power: American Diplomacy in the Carter Years* (New York: Hill and Wang, 1986).

259. On Reagan's strategy of rollback, which was a more assertive form of containment, see Stephen M. Walt, "The Case for Finite Containment: Analyzing U.S. Grand Strategy," *International Security* 14, No. 1 (Summer 1989), pp. 5–49; George Liska, "The Reagan Doctrine: Monroe and Dulles Reincarnate?" *SAIS Review* 6, No. 2 (Summer–Fall 1986), pp. 83–98; Fareed Zakaria, "The Reagan Strategy of Containment," *Political Science Quarterly* 105, No. 3 (Autumn 1990), pp. 373–395; William M. LeoGrande, "Rollback or Containment? The United States, Nicaragua, and the Search for Peace in Central America," *International Security* 11, No. 2 (Fall 1986), pp. 89–120.

260. Daniel Yankelovich and Larry Kaagan, "Assertive America," *Foreign Affairs* 59, No. 3 (January 1980), p. 696.

261. On the themes in Reagan's grand strategy, cf. William Kristol and Robert Kagan, "Toward a Neo-Reaganite Foreign Policy," *Foreign Affairs* 75, No. 4 (July–August 1996), pp. 18–32; Robert W. Tucker, Reagan's Foreign Policy," *Foreign Affairs* 68, No. 1 (*America and the World 1988/89*), pp. 1–27; Robert Gilpin, "American Policy in the Post-Reagan Era," *Daedalus* 116, No. 3 (*Futures*, Summer 1987), pp. 33–67; Tamar Jacoby, "The Reagan Turnaround on Human Rights," *Foreign Affairs* 64, No. 5 (Summer 1986), pp. 1066–1086; Robert J. McMahon, "Making Sense of American Foreign Policy during the Reagan Years," *Diplomatic History* 19, No. 2 (1995), pp. 367–384; Robert E. Osgood, "The Revitalization of Containment," *Foreign Affairs* 60, No. 3 (*America and the World 1981*), pp. 465–502.

262. John Lewis Gaddis, *Strategies of Containment* (New York: Oxford University Press, 2005), p. 350.

263. Richard V. Allen, "The Man Who Won the Cold War," *Hoover Digest*, No. 1 (January 30, 2000), *The Fall of Communism*, at www.hoover.org/publications/hoover-digest/article/7398. "In January 1977, I visited Ronald Reagan in Los Angeles. During our four-hour conversation, he said many memorable things, but none more significant than this. 'My idea of American policy toward the Soviet Union is simple, and some would say simplistic,' he said. 'It is this: We win and they lose. What do you think of that?' One had never heard such words from the lips of a major political figure; until then, we had thought only in terms of *managing* the relationship with the Soviet Union."

264. John Lewis Gaddis, *Strategies of Containment* (New York: Oxford University Press, 2005), p. 351.

265. See "U.S. Relations with the USSR," *National Security Decision Directive, NSDD-75*, dated January 17, 1983, pp. 1, 3.

266. Ronald W. Reagan, *An American Life* (New York: Simon & Schuster, 1990), p. 267.

267. Francis Marlo, "The Intellectual Roots of Reagan's Strategy," Fletcher PhD Thesis (April 2006), p. 39.

268. John Lewis Gaddis, *Strategies of Containment* (New York: Oxford University Press, 2005), pp. 352, 355.

269. "U.S. National Security Strategy," *National Security Decision Directive*, NSDD-32, May 20, 1982, p. 1.

270. "U.S. National Security Strategy," *National Security Decision Directive*, NSDD-32, May 20, 1982, pp. 1–2.

271. "U.S. National Security Strategy," *National Security Decision Directive*, NSDD-32, May 20, 1982, p. 1.

272. "U.S. National Security Strategy," *National Security Decision Directive*, NSDD-32, May 20, 1982, p. 2.

273. For the principles defining his economic and political reforms, see Mikhail S. Gorbachev, *Perestroika: New Thinking for Our Country and the World* (New York: HarperCollins, 1987).

274. For arguments about the Soviet Union's collapse, see Stephen M. Kotkin, *Armageddon Averted: The Soviet Collapse, 1970–2000* (New York: Oxford University Press, 2008); N. K. Chandra, "Was Collapse of CPSU Inevitable? A Polemical Essay," *Economic and Political Weekly* 28, No. 5 (January 30, 1993), pp. PE23–PE27, PE30–PE36f. For political and economic explanations, see D. N., "What Collapsed in the Soviet Union?" *Economic and Political Weekly* 28, No. 45 (November 6, 1993), pp. 2443–2444. On the role of the war in Afghanistan, see Rafael Reuveny and Aseem Prakash, "The Afghanistan War and the Breakdown of the Soviet Union," *Review of International Studies* 25, No. 4 (October 1999), pp. 693–708. For explanations related to international-relations theory, see Richard K. Herrmann, "Policy-Relevant Theory and the Challenge of Diagnosis: The End of the Cold War as a Case Study," *Political Psychology* 15, No. 1 (special issue: *Political Psychology and the Work of Alexander L. George*, March 1994), pp. 111–142. On the role of China, see Nancy Bernkopf Tucker, "China as a Factor in the Collapse of the Soviet Empire," *Political Science Quarterly* 110, No. 4 (Winter 1995–1996), pp. 501–518. For leadership and institutional explanations, see Seweryn Bialer, "The Death of Soviet Communism," *Foreign Affairs* 70, No. 5 (Winter 1991), pp. 166–181. As for the influence of U.S. policies, see Robert D. Schulzinger, "The End of the Cold War, 1961–1991," *OAH Magazine of History* 8, No. 2 (*Rethinking the Cold War*, Winter 1994), pp. 13–18; James Mann, *The Rebellion of Ronald Reagan: A History of the End of the Cold War* (New York: Viking, 2009). For more information regarding America's strategies at the end of the Cold War, see Thomas Mahnken, *Competitive Strategies for the 21st Century: Theory, History, and Practice* (Stanford, CA: Stanford University Press, 2012).

275. *National Security Decision Directive 75*, January 17, 1983, p. 7.

276. *National Security Decision Directive 75*, January 17, 1983, p. 1. On leadership transition, see Raymond L. Garthoff, ed., *The Great Transition: American-Soviet Relations and the End of the Cold War* (Washington, DC: The Brookings

Institution, 1994); Stephen White, Graeme Gill, and Darrell Slider, *The Politics of Transition: Shaping a Post-Soviet Future* (New York: Cambridge University Press, 1993); Archie Brown and Lilia Shevtsova, eds., *Gorbachev, Yeltsin, and Putin: Political Leadership in Russia's Transition* (Washington, DC: Carnegie Endowment for International Peace, 2001).

277. *National Security Decision Directive 75*, January 17, 1983, p. 2. The "functional" included "military strategy," "economic policy," and "political action"; the "geo-political" focused on "industrial democracies," "third world," "Soviet Empire," "China," and "Yugoslavia." The areas for the pursuit of "bilateral relationship" were "arms control," the "official dialogue," and "U.S.-Soviet Cooperative Exchanges."

278. *National Security Decision Directive 75*, January 17, 1983: "Effective opposition to Moscow's efforts to consolidate its position in Afghanistan. Blocking the expansion of Soviet influence in the critical Middle East and Southwest Asia regions. Maintenance of international pressure on Moscow to permit a relaxation of the current repression in Poland and a longer-term increase in diversity and independence throughout Eastern Europe. Neutralization and reduction of the threat to U.S. national security interests posed by the Soviet-Cuban relationship" (emphasis added).

279. *National Security Decision Directive 75*, January 17, 1983, p. 9.

280. James Mann, *The Rebellion of Ronald Reagan* (New York: Viking Penguin, 2009), p. xvi.

281. John Lewis Gaddis, *Strategies of Containment* (New York: Oxford University Press, 2005), p. 369.

282. Ronald Reagan, "Remarks to the National Association of Evangelicals," *Tear Down This Wall: The Reagan Revolution* (New York: Continuum International Publishing, 2004), p. 36.

283. John Lewis Gaddis, *Strategies of Containment* (New York: Oxford University Press, 2005), p. 370.

284. See *The Iran-Contra Report*, November 18, 1987, at www.presidency.ucsb.edu/PS157/assignment%20files%20public/congressional%20report%20key%20sec tions.htm.

285. "U.S. National Security Strategy," *National Security Decision Directive, NSDD-32*, dated May 20, 1982, pp. 1. Cf. John Lewis Gaddis, *Strategies of Containment* (New York: Oxford University Press, 2005), p. 144.

286. Ronald W. Reagan, *An American Life* (New York: Simon & Schuster, 1990), p. 239.

287. Reagan, *An American Life* (New York: Simon & Schuster, 1990), p. 450.

288. John Lewis Gaddis, *Strategies of Containment* (New York: Oxford University Press, 2005), p. 371.

289. Jack F. Matlock Jr., *Reagan and Gorbachev* (New York: Random House, 2004), p. 66.

290. Matlock, *Reagan and Gorbachev* (New York: Random House, 2004), p. 67.

291. Matlock, *Reagan and Gorbachev* (New York: Random House, 2004), p. 51.

292. Ronald W. Reagan, *An American Life* (New York: Simon & Schuster, 1990), p. 13. Also, Paul Lettow, *Ronald Reagan and His Quest to Abolish Nuclear Weapons* (New York: Random House, 2005).

293. Ronald W. Reagan, *An American Life* (New York: Simon & Schuster, 1990), p. 14.

294. Reagan, *An American Life* (New York: Simon & Schuster, 1990), p. 13.

295. Jack F. Matlock Jr, *Reagan and Gorbachev* (New York: Random House, 2004), p. 11.

296. President Ronald Reagan, "Address to the Nation on Defense and National Security," March 23, 1983, at http://www.presidency.ucsb.edu/ws/index.php?pid=41093&st=&st1=

297. Jack F. Matlock Jr, *Reagan and Gorbachev* (New York: Random House, 2004), p. 59.

298. See Ashton B. Carter and David Schwartz, *Ballistic Missile Defense* (Washington, DC: The Brookings Institution, 1983).

299. Lou Cannon, *President Reagan: The Role of a Lifetime* (New York: PublicAffairs, 1991), p. 673.

300. Ronald W. Reagan, *An American Life* (New York: Simon & Schuster, 1990), p. 708.

301. Anatoly Dobrynin, *In Confidence: Moscow's Ambassador to Six Cold War Presidents (1962–1986)* (New York: 1995), p. 563. Cf. John Lewis Gaddis, *Strategies of Containment* (New York: Oxford University Press, 2005), p. 361.

302. Ronald W. Reagan, *An American Life* (New York: Simon & Schuster, 1990), p. 634.

303. John Lewis Gaddis, *Strategies of Containment* (New York: Oxford University Press, 2005), p. 364–369.

304. Gaddis, *Strategies of Containment* (New York: Oxford University Press, 2005), p. 367.

305. George Shultz, *Turmoil and Triumph: My Years as Secretary of State* (New York: Charles Scribner's Sons, 1993), p. 586.

306. Ronald W. Reagan, *An American Life* (New York: Simon & Schuster, 1990), p. 708.

307. John Lewis Gaddis, *Strategies of Containment* (New York: Oxford University Press, 2005), p. 370.

308. For one explanation of why the Soviet Union would ultimately collapse, see Karl W. Deutsch, *The Analysis of International Relations* (Englewood Cliffs, NJ: Prentice Hall, 1968), p. 139: "This is one reason, in Riker's view, why empires decline, and why the United States and the Soviet Union will lose in the future a large part of the power they now hold in world politics: sooner or later they will be weakened by this fatal tendency of coalition leaders to overspend on allies." Deutsch cites the work of William H. Riker, *The Theory of Political Coalitions* (New Haven, CT: Yale University Press, 1967), pp. 29–31, 174.

309. Henry Kissinger, *Diplomacy* (New York: Simon & Schuster, 1994), pp. 764–765: "Reagan might well have had only a few basic ideas, but these also happened to be the core foreign-policy issues of his period, which demonstrates that a sense of direction and having the strength of one's convictions are the key ingredients of leadership."

310. John Lewis Gaddis, *Strategies of Containment* (New York: Oxford University Press, 2005), p. 376.

10 *Drifting between Principles: Bush to Obama*

1. Walter Russell Mead, *Special Providence: American Foreign Policy and How It Changed the World* (New York: Knopf, 2001); Earl C. Ravenal, "The Case for Adjustment," *Foreign Policy* 81 (Winter 1990–1991), pp. 3–19; William G. Hyland, "America's New Course," *Foreign Affairs* 69, No. 2 (Spring 1990), pp. 1–12; See Terry L. Deibel, *Foreign Affairs Strategy: Logic for American Statecraft* (New York: Cambridge University Press, 2007).

2. For background on Bush, see Herbert S. Parmet, *George Bush: The Life of a Lone Star Yankee* (New Brunswick, NJ: Transaction Publishers, 2001); Tom Wicker, *George Herbert Walker Bush* (New York: Viking, 2004); George H. W. Bush and Brent Scowcroft, *A World Transformed* (New York: Knopf, 1998); Linda O. Valenty and Ofer Feldman, eds., *Political Leadership for the New Century: Personality and Behavior among American Leaders* (Westport, CT: Praeger Publishers, 2002), pp. 51–64; Robert Green, *George Bush: Business Executive and U.S. President* (Chicago: Ferguson Publishing, 2000); Ryan J. Barilleaux and Mark J. Rozell, *Power and Prudence: The Presidency of George H. W. Bush* (College Station: Texas A&M University Press, 2004).

3. On Bush's grand strategy, see Bob Woodward, *The Commanders* (New York: Simon & Schuster, 1991); Lawrence F. Kaplan and William Kristol, eds., *The War Over Iraq: Saddam's Tyranny and America's Mission* (San Francisco: Encounter Books, 2003); George H. W. Bush and Brent Scowcroft, *A World Transformed* (New York: Knopf, 1998); Steven Hurst, "The Rhetorical Strategy of George HW Bush during the Persian Gulf Crisis 1990–91: How to Help Lose a War You Won," *Political Studies* 52, No. 2 (2004), pp. 376–392.

4. William C. Martel, "Grand Strategy of 'Restrainment,'" *Orbis* 54, No. 3 (Summer 2010), pp. 356–373, p. 357.

5. George H. W. Bush, Inaugural Address, January 20, 1989, at www.bartleby.com/124/pres63.html.

6. See Kenneth Oye, Robert Leiber, and Donald Rothchild, eds., *Eagle in a New World: American Grand Strategy in the Post-Cold War Era* (New York: HarperCollins, 1992), p. ix; Josef Joffe, "'Bismarck' or 'Britain'? Toward an American Grand Strategy after Bipolarity," *International Security* 19, No. 4 (1995), pp. 94–117.

7. George H. W. Bush, *National Security Strategy of the United States*, August 1991, at www.fas.org/man/docs/918015-nss.htm.

8. Bush, *National Security Strategy of the United States*, March 1990, at www.fas.org/man/docs.

9. Bush and Brent Scowcroft, *A World Transformed* (New York: Knopf, 1998), pp. viii–ix; William C. Wohlforth "Realism and the End of the Cold War," *International Security* 19, No. 3 (1994), pp. 91–129; Raymond L. Garthoff, ed., *The Great Transition: American-Soviet Relations and the End of the Cold War* (Washington, DC: The Brookings Institution Press, 1994); Meenekshi Bose and Rosanna Perotti, eds., *From Cold War to New World Order: The Foreign Policy of George HW Bush* (Westport, CT: Greenwood Publishing Group, 2002); Christopher Maynard, *Out of the Shadow: George HW Bush and the End of the Cold War* (College Station: Texas A&M University Press, 2008).

10. Bush and Scowcroft, *A World Transformed* (New York: Knopf, 1998), pp. 180–181.

11. George H. W. Bush, *National Security Strategy of the United States*, March 1990, at www.fas.org/man/docs.

12. On grand strategy during the Bush administration, see Walter Russell Mead, "The Bush Administration and the New World Order," *World Policy Journal* 8, No. 3 (Summer 1991), pp. 375–420; Raymond Taras and Marshal Zeringue, "Grand Strategy in a Post-Bipolar World: Interpreting the Final Soviet Response," *Review of International Studies* 18, No. 4 (October 1992), pp. 355–375; Walter Russell Mead, "An American Grand Strategy: The Quest for Order in a Disordered World," *World Policy Journal* 10, No. 1 (Spring 1993), p. 9, who described the "false dawn of a new world order." Also, Jeremi Suri, "American Grand Strategy from the Cold War's End to 9/11," *Orbis*, Fall 2009, pp. 616–621; William C. Martel, "Grand Strategy of 'Restrainment,'" *Orbis* 54, No. 3 (Summer 2010), p. 358.

13. "1989: Massacre in Tiananmen Square," *BBC*, at http://news.bbc.co.uk/onthisday/hi/dates/stories/june/4/newsid_2496000/2496277.stm.

14. George H. W. Bush and Brent Scowcroft, *A World Transformed* (New York: Knopf, 1998), p. 89.

15. George H. W. Bush, *National Security Strategy of the United States*, March 1990, at www.fas.org/man/docs.

16. George H. W. Bush, "Announcing the War against Iraq," at www.historyplace.com/speeches/bush-war.htm: "a world where the rule of law, not the law of the jungle, governs the conduct of nations. When we are successful – and we will be – we have a real chance at this new world order, an order in which a credible United Nations can use its peacekeeping role to fulfill the promise and vision of the U.N.'s founders."

17. George H. W. Bush, *National Security Strategy of the United States*, August 1991, at www.fas.org/man/docs/918015-nss.htm.

18. Cf. William Schneider, "The Old Politics and the New World Order," in Kenneth Oye, Robert Leiber, and Donald Rothchild (eds.), *Eagle in a New World: American Grand Strategy in the Post-Cold War Era* (New York: HarperCollins, 1992), p. 61; H. W. Brands, "George Bush and the Gulf War of 1991," *Presidential Studies Quarterly* 34, No. 1 (*Going to War*, March 2004), pp. 113–131.

19. President George H. W. Bush, "Address before a Joint Session of the Congress on the Persian Gulf Crisis and the Federal Budget Deficit," September 11, 1990, at www.millercenter.org/president/speeches/detail/3430: President Bush outlined "his four objectives in the Gulf, and then later [spoke] in sweeping historical language about the emergence of a new world order – as if these were separate things." Also, Christian Alfonsi, *Circle in the Sand: The Bush Dynasty in Iraq* (New York: Vintage Books, 2006), p. 110: "Not only an objective, but the objective."

20. President George H. W. Bush, "Address before a Joint Session of the Congress on the Persian Gulf Crisis and the Federal Budget Deficit," September 11, 1990, at www.millercenter.org/president/speeches/detail/3430: "An era in which the nations of the world, East and West, North and South, can prosper and live in harmony.... A world where the rule of law supplants the rule of the jungle. A world in which nations recognize the shared responsibility for freedom and justice."

21. George H. W. Bush and Brent Scowcroft, *A World Transformed* (New York: Knopf, 1998), p. 388.

22. Bush and Scowcroft, *A World Transformed* (New York: Knopf, 1998), p. 400.

23. President George H. W. Bush, "Address before a Joint Session of the Congress on the Persian Gulf Crisis and the Federal Budget Deficit," September 11, 1990, at http://www.presidency.ucsb.edu/ws/index.php?pid=18820&st=&st1=

24. President George H. W. Bush, *National Security Strategy of the United States*, August 1991, at www.fas.org/man/docs/918015-nss.htm: "less hobbled by the ritualistic anti-Americanism that so often weakened its credibility."

25. George H. W. Bush and Brent Scowcroft, *A World Transformed* (New York: Knopf, 1998), p. 303.

26. William Schneider, "The Old Politics and the New World Order," in Kenneth Oye, Robert Leiber, and Donald Rothchild (eds.), *Eagle in a New World: American Grand Strategy in the Post-Cold War Era* (New York: HarperCollins, 1992), p. 62.

27. Colin Powell, *My American Journey* (New York: Random House, 1995), p. 434: "The lessons I had absorbed from Panama confirmed all my convictions over the preceding twenty years, since the days of doubt over Vietnam. Have a clear political objective and stick to it. Use all the force necessary, and do not apologize for going in big if that is what it takes. Decisive force ends wars quickly and in the long run saves lives."

28. Excerpts from the Weinberger speech appearing in the above and following paragraphs are drawn from "The Uses of Military Power" speech before the National Press Club, Washington, DC, November 28, 1984, reprinted in Michael I. Handel, *Masters of War: Classical Strategic Thought* (Portland, OR: Frank Cass, 2000), pp. 329–335. "1) If we decide that it is necessary to put combat troops into a given situation, we should do so wholeheartedly and with the clear intention of winning. 2) If we do decide to commit to combat overseas, we should have clearly defined political and military objectives. 3) The relationship between our objectives and the forces we have committed – their size and composition – must be continually reassessed and adjusted if necessary. 4) Before the U.S. commits combat forces abroad, there must be some reasonable assurance [that] we will have the support of the American people and their elected representatives in Congress." Cf. Jeffrey Record, "Back to the Weinberger-Powell Doctrine," *Strategic Studies Quarterly*, Fall 2007, at www.au.af.mil/au/ssq/2007/fall/record.pdf.

29. William Schneider, "The Old Politics and the New World Order," in Kenneth Oye, Robert Leiber, and Donald Rothchild (eds.), *Eagle in a New World: American Grand Strategy in the Post-Cold War Era* (New York: HarperCollins, 1992), p. 67.

30. George [H. W.] Bush, "A Nation Blessed," adapted from a commencement address to the Naval War College, June 15, 2001, *Naval War College Review* 54.4 (Autumn 2001), pp. 135–140, at p. 139.

31. George H. W. Bush, *National Security Strategy of the United States*, August 1991, at www.fas.org/man/docs/918015-nss.htm.

32. President George H. W. Bush, *National Security Strategy of the United States*, March 1990, at www.fas.org/man/docs.

33. President George H. W. Bush, "Address before a Joint Session of the Congress on the Persian Gulf Crisis and the Federal Budget Deficit," September 11, 1990, at http://www.presidency.ucsb.edu/ws/index.php?pid=18820&st=&st1=:   "That's why Secretary Baker and Treasury Secretary Brady have met with many world leaders to underscore that the burden of this collective effort must be shared."

34. Kenneth Oye, Robert Leiber, and Donald Rothchild, eds., *Eagle in a New World: American Grand Strategy in the Post-Cold War Era* (New York: HarperCollins, 1992), p. 27.

35. President George H.W. Bush, *National Security Strategy of the United States*, August 1991, at www.fas.org/man/docs/918015-nss.htm.

36. See Kenneth Oye, Robert Leiber, and Donald Rothchild, eds., *Eagle in a New World: American Grand Strategy in the Post-Cold War Era* (New York: HarperCollins, 1992), pp. 26–27.

37. For background on Clinton, see David Maraniss, *First in His Class: A Biography of Bill Clinton* (New York: Simon & Schuster, 2008); Martin Walker, *The President We Deserve: Bill Clinton, His Rise, Falls, and Comebacks* (New York: Crown Publishers, 1996); John F. Harris, *The Survivor: Bill Clinton in the White House* (New York: Random House, 2006); Meredith L. Oakley, *On the Make: The Rise of Bill Clinton* (Washington, DC: Regnery Publishing, 1994); Fred I. Greenstein, "The Presidential Leadership Style of Bill Clinton: An Early Appraisal," *Political Science Quarterly* 108, No. 4 (1993), pp. 589–601; George Stephanopoulos, *Bill Clinton, All Too Human: A Political Education* (Boston: Little, Brown, 1996).

38. On Clinton's grand strategy, see Colin Dueck, "New Perspectives on American Grand Strategy: A Review Essay," *International Security* 28, No. 4 (2004), pp. 197–216; Mark Schafer and Stephen G. Walker, "Democratic Leaders and the Democratic Peace: The Operational Codes of Tony Blair and Bill Clinton," *International Studies Quarterly* 50, No. 3 (2006), pp. 561–583; Christopher Layne and Benjamin Schwarz, "American Hegemony: Without an Enemy," *Foreign Policy* 92 (1993), pp. 5–23; Christopher Layne, "Rethinking American Grand Strategy: Hegemony or Balance of Power in the Twenty-First Century?" *World Policy Journal* 15, No. 2 (1998), pp. 8–28; Robert Kagan, "The Benevolent Empire," *Foreign Policy* (1998), pp. 24–35.

39. See Bill Clinton, First Inaugural Address, January 20, 1993, at www.bartleby.com/124/pres64.html.

40. I. M. Destler, "Foreign Economic Policy Making under Bill Clinton," in James M. Scott (ed.), *Making U.S. Foreign Policy in the Post-Cold War World* (Durham, NC: Duke University Press, 1998), p. 89.

41. Peter Trubowitz, *Politics and Strategy: Partisan Ambition and American Statecraft* (Princeton, NJ: Princeton University Press, 2011), p. 120.

42. David Halberstam, *War in a Time of Peace: Bush, Clinton, and the Generals* (New York: Simon and Shuster, 2001), p. 168.

43. Lawrence J. Korb, Laura Conley, and Alex Rothman, "A Historical Perspective on Defense Budgets: What We Can Learn from Past Presidents about Reducing Spending," *Center for American Progress*, July 6, 2011, at www.americanprogress.org/issues/budget/news/2011/07/06/10041/a-historical-perspective-on-defense-budgets/.

44. Peter Trubowitz, *Politics and Strategy: Partisan Ambition and American Statecraft* (Princeton, NJ: Princeton University Press, 2011), p. 120: "Still Clinton was less disciplined in this regard than either Van Buren or Hoover, or than my theory of the determinants of grand strategy would predict." Cf. Iwan Morgan, "Jimmy Carter, Bill Clinton, and the New Democratic Economics," *The Historical Journal* 47, No. 4 (2004), pp. 1015–1039.

45. Trubowitz, *Politics and Strategy: Partisan Ambition and American Statecraft* (Princeton, NJ: Princeton University Press, 2011), p. 121.

46. The origins of Clinton's Engagement and Enlargement national security strategy were outlined in William J. Clinton, "Statement on the National Security Strategy Report, July 21, 1994," at The American Presidency Project: William J. Clinton: Statement on the National Security Strategy Report, at www.presidency.ucsb.edu/ws/index.php?pid=50525#ixzz1pIqNMSYK.

47. See William J. Clinton, A *National Security Strategy of Engagement and Enlargement* (Washington, DC: The White House, February 1995), p. 2, at www.au.af.mil/au/awc/awcgate/nss/nss-95.pdf: However, "as the world's premier economic and military power, the United States is indispensable to the forging of stable political relations and open trade."

48. See Douglas Brinkley, "Democratic Enlargement: The Clinton Doctrine," *Foreign Policy*, No. 106 (Spring 1997), pp. 110–127; Charles William Maynes, "A Workable Clinton Doctrine," *Foreign Policy*, No. 93 (Winter 1993–1994), pp. 3–21; John Dumbrell, "Was There a Clinton Doctrine? President Clinton's Foreign Policy Reconsidered," *Diplomacy and Statecraft* 13, No. 2 (2002), pp. 43–56.

49. See Michael Klare, "The Clinton Doctrine," *The Nation*, April 1, 1999, at www.thenation.com/article/clinton-doctrine#axzz2c3EFUGsk.

50. See William J. Clinton, A *National Security Strategy of Engagement and Enlargement* (Washington, DC: The White House, February 1995), p. 22, at www.au.af.mil/au/awc/awcgate/nss/nss-95.pdf: "We must focus our efforts where we have the most leverage. And our efforts must be demand-driven – they must focus on nations whose people are pushing for reform or have already secured it."

51. See Clinton, A *National Security Strategy of Engagement and Enlargement* (Washington, DC: The White House, February 1995), p. 24, at www.au.af.mil/au/awc/awcgate/nss/nss-95.pdf: ". . . our greatest strength is the power of our ideas, which are still new in many lands. Across the world, we see them embraced – and we rejoice. Our hopes, our hearts, our hands, are with those on every continent who are building democracy and freedom."

52. See Clinton, A *National Security Strategy of Engagement and Enlargement* (Washington, DC: The White House, February 1995), p. 7, at www.au.af.mil/au/awc/awcgate/nss/nss-95.pdf: "We must also use the right tools – being willing to act unilaterally when our direct national interests are most at stake; in alliance and partnership when our interests are shared by others; and multilaterally when our interests are more general and the problems are best addressed by the international community."

53. Peter Trubowitz, *Politics and Strategy: Partisan Ambition and American Statecraft* (Princeton, NJ: Princeton University Press, 2011), p. 120: "Militarily, the United

States was spending more than the combined sum spent by all of its potential adversaries, and more than all its main allies combined. The U.S. defense budget of roughly $280 billion was well over three times the total of Russia and China together."

54. For more scholarship on dramatic shifts in power, see Paul Kennedy, *The Rise and Fall of Great Power: Economic Change and Military Conflict from 1500 to 2000* (New York: Random House, 1987); Robert Gilpin, *War and Change in the World* (New York: Cambridge University Press, 1981). On the implications for grand strategy, see Joseph S. Nye Jr. "Soft Power," *Foreign Policy*, No. 80 (*Twentieth Anniversary*, Autumn 1990), pp. 153–171; Christopher Layne, "Rethinking American Grand Strategy: Hegemony or Balance of Power in the Twenty-First Century," *World Policy Journal* 15, No. 2 (Summer 1998), pp. 8–27.

55. See Bill Clinton, First Inaugural Address, January 20, 1993, at www.bartleby.com/124/pres64.html.

56. Peter Trubowitz, *Politics and Strategy: Partisan Ambition and American Statecraft* (Princeton, NJ: Princeton University Press, 2011), p. 123. As a practical matter, "Clinton, though generally supportive of multilateral diplomacy, especially in foreign economic affairs, temporized when public support for a growing reliance on cost-sharing multilateral partnerships faltered in other areas."

57. Trubowitz, *Politics and Strategy: Partisan Ambition and American Statecraft* (Princeton, NJ: Princeton University Press, 2011), pp. 123–124.

58. Bill Clinton, *My Life* (New York: Knopf, 2004), p. 593, who admits that "the failure to try to stop Rwanda's tragedies became one of the greatest regrets of my presidency."

59. Peter Trubowitz, *Politics and Strategy: Partisan Ambition and American Statecraft* (Princeton, NJ: Princeton University Press, 2011), p. 127: Clinton was "ambivalent about reversing U.S. grand strategy and only partially committed to retrenchment."

60. Garry Wills, "The Clinton Principle," *New York Times Magazine*, January 19, 1997, p. 44; Richard N. Haass, "Fatal Distraction: Bill Clinton's Foreign Policy," *Foreign Policy*, 1997, pp. 112–123.

61. For background on Bush, see George W. Bush, *Decision Points* (New York: Crown Publishers, 2010); Stanley A. Renshon, *In His Father's Shadow: The Transformations of George W. Bush* (New York: Palgrave Macmillan, 2004).

62. On Bush's grand strategy, see Andrew J. Bacevich, "Bush's Grand Strategy," *The American Conservative* 4 (November 2002); John Lewis Gaddis, "A Grand Strategy of Transformation," *Foreign Policy* 133 (November–December, 2002), pp. 50–57; Robert Jervis, "Understanding the Bush Doctrine," *Political Science Quarterly* 118, No. 3 (Fall 2003), pp. 365–546; Edward Rhodes, "The Imperial Logic of Bush's Liberal Agenda," *Survival* 45, No. 1 (2003), pp. 131–154; Niall Ferguson, "Hegemony or Empire?" *Foreign Affairs* 82, No. 5 (September–October, 2003), pp. 154–161; Alexander Moens, *The Foreign Policy of George W. Bush: Values, Strategy and Loyalty* (Surrey, UK: Ashgate Publishing, 2004); Lloyd E. Ambrosius, "Woodrow Wilson and George W. Bush: Historical Comparisons of Ends and Means in Their Foreign Policies," *Diplomatic History* 30, No. 3 (2006), pp. 509–543; Ivo H. Daalder and James M. Lindsay, *America Unbound: The Bush Revolution in Foreign Policy* (New York: Wiley, 2005).

63. See Karl Rove, *Courage and Consequence: My Life as a Conservative in the Fight* (New York: Simon & Schuster, 2010), pp. 134–135: "He [Bush] said his goal was to help 'usher in the responsibility era ... that stands in stark contrast to the last few decades, when the culture clear said: If it feels good, do it.' He talked about tax cuts, Social Security, and education reform, his faith-based initiative, and the need for increased defense spending."

64. Ryan J. Barilleaux and David Zellers, "How George W. Bush Remade American Foreign Policy," in Mark J. Rozell and Gleaves Whitney (eds.), *Testing the Limits: George W. Bush and the Imperial Presidency* (Lanham, MD: Rowman & Littlefield Publishers, 2009).

65. John Lewis Gaddis, "A Grand Strategy of Transformation," *Foreign Policy* 133 (November–December 2002), pp. 50–57, at p. 50.

66. John W. Dietrich, ed., *The George W. Bush Foreign Policy Reader: Presidential Speeches with Commentary* (Armonk, NY: M. E. Sharpe, Inc., 2005), p. 6.

67. See Karl Rove, *Courage and Consequence: My Life as a Conservative in the Fight* (New York: Simon & Schuster, 2010), p. 142.

68. George W. Bush, *Decision Points* (New York: Crown Publishers, 2010), p. 307.

69. John W. Dietrich, ed., *The George W. Bush Foreign Policy Reader: Presidential Speeches with Commentary* (Armonk, NY: M. E. Sharpe, 2005), p. 7.

70. Mackubin Thomas Owens, "The Bush Doctrine: The Foreign Policy of Republican Empire," *Orbis*, Winter 2009, p. 24.

71. See "Bush, Gore Spar Politely in Round Two," *ABC News*, October 11, 2000, at www.abcnews.go.com/Politics/story?id=122722.

72. Mackubin Thomas Owens, "The Bush Doctrine: The Foreign Policy of Republican Empire," *Orbis*, Winter 2009, p. 24.

73. John W. Dietrich, ed., *The George W. Bush Foreign Policy Reader: Presidential Speeches with Commentary* (Armonk, NY: M. E. Sharpe, 2005), pp. 22–23.

74. Dietrich, ed., *The George W. Bush Foreign Policy Reader: Presidential Speeches with Commentary* (Armonk, NY: M. E. Sharpe, 2005), p. 24.

75. Dietrich, ed., *The George W. Bush Foreign Policy Reader: Presidential Speeches with Commentary* (Armonk, NY: M. E. Sharpe, 2005), p. 28: "An American president should work with our strong democratic allies in Europe and Asia to extend the peace. He should promote a fully democratic Western Hemisphere, bound together by free trade. He should defend America's interests in the Persian Gulf and advance peace in the Middle East, based upon a secure Israel. He must check the contagious spread of weapons of mass destruction, and the means to deliver them. He must lead toward a world that trades in freedom. And he must pursue all these goals with focus, patience and strength."

76. Dietrich, ed., *The George W. Bush Foreign Policy Reader: Presidential Speeches with Commentary* (Armonk, NY: M. E. Sharpe, 2005), p. 133.

77. See Karl Rove, *Courage and Consequence: My Life as a Conservative in the Fight* (New York: Simon & Schuster, 2010), p. 160: Bush called for "an end of the Anti-Ballistic Missile (ABM) Treaty now that the Soviet Union had collapsed ..."

78. George W. Bush, *Decision Points* (New York: Crown Publishers, 2010), p. 342: "I told Vladimir [Putin] I planned to give him the required six-months' notice that America would withdraw from the Anti-Ballistic Missile Treaty, so that we could

both develop effective missile defense systems.... 'The Cold War is over,' I told Putin. 'We are no longer enemies.'"

79. The exact death toll was 2,977, not including the 19 hijackers. Notably, this was more than the 2,402 Americans who were killed during the Japanese attack on Pearl Harbor seventy years earlier, on 7 December 1941.

80. Howard Jones, *Crucible of Power: A History of American Foreign Relations From 1945* (Plymouth, UK: Rowman & Littlefield Publishers, 2009), p. 332.

81. John W. Dietrich, ed., *The George W. Bush Foreign Policy Reader: Presidential Speeches with Commentary* (Armonk, NY: M. E. Sharpe, 2005), p. 52.

82. Dietrich, ed., *The George W. Bush Foreign Policy Reader: Presidential Speeches with Commentary* (Armonk, NY: M. E. Sharpe, 2005), p. 61; George W. Bush, State of the Union Address, January 29, 2002, at www.washingtonpost.com/wp-srv/onpolitics/transcripts/sou012902htm.

83. Dietrich, ed., *The George W. Bush Foreign Policy Reader: Presidential Speeches with Commentary* (Armonk, NY: M. E. Sharpe, 2005), p. 63. As Bush said, "We will defend the peace against threats from terrorists and tyrants.... And we will extend the peace by encouraging free and open societies on every continent."

84. Dietrich, ed., *The George W. Bush Foreign Policy Reader: Presidential Speeches with Commentary* (Armonk, NY: M. E. Sharpe, 2005), p. 64 (emphasis added).

85. On preemption, see William H. Taft and Todd F. Buchwald, "Preemption, Iraq, and International Law," *American Journal of International Law* 97.3 (2003), pp. 557–563; David B. Rivkin Jr., Lee A. Casey, and Mark Wendell DeLaquil, "Preemption and Law in the Twenty-First Century," *Chicago Journal of International Law* 5 (2004), p. 467; Betty Glad and Chris J. Dolan, eds., *Striking First: The Preventive War Doctrines and the Reshaping of US Foreign Policy* (New York: Palgrave Macmillan, 2004).

86. George W. Bush, *The National Security Strategy of the United States of America*, September 17, 2002, p. 15, at www.nssarchive.us/NSSR/2002.pdf: "For centuries, international law recognized that nations need not suffer an attack before they can lawfully take action to defend themselves against forces that present an imminent danger of attack. Legal scholars and international jurists often conditioned the legitimacy of preemption on the existence of an imminent threat – most often a visible mobilization of armies, navies, and air forces preparing to attack."

87. George W. Bush, *The National Security Strategy of the United States of America*, September 17, 2002, at www.nssarchive.us/NSSR/2002.pdf, p. 15: "They know such attacks would fail. Instead, they rely on acts of terror and, potentially, the use of weapons of mass destruction – weapons that can be easily concealed, delivered covertly, and used without warning."

88. John Lewis Gaddis, "A Grand Strategy of Transformation," *Foreign Policy* 133 (November–December 2002), pp. 50–57, at p. 51.

89. George W. Bush, *The National Security Strategy of the United States of America*, September 17, 2002, p. iv, at www.nssarchive.us/NSSR/2002.pdf. Cf. John Lewis Gaddis, "A Grand Strategy of Transformation," *Foreign Policy* 133 (November–December 2002), pp. 50–57, at p. 51.

90. George W. Bush, *The National Security Strategy of the United States of America*, September 17, 2002, p. 5, at www.nssarchive.us/NSSR/2002.pdf.

91. Bush, *The National Security Strategy of the United States of America*, September 17, 2002, p. 15, at www.nssarchive.us/NSSR/2002.pdf.

92. Bush, *The National Security Strategy of the United States of America*, September 17, 2002, p. 6, at www.nssarchive.us/NSSR/2002.pdf.

93. John Lewis Gaddis, "A Grand Strategy of Transformation," *Foreign Policy* 133 (November–December 2002), pp. 50–57.

94. See Ivo H. Daalder and James M. Lindsay, *America Unbound: The Bush Revolution in Foreign Policy* (New Work: Wiley, 2005); Robert Jervis, "Understanding the Bush Doctrine," *Political Science Quarterly* 118, No. 3 (2003), pp. 365–388; Michael Cox, "Empire, Imperialism and the Bush Doctrine," *Review of International Studies* 3, No. 4 (2004), pp. 585–608; Mackubin Thomas Owens, "The Bush Doctrine: The Foreign Policy of Republican Empire," *Orbis*, Winter 2009; Jacob Shively, "The Constraints of Grand Strategy: The Bush Doctrine and Great Power Reactions to Crisis," World International Studies Conference, Porto, Portugal, August 17–20, 2011; Sean D. Murphy (ed.), "U.S. Adoption of New Doctrine on Use of Force," *American Journal of International Law* 97, No. 1 (January 2003), pp. 203–205; Jonathan Monten, "The Roots of the Bush Doctrine: Power, Nationalism, and Democracy Promotion in U.S. Strategy," *International Security* 29, No. 4 (Spring 2005), pp. 112–156.

95. George W. Bush, *Decision Points* (New York, New York: Crown Publishers, 2010), pp. 396–397.

96. See George W. Bush, "President's State of the Union Address," January 29, 2002, at http://www.presidency.ucsb.edu/ws/index.php?pid=29644&st=&st1=; International Institute for Strategic Studies, "Towards Stability in Afghanistan: Qualified Progress?" *Strategic Comments* 10.4 (May 2004), pp. 1–2, at www.iiss .org/stratcom.

97. See "Operation Enduring Freedom: One Year of Accomplishments" (October 7, 2002), available at www.whitehouse.gov/infocus/defense/enduringfreedom.html. See also Kimberly Marten, "Warlordism in Comparative Perspective," *International Security* 31, No. 3 (Winter 2006/2007), pp. 41–73.

98. See Bob Woodward, *Bush at War* (New York: Simon & Schuster, 2002), p. 334. Some two dozen Afghans, meeting under UN auspices, would produce the Bonn Agreement of December 5, 2001, regarding setting up a new government, at www .afghan-web.com/politics/bonn_agreement_2001.html.

99. Woodward, *Bush at War* (New York: Simon & Schuster, 2002), p. 275.

100. Woodward, *Bush at War* (New York: Simon & Schuster, 2002), p. 241, who quoted Bush as saying this.

101. See Raymond W. Copson (coord.), "Iraq War: Background and Issues Overview," *CRS Report for Congress*, April 22, 2003), pp. 1–4, at www.fas.org/man/crs/ RL31715.pdf; Patrick E. Tyler, "Bush Signal: Time Is Now," *New York Times*, November 8, 2002, p. A1. Some date the onset of planning from Defense Secretary Rumsfeld's demand on 9/11 for "best info fast. Judge whether good enough hit S. H. [Saddam Hussein] at same time. Not only UBL [bin Laden]." See "Plans for

Iraq Attack Began on 9/11," *CBS News*, September 4, 2002, at www.cbsnews.com/stories/2002/09/04/september11/main520830.shtml.

102. "We know he's been developing weapons of mass destruction." Cf. "President Holds Prime Time News Conference," The White House, October 11, 2001, at http://www.hsdl.org/?view&did=474848. See "President's State of the Union Message to Congress and the Nation," *New York Times*, January 29, 2003, pp. A12–A13: "The world has waited 12 years for Iraq to disarm. America will not accept a serious and mounting threat to our country, our friends and our allies." Richard W. Stevenson, "Bush Warns Iraq It Has Only Weeks to Yield Weapons," *New York Times*, January 31, 2003, p. A1; "Powell's Address, Presenting 'Deeply Troubling' Evidence on Iraq," *New York Times*, February 6, 2003, p. A14: "Indeed, the facts and Iraq's behavior show that Saddam Hussein and his regime are concealing their efforts to produce more weapons of mass destruction."

103. Bob Woodward, *Plan of Attack: The Definitive Account of the Decision to Invade Iraq* (New York: Simon & Schuster, 2004), p. 1. As President Bush asked Rumsfeld, "What kind of a war plan do you have for Iraq? How do you feel about the war plan for Iraq?" See also Glenn Kessler, "U.S. Decision on Iraq Has Puzzling Past," *Washington Post*, January 12, 2003, p. A1; Douglas Jehl, "British Memo on U.S. Plans for Iraq War Fuels Critics," *New York Times*, May 20, 2005, p. A8; Daniel Byman, "Iraq after Saddam," *Washington Quarterly* 24.4 (Autumn 2001), pp. 151–162; George C. Wilson, "Toppling Saddam with Quick Strikes," *National Journal*, December 21, 2002, pp. 37–42; and David Hastings Dunn, "Myths, Motivations and 'Misunderestimations': The Bush Administration and Iraq," *International Affairs* 79, No. 2 (March 2003), pp. 279–297.

104. See Cover Letter, The Commission on the Intelligence Capabilities of the United States Regarding Weapons of Mass Destruction, *Report to the President of the United States* (Washington, DC: March 31, 2005) (aka Robb-Silberman Report, at www.gpoaccess.gov/wmd/pdf/full_wmd_report.pdf.), p. 1: "The Intelligence Community was dead wrong in almost all of its prewar judgments about Iraq's weapons of mass destruction. This was a major intelligence failure." Further, "Its principal causes were the Intelligence Community's inability to collect good information about Iraq's WMD programs, serious errors in analyzing what information it could gather, and a failure to make clear just how much of its analysis was based on assumptions, rather than good evidence."

105. See *The National Security Strategy of the United States of America* (Washington, DC: The White House, September 2002), at http://georgewbush-whitehouse.archives.gov/nsc/nss/2002/, p. 14; George W. Bush, "The President's State of the Union Address," January 29, 2002, at www.whitehouse.gov/news/releases/2002/01/20020129-11.html; Michael Klare, "The Rise and Fall of the "Rogue Doctrine": The Pentagon's Quest for a Post–Cold War Military Strategy," *Middle East Report*, No. 208 (*US Foreign Policy in the Middle East: Critical Assessments*, Autumn 1998), pp. 12–15, 47.

106. "Vice President Speaks at VFW 103rd National Convention," The White House, August 26, 2002, at http://georgewbush-whitehouse.archives.gov/news/releases/2002/08/20020826.html: "The Iraqi regime has in fact been very busy enhancing its capabilities in the field of chemical and biological agents. And they continue to

pursue the nuclear program they began so many years ago. These are not weapons for the purpose of defending Iraq; these are offensive weapons for the purpose of inflicting death on a massive scale, developed so that Saddam can hold the threat over the head of anyone he chooses, in his own region or beyond." See Stephen Fidler and David White, "Intelligence Report Says Baghdad Is Ready to Use Chemical and Biological Weapons," *Financial Times*, September 25, 2002, p. 2.

107. For the CIA's view of Iraq's noncompliance with specific UNSCRs, see *Iraq's Weapons of Mass Destruction Programs* (Washington, DC: CIA, October 2002). For a UN view of U.S. noncompliance with the Security Council, see "Iraq War Illegal, Says Annan," *BBC News*, September 16, 2004.

108. "Security Council, 15–0, Votes a Tough Resolution Telling Hussein to Disarm," *New York Times*, November 9, 2002, p. A1.

109. "President Says Saddam Hussein Must Leave Iraq within 48 Hours; Remarks by the President in Address to the Nation," The White House, March 17, 2003; at http://georgewbush-whitehouse.archives.gov/news/releases/2003/03/20030317-7 .html. See Raymond W. Copson (coord.), "Iraq War: Background and Issues Overview," *CRS Report for Congress*, April 22, 2003), pp. 6–7, at www.fas.org/ man/crs/RL31715.pdf.

110. See "President Bush Addresses the Nation," March 19, 2003, at http://georgew bush-whitehouse.archives.gov/news/releases/2003/03/20030319-17.html.

111. Quoted in Bob Woodward, *Plan of Attack: The Definitive Account of the Decision to Invade Iraq* (New York: Simon & Schuster, 2004), pp. 154–155. A working draft was reviewed at a principals' meeting on August 14, 2002. Bush signed it on August 29, 2002 (ibid., p. 228).

112. Raymond W. Copson (coord.), "Iraq War: Background and Issues Overview," *CRS Report for Congress*, April 22, 2003), p. 7, at www.fas.org/man/crs/RL31715.pdf. For the speech, see "President Discusses the Future of Iraq," February 26, 2003, at http:// georgewbush-whitehouse.archives.gov/news/releases/2003/02/20030226-11.html.

113. See "President Bush Addresses the Nation," March 19, 2003; "President Discusses Beginning of Operation Iraqi Freedom," March 22, 2003, at http://georgewbush-whitehouse.archives.gov/news/releases/2003/03/20030319-17.html.

114. Bob Woodward, *Plan of Attack* (New York: Simon & Schuster, 2004), p. 10. See also "President Bush Outlines Iraqi Threat," October 7, 2002, at http:// georgewbush-whitehouse.archives.gov/news/releases/2002/10/20021007-8.html, where Bush notes that "two administrations – mine and President Clinton's – have stated that regime change in Iraq is the only certain means of removing a great danger to our nation." Cf. "Transcript: Confronting Iraq Threat 'Is Crucial to Winning War on Terror,'" *New York Times*, October 8, 2002, p. A12.

115. Cf. David Mitchell and Tansa George Massoud, "Anatomy of Failure: Bush's Decision-Making Process and the Iraq War," *Foreign Policy Analysis* 5, No. 3 (July 2009), pp. 265–286.

116. Neela Banerjee, "Stable Oil Prices Are Likely to Become a War Casualty, Experts Say," *New York Times*, October 2, 2002, p. A13.

117. See also, Walter Russell Mead, *Power, Terror, Peace, and War: America's Grand Strategy in a World at Risk* (New York: Vintage Books, 2005), p. 42: "Providing the

'international public good' of a secure oil supply not only helps ensure *America's* oil supply, it helps make the United States the lone global superpower in a world of regional powers, and it also reinforces the widespread (though by no means universal) belief that American power helps underwrite and secure world peace" (emphasis in original).

118. George W. Bush, Second Inaugural Address, January 20, 2005, at www.bartleby .com/124/pres67.html.

119. John Lewis Gaddis, "Ending Tyranny: The Past and Future of an Idea," *American Interest* 6, No. 1 (September/October 2008), pp. 6–15.

120. See Dan Balz and Jim VandeHei, "Bush Speech Not a Sign of Policy Shift, Officials Say: Speech Said to Clarify 'the Values We Cherish,'" *Washington Post*, January 22, 2005, p. A01, at www.washingtonpost.com/wp-dyn/articles/A27672-2005Jan21.html.

121. George W. Bush, *The National Security Strategy of the United States of America*, March 16, 2006, p. ii, at www.presidentialrhetoric.com/speeches/nss2006.pdf.

122. Bush, *The National Security Strategy of the United States of America*, March 16, 2006, p. 49, at www.presidentialrhetoric.com/speeches/nss2006.pdf.

123. Peter Trubowitz, *Politics and Strategy: Partisan Ambition and American Statecraft* (Princeton, NJ: Princeton University Press, 2011), p. 97.

124. George W. Bush, *The National Security Strategy of the United States of America*, March 16, 2006, p. i, at www.presidentialrhetoric.com/speeches/nss2006.pdf: ". . . fully revealed to the American people on September 11, 2001."

125. Cf. Stephen G. Brooks and William C. Wohlforth, "International Relations Theory and the Case against Unilateralism," *Perspectives on Politics* 3, No. 3 (2005), p. 509.

126. See William J. Broad, "U.S. Rethinks Strategy for the Unthinkable," *New York Times*, December 10, 2010, at www.nytimes.com/2010/12/16/science/16terror .html: "In late 2001, a month after the Sept. 11 attacks, the director of central intelligence told President George W. Bush of a secret warning that Al Qaeda had hidden an atom bomb in New York City. The report turned out to be false. But atomic jitters soared."

127. Cf. Stephanie Craft, "U.S. Public Concerns in the Aftermath of 9–11: A Test of Second Level Agenda-Setting," *International Journal of Public Opinion Research* 16, No. 4 (2004), pp. 456–463.

128. George W. Bush, *The National Security Strategy of the United States of America*, March 16, 2006, p. 36, at www.presidentialrhetoric.com/speeches/nss2006.pdf.

129. Cf. Melvyn P. Leffler, "9/11 in Retrospect: George W. Bush's Grand Strategy, Reconsidered," *Foreign Affairs* 90 (2011), p. 33.

130. For background on Obama, see Barack Obama, *Dreams from My Father: A Story of Race and Inheritance* (New York: Broadway Books, 2004); Barack Obama, *The Audacity of Hope: Thoughts on Reclaiming the American Dream* (New York: Vintage Books, 2007); Hark Halperin and John Heilemann, *Game Change: Obama and the Clintons, McCain and Palin, and the Race of a Lifetime* (New York: Harper, 2010).

131. On Obama's grand strategy, see Christopher Layne, "America's Middle East Grand Strategy after Iraq: The Moment for Offshore Balancing Has Arrived,"

Review of International Studies 35, No. 1 (2009), pp. 5–25; Brendan Taylor, *Sanctions as Grand Strategy* (New York: Routledge, 2012); Rosa Brooks, "Obama Needs a Grand Strategy," *Foreign Policy*, January 23, 2012; Nicholas Kitchen, "The Obama Doctrine–Détente or Decline," *European Political Science* 10, No. 1 (2010), pp. 27–35; Sarah Kreps, "American Grand Strategy after Iraq," *Orbis* 53, No. 4 (2009), pp. 629–645.

132. See Barack Obama, First Inaugural Address, January 20, 2009, at www.bartleby.com/124/pres68.html: "For everywhere we look, there is work to be done. The state of our economy calls for action, bold and swift, and we will act – not only to create new jobs, but to lay a new foundation for growth. We will build the roads and bridges, the electric grids and digital lines that feed our commerce and bind us together. We will restore science to its rightful place, and wield technology's wonders to raise health care's quality and lower its cost. We will harness the sun and the winds and the soil to fuel our cars and run our factories. And we will transform our schools and colleges and universities to meet the demands of a new age."

133. See Obama, First Inaugural Address, January 20, 2009, at www.bartleby.com/124/pres68.html.

134. See Barack Obama, *National Security Strategy 2010* (Washington, DC: The White House, May 2010), p. 2, at www.whitehouse.gov/sites/default/files/rss_viewer/national_security_strategy.pdf.

135. See *Rasmussen Reports*, "53% Favor Immediate Withdrawal of All U.S. Forces From Afghanistan," March 19, 2012, at www.rasmussenreports.com/public_content/politics/current_events/afghanistan/53_favor_immediate_withdrawal_of_all_u_s_forces_from_afghanistan; *Rasmussen Reports*, "67% Favor Ending U.S. Combat Role in Afghanistan by Next Year," February 7, 2012, at www.rasmussenreports.com/public_content/politics/current_events/afghanistan/67_favor_ending_u_s_combat_role_in_afghanistan_by_next_year.

136. Peter Trubowitz, *Politics and Strategy: Partisan Ambition and American Statecraft* (Princeton, NJ: Princeton University Press, 2011), p. 13.

137. "Full Transcript: President Obama's Speech on Afghanistan Delivered at West Point," *ABCNews.com*, December 1, 2009, at www.abcnews.go.com/Politics/full-transcript-president-obamas-speech-afghanistan-delivered-west/story?id=9220661#.T4x9KO1c_dk.

138. See John T. Bennett, "Thousands of US Troops Likely in Afghanistan beyond 2014 Withdrawal Date," *U.S. News & World Report*, April 26, 2012, at www.usnews.com/news/blogs/dotmil/2012/04/26/thousands-of-us-troops-likely-in-afghanistan-beyond-2014-withdrawal-date.

139. Daniel W. Drezner, "Does Obama Have a Grand Strategy?" *Foreign Affairs* 90, No. 4, July/August 2011, p. 58.

140. For the origins of the phrase, see Ryan Lizza, "Leading from Behind," *The New Yorker*, April 27, 2011, at www.newyorker.com/online/blogs/newsdesk/2011/04/leading-from-behind-obama-clinton.html: "You take the front line when there is danger. Then people will appreciate your leadership." Also, Daniel W. Drezner, "Does Obama Have a Grand Strategy?" *Foreign Affairs* 90, No. 4 (July/August 2011), p. 48: "It is this vacuum of interpretation that the administration's critics have rushed to fill. Unless and until the president and his advisers define explicitly

the strategy that has been implicit for the past year, the president's foreign policy critics will be eager to define it – badly – for him."

141. Drezner, "Does Obama Have a Grand Strategy?" *Foreign Affairs* 90, No. 4 (July/ August 2011), p. 64.

142. See "Weekly Security Update," *Iraq Business News*, August 15, 2012. Also, see James Dao and Andrew Lehren, "In Toll of 2,000, New Portrait of Afghan War," *New York Times*, August 22, 2012, at www.nytimes.com/2012/08/22/us/war-in-afghanistan-claims-2000th-american-life.html.

143. See Nicholas Kitchen, "The Obama Doctrine–Détente or Decline," *European Political Science* 10, No. 1 (2010), pp. 27–35; Joseph M. Parent and Paul K. MacDonald, "The Wisdom of Retrenchment," *Foreign Affairs* 90, No. 6 (November/December 2011), pp. 32–47: "Today, however, U.S. power has begun to wane.... In addition to fiscal discipline, Washington appears to have rediscovered the virtues of multilateralism and a restrained foreign policy" (pp. 32–33). Cf. Kyle Haynes, William R. Thompson, Paul K. MacDonald, and Joseph Mr. Parent, "Correspondence: Decline and Retrenchment: Peril or Promise?" *International Security* 4, No. 36 (Spring 2012), pp. 189–203.

144. Cf. Barack Obama, "Renewing American Leadership," *Foreign Affairs* 86, No. 4 (July–August, 2007), pp. 2–16; Bob Woodward, *Obama's Wars* (New York: Simon & Schuster, 2010); Barack Obama, "Remarks by the President on a New Strategy for Afghanistan and Pakistan" (Washington, DC: March 27, 2009), at http://usun.state .gov/briefing/statements/2009/march/131656.htm; Michael R. Gordon, "Afghan Strategy Poses Stiff Challenge for Obama," *New York Times*, December 2, 2008, at www.vfp143.org/lit/Afghanistan/NYTimes-Afghan_Strategy_Poses_Stiff_Challenge_ for_Obama.pdf.

145. Foon Rhee, "Obama: Afghanistan, Not Iraq, Should Be Focus," *Boston.com*, July 15, 2008: "Osama bin Laden and Ayman al-Zawahari are recording messages to their followers and plotting more terror."

146. Foon Rhee, "Obama: Afghanistan, Not Iraq, Should Be Focus," *Boston.com*, July 15, 2008.

147. Barack Obama, "Renewing American Leadership," *Foreign Affairs* 86, No. 4 (July–August, 2007), pp. 2–16.

148. *Agreement between the United States of America and the Republic of Iraq on the Withdrawal of United States Forces from Iraq and the Organization of Their Activities during Their Temporary Presence in Iraq*, at http://www.state.gov/docu ments/organization/122074.pdf.

149. "Full Transcript: President Obama's Speech on Afghanistan Delivered at West Point," *ABCNews.com*, December 1, 2009, at www.abcnews.go.com/Politics/full-transcript-president-obamas-speech-afghanistan-delivered-west/story? id=9220661#.T5Bryu1c_dk. Cf. William C. Martel, *Victory in War: Foundations of Modern Strategy* (New York: Cambridge University Press, 2011), pp. 300–306, for an analysis of President Obama's 2009 Afghan policy review.

150. "Full Transcript: President Obama's Speech on Afghanistan Delivered at West Point," *ABCNews.com*, December 1, 2009, at www.abcnews.go.com/Politics/full-transcript-president-obamas-speech-afghanistan-delivered-west/story?id=9220661# .T5Bryu1c_dk.

151. "Full Transcript: President Obama's Speech on Afghanistan Delivered at West Point," *ABCNews.com*, December 1, 2009, at www.abcnews.go.com/Politics/full-transcript-president-obamas-speech-afghanistan-delivered-west/story?id=9220661#.T5Bryu1c_dk.

152. Peter Trubowitz, *Politics and Strategy: Partisan Ambition and American Statecraft* (Princeton, NJ: Princeton University Press, 2011), 146.

153. Ryan Lizza, "The Consequentialist," *New Yorker*, May 2, 2011, at www.newyorker.com/reporting/2011/05/02/110502fa_fact_lizza: "Pursuing our interests and spreading our ideals thus requires stealth and modesty as well as military strength."

154. Cf. Barack Obama, "Remarks by the President in Address to the Nation on Libya," National Defense University (Washington, DC: March 28, 2011); Bruce D. Jones, "Libya and the Responsibility of Power," *Survival* 53, No. 3 (2011), pp. 51–60; Anne-Marie Slaughter, "Interests vs. values? Misunderstanding Obama's Libya Strategy," *New York Review of Books* 30 (2011).

155. Ryan Lizza, "News Desk: Leading From Behind," *New Yorker*, April 27, 2011, at www.newyorker.com/online/blogs/newsdesk/2011/04/leading-from-behind-obama-clinton.html: "It was just a total cacophony of contradiction. And part of my goal is to move people toward having to take responsibility, to begin to match words and actions." Also, "The United States should do something, but don't bomb anybody."

156. Lizza, "News Desk: Leading From Behind," *New Yorker*, April 27, 2011, at www.newyorker.com/online/blogs/newsdesk/2011/04/leading-from-behind-obama-clinton.html: In Clinton's words, "That is a significant difference."

157. David Rohde, "The Obama Doctrine," *Foreign Policy*, February 27, 2012, at www.foreignpolicy.com/articles/2012/02/27/the_obama_doctrine.

158. Rohde, "The Obama Doctrine," *Foreign Policy*, February 27, 2012, at www.foreignpolicy.com/articles/2012/02/27/the_obama_doctrine.

159. See William C. Martel, *Victory in War: Foundations of Modern Strategy* (New York: Cambridge University Press, 2011), pp. 278–311, for an analysis of victory in the intervention against Afghanistan.

160. Cf. Irving Louis Horowitz, "Political Indecision and Military Muddle in an Age of Grand Strategy," *The Forum* 9, No. 3 (October 2011), p. 4; Daniel S. Morey, Clayton L. Thyne, Sarah L. Hayden, and Michael B. Senters, "Leader, Follower, or Spectator? The Role of President Obama in the Arab Spring Uprisings," *Social Science Quarterly* 93, No. 5 (December 2012), pp. 1185–1201. See Richard N. Haass, "The U.S. Should Keep Out of Libya," *Wall Street Journal*, March 8, 2011, p. A8.

161. "The Second Presidential Debate," October 7, 2008, at http://elections.nytimes.com/2008/president/debates/second-presidential-debate.html.

162. Nicholas Schmidle, "Getting Bin Laden," *New Yorker*, August 8, 2011, at www.newyorker.com/reporting/2011/08/08/110808fa_fact_schmidle.

163. See Alissa J. Rubin, "Afghan Pact Vows U.S. Aid for a Decade," *New York Times*, April 23, 2012, p. A1.

164. See Aliya Robin Deri, "'Costless' War: American and Pakistani Reactions to the U.S. Drone War," *Intersect* 5 (Stanford University, 2012); and Salman Masood, "Drone Strikes Continue in Pakistan as Tension Increases and Senate Panel Cuts Aid," *New York Times*, May 24, 2012.

165. See "The Year of the Drone," *New America Foundation: Counterterrorism Strategy Initiative,* at http://www.newamerica.net/publications/policy/the _year_of_the_drone.

166. David Rohde, "The Obama Doctrine," *Foreign Policy,* February 27, 2012, at www .foreignpolicy.com/articles/2012/02/27/the_obama_doctrine.

167. Ian Johnson and Jackie Calmes, "As U.S. Looks to Asia, It See China Everywhere," *New York Times,* November 15, 2011. Cf. Kenneth Lieberthal, "The American Pivot to Asia: Why President Obama's Turn to the East Is Easier Said than Done," *Foreign Policy,* December 21, 2011; Mark E. Manyin (coord.), *Pivot to the Pacific?: The Obama Administration's "Rebalancing" toward Asia* (Washington, DC: Congressional Research Service, Vol. R42448, March 28, 2012). On the origins of "pivot" in geopolitics, see Halford J. Mackinder, "The Geographical Pivot of History," *Geographical Journal* 23, No.4 (1904), pp. 421–437. President Barack Obama, "Text – Obama's Remarks on Military Spending," *New York Times,* January 5, 2012, at www.nytimes.com/2012/01/06/us/text-obamas -remarks-on-military-spending.html.

168. Obama, "Text – Obama's Remarks on Military Spending," *New York Times,* January 5, 2012, at www.nytimes.com/2012/01/06/us/text-obamas-remarks-on-mili tary-spending.html.

169. Matt Siegel, "As Part of Pact, U.S. Marines Arrive in Australia, in China's Strategic Backyard," *New York Times,* April 4, 2012, at www.nytimes.com/2012/04/05/world/ asia/us-marines-arrive-darwin-australia.html.

170. Mark E. Manyin, Stephen Daggett, Ben Dolven, Susan V. Lawrence, Michael F. Martin, Ronald O'Rourke, and Bruce Vaughn, *Pivot to the Pacific? The Obama Administration's "Rebalancing" toward Asia* (Washington, DC: United States Congressional Research Service, Vol. R42448, March 28, 2012), p. 4, at www .fas.org/sgp/crs/natsec/R42448.pdf: "With the exception of the Korean Peninsula, Asia is seen mainly as a naval theater of operations, while the decision not to cut the Navy as sharply as other services reflects a dramatic shift in priorities, which is unusual in year-to-year defense planning."

171. Hillary Clinton, "America's Pacific Century," *Foreign Policy,* November 2011, at www.foreignpolicy.com/articles/2011/10/11/americas_pacific_century: "We know that these new realities require us to innovate, to compete, and to lead in new ways."

172. Clinton, "America's Pacific Century," *Foreign Policy,* November 2011, at www .foreignpolicy.com/articles/2011/10/11/americas_pacific_century. For Clinton, the U.S. strategy in the Pacific "will proceed along six key lines of action: strength-ening bilateral security alliances; deepening our working relationships with emerg-ing powers, including with China; engaging with regional multilateral institutions; expanding trade and investment; forging a broad-based military presence; and advancing democracy and human rights."

173. Mark E. Manyin (coord.), *Pivot to the Pacific? The Obama Administration's "Rebalancing" toward Asia* (Washington, DC: United States Congressional Research Service, Vol. R42448, March 28, 2012), p. 4, at www.fas.org/sgp/crs/ natsec/R42448.pdf: This includes "Congress's oversight and appropriations roles, as well as its approval authority over free trade agreements, [all of which] will help

determine to what extent the Administration's plans are implemented and how various trade-offs are managed." This is occurring "as China [becomes] an ever-more influential regional power."

174. Peter Trubowitz, *Politics and Strategy: Partisan Ambition and American Statecraft* (Princeton, NJ: Princeton University Press, 2011), p. 97.

175. Cf. William C. Martel, "For America, Decline Is a Choice," *The Diplomat*, March 15, 2013, at www.thediplomat.com/2013/03/15/for-america-decline-is-a-choice: "We already are seeing deepening weariness on the part of the American people to support the costs and burdens of global leadership."

176. Cf. Henry R. Nau, "Obama's Foreign Policy," *Policy Review* 160 (2010), pp. 27–47; Thomas Wright, "Toward Effective Multilateralism: Why Bigger May Not Be Better," *Washington Quarterly* 32, No. (2009), pp. 163–180; Henry A. Kissinger, "Obama's Foreign Policy Challenge," *Washington Post*, April 22, 2009; Thomas G. Weiss, "Toward a Third Generation of International Institutions: Obama's UN Policy." *Washington Quarterly* 32, No. 3 (2009), pp. 141–162.

177. See Barack Obama, *National Security Strategy 2010* (Washington, DC: The White House, May 2010), p. 3, at www.whitehouse.gov/sites/default/files/rss_viewer/natio nal_security_strategy.pdf. Cf., Christopher Hemmer, "Continuity and Change in the Obama Administration's National Security Strategy," *Comparative Strategy* 30, No. 3 (2011), pp. 268–277; Kenneth Roth, "Empty Promises-Obama's Hesitant Embrace of Human Rights," *Foreign Affairs* 89, No. 2 (March/April 2010), pp. 10–16.

178. Obama, *National Security Strategy 2010* (Washington, DC: The White House, May 2010), p. 9, at www.whitehouse.gov/sites/default/files/rss_viewer/national_se curity_strategy.pdf.

179. Obama, *National Security Strategy 2010* (Washington, DC: The White House, May 2010), p. 11, at www.whitehouse.gov/sites/default/files/rss_viewer/national _security_strategy.pdf.

180. Cf. Walter Russell Mead, "The Failed Grand Strategy in the Middle East," *Wall Street Journal*, August 24, 2013, p. C1; Nicholas Kitchen, "The Obama Doctrine–Détente or Decline," *European Political Science* 10, No. 1 (2010), pp. 27–35; Michael O'Hanlon, Bruce Reidel, "Plan A-Minus for Afghanistan," *Washington Quarterly* 34, No. 1, 2011, pp. 123–132; Frida Ghitis, "Obama's Foreign Policy in a Tailspin," *CNN Opinion*, August 9, 2013, at www.cnn.com/ 2013/08/09/opinion/ghitis-obama-mideast. Cf. James M. Lindsay, "George W. Bush, Barack Obama and the Future of US Global Leadership," *International Affairs* 87, No. 4 (2011), pp. 765–779.

181. Cf. Hillary Clinton, "America's Pacific Century," *Foreign Policy* 189.1 (2011), pp. 56–63: "With Iraq and Afghanistan still in transition and serious economic challenges in our own country, there are those on the American political scene who are calling for us not to reposition, but to come home. They seek a downsizing of our foreign engagement in favor of our pressing domestic priorities. These impulses are understandable, but they are misguided. Those who say that we can no longer afford to engage with the world have it exactly backward – we cannot afford not to."

182. Peter Trubowitz, *Politics and Strategy: Partisan Ambition and American Statecraft* (Princeton, NJ: Princeton University Press, 2011), p. 97.

183. George W. Bush, *The National Security Strategy of the United States of America*, March 16, 2006, p. i, at www.presidentialrhetoric.com/speeches/nss2006.pdf: "This strategy reflects our most solemn obligation: to protect the security of the American people."

184. George W. Bush, *Decision Points* (New York: Crown Publishers, 2010), pp. 436–37: "In 2001, the region saw terrorism on the rise, raging violence between Palestinians and Israelis, the destabilizing influence of Saddam Hussein, Libya developing weapons of mass destruction, tens of thousands of Syrian troops occupying Lebanon, Iran pressing ahead unopposed with a nuclear weapons program, widespread economic stagnation, and little progress toward political reform. . . . By 2009, nations across the Middle East were actively fighting terrorism instead of looking the other way. . . . Throughout the region, economic reform and political openness were beginning to advance." As Bush wrote, the "most dramatic advances for freedom came in the Middle East."

185. See William J. Broad, "U.S. Rethinks Strategy for the Unthinkable," *New York Times*, December 10, 2010, at http://www.nytimes.com/2010/12/16/science/16ter ror.html?pagewanted=all.

186. Peter Trubowitz, *Politics and Strategy: Partisan Ambition and American Statecraft* (Princeton, NJ: Princeton University Press, 2011), p. 97.

187. See Barack Obama, *National Security Strategy 2010* (Washington, DC: The White House, May 2010), p. 7, at www.whitehouse.gov/sites/default/files/rss_viewer/natio nal_security_strategy.pdf.

188. See Anne Lowrey, "Change in Paris May Better Fit U.S. Economic Positions," *New York Times*, May 8, 2012, p. A9.

189. See Barack Obama, *National Security Strategy 2010* (Washington, DC: The White House, May 2010), p. 2, at www.whitehouse.gov/sites/default/files/rss_viewer/natio nal_security_strategy.pdf.

190. See Obama, *National Security Strategy 2010* (Washington, DC: The White House, May 2010), p. 3, at www.whitehouse.gov/sites/default/files/rss_viewer/natio nal_security_strategy.pdf.

191. See Gideon Rose, "Neoclassical Realism and Theories of Foreign Policy," *World Politics* 51 (1998), pp. 144–172; Margaret G. Hermann, "How Decision Units Shape Foreign Policy: A Theoretical Framework," *International Studies Review* 3, No. 2 (Summer 2001), pp. 47–81; Ole R. Holsti, *Public Opinion and American Foreign Policy* (Ann Arbor: University of Michigan Press, 2009).

192. Cf. David E. Sanger, "Deficits May Alter US Politics and Global Power," *New York Times*, February 2, 2010, p. A2.

193. Cf. William C. Martel, "An Authoritarian Axis Rising?" *The Diplomat*, June 29, 2012, at www.thediplomat.com/2012/06/29/an-authoritarian-axis-rising/.

194. On grand strategy during the Bush administration, see Walter Russell Mead, "The Bush Administration and the New World Order," *World Policy Journal* 8, No. 3 (Summer 1991), pp. 375–420; Raymond Taras and Marshal Zeringue, "Grand Strategy in a Post-Bipolar World: Interpreting the Final Soviet Response," *Review of International Studies* 18, No. 4 (October 1992), pp. 355–375; Walter Russell Mead, "An American Grand Strategy: The Quest for Order in a Disordered World," *World Policy Journal* 10, No. 1 (Spring 1993), p. 9, who

described the "false dawn of a new world order." Also, Jeremi Suri, "American Grand Strategy from the Cold War's End to 9/11," *Orbis*, Fall 2009, pp. 616–621.

195. On principles governing Clinton's foreign policy, see Charles William Maynes, "A Workable Clinton Doctrine," *Foreign Policy*, No. 93 (Winter 1993–1994), pp. 3–21; Joseph S. Nye Jr., "The Case for Deep Engagement," *Foreign Affairs*. 74, No. 4 (July–August 1995), pp. 90–102; Michael Mandelbaum, "Foreign Policy as Social Work," *Foreign Affairs* 75, No. 1 (January–February 1996), pp. 16–32; Richard N. Haass, "What to Do with American Primacy," *Foreign Affairs* 78, No. 5 (September–October 1999), pp. 37–49; Stephen M. Walt, "Two Cheers for Clinton's Foreign Policy," *Foreign Affairs* 79, No. 2 (March–April 2000), pp. 63–79; Samuel R. Berger, "A Foreign Policy for the Global Age," Foreign Affairs 79, No. 6 (November–December 2000), pp. 22–39; "Clinton's Foreign Policy," Foreign Policy, No. 121 (November–December 2000), pp. 18–20, 22, 24, 26, 28–29; President William Clinton, *A National Strategy of Engagement and Enlargement* (Washington, DC: U.S. Government Printing Office, 1994); President William Clinton, *A National Security Strategy for a Global Age*, The White House, December 2000. On formulating grand strategy, see Jeremi Suri, "American Grand Strategy from the Cold War's End to 9/11," *Orbis*, Fall 2009, pp. 621–626.

196. On principles governing the Bush administration's policies, see Condoleezza Rice, "Promoting the National Interest," *Foreign Affairs* 79, No. 1 (January–February, 2000), pp. 45–62; George W. Bush, *The National Security Strategy of the United States of America*, The White House, March 2006.

197. See, for example, Robert Kagan, "Bipartisan Spring: Washington May Be Deeply Polarized on Domestic Matters, but When It Comes to Foreign Affairs, a Remarkable Consensus Is Taking Shape," *Foreign Policy*, March 3, 2010, at www.foreignpolicy.com/articles/2010/03/03/bipartisan_spring: "The Obama administration took office guided by the philosophy that whatever Bush did, it should do the opposite, and this policy of 'un-Bush' dominated the first months."

11 *The Making of Future American Grand Strategy*

1. For example, see Terry L. Deibel, *Foreign Affairs Strategy: Logic for American Statecraft* (New York: Cambridge University Press, 2007).

2. William C. Martel, "Why America Needs a Grand Strategy," *The Diplomat*, June 18, 2012, at www.thediplomat.com/2012/06/18/why-america-needs-a-grand -strategy.

3. Paul Kennedy, *The Rise and Fall of the Great Powers* (New York: Random House, 1987).

4. For the argument that the "relationship between ends and means is the all-important center, the iron linkage of [all] strategic thought," see John Lewis Gaddis, "Containment and the Logic of Strategy," *National Interest* 10 (Winter,1987–1988), p. 29.

5. See John Lewis Gaddis, *We Now Know: Rethinking the Cold War* (New York: Oxford University Press, 1997), p. 88, on the U.S. unwillingness to exploit its nuclear advantage.

6. See Adam Quinn, "The Art of Declining Politely: Obama's Prudent Presidency and the Waning of American Power," *International Affairs* 87, No. 4 (2011), pp. 803–824.

7. On principles in American foreign policy, see George F. Kennan, "On American Principles," *Foreign Affairs*, 1995, pp. 116–126.

8. *Political culture* is defined as "the set of attitudes, beliefs and sentiments that give order and meaning to a political process and which provide the underlying assumptions and rules that govern behavior in the political system." On political culture, see Charles Andrain, *Political Life and Social Change* (Belmont, CA: Duxbury Press, 1974); Talcott Parsons, "Culture and Social Systems Revisited," *Social Sciences Quarterly* 53 (September 1972), pp. 253–266; and Karl Deutsch, "Symbols of Political Community," in Lyman Bryson et al., *Symbols and Society* (New York: Harper and Row, 1953).

9. See William C. Martel, "Why America Needs a Grand Strategy," *The Diplomat*, June 18, 2012, at www.thediplomat.com/2012/06/18/why-america-needs-a-grand-strategy.

10. See Peter Feaver, "Debating American Grand Strategy after Major War," *Orbis* 53, No. 4 (Fall 2009), pp. 547–552; William C. Martel, "America's Dangerous Drift," *The Diplomat*, February 25, 2013, at http://thediplomat.com/2013/02/americas-dangerous-drift/; Jeremi Suri, "American Grand Strategy from the Cold War's End to 9/11," *Orbis*, Fall 2009, pp. 621–626.

11. See William C. Martel, "Grand Strategy of the Authoritarian Axis," *The Diplomat*, July 24, 2012, at www.thediplomat.com/2012/07/24/grand-strategy-of-the-authoritarian-axis/.

12. See David W. Moore, "Public Overwhelmingly Backs Bush in Attacks on Afghanistan," *Gallup*, October 8, 2001, at www.gallup.com/poll/4966/Public-Overwhelmingly-Backs-Bush-Attacks-Afghanistan.aspx.

13. See "Most Favor Afghanistan Withdrawal by 2014 But Fear U.S. Will Stay Too Long," *Rasmussen Reports*, May 4, 2013, at www.rasmussenreports.com/public_content/politics/current_events/afghanistan/most_favor_afghanistan_withdrawal_by_2014_but_fear_u_s_will_stay_too_long. Cf. Richard C. Eichenberg, "Victory Has Many Friends: US Public Opinion and the Use of Military Force, 1981–2005," *International Security* 30, No. 1 (2005), pp. 140–177.

14. President George H. W. Bush, *National Security Strategy of the United States*, March 1990, at www.fas.org/man/docs.

15. See Kenneth Lieberthal, "The American Pivot to Asia: Why President Obama's Turn to the East Is Easier Said than Done," *Foreign Policy*, December 21, 2011; Mark E. Manyin (coord.), *Pivot to the Pacific? The Obama Administration's "Rebalancing" Toward Asia* (Washington, DC: Congressional Research Service, Vol. R42448, March 28, 2012).

16. For analyses of the role of selective service in shared responsibility, see Dale R. Herspring, *Civil-Military Relations and Shared Responsibility: A Four-Nation Study* (Baltimore: Johns Hopkins University Press, 2013).

17. Walter Russell Mead, *Providence: American Foreign Policy and How It Changed the World* (New York: Knopf, 2001), pp. 47–48.

18. See Leslie H. Gelb, "GDP Now Matters More Than Force – A US Foreign Policy for the Age of Economic Power," *Foreign Affairs* 89 (November–December 2010), pp. 35–43.

19. See Francis Fukuyama, "The End of History," *The National Interest* 31, 1989, pp. 3–18.

20. See Leslie H. Gelb, "In Defense of Leading from Behind: So What If It's a Terrible Slogan? It's Still the Right Strategy," *Foreign Policy*, April 29, 2013, at www.foreignpolicy.com/articles/2013/04/29/in_defense_of_leading_from_behind.

21. See Michael R. Gordon, "Kerry Cites Clear Evidence of Chemical Weapon Use in Syria," *New York Times*, August 26, 2013, at www.nytimes.com/2013/08/27/world/middleeast/syria-assad.html.

22. For example, see "Netanyahu Proposes New 'Marshall Plan' for Egyptian Economy to Support Coup," *Middle East Monitor*, July 26, 2013, at www.middleeastmonitor.com/news/middle-east/6680-netanyahu-proposes-new-qmarshall-planq-for-egyptian-economy-to-support-coup#sthash.BpArWyku.dpuf.

Index